THE
BATTLE
FOR
HELL'S ISLAND

THE
BATTLE
FOR
HELL'S ISLAND

HOW A SMALL BAND
OF CARRIER DIVE-BOMBERS HELPED
SAVE GUADALCANAL

STEPHEN L. MOORE

NAL
CALIBER

NAL
CALIBER

Published by New American Library,
an imprint of Penguin Random House LLC
375 Hudson Street, New York, New York 10014

This book is an original publication of New American Library.

First Printing, November 2015

For more information about Penguin Random House, visit penguin.com.

LIBRARY OF CONGRESS CATALOGING-IN-PUBLICATION DATA:
Moore, Stephen L.
The battle for Hell's Island: how a small band of carrier dive-bombers helped save Guadalcanal/Stephen L. Moore.
p.   cm.
ISBN 978-0-451-47375-2 (hardback)
1. Allied Air Forces in the Solomons.   2. Guadalcanal, Battle of, Solomon Islands, 1942–1943.
3. World War, 1939–1945—Aerial operations.   4. United States. Army Air Forces. Air Force, 13th.
I. Title.
D767.98.M66   3015
940.54'265933—dc23   2015016506

Printed in the United States of America
10 9 8 7 6 5 4 3 2 1

Penguin
Random
House

CONTENTS

MAPS

THE
BATTLE
FOR
HELL'S ISLAND

PREFACE

"If you're going to miss with your bomb, you might as well stay home and let a *good* pilot take your place."

The sharp words still sizzled in Lieutenant Birney Strong's mind as he looked at the perfect scene playing out before him. Fourteen thousand feet below on the blue Pacific surface were the distinctive flat lines of two Japanese aircraft carriers. Birney had a determined calm about him as he briefly eyed the thin white wakes streaming behind the gleaming yellow-hued hardwood flight decks far below his dive-bomber.

I couldn't ask for a better setup, he thought. *A dive-bomber pilot's dream.*

He had not felt as happy the night before as he sat in the carrier *Enterprise*'s wardroom. The ship's air officer, Commander John Crommelin, had lectured his aviators about what he expected from them the following day. Birney puffed on his cigarette and gulped black coffee as the commander barked, "The Japs are determined to drive us out of the south Pacific. If they get through to Guadalcanal with their carriers tomorrow, the Japs will take it. If Guadalcanal falls, our lifeline to Australia will be menaced."

Crommelin emphasized that his aviators were to concentrate on knocking out the enemy's carriers. The comment about letting a good pilot take your place if necessary had particular harshness for Birney Strong that was not felt by the more junior aviators. Just two months before, he had sighted and reported a Japanese carrier force off the Solomon Islands. Instead of attacking, he had led his wingman home, a decision he had regretted for weeks. Crommelin had of course chastised Strong for his decision not to attack. Since that day, most of Strong's squadron had been granted leave back to the States, but not Birney. He had been ordered right back out to the Pacific war zone to continue the fight for Guadalcanal. Now the third senior pilot of a new scout-bombing carrier squadron, he had one goal: to prove his valor to Commander Crommelin by blasting the next Japanese carrier he faced.

In his own mind, however, Birney had nothing to prove to himself. He had been involved in almost every major Pacific offensive since the start of World War II ten months ago. The handsome, blond-haired, blue-eyed pilot had a swagger of confidence that he had earned. In February, he was one of the first pilots to attack Japanese shipping in the Gilbert Islands. In March, he had attacked Japanese shipping in the New Guinea harbors of Lae and Salamaua. In early May, he made three more attacks against Japanese ships in Tulagi Harbor in the Solomons. Strong dive-bombed the Japanese carrier *Shoho* three days later during the Coral Sea carrier battle and then used his SBD Dauntless dive-bomber like a fighter to battle Japanese Zero fighters attacking his own task force.

Lieutenant Strong was a top-notch pilot who had racked up eight hundred flight hours since graduating from the U.S. Naval Academy in 1937. His awards already included a Navy Cross, an honor second only to a Medal of Honor. He was good at what he did, and was not afraid to let others know of his confidence. He knew that some considered him to be arrogant. But the cocky scout pilot from Washington, DC, needed more than his impressive record to restore the goodwill of his air officer. Strong's failure to attack the Japanese carrier in August off the Eastern Solomons was a personal mission to correct.

Now, on the morning of October 26, 1942, was his fresh chance. High above the Pacific, Birney Strong was leading one of the eight teams of SBDs on the early scout-strike mission. He was fired up and ready to make his bomb count. "I think you'll find the yellowbellies are in your sector," Birney told his squadron skipper before takeoff. "When you find them, call out loud."

His skipper had indeed located the enemy and Strong moved in quickly with his wingman, Ensign Chuck Irvine. They soon spotted the Japanese carriers *Shokaku* and *Zuiho* emerging from under a layer of clouds far below their dive-bombers. "Uncle John" Crommelin's speech the previous evening left little doubt in Birney's mind. His mission was to turn back the Japanese carriers that threatened thousands of U.S. Marines on Guadalcanal and the course of America's first Pacific offensive. Uncle John had made it clear that the aviators should "knock the sons of bitches off the face of the earth."

Lieutenant Birney Strong of VS-5.

Birney glanced over to Irvine's nearby SBD. He planned to dive on the nearest flattop, so he patted the top of his leather flight helmet. *I've got it*, Birney signaled to Ensign Irvine. *Follow me.*

Birney activated his dive flaps; Irvine instinctively slid his Dauntless away to allow the proper spacing interval. The pair nosed over two and three-quarter miles above their prey to begin the thirty-second plunge to the release point.

The teakwood deck of *Zuiho* grew closer by the second. The big red circle painted forward on the Japanese aircraft carrier's flight deck looked like the bull's-eye on a dartboard. Birney Strong had no intention of drawing the scorn of Commander Crommelin again. He would nail this bastard with his bomb or die trying.

ONE

"It's All Exciting as Hell"

Damn my luck.

Warm salt spray hit Robert John Henry Weinzapfel's face as he watched another dive-bomber hurtle forward down the teak-covered flight deck. It was not uncommon for off-duty sailors to gather topside in "Vulture's Row" on the island superstructure to watch aircraft departing from and landing on their massive carrier. The seaborne airfield was only 90 feet wide but stretched 880 feet, nearly three football fields long. One by one, the blue-gray-colored warplanes roared skyward.

The smell of tropical flora was in the air and the Hawaiian Islands were breaking the horizon in the distance. The seas were rough. "The ship was rolling something awful, and a few of the boys furnished us with some thrills in taking off," Weinzapfel wrote that night.[1]

He watched as some of his squadron's junior pilots—Ensigns Tony Quigley, Marvin Haschke, Richard Neely, Jack Leppla, and Roy Hale—launched. Even Harry Wood, the newest pilot who had joined a month after Robert, was now en route to liberty on Oahu.

The date was October 18, 1941, and Ensign Weinzapfel looked on with envy as the planes soared away. After eighteen months in flight training, he was now grounded. He massaged the injured ear that had taken him off active flight duty and cursed his own poor luck.

His fellow pilots had lifted off from the deck of the U.S. Navy's aircraft carrier *Lexington* (CV-2). She and her sister *Saratoga* (CV-3) were the largest warships afloat, each nearly nine hundred feet in length and in service since 1927. Named for American Revolution battles, *Lexington* and *Saratoga* had been laid down on the hulls of battle cruisers, and each behemoth would displace fifty thousand tons when fully loaded. Many of their sailors had affectionately nicknamed the sibling flattops "Lady Lex" and "Sister Sara." Each could operate ninety aircraft and sported only two aircraft elevators, as opposed to three on the newer carriers being built. By 1941, however, both carriers were effectively restricted to a single elevator, as neither used the smaller elevators at all during daylight operations.

As of late 1941, each Navy fleet carrier operated two dive-bomber squadrons. The carriers *Ranger* (CV-4) and *Wasp* (CV-7) were on duty in the Atlantic, handling neutrality patrols against Nazi U-boats. The Navy's newest carrier, *Hornet* (CV-8), was nearing completion and would soon begin operating its own air group in early 1942. For the moment, most of the new pilots that made it to fleet duty were assigned to *Lexington*, *Saratoga*, *Yorktown* (CV-5), or *Enterprise* (CV-6).

Ensign Weinzapfel was one of twenty-one pilot officers assigned to *Lexington*'s Scouting Squadron Two (VS-2). The dark-haired, boyish-faced twenty-four-year-old from north Texas was a recent graduate of the Navy's flight-training program. Born in the small town of Scotland, he was the oldest of eight children. As a youth, Robert and his devout Catholic family had moved a short distance from Windthorst, Texas, east to the rural town of Muenster when his father, Joseph, and business partner, John Meurer, started the Muenster State Bank there in 1923.

In school, Robert had excelled in both athletics and academics, and he graduated at the

Courtesy of Henry Weinzapfel

Ensign Robert John Henry Weinzapfel of *Lexington*'s VS-2.

top of his class. Following college at St. Mary's in San Antonio, he had gone to an Army Air Force recruiter to pursue his interest in aviation. He expressed some doubts, however, about his own ability to shoot down another plane in combat—thus taking someone else's life—and the Army recruiter turned him down. Robert remained unfazed, conferred next with a Navy recruiter, and was accepted right away.

Ensign Weinzapfel's elimination flight training began in April 1940 in naval trainers, first in San Antonio and soon migrating to Opa-Locka, Florida, by July. His first solo flight came on August 1, 1940, in an N3N-3 biplane naval trainer—nicknamed the "Yellow Peril" by pilots both for its bright color and for the high number of aviation cadets who washed out of flight training. In September, Robert had the thrill of flying again back in Texas, including his hometown of Muenster, where he gave short flights to his father and to siblings Joe, Henry, Thomas, and Juanita.

During early 1941, Weinzapfel flew the Stearman N2S biplane trainer at Pensacola Naval Air Station (NAS). He progressed in April to the next training level at NAS Miami, and in May was assigned to Scouting Squadron Three under Lieutenant Commander Robert C. Sutliff on board the carrier *Saratoga*. Weinzapfel's training progressed on instrument flying, navigation, section tactics, and practice carrier landings. During June and July, he often swapped flying and riding rear seat with fellow trainees Horace Proulx, Bob Elder, Charlie Lane, Wesley Osmus, Leonard Thornhill, Corwin Morgan, and Jack Leppla as they became carrier-qualified.

John Arthur "Jack" Leppla, a Purdue University graduate from Lima, Ohio, became Weinzapfel's best friend and roommate throughout flight training. Jack was of Mediterranean ancestry, with dark hair, bushy eyebrows, and a dark complexion. Aviation was in the Leppla blood. Jack's brother Paul was an Army Air Force mechanic and his other brother, George, was flying Pan American Clipper planes in the Pacific Zone. Jack possessed an outgoing personality and competitive nature. During flight training at Pensacola, he fell back on his high school football abilities by playing on the NAS team. He narrowly escaped death in February 1941 when he and fellow trainee Ensign Robert F. Fenley's naval trainers collided at fifteen hundred feet above Bayou Grande near Pensacola.

Both ensigns jumped from their crippled planes in parachutes but Fenley drowned after splashing down.[2]

Weinzapfel and Leppla were inseparable during the fall of 1941. They had roomed together through flight training in both Pensacola and in Miami. When *Saratoga* moved to San Diego, they became roommates again there. Both pilots were reassigned from VS-3 and moved ashore to the North Island NAS at San Diego. That summer, Mrs. Leppla and Robert Weinzapfel's parents paid their sons a visit. The young pilots took great pride in showing their parents around the air station and enjoyed a meal together.

Leppla and Weinzapfel were reassigned from Scouting Three into VS-2 at North Island on August 13, 1941. The organization of their new *Lexington* Air Group was similar to what they had become accustomed to on Sister Sara. There was a fighter squadron, VF-2, and a torpedo squadron, VT-2, along with two dive-bomber squadrons flying the Douglas SBD. All of the *Lexington* airmen fell under the charge of Lieutenant Commander William Bowen Ault of Enterprise, Oregon. To young men like Weinzapfel and Leppla, Bill Ault was a fatherly figure at age forty-three. A 1922 Naval Academy graduate, Ault had flown in the aviation unit of the cruiser *Cincinnati* and with Patrol Squadron (VP) 10-S on the old aircraft tender *Wright* (AV-1). He had also served on the carriers *Lexington*, *Enterprise*, and *Yorktown*, before returning to *Lexington* in July 1941 to become her senior aviator. As the commander of the *Lexington* Air Group, Bill Ault was known by the moniker "CLAG" to his pilots.

U.S. Navy

Dauntless pilot Jack Leppla of *Lexington*'s Scouting Two, wearing his golden wings naval aviator insignia.

Commander Ault was tall

and lean, with an easygoing personality. He was not one to direct from the tarmac, however. Ault jumped in his cockpit and participated alongside his newer pilots in simulated attacks as his air group became more seasoned at NAS North Island. The squadrons began receiving the new Douglas SBD Dauntless dive-bomber during this training period. Each of the *Lexington* squadrons, Bombing Two and Scouting Two, was designed to operate eighteen SBDs, with a few spare pilots each to fill in for anyone sick or injured.

Weinzapfel practiced flying instrument training flights with fellow rookies Roy Hale and Tony Quigley, the young VS-2 pilots alternating between rear seat and pilot's cockpits to help each other. Scouting Two was under Lieutenant Commander Robert Ellington Dixon, a 1927 academy graduate from the little Georgia town of Richland, south of Atlanta. Like Bill Ault, thirty-five-year-old Bob Dixon was quiet but confident in his own abilities. Dixon's squadron was equally split between regular Naval Academy graduates and newly commissioned ensigns fresh from flight school. Six other officers had graduated from Annapolis: Edward Allen, Hoyt Mann, John "Pappy" Hunter, Thomas "Bobby" Edwards, Roy Hale, and Evan Peter "Pete" Aurand.

Some of the academy boys had no more flight time than VS-2's younger ensigns. Lieutenant (j.g.) Pete Aurand had earned his golden wings only in February 1941, but it would be his second tour of duty on the carrier *Lexington*. He had served as a junior gunnery officer on the carrier during his mandatory two years of surface duty after graduating from the academy.

Born in New York City, Pete was the son of Major General Henry S. Aurand, head of the Army's Sixth Service Command. An uncle and a cousin had joined the Navy, and Pete also found a calling for sea duty, although his younger brother followed in their father's footsteps by graduating from West Point. Pete racked up various behavior demerits while at Annapolis but graduated in 1938 and eventually became part of Bob Dixon's Scouting Two. "There was a distinction prewar between scouting squadrons and bomber squadrons, even though they had the same airplane," he said later. "In the scouting squadron, you did air-to-air gunnery, dive-bombing, scouting, and so forth. The dive-bomber guys concentrated on bombing. I decided that the scouting squadron did everything: air-to-air gunnery and the whole bit. I asked for and got Scouting Squadron Two. If I knew then what I know now, I'd probably have asked for a fighter squadron, but it seemed to me that that was the best of all worlds."[3]

Robert Weinzapfel, Jack Leppla, Pete Aurand, and the other new VS-2 pilots soon blended in with the older academy men. Dixon drilled his airmen on training and bombing practices until *Lexington* departed the West Coast on October 14, 1941, for Hawaii. Weinzapfel, an accomplished musician, stored his prized violin with some of Leppla's buddies until his carrier could return to California. Three days before Lady Lex departed San Diego, Weinzapfel had gone through high-altitude dive-bombing practice with a head cold. "As a result, my left ear became sore and became infected," he wrote. "After I spent a couple of days on the ground doctoring it, the doctor had to lance my eardrum." When *Lexington* steamed into the Hawaiian Islands on October 18, he was a mere sightseer as Leppla and his other buddies launched ahead of the ship for Ford Island.[4]

Robert's disappointment in being grounded was overcome when his automobile arrived in Hawaii the next week. He had purchased a Model A Ford in San Diego for the bargain price of forty-five dollars, then arranged to have it shipped by a cargo vessel to a PBY aviator buddy stationed in Honolulu who was entitled to a car. "I bought some paint and had my squadron painter put it on for me with his spray gun," he related. Weinzapfel became quite popular among his VS-2 buddies, as he was the only one on Oahu with a vehicle.[5]

Lexington operated near the Hawaiian Islands during November. Weinzapfel was relieved when the flight surgeon returned him to flight status midmonth. During his ship's stays in port, he purchased an 8mm movie camera and took up sport fishing with a spear gun. During the early days of December 1941, war with Japan was the furthest thing from his mind.

The opening days of the Pacific War caught *Yorktown* (CV-5) docked at Norfolk, *Saratoga* completing an overhaul in the Bremerton Navy Yard in Washington State, and the carriers *Ranger* and *Wasp* on Atlantic duty. *Yorktown*'s sister carrier, *Enterprise*, was returning to Pearl Harbor one day later than scheduled and narrowly avoided a full confrontation with the Japanese carriers. Still, her inbound air group was caught in the surprise attack and suffered a number of SBD and F4F aviators killed. More than two thousand Americans perished in the attack on Hawaii.

Lexington, the only other carrier in the immediate area at the time, had put to sea from Hawaii on December 5, bound for Midway to deliver eighteen Vought SB2U-3 Vindicator scout bombers for Marine Scouting Squadron 231. *Lexington*'s Task Group 12 was operating near Midway on the morning of December 7. Word of the attack changed everything, and TF-12 was ordered to intercept the Japanese raiding force, if possible.

"The flight deck crew began the slow and tedious respotting of the flight and hangar decks," recalled Ensign Charles E. Roemer, *Lexington*'s assistant landing signal officer (LSO). "Spotting in those days consisted of the 'taxi forward, push 'em back by hand' method." Scouting Two took off at about 1000, all pilots except Lieutenant (j.g.) Joe Smith and Ensigns Marvin Haschke and Robert Weinzapfel. Her SBDs flew three-hundred-mile scouting missions with only a brief flurry of excitement when one of her pilots thought he had spotted his new enemy. The "Japanese ship" soon proved to be a small reef near French Frigate Shoals.[6]

By late afternoon, most of Scouting Two and Bombing Two—the latter launched at 1400—had been recovered. However, several VS-2 pilots were unable to locate *Lexington* during the late hours of December 7. Among them were Ensigns Lincoln Curtis Koch and Harry Wood. Koch had been born in Calcutta, India, while his Methodist missionary parents were serving overseas. He and his eight siblings returned to Denver with their family and then settled in Clayton, New Mexico. "Linc" Koch graduated from the University of New Mexico and was intent upon earning his master's degree before the state of the economy prompted him to join the Navy.

When he arrived at Point Option—the pre-designated position where *Lexington* was supposed to be—Linc Koch found "no ship, no task force. Scattered rain showers reduced visibility somewhat and there was a ceiling of about twelve hundred feet. I started a square search and instituted a spartan fuel conservation program." As his fuel dwindled, Linc's thoughts drifted toward his girlfriend, Jean, a young woman whom he planned to soon marry who worked for a hotel in Honolulu.[7]

Neither Wood nor Koch had the new YE/ZB homing system in their SBDs as they groped for hours through the deteriorating weather for their carrier. Finally, Koch heard VB-2's Lieutenant (j.g.) Ralph Cousins, who was also searching for the ship, break radio silence and ask for a searchlight. "I kept flying expanding squares and I finally called the ship," Cousins recalled. "We weren't supposed to break radio silence unless it was an emergency."[8]

Cousins, an academy graduate who hailed from Ironwood, Michigan, had survived a plane crash during flight training at Pensacola and a subsequent ditching at sea when his engine failed during bombing practice on the target ship *Utah* with VB-2. Now, on the first day of war, Cousins found himself "totally lost" and facing the prospect of ditching again. Knowing that *Lexington* had a "new gadget" called radar, he asked that they use it, "locate me and give me a vector." Climbing to altitude, Cousins picked up *Lexington*'s signal and made it back to the ship. "It was a welcome sight," he recalled.

"I owe my life to this breach of radio silence," Linc Koch admitted. Skipper Bob Dixon and other pilots remained topside, straining their eyes for signs of the missing SBDs on the darkening horizon. Robert Weinzapfel of VS-2 was praying for their safe return. "If they'd go down, we would never go after them and they would be goners," he jotted in his diary that night. Weinzapfel felt, "It's all exciting as hell, our first day of war."

After spotting *Lexington*'s searchlight, Linc Koch found the shimmering luminescence of the carrier's wake and finally made it into the groove well after dark. "My engine coughed to a stop as I cleared the arresting gear," he related. Harry Wood's engine died as he landed on board. "Their marathon flight of more than eight hours was safely completed— probably an unintended record for this aircraft," recalled the assistant LSO Roemer. "I was so emotionally drained that I required assistance to get out of the cockpit," said Koch. "A good friend and fellow pilot, Ensign Tony Quigley, was first up on the wing to welcome me and help me get out of the plane."[9]

By the morning of December 8, the Japanese fleet was assumed to be heading toward the island of Jaluit in the Marshalls. The sudden war brought apprehension to some, strengthened bonds with others, and created a special pact between four close friends of *Lexington*'s Scouting Two.

Aviation Radioman Third Class (ARM3c) Wayne Carson Colley had joined the *Lexington* scout unit in its early months. Colley was born December 13, 1921, in Clintwood, Virginia, a hillside hamlet snuggled up next to the Kentucky border. Many of the Colley line who settled in this little farming community had fought in the Civil War. Wayne was a tall, lanky kid of six feet two inches, with dark hair, light ice-blue eyes, and classic good looks. Nicknamed "Slim" by his peers, the young man with the strong Virginia accent had a love for the outdoors. His hunting and fishing skills put food on the table at the Colley home, where he was raised with a sister and five brothers.

His father, Jasper Colley, insisted that young Wayne would not follow the Colley tradition of working in coal mines. Jasper, a schoolteacher, had lost a leg after an explosion in the mines, and he loved to show students his artificial limb. Wayne joined the Civilian Conservation Corps (CCC) just short of graduating from high school. In 1939, he enlisted in the Navy and went through boot camp at Norfolk. During his early service in the military, he was able to complete high school and earn his diploma.

Slim Colley was shipped out to San Diego after boot camp and assigned to Scouting Two. When word was passed of open spots for radiomen, he jumped at the chance. In order to become carrier-qualified, it was important to be not only a master of Morse code but also a proficient aerial gunner. "The Navy kept grabbing radiomen and sending them off to other ships," Colley explained. "Once you qualified, you had the rate 'radioman-qual-air,' and that kept them from sending you to some ship as a radioman."[10]

During the months of training, Colley became close with three other radiomen: Lawrence Sargent Craft, Lanois Mardi Wheeler, and James Buford Jewell. The quartet had gone through boot camp together in December 1939, progressed through radio training, and been assigned to Scouting Two together in early 1940. Good-natured Lanny Wheeler came from Roscoe, Illinois, just outside of Chicago. Jewell came from the little town of Horse Cave, Kentucky, located northeast of Nashville and just east of Mammoth Cave National Park. Known to his tight-knit group simply as J.B., Jewell and his brother joined the Navy, leaving their mother to manage the family's large bluegrass country farm.

Larry Craft, the youngest son of a poor, twelve-child family from Winnsboro, South Carolina, was the only married one of the VS-2 quartet. Known from a young age as "Lefty," Craft was a wiry, five-foot-eight farm boy of Dutch and Native American ancestry. He was dark complected, with black hair and dark eyes. Although of small stature, with small feet and hands, Lefty had an oversize "large and in-charge" personality.

He met his future wife, Beatrice McLendon, during a visit to the local mercantile store to buy farm supplies in 1939. Lefty became quite fond of the young store bookkeeper he called "Bee Bee," but he was intent upon fulfilling boyhood dreams of joining the Navy to see the world. He enlisted on December 12 at Norfolk, and was ordered to San Diego for boot camp. Bee Bee accompanied him to Georgia when he said his good-byes to his sister Geneva. In their parting hours, Lefty surprised Bee Bee by saying, "Let's get married." She agreed and they began plans for a future wedding when he had leave from the Navy.

As the group progressed through radio training at San Diego and on to *Lexington*, Lefty, J.B., Slim, and Lanny were inseparable. They shared chow time, shore leaves, and idle time on board ship when they were not flying. "We were like brothers," said Colley.

Lexington returned from maneuvers to San Diego at the end of August 1940 and Lefty was given leave to visit home in Winnsboro. He married Bee Bee McLendon on September 6, and she soon flew to California to start a home in nearby Coronado. Bee Bee got to know Jewell, Colley, and Wheeler, who were often guests at the Craft dinner table. However, as Scouting Two took shape during 1941, flight duties and sea excursions became more frequent.

Among the tests the dive-bomber crews endured was how many G's (G-force) their bodies could withstand. Bob Dixon's aviators flew as many as four flights in a twenty-four-hour period. While operating from the Hawaiian Islands, the old target ship *Utah* was often the victim of their practice bombing attacks. The SBC-4s that Colley and company flew had two miniature bomb racks on each wing, capable of carrying five small bombs each. From an altitude of about fifteen thousand feet, the pilots would dive to release one small dummy bomb against the target ship. Then they would climb back to altitude and repeat the process nine more times until all their practice bombs were expended.

"We did this till we couldn't walk, sleep, or eat," said Colley. "We were just zombies." With as many as forty practice dives in a single day, the pilots and their rear-seat gunners had little time to even use the head. When Colley finally found some sack time, he was practically delirious. "You'd crawl in the sack after that and the bunk would go every which way—up, down, sideways."[11]

Scouting Two's senior radioman, twenty-eight-year-old Ferdinand John "Fred" Sugar, worked his new gunners to the point of perfection. Aside from bombing and gunnery drills, the airmen mastered the art of operating from the tight confines of a carrier flight deck. The giant *Lexington* even carried arresting gear forward, in addition to the usual aft-mounted wire traps, so that she could land aircraft on her bow in an emergency. "About every three months, we'd go out for operations where we had to take off over the stern," Colley said. "The ship would be backing down; it could do fifteen to twenty knots, and we'd take off and then land on the bow."

The early Curtiss SBC-4 was a rugged aircraft, even under extreme tests. Colley was in the rear seat for one flight in which the biplane was put through a G-force test from twenty thousand feet without any flaps. "We pulled eleven and a half G's on the pullout," he recalled of his pilot's front cockpit meter reading. "That tore me up. I spit up blood for a week after that. Every damn tooth in my head ached on the pullout but the plane held together."

Colley, Craft, Jewell, and Wheeler found themselves in good company with Scouting Two. Chief Sugar's enlisted men were solid and well trained. Among them was Aviation Radioman Third Class (ARM3c) John Liska, from Van Nuys, California. For him, the Navy was a chance to make something of himself and to help provide for his family. Born in Coaldale, Pennsylvania, John had moved at an early age to California, where he was raised with two brothers and two sisters. His father worked for a power company, but was crippled by an industrial accident that left his wife to raise their children on a chicken farm.

At age twelve, Johnny began tinkering with radios by building crystal sets and then tube sets, eventually turning the family's old chicken house into his workshop to dabble in shortwave sending and receiving. He was an all-around athlete and gymnast in high school and also helped his brother in a floor-laying business. In February 1941, John Liska had his mother sign his enlistment papers when he was seventeen so that he could join the Navy while still in high school. Although mild-mannered and humble by nature, John was a five-foot-ten weight lifter with powerful hands and, according to his son's description, was "built like a brick shithouse." His regular letters written to his brothers and sisters helped inspire his brother Frank to join the Navy in 1941, while his younger brother Steve hoped to join after finishing high school. Frank also became an enlisted radioman, but was later killed in a VP-117 patrol plane crash. Johnny Liska became one of the brothers of VS-2 and in due time would find his chance to shine.

The onset of war was something J. B. Jewell, Lefty Craft, Slim Colley, and Lanny Wheeler talked about for long hours. "We all had an agreement—the four of us—that if any of us got killed, whoever survived would try and see the others' folks," Colley said. Each of their families had already gotten to know the other young men. As for their survival pact, Colley and his buddies hoped it was something they would never have to fulfill.

The second day of war was passed with scouting missions conducted by the SBD squadrons. *Lexington* launched sixteen Dauntlesses of VS-2 to search out to 315 miles. Lieutenant (j.g.) Jack "Pappy" Hunter, the squadron's gunnery officer, in 2-S-7, radioed that he was being forced to make a water landing. He announced to wingman Tony Quigley that his engine had failed. At 0840, Hunter landed his SBD in the ocean, and he had climbed into his rubber raft with rear-seat man Radioman Second Class Earl Willard Lang. Quigley got a thumbs-up signal from Hunter and then held station over the pair to radio information on their coordinates.[12]

Admiral Newton dispatched the destroyer *Drayton* to rescue the downed VS-2 aviators. In the interim, Task Force 12 received word at 0900 that the Japanese strike force had retired from the Hawaiian Islands area and that *Lexington* should proceed toward Oahu. It was a somber group of pilots that gathered in the ready room that night to mourn the missing Pappy Hunter. Robert Weinzapfel found comfort in prayer before any mission. "But, to pray for help in finding the enemy so I can bomb him and kill as many men as possible," he wrote in his diary on December 8, "well, it's just hard to do. I began to complain that I wasn't getting to fly any, so I was put on a submarine patrol hop this afternoon." *Drayton* and another destroyer, *Lamson*, searched for Hunter's crew into the following day.[13]

Scouting Two's misfortunes continued on December 9 during recovery of a dozen scouts at 1230, when Robert Weinzapfel fell victim to a mishap. As he was bringing his plane, number 2-S-17, in for a landing, his Dauntless veered over the starboard side and crashed into the ocean.

"We were landing but he took a wave-off and we stalled and spun in," said Radioman Third Class Raymond Eugene Reames, his rear gunner. It was the first flight the two had made together. Reames was another Texan, from the central Texas town of Cisco. Reames, twenty-two, had joined the navy in July 1940, after graduating from Cisco High School, and had been the honor man of his company during training at San Diego. The force of the impact knocked Reames unconscious for a moment, but he quickly came to as the ocean rushed into his cockpit.

Reames kicked free of his rear seat as their Dauntless bubbled under the waves nose first. The tail section rose into the air, and this was all that was visible when the young gunner freed himself. "Immediately, I tried to get to him but the tail fell on top of me," Reames reported. Ensign Weinzapfel remained in the cockpit as the SBD plunged beneath the waves. The crash had likely driven the pilot into his bombsight or other instruments, knocking him unconscious. Reames was mortified to watch their bomber disappear with his fellow Texan trapped inside. "He was one swell fellow," Reames recalled.

Lexington's plane guard destroyer, *Flusser*, fished Reames out of the ocean, but Ensign Weinzapfel was gone. His longtime roommate, Jack

U.S. Navy

Scouting Squadron Two (VS-2) pilots on *Lexington*'s flight deck on December 24, 1941: (*front row, left to right*) Ensign Johnny Leppla, Ensign "Roscoe" Neely, Lieutenant Commander Bob Dixon, Lieutenant Evan Aurand, and Ensign Linc Koch; (*back row, left to right*) Lieutenant (j.g.) Tommy Edwards, Lieutenant Hoyt Mann, Lieutenant (j.g.) Roy Hale, Ensign Harry Wood, Ensign Marvin Haschke, Ensign Everleigh Willems, Ensign Art Schultz, Ensign Tony Quigley, Lieutenant Joe Smith, Lieutenant (j.g.) Chandler Swanson, and Lieutenant Edward Allen.

U.S. Navy photo, courtesy of Colleen Colley

Scouting Squadron Two gunners on *Lexington*'s flight deck on December 24, 1941: (*front row, left to right*) Fred Sugar, Larry Craft, Bruce Rountree, Wayne Colley, Lanny Wheeler, and Cyril Huvar; (*back row, left to right*) Clarence Garlow, John Liska, John Edwards, Robert Wheelhouse, Charles Rouser, and James Jewell.

Leppla, wrote to the Weinzapfel family back in Muenster, Texas, to express his deep grief. "To me, Robert was like a brother and the best friend I ever had," Leppla wrote. "Robert was either killed instantly or rendered unconscious by the impact and therefore could not free himself from the plane. His courage was well known and I know he had no fear of death."[14]

The family also received correspondence from VS-2 skipper Bob Dixon. The Weinzapfel family and the Leppla family would remain in contact throughout the war. When Mrs. Weinzapfel wrote to Ensign Leppla in January 1942, she sent the following wish: "Do a good fight, John. Do your part and Robert's also. His spirit is with you."[15]

Jack Leppla would certainly carry on for his brave friend. In due time he would prove that he possessed a fighting spirit that the Japanese would prefer to avoid.

Lexington retained her Marine scout bombing squadron instead of sending it to Midway. As the carrier approached Oahu on the morning of December 10, the Vindicators were launched ahead for Ewa Field. *Lexington* spent the next days operating to the southwest of Oahu, sending out search planes and combat air patrols to guard against a return of Japanese strikers. *Lexington* finally steamed into the channel of Pearl Harbor late in the afternoon of December 13. Her planes had not managed to attack anything Japanese, and the new war had already cost her two precious dive-bombers and three airmen.

Scouting Two flew ashore to Ford Island. Bob Dixon reported that his aviators "went on the alert until one and a half hours after sunset and again went on the alert one hour before sunrise the following morning." The air still smelled of ashes and burned paint while rescue crews continued to try to save men trapped in the overturned battleship *Oklahoma*. Ensign Mark Whittier and two other VB-2 pilots were scrambled in their SBDs after lunch to investigate a report of a Japanese submarine between Oahu and Molakai, but they found only debris in the ocean.[16]

The submarine scare kept Pearl Harbor's command on edge all night. "They arranged for us to have a night at the Royal Hawaiian Hotel, but in the middle of the night we got a knock on the door and were told to return to the base immediately," recalled Ensign Norm Sterrie of Torpedo

Two. The pilots were told that *Lexington* was heading out to sea because of evidence of a Japanese sub in the harbor. "We got out to the ship in a fly-by-night episode at rapid speed without lights across the island and then to the ship," Sterrie related, "but they decided not to go out that night."[17]

Pete Aurand of VS-2 found that his girlfriend, Patricia Riley, had narrowly survived the Pearl Harbor attack. She was standing in her sister's yard, snapping a photo of the exploding battleship *Arizona*, when a Japanese plane swooped in low. Her brother pulled Patricia to safety before machine-gun bullets chewed up the sod where she had been standing. Ashore on leave, Pete proposed to his girlfriend next to the burned hulk of an aircraft. She accepted, but their ceremony would have to wait until *Lexington* was back in port for a longer period of time.[18]

When *Lexington*'s Task Force 11 sortied from Pearl Harbor the next day, December 14, she was under command of Vice Admiral Wilson Brown with orders to conduct an offensive mission. After clearing the harbor channel, she landed all of her planes: twenty-one Brewster Buffalo F2A fighters, thirty-two SBDs, and fifteen TBD Devastators. Two days later, Ensigns Mark Whittier and Clem Connally of VB-2 reported what they believed to be a Japanese carrier about ninety-five miles from Point Option. They made dive-bombing attacks and headed back for their carrier while Captain Ted Sherman launched a strike force of three dozen planes to follow up. Fortunately, the young pilots' marksmanship was as poor as their ship-recognition skills. Their carrier turned out to be a derelict dynamite barge that had been cut loose during the Pearl Harbor attack by the tugboat that was hauling it toward Palmyra Island. Connally and Whittier, teased by their squadron mates for bombing the derelict "carrier," could well have blown their SBDs from the skies had they landed direct hits.[19]

Ensign Whittier had been with Bombing Two since August 1938. During his college years at the University of Minnesota, he had planned to attend medicine school after completing his first two years of basics. His grades were not high enough to make the cut to med school, so Whittier opted to enlist in the Navy, become an aviator, and then resume his medical schooling after his service. Bombing Two's pilots became a tight bunch as their training progressed. "We flew together, worked together, drank together, and, all too frequently, mourned together," wrote Whittier. To lighten the strain, VB-2's pilots created the "Flying Jack-Ass Medal" award, to be worn around the neck by anyone who pulled a complete aerial moment of ignorance. "He was the exalted keeper of this 'trophy' until such time, in his judgement, someone deserved it more."[20]

Whittier earned the Flying Jack-Ass Medal during aerial gunnery practice one day by pressing home his attack on the tow plane so close that his prop shredded the tow sleeve. The next "victim" was none other than his skipper, Lieutenant Commander Harry "Don" Felt. During an early-morning takeoff from *Lexington*, Felt spun his SBD into the ocean and suffered a broken arm and broken ribs in the crash. Transferred back to his carrier via a high-line basket, Felt was resting comfortably in his stateroom when wingman Mark Whittier paid him a visit. Whittier wished him a painless recovery and departed without a word, leaving the Flying Jack-Ass Medal on the doorknob.[21]

In the wake of Whittier's "carrier" sighting, *Lexington*'s task force refueled at sea during the next few days. The air group was anticipating an offensive strike, but word was received on December 20 that the mission was canceled. The weather was rough on December 23 as *Lexington* tried in vain to refuel from the tanker *Neosho*. Lieutenant (j.g.) Joel Davis Jr., flying a VB-2 Dauntless on a routine scouting patrol, crashed into the ocean fourteen miles north of the carrier. *Lexington* and her plane guard ships raced to the scene, but Davis and his gunner, Radioman Third Class Vernon Schmidt, apparently did not escape their sinking plane. It was *Lexington*'s third SBD loss of the month.[22]

Task Force 11 returned to Pearl Harbor on December 27. Bob Dixon's VS-2 and Don Felt's VB-2 squadrons overhauled their planes at Ford Island during the next two days. Pete Aurand of VS-2 took the opportunity ashore that afternoon to quickly marry his fiancée, Patricia. *Lexington*'s dive-bomber squadrons picked up new rookie ensigns to make up for their December losses. Scouting Two added Ensigns John Wingfield and Joe Johnson, while Bombing Two gained five new pilots—Ensigns Frank McDonald, Russell Lecklider, Don Wakeham, Joseph Riley, and William Edwards.[23]

After two days in port, *Lexington* ventured out on December 29 for a short cruise southwest of the Hawaiian islands. She returned to Pearl on January 3, 1942, for several days of overhaul while her air group returned to the local bases. The first month of war had been frustrating in that there had been no enemy action for the *Lexington* aviators, and it had been costly in terms of lost aircraft.

TWO

Rocky, Swede, and "the Master"

The surprise attack on Pearl Harbor created an equally intensive mobilization for war among the carrier *Yorktown*'s air group.

Her airmen were based on and around the Norfolk, Virginia, naval air base. The pilots had returned from a training cruise on December 3, and they were eager for some downtime. The Norfolk *Virginian-Pilot* headlines hinted at escalating tensions in the Far East and that war in the Pacific was looming on the horizon. Nonetheless, lively festivities and celebrations were in order.[1]

Several pilots used their liberty time to get hitched. *Yorktown* fighter pilot Leslie Knox was married on Saturday, December 6, at Our Lady of Victory Chapel at NOB Norfolk. He was preceded in holy matrimony by two other *Yorktown* aviators. Both Ensign Lavell "Jeff" Bigelow of VB-5 and Lieutenant Roger Blake Woodhull of VS-5 were joined with their significant others the previous afternoon. Scouting Five's officers threw a big cocktail party at the base officers' club in honor of Woodhull and his new bride, Jean Maxwell Brown Woodhull.

Woodhull was celebrating life as much as he was his new marriage. He had narrowly escaped a midair tragedy just weeks prior during training exercises in Louisiana. His Scouting Five had been one of four Navy squadrons selected to participate in the September 1941 "Louisiana Maneuvers," the largest joint Army-Navy exercise ever held.

More than seventy thousand Army soldiers had participated in mock war exercises in Louisiana during May 1940. The following summer, General George C. Marshall had organized another, larger version of the war games in the Bayou State. More than four hundred thousand troops congregated during late August 1941 for the so-called Louisiana Maneuvers, designed to evaluate U.S. training, logistics, doctrine, and commanders. This time, the military exercises included aerial support from both Army and Navy squadrons to enhance the training. The Navy's contribution was two fighter squadrons, plus Scouting Five from *Yorktown* and VB-2 from *Lexington*.

Roger Woodhull and seventeen other VS-5 crews had flown from Norfolk on September 9, 1941, for Louisiana. He made the six-hour flight to Lake Charles via New Orleans through hurricane-induced foul weather in an aircraft that was brand-new to him. Scouting Five had just traded in their old biplane Curtiss SBC bombers for new model Douglas SBD Dauntless dive-bombers. The SBDs were certainly a vast improvement, with greater dive performance, range, and speed than their predecessor. The SBD-3 model had a top speed of 216 knots, or 250 mph, from each plane's thousand-horsepower Wright Cyclone engine, although actual cruising speed on combat missions was normally 140 to 160 knots to preserve fuel. The range of an SBD with a thousand-pound bomb was safely between 200 and 225 miles or 250 and 275 miles with a five-hundred-pound bomb.

For the Louisiana war games, Woodhull's squadron took up residence at the crude Lake Charles airfield. "Our previous training had not included sleeping in a tent and operating off a gravel strip," said Lieutenant (j.g.) Bill Christie, one of a few VB-5 pilots who joined VS-5 for the training. The Navy pilots and rear gunners were resigned to bucket baths and swatting mosquitoes while roughing it in sweltering weather in Army tents. One of Scouting Five's senior aviators, Lieutenant (j.g.) Charlie Ware, a 1940 Naval Academy graduate from Knoxville, found the conditions at Lake Charles to be "rugged" but "a lot of fun with the Army."[2]

The troops of the Louisiana Maneuvers had been divided into two fictitious countries. Ware, Woodhull, and their VS-5 companions were assigned to the "Blue Army," more than two hundred thousand men of General Walter Krueger's Third Army. The Blue Army was called *Almat*—an acronym for Arkansas, Louisiana, Mississippi, Alabama, and Tennessee—and it was to act as a foreign army that had invaded Lousiana's coast. They were to attack the "Red Army" of the made-up country *Kotmk* (Kansas, Oklahoma, Texas, Missouri, and Kentucky). The Red Army, commanded by Lieutenant General Ben Lear, would be deployed in an egg-shaped area in northwest Louisiana near Shreveport.[3]

The Red Army opened the maneuvers before dawn on Monday, September 15, by advancing an armored division across the Red River. Brigadier General George S. Patton's armored division of tanks, mobile infantry, and artillery followed. Many of the Army officers present— Patton, Omar Bradley, Mark Clark, Dwight D. Eisenhower, and Lesley J. McNair—would later rise to very senior roles in World War II. The first mission for *Lexington*'s VB-2 and *Yorktown*'s VS-5 was a predawn surprise air attack against the Barksdale Army Air Base at Shreveport that day. Skippers Don Felt and Bill Burch led their SBD squadrons in a night takeoff and then flew north. The units circled Barksdale to prepare to hit from both the northwest and the northeast at the same time— twenty minutes before sunrise.

The Blue Army's navy dive-bombers caught the Red Army's fighter planes parked on the runway. Burch's and Felt's pilots swooped in so that their rear-seat gunners could toss six-ounce sacks of wet flour to simulate bomb drops. "Rows of parked army airplanes were our objective and we decommissioned them in short order," said Mark Whittier. The ground umpires, however, failed to rule on the success of the Navy's bombardment as the SBDs retired from Barksdale. Embarrassed Army fighter pilots quickly manned their P-40s and took off. "The Army fighters overtook our retirement and sliced through our formation," said Lieutenant Commander Felt.[4]

The results were nearly fatal for VS-5's Lieutenant Woodhull and his gunner, Aviation Radioman Third Class Albert Woodrow Garlow. Woodhull, two weeks shy of his twenty-eighth birthday, was the nephew of a San Antonio judge. In 1937, he had graduated seventh in his class of 365 at the Naval Academy, where he had participated in boxing, soccer, and lacrosse. Known to his classmen as "Rog" or "Woody," he then served on surface ships until starting his pilot training in 1940 at NAS Pensacola.

Woodhull served on the carriers *Wasp* and *Ranger* before being assigned to *Yorktown*'s Scouting Five in January 1941. By September, he and gunner Al Garlow had been flying as a pilot-radioman team for several months.

Garlow was a hard-luck youth who had found his calling in the U.S. Navy. He was raised in rural Nebraska, but his parents divorced when he was thirteen. Al packed his bags and went to work on a farm while he attended high school. He hitchhiked to San Diego after his senior year and enlisted in the military in 1937. Al worked as a mess cook during his early months on *Lexington*. He often served the aviators, who took notice of the young man's personable disposition. He soon got the chance to go through radioman training and began flying with Torpedo Two, where he remained until early 1941. Garlow stood only five feet seven and was very slight of frame. He had grown up in a real cowboy town but his friends chided him that he was more likely to end up a jockey than a cowboy. He was assigned to *Yorktown* in June 1941 and became part of Scouting Five the following month.

Garlow was facing aft as his Dauntless roared away from the Blue Army's field at Barksdale shortly after daybreak. Behind him, the excited Army Eighth Pursuit Group fighter pilots began making continuous dives and swoops on the fleeing Navy bombers to try to convince the ground spotters that they were making "kills" against their adversaries. One of the Curtiss P-40s dived straight down on Woodhull and then pulled up for altitude in between Woodhull and the SBD ahead of him.

The P-40 plowed right into the SBD with a frightful explosion. Woodhull's prop slashed off the tail section of the fighter in the midair collision. The P-40 of Second Lieutenant John Ward Bobrowski from Racine, Wisconsin, plunged toward the earth, minus its tail. Witnesses said that Bobrowski was unable to parachute from his flaming plane. Woodhull hollered over the intercom, "Bail out! I'm going to try and land the plane, but you bail out now!"[5]

Garlow had blind faith in his pilot. He also knew better than to question orders. He unbuckled his seat belt harness and flung himself over the side of the SBD's rear cockpit from a mere six hundred feet. His parachute scarcely had time to deploy but it did the trick. Garlow landed in a cotton field near the Coushatta crossing of the Red River, fortunate to be alive, but spent two days working his way back to the Blue Army base.[6]

Woodhull found to his surprise that he still had some control of his SBD. He finally thought to tell Garlow, "Never mind," but when he glanced backward, his rear-seat man was gone. All three blades of his dive-bomber's prop were bent, and the propeller itself was slammed six inches out of line. Woodhull's cowling was smashed up against the engine, one tire was punctured, his bomb rack was torn off, half the underside of one wing had been carried away, and his SBD's fuselage was torn. His engine vibrated so badly because of the bent prop that the tail vibrated out of line by two feet. Woodhull's entire engine mount was twisted five inches out of alignment, and yet he was still flying.

He nursed his crippled war bird some 110 miles back to the Blue Army's airfield, escorted by his VS-5 companions. Even with one blown tire on his landing gear, Woodhull managed to crash-land his Dauntless without injury. "We acquired a healthy respect for that airplane and its ability to take punishment and still get back," said squadron skipper Bill Burch. "We knew we were flying a rugged airplane, and I think that confidence had a lot to do with the things we were able to do with it later on in the Pacific."[7]

By the time the war games ended on September 28, twenty-six men had been killed—some from drowning, some from vehicle accidents, five in airplane crashes, and one soldier who was struck by lightning. Scouting Five departed Louisiana on September 29 to begin another cross-country flight back to Norfolk, where they arrived on October 1. For their part in the maneuvers, VS-5's pilots and gunners were praised by both Navy and Army leaders. They had received an important indoctrination in aerial support of land warfare. Roger Woodhull and some of his fellow Dauntless aviators—Al Garlow, Willard Glidewell, Turner Caldwell, Swede Vejtasa, and Jim Cales—could not imagine that in less than a year's time, this service would be invaluable to their survival when they found themselves flying from a sweltering Pacific island called Guadalcanal.

The first week of December 1941 was a more joyous time for Woodhull as he celebrated both his survival and his new bride, Jean. Any thoughts of war were clouded and far removed from most of the *Yorktown* pilots' minds when they finally stumbled back to their quarters on the Norfolk base in the wee hours of December 7, 1941.

Rocky Glidewell, Scouting Five's senior enlisted man, was a popular guy. His fun-loving spirit endeared him to his junior radiomen. His determination and prowess with machine guns gave his air group officers confidence in selecting him to fly with the most senior aviators.

On the afternoon of December 7, Glidewell picked up his Plymouth convertible that he kept just off the Norfolk naval base. Two shipmates and their girlfriends piled in, and Rocky's girl took her usual seat alongside him in the front. Christmas was less than three weeks away as they set out with the top down, intent on finding the perfect Norfolk pine to decorate for the holidays. Rocky's car radio belted out the latest popular music. Glenn Miller's orchestra swing tune "Chattanooga Choo Choo" was just climbing the charts to the top position.

Tall and handsome, Rocky was solidly built. He was a first-class petty officer with twelve years in the U.S. Navy. Behind his warm smile and bright eyes was a serious man who was not known to back down from a fight. The nickname he had earned in the boxing rings fit like a glove. To his parents, he was Willard Ellis Glidewell, who entered the world in 1912 in Jackson County, Illinois. His father was a railroad man who died when he was ten, leaving him and his older brother to work the farm and care for his mother and two sisters. Although his mother remarried, Glidewell found himself "doing a man's work" as a teenager, laboring on another man's farm, plowing, tending fields, threshing, and tending to livestock.[8]

He first tried to enlist in the Navy in the fall of 1929, but failed the physical because of a deviated septum caused by a farm horse that gave him a busted nose. Glidewell took the recruiter's advice to have his nose repaired and diligently saved his earnings from working at a bowling alley that winter. Fresh from nasal surgery and eighteen years old, Willard Glidewell went to the recruiting station at Chicago again in 1930 and secured an enlistment.

During his five months at the Great Lakes training station, Glidewell pursued amateur boxing. Although he weighed only 134 pounds at the time, he had a real fighting spirit. His given name, Willard, did not sound like a particularly tough ring name, so Glidewell adopted the soubriquet "Rocky," a nickname that would follow him for life. During his first boxing match, Rocky broke his thumb because his gloves were too loose, but he still managed to win the fight.

Rocky Glidewell earned top marks on his boot camp test, which only a dozen men passed. He was assigned to the radio communications division aboard the USS *Idaho*, where he learned Morse code and progressed rapidly in his skills. He joined the destroyer *Overton* (DD-239) in 1932 and sailed with her for duty in the Panama Canal Zone as a showing of American presence. Rocky boxed off and on in Panama,

U.S. Navy

Willard "Rocky" Glidewell,
Scouting Five's senior radioman.

representing the Navy's featherweight division against both Army and Army Air Force opponents. In the fall of 1937 Glidewell finally moved toward naval aviation by being assigned at Norfolk to the carrier *Yorktown*'s Scouting Squadron Five as an aviation mechanic. Christened by Mrs. Franklin D. Roosevelt in 1936, the $25 million *Yorktown* landed her first aircraft on November 10, 1937. Displacing 25,500 tons when fully loaded, *Yorktown*, at 809 feet in length, was smaller than the giant *Lexington* and *Saratoga*. Still, she sported a top speed of 32.5 knots and could operate ninety aircraft at sea, making her a leaner, equally deadly combat vessel in terms of striking power.

When a slot came open for competition to attend radio school, Rocky passed the test with flying colors. By December 1941, Glidewell had advanced to first-class radioman and was senior among his Scouting Five peers. He flew as Lieutenant Commander William L. Rees's regular gunner from August 1940 until his transfer in June 1941. Glidewell flew hops with a number of VS-5's other pilot officers but soon settled in as new Air Group Commander Curtis Stanton Smiley's regular gunner.

During twelve years of naval service, he had become familiar with many island chains of the Pacific. The Hawaiian Islands were thus more familiar to Rocky than to most Americans when they rose to the forefront of everyone's attention. The passengers in his Plymouth did not know how to take the news at first. Crackling from the convertible's radio came the shocking announcement that Pearl Harbor had been attacked.

Japanese warplanes carried out a surprise attack at Oahu, destroying many of the Pacific Fleet's mighty battleships. Glidewell turned his car toward Norfolk and gunned his engine. Dropping off the girls at their homes, he and his shipmates raced back to the base. *Yorktown*'s sailors were immediately restricted to the base and to their ship. Air Group Commander Smiley was charged with a multitude of details to prepare his squadrons and their aircraft for war. Rocky Glidewell, as senior enlisted petty officer of his scout bombing squadron, was similarly tasked with getting his personnel prepared. The devastating truth soon came out. Six Japanese aircraft carriers had pummeled Hawaii, killing more than two thousand sailors, soldiers, and civilians alike. *This is it,* thought Rocky. *An eye for an eye. Time to show 'em what America is made of.*

Most of Glidewell's enlisted men were eager for action on the high seas. There was nineteen-year-old Harold Wilger, fresh out of high school from Willmar, Minnesota. Another newcomer was Tony Brunetti, whose mother had campaigned in Hartford, Connecticut, to allow early graduation to hometown boys who wanted to join the military. Other VS-5 radiomen had more Navy tenure. Joe Roll from Detroit and Missourian Carl Russ each had more than five years of military service under their belts. Jim Cales, who hailed from the coal-mining state of West Virginia, had enlisted in the Navy exactly two years earlier, on December 7, 1939. Glidewell's closest peer was Chief Radioman Oliver Grew, who was known for his long, waxed mustache and as skipper Bill Burch's regular gunner.[9]

With nineteen dive-bombers assigned to his squadron, Glidewell carried an average of twenty-two radiomen-gunners in order to man all aircraft, with a few spares. He knew that with war would come losses, and that as time went on he would be forced to train replacements. Fortunately, there were ample trained radiomen amongst the ship's company.

One such individual was Clay Strickland, born the sixth of nine children on a rented farm near Clifton, Texas. Clay graduated from high school in nearby Kopperl, Texas, in May 1937, and worked on the family farm until age twenty-one. He enlisted in the Navy in July 1940. Seaman Second Class Strickland was assigned to the K-Division with the ship's radio gang, decoding and coding messages. Two months later, he was assigned to VB-5 as a radioman striker, where he would spend the early months of 1942 climbing the totem pole toward active flight duty. In due time, Clay Strickland would become integrated into VS-5 and become another of Glidewell's charges.[10]

Scouting Five skipper Bill Burch was in disbelief when he heard the news about Pearl Harbor from one of his pilots that afternoon. Burch, confused, could only think to ask how they knew the attackers were Japanese.[11]

Many of his pilots were recovering from the late cocktail party thrown in honor of Roger Woodhull's wedding. Ensign Lavell "Jeff" Bigelow, a twenty-four-year-old Brigham Young graduate from Provo, Utah, heard the news over the radio. The Bombing Five pilot and his bride of two days were packing their bags for their honeymoon. "I took off my civilian clothes, put on my uniform, and checked into the USS *Yorktown*," Bigelow recalled of his sudden status change. Link Traynor of VS-5 was just unpacking in his new Norfolk apartment when he heard of the attack on the radio. Two hours later, a duty officer rapped on his door and announced, "Traynor, I'll give you two hours to get to the squadron with your luggage ready to go."[12]

Lieutenant (j.g.) Stanley Winfield Vejtasa and his wife of two years, Irene Funk Vejtasa, had rented a house in Norfolk for themselves and their one-year-old son, Gene. Stan believed that war with Japan was imminent, but he was not expecting the phone call he received that afternoon. "Get your ass down here," an officer demanded. "Pearl Harbor has just been bombed. Get down to the squadron!"[13]

Stan Vejtasa had also been with VS-5 since its beginnings in 1940. The six-foot-two, blue-eyed, blond-haired young man of mixed European ancestry hailed from the farmlands of Circle, Montana. His grandparents, Frank and Frances Svoboda Vejtasa (originally Vejtasovych), had been born in Moravia, now part of the Czech Republic. Frank came to Omaha, Nebraska, in 1880 and drove a one-horse streetcar there for two years. He saved enough money by 1884 that he and Frances could start a homestead east of present Fairdale, North Dakota, just a half mile from an Indian camp.[14]

The Vejtasas raised seven boys and four girls while farming the Walsh County, North Dakota, land where the buffalo and Indians still roamed freely. Times were tough, but their oldest son, John Vejtasa, put himself through college in Minnesota, becoming one of the first in his family to achieve this distinction. John married Inga Rinnhaugen of Minnesota, whose parents who had emigrated from Norway. Their first daughter, Mildred, was born in 1911 and three years later, their first son, Stanley Vejtasa, was born in Paris, Montana. John had decided to take advantage of the 1909 Enlarged Homestead Act, which provided 320 acres to farmers who accepted marginal lands in the Great Plains that could not be easily irrigated.[15]

Young Stan Vejtasa was raised on his family's land in the rugged backcountry of eastern Montana, where he and his sister Mildred helped with their younger siblings. Stanley followed in his father's footsteps by attending college both at the Montana State College in Bozeman and at the University of Montana in Missoula. Vejtasa enlisted in the U.S. Naval Reserves on September 15, 1937, was appointed an Aviation Cadet in July 1938, and had earned his gold wings one year later. He was commissioned as an ensign in August 1939, and was assigned to Scouting Five. During his first eighteen months of flying, Stan Vejtasa proved his abilities to skipper Curt Smiley and then Bill Burch. By the end of 1941, twenty-seven-year-old Vejtasa had racked up nearly thirteen hundred hours of flight time.[16]

The only real problem he had was with his European name. The pronunciation of Vejtasa (VAY-tuh-suh) would give Stan trouble all his life. Even during training at Norfolk, skipper Burch could not master it. In front of the squadron, Burch once quipped, "He's blond. He must be a Swede." In his office, the skipper later admitted to Vejtasa that he found his name too difficult to pronounce.

"So," he said, "you are now Swede." And with that, Stanley Vejtasa became known to all who flew with him as "Swede" from that day forward.

Swede had no problem with the new nickname. In fact, he had his own for Bill Burch—"the Natural." "There was no aviator in the world like Bill Burch," he said. "I don't give a damn what it was, he could fly that airplane and it was just like it was second nature to him." Vejtasa flew the number-two position on Lieutenant Commander Burch quite often. Burch was the ultimate teacher, showing Swede various maneuvers, such as how to utilize the sun, wind, and clouds when approaching a target. "It was automatic with Burch," Swede said. He could instantly size up a weather formation and determine the best direction from which to achieve the element of surprise with his dive-bomber.[17]

Lieutenant Commander William Oscar Burch Jr. was a Kentucky native who had graduated in 1927 from the Naval Academy in Annapolis, Maryland. One of his junior pilots described the thirty-seven-year-old Burch as a tall, slim man "with thinning blond hair and piercing, pale blue eyes. He had an intense yet mild manner and normally talked in a low voice, which would increase in intensity and volume as he became excited." Burch had first been assigned to VS-5 on March 29, 1940, as the unit's operations officer. He advanced to executive officer (XO), and in May 1941 he took the position of Curt Smiley, his former commanding officer (CO). Smiley had been elevated to the command of the entire *Yorktown* Air Group, replacing outgoing Bill Rees.[18]

When Scouting Five traded its obsolete Curtiss SBC-4 biplane scout bombers for eighteen new monoplane SBD-3 Dauntless dive-bombers in July 1941, it was a whole new game for Burch. Swede felt that the SBD "was a helluva fine airplane." He learned from his instructor how to utilize this new dive-bomber in combat situations. "Normally you'd think that sort of thing would be applicable to fighter squadrons only, but that didn't bother him a bit," Swede said of Burch. "He felt that with any airplane in every formation you had to be able to protect yourself."

Burch drilled wingman Vejtasa endlessly on the best ways to duck and dodge opponents with his SBD and how to bring them into a line of fire. "Bill could maneuver that airplane and he was always telling me where to fly on him so that he could maneuver," said Swede. "This was the trick and we did it, time and again. In individual combat, he was an artist."

Scouting Five had returned from a cruise on the carrier *Ranger* when Bill Burch took command. His squadron spent the next two months

at Norfolk before participating in the September Lousiana war
There, Burch taught his VS-5 pilots to fly aggressively—counter-
maneuvering and even dogfighting—against the opposing Red Army
aviators. Whether flying with a full division or only with a wingman, he
was known to taunt his fellow fighter pilots. In early 1941, the fighter
boys had F3F biplanes, while the bomber squadrons had old SBC biplanes. "Attack us at any time!" Burch would advise his fighter escorts,
who were enthusiastic to partake of the opportunity. "I don't give a damn
what it was, I never saw him get trapped. He was watching all the time,"
Vejtasa said of his skipper.[19]

Swede flew in Bill Burch's section during the Louisiana war games.
"Every mission was simulated combat of some sort, searching, attacking
tanks, vehicle trains, enemy troops and repelling enemy fighters," said
Swede. "I learned more of the art of handling a number of aircraft,
achieving the most advantageous position, executing the attack maneuver and rendezvousing the group expeditiously." To Vejtasa, the most
interesting aspect of flying with Burch was the timing and execution of
the proper Dauntless counteraction against enemy fighters. "Bitching the
VF was the name of the game," said Swede, "and I was learning from the
master."[20]

Scouting Five had returned to Norfolk by October 1, whereupon Burch
and his capable executive officer, Lieutenant Wally Short—a 1932
Naval Academy graduate from New York—began solidifying the pilot
base they would take to war.

They had a solid core of senior pilot officers. Third in seniority of
VS-5 as flight officer (FO) was Lieutenant Turner Foster Caldwell Jr., a
twenty-eight-year-old originally from Pennsylvania who had graduated
from the academy three years after Short. Next in seniority came Lieutenant Elbert Miller "Steve" Stever, a dark-haired New Yorker with boy-
ish good looks who was a 1935 academy classmate of Caldwell. Rounding
out VS-5's full lieutenants were Charlie Ware, Roger Woodhull, and
Stockton Birney Strong, the latter two 1937 academy graduates. *Lucky
Bag*, the yearbook of the Naval Academy, described six-foot-tall, blond-
haired, handsome bachelor Birney Strong as possessing great self-control,
an "infectious smile," and "good common sense."

Eight other seasoned pilots had been with the squadron since March 29, 1940: Lieutenants (j.g.) Swede Vejtasa, Earl Johnson, Art Downing, Frederic Faulkner, and Ensigns Walton Austin, Hugh Nicholson, Bill Hall, and Thomas Reeves. One day after returning from Louisiana, Burch began receiving ensigns freshly graduated from NAS Miami and Jacksonville. Each sported brand-new gold wing insignias on his uniform, but most of them had little or no experience flying Dauntless dive-bombers. It would be up to "the Natural" and his seasoned pilots to break them in during late 1941.

First to arrive on October 2 were Ensigns Samuel Jackson Underhill, Kendall Carl Campbell, and Walter Wesley Coolbaugh. Campbell, who hailed from Garden City, Kansas, had earned his wings on August 19. Coolbaugh and Underhill were more recent graduates, just one day out of Florida training when they were ordered to VS-5. Walt Coolbaugh was raised on Skyline Farm, near Clarks Summit, Pennsylvania. He had been a student in the first CPTP (civilian pilot training program) at Keystone Junior College and was attending American University in Washington, DC, on a scholarship in 1940 when he received his appointment as an aviation cadet. Sam Underhill was an Ivy Leaguer from Jericho, New York. He earned his bachelor's degree from Yale and was attending Harvard Law School when he enlisted in the Naval Reserve in November 1940.

Scouting Five added five more rookie pilots during the next six weeks. Ensign Harry Travers joined on October 6, followed three weeks later by Ensign Elmer Maul of Eaton, Colorado. Ensign Edward Blaine Kinzer from Rock, West Virginia, earned his wings on October 20 and joined VS-5 on November 12. Rounding out Bill Burch's new pilots were Ensigns Lawrence Gilworth Traynor and John Harry Jorgenson, who joined the squadron on November 23.

Larry Traynor was the youngest of three brothers born in the Adirondacks of New York. His mother died of cancer when he was six and his father was killed five years later by a hit-and-run driver. Ray, Harry, and Larry Traynor were shuffled between family members, and Larry even spent one stretch of his young life sleeping in a hayloft. The Traynor boys were taken in by an uncle who became their permanent guardian, and young Larry graduated from St. Lawrence University in 1940. His brother

U.S. Navy

Ensign Larry "Link" Traynor of VS-5.

Harry enlisted in the U.S. Army while Ray and Larry joined the Navy to become aviators.[21]

During college, Larry was a star hockey, football, and baseball player—and good enough as a shortstop to consider going pro. His nickname was "Pie," in honor of Hall of Fame third baseman Harold "Pie" Traynor of the Pittsburgh Pirates. His nickname changed to "Link" Traynor during his 1941 aviation cadet program because of the Link Aviation Devices pilot flight simulator known as a Link Trainer. The rotating machine, also called the "blue box," had a bright blue fuselage with yellow wings and tail sections that responded to a pilot's controls. Link received his gold wings and commission on November 1 and was sent from Florida straight to advanced carrier training groups (ACTG) in Norfolk. "I had not qualified in the SBD aboard a carrier," Link admitted. "I had qualified in an SNJ during training."

Such was the state of *Yorktown*'s VS-5—a mixed bag of veterans and green rookies—when Hawaii was assaulted on December 7. Captain Elliott Buckmaster received orders the next day to prepare his carrier for war. During the next week, *Yorktown* was overhauled as Norfolk Navy Yard personnel added heavier antiaircraft guns to the ship. Torpedo Five (VT-5) was ordered to reduce its number from eighteen to twelve Douglas TBD Devastator torpedo planes in order to make room for another half dozen dive-bombers.

The skipper, Lieutenant Commander Joseph Franklin Taylor, was as tough as they came. Three days after he had taken command of VT-5 on June 3, 1941, he suffered a horrific crash while landing his unlucky 5-T-13 on *Yorktown*. His Devastator hit the ramp and cartwheeled into the ocean, taking his copilot down with it. Joe Taylor broke through his canopy as the TBD sank toward the depths. He and his radioman were hauled aboard by an escorting destroyer and transferred back to *York-town*. Taylor was a mess. Broken bones protruded through his hands, his arms were gashed open, his face was lacerated, and his pelvis was broken in two places. Taylor was hospitalized at Portsmouth, where doctors gave him little hope to fly again. The persistent aviator, however, was back in command of VT-5 in a mere three months. No pilot who flew a TBD with Taylor would ever question his determination or abilities.[22]

Yorktown's fighter squadron was Fighting Forty-Two, which flew the F4F-3 Wildcat fighter plane. Her original VF-5 had been replaced by VF-42 in 1941 due to the former squadron's still sporting older biplane fighters. Normally, each of the carrier's squadrons sported the carrier's hull number—the numeral 5 in *Yorktown*'s case—but VF-42 on CV-5 proved to be an exception heading into World War II. The other half of the *Yorktown* Air Group, Bombing Five and Scouting Five, flew Dauntless dive-bombers.[23]

Yorktown finally departed Hampton Roads on the night of December 16 with four destroyers, bound for the Panama Canal and the Pacific. Commander Curt Smiley's air group flew ashore at Panama while their carrier transited the canal locks on December 21. Link Traynor, Henry Travers, Elmer Maul, and other VS-5 rookies were carrier-qualified in the SBD during this voyage.

Yorktown's SBDs landed at the Army's Albrook Field in the seaport of Colón on Manzanillo Island. Roger Woodhull damaged his SBD upon landing and spent his time helping ground crews change his crumpled left wing. The dirt airfield was saturated with rain, and Lieutenant Wally Short inadvertently led a train of his VS-5 pilots through a mud hole that buried their landing gear. "If there had existed any doubt as to whether VS-5 pilots would follow their leaders through 'hell and high water,' all fears as to the high water were proven groundless," wrote Lieutenant (j.g.) Art Downing.[24]

Rocky Glidewell used his weight of a dozen years of naval service to convince Army personnel to put extra effort into quickly servicing every aircraft of his group. Commander Smiley's air group departed Panama the next day and landed back on board their carrier as *Yorktown* entered the Pacific Ocean.[25]

The only mishap en route occurred on December 23, when Charlie

Ware of VS-5 crashed his SBD in the drink during takeoff. The plane-guard destroyer *Russell* quickly retrieved Ware and radioman Joe Roll without serious injury and the task group reached San Diego on December 30. There, *Yorktown*'s task force officially became known as Task Force 17 (TF-17), and Rear Admiral Frank Jack Fletcher came on board on New Year's Day 1942 to command these ships. Fletcher, a fifty-six-year-old non-aviator, had previously commanded cruiser task groups but soon proved willing to go the extra mile for his aviators. His TF-17 was assigned to safeguard the passage of the 2nd Marine Division to the Pacific island of Samoa. *Yorktown* made final preparations for war during the ensuing week at San Diego. When she departed the West Coast on January 6, she was in company with two cruisers, four destroyers, a tanker, and three transport ships filled with Marines. *Yorktown* additionally carried thirty-two spare aircraft for delivery to Pearl Harbor.[26]

The trip toward Samoa took more than a week. Bill Burch found the voyage to be "one of continuous patrol and scouting" for his VS-5 bunch. The monotony was broken only by the traditional crossing of the equator ceremony on January 14. Pollywogs were converted to "shellbacks" during a day of bizarre rituals to indoctrinate the lowly newbies. Art Downing found that "necessary watches 'for the line,' gooney-bird patrols, anti-mermaid squads, and King Neptune–welcoming committees" were among the assignments he and other VS-5 pollywogs faced.[27]

Yorktown approached within 275 miles of Samoa on January 19, whereupon Admiral Fletcher sent the troop transports and their escort ships ahead for their landings. The following day, *Yorktown* provided air cover as the Marines landed. Fletcher received word from Admiral Halsey that day that his TF-17 and Halsey's TF-8 were to make offensive air strikes against Japanese-held positions in the Marshall and Gilbert Islands about a week after the Samoan landings were completed.

The carrier strikes were scheduled to occur around February 1. These actions by *Yorktown* and her sister carrier, *Enterprise*, would mark the first showing of offensive force against the Japanese since the Pearl Harbor attack nearly two months prior. Admiral Nimitz's plan called for each carrier group to approach its target islands separately but to launch simultaneous attacks. Nimitz had only two other fleet carriers in the Pacific by late January, the larger sister flattops *Lexington* and *Saratoga*.

Captain Ted Sherman's *Lexington* put to sea on January 7 from Hawaii, flying the flag of Vice Admiral Wilson Brown's Task Force 11, with orders to patrol near Johnston Island. *Lexington* was spotted by a Japanese submarine two days later, and several I-boats were pulled from Hawaiian waters to pursue her.

Lady Lex's good-luck charm was apparently more potent that that of Sister Sara. On January 11, *Saratoga* was slammed by a torpedo amidships from the submarine *I-6*. She struggled back to Pearl Harbor a week later with serious damage. The lion's share of her air group was retained at Oahu as replacements for other carrier groups, while *Saratoga* was sent stateside for full torpedo-damage repairs and modernization. On January 21, Admiral Brown's TF-11 was notified that the *Lexington* Air Group was to make a strike against Japanese forces on Wake Island. Admiral Nimitz sent the tanker *Neches* to refuel the task group en route to the strike area. The planned raid was foiled by another Japanese submarine, which sank *Neches* just 135 miles southwest of Oahu on January 23. *Lexington*'s air group would not be able to make the Wake strikes and fight its way back out without fuel. The dejected aviators learned that they were once again heading back to Hawaii to refuel, having contributed little to slow the Japanese war machine in two full months of battle cruising.[28]

The Marshalls–Gilberts raids were thus entrusted to *Yorktown* and *Enterprise*. The *Enterprise* Air Group would concentrate on Wotje, Maloelap, and Kwajalein in the Marshalls. The *Yorktown* Air Group would hit Jaluit and Mili in the southern Marshalls and also the new Japanese conquest of Makin Atoll in the northern Gilbert Islands. The weather turned nasty as *Yorktown* approached the Marshalls and Gilberts on January 31. Staff aerologists predicted foul weather again the following morning, but the *Yorktown* and *Enterprise* strikers were committed to America's first offensive carrier strikes, good weather or bad.

THREE

"Hit-and-Run Attack in Impossible Weather"

Breakfast came early for Chief Rocky Glidewell on February 1. He and his fellow *Yorktown* aviators were roused at 0300 for coffee and scrambled eggs. Bill Burch gathered Scouting Five's aviators in their ready room for last-minute reviews of their strike objectives. Cigarette smoke hung heavy in the air as pilots scribbled important data on their chart boards. It was crucial for all involved to understand Point Option—the place in the ocean where their carrier was expected to be upon returning from their strikes.

Yorktown's deck trembled beneath Glidewell's feet as she raced ahead at 25.5 knots with the cruisers *Louisville* and *St. Louis* close by. Task Force 17's destroyers trailed at a more fuel-conserving pace, while the other three warships dashed toward the launch point. Glidewell made his way to the flight deck early to ensure that everything was in order with air group commander Curt Smiley's command SBD.

Flight crews scurried about in the rain-whipped darkness as they checked aircraft engines, guns, and bomb loads. Shortly after 0415, the loudspeakers blared, "Pilots, man your planes!"

Thirty-two planes erupted into a series of bright blue exhaust flames as engines were cranked over. Four Wildcats for combat air patrol (CAP) were first off the deck at 0452. Dark clouds obscured the horizon and lightning flashed ominously to the northwest, in the direction of Jaluit. Commander Smiley and Rocky Glidewell were next off the deck, leading

Yorktown's first strike group of seventeen SBDs and eleven TBDs. The island structure catwalks—known as "Vulture's Row"—were packed with spectators to watch the first battle launch against Japanese-held territory.[1]

Lieutenant Commander Bob Armstrong, skipper of Bombing Five, followed with sixteen of his squadron. Fighting Forty-Two was retained for task force protection, leaving the bombers and torpedo bombers unescorted for their strike. Bob Armstrong had been reared on farms in Nebraska, Oklahoma, and Illinois, where he made spare money trapping beaver and muskrat for pelts to sell. He graduated from the Naval Academy in 1926 along with Lieutenant Commander Bill "Holly" Hollingsworth. The two buddies later became brothers-in-law by marrying sisters Thelma and Mildred Stallworth. Bob Armstrong took command of *Yorktown*'s VB-5 in early 1941, when Murr Edward Arnold moved up to become *Yorktown*'s air officer. Approaching thirty-eight years of age, Armstrong was nicknamed "Pappy" by his younger pilots and enlisted men. As fate would have it, Pappy and his brother-in-law, Holly Hollingsworth, were both leading their respective dive-bomber squadrons from *Yorktown* and *Enterprise* into the predawn skies on February 1 to finally strike back against the powerful Imperial Japanese Navy.[2]

Each SBD throttled down the darkened flight deck and pulled up into complete darkness, switching to instruments as soon as the plane was in the air. Armstrong's dive-bombers were followed by eleven TBDs of Torpedo Five—all loaded with three five-hundred-pound bombs versus the usual torpedo load. It was by far the worst weather the *Yorktown* Air Group had ever launched in. "It was impossible for the group and squadron leaders to determine whether all planes were in formation on departure," Smiley noted. *Yorktown*'s crews respotted her deck with fourteen SBDs of Bill Burch's VS-5, slated to launch right behind Smiley's lead bunch.[3]

Armstrong spent forty-five minutes sweeping around the carrier in gentle turns to allow his bombers to form on him. He took departure from *Yorktown* about 0535, at a 110-knot cruising speed in order not to outdistance Joe Taylor's slower Devastators. About a half hour out from the ship, they encountered a nasty squall, which further divided the squadrons and blocked their aproach to Jaluit. "Lousy luck to come this far to try to crank up the Navy's and the country's morale only to have this kind of weather," wrote Seaman Second Class Lynn Forshee, an Iowan rear gunner flying with VB-5's Ensign Jim Crawford.[4]

As low as fifty feet, the scattered SBD pilots relied on instruments to navigate to Jaluit through the powerful storm. Two of the circling SBDs, belonging to VB-5 executive officer Lieutenant George Bellinger and Ensign Mike Fishel, collided in midair near Jaluit. Also lost in this tragedy were Bellinger's radioman, Radioman First Class Donald MacKillop, and Fishel's gunner, Radioman Second Class Leonard Wilson Costello. All Pappy Armstrong saw were two bright flashes, which he presumed to be lightning.[5]

Others had near-fatal bouts with disorientation and vertigo in the storm. Bill Christie and Jeff Bigelow each nearly spun into the ocean before regaining control of their SBDs. Smiley climbed to a higher altitude to help direct his air group's attacks. His rear-seat man, Rocky Glidewell, was blessed with excellent vision, and he helped to point out the targets of opportunity. "Our aerial opposition this day was not fighters but flak," Glidewell recalled. "This was where they started separating the men from the boys. Older pilots were not as aggressive as younger pilots, I realized, because I flew with an older pilot."[6]

Once it was light enough to see, the pilots still struggled with finding enough breaks in the clouds to zero in on their targets in Jaluit's harbor. Armstrong made his dive at 0725 from nine thousand feet. He and wingmen Johnny Nielsen and John "Jo Jo" Powers missed a large merchant ship due to fogged windscreens and bombsights. Lieutenant Sam Adams and his second section bombed various merchant ships. "We couldn't see anything, and I didn't have the slightest idea where I was diving," Ensign Dave Berry admitted.[7]

Lieutenant Keith Taylor, unable to find his objective in the overcast, finally returned to the ship with two VT-5 pilots. Jeff Bigelow landed his bomb seventy-five feet off the after port side of a large, undamaged freighter in the anchorage. Ensign Ben Preston and gunner Harry Cowden spotted a tanker through the overcast, but had to circle for half an hour before they could find a large enough break in the clouds to dive through. Facing antiaircraft fire from the Japanese sailors below, Preston achieved only a near miss ahead of the tanker.[8]

Lieutenant Bill Guest and Ensign Hank McDowell attacked the 8,600-ton transport *Kanto Maru*. Guest's five-hundred-pounder struck her stern and created a large fire. Rear gunners Otto Phelps and Clay Strickland strafed ships and Japanese structures on the shore as Guest and McDowell retired. Bill Christie made a near miss on *Kanto Maru* while Ensign Orest Houghton started a fire near a small building with his bombs. Jim Crawford released at two thousand feet on an administrative building. "Debris, smoke, and flames shot up," said his gunner, Lynn Forshee. "On our pullout we passed over a ship in the harbor and Mr. Crawford strafed with his 50s. I began strafing with the .30-caliber. Mr. Crawford thought my tracers were enemy fire and banked to take me off target."[9]

Joe Taylor's Torpedo Five had even worse luck over Jaluit. Only Lieutenant (j.g.) Tom Ellison claimed a hit on a merchant ship. Two VT-5 Devastators were damaged by flak and were forced to ditch alongside one of the northwestern islands of Jaluit. Lieutenant Harlan "Dub" Johnson and Ensign Herbie Hein took to their rubber rafts with their crewmen and rowed ashore to one of the little islands. They were taken in by natives, but the six airmen were captured by a Japanese patrol two days later. They would spend the rest of the war as POWs.[10]

Commander Smiley's first *Yorktown* strike group had only damaged the transport *Kanto Maru* with one direct hit, and caused minor damage to the transport *Daido Maru* from near misses. His pilots had also strafed a radio station, shore installations, and various shipping, but lost two SBDs and four TBDs in action. Only six of the sixteen aviators aboard these planes had survived, and they had fallen into enemy hands.[11]

Bill Burch's Scouting Five was next into action on February 1. He launched from *Yorktown* at 0537, less than twenty minutes after Smiley's first strike group. His nine SBDs, all armed with five-hundred-pound bombs, were under orders to attack Makin Island. Burch's group made an effective rendezvous on *Yorktown*'s starboard side and headed out for their target area by 0600.

Lieutenant Turner Caldwell, leading Burch's second section of the first division, was a realist. The Navy had not yet developed air-sea rescue operations for downed pilots in early 1942, so "every flight was potentially your last." Swede Vejtasa, flying the tail-end section for this strike, had trust in Burch's ability to get them through the mission. "He seemed like he knew everything and did everything right immediately and I don't know why because he had no more combat experience than the rest of us," he said. As the Japanese-held island appeared on the horizon, Vejtasa was eager to put his SBD through the paces against the enemy.[12]

Gunner Al Garlow kept a sharp eye out for Makin from the rear cockpit of Roger Woodhull's third section SBD. At about 0645, he could clearly see the Japanese-held island from VS-5's low altitude of seven hundred feet. The weather was better than what the Jaluit strikers had experienced. Bill Burch led his nine dive-bombers in a climb to twelve thousand feet to attack. "There was one large ship that looked like a seaplane tender near the north end of the anchorage," said Garlow. "At the southeast end were two four-engine patrol planes in the water." Garlow had spotted a pair of floating Kawanishi H6K Type 97 flying boats and the 2,900-ton aircraft transport/gunboat *Nagata Maru*, riding at anchor.[13]

Burch pushed over first shortly before 0700. "It appeared that the ship had sighted us and was trying to get under way," said his gunner, Oliver Grew. Photographer John Pflaum, flying in Tom Reeves's 5-S-2, noted a large cloud of black smoke rising from the ship's stack "and a small wake appeared at her stern" as *Nagata Maru* headed for shallow water. Grew and others agreed that the skipper landed his bomb on the seaplane tender's afterdeck. The next pilot down was Birney Strong. His gunner, Radioman Second Class John Hurley from Boston, saw "a sheet of flame 100 feet high" leap from the ship as Burch's bomb hit, followed by the explosion of his own pilot's bomb. *Nagata Maru* was covered with spray as fires broke out, destroying her planes on deck.[14]

Behind Strong, Tom Reeves and Turner Caldwell added near misses alongside the maneuvering seaplane tender. The next to dive were Fritz Faulkner and his wingman, Ensign Bill Hall, who had majored in music at Redlands University in California before joining the Navy in 1938. Diving toward the Makin anchorage, Ensign Hall struggled to see through his fogged-over inner windshield. He saw at least two bombs ahead of him fall a little wide and aft of the seaplane tender. Hall found that "antiaircraft fire was practically nil" through much of the action although his gunner, Onni Kustula, reported one gun had fired at them during their bombing run.[15]

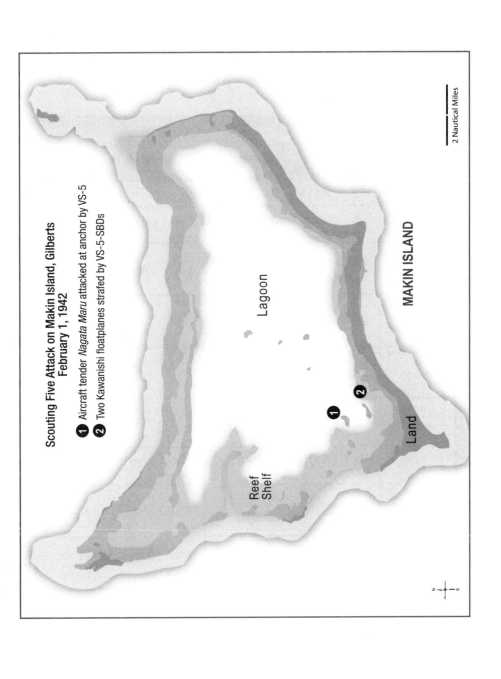

Scouting Five Attack on Makin Island, Gilberts
February 1, 1942

① Aircraft tender *Nagata Maru* attacked at anchor by VS-5
② Two Kawanishi floatplanes strafed by VS-5-SBDs

Reef
Shelf

Lagoon

Land

MAKIN ISLAND

2 Nautical Miles

Roger Woodhull, seventh to dive, saw a dark red flame shooting up from the ship's stern where his comrades had already landed at least one bomb. Swede Vejtasa was the last to dive on the tender. He saw smoke and fire from Burch's bomb hit but was plagued with a fogged-over windshield and bombsight. He could not tell where his bomb had landed, but

Yorktown's Gilbert Islands Strikes February 1, 1942		
Makin Island Strike, VS-5 (9 SBDs)		
PLANE	**PILOT**	**REAR-SEAT GUNNER**
5-S-1	Lt. Cdr. William Oscar Burch Jr.	CRM Oliver Wendell Grew
5-S-5	Lt. Stockton Birney Strong	RM2c John F. Hurley
5-S-2	Ens. Thomas A. Reeves	Pho2c John V. Pflaum
5-S-6	Lt. Turner Foster Caldwell Jr.	RM2c Leon Hall
5-S-7	Lt. (j.g.) Frederic Lewis Faulkner	Sea2c Charles Joseph Bonness
5-S-8	Ens. William Edward Hall	RM3c Onni Emil Kustula
5-B-1	Lt. Roger Blake Woodhull	RM2c Albert Woodrow Garlow
5-B-2	Lt. (j.g.) Stanley Winfield Vejtasa	Sea1c Frank Barton Wood
5-B-5	Ens. Walton Anderson Austin	RM3c Woodrow Andrew Fontenot

	Yorktown's Mili Island Strike Scouting Five SBDs: February 1, 1942	
PLANE	PILOT	REAR-SEAT GUNNER
5-S-17	Lt. Wallace Clark Short Jr.	RM1c Carl Edgar Russ
5-B-11	Lt. Charles Rollins Ware	RM2c Joseph Ellsworth Roll
5-B-7	Lt. (j.g.) Arthur Latimer Downing	RM2c Elmer C. Jones
5-B-10	Lt. (j.g.) Earl Vincent Johnson	Sea1c Edgar W. Adams
5-B-13	Ens. Hugh Wilbur Nicholson	RM3c James Hedger Cales

upon pullout, he saw muddy patches where several bombs had struck close to the ship just off the starboard quarter.

Burch pulled out to the left and climbed to make strafing runs on the two big seaplanes anchored in the harbor. As he dropped to three thousand feet, he opened up with his forward .50-caliber guns on the Kawanishi floating to the right. "Tracers streaked down into it, and when I got down to 1,000 feet, it blew up right in the sights," Burch said.[16]

His other pilots took their turns at strafing the other Japanese flying boat but failed to set it on fire. Vejtasa's plane came under fire from batteries aboard *Nagata Maru* as he strafed the second Kawanishi. His gunner, Seaman First Class Barton Wood, stated, "One shell burst near us and jarred us slightly. We then gained altitude and strafed the second plane." Next in line was Ensign Walton "Red" Austin. Born in Stevenson, Alabama, Red Austin was one of four brothers who had all entered military service. He graduated from Georgia Tech in 1934 and had been an

ARM1c Jim Cales (*in the rear cockpit of his VS-5 Dauntless*) with pilot Red Austin in September 1941 during the Louisiana Maneuvers.

instructor at the Tennessee Military Institute in Sweetwater before joining the Navy. In 1936, Austin had set a national speed and distance record in swimming from Hales Bar, Tennessee, to Guntersville—a distance of eighty-seven miles in twenty-nine hours and thirteen minutes. Now Austin lined up on the second Kawanishi and poured a multitude of tracers into it. The big flying boat, however, stubbornly refused to catch fire.

"I got on the radio and asked if anyone had any ammunition left," Burch stated. "Turner Caldwell said he had."

Scouting Five's skipper then called, "Get that plane!"

As Caldwell made another run on the Kawanishi, the flying boat's crew opened fire on the SBD. "After two short sighting-in bursts, I fired a string of about twenty shots into the plane, which immediately burst into a large ball of fire," Caldwell reported. "An enemy gunner was firing at me from a turret aft of the wing until I started to shoot." The big seaplane blew up in what Burch deemed "a tremendous explosion."[17]

Scouting Five's bombing and strafing of *Nagata Maru* left her running for shallow water to beach herself. Chief Grew in Burch's rear seat believed that the tender, when last seen, was settling badly at the stern. Burch's nine SBD crews soon rendezvoused, and all had landed safely back on board *Yorktown* by around 0800.

The third contingent of *Yorktown* SBDs to launch on February 1 had been that of VS-5's executive officer, Lieutenant Wally Short. His five-plane group, lined up right behind Bill Burch's SBDs at about 0600, was assigned to attack Mili, seventy miles northeast of their ship.[18]

Short found the lagoon without shipping, so he led his SBDs down to three thousand feet for a closer inspection of Mili's potential targets.

He found only a large barn-shaped storehouse on the island west of Tokawa Island. He led the first three-plane section to attack it, but Short missed the mark with his bomb. Charlie Ware circled overhead to reconnoiter the first section's attack while his rear-seat man, Joe Roll, snapped pictures of the attack. Second to dive was Ensign Hugh "Nick" Nicholson, a thirty-year-old graduate of Indiana University who had been a schoolteacher in Bloomington before becoming an aviation cadet. His bomb also missed the warehouse.

Earl Johnson was close on Nick's heels. Johnson, the "perennial Don Juan" of Scouting Five, per his buddy Art Downing, hailed from Winthrop, Minnesota, and was the eldest son of a doctor. Johnson and gunner Edgar Adams missed with their bombs, and Ware was stuck with a dud bomb. Art Downing moved south to Mili after losing his division's other four planes. Described by one of his junior pilots as "tall and dark, with rugged, handsome features," Downing had been nicknamed "Goocher" for his strong sense of "subtle humor." He dropped his bomb toward a pair of small tanks behind a little village. "I observed no fires so concluded I had destroyed the natives' supply of fresh water," Downing said. His gunner, Elmer Jones, saw the inhabitants "fleeing in all general directions."[19]

Wally Short's division, although last to depart *Yorktown* that morning, was the first to return due to their shorter flying distance. Bob Armstrong's Jaluit strikers straggled back and began landing at 0858—after Burch's and Short's groups had already landed. *Yorktown*'s deck crews refueled and rearmed an anti-torpedo-plane patrol drawn from fourteen of the VS-5 SBDs of the newly returned Mili and Makin attack groups. As these planes took off, a violent thunderstorm reduced visibility and produced winds gusting up to fifty knots.[20]

Tom Reeves, flying the VS-5 anti-torpedo-plane patrol, crashed at 0940 during the heavy squall, close aboard on *Hughes*'s port quarter. He had been flying at two hundred feet in blinding rain when the engine of his 5-S-2 cut out. Reeves and his gunner, Seaman Second Class Lonnie Gooch, took to their rubber boat as the destroyer *Walke* moved in. At 1003, her motor whaleboat picked up Reeves, who was suffering from a severe scalp wound. Gooch seemed to be injured internally. At 1108, after *Walke*'s pharmacist's mate stitched up Reeves's head and tried to ease Gooch's pain, both aviators were transferred to the cruiser *Louis-ville* for further treatment.[21]

One of the surviving Kawanishi flying boats from Jaluit pestered the destroyers searching for downed aviators until *Yorktown*'s CAP was called in. Fighting 42's ensigns Elbert Scott McCuskey and Johnny Adams pursued the Japanese plane as it approached *Yorktown*. Moments later, they blew it apart, and its flaming wreckage crashed into the sea. A jubilant McCuskey broke radio silence to whoop, "We just shot his ass off!" McCuskey and Adams were mobbed by the flight deck crew upon their return at 1430. They had scored the carrier's first aerial victory against a Japanese aircraft.[22]

The foul weather and plane losses compelled Fletcher to cancel a second strike against Jaluit that he had contemplated. The task force withdrew toward Pearl Harbor, with VT-5 mourning the loss of a dozen aviators and VB-5 down over the loss of two pilots and two gunners. Scouting Five's Birney Strong felt, "The weather was very, very rotten. It was not any fun flying but it was an excellent attack to introduce a combat unit into war."[23]

Yorktown reached Pearl Harbor at noon on February 6 and for the first time her crew saw the results of the Pearl Harbor attack. Tony Brunetti of VS-5 recalled, "The crew, mostly up on the flight deck, was deathly silent as we counted the seven sunken battleships and the still-smoking wreckage of installations on the beaches." The images would haunt young Brunetti for years. He developed a hatred for his country's enemy and longed for *Yorktown*'s next opportunity to strike back.[24]

The *Yorktown* Air Group flew ashore to a warm welcome at the Marine base on Ewa Field. "As we cut engines, a bus drove up to the planes and we were handed a paper welcoming us and 'ordering' us to the Royal Hawaiian Hotel for a forty-eight-hour rest," recalled Lieutenant Commander Burch. Swede Vejtasa saw the devastated battleship *Pennsylvania* and the destroyer *Shaw*, smashed in her dry dock. As soon as Swede landed at Ewa, he and other pilots grabbed brooms to clean off the runway. "There was so much brass and empty shells and bullets on the runway that we couldn't operate, so we had it swept down," he said.[25]

Art Downing found only a few flies in the ointment on Oahu: "Liquor had gone, and an eight o'clock curfew was enforced for all hands."

During the stay in port, VS-5 lost three veteran pilots. Charlie Ware was assigned to *Enterprise*'s VS-6, Bill Hall was assigned to the air station pending a transfer to *Lexington*'s VS-2, and Tommy Reeves remained at the air station to recover from his scalp wounds.[26]

Yorktown pilot Johnny Nielsen swapped tales at the Royal Hawaiian with some of the newly returned *Enterprise* SBD pilots. He learned their weather had been good enough for multiple strikes to be flown, far different from the opportunities afforded his own carrier. The first combat against Japanese-held soil had been far less satisfying for *Yorktown*'s air group than it had been for the Big E's air group. "We had made a hit-and-run attack in impossible weather," said Nielsen.[27]

FOUR

"I Wanted to Hit 'em Hard"

Lexington, officially the flagship of Vice Admiral Wilson Brown's Task Force 11, set sail again from Pearl Harbor on January 31, 1942. Lieutenant Commander John Smith "Jimmy" Thach's Fighting Three—laid up in Oahu since *Saratoga* was torpedoed—stepped in as temporary replacements for Lieutenant Commander Paul Ramsey's VF-2 for this cruise.

The Lady Lex passed over the equator on February 5, and Captain Ted Sherman allowed his crew to celebrate the age-old naval custom of conducting a line-crossing ceremony. "A little thing like war did not stop us from carrying on an old tradition," said VB-2's Ensign Arthur Behl, who was known as "Junior" back in his hometown of Lanark, Illinois. Behl's gunner was Aviation Radioman Third Class Joe Teyshak, who had been raised by his mother in the little town of Streater, Illinois, after his father died at an early age. As pollywogs, both Behl and Teyshak together endured the odd festivities of being transformed into veteran "shellbacks." Pollywogs were given bizarre haircuts, forced to run gauntlets of electric paddles, and forced to eat bizarre concoctions. Initiates went before the Royal Court for "sentencing" to receive their punishment for being a lowly pollywog. The Royal Jury included Commander Bill Ault, Bob Dixon, and Weldon Hamilton from the *Lexington* Air Group.[1]

Lexington received orders to help destroy Japanese advances toward the New Hebrides and key installations along the communication line between Australia and Pearl Harbor. Admiral Brown proposed using his air group to make a bombing raid at daybreak on February 21 on the base of Rabaul, where Japanese shipping and aircraft had been detected. TF-11 moved from the New Hebrides into the waters northeast of the Solomon Islands by February 19 and was soon paralleling the coast of Bougainville. On the morning of February 20, six of Bob Dixon's scouts were sent on a precautionary three-hundred-mile search mission.

Before the scouts returned, Jimmy Thach and his wingman shot down a big Kawanishi Type 97 four-engine flying boat coming out of Rabaul. It crashed and burned on the water within sight of *Lexington*. Admiral Brown decided to call off the strike two hours later, when VF-3 downed another snooper. By late afternoon, nine Rabaul bombers— Mitsubishi G4M1 "Bettys" with seven-man crews—moved in to attack the departing *Lexington* force. Lieutenant Noel Gayler's Wildcat division splashed three of the bombers as crews raced to man eleven fully fueled VS-2 dive-bombers still spotted on the flight deck. The Betty bombers were in sight on the horizon as the last of Bob Dixon's scouts scrambled aloft.[2]

The remaining Japanese bombers dropped their bombs on *Lexington*, but Captain Sherman ably dodged their efforts with violent maneuvers. One of the crippled Bettys, with one engine completely shot away, made a beeline for Lady Lex. Gunner Forest Stanley, seated in Mark Whittier's VB-2 Dauntless still spotted on deck, joined the ship's gunnery department in blazing away at the would-be kamikaze. The bomber slammed into the ocean just seventy-five yards astern of *Lexington* with an orange explosion and a black plume of smoke. Wayne Colley was similarly stranded in Ensign Art Schultz's VS-2 bomber. He managed to fire a few rounds of his .30-caliber machine gun before his wing was disabled by rounds from the ship's AA gunners. Colley, from that point, "had to sit in my cockpit and watch the fight."[3]

Lieutenant Edward Allen, the exec of Scouting Two, finished off another Betty near the task force with his twin nose guns. He became the first SBD pilot of the war to down an enemy bomber. Allen and his rear gunner, Aviation Radioman First Class Bruce Rountree, then shared in the kill of a second Betty. Not to be outdone, Lieutenant Walter Henry of VB-2 pursued the last departing Betty and blasted it into the ocean about eighty miles west of the task force.[4]

Lexington's radar showed a second wave of Japanese strikers inbound at 1649, and fighters were vectored out to intercept. These eight Betty bombers were engaged by Lieutenant (j.g.) Edward Henry "Butch" O'Hare and his VF-3 wingman a few miles astern of the task force. In his first pass, O'Hare destroyed two Bettys. He quickly shot down three more, becoming the Navy's first "ace" in one day, before exhausting his ammunition while firing on a sixth bomber. Of the Bettys that survived, the closest bomb to *Lexington* landed a hundred feet astern.[5]

Lexington's Wildcat and Dauntless aviators claimed as many as twenty Japanese planes destroyed in the day's action. In fact, fifteen of the seventeen Betty bombers either had been shot down or were forced to ditch due to battle damage. For their work as fighter pilots in dive-bombers, Lieutenants Henry and Allen became the first *Lexington* SBD pilots to receive the Navy Cross. Fighter pilot Butch O'Hare would soon be pinned with a Medal of Honor for helping to save *Lexington* from serious damage on February 20.

Task Force 11's Rabaul raid was canceled due to the heavy aerial opposition, forcing *Lexington* to withdraw to refuel. Wilson Brown sent a dispatch to Admiral Nimitz recommending that another carrier task group join his before another offensive was attempted. Thus were the wheels set in motion for Rear Admiral Fletcher's TF-17 to join with *Lexington* to conduct the next counterattack on Japanese bases.

Yorktown's Task Force 17 had already put to sea from Pearl Harbor on February 16 for southern waters and more action. Commander Curt Smiley's air group landed on the carrier that afternoon, fresh from several days ashore at Oahu. As *Yorktown* sailed south, her aviators were consumed with the usual training flights and daily searches and inner air patrols.

Lieutenant Johnny Nielsen of VB-5 ran out of fuel on February 21, north of Canton Island. He injured his face in the ensuing water landing, but he and gunner Dean Straub were rescued by the plane guard destroyer *Walke*. Three days later, on February 24, Lieutenant Steve Stever of VS-5 crashed over *Yorktown*'s port bow during takeoff. Stever's SBD smashed into the ocean on its back, and his arm was broken in the crash. Lieutenant Commander Thomas E. Fraser, skipper of the *Walke*, inducted Stever and his gunner into the "First Destroyer Aircraft Squadron," an organization comprising the four *Yorktown* pilots and gunners rescued by his ship. Nielsen and the two enlisted men were returned to their squadrons via the bosun's chair a week later during *Yorktown*'s refueling at sea. Johnny Nielsen was grounded due to his facial injuries, but Lieutenant Stever was sent to Pearl Harbor on board the oiler *Kaskaskia* for treatment.[6]

For Swede Vejtasa of VS-5, this period was marked by endless patrol flights. "This became a way of life," he recalled. There were scouting flights in the afternoons and anti-submarine patrols. The first thing he noticed was how much warmer it was operating close to the equator in SBD cockpits that had no air-conditioning. "Most of the boys got their faces and cheeks sunburned. The docs had us putting calamine lotion on there trying to help a bit. A few of the boys even sewed visors on their helmets."[7]

Yorktown's force rendezvoused with Vice Admiral Brown's carrier group on March 6 as plans for a joint carrier group raid on Rabaul began to take shape. Fletcher and Brown's offensive was modified two days later when word was received that Japanese armed forces had landed on the northeast coast of New Guinea. Intelligence placed a number of transports and other Japanese ships in the Gulf of Papua, near Port Moresby, where enemy troops had seized the coastal New Guinea towns of Lae and Salamaua. In the interim, Bill Halsey's *Enterprise* air group had pounded the recently conquered base at Wake Island on February 24 and followed up with a strike against Marcus Island on March 4.[8]

The U.S. Navy had a golden opportunity to strike the military forces and assembled shipping at Lae and Salamaua before they could be fully consolidated. *Lexington* Air Group commander Bill Ault and another SBD pilot flew to the air base at Townsville in northeastern Australia on March 9 to gather maps and more data on the area. He learned that his pilots would have to fly over the rugged 13,000-foot Owen Stanley Range to reach the Japanese shipping off New Guinea. The mountains had a

7,500-foot pass that lay almost on the direct line between the Gulf of Papua (on the western coast of New Guinea) and Salamaua. Ault returned to *Lexington* with this valuable data and hastily gathered maps, which gave Admiral Brown and Captain Sherman the confidence to proceed with the raid.[9]

Ted Sherman, directing the aerial assault, decided that his *Lexington* would launch her warplanes first, followed quickly by attack waves from *Yorktown*. He opted to arm Lieutenant Commander Jimmy Brett's VT-2 Devastators with two-thousand-pound aerial torpedoes for the tricky flight through the high-elevation mountain pass. As insurance, *Yorktown*'s VT-5 would carry only half the weight, in the form of two five-hundred-pound bombs per TBD. The two carriers would launch a total of 104 strike planes, 52 each, from a distance of about forty-five miles off the coast of New Guinea, from a point west of Port Moresby.

The weather was excellent in the Gulf of Papua as general quarters sounded on *Yorktown* at 0545 on March 10. After a quick breakfast, the aviators settled into their respective ready rooms for final briefings and to await the calls to man their aircraft. Shortly after *Yorktown* had launched an early CAP and four VS-5 Dauntlesses for anti-torpedo-plane patrol, *Lexington* began sending up her strike force at 0749.

Scouting Two's gunners had completed their preflight checkouts by the time their pilots raced across the flight deck to climb into their cockpits. Buddies Wayne Colley, J. B. Jewell, Lanny Wheeler, and Larry Craft were eager to put their two-plus years of training to the test. This was it—a real combat strike against the enemy at long last. Each of the friends silently hoped for the best. If any of the quartet was lost in action, the survivors had pledged to pay hometown visits to the families of those lost to pay their proper respects.

As *Lexington*'s air group prepared to launch, Mark Whittier of Bombing Two noticed "a single albatross soaring with grace and languid ease over our wake, a sign of good luck for any ship." Lieutenant Commander Jimmy Thach's eight VF-3 Wildcat escorts were followed off by eighteen SBDs of Bob Dixon's VS-2, CLAG Bill Ault, and another dozen VB-2 Dauntlesses under Weldon Hamilton. Last to launch were Jimmy Brett's thirteen torpedo-armed TBDs. Lieutenant Warren Welch's VB-2 division remained behind to handle Inner Air Patrol (IAP) duties for the task group.[10]

Yorktown delayed her launches in order to give the *Lexington* planes ample time to reach the target area first. Plane handlers had spotted the first twenty-five planes on deck—thirteen SBDs from Scouting Five and a dozen bomb-armed TBDs of Torpedo Five. Some planes had messages chalked on them, such as "Heads Up Below," and on the bombs phrases such as, "A Present from FDR."[11]

Yorktown turned into the wind at 0803 to begin launching. Bill Burch's Scouting Five was first off, followed by Joe Taylor's VT-5 TBDs. Lieutenant Commander Bob "Pappy" Armstrong next led up seventeen VB-5 Dauntlesses, followed by Lieutenant Commander Oscar Pederson with a ten-plane fighter group. *Yorktown*'s Dauntlesses were armed with a single five-hundred-pound bomb and a pair of hundred-pound wing bombs to use on ships in the Huon Gulf.

Bill Ault shepherded the two carrier strike groups through the high mountain pass between Mounts Chapman and Lawson on the New Guinea coast. Ensign Tom Ball from South Carolina, flying near the tail of Jim Newell's VB-2 division, was apprehensive as he approached with his bomb load. "I could see all that green below and I was really worried about making it over the pass," he said. Ball cleared the pass with more than a thousand feet to spare. Bombing Two and VS-2's Dauntlesses then commenced the forty-five-mile run to Lae and Salamaua on the coast of Huon Gulf.[12]

Salamaua Harbor was dead ahead, and Lae about twenty miles to the left. The *Lexington* Air Group caught sixteen ships of the Japanese invasion force without air cover. There were two army transports, *Yokohama Maru* and *China Maru*, off Salamaua. Off Lae, they found navy transports *Tenyo Maru* and *Kokai Maru*, along with the armed merchant cruiser *Kongo Maru*. These ships were screened by two Japanese destroyers, *Mutsuki* and *Yayoi*. In Huon Gulf lay the light cruiser *Yubari*, flagship of Rear Admiral Kajioka Sadamichi. Also present in this gulf were the large minelayer *Tsugaru* and three destroyers—*Yunagi*, *Oite* and *Asanagi*. Some twenty-five miles to the east of Lae was the air support force near Hanisch Harbor, composed of the seaplane tender *Kiyokawa Maru* and her escorting destroyer *Mochizuki*.[13]

Just after 0920, Bob Dixon's Scouting Two singled out the three transports at Lae to attack. These were the armed merchant cruiser *Kongo Maru*, moored alongside the dock at Lae, and the transports *Tenyo Maru* and *Kokai Maru*, anchored about a half mile offshore. Lieutenant Commander Dixon, Joe Smith, and Richard "Roscoe" Neely attacked *Kongo Maru*, and Ensign Neely was credited with scoring a direct hit. Lieutenant Bobby Edwards from Corpus Christi, Texas, was hampered by severe fogging of his inner windshield and gun sight as his section was next to dive. Edwards missed and wingman Pete Aurand was unable to get his five-hundred-pounder to release but Jack Leppla, flying tail-end Charlie for the first division, slammed home a direct hit.[14]

Scouting Two's second division—Lieutenant Edward Allen with Tony Quigley, Joe Johnson, Chandler Swanson, Harry Wood, and Art Schultz—was next to dive. Allen recorded one direct hit on a transport by Quigley, four near misses, and one bomb that failed to release. In the heat of action, Ensign Schultz also felt sure that his five-hundred-pounder was a direct hit. His rear gunner, Slim Colley, was more concerned with surviving his first combat mission. *So far, so good*, he thought. Schultz recovered from his dive and began closing on a division mate's Dauntless to join up. From his vantage point, Colley made out the side designation of 2-S-8. He knew in an instant it was Ensign Johnson's plane, in which his buddy J. B. Jewell was flying rear seat.[15]

Johnson was low on the water at two hundred feet as Schultz's dive-bomber approached. As they came within two hundred yards of each other, Colley waved excitedly to Jewell, who waved back. And then it happened.

A five-inch shell from a Japanese coastal battery slammed into Johnson's low-flying Sail-Eight plane, directly where Jewell was sitting. "I was looking at him and all of a sudden the plane just disintegrated," said Colley. The SBD split in half and plunged straight into the ocean, killing both Ensign Johnson and Aviation Radioman Third Class Jewell. As Colley stared at the crash site, Art Schultz swung their SBD back around and unleashed his remaining wing bombs against the transport.[16]

Although Schultz claimed a hit, Colley angrily felt that "the tactics were all wrong" on this first strike. In the process of first dropping their big bomb and then circling to make secondary runs with their small wing bombs, the Dauntless aircrews remained in positions of peril over a stirred-up enemy lagoon for upwards of a half hour. *They are shooting the dickens out of us,* thought Colley. *We should just salvo our bombs and get the hell out of here!*[17]

Scouting Two's third division was headed by Lieutenant Hoyt Mann, an Alabama native who had been a tennis star and choir singer during his academy days. His group—Max Woyke, Everleigh Willems, Roy Hale, Marvin Haschke, and John Wingfield—attacked the other transport anchored a half mile offshore. Although the rest of the group scored several near misses, Ensign Haschke was credited with planting his bomb right on the money. *Kongo Maru, Tenyo Maru,* and *Kokai Maru* all suffered damage from *Lexington's* first bombing strike, although none were directly sunk.[18]

Scouting Two's seventeen surviving SBDs made secondary drops on the various ships, including an auxiliary minelayer, which was also strafed by the pilots. Bobby Edwards made his secondary dive on the light cruiser *Yubari* with Pete Aurand tucked in behind him. Heavy anti-aircraft fire filled the sky with black puffs of smoke as concussions rocked their Dauntlesses. The warship managed to avoid Edwards's bomb but her gunners stayed locked in on his SBD. This break in the heavy flak allowed Aurand to concentrate on his target, and this time his bomb released as planned. His five-hundred-pounder was seen by others to strike *Yubari* squarely abaft her second stack.[19]

Bob Dixon credited hundred-pound bomb hits on various ships to VS-2 pilots Allen, Mann, Hale, Aurand, Schultz, Smith, Wood, Leppla, and Wingfield. For their successful first strike against Japanese shipping, six Scouting Two pilots would later be pinned with a Navy Cross: Dixon, Aurand, Quigley, Neely, Leppla, and Haschke.[20]

Weldon Hamilton's Bombing Two moved in next at 0928 against what he deemed to be a *Mogami*-class cruiser, actually the big minelayer *Tsugaru*. Hamilton and wingman Clem Connally missed, but Lieutenant (j.g.) Mark Whittier's bomb plunged through *Tsugaru's* afterdeck, smashing her stern portion. Lieutenant Ralph Cousins managed only a portside miss on *Tsugaru*, but Lieutenant (j.g.) Brink Bass landed a damaging near miss just twenty feet astern of the warship. VB-2 believed they left the ship sinking from Bass and Whittier's thousand-pounders, but Japanese records show *Tsugaru* was merely damaged by near misses from the *Lexington*'s dive-bombers.[21]

Lieutenant Jim Newell and Lieutenant (j.g.) Jack Sheridan led sections of VB-2 against the transport *China Maru*, anchored off Salamaua. Two direct hits were claimed on the port side amidships, one by Bob "Buck" Buchan, but Japanese records again failed to bear out any direct hits. Bombing Two escaped with only one SBD slightly damaged from ground fire. Scouting Two suffered two aviators lost, one Dauntless downed, and seven SBDs that returned with one or more Japanese bullet holes. Jimmy Brett's TBDs returned intact, although several of their torpedoes had either run deep or otherwise malfunctioned. At least one war-fish did slam into the transport *Yokohama Maru*, causing her to settle on the muddy harbor bottom off the coast of Salamaua.[22]

Lexington's portion of the Lae–Salamaua raid was over in about twenty minutes. The Japanese had only minutes to recover before the *Yorktown* air group landed a second punch.

Rocky Glidewell was marking his first combat mission as rear gunner for Scouting Five's skipper, Bill "Willie" Burch. Rocky had made three previous flights with Burch in 1941, but prior to February 18 he had been Air Group Commander Curt Smiley's regular radioman. The former amateur boxer took such changes in stride, for Glidewell and Burch were old hunting buddies. In the skies, the pair would prove to be a deadly combination.

In the air, Burch's pilots maintained radio silence until they were in action over the harbor. Then they called to each other by their nicknames to avoid using their real names. The pilots' handles were "Stinky" Caldwell, "Swede" Vejtasa, "Fritz" Faulkner, "Yogi" Jorgenson, "Goocher" Downing, "Link" Traynor, and so on. During the first fifty miles of their outbound leg, Burch's VS-5 and Pappy Armstrong's VB-5 climbed for altitude in order to clear the mountains. "I almost put a 1,000-pound bomb on my plane against the captain's order," Burch recalled. "I wanted to hit 'em hard, and I didn't think we'd have any real trouble getting over the mountains."[23]

Yorktown's strikers arrived over Lae and Salamaua around 0945, less than twenty minutes after the *Lexington* group had commenced its attacks. Pappy Armstrong pushed over first on the Japanese convoy commander's flagship, the light cruiser *Yubari*. This cruiser's skipper spun his warship on a dime, causing the bombs of Pappy, Johnny Nielsen, and Jo Jo Powers to explode in *Yubari*'s wake. Ben Preston and Keith Taylor missed with their big bombs, but during secondary dives were each credited with hits with their smaller wing bombs. Lieutenant Sam Adams, Dave Berry, and Jeff Bigelow of VB-5's second division each toggled all three of their bombs at once against *Yubari*. "Not one of those nine bombs hit the water," said Berry. "Every one hit the ship." Berry saw Bigelow's five-hundred-pounder "blow the stack off." *Yubari* made a half turn and commenced to burn.[24]

After making his drop against *Yubari*, Lieutenant (j.g.) Floyd Moan suddenly found that his errant engine had died. He and his gunner, Bob Hodgens, narrowly avoided a water landing when Moan was able to restart his engine. He made another dive to unleash his wing bombs against a destroyer and then made several strafing runs against the Japanese vessels. Lieutenant Bill Guest's third division achieved three near misses on *Yubari*. In their secondary dives on the destroyers *Yunagi* and *Asanagi*, they claimed two hits and a possible with small bombs. Guest's division also strafed a small gunboat, setting it afire. Ensign Jim Crawford strafed an airfield while his gunner Lynn Forshee shot up a radio station and even lobbed a hand grenade from his rear cockpit. Joe Taylor's Torpedo Five made bombing attacks on the seaplane tender *Kiyokawa Maru*, but scored only one direct hit out of two dozen bombs.[25]

Next in were the thirteen Dauntlesses of Scouting Five. When Burch approached Salamaua Harbor, he saw that "ships were frantically steaming away in all directions with some as far as thirty miles at sea." His first division—including Birney Strong, Sam Underhill, Fritz Faulkner, Turner Caldwell, Yogi Jorgenson, and Swede Vejtasa—spotted three transportcargo ships near Lae at 1005. They were the armed merchant cruiser *Kongo Maru*, moored alongside the dock, and the transports *Tenyo Maru* and *Kokai Maru*, under way, close to shore and already damaged by *Lexington*'s bombers. Calling back to Wally Short's second division, Burch directed five planes each against the two larger ships while three pilots were to take on the auxiliary vessel.[26]

Scouting Five claimed direct hits on each of the larger ships closer to

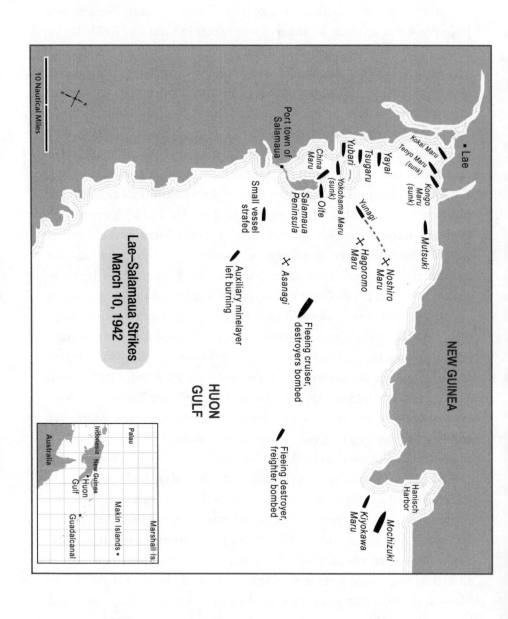

**Lae–Salamaua Strikes
March 10, 1942**

10 Nautical Miles

Port town of
Salamaua

Kokai Maru

Tenyo Maru
(sunk)

• Lae

Kongo
Maru
(sunk)

Yayai

Yubari

Tsugaru

China
Maru

Yokohama Maru
(sunk)

Olte

Mutsuki

Yunagi

Noshiro
Maru

Salamaua
Peninsula

Hagoromo
Maru

Small vessel
strafed

Asanagi

NEW GUINEA

Auxiliary minelayer
left burning

Fleeing cruiser,
destroyers bombed

HUON
GULF

Fleeing destroyer,
freighter bombed

Hanisch
Harbor

Kiyokawa
Maru

Mochizuki

Palau

Indonesia

Australia

New Guinea

Huon
Gulf

Makin Islands •

Marshall Is.

Guadalcanal

shore. Burch found that an error in his arming device caused both his large bomb and his pair of wing bombs to drop in unison. As he pulled out of his dive, he attempted to close the flaps but accidentally grabbed his landing gear handle instead, dropping his wheels in the process. "Several of my squadron, seeing a plane with wheels and thinking I was a Jap, started to attack me," Burch said. "They were making an approach when they recognized me, but they told me later they had a hard time keeping their gunners from shooting."[27]

Lieutenant Short, Art Downing, and Kendall Campbell of the third division were credited with hits on the third ship as well, leaving it on fire and sinking. Jim Cales, rear gunner for Ensign Underhill, thought highly of his pilot but was less than impressed with his dive-bombing skills, as young Underhill missed his ship by a wide mark.[28]

Swede Vejtasa released his big bomb and attempted to drop his hundred-pounders during his first attack. Upon rejoining the formation, one of his wingmen announced, "Swede, you've got a hung bomb." Bill Burch, who had no bombs left, climbed his squadron back up to seven thousand feet so that those with wing bombs remaining could deliver them. Vejtasa dived on one of the transports that was getting under way while gunner Barton Wood strafed the harbor during their pullout. Several members of VS-5 witnessed Swede's last hundred-pounder explode right on the bow of the ship. Other pilots individually strafed ships and gun emplacements. Yogi Jorgenson made repeated runs at Japanese foot soldiers, chasing them along the beach as his .50-caliber bullets kicked up sand behind their feet. Burch then collected his flock and started for the mountains, leaving *Kongo Maru, Tenyo Maru,* and *Kokai Maru* beached and burning.[29]

Pappy Armstrong circled around the area during Scouting Five's attacks to observe the results. As he headed south to climb back over the Owen Stanley Range, he saw at least five ships steaming out of the gulf at high speed. Armstrong eagerly sent word to the brass on *Yorktown,* "Recommend second attack immediately."[30]

The air groups began landing around 1050, and all had returned save VS-2's one loss. Ensign Art Schultz was disturbed to find that Joe Johnson was officially listed as missing in action. He had clearly seen the SBD torn apart by a direct hit that sent the two airmen plunging to their

deaths in the ocean. Schultz felt that such an official status would un-
necessarily leave their families clinging to a false sense of hope.[31]

Yorktown and *Lexington*'s first coordinated attack had sunk *Kongo
Maru*, *Tenyo Maru*, *Yokohama Maru*, and the minesweeper *Tama Maru
No. 2*. The cruiser *Yubari* was damaged and had lost thirteen men killed
and fifty-four wounded. In addition, the destroyers *Asanagi, Yunagi,* and
Oite had been damaged, as had the seaplane tender *Kiyokawa Maru*.
Japanese counts placed their dead at 130 men and their wounded at
245 men, the most damage inflicted on a Japanese fleet since the start of
the war. The damage also caused Vice Admiral Shigeyoshi Inoue to postpone planned invasions of Port Moresby and Tulagi by a month.[32]

Yorktown and *Lexington* withdrew southeastward into the Coral
Sea on March 11. The task forces refueled during retirement, and *Lexington* parted ways on March 16 to head for Pearl Harbor. She arrived
on March 26, where she would undergo a short overhaul. *Yorktown*'s
Task Force 17 remained at sea to guard the line of communication between the United States and Australia.

The increased level of harassment raids being carried out by the
American carrier air groups would not go unnoticed by Japanese high
command. Plans were being formulated for more offensive advances by
the Japanese, making a major clash between her carrier groups and the
U.S. task forces inevitable.

FIVE

Deck Dodgers Find a Home

Thousands of young men aspired to become naval aviators in the early 1940s. The process consumed the better part of a year, during which the aviation cadets faced injury, death, or washout nearly every day. The prize for possessing "the stuff" to make it through the program was being pinned with golden wings and being commissioned as an ensign in the U.S. Navy. Two such aviation cadets, Bob Gibson and Hal Buell, first met at their elimination base ("E-base") training, and were destined to see more of each other during 1942.

Harold Lloyd "Hal" Buell was ahead of the curve at E-base in that he had had some flight time. An orphan from Ottumwa, Iowa, he had been enamored with aviation since seeing his first pilot close up at age nine. Hal lived with a guardian family on a small farm until he entered college in September 1938 in Fairfield, Iowa. He was accepted into a college flight training course in 1939 and was given instruction on flying a Piper Cub two-seater, sixty-five-horsepower-engine aircraft. Buell had earned his private pilot's license by early 1940 but was unable to join the Navy's flight program yet because he did not have two full years of college credit.[1]

Hal contemplated volunteering for the Royal Canadian Air Force (RCAF) while continuing to attend Parsons College. He instead received an invitation shortly after his twenty-first birthday to report to the U.S. Naval Reserve Aviation Base in Robertson, Missouri, for E-base flight training. Thirty young men gathered at the Missouri base in cold,

U.S. Navy

Ensign Harold "Hal" Buell.

bleak weather on January 6, 1941. Each prospective airman had enlisted in the Navy and was rated as a seaman, second class. Hal and his companions received ten hours of training during four to six weeks in the open-cockpit Stearman Model 75 "Yellow Peril" biplanes. Buell passed his solo flight in short order and presented his instructor with a traditional gift of a fifth of Ballantine's scotch.[2]

One of Buell's companions at the Missouri E-base was Robert Douglas Gibson from Unionville, Missouri. He also had the advantage of having taken a college flight training program in a Piper Cub. Bob Gibson had graduated from the University of Missouri in Columbia in June 1940 but found that his job as a high school music teacher was not satisfying. Looking out his classroom windows, he could see airplanes across the Mississippi River flying from Parks Air College. "I became curious about aviation," Bob said. He and another teacher signed up for pilot CPT (civilian pilot training) and began taking flight lessons.[3]

"Learning to fly was a snap," Bob said. At the end of his training program, he and three flying school buddies decided to seek further adventures by joining a military service in which they could really develop their flight careers. They picked the Navy, with twenty-year-old Bob obtaining his father's permission to sign up. His teaching career would have to wait. "The superintendent of schools was a German, and he raised hell," said Gibson. "He said, 'I'll see that you never get another job!'"[4]

Bob was the son of a sheriff who had taught him to become an excellent marksman from the age of ten. His nickname during flight school quickly became "Hoot," in reference to the American rodeo champion and pioneer cowboy film actor Edmund "Hoot" Gibson. Hoot, one of the largest box-office draws in western films, appeared in his own books and even flew airplanes, so Bob Gibson's nickname just seemed to fit.

Hoot Gibson met Hal Buell and twenty-eight other potential aviators at the St. Louis E-base training. His first instructor was a former dive-bomber pilot named Bruce Weber. "Bruce let me know in short order that I knew 'zilch' about flying," said Gibson. "And I was smart enough to answer, 'Aye, aye, sir!'" His CPT training was more than enough to get him through E-base and on to his next training assignment in Jacksonville, Florida. Hoot and three E-base buddies—Bill Branham, Mark Boyer, and Dave Chaffee—piled into Gibson's car and set out for Florida. Gibson was particularly close with Chaffee, a wavy, red-haired graduate of Baldwin-Wallace University in Ohio. Dave's good looks, cheerful personality, and strong singing voice helped charm the ladies wherever the quartet roamed in the ensuing months.[5]

Gibson's flight class was put on hold for a month before they were assigned to begin training at the Pensacola Naval Air Station. Hal Buell also began his naval aviation training at Pensacola about a month later in April 1941. Here, the wannabe pilots were discharged as seamen and appointed as aviation cadets, USNR. The first stage of basic instruction was called Squadron One, which consisted of considerable classroom time and flight hours in Stearman N3Ns or N2S aircraft. Those cadets who didn't wash out of Squadron One advanced to Squadron Two training in old service aircraft—O3Us, SBUs, and the like.

In Squadron One, two of Hoot Gibson's buddies

Courtesy of Robert Gibson Jr.

Lieutenant (j.g.) Bob "Hoot" Gibson of VB-10 beside his SBD.

struggled with making the proper tail-first landing approach necessary for future carrier operation. One was E-base buddy Dave "Red" Chaffee, and the other was Steve Czarnecki, a young aviator from Cleveland who lived in the same hall of Gibson's barracks. Hoot had thus far aced his check flights with Marine instructor Marion Carl, who was later a leading fighter pilot at Guadalcanal. "I spent many hours giving both Dave and Steve encouragement to conquer their devils of flight," said Gibson. His ability to push both rookie pilots through would later cause Hoot great guilt.[6]

"If you didn't get killed in Squadron Two, then you went into the third squadron—instruments," said Gibson. The cadets were selected for more advanced training in one of three types of fleet naval aviator billets: VC, the most coveted carrier-type squadron assignment; VP, multi-engined seaplane or transport duty; or VO-VS, seaplane duty on battleships or cruisers. Buell was elated to find his name on the VC list, along with some of his friends: Hoot Gibson, Dave Chaffee, Ed Kinzer, Herbert Shonk, Steve Czarnecki, and others. They were one step closer to flying from an aircraft carrier.[7]

The more advanced VC training of Squadron Three was conducted at Opa-Locka Field at Miami NAS. The cadets were introduced to dive-bombing, fighter tactics, aerial navigation, gunnery, and fleet-type formation flying. Buell and Gibson were both selected for dive-bombers. At first, Gibson found a lot of the dive-bombing "was just by guess and by God." He learned from fellow cadet Joe Doyle to always stick to his target ship during a dive and corkscrew his plane to stay with his ship. The aviators dropped aluminum two-and-a-half-pound bombs with shotgun shells that produced a puff of smoke when they hit. Gibson achieved four hits for four drops by twisting with his target and releasing his dummy bombs at low altitude.[8]

Hoot Gibson graduated from Opa-Locka on September 1, 1941, and received both his gold wings and his commission as an ensign in the U.S. Navy. Hal Buell followed suit two months later, on November 1. Buell received orders to Scouting Squadron 71 (VS-71) on the carrier *Wasp* (CV-7), while Gibson was assigned to *Lexington*'s VB-2. In order to fully integrate into these units, the newly commissioned pilots had to first become carrier-qualified.

Ensign Gibson was sent to NAS North Island near San Diego with thirty other new pilots. Since they were required to be single for another year, they lived up their off-duty hours in true bachelor fashion. Gibson shuttled buddies with his car to the hottest bars to sip on popular drinks of the day such as "stingers" and "French 75s," champagne-and-cognac concoctions. "We thirty pilots were elated and loved every minute of it and thought we were in the big leagues," he said.[9]

After earning his gold wings, Ensign Buell was assigned to the Norfolk Naval Base as part of one of the Navy's two advanced carrier training groups (ACTG). This temporary assignment consisted of flight training exercises in older-model scout bombers until such time as the aircraft carrier to which the new pilots were to be assigned arrived from sea.

On February 8, Buell became carrier-qualified by making three arrested landings on the tiny flight deck of the squatty escort carrier *Long Island* in Chesapeake Bay. The accomplishment was cause for celebration for Buell and many of his ACTG rookies who were still waiting for their assigned carriers to arrive. His companions included many young men who would soon see Pacific service flying the SBD Dauntless: Johnny Lough, J. Q. Roberts, Gene Greene, John Ammen, Carl Peiffer, Roger Scudder, Walt Brown, Elmer Conzett, Henry Ervin, and Dave Chaffee. The newly carrier-qualified ensigns threw a huge party at the base officers' club and dubbed their private group the "Norfolk Deck Dodgers."[10]

One week later, twenty-two Norfolk Deck Dodgers were ordered to ship out immediately to the Pacific. Buell was assigned to *Yorktown*'s VS-5, and found that he had a mere six days to get himself cross-country to San Francisco. He and fellow pilot Lough took his 1938 Ford convertible coupe as far as Illinois before catching a passenger train to California. Buell and other ACTG pilots sailed on the transport ship *Castor* under the Golden Gate Bridge on February 23, bound for Pearl Harbor.[11]

They arrived in Hawaii eight days later and were stunned by the signs of devastation still evident. Buell and the first group of replacement carrier pilots were temporarily assigned to Lieutenant Commander Max Leslie's VB-3 on March 4. Bombing Three had been based at Kaneohe

Bay, across Oahu, since the torpedo damage to *Saratoga* had left them stranded in January.

Hoot Gibson was not far behind his buddy Buell in reaching the Pacific theater. Gibson had been attached to the Navy's other ACTG in San Diego in early 1942, and his group was the second class sent to the Pacific. To his buddies, Gibson was called simply "Gibby" or "Hoot," and the fact that he had a car made him all the more popular. The Navy's newest carrier, *Hornet*, finally arrived in port and Gibson successfully carrier-qualified with his successful "traps" on March 23. Gibson and thirty-two other ACTG rookies boarded the troop transport *President Grant* on April 8 and made the eight-day voyage to Pearl Harbor to join the Pacific fleet.

Gibson was assigned to the officers' quarters on Ford Island, right near where the battleship *Arizona* had been blown apart. Several days later, he was assigned to the orphaned Bombing Three at Kaneohe. He, Hal Buell, and other Norfolk Deck Dodgers who had yet to serve on an aircraft carrier became very close. They got to know more senior pilots in the meantime as air groups came in and out of port. Gibson found naval aviators to be a generally fatalistic bunch. "They thought the odds were against us. I never entertained those thoughts, but a lot of people talked about it. Even so, when you were off duty, you immediately struck strong friendships because of that. We were all in the same boat together."[12]

The new ACTG pilots were godsends to offset losses in the Pacific carrier air groups. Admiral Fletcher's TF-17 remained at sea following the Lae–Salamaua strikes as *Yorktown* continued to safeguard the line of communications between the United States and Australia. Admiral Brown's TF-11 returned to Pearl Harbor on March 26. The *Lexington* Air Group flew ashore to Oahu, where the airmen learned that they would enjoy the luxury of a week's leave at the famed Royal Hawaiian Hotel. Lady Lex spent time in the Navy yards for an overhaul, which included the replacement of some of her outdated antiaircraft guns. Her air group was revamped during the interim and Paul Ramsey's Fighting Two reported back on board for duty.

Lieutenant Pete Aurand and Ensign Linc Koch of VS-2 received new assignments while in port. Pete was promoted to lieutenant commander and was transferred back stateside to help establish the new Escort Scouting Squadron 28 (VGS-28). In exchange, Bob Dixon took on three new ensigns fresh from ACTG—Jesse Walker, Bob Smith, and Carl Thomas—plus a more veteran pilot in the form of Lieutenant (j.g.) Bill Hall. The latter had flown with *Yorktown*'s VS-5 for the February 1 Makin strike, and had then been loaned out to *Enterprise*'s VS-6 for the Wake and Marcus Island raids. Hall finally arrived in the *Lexington* wardroom as the scout bomber pilot with the most combat strikes of 1942. His new VS-2 comrades dubbed him "Pappy" Hall.[13]

Weldon Hamilton's VB-2 lost three pilots to transfers, including gunnery officer Warren Welch, and gained new ACTG rookie ensigns Warren Schoen, Herbert Shonk, and Roger Scudder. In the meantime, *Enterprise* put to sea on April 8 to join forces with the new carrier *Hornet*. They were assigned to escort Lieutenant Colonel Jimmy Doolittle's B-25 Army bombers to Tokyo, and Max Leslie's VB-3 went aboard the Big E on temporary duty. Leslie left behind many of his rookie ensigns who had recently joined the squadron from their ACTG classes. Several weeks later, a group of the new pilots finally got their chance to be assigned to *Yorktown* and *Lexington*.

"A flight of us were up and apparently they needed five pilots immediately for the South Pacific," recalled Bob Gibson. "Officials at the Kaneohe Air Station decided to send the first five that landed. I was the sixth plane and I was always disappointed thereafter. I was totally eager to get into action, feeling that the U.S. couldn't win the war without me." Gibson remained behind, while Hal Buell and other new ensigns headed out the following morning. Among them was Dave Chaffee, Gibson's close friend whom he had coached through the tough training days at Pensacola.[14]

Ten ACTG pilots gathered on Hickam Field in the predawn darkness on April 24. They boarded an Army Air Corps B-17 with their gear and were airborne at 0700. They landed eight hours later on Christmas Island and spent a restless night sleeping in tents. The new dive-bomber pilots were next flown to remote Canton Island and then on to Viti Levu in the Fiji Islands. They were then flown to the dock area of the capital city of Suva, where the destroyer *Sims* waited to ferry them out to their new carrier, *Yorktown*.[15]

A fter the Lae strike, *Yorktown* continued long weeks of battle cruising in company with two heavy cruisers and five destroyers. By April
1, her TF-17 was about a hundred miles off New Caledonia. Scouting
Five's airmen flew daily scouting missions and inner air patrols but found
little of interest during their many hours in the skies. During off-duty
hours, they played volleyball or cards, or wrote letters.

"We crossed and recrossed the Coral Sea until we knew the flying fish
by name," wrote pilot Art Downing. Scouting Five took up a cribbage
tournament, with the finals coming down to pilots "Easy Victor" Johnson and Red Austin. Per Downing, "Red's simple, unenlightened game
was no match for Easy Victor's treacherous and ruthless tactics."[16]

The battle cruising had already hit six weeks in duration, and by
April 5, Easter Sunday, *Yorktown*'s stores were even out of powdered
eggs. Task Force 17 operated in the Coral Sea, about three to four hundred miles southwest of Guadalcanal, during the next several days. By
April 10, the commissary was so depleted that *Yorktown*'s crew bought
raffle tickets to win the last steak still on board.[17]

On April 14, Admiral Fletcher finally advised Admiral Nimitz that he
planned to withdraw to Tongatabu in the Tonga Islands to facilitate some
repairs on his fighter planes. One week later, *Yorktown* weighed anchor
in the remote port and her air group was flown ashore to operate from the
dirt airstrip at Tonga Airfield. "We lived in the islands with the natives in
grass shacks with sides made of bamboo," said Rocky Glidewell. The
pilots frequented the local Nuku'alofa Club in the evenings, played baseball, went swimming, and ate their fair share of island fruits.[18]

There were significant changes to the air group before *Yorktown* put
to sea again. Air Group Commander Curt Smiley had new orders and his
place as CYAG was taken by Lieutenant Commander Pete Pederson, for-
merly the skipper of VF-42. Bombing Five's skipper, Pappy Armstrong,
was promoted to a new role with the air staff. Command of the bomber
unit was handed to Lieutenant Wally Short, the XO of Scouting Five.

The squadron shifting of Short to VB-5 was due to Captain Buckmaster and Dixie Kiefer's desire to have a strong individual who they
believed would get results to fill Armstrong's shoes. Some of VB-5's senior pilots reacted to the change "with a bit of coolness," as they favored

Sam Adams—three years Short's junior—over a non-squadron man taking over. Short, however, "turned out to be a good man," per pilot Bill Christie. Short was quick to make changes. For one, all pilots would fly their missions as assigned by the operations officer, Lieutenant Adams. There would be no ducking of obligations; even the skipper would fly every scout mission, as per Adams's assignment of the day.[19]

Lexington's Task Force 11, now under Rear Admiral Aubrey W. Fitch, departed Pearl Harbor on April 15 and sent Marine Fighting Squadron 211's Buffalo fighters off to remote Palmyra Island three days later. *Lexington* crossed the equator and held another shellback initiation on April 20. The following day, Fitch received orders to rendezvous on May 1 with Fletcher's TF-17 about 250 miles northwest of New Caledonia. *Yorktown* weighed anchor at 0900 from Tongatabu on April 27 and put to sea, headed for the Coral Sea again.

Rocky Glidewell, normally the rear gunner for VS-5 skipper Bill Burch, found himself flying with Lieutenant (j.g.) Art Downing during the fly-out from Tongatabu to the carrier. Scouting Five was detailed with searching north of the islands before landing on their ship. Just over half an hour into their flight, Glidewell was peering out over his canopy at the ocean below. As he pulled his head back in from the slipstream, he casually wiped the fog off his goggles. "I wiped it off on my flight gear and there was oil," he said. He and Downing then watched their engine's oil pressure drop from ninety—lower than normal for scout cruising—down to seventy.[20]

Glidewell took action as oil spattered their windshield. "I took out the searchlight I carried in the plane for signaling purposes and aimed it back toward the fleet at Nupanoma Harbor, about twenty miles away," he said. Glidewell could see *Yorktown*'s superstructure and several destroyers under way ahead of her. He blinkered out a blind message, not following the usual procedure of making a preliminary call and waiting for a receipt. "Forced landing in the water," he signaled.

Glidewell then turned around to hang on as their engine quit at two thousand feet. Downing brought his SBD down in a dead-stick landing in the smooth seas. The bomber bounced once, skipped back into the air, and then plowed in nose first at a forty-five-degree angle. The second impact slammed the pilot's face into the controls. Glidewell scrambled to retrieve the plane's life raft as their Dauntless bobbed up and down in the gentle swells. He maneuvered the raft to the front cockpit, where he saw Downing slumped over, with water up to his shoulders.

Glidewell pulled the toggles on Downing's life vest, hauled him into the raft, and paddled away from the sinking dive-bomber. Glidewell paddled earnestly for the barrier coral reef he saw about two miles away. Downing sat quietly in the raft, seeming rather dazed and distant. At length, he asked Glidewell thickly, "Is there anything wrong with my face?"

"You look fine," Glidewell replied. When Downing opened his mouth to speak again, his gunner spotted the problem. "You don't have any upper teeth," Rocky announced. The force of the impact had been so great that Downing's face was shoved into the controls, and some of his upper teeth had been broken out.

Rocky spotted the destroyer *Walke* racing toward them with a high bow wave. He would learn that one of the quartermasters on her bridge had picked up his blind signal by chance and had relayed it to the destroyer's skipper. "I would say that happened to be an act of God that he happened to be up there, looking toward me twenty miles away to see a flashing message with no preliminary call," Glidewell felt. "That was divine intervention when he picked up my blind signal."[21]

Walke hauled the pair aboard with a Jacob's ladder. Downing and Glidewell were soon transferred back to *Yorktown* in exchange for the usual payment of ice cream for having rescued aviators. "The pilot was good for fifteen gallons of ice cream and I was good for ten gallons," Glidewell recalled.

Two days out, on the morning of April 29, *Yorktown* lowered a motor launch. The destroyer *Sims* had come out from Sura with ten new ACTG ensigns. Half were slated to be transferred to the *Lexington* Air Group as replacements, three to Bombing Two, and two to Scouting Two. They were Hal Buell, Walter E. Brown Jr., Ralph Hays Goddard, Richard Kenneth Batten, Henry Nichols Ervin, Davis Elliott "Dave" Chaffee, Thomas Eugene Brown, Robert Frederick Edmondson, John Neville Ammen Jr., and Harry Alvin Frederickson.[22]

Since conflict with Japanese invasion forces was expected, Captain

Buckmaster retained the new pilots instead of sending them to their designated *Lexington* units. Five were added to Bill Burch's VS-5 roster. The other half—Chaffee, Tom Brown, Edmondson, Ammen, and Frederickson—would fill slots vacated in Bombing Five by the recent transfers of pilot Orest Houghton and others. Houghton, according to his gunner, Joe Lynch, had "become a conscientious objector" to the war who "could not dive-bomb people anymore."[23]

Ensign Buell was eager, but he found that his new skipper Burch did not plan to fly his new recruits unless circumstances made it absolutely necessary. His daily duties involved little more than manning standby planes to warm their engines or help spot them on deck. Buell's morale was further bruised when he learned that his other ACTG buddies were told by Wally Short they would fly in rotation with Bombing Five.[24]

Buell, Goddard, Ervin, Batten, and Walt Brown pressured the older VS-5 pilots to work on Burch to allow them to also join the rotations. Burch finally relaxed enough to allow his rookies to fly antisubmarine patrols within sight of the task force. Buell's first flight as wingman was for Goocher Downing, an aggressive pilot who made it challenging for young wingmen. Knowing that his job was to stay in formation no matter what, Buell "hung on like a pit bull" with each of Downing's maneuvers. Buell was assigned as the roommate to Ed Kinzer, another Norfolk Deck Dodger he had trained with at Pensacola in 1941. "Unfortunately," Buell recalled, "I was going to know some of them for only a week, including my new roommate."[25]

As *Lexington*'s Task Force 11 approached its rendezvous with the *Yorktown* force, Scouting Two lost an SBD on April 30 when Lieutenant (j.g.) Roy Hale was forced to ditch his 2-S-7. He and his gunner were recovered, and the carrier task groups drew within sight of each other after daybreak on May 1.

On May 2, Swede Vejtasa and gunner Leon Hall made a submarine sighting at 1527 only thirty-two miles from the task force. It was the Japanese submarine *I-21*, four days out of Truk Atoll with orders to patrol off Nouméa. "I charged my guns and immediately began to climb, staying on the up sun side," Vejtasa said. He felt that the sub's lookouts had spotted the SBDs, as *I-21* suddenly made a crash dive. Vejtasa could make out the outline of the submerged submarine just ahead of the boiling water. He and new pilot Skip Ervin circled over the area, carefully noting the I-boat's course and position.[26]

They maintained radio silence and returned to their carrier, where Vejtasa dropped their sighting report at 1536 via a weighted beanbag message. Lieutenant (j.g.) Tom Ellison led three *Yorktown* TBDs out to attack, and they dropped six depth bombs as *I-21* made a crash dive. Captain Buckmaster feared that the submarine may have gotten off a contact report of carrier planes attacking her, but *I-21* merely reported that she had been attacked by planes.[27]

Task Force 17 refueled from the tanker *Neosho* on May 3. During the refueling process, intelligence from Army pilots showed that the Japanese had an invasion force off the south coast of Santa Isabel Island, believed to be heading toward Tulagi in the Solomon Islands. Admiral Fletcher left *Neosho* behind with a destroyer and headed toward Tulagi, intent upon making a strike there on the morning of May 4.

The Japanese invasion of the Solomon Islands was a serious offensive to shut down the Allies in the Pacific. Japan planned to advance south and sever the lines of communication between the United States and Australia. This effort would be boosted with a new air base and garrison on the island of Guadalcanal, located five hundred miles east of New Guinea and a thousand miles northeast of Australia. Operation MO, or the Port Moresby Operation, was supported by Admiral Isoroku Yamamoto, the commander in chief of the Combined Fleet. His plan was to take control of the Australian territories of New Guinea and Papua to support the capture of Port Moresby, the capital and largest city of Papua, on about May 7. This effort was to be preceded by the occupation of Tulagi Island, near Guadalcanal, where his military would establish a seaplane base and garrison for operations in the Coral Sea area.

The Tulagi invasion task force was under Rear Admiral Kiyohide Shima's 19th Division. His force included his flagship, the large mine-layer *Okinoshima*, two troop transports, two destroyers, three converted minesweepers, two subchasers, a minelayer, and two auxiliary mine-sweepers. The landing operation commenced during the early-morning hours of May 3 as troops moved ashore on Tulagi and the small islet of Gavutu, lying just off Florida Island. Within hours, forces had also occupied Gavutu's sister islet of Tanambogo. The occupation of these

Solomon islands was well under way as Admiral Fletcher's TF-17 moved in on the Guadalcanal and Tulagi areas.

On the night of May 3, *Yorktown* pilots, gunners, and mechanics all put in many hours checking equipment, calibrating ammunition, and arming their planes. It had been almost two months since their combat over Lae and Salamua. Wally Short and Bill Burch lectured their aircrews on their assignments for the following morning, coaching in particular the newly received pilots on their roles. With dawn would come a fresh chance to hand out some vengeance.

SIX

First Strikes in the Solomons

Bill Burch was ready for action. After weeks of endless battle cruising, his Scouting Five would be the first ordnance-bearing strike planes to launch on May 4. After a quick breakfast in the predawn hours, his pilots assembled in the ready room for final instructions. "We had been at sea for quite a long time, and morale was pretty low," Burch said. "It was good news that we were heading in for an attack."[1]

Burch explained that the *Yorktown* Air Group would be making the strike without Lady Lex's air group. They would launch from about a hundred miles south of Guadalcanal to attack Japanese shipping gathered in Tulagi Harbor. Tulagi—only four thousand yards long and never more than a thousand yards wide—was a tiny island nestled below the larger Florida Island, just north of Guadalcanal. Japanese troops had occupied Tulagi and Florida, and the shipping in Tulagi's harbor was ripe for the picking.[2]

Six CAP Wildcats were launched at 0631, followed by Lieutenant Commander Burch's scouts—each loaded with a thousand-pound bomb. Joe Taylor's twelve TBDs needed the entire flight deck to gain altitude with their loads of aerial torpedoes—marking this as the first time they were used in combat. Lieutenant Wally Short's fifteen VB-5 SBDs were quickly lifted up on the elevators from the hangar deck and launched at the tail of the procession. Each squadron made its way independently to Tulagi through rainsqualls.[3]

At 0702, the last of the strikers was airborne. Scouting Five, being much faster than Taylor's obsolete torpedo planes, flew a sweep to the north toward Rabaul to look for shipping coming from that direction. Burch's squadron had a special passenger this day in the person of Lieutenant Commander Walter "Butch" Schindler, Admiral Fletcher's staff gunnery officer. Schindler was qualified in aerial observation, and he finally convinced his boss the previous evening that his skills would come in handy in spotting the better shipping targets. He took over the rear-seat position for Lieutenant (j.g.) Nick Nicholson, one of Burch's wingmen.[4]

Burch saw only one ship in his sweep toward Rabaul. It appeared to be a destroyer, heading north. By the time he had led VS-5 back to Tulagi, shortly after 0800, Torpedo Five and Bombing Five were arriving on the scene. A layer of thin, broken overcast at six thousand feet obscured much of the shipping in Tulagi Harbor. "The weather became a problem," said Swede Vejtasa, leading the second section of VS-5's first division. From his high vantage point, Vejtasa began making out an abundance of Japanese ships below. "They had a devil of a lot of ships, which were off-loading and loading gear."[5]

The Japanese ships near Tulagi were part of an invasion force under Rear Admiral Kiyohide Shima. The older destroyers *Yuzuki* and *Kikuzuki* were moored alongside Shima's flagship *Okinoshima* for fueling. The large transports *Azumasan Maru* and *Koei Maru* were busy unloading supplies, while two small patrol craft were under way in the harbor. Numerous small craft and two small subchasers were also in Tulagi's harbor. Three auxiliary minesweepers steamed northeastward from the harbor, one likely the "destroyer" seen by Burch.[6]

From twenty thousand feet, Burch scanned the available targets. He radioed for Wally Short's VB-5 pilots to take the northernmost shipping while he would attack the ships to the south. Joe Taylor reported in at 0815 that his Torpedo Five was ready, so Burch organized his scouts for attack. Eight of his pilots—Nick Nicholson, Swede Vejtasa, Birney Strong, Art Downing, Fritz Faulkner, Turner Caldwell, Red Austin, and Earl Johnson—had made attacks in the Marshalls, and most had also made the New Guinea raid. Three others—John Jorgenson, Sam Underhill, and Link Traynor—had only made the New Guinea strike. Ed Kinzer was still a combat virgin.

Burch picked a merchantman for his lead section and ordered Strong and Caldwell to take their groups against a different ship. Halfway down in his dive, the skipper called for a change. He suddenly had a more complete view of Tulagi Harbor as he broke free of the cloud layer. Burch radioed for his divisions to switch from merchant ship targets to the warship cluster. Some of the pilots missed this call, however, and attacked their previously assigned targets.[7]

The majority of VS-5's pilots made their attacks on flagship *Okinoshima* and the destroyers *Kikuzuki* and *Yuzuki* moored alongside. They achieved complete surprise, as the Japanese ships put up no antiaircraft fire until the American strikers were pulling out of their dives to rendezvous. Burch's scouts claimed four hits and a "probable," but their claims were overly optimistic. None of the warships were hit directly. The poor marksmanship of VS-5 was due to a familiar problem: passing from high-altitude, cooler air into the warmer air at low altitudes during their dives, the pilots suffered from fogged inner windshields and telescopic sights. Burch compared it to "putting a white sheet in front of you and you have to bomb from memory." His pilots had to stick their heads out of the sides of their cockpits and aim down the side of the target ship.[8]

"You couldn't see a damn thing," said Vejtasa, fourth to dive. Swede opened his canopy to help adjust for the temperature change, but his windshield and bombsight fogged over badly. As he pulled out, he quickly tried to get his bearings to avoid crashing into the sea, or another diving plane, or a Japanese warship. Burch rendezvoused his scouts over Tulagi and moved on. Only one plane had suffered damage to its bomb racks from an AA burst. The only other opposition for VS-5 was a Japanese floatplane, which was chased off by their rear gunners.

Joe Taylor's TBDs had crossed the west end of Guadalcanal and circled north before coming in on the anchorage from the northeast at 0850. Each Devastator carried a Mark 13, Model 0, torpedo under its belly set to run at ten feet. Only 156 of the Mod 0 torpedoes—featuring propellers in front of their rudders—were ever produced, and as of May 1942, only *Yorktown*'s VT-5 was equipped with them. The newer Mod 1 Mark 13s supplied to most torpedo squadrons would prove to be far less reliable.[9]

Three TBDs attacked the transport *Azumasan Maru*, but their tor-

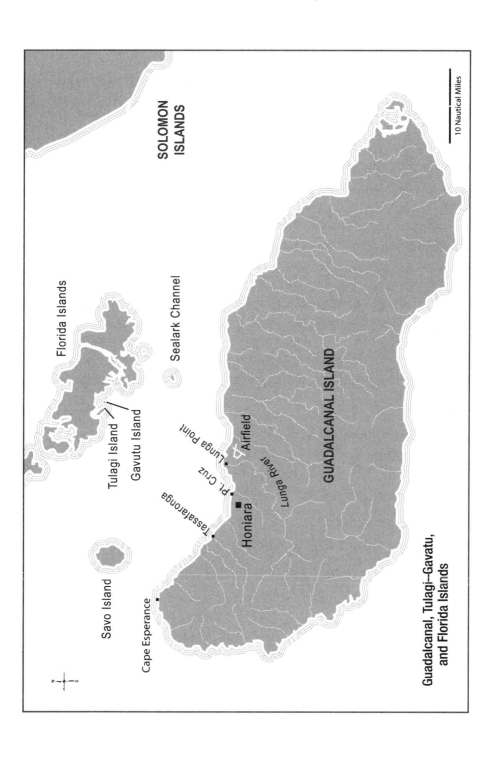

Guadalcanal, Tulagi–Gavutu,
and Florida Islands

SOLOMON
ISLANDS

Florida Islands

Tulagi Island
Gavutu Island

Sealark Channel

Savo Island

Cape Esperance

Tassafaronga

Honiara

Pt. Cruz

Lunga Point

Airfield

Lunga River

GUADALCANAL ISLAND

10 Nautical Miles

N
S

pedoes churned harmlessly underneath her and exploded on the beach beyond. Seven other TBDs attacked the nest of *Okinoshima* and the destroyers alongside her. The pilots reported that of six fish that were released, three scored hits on a light cruiser, actually the destroyer *Kikuzuki*. Taylor's pilot did put one torpedo into *Kikuzuki*'s engine room, forcing the destroyer's crew to ground her before she could sink. The last two planes of VT-5 claimed hits on the cargo ship *Koei Maru* and headed back to *Yorktown* under heavy AA fire.[10]

Last in to attack Tulagi was Wally Short, with three five-plane divisions of Bombing Five. At 0900, he led Johnny Nielsen, Leif Larsen, Jo Jo Powers, and Ben Preston in an attack on the minesweeper *Tama Maru*. The closest near miss by Powers was thirty feet off its mark. A Mitsubishi F1M2 floatplane attempting to get airborne near Makamo Island was burned by the first division SBDs. Lieutenant Sam Adams led his second VB-5 division—Dave Berry, Jeff Bigelow, Bill Christie, and Win Rowley—down on the minelayer *Okinoshima*, which was beginning to get under way. Gunner Lynn Forshee—flying rear seat for Lieutenant (j.g.) Christie since his regular pilot, Jim Crawford, had developed pneumonia and was transferred back to Pearl Harbor from Tongatabu—noted that Christie achieved a near miss. Only one of their division mates was credited with a hit. Of three bombs dropped on *Okinoshima*, Lieutenant Keith Taylor, with Floyd Moan and Rockey Dickson of his third division, claimed one hit and a possible. Bill Guest and Hank McDowell attacked *Tama Maru* and the destroyer *Yuzuki*, but failed to make any hits.[11]

The excited SBD and TBD pilots exaggerated the results of their attack. The only ship to sustain significant damage had been the destroyer *Kikuzuki*, hit by Torpedo Five. Bill Burch was first to land on *Yorktown*, around 0930, and he raced for the bridge to report to Captain Buckmaster and Admiral Fletcher. The planes of Scouting Five and Torpedo Five were quickly hauled below to the hangar deck for rearming and refueling. Once the flight deck was cleared, Wally Short's fifteen VB-5 SBDs were landed, the last at 0954.

Three SBDs had been hit, including that of Short, who suffered a four-inch hole in his vertical stabilizer. Two other planes were so damaged that they were unable to make another strike. "We landed aboard and grabbed sandwiches and hot coffee as the planes were rearmed with another 1,000-lb. package of cheer for Admiral Tojo," wrote VS-5's Art Downing.[12]

Wally Short raced for the bridge to add his input to what Burch was already laying out for the command staff. Burch admitted to Admiral Fletcher that his first strike "didn't do any good," and that he was eager to go back in. "All right, get in your plane," Captain Buckmaster told him. Thrilled, Burch later quipped that he barely had time to "get a cup of coffee" before his planes were ready to go again.[13]

I t was just over one hour from the time the first strike had begun to land that they were in the air again. Wally Short borrowed Bill Guest's SBD, cutting his VB-5 contribution to the second strike to fourteen SBDs. Also included as a substitution plane for one of those damaged was VB-5 rookie pilot Dave Chaffee. Lynn Forshee, having made the first strike, was ordered to join Ensign Leif Larsen, a tall, athletic-looking Swede from Deadwood, South Dakota. Larsen's regular gunner, Seaman Bill "Moose" Mohler, was suffering from a sinus problem that caused painful pressure during his plane's morning dive-bombing attack.[14]

At 1036, Wally Short was off the deck, with orders to scout west and northwest of Florida Island before turning back south for Tulagi. His squadron was followed a half hour later by thirteen SBDs of Bill Burch's VS-5, with Commander Butch Schindler again riding in a rear seat as an aerial observer. Ensign Walt Coolbaugh joined the procession in his reserve SBD to replace a dive-bomber that had been damaged in the earlier strike. Joe Taylor's Torpedo Five, down to eleven TBDs, followed, with Ensign George Bottjer's damaged plane kept aboard.[15]

The three *Yorktown* squadrons proceeded independently. The SBDs were hampered by poor radio performance and their longer scouting legs failed to provide any new data for the TBD crews. First of the second strike group to arrive, Scouting Five found the merchant ship *Azumasan Maru* still at anchor. The other transport, *Koei Maru*, was now standing out of the harbor while the torpedoed destroyer *Kikuzuki* had been beached. Off Savo Island, the minelayer *Okinoshima* and destroyer *Yuzuki* were under way in a northwesterly direction. Burch's squadron also sighted what they took to be a column of three gunboats, actually mine-sweepers, northeast of Savo Island, heading west.[16]

Believing the fleeing *Okinoshima* to be a heavy cruiser, Burch led his squadron into seventy-degree dives at 1210. Swede Vejtasa found the results more favorable, although the fogging problem plagued him again during the dive. Scouting Five claimed two thousand-pound bomb hits and one probable on *Okinoshima*, although her smart maneuvering and twenty-knot speed helped her avoid any direct hits. In return, heavy and accurate AA fire damaged two SBDs.[17]

Vejtasa's inner windshield fogging over was just as frustrating this time as it had been during his first strike that morning. *I'm not going to waste my bombs without some kind of aim,* he thought. Swede announced to his gunner that he would make another approach. For his second flight, he had picked up another gunner in place of Leon Hall, who had been with Swede on his first hop against Tulagi Harbor. It was not unusual for VS-5's junior pilots to have different radiomen for different flights. In the scrambling between the strikes against Tulagi, Swede was paired with a teenage junior gunner with whom he was unacquainted, Seaman First Class Lovelace Mark Broussard, who hailed from a small town in southern Louisiana.

Swede pulled up and banked around to make another approach after the drop in altitude allowed his windshield to clear up. He pushed over on *Okinoshima* again, and this time his view was much less hazy. Swede was feeling good about his aim as he pulled out. Over the intercom, he suddenly found that "the Frenchman was going crazy."[18]

Broussard had spotted a Japanese fighter coming in fast on their tail. The rattled rookie gunner momentarily burst into his native Cajun tongue. "When he got excited, he never spoke English," recalled Vejtasa. "He only spoke French." Swede had not noticed the fighter that Broussard was calling out. "Instead of shooting at him, he was trying to get my attention," said Swede. "Well, he got my attention, all right!"

Glancing back, Vejtasa saw a seaplane fighter with floats coming up on his tail. He turned underneath his opponent to gain a firing position while Broussard recovered his composure. The alert Japanese pilot immediately countered Swede's maneuver. "I knew what to do, how to counter that guy," said Vejtasa. The floatplane and SBD twisted in back-and-forth scissor maneuvers for several wild minutes. Swede found his opponent "remarkably maneuverable. I'd fire as we could and he'd fire at me. I could see tracers coming all the time." After perhaps the fourth turn, Swede was hoping for a head-on run against the floatplane. He waited until the Japanese pilot bypassed him with his faster speed. As the Zero broke away into a turn for another pass, Swede gunned his throttle and climbed onto his opponent's tail. This time, the twin .50-caliber shots he fired through his prop peppered the floatplane and set it afire.

The fighter dived toward the water to escape, trailing smoke. As Swede narrowed the distance to finish things off, his vision suddenly went dark. *What the hell has happened here?* he thought. Vejtasa realized the Japanese pilot had scored some hits on his SBD, cutting one of his oil lines. Somewhere in the twisting fight, the fighter "had hit me, had gotten in some arrows." His fouled windshield prevented him from continuing the fight but Swede was given shared credit for the kill when his squadron mates finished off the fighter.

Turner Caldwell, pulling out of his dive on *Okinoshima*, saw the Japanese biplane seaplane maneuvering against Vejtasa's SBD ahead of him. "Several of us made runs at him, but he was extremely maneuverable," Caldwell said. "Despite his very expert tactics, we proved too many for him," said Art Downing, who made the first strafing run. He saw the damaged floatplane drop toward the harbor and land in the water, where the pilot jumped overboard and swam for nearby Florida Island's beach. Yogi Jorgenson saw the rear-seat gunner of the floatplane slumped over, apparently dead, in the rear cockpit.[19]

Swede was left with oil spraying out of his engine and onto his windshield. "I had to open the canopy and look over the side and was getting my goggles covered," he said. "I decided real quick I was not going to land there or land on Guadalcanal. I was going to try to make it aboard ship." As he cleared the area of enemy shipping, a squadron mate flew alongside and radioed, "Swede, you're smoking."

While some pilots strafed small launches in Tulagi Harbor, Bill Burch called in Joe Taylor's TBDs to attack his wounded "cruiser" target, *Okinoshima*. Taylor and Lieutenant Eb Parker split their divisions to make drops from either side of *Okinoshima*, but the nimble minelayer dodged them all. While making his second run, Lieutenant Leonard

"Spike" Ewoldt became separated from VT-5. His efforts to return to *Yorktown* would be in vain.[20]

Wally Short's VB-5 found what appeared to be three unidentified gunboats five miles east-northeast of Savo Island. These were the special-duty minesweepers *Wa 1* and *Wa 2*, in company with the 264-ton converted whale catcher *Tama Maru*. Lieutenant Short assigned one "gunboat" to each division. From his division, Johnny Nielsen or Jo Jo Powers planted a thousand-pound bomb squarely on the rearmost minesweeper's deck and blew the little ship into pieces. Sam Adams pushed over against the next gunboat, followed by Berry, Bigelow, Rowley, Christie, and Chaffee. "When the smoke and debris subsided, there were a few crates in the water, a big, reddish-brown splotch, but no ship," said Dave Berry. "Rowley's bomb blew that gunboat into a thousand pieces, and she just disappeared." Minesweepers *Wa 1* and *Wa 2* had been obliterated.[21]

Keith Taylor's third division dived on *Tama Maru*, whose sharp evasive turns caused three bombs to splash all around her. The fourth pilot shifted to *Okinoshima*, landing his bomb within twenty feet off the port side. Adams's and Short's divisions strafed the last minesweeper, leaving it sinking near Vatilau Island. These were small targets for such big bombs later in the war. U.S. submarines did not even receive official credit during the war for sinking a merchant ship of less than five hundred tons.[22]

Swede Vejtasa struggled to keep his damaged SBD aloft for the return flight. "My engine was still kicking over, doing all right at slow speed," he related. "Oil was still running out all over my canopy and the windshield." Vejtasa had nothing to wipe his windshield with, so he straggled for home with limited visibility. Reaching the squadron rendezvous point, Swede found that Bill Burch had circled back around with his division to await any stragglers. The skipper could see his best wingman was in trouble. He selflessly signaled Turner Caldwell to take the rest of the scouts home. "That's what kind of a guy Bill Burch was," recalled Swede. The other SBDs soon became specks on the horizon. Vejtasa suffered through a long flight, peering out the side of his oily cockpit. *I'm in serious danger of having to land in the water,* he thought.[23]

All the while, the Scouting Five skipper flew tight wing on Vejtasa and monitored his progress. At long last, the welcome sight of their task force appeared on the distant horizon. Burch then signaled to his junior pilot, *Go straight in.* Burch alerted *Yorktown* LSO Soupy Campbell that Swede needed to make an emergency landing. Mentally exhausted from fighting his crippled bird, Swede successfully chopped his engine and caught an arresting wire. Eager plane crews helped him and his excited Cajun gunner Broussard from their plane. After reaching the ready room, Swede was told by the deckhands that his engine was exhausted of oil. "When I taxied to the Number One elevator, I cut the engine and it just quit." Vejtasa's Dauntless was out of service but VS-5's able mechanics would have it back in commission the following day.

Swede had long held Willie Burch in high regard, but Burch rose in Swede's esteem after his skipper shepherded him home.[24]

When *Yorktown*'s second strike landed, they reported the Japanese floatplanes that had troubled them. Admiral Fletcher responded by launching four Wildcats to scour the Tulagi area. Lieutenant (j.g.) Bill Leonard quickly splashed one and Ensign Edgar "Red" Bassett flamed another. The *Yorktown* fighters then strafed the fleeing destroyer *Yuzuki*, killing ten men and wounding twenty others. They also so thoroughly shot up the fleeing minelayer *Tama Maru*—already damaged by VB-5— that her captain ran her aground on Florida Island, where she sank two days later.[25]

At 1300, while VF-42 was in action, *Yorktown* started landing her second wave of strikers. Admiral Fletcher spoke with returning VB-5 pilot Floyd Moan, who described his squadron's attack on the gunboats and urged the admiral to let them make another strike. While Moan felt Fletcher seemed reluctant, no sooner had he reached his ready room than he learned that a third wave had been ordered.[26]

With Nielsen and Vejtasa's SBDs out of action due to damage, the third Tulagi strike group consisted of only twelve VS-5 SBDs and nine VB-5 planes. Some aircrews who had not made the morning attacks rotated into the strike schedules, including Lieutenant Roger Woodhull and Ensign Kendall Campbell of Scouting Five. From Bombing Five, all nine aircrews—those of Short, Powers, Preston, Adams, Berry, Rowley, Taylor, Dickson, and Moan—had already flown the first two missions of the day.

"I never got so tired of flying in my life," Seaman Second Class Wilburn Dayton Harp admitted to his parents. Raised in Lakeland, Florida, Harp had been named in 1940 the most athletic boy of his high school, where he had played basketball and baseball. "We landed hardly long enough to get a cup of java, till we were ready to go again." The constant flights and concern about enemy antiaircraft fire would cause the hearty teenager to lose ten pounds during the next week in the Coral Sea.[27]

The twenty-one third-wave Dauntless crews were airborne by 1400 and headed for Tulagi to finish off any undamaged shipping. Bill Burch attacked the anchored, undamaged transport *Azumasan Maru* around 1430. This time the AA fire was lighter and less accurate. Scouting Five claimed one hit and several near misses, although none of their bombs struck this transport directly. The dozen pilots then made strafing runs on a small subchaser in Tulagi Harbor until it sank. "It was the only ship we saw go down," said Burch. Art Downing added, "It received a merciless pounding, finally sinking from sheer weight of lead, no doubt."[28]

Bombing Five found an oil slick and followed it toward its source, the damaged destroyer *Yuzuki*. Wally Short passed her by for bigger game, the big minelayer *Okinoshima*. His division and that of Sam Adams attacked around 1515, but achieved only two close near misses. *Yorktown* lost several planes during the Tulagi strikes, including Spike Ewoldt of Torpedo Five, who had become lost following the second strike. He eventually ran into Scott McCuskey and Johnny Adams from VF-42. They stayed with the VT-5 pilot until around 1605, when Ewoldt ditched his TBD some forty miles off Guadalcanal. Low on fuel, McCuskey and Adams landed their Wildcats at Cape Henslow, on the south coast of Guadalcanal. The destroyer *Hammann* closed the coast that evening and sent a motor whaleboat to rescue the two fighter pilots. Ewoldt and his gunner, Ray Machalinski, rowed their life raft ashore on Guadalcanal and became the third and fourth U.S. military men to step foot on the island. Aided by Coastwatchers, the VT-5 airmen made it back to Pearl Harbor on June 16, six weeks after their loss.[29]

Six SBDs and two TBDs were damaged and three aircraft were lost on May 4. Birney Strong, who had made three strikes with VS-5, considered the day's work "an excellent raid" that "really gave us the confidence in our own ability to do any task." The *Yorktown* Air Group claimed to have demolished two destroyers, a cargo ship, and four small gunboats, and had forced a light cruiser aground while heavily damaging a seaplane tender and also damaging a light cruiser and a large cargo ship. In reality, *Yorktown*'s pilots had forced the destroyer *Kikuzuki* to beach herself with torpedo damage, sunk three small minelayers, destroyed four observation seaplanes, and damaged the minelayer *Okinoshima*, the transport *Azumasan Maru*, and the destroyer *Yuzuki*.[30]

Ensign Harry Frederickson, who had just joined VB-5 the previous week, noted in his diary that the crew was "proud of the way Admiral Fletcher and Captain Buckmaster ran the affair." The command staff and senior aviators, however, were less impressed with their results. Staff officer Butch Schindler, who had flown three observation missions with VS-5, deemed the bombing accuracy as "poor." Only eleven of seventy-six bombs and five of twenty-two torpedoes were thought to have been hits, and even this was inflated.[31]

Sixteen of twenty-two Scouting Five pilots had taken part in the day's strikes. Turner Caldwell felt the fogged telescopic sights had been a big problem for the pilots. "It had forced us to dive from lower altitudes after the first attack and our bombing was much less accurate," Caldwell stated. "We were very disappointed."[32]

Yorktown's task force retired from Tulagi during the late afternoon of May 4, while *Lexington*'s SBDs conducted a search to ensure they were not being stalked. Admiral Fletcher's TF-17 steamed toward a planned rendezvous with Admiral Fitch's TF-11, built around *Lexington*, and Rear Admiral John Crace's TF-44. Admiral Nimitz's intelligence following the Tulagi raid showed that the Japanese were at sea with a heavy force. Eleven troopships, escorted by destroyers, were heading toward Port Moresby, covered by the light carrier *Shoho*, four heavy cruisers, and a destroyer. Another carrier force—built around the heavier carriers *Zuikaku* and *Shokaku*—was close by with a screen of heavy cruisers and destroyers.

Shokaku and *Zuikaku*, at thirty-two thousand tons fully loaded, were larger than *Yorktown*, each being 844 feet in length and capable of operating seventy planes. The smaller *Shoho* was 674 feet in length and displaced 14,200 tons fully loaded, but she carried a mere eighteen aircraft into the Coral Sea. The three carriers had 127 operational aircraft, fairly evenly matched with the 134 planes on board *Yorktown* and *Lexington* as of dawn on May 7.[33]

Rookie VS-5 pilot Hal Buell finally got his chance to fly a mission other than anti-submarine patrol (ASP) duty on May 5, even if it was by accident. Buell was assigned by flight officer Roger Woodhull to man an extra Dauntless and start its engine and taxi it onto the deck. As the launch proceeded, one of the scheduled search patrol pilots was given a "down" signal—his aircraft was not performing. The plane deck director signaled to Buell to move his aircraft and taxi forward for takeoff. Seconds later, Buell—with rear gunner Barton Wood—roared down the deck and lifted up over the Coral Sea on his first combat flight.[34]

At 0808, one of Scouting Five's patrol pilots reported a Japanese submarine only 150 miles from the task force. Although VT-5 TBDs, armed with depth bombs, that had been sent out to attack failed to find the I-boat, VF-42 fighter pilots did dispose of a Kawanishi Type 97 flying boat out of Tulagi, jumping it only twenty-five miles from their carrier. Task Forces 17 and 11 made contact with each other shortly after 0800, and Admiral Fletcher began refueling his ships from the fleet oiler *Neosho*. When *Yorktown* took her turn, seven men rode the bosun's chair over the water to *Neosho*, all men designated to move on to other assignments. Among those departing *Yorktown* were VB-5 rear-seat man Radioman First Class George Mansfield and ACRM Harrison Schilling Nobbs, the longtime rear gunner for VT-5 skipper Joe Taylor.[35]

Swede Vejtasa and Fritz Faulkner, VS-5's engineering officer, had received orders to join a new fighter squadron organizing in San Diego. They were also scheduled to ride the bosun's chair over to *Neosho* for transportation back to the mainland. A number of Scouting Five's pilots had gathered topside to joke with Vejtasa and Faulkner and wish them good luck on their new fighter pilot odyssey. The group was joined by Bill Burch and the air group boss, Murr Arnold. There was a last-minute round of serious discussions concerning the expected rendezvous with the Japanese carriers. Finally, Commander Arnold said, "We're expecting some action within the week. We really need every pilot we can get, particularly you guys with experience. How would you guys like to stay aboard?"[36]

As an aviator without other duties on board a fuel tanker, Swede expected to stand many long watches on the bridge. "I'll stay," said Vejtasa. "I don't want to make that long trip on the *Neosho* anyway."

Fritz Faulkner was just as eager to see some more action. He and Vejtasa watched *Neosho* finish her fueling and cast off the lines. Swede was eager for the chance to train as a fighter pilot but he was fully prepared to wait just a few more days. He would find that opting out of the *Neosho* voyage might well have saved his life.

Lexington's air group handled scouting duties the following day, May 6. Neither her morning nor her afternoon search flights made contact with Japanese ships, although the opposing forces were only a few hundred miles apart. Admiral Fletcher finally dismissed the tanker *Neosho* with the destroyer *Sims* in the afternoon. He believed that his carriers would see action the following day.

Fletcher had placed Admiral Aubrey Fitch in tactical command of the two American carriers' air groups for the expected battle, and issued orders for the following day. As the duty carrier for May 7, *Yorktown* was to launch ten scout SBDs in the predawn hours to search 250 miles northwest to northeast in the direction of Bougainville. *Lexington* was to ready a full strike force, awaiting word from the searchers, while holding back seven SBDs for anti-torpedo-plane patrol duties. *Yorktown* would follow shortly thereafter with her own strike group.[37]

Yorktown air officer Murr Arnold started loading thousand-pound bombs on all of his VS-5 and VB-5 SBDs. Admiral Fitch's orders, however, came over on the evening of May 6 for all scout planes to be equipped with five-hundred-pound bombs and hundred-pound wing bombs. Arnold protested the orders to Admiral Fletcher and Captain Buckmaster, who ultimately let him keep the thousand-pound bombs on his planes, with the exception of the ten dawn searchers.

"We knew for certain that something would happen the next day," said Turner Caldwell. "We all went to bed early with a feeling of expectancy. This was to be the real thing." Caldwell was confident that the following day would bring the first full-scale battle of World War II between carrier task forces. He would not be disappointed.[38]

Dawn of May 7, 1942, found *Yorktown* and *Lexington* prepared for battle with 136 total aircraft, of which 127 were operational for combat on their flight decks and hangar decks. This total included sixty-six Dauntless dive-bombers in good working order. *Yorktown* turned into the wind at 0619 to launch ten VB-5 search planes, each with the lighter bomb loads. Bombing Five was to fly single-plane searches out 250 miles to the north and east of the Louisiades. Keith Taylor, the VB-5 executive officer, departed with Dickson, Adams, Nielsen, Guest, Moan, McDowell, Berry, Preston, and Bigelow. Bad weather caused Hank McDowell to return to the ship after flying out only 165 miles, but the other nine Dauntless crews carried out their search missions.[39]

During the waiting period, *Lexington* turned into the wind at 0703 to launch four VF-2 Wildcats for combat air patrol (CAP) duties, along with six SBDs for the anti-torpedo-plane patrol. Ensigns Tom Ball and John Clarke from VB-2 made up one section, along with four planes from VS-2, piloted by Hoyt Mann, Max Woyke, Roy Hale, and John Wingfield.

Ensign Wingfield's rear gunner was Seaman Second Class Kenneth James Garrigan, a young man born in Pennsylvania who had finished high school in Columbus, Ohio. The wiry youngster worked in the forestry service until he gained enough weight to meet the Navy's minimum requirements in 1941. Scouting Two's senior radioman, Fred Sugar, put Garrigan on the flight schedule shortly after the New Guinea raid in March. He was eager for action and happy to be in the air, even if was just for a four-hour anti-torpedo-plane patrol around the task force.

At 0735, a little over an hour after VB-5's dawn searchers departed, Lieutenant Taylor reported to *Yorktown* that there were two heavy cruisers northwest of Rossel Island, about 170 miles northwest of TF-17. Admiral Fletcher continued to hold back his strike groups, waiting to hear word on the Japanese carriers. The ships spotted by Taylor were the heavy cruisers *Furutaka* and *Kinugasa*, whose floatplanes had been dispatched to locate the American carriers.[40]

About 0800, Lieutenant Johnny Nielsen spotted one of *Furutaka*'s twin-float Kawanishi E7K2 Type 94 reconnaissance floatplanes, known to the Allies as an "Alf." Nielsen chased the Alf toward Misima Island and shot it down. *Yorktown* scout Jeff Bigelow sighted another Type 94 from *Kinugasa* a short while later. In a lengthy series of attacks, Bigelow expended 225 rounds of .50-caliber bullets and dropped the flaming cruiser plane into the ocean. Nielsen next spotted two cruisers and four destroyers, but, according to radioman Dean Straub's continuous-wave transmission report, received at 0845 on *Yorktown*, there were "two carriers and four cruisers." Only when he was back on board would Nielsen realize his error. New sheets had been placed in the confidential pad he used to make his report. The system of pegs and holes necessary to create the report was coded improperly due to the sheets' not being properly aligned.[41]

Going by Nielsen's erroneous report of carriers, Admiral Fletcher ordered both the *Yorktown* and *Lexington* air groups to launch full strikes. He assumed that Nielsen had discovered the carrier division, including *Shokaku* and *Zuikaku*, two of the carriers that had struck Pearl Harbor on December 7. Rear Admiral Chuichi Hara, commander of the Japanese 5th Carrier Division, was in the meantime making his own mistaken launch from *Shokaku* and *Zuikaku*, about 225 miles to the northwest. The crew of a *Shokaku* scouting plane radioed at 0745 that they had spotted American ships, including a carrier, a cruiser, and three destroyers about 150 miles to the south. Admiral Hara responded around 0800 by launching eighteen fighters, thirty-six dive-bombers, and twenty-four torpedo planes to hit this American force, unaware that his own searchers had erred badly in their reports. Instead of finding one of the American carriers, the Japanese scouts had stumbled across the tanker *Neosho* in company with *Sims*, her escorting destroyer.[42]

By late morning, the *Shokaku* and *Zuikaku* aviators were forced to attack the only prey in their grasp, the luckless oiler and destroyer. Holding back on their torpedoes, the Japanese group pounded the destroyer *Sims* with four bombs, which quickly put her under the waves. *Neosho* was torn apart by seven bombs and a flaming *Zuikaku* bomber. She was further damaged by eight near misses but would remain stubbornly afloat for days. Among those perishing aboard *Neosho* were four recently transferred *Yorktown* sailors, including VT-5's Harrison Nobbs and VB-5's George Mansfield.[43]

Thus began the world's first naval battle between opposing aircraft carrier forces, in the Coral Sea, with each side acting according to mistaken contact reports. The Japanese had spent their main striking power pounding a fuel tanker and a destroyer. The luck of the American carriers' air groups, which had also launched against phantom carrier targets, remained to be seen.

SEVEN
"Scratch One Flattop!"

Lefty Craft was pacing around like an expectant mother. After the morning scouts departed, *Lexington*'s flight deck had been respotted with strike planes. Lefty had double-checked all of his SBD's equipment, and now all he had to do was wait for news from the searchers.

Admirals Fletcher and Fitch continued closing the enemy force before committing a full strike based on John Nielsen's contact report. At around 0915, Fitch finally told carrier captains Ted Sherman and Elliott Buckmaster to proceed. Lady Lex's flight deck came to life with roaring engines. "Everyone was excited," said Craft.

Radioman Second Class Harold Sidney Nobis eagerly buckled himself into the rear seat of his Dauntless. The young native of Lisbon, North Dakota, had been part of Bombing Two for seven months. *Is this my last ride or will I live to make another attack?* Nobis wondered. His pilot, Brink Bass, told him that their objective was two Japanese carriers. Nobis feared that he or some of his buddies would not be coming back. *We will probably receive a hot reception in the form of fighter planes.*[1]

Lexington was the first to begin launching at 0926. Scouting Two's SBDs were cued up to go as the morning's CAP fighters took to the skies. Lefty Craft excitedly gave the thumbs-up to some of his buddies in their rear cockpits—Slim Colley, Johnny Liska, Ralph Gowling, and Charles Rouser. They all grinned and signaled back. Pilot Joe Smith asked Craft if everything was in order. Lefty responded affirmatively, and Smith gunned their Dauntless to the starting line.

Bob Dixon's VS-10 contributed only ten SBDs aside from one other that had been mixed in the CLAG section. The balance of Dixon's crews were being held back for anti-torpedo-plane duties. Air group commander Bill Ault was next to launch with his two wingmen, Alva Simmons of VB-2 and Art Schultz of VS-2. Weldon Hamilton followed in 2-B-1, ahead of fourteen more of his VB-2 pilots. Ensigns Tom Ball and John Clarke were left on standby for anti-torpedo-plane patrol duties. The remaining VB-2 junior pilots—Ensigns Junior Behl, William "Buddy" Edwards, Warren Schoen, Roger Scudder, and Herb Shonk—were left to ride out the battle in their ready room. The *Lexington* strike group totaled fifty aircraft, including ten escorting Wildcat fighters under Lieutenant Commander Paul Ramsey and a dozen TBDs led by Lieutenant Commander Jimmy Brett. The squadrons formed above the carrier and left as a group at 0947, with the slower torpedo planes bringing up the rear. Ault's CLAG section stayed at a medium height of around ten thousand feet to orchestrate the whole show.[2]

In *Yorktown*'s ready rooms, the pilots made final preparations. Swede Vejtasa scribbled down the all-important data on his chart board in Scouting Five's room. He plotted their flight plan and Point Option, where CV-5 was expected to be found again upon their return. As he finished, Commander Butch Schindler strode into their room. He had made combat strikes two days prior at Tulagi, and Schindler was eager to go up again. *What a brave fellow he is to jump into the back of a dive-bomber*, thought Swede.[3]

Schindler spoke with Lieutenant Commander Burch for several moments. Then Burch turned to his trusted wingman and announced, "Okay, Swede, you take him."

As the speakers blared the orders for, "Pilots, man your planes," Vejtasa turned to the admiral's commander. "Okay, sir, let's go."

Schindler and Vejtasa scrambled up the steel ladder to the flight deck and trotted to their SBD. It was spotted fourth in the VS-5 order. They would be flying at high altitude, so Swede gave Schindler a refresher on the use of the oxygen mask and the radio gear. Swede swung into his cockpit, strapped himself in, and made a quick check of his instruments. As he gunned his engine, everything seemed in order. He gave the launch officer the required thumbs-up that all was in order. Releasing his brakes, he rolled forward toward the takeoff position. Ahead, he watched other SBDs racing one by one down the flight deck.

Battle of the Coral Sea: May 7, 1942		
USS Lexington Strike Force		
CLAG SECTION: 3 SBDS		
PLANE	**PILOT**	**REAR-SEAT GUNNER**
CLAG	Cdr. William Bowen Ault	ARM1c William Thomas Butler
2-B-12	Ens. Alva Alton Simmons	ARM3c Joseph George Teyshak
2-S-4	Ens. Arthur Joseph Schultz Jr.+	ARM3c Wayne Carson Colley
SCOUTING TWO (VS-2): 10 SBDS		
PLANE	**PILOT**	**REAR-SEAT GUNNER**
2-S-1	Lt. Cdr. Robert Ellington Dixon	ARM1c Ferdinand John Sugar
2-S-2	Lt. (j.g.) Joseph Grant Smith	ARM3c Lawrence Sargent Craft
2-S-3	Ens. Richard Franklin Neely	RM3c Ralph Arthur Gowling
2-S-13	Lt. Thomas Elbert Edwards Jr.	ARM1c Clarence Halman Garlow
2-S-12	Ens. John Arthur Leppla	ARM3c John (n.) Liska

(continued)

Battle of the Coral Sea: May 7, 1942

USS Lexington *Strike Force*

SCOUTING TWO (VS-2): 10 SBDS

PLANE	PILOT	REAR-SEAT GUNNER
SECOND DIVISION		
2-S-10	Lt. Edward Henry Allen*	ARM3c Charles Wayne Rouser*
2-S-9	Ens. Anthony Joseph Quigley	ARM3c Robert Earl Wheelhouse
2-S-8	Lt. (j.g.) William Edward Hall	ARM3c Doyle C. Phillips
2-S-16	Lt. (j.g.) Chandler Waterman Swanson	ARM2c John Owen Edwards
2-S-17	Ens. Harry Wood	ARM3c Cyril Frederick Huvar Jr.

BOMBING TWO (VB-2): 15 SBDS

PLANE	PILOT	REAR-SEAT GUNNER
2-B-1	Lt. Cdr. Weldon Lee Hamilton	ACRM Gordon Chester Gardner
2-B-17	Ens. Clem Brandon Connally	RM3c Roy J. Haas
2-B-3	Ens. Frank Ronald McDonald	RM3c Charles Harold Owen Hamilton
2-B-4	Lt. Ralph Wynne Cousins	ARM1c James Riley Woods
2-B-6	Ens. Joseph Archer Riley	RM3c George Eldo Eiswald

SECOND DIVISION		
2-B-7	Lt. Walter Franklin Henry	ARM2c Michael Maciolek
2-B-8	Lt. (j.g.) George Orr Wood	ARM2c Clifford Ernest Schindele
2-B-9	Ens. J. Donald Wakeham	RM3c James Warren Nelson
2-B-10	Lt. (j.g.) Harry Brinkley Bass	ARM2c Harold Sidney Nobis
2-B-11	Ens. Robert Pershing Williams	Sea1c Charles John Young
THIRD DIVISION		
2-B-13	Lt. James Harold Newell	Sea1c Robert C. Hynson
2-B-14	Lt. (j.g.) Robert Boone Buchan	ARM2c Forest Glen Stanley
2-B-18	Ens. Russell Paul Lecklider	RM3c Otis Allan Bowling
2-B-16	Lt. (j.g.) John Gracie Sheridan	ARM2c Arthur Silvia Margarido
2-B-5	Lt. (j.g.) Paul Joseph Knapp	ARM3c Leonard A. DeSalvo
TORPEDO TWO (VT-2): 12 TBDs, Lt. Cdr. James Henry Brett Jr.		
FIGHTING TWO (VF-2): 10 F4Fs, Lt. Cdr. Paul Hubert Ramsey		
		50 aircraft total

* Lost in action
+ Wounded in action

Battle of the Coral Sea: May 7, 1942	
USS Yorktown *Strike Force*	
BOMBING FIVE (VB-5): 8 SBDS	
PILOT	**REAR-SEAT GUNNER**
Lt. Wallace Clark Short Jr.	ACRM John Warren Trott
Ens. John Neville Ammen Jr.	RM3c Joseph Michael Lynch
Ens. John Windsor Rowley*	ARM3c Desmond Christopher Musgrove*
Lt. (j.g.) William Francis Christie	Sea1c Lynn Raymond Forshee
Ens. Leif Walther Larsen	Sea2c Wilburn Dayton Harp
Ens. Harry Alvin Frederickson	Sea1c John Michael Iacovazzi
Lt. John James Powers	ARM2c Everett Clyde Hill
Ens. Thomas Eugene Brown	Sea2c Robert John Hodgens
SCOUTING FIVE (VS-5): 17 SBDS	
PILOT	**REAR-SEAT GUNNER**
Lt. Cdr. William Oscar Burch Jr.	ARM1c Willard Ellis Glidewell
Ens. John Harry Jorgenson	ARM2c Anthony William Brunetti

Lt. (j.g.) Hugh Wilbur Nicholson	RM3c Onni Emil Kustula
Lt. (j.g.) Stanley Winfield Vejtasa	Cdr. Walter Gabriel Schindler
Ens. Arthur Latimer Downing	RM2c Elmer C. Jones
Lt. (j.g.) Frederic Lewis Faulkner	RM2c Charles A. Jaeger
SECOND DIVISION	
Lt. Turner Foster Caldwell Jr.	ARM2c Leon (n.) Hall
Ens. Walton Anderson Austin	ARM2c Joseph Ellsworth Roll
Ens. Elmer Maul	RM3c Jack R. McLain
Lt. Stockton Birney Strong	RM2c John F. Hurley
Ens. Edward Blaine Kinzer	Sea1c Charles Joseph Bonness
Ens. Kendall Carl Campbell	RM3c Harold Joseph Wilger
THIRD DIVISION	
Lt. Roger Blake Woodhull	RM2c Albert Woodrow Garlow
Ens. Samuel Jackson Underhill	RM3c Woodrow Andrew Fontenot

(continued)

Battle of the Coral Sea: May 7, 1942	
USS Yorktown *Strike Force*	
SCOUTING FIVE (VS-5): 17 SBDS	
PILOT	**REAR-SEAT GUNNER**
THIRD DIVISION	
Ens. Walter Wesley Coolbaugh	Sea1c Lovelace Mark Broussard
Lt. (j.g.) Earl Vincent Johnson	ARM3c Franklin Delano Richesin
Ens. Lawrence Gilworth Traynor	ARM1c James Hedger Cales
TORPEDO FIVE (VT-5): 10 TBDs, Lt. Cdr. Joseph Franklin Taylor	
FIGHTING FORTY-TWO (VF-42): 8 F4Fs, Lt. Cdr. James Henry Flatley Jr.	
	43 total

* Ditched following strike. Aircrew later recovered. Strike composition from the research of Mark E. Horan, with additional aircrew information from James C. Sawruk.

Yorktown's air group launched about twenty minutes behind that of *Lexington*. The carrier's executive officer, Dixie Kiefer, paid a last-minute visit to his old friend Joe Taylor, the VT-5 skipper. Kiefer had been Taylor's instructor during flight school at Pensacola, and Taylor had subsequently served under Kiefer in two squadrons during the 1930s. Commander Kiefer climbed up on the wing of Taylor's TBD and taped a cellophane good-luck tag on his instrument panel. In the tag was a single strand of lady's hair and a four-leaf clover.[4]

"Joe, if that won't bring you back, nothing will," Kiefer said.

At 0944, Wally Short launched first, with eight VB-5 SBDs, followed by seventeen of Burch's VS-5 planes. As he gathered speed down the flight deck, Swede Vejtasa was struck with a sudden realization: the *Yorktown* strikers were being led into battle by four squadron leaders he considered "superb"—Bill Burch, Wally Short, Joe Taylor, and Jimmy Flatley. Yet they were more qualified than he was only by rank and years of service. *They have no more combat experience than I do,* he thought.

Ensign Win Rowley of VB-5 struggled with a faulty engine, but finally coaxed it to life and raced to catch up with his squadron. Scouting Five rookies Hal Buell, Skip Ervin, Walt Brown, and Ralph Goddard returned to a deserted ready room to await the results of the strike. The dive-bombers slowly climbed to eighteen thousand feet and circled the task force as Taylor's ten Devastators lumbered into the air with torpedo loads. Taylor's slow TBDs departed immediately at five hundred feet, while the *Yorktown* SBDs and F4Fs departed the task force at 1013. Counting *Yorktown*'s forty-three planes, the number launched from the two carriers to attack the carrier *Shoho* was ninety-three strikers.[5]

Minutes later, Admiral Fletcher received new intelligence that made his blood boil. First, an Australian-based B-17 reported an aircraft carrier, ten transports, and sixteen other vessels thirty miles south of the force reported by Lieutenant Nielsen. Then Nielsen arrived over *Yorktown* and had gunner Dean Straub toss down a weighted beanbag message. His correct report of two cruisers and four destroyers caused considerable excitement with Fletcher's staff—who had just dispatched two carriers' worth of strike groups based on a false report. According to Lieutenant Forrest R. Biard, an intelligence officer of the admiral's staff, Nielsen was told that he had just cost the United States two aircraft carriers.[6]

It was too late to stop the outbound strike group, so *Yorktown* radioed the corrected composition of the enemy task force in plain language. During this time, a Japanese snooper plane from the cruiser *Kinugasa* spotted the American carriers and reported their presence. *Yorktown* fighter pilots soon disposed of a Kawanishi flying boat that was lurking close to the American task force. The unfolding drama of May 7 in the Coral Sea was not at all playing out as Fletcher and Fitch desired.

Lefty Craft peered down from his cockpit. Churning white breakers swirling like whipped cream were visible off the northwestern tip of Tagula Island. *Lexington*'s dive-bombers passed along the green shorelines and then over the eastern tip of Misima Island. Bombing Two skipper Weldon Hamilton swept the horizon with his powerful 7x50 binoculars over the area where the Japanese carrier had been reported. Visibility was excellent. Ham finally picked out a number of thin white hairs on the blue sea. From his rear cockpit farther back in VS-2, Craft knew instantly that they had found the enemy's fleet.[7]

Gunner Harold Nobis's flight goggles were fogging over from the cold air at high altitude. His pulse quickened once the radio crackled to life: an enemy flattop had been sighted in the distance. Nobis suddenly realized that he was shivering, "but whether from the cold or excitement" he could not tell. Lieutenant Commander Hamilton ordered Bob Dixon's scouts to take the lead while he coached Jimmy Brett's torpedo planes in on the enemy fleet. Hamilton recognized *Shoho* from the sun reflecting off her light-colored flight deck, and he radioed, "I see one flattop bastard."[8]

Shoho—which in Japanese meant "happy phoenix"—was screened by heavy cruisers *Kako*, *Aoba*, *Furutaka*, and *Kinugasa*, and the destroyer *Sazanami*. Bill Ault and his two wingmen came under heavy antiaircraft fire as they approached from ten thousand feet. *Shoho* was caught completely off guard. She had just launched three Zeros for task force protection and landed five other aircraft. On one of her hangar decks, torpedo planes were being armed for a strike when lookouts at 1050 shouted that American planes were approaching from off *Shoho*'s port bow. Commander Ault headed in to attack while Scouting Two prepared to follow.[9]

At 1110, Ault became the first American pilot in World War II to dive on a Japanese carrier. Shells burst close enough to make his plane bounce around. "The shooting could hardly have been better," Ault admitted. The heavy AA fire served to throw off their aim, for Ault, Simmons, and Schultz managed only near misses. *Shoho*'s skipper, Captain Ishinosuke Izawa, watched them coming in and ordered a sharp turn to port. The first three SBDs missed, although Ault claimed one hit. "I didn't have a chance to look back and see if I had scored a hit, but my rear gunner, Slim Colley, told me I had scored," said Art Schultz.[10]

Bob Dixon's scouts, each carrying a five-hundred-pound bomb and a pair of hundred-pound wing bombs, were next. Dixon noted Japanese fighters in the air but his planes were unmolested as they approached. Two Zeros flashed past Dixon's lead section as he opened his dive brakes in his initial ninety-degree plunge. Some of the *Lexington* fighter pilots believed Dixon landed his big bomb amidships, wrecking the flight deck. In reality, Captain Izawa had continued to swing *Shoho* hard to port in a full circle, presenting only her narrow beam as a smaller target to VS-2. Ensign Roscoe Neely missed to port, but the blast tossed two burning planes from *Shoho*'s deck into the sea.[11]

Lieutenant (j.g.) Joe Smith was third in Dixon's section. In his rear seat, Lefty Craft saw two Zeros slide onto his tail as they approached the push-over point. "I aimed for the nearest and pressed the triggers," he said. Lefty unleashed about seventy rounds of .30-caliber, enough to convince the Zero to seek a new target. The second Zero started in toward Smith's plane. Lefty was pleased when the firepower from Ralph Gowling, in Neely's rear seat, drove that fighter away as well. Smith's bomb exploded close enough to *Shoho*'s starboard side to blow three more airplanes overboard. As his Dauntless pulled out of its dive, Craft chewed up the carrier's decks with his machine gun. "I had the pleasure of seeing one antiaircraft crew take cover, leaving their gun as I threw a deadly stream on them," he said.

Bobby Edwards, next in formation, also missed. Eighth in total dive order and fifth down from Scouting Two was Jack Leppla, who was attacked by Zeros as he went into his dive. He saw one fighter flash past him and shoot at Smith's SBD ahead of him. Leppla momentarily took his eye off the carrier, sighted in the Zero ahead

U.S. Navy

Lieutenant Commander Bob Dixon, skipper of Scouting Two.

of him, and opened fire with his fixed .50-calibers. The Zero appeared to fall away and Leppla claimed it as a kill. "This Jap never came out of its dive and crashed into the sea," he said. Returning his sights to *Shoho*, he released his five-hundred-pound bomb.[12]

His rear gunner, Johnny Liska, saw Zeros follow their SBD down throughout its dive. He noticed bombs splashing in the water around *Shoho* and then Leppla's bomb appeared to land "close off the carrier's port quarter." Antiaircraft fire burst all around Liska's rear cockpit as his pilot banked around to make another run on one of the escort cruisers. Two Zeros followed Leppla, and every time they came in close, Liska gave them a burst with his .30-caliber. Leppla proceeded to dump his two wing bombs on the escort ship. "The Zeros were on us and I was a little too busy to see whether we hit it," admitted Liska.[13]

Dixon's game plan had been for each pilot to make secondary dives on the screening ships to drop their smaller bombs, but Leppla was the only pilot able to shake Zeros long enough to do so. Leppla saw one Zero fall away toward the ocean and he chalked it up as a kill for his young gunner. Liska's Browning then jammed up momentarily. He struggled to free the gun while Leppla twisted and turned under fire from another fighter. Liska could see only one Zero behind him by the time he cleared his gun. He fired a burst and saw his tracers walking into the Mitsubishi. "On looking up again, the Zero had disappeared," said Liska. "Perhaps the pilot was wounded, for I could see no other reason for him to quit the fight."[14]

Dixon credited Leppla with one fighter kill and Liska with downing two more Zeros. Lieutenant Edward Allen's second division of VS-2 received equal attention during their dives. Lefty Craft looked back and saw Allen's SBD being worked over by fighters. He felt that gunner Charles Rouser was handing out his share of damage, but the fight was short-lived. Allen's 2-S-10 was hammered by Zeros after he dropped his bomb. Lefty saw the crew perish as Allen's Dauntless slammed into the ocean near *Shoho*.

Ensign Tony Quigley nearly had his control cables shot away by the Zeros. The fighters then shifted to the final section led by Lieutenant (j.g.) Pappy Hall—a veteran of *Enterprise* and *Yorktown* combat during the early months of the war. Bullets penetrated Hall's self-sealing gas tanks. Another slug entered his SBD from the front through the side panel of the windshield and ripped into the shoulder of his rear-seat gunner, Doyle Phillips. The fighter opposition was enough to spoil the aim of Hall and his wingmen, Chandler Swanson and Harry Wood.

Scouting Two's SBDs had to fight their way out from the *Shoho* task group. Lefty Craft saw bullets ripping through his left wing as Zeros latched onto the tail of Joe Smith's bomber. Smith alertly snapped his SBD sharply around to fire at one of the Zeros. "Look out!" he yelled back to Craft. "Here come two more from below!"

Lefty swung his .30-caliber to bear on the incoming fighters. "I gave my trigger a squeeze and saw the second fighter break off and wobble like he was hit," he said. Craft's gun was empty, so he worked quickly to load another canister of a hundred rounds. In the brief interim, the second Zero pounded his momentarily helpless Dauntless. A bullet ripped through Lefty's rear cockpit, missing him but shattering his radio gear. Smith nosed his SBD into a dive to escape while his gunner finished switching ammo cans.

Lefty looked over to his side and saw his buddy Slim Colley open fire on the incoming Zero. Colley's pilot, Art Schultz, found their dive-bomber was also under heavy fire since pulling out from their dive on *Shoho*. Lefty believed that Colley had downed the Zero with one strong burst, and he was indeed credited with a fighter kill by his squadron. Schultz escaped with twenty-nine bullet holes in his 2-S-4 and superficial shrapnel wounds in his right arm and right thigh. Lieutenant Commander Dixon credited VS-2 with downing several Zeros and making several bomb hits during its attack on *Shoho*—although Japanese records do not credit any direct hits.[15]

Weldon Hamilton's Bombing Two was next to attack the nimble 11,262-ton *Shoho*. He had watched VS-2's attacks from sixteen thousand feet but could see no smoke or fires on the flattop. At 1118, he gave his pilots the signal to go in.

"It was a dive-bomber's dream," said Hamilton. "We were hidden in the sun and dived fast downwind." Hamilton and Paul Ramsey, skipper of VF-2, saw a tremendous explosion in the middle of *Shoho*'s flight deck as one of the first VB-2 thousand-pounders slammed home. As Hamilton released his bomb, he inadvertently squeezed the bomb-release trigger too hard and fired his forward .50-calibers. Thereafter, his Wright Cyclone engine began to run rough. Only after landing did he realize that the synchronization gear on one machine gun had slipped, causing him to perforate his own prop with slugs.[16]

In the rear seat, gunner Gordon "Skip" Gardner had his hands full. A Madison, Wisconsin, native who used to sneak into Badgers football games with his brother, Gardner reported to Hamilton that a Zero had followed them into their dive and was still in pursuit. He ripped off eighty rounds of ammunition but could not get a clean shot. Gardner hollered to Hamilton, "Bring up her nose!"[17]

By dipping their SBD's tail down, Gardner hoped to find a better mark on the pursuing Zero. He fired on the fighter during each of its three attack runs. The Zero apparently had jammed guns or was out of ammunition, as Gardner did not see any evidence of him firing. Gardner believed that he finally disabled the Zero with the last of his own ammunition.[18]

Lieutenants Walt Henry and Jim Newell's divisions followed that of Hamilton. They claimed four more bomb hits, all aft and around the area of Hamilton's hit. *Shoho* erupted into smoke and flames, which obscured the carrier and made it virtually impossible to properly assess hits versus misses. Eighth down was Ensign Don Wakeham, son of an Anaheim, California, orange grower. He felt that he hit *Shoho* "smack amidships." Wakeham saw the Japanese carrier "open up like a red rose—flames leaping five hundred feet high."[19]

Lieutenant (j.g.) Brink Bass was right behind Wakeham. In his rear seat, Harold Nobis glanced forward and saw that *Shoho* was already "hit and burning in two places." As Bass made his drop and leveled off, the VB-2 radioman felt "great. But only for a moment." Nobis spotted Zeros up above, one of which peeled off as if to make a pass. Fortunately, the Japanese fighter pilot shifted his aim and swung away from Bass's 2-B-10.[20]

Lieutenant (j.g.) Buck Buchan's gunner, Forest Stanley, opened up on a pursuing Zero, observed it crash into the sea, and was given credit for a kill. Six Dauntlesses from VB-2 suffered bullet holes and shrapnel damage in their attacks. At least two of their thousand-pound bombs created tremendous damage in *Shoho*'s hangars, where armed and fueled aircraft burned with thick, black smoke that hid the carrier's stern. Harold Nobis noted with pride that the flattop was "burning from stem to stern."[21]

Lieutenant Commander Brett's Torpedo Two was making torpedo drop approaches as VB-2 completed its attack. They claimed five hits, and Chief Aviation Pilot Melvin Georgius's rear gunner, Roy Ghilardi, shot up a Zero pilot during their departure. Gunner Harley Talkington scored a direct torpedo hit, aft of amidships on *Shoho*'s starboard side. The explosion sent seawater mushrooming high above the carrier's flight deck—a scene caught spectacularly on film. *Shoho* was smothered in a matter of minutes, struck by two bombs and at least five torpedoes. Her engineering spaces were destroyed and she rapidly began to lose speed.[22]

"We were at the end of our scouting range when we found her," said Scouting Five's senior gunner Rocky Glidewell. He was the old man of the squadron, having surpassed a thousand flying hours with this day's launch—more flight time than any other radioman and more than most pilots of his *Yorktown* squadron. He had flown with skipper Willie Burch during the past three months, and the two had gained great respect for each other. "He was Willie and I was Rocky, although you didn't call him Willie to his face," Glidewell related. "We only called him Willie among our group. He was an A–number one pilot."[23]

As Burch approached *Shoho* around 1100, he noticed splashes all around the carrier, an indication that she was under attack by *Lexington*'s aircraft. Burch tried to coach in academy classmate Joe Taylor with his VT-5 torpedo planes for a simultaneous attack, but at 1125 he noted *Shoho* turning into the wind to launch additional fighters. He radioed Taylor that he would wait no longer. Burch followed a fighter all the way down the deck through his telescopic sight as he dived to fifteen hundred feet before pulling out. "It was the best attack I ever made in my life," Burch said. Swede Vejtasa, following the skipper, saw the carrier wiggle a bit as Burch's ordnance erupted in the middle of *Shoho*'s flight deck. Swede reached two thousand feet before releasing his own bomb.[24]

He noticed only one Zero in the area as he pulled out. "He was firing at the CO but at a considerable distance," he said. "He was quite a ways from me but I fired a few rounds so he could see some tracers." Swede, who had temporarily traded his chance to become a Wildcat fighter pilot, succeeded in forcing the Zero to peel away from Burch's plane.

Schindler and Vejtasa believed that many of Scouting Five's trailing planes, including those of Nick Nicholson and Art Downing, landed hits as well. One VS-5 pilot accidentally jettisoned his ordnance prior to diving, but fifteen of seventeen bombs were dropped on *Shoho*. Turner Caldwell, leading the second division, felt "it was a perfect setup." The good weather this day saved his telescope from fogging and, better yet, he had not encountered any fighter resistance. It was only after Caldwell was into his dive that he heard radioman Leon Hall of Dallas, Texas, say that he had spotted Zeros astern. Caldwell watched Burch's bomb explode and "after that every bomb seemed to be a hit. I released with my sight dead on; couldn't possibly miss." One of Caldwell's wingmen, twenty-six-year-old Ensign Elmer Maul, said, "On my way down I saw three hits before I let mine go."[25]

Skipper Burch banked around to allow Glidewell in the rear seat to photograph the attack. "I was carrying a K-35 camera with about thirty-six frames in it," Glidewell said. Using one of the handles to cock the camera and advance the frames, he snapped pictures of the burning *Shoho*. "The flak wasn't too rough. I took pictures of the flotsam and jetsam of what was left of the carrier."[26]

Roger Woodhull, with young wingmen Sam Underhill and Walt Coolbaugh, led in VS-5's third division next. Lieutenant Woodhull was credited with making a direct hit. Al Garlow was hanging on to his machine gun as they pulled out right past one of *Shoho*'s escorting cruisers. One large-caliber shell passed so close, Garlow could hear it roar by. Glancing over his shoulder, he saw it fountain in the sea ahead of his plane.

The last VS-5 section to dive was that of Lieutenant (j.g.) Earl Johnson and wingman Link Traynor. *Shoho* was blazing so heavily and pouring forth so much black smoke that Traynor could not even see the carrier as he started his dive. He then had to toggle his bomb into the ocean when he found it would not release during his dive. Willie Burch's excited pilots claimed nine hits and two damaging near misses. Again, it was virtually impossible to accurately assess their true hit ratio due to how severely the carrier was being pounded.

At around 1130, Wally Short's eight VB-5 pilots pushed over on the heels of Burch's scouts. Short, Win Rowley, and Bill Christie were believed to have scored, followed by Ensign Leif Larsen. Sixth to dive on *Shoho* was Ensign Harry Frederickson, who had joined the squadron the previous week. He was also flying with a rookie radioman, Seaman First Class John Michael Iacovazzi, who had never flown a combat mission. A native of Endicott, New York, Iacovazzi had joined the squadron in November 1941, fresh out of radio school with buddies Bob Hodgens and Gerald Hollingsworth. Iacovazzi felt no sense of fear. "I was just doing my job," he said. "Frederickson never pulled out of the dive but took us right to the water." As their SBD skimmed low on the water, dodging flak bursts, Iacovazzi was relieved the Zeros he could see in the vicinity had left his plane alone.

Last in were Lieutenant Jo Jo Powers and Ensign Tom Brown, a Deck Dodger rookie received just one week prior. As Powers planted another thousand-pound bomb through *Shoho*'s flight deck, Brown decided the carrier was totaled. Japanese records show three big bombs from *Yorktown*'s SBDs landed in quick succession against her bow and forward flight deck, while others exploded farther along her length. The flight deck became a raging inferno and the Japanese counted perhaps eleven direct bomb hits from the two *Yorktown* squadrons.[27]

Brown shifted to a screening warship and believed his big bomb scored a devastating direct hit. Bill Burch was looking down on the ship when "I saw a tremendous explosion on the quarterdeck." Brown's target was likely the *Sazanami*, which was not hit. Still, the excitement of the moment led several *Yorktown* aviators to believe that Brown had single-handedly taken out a cruiser. Even Butch Schindler, the trained aerial observer flying rear seat with Swede Vejtasa, believed that he saw a warship capsize and sink.[28]

"There wasn't enough of the flight deck of the carrier *Shoho* visible to make a good target so we broke off and took a cruiser," said Lynn Forshee, gunner for Bill Christie. Similarly, Turner Caldwell saw that

Shoho was "in bad shape," burning "from bow to stern, and settling in the water." Art Downing felt *Shoho* had collected so many hits that she was "the most sunk ship in the history of naval warfare."[29]

Joe Taylor's Devastators moved in from either bow as the SBDs were pulling out. Pilot Tom Ellison felt, "There never was so successful a torpedo pattern in the entire war." All ten of the TBD pilots made successful drops and all claimed hits. Japanese records indicate that at least two torpedoes struck *Shoho*'s starboard bow, and others probably detonated further aft. For this strike, VT-5 had expended the last of its more effective Mark 13 Model 0 aerial torpedoes. Link Traynor of VS-5 felt, "It was really an example of a perfectly coordinated air strike."[30]

Six minutes after *Yorktown*'s planes completed their attacks, word went out on board *Shoho* at 1131 to abandon ship. She had absorbed at least thirteen bomb hits and seven torpedoes before it became futile to keep records. Only about two hundred of the carrier's eight-hundred-man crew were ultimately retrieved from the sea.[31]

"I looked at the *Shoho* target and I saw this huge black cloud of smoke but there was nothing under it," Swede Vejtasa said. From his rear seat, Schindler remarked, "Seven minutes, and she's gone!" Birney Strong felt that the disappearance of *Shoho* "was really a beautiful sight to watch." At 1210, as *Lexington*'s air group departed the scene, Bob Dixon radioed a prearranged message to Task Force 17: "Scratch one flattop! Signed Bob."[32]

Win Rowley and Bill Christie of VB-5 were jumped by Zeros while retiring from *Shoho*. Gunner Lynn Forshee's machine gun jammed, so he stood and fired his .45-caliber pistol at a passing fighter. Christie and Rowley next fought off a Japanese floatplane fighter that appeared on their tails. Forshee had cleared the stoppage and rejoined the fight. At length, all three opponents ran short of ammunition before the Zero could be damaged. Forshee saw the Japanese pilot take a parting shot with his Very signaling pistol.[33]

Tony Quigley's VS-2 Dauntless had suffered a damaged left aileron during his attack. He made it as far as Rossel Island, about sixty miles away, before he had to ditch inside a reef just off the island. He and gunner Robert Wheelhouse rowed ashore. Natives helped them to a local missionary, who sheltered them until they were eventually rescued by a Royal Australian Air Force patrol plane.[34]

Jack Leppla and gunner Johnny Liska encountered a lone Japanese seaplane on their way home. Leppla banked toward it and closed the distance. The Japanese pilot turned to fight, and a short dogfight ensued. Leppla poured on the lead, slamming hits into the determined floatplane until he saw it tumble toward the sea. The VS-2 pilot and gunner had thus claimed kills for the day to the tune of four Japanese planes. As they approached *Lexington*, Liska felt very much relieved to see that his carrier was still intact.[35]

The returning *Lexington* and *Yorktown* SBDs tuned in their Zed Baker homing receivers and picked up the signal from their carriers as far as seventy-five miles away. "About thirty miles from the target, we ran into pretty solid weather," recalled Swede Vejtasa. "We were all tucked in pretty close together." Burch took Scouting Five down to about a thousand feet above the ocean. Swede could occasionally make out the ocean surface, choppy from the high winds. He was doing his own navigation, to be sure. *I need to know where I am,* he thought. *I trust the skipper implicitly. This guy is like a homing pigeon, but in case I get separated, I need to know where the ship is.*[36]

Vejtasa was impressed with his skipper's dead-on navigation, because the next time he could see the ocean through a cloud break, he found that Burch had put them right above their own task force. "He had us trained for inclement-weather carrier landings and approaches, so we broke up in our three main divisions and made for the carrier." Bob Dixon's Scouting Two also homed in on their flight deck through the weather front. "We were certainly relieved to see the old *Lexington* steaming along with no damage," said Lefty Craft. *Lexington* cleared her deck of fighters and also launched seven SBDs on anti-torpedo-plane patrol to make room for her returning warriors. Between 1239 and 1316, her air group completed its landings. Weldon Hamilton made it back with a vibrating engine and holes in his propeller. War correspondent Stanley Johnston found that Jack Leppla's Dauntless "looked like my wife's colander. There were bullet holes in the wings, fuselage, the tail, the ailerons."

Johnston saw other bullets had gone through the Plexiglas cockpit covers, missing the pilot and gunner by inches. One bullet had smashed into the instrument panel, while another tore the heel of Leppla's right shoe. Yet another bullet had "buzzed around the cockpit like a bee" and ripped through the leg of Leppla's flying suit, to remain in the knee of his trousers.[37]

Leppla sustained many superficial wounds to his left arm and hand from fragments of an explosive shell that had struck his Dauntless. Two other members of VS-2 had been wounded: Ensign Art Schultz, with superficial shrapnel wounds to his right arm and right thigh, and radioman Doyle Phillips with a bullet in his left shoulder.

Yorktown's air group landed between 1309 and 1338. Swede Vejtasa led Art Downing and Fritz Faulkner through a series of turns above the carrier before they made their final individual landing approaches. As he came into the groove through the foul weather, Swede could see LSO Soupy Campbell standing aft on the flight deck with his lighted wands. The first of the scouts to land were from Burch's section, followed by Vejtasa's. As soon as Swede caught a wire and taxied forward, Commander Schindler was unbuckling himself from the rear seat. The staff officer quickly jumped down to the flight deck and raced for the island structure to report to Admiral Fletcher on the success of their carrier strike.

Only three TBDs of VT-5 had taken hits—minor bullet and shrapnel holes in wings, tail and fuselage. One SBD failed to return, that of Ensign Win Rowley, who had attempted a dogfight with a Japanese plane after his attack on *Shoho*. In so doing, he became separated from the rest of VB-5. He headed for Port Moresby but ditched from fuel exhaustion before making it. Rowley and gunner Desmond Musgrove rowed ashore in their rubber boat. Natives moved them to an Australian outpost on New Guinea, where their journey back to friendly hands was expedited.[38]

The *Yorktown* and *Lexington* SBD squadrons claimed nine enemy aircraft destroyed in aerial combat, although later examinations of Japanese records would not bear out these claims. On their return, one SBD crew from each American carrier had been forced to ditch, but were later recovered. A third SBD to be lost was that of Lieutenant Edward Allen and his VS-2 radioman, who had been killed in action over the Japanese force.[39]

However, the American pilots had sunk the carrier *Shoho* and forced the Port Moresby Invasion Force to turn back. The *Yorktown* group returned with much celebration. Photos taken from Torpedo Five's Devastators, in which the full devastation to *Shoho* was apparent, were developed and rushed to the bridge. Joe Taylor found Captain Buckmaster, Commander Kiefer, and Admiral Fletcher wildly excited, as they "threw their arms around Bill Burch and me and hugged us."[40]

Lieutenant Edward Henry Allen, the XO of Scouting Two.

The intelligence officers gathered information from the strikers. One mystery was who from Bombing Five had made the solo attack on the cruiser that was believed to have blown up and sunk. "Brown thought that a little old cruiser wasn't worth mentioning," Lieutenant Commander Burch related. "Finally, he admitted his one bomb sinking, and from then on he was known as 'Bomber Brown.'"[41]

Admirals Fletcher and Fitch contemplated launching a second strike against Japanese forces near the Deboyne area, but the plans were scrapped due to foul weather and lack of information on the whereabouts of the other Japanese aircraft carriers.

While the *Lexington* and *Yorktown* air groups were working over *Shoho*, Japanese strike groups had been launched from *Zuikaku* and *Shokaku*. The early Japanese carrier group had attacked *Neosho* and *Sims* instead of U.S. carriers, but at 1615 Admiral Hara launched another twelve bombers and fifteen Zeros to search for the American carrier forces.

At 1747, a snooper was picked up by *Lexington*'s radar, and fighters both carriers were vectored out to intercept. Skippers Paul Ramsey of VF-2 and Jimmy Flatley of VF-42 led their Wildcats into action and claimed eight kills against the *Shokaku* and *Zuikaku* carrier planes. By 1830, the sun had set and the F4F pilots made their approaches on the *Lexington* and *Yorktown* landing circles.

While recovering fighters, Task Force 17 experienced one of the stranger events of the Pacific War. Three Japanese dive-bomber pilots, disoriented from their brush with the U.S. fighters, approached *Yorktown*'s landing circle at 1850, well after dark. Flashing the code letter F, the Japanese pilots attempted to use recognition signals to ensure that they had found their own carriers. *Yorktown*'s LSO, Lieutenant Campbell, was bringing aboard some of VF-42's Wildcats when he noticed other pilots in the landing circle who seemed unaware of U.S. Navy doctrine.[42]

Swede Vejtasa, topside watching the landings, felt there was something different about these planes. Looking up at one, he thought: *Funny, that guy should be on the port side, not on the starboard.* The plane buzzed right by at bridge level. Swede was puzzled, unable to recognize it immediately. *The color isn't right. It looks like some dark blue kind of color.* And then he spotted the telltale emblem. On its side, he saw the biggest rising sun he had ever seen.

Obviously a Jap aircraft! Where in the hell did this guy come from?

Right behind the first Japanese plane, he spotted another one coming in even lower. This one appeared to be at flight-deck level. "How the hell he escaped without catching a wire, I don't know," he said. Vejtasa watched the enemy pilot gun his engine and race away at low altitude. Lieutenant Commander Ernie Davis, *Yorktown*'s gunnery officer, called over the bullhorn that these planes were not "friendlies." Pappy Armstrong followed with his own announcement: "Stand by to repel boarders!" Around the task force, several destroyers and then the cruiser *Minneapolis* opened fire on any plane in the vicinity.[43]

Yorktown's gunners did not bring down any of the confused Japanese pilots, but succeeded in shooting .50-caliber holes through the F4F of VF-42's Ensign Bill Barnes. Another *Yorktown* fighter pilot, Ensign John Drayton Baker, became lost in the darkness while engaging

Japanese planes. *Yorktown* tracked him by radar until 2028 and finally gave the lost pilot a course toward the nearest land, Tagula, although Baker was never heard from again. By strange coincidence, another pilot named Baker—Lieutenant (j.g.) Paul Baker of *Lexington*'s VF-2—had been lost in the late-afternoon fighter action. Unaware that Paul Baker had already perished, *Lexington*'s fighter-director officer and his fellow communicators struggled to determine which lost Baker was on their radar. John Baker faded from the radar screens and the strange events of the evening of May 7 finally came to a close.

Link Traynor ran into F4F pilot Bill Barnes in the wardroom that night. He heard how Barnes had narrowly made it down with a severed oil line, bullet holes in his cockpit, and a slug in his parachute pack. "He actually had two holes in his sleeves from our fire," said Traynor.[44]

Admiral Fletcher contemplated intelligence on the Japanese force in making a night strike against them. Scouting Five's Bill Burch was in favor of the SBDs and TBDs being sent out on a night mission to inflict further damage on the Japanese. Fletcher decided to save his aircraft until dawn, when he could launch another strike with better odds of returning. This decision had been put to his Air Group Five pilots, most of whom had no night combat training. Burch's XO, Turner Caldwell, was pleased with the decision. "Some of us would have been surely lost," he reflected.[45]

On *Lexington* that evening, Scouting Two's Lefty Craft felt good about the bombing damage and enemy planes they had claimed. "Our pilots and gunners really had a field day," he said. Craft believed they would have another long day of action starting early the next morning. Al Garlow of *Yorktown*'s VS-5 crawled into his bunk and tried to get some sleep. Many of his fellow gunners were apprehensive about facing Japan's finest aviators again. One of Garlow's buddies, Seaman Charles Bonness, approached him and said he had a bad feeling about the next day. Garlow, feeling a little apprehensive himself, tried to offer reassurance.

In Bombing Five's ready room on *Yorktown*, preparations were made for the following morning's strike. Flight officer Jo Jo Powers lectured on point-of-aim and bombing techniques for his pilots. He advocated a low-level release to ensure a direct hit, but warned his fellow pilots that this might subject them to the risks of heavy AA fire, a pullout from an altitude too low from which to safely recover, and the possibility of getting caught in their own bomb blast. Lieutenant Powers, for one, made it clear to his roommate, Johnny Nielsen, that he intended to follow this course the following day to guarantee a hit with his bomb.[46]

Radioman Lynn Forshee offered, "I'm quite sure that his rear-seat man, Hill, would not have found much reassurance in that."[47]

EIGHT

"I Am Going to Get a Hit"

Lefty Craft and his fellow *Lexington* radiomen were awakened at 0400 on May 8. "We dashed up to the flight office to see who had the early-morning hop," Craft said. "The schedule was on the bulletin board and I found that my pilot and I had the early flight."

On *Yorktown*, Swede Vejtasa scanned the flight schedule posted on the plotting board in VS-5's ready room. Flight quarters was scheduled for 0540, but he was not pleased with what he saw. In the previous four days, Vejtasa had bombed Japanese shipping at Tulagi and the carrier *Shoho*. This time, Swede's name was not listed for the strike group. Half of VS-5 had drawn "anti-VT" assignments, while skipper Bill Burch and another small group were posted on the strike roster to go out against the Japanese warships. Vejtasa and seven others would be sent out on task force patrol to potentially battle incoming enemy aircraft. He felt this was "one of the stupidest things that was ever done. Instead of a good possibility of getting some hits on their carriers," Vejtasa and half of his squadron would be flying station off the bows of the American carriers.

The fact that Scouting Five had fifteen serviceable SBDs for morning duty was no small task. Harry Bobbitt and five other mechanics had been awake all night under the direction of Chief Jake Ulmer in order to change out engines on two of the *Yorktown* squadron's Dauntlesses.[1]

On the morning of May 8, the scouting duties fell to *Lexington*. Admiral Fitch had 128 aircraft at his disposal, with 117 in flyable condition.

He opted to send eighteen SBDs on the hunt, using a dozen from VS-2 to search the northern sections as far out as two hundred miles. Bob Dixon took off with Joe Smith, Roscoe Neely, Everleigh Willems, Art Schultz, Chandler Swanson, Roy Hale, Hoyt Mann, Pappy Hall, Jack Leppla, Bobby Edwards, and Max Woyke to cover the farther extremes. Lieutenant (j.g.) Bob Buchan with Bob Williams, John Clarke, Frank McDonald, Junior Behl, and Paul Knapp of VB-2 left to search 150 miles to the south. Upon their return, these dive-bombers would be refueled and used as anti-torpedo-plane patrol planes. At 0635, *Lexington* turned into the wind and began launching her CAP and the scout planes. *Yorktown* had the duty of most CAPs for the morning, as well as eight SBDs for anti-torpedo-plane patrol. She commenced launching these at 0724.[2]

Lexington's scout planes faced heavy cloud cover as they flew toward the Japanese carrier force. Lefty Craft was flying with his regular pilot, Lieutenant (j.g.) Joe Smith, a University of Utah graduate. Suddenly, through a break in the overcast, Craft spotted something on the surface below. At 0820, Smith climbed several hundred feet, where he was able to make out Admiral Hara's Port Moresby (MO) Striking Force ships below. Smith then ordered Craft to send the contact report by voice immediately while he ducked low through the cloud cover.

Lefty announced to *Lexington* that they had found two carriers, four cruisers, and three destroyers about 120 miles from Point Zed, their point of launch. Five minutes later, Craft sent a clarifying report of two Japanese carriers, four cruisers and "many destroyers" at a distance of 175 miles. There was a delay in transmission as Smith maneuvered his 2-S-2 into a more favorable position and dodged Japanese Zeros. Craft felt certain that both he and Smith had caused some damage to the enemy fighters in the exchange. Twenty minutes later, he got off a second contact report, but much of the transmission was garbled. The men in *Lexington*'s radio shack could not get the true distance from Smith's point of launch.[3]

At about the same time, a Japanese aircraft was detected on radar about twenty-two miles from *Lexington*. The *Shokaku* pilot radioed his fleet at 0822 that he had found the American carriers. The snooper lurked undetected near Task Force 17, continuing to send information.

Admiral Hara readied a strike force, and by 0910 *Zuikaku* and *Shokaku* were launching sixty-nine fighters, dive-bombers, and torpedo planes to hit the Americans.[4]

The American force would launch at almost the same time. Once Joe Smith's contact report was received, the strike groups were prepared. In Bombing Five's ready room, Lieutenant Jo Jo Powers told his fellow pilots, "Remember, the folks back home are counting on us." He still planned on pressing home his attack beyond the normal safe dropping distance. "I am going to get a hit," he declared, "if I have to lay it on their own flight deck."[5]

In the meantime, Joe Smith had received no acknowledgment of his report to *Lexington*. Lefty Craft found that their radio receiver was out of commission, so they headed for home. Scouting Two skipper Bob Dixon, covering the adjoining subsector to the west, heard Smith's report and also the carrier asking him to repeat his calls. The silence from Smith made Dixon assume that he might need help. Dixon relayed Smith's report to the task force and then headed east to help establish the carrier contact. Another alert VS-2 pilot, Everleigh Willems, also had his gunner, Lanny Wheeler, relay Smith's sighting to TF-17. Roscoe Neely, flying the next sector, similarly had radioman Ralph Gowling go on the air to rebroadcast Smith's vital carrier contact report.[6]

Admiral Fitch, given command decisions for the two carriers' air groups, hesitated on whether to send in the torpedo squadrons. Captain Buckmaster suggested that the carriers should steam toward the Japanese targets to reduce the Point Option—the spot in the ocean where the aviators could expect to find their flight decks after the mission. Fletcher and Fitch agreed, and the TBDs were added. At launch time, the distance to the Japanese fleet was about 210 miles, but as the U.S. and Japanese groups steamed toward each other, the return distance would be narrowed.[7]

Yorktown's flight deck came to life as engines sputtered and then roared. At 0900, she began launching, with six Wildcats under Lieutenant Commander Chas Fenton, two to cover the SBDs and four to escort the slower TBDs. Two dozen Dauntlesses were next, each loaded with a thousand-pound bomb. Due to anti-torpedo-plane patrol duty, Bill Burch contributed only seven VS-5 SBDs to the strike, all of them manned by aircrews who had made the *Shoho* strike.

Bombing Five, having sent only eight planes on the previous day's strike, would send all seventeen of its SBDs out this day. Twelve VB-5 pilots would be making potentially their first attack against an enemy flattop. As Wally Short's pilots began launching, Bill Christie found his usual 5-B-16 plane spotted in the wrong order. Instead of joining the wrong division, he simply took Dave Chaffee's 5-B-7, which had been spotted where his own SBD should have been. Climbing into Christie's rear seat, radioman Lynn Forshee noted that his buddy Johnny Kasselman had left his .45 automatic pistol in Chaffee's normal rear cockpit. "I now had two and I hoped that Johnny would not have need for his," he recalled.[8]

With CYAG Pete Pederson grounded again to control fighter operations, Bill Burch took acting command of the *Yorktown* bunch. Last off the deck were nine TBDs of VT-5 under the command of Joe Taylor. As the SBDs effected their rendezvous over the task force, the presence of Japanese snoopers kept the CAP on edge. Turner Caldwell noted "a spirited conversation going on over the fighter director circuit" during this time. As Scouting Five headed out, Art Downing, flying just ahead of Caldwell, noticed the cloudy skies were thickening: "Conditions were as bad [this] day as they had been good the preceding."[9]

Battle of the Coral Sea: May 8, 1942	
USS Yorktown *Strike Force*	
BOMBING FIVE (VB-5): 17 SBDs	
PILOT	**REAR-SEAT GUNNER**
Lt. Wallace Clark Short Jr.	ACRM John Warren Trott
Lt. John Ludwig Nielsen	ARM2c Walter Dean Straub

Lt. Harlan Rockey Dickson	Sea1c Gerald E. Hollingsworth
Lt. John James Powers*	ARM2c Everett Clyde Hill*
Ens. Leif Walther Larsen	Sea2c Wilburn Dayton Harp
Ens. Benjamin Gifford Preston	RM2c Harry R. Cowden
SECOND DIVISION	
Lt. Samuel Adams	RM2c Alvin Arthur Sobel
Ens. Lavell Meldrum Bigelow	ARM3c John F. Gardner
Ens. David Render Berry	RM3c Ernest Alwyn Clegg
Lt. (j.g.) William Francis Christie	Sea1c Lynn Raymond Forshee
Ens. Davis Elliott Chaffee*	Sea1c John Anthony Kasselman*
Ens. Harry Alvin Frederickson	RM2c Joseph Michael Lynch Jr.
THIRD DIVISION	
Lt. William Selman Guest	ARM3c Henry P. McGowan Jr.
Lt. (j.g.) Henry Martin McDowell	RM3c Eugene Clay Strickland

(continued)

Battle of the Coral Sea: May 8, 1942

USS Yorktown *Strike Force*

BOMBING FIVE (VB-5): 17 SBDs

PILOT	REAR-SEAT GUNNER
THIRD DIVISION	
Ens. Robert Frederick Edmondson	Sea2c William Johnson
Lt. Keith Eikenberry Taylor	RM2c Joseph John Karrol
Lt. (j.g.) Floyd Edward Moan	Sea2c Robert John Hodgens

SCOUTING FIVE (VS-5): 7 SBDs

PILOT	REAR-SEAT GUNNER
Lt. Cdr. William Oscar Burch Jr.	ARM1c Willard Ellis Glidewell
Ens. John Harry Jorgenson	ARM2c Anthony William Brunetti
Lt. (j.g.) Hugh Wilbur Nicholson	RM3c Onni Emil Kustula
Lt. (j.g.) Frederic Lewis Faulkner	RM2c Charles A. Jaeger
Ens. Arthur Latimer Downing	RM2c Elmer C. Jones

Lt. Turner Foster Caldwell Jr.	Cdr. Walter Gabriel Schindler
Ens. Elmer Maul	RM3c Jack R. McLain

TORPEDO FIVE (VT-5): 9 TBDs, Lt. Cdr. Joseph Franklin Taylor
FIGHTING FORTY-TWO (VF-42) 6 F4Fs, Lt. Cdr. Charles Rudolph Fenton
39 aircraft total

* Lost in action during May 8 carrier strike. Strike composition according to the research of Mark E. Horan, with additional aircrew information from James C. Sawruk.

Battle of the Coral Sea: May 8, 1942		
USS Lexington *Strike Force*		
CLAG SECTION: 4 SBDs		
PLANE	**PILOT**	**REAR-SEAT GUNNER**
2-S-11	Cdr. William Bowen Ault+*	ARM1c William Thomas Butler+*
2-S-4	Ens. John Davis Wingfield*	AOM3c William Priere Davis*
2-S-5	Ens. Harry Wood++	ARM3c Cyril Frederick Huvar Jr.++
2-S-17	Ens. Marvin Milton Haschke	Sea2c Jack Lilley

(continued)

Battle of the Coral Sea: May 8, 1942		
USS Lexington *Strike Force*		
BOMBING TWO (VB-2): 11 SBDs		
PLANE	**PILOT**	**REAR-SEAT GUNNER**
2-B-3	Lt. Cdr. Weldon Lee Hamilton	ACRM Gordon Chester Gardner
2-B-2	Ens. Clem Brandon Connally	RM3c Roy J. Haas
2-B-11	Lt. (j.g.) John Gracie Sheridan	ARM2c Arthur Silvia Margarido
2-B-7	Lt. Walter Franklin Henry	ARM2c Michael Maciolek
2-B-8	Lt. (j.g.) George Orr Wood	ARM2c Clifford Ernest Schindele
2-B-9	Ens. J. Donald Wakeham	RM3c James Warren Nelson
SECOND DIVISION		
2-B-12	Lt. James Harold Newell	Sea1c Robert C. Hynson Jr.
2-B-14	Lt. Ralph Wynne Cousins	ARM1c James Riley Woods
2-B-18	Ens. Russell Paul Lecklider	RM3c Otis Allan Bowling
2-B-10	Lt. (j.g.) Harry Brinkley Bass	ARM2c Harold Sidney Nobis

| 2-B-17 | Ens. William Clarence Edwards Jr. | ARM3c Ralph H. Horton Jr. |

TORPEDO TWO (VT-2): 12 TBDs, Lt. Cdr. James Henry Brett Jr.

FIGHTING TWO (VF-2): 9 F4Fs, Lt. Noel Arthur Meredyth Gayler

36 aircraft total

* Lost in action
+ Wounded in action
++ Ditched, later recovered.
Strike composition according to the research of Mark E. Horan. Additional aircrew information from James C. Sawruk.

Minutes later, at 0907, *Lexington* began launching, with three dozen strikers. There were some last-minute assignment changes as the deck crews spotted the aircraft. Twelve VS-2 aircrews had been sent out on the morning strike, while others waited for additional orders. Three junior pilots—Ensigns John Wingfield, Robert Smith, and Jesse Walker—had been assigned as standby attack group aviators. Air Group Commander Bill Ault hurriedly organized a four-plane CLAG section of VS-2 ensigns Harry Wood, Marvin Haschke, and standby pilot Wingfield.

Wingfield's regular gunner, Ken Garrigan, was caught off guard in the shuffle. "I hadn't had anything to eat, so Wingfield told me to go find something to eat," he recalled. When he returned topside, Garrigan saw Texas-born Bill Davis in his rear cockpit as a fill-in as Wingfield launched. "They never came back," he said, reflecting on how his quick meal ended up sparing his life that day. "No question, somebody was always looking out for me," said Garrigan.

Yorktown's strike group left the task force at 0915, with *Lexington*'s group departing ten minutes later. The eighty-two planes had an estimated 175-mile flight to the Japanese carriers. It would take them a little over an hour to arrive. Weldon Hamilton's eleven VB-2 SBDs, armed with thousand-pound bombs, climbed to eighteen thousand feet as the *Lexington* force departed. Their fuel capacity of 250 gallons was cut down by 30 gallons due to the doctrine of dropping at least 22 gallons for such a heavy load, to avoid limiting their flight time.[10]

The *Yorktown* and *Lexington* strike groups proceeded independently toward the Japanese carriers, facing low visibility, rainsqualls, and the knowledge that once again they would not attack simultaneously.

Bob Dixon had headed for the position where Joe Smith had reported the Japanese carriers. His low-altitude search through the rain clouds was like "looking for a deer in a forest." At around 0930, he finally spotted two carriers and two destroyers through a clear spot. Dixon reported to *Lexington* that the Japanese were heading south at an increased speed of twenty-five knots about forty miles south of where Smith first reported them.[11]

For the next seventy-five minutes, Dixon shadowed the Japanese carriers through the cloud cover. He carefully dodged Japanese aircraft while counting fourteen ships below, including the two carriers. The Japanese actually had only twelve ships: *Shokaku*, *Zuikaku*, six destroyers, and four cruisers. Dixon monitored the carrier force until 1045, while Chief Sugar in the rear seat occasionally opened fire on Zeros that pressed too close.[12]

Joe Smith, far ahead of Dixon, came upon the outbound *Yorktown* strike group and reversed course to fly up beside Joe Taylor's TBD. Smith and Craft signaled the last known position of the Japanese fleet and then headed for home. *Lexington*'s strike group, trailing that of *Yorktown*, became separated in the rough weather. Weldon Hamilton's VB-2 lost track of Jimmy Brett's torpedo planes and Commander Ault's lead SBD section. Hamilton could only try to match their course changes from radio information without ever having them in sight.[13]

Bill Burch led Scouting Five in a gradual climb toward the area of the Japanese fleet. He had reached about 17,500 feet when he noticed a large group of Japanese dive-bombers passing several thousand feet below on an opposite course. "I reported them by voice, giving position, course, speed, and altitude," he stated. "I heard Joe Taylor report a large group of torpedo planes approaching in that same direction." The aviators could only wonder what would become of their own fleet during their absence.[14]

At 1032, Art Downing looked down at a welcome sight: eighteen thousand feet below, scrawled across the blue ocean, were the telltale white wakes of warships. It was Vice Admiral Takeo Takagi's MO Striking

Force, including the heavy carriers *Shokaku* and *Zuikaku*. After flying only one and a quarter hours, *Yorktown*'s air group was first to happen upon its quarry. Downing called to Burch, but there was no reply. Turner Caldwell, the VS-5 XO, announced, "Ships on our left—looks like a carrier!"[15]

Far below lay what appeared to be a battleship, three heavy cruisers, and four light cruisers or destroyers near the carrier, all making about twenty knots. Burch circled to the left to organize his dive-bombers while he waited for Taylor's slower TBDs. A broken layer of clouds lay below them, and the Japanese ships were just to the north of a large storm front. Art Downing was first to spot *Zuikaku*, about two miles directly beyond the first carrier, *Shokaku*. Burch called to Taylor to check his progress while continuing to circle the fleet. A voice came over the radio advising the bombers to hold up their attack, but Burch quickly realized the Japanese were trying to jam up their radio circuit.

From Dave Chaffee's VB-5 Dauntless, Johnny Kasselman exchanged last-minute signals with his buddy Lynn Forshee. "Johnny, who was my wingman, sent me a message, tapping it out on his helmet, 'IAS,'" recalled Forshee, who was flying in Bill Christie's rear seat. Forshee checked with Christie and tapped back their indicated airspeed. "MOPA" was the signaled fired back by Kasselman. "Johnny wanted to check the setting on the radio with mine," said Forshee. "I gave him the master oscillator and power amplifier settings and we circled while the carrier *Zuikaku* headed into a rainsquall to hide."[16]

Burch's SBDs circled about the Japanese fleet for seventeen minutes while Torpedo Five caught up. He radioed Joe Taylor to take the northernmost carrier while he divided his SBD squadrons. During these minutes, Turner Caldwell could see *Shokaku* turning into the wind to launch planes as *Zuikaku* headed for the nearby rainsquall. *It's now or never!* he thought. Antiaircraft fire began reaching for the American planes. At 1057, Taylor finally radioed his classmate: "Okay, Bill, I'm starting in."[17]

Japanese fighters were climbing up toward the SBDs. "They were ready for us," said the skipper's gunner, Rocky Glidewell. Willie Burch gave the crossover signal to Bombing Five by raising his arm and wiggling his ailerons. The trailing VB-5 pilots opened out while Burch's VS-5 peeled off in a right flipper turn to attack. Burch pushed over into his dive so abruptly that wingmen Yogi Jorgenson and Hugh Nicholson had to pour on the throttles to keep up. His sights fogged up again but he doggedly stuck his head over the side of the cockpit to keep the big carrier lined up properly. He saw *Shokaku* "maneuvering frantically, turning and zigzagging" during his dive. At fifteen hundred feet, Burch yanked the bomb release lever as he pulled out.[18]

"We ran into a whole formation of Japanese fighters," gunner Glidewell noted as Burch pulled out of his dive. Ensign Jorgenson was right on the skipper's heels, pushing through the intense AA fire. He released at two thousand feet, and was just recovering when his Dauntless was slammed by a heavy shell. Gunner Tony Brunetti felt his plane shudder violently and saw a large hole in their left wing and aileron. Jorgenson's SBD lurched and started into a left spin. Yogi shouted at Brunetti to help him right their crippled war bird by using his rear-seat control stick.[19]

"About the time I considered turning around and putting the stick in, I saw two Zeros coming on fast," Brunetti related. Jorgenson wrestled back control of his plunging SBD, but saw heavy shell damage to his wing. "Fabric quickly ripped off and wiring and tubing protruded," he said. The Mitsubishis closed in fast on their tail and opened fire. At first Brunetti could not bring his gun to bear on the Zeros without hitting his own plane's horizontal stabilizers. As 7.7mm machine-gun bullets ripped through their plane, Jorgenson shouted back, "Brunetti, are you dead? Why aren't you firing?"[20]

Bullets smashed into Jorgenson's cockpit instruments and thumped into his seat-back armor. Others passed over his right shoulder, tearing away part of his telescopic sight. One slug sliced the oxygen tube lying on his forearm, causing it to smoke. "Several 7.7mm bullets passed between my legs and hit the pilot's leg," said Brunetti. Jorgenson's right leg was grazed in three places, and his foot and toes were injured by shrapnel or powder burns. At this moment, as one of the Zeros pulled up, Brunetti found a clean shot. Brunetti's stream of lead laced the Zero's canopy, riddling the pilot and immediately causing the fighter to fall off toward the ocean.[21]

Brunetti could not see the Japanese cockpit as the Zero fell away but Jorgenson shouted over the intercom, "You just shot his head off!"

Another Zero began firing on their SBD from about a hundred yards back, just below their tail. Brunetti called to Jorgenson to climb to give him a clear shot. As the SBD's nose rose, the Zero slid into Brunetti's sights, and he let loose with his .30-caliber Browning. Brunetti's gun jammed, and as he worked frantically to clear it, the Zero pounded their Dauntless with his 20mm cannons. Brunetti charged his gun again and again, but it was stuck. The white scarf streaming out of his flight jacket became so irritating as he struggled to fix the guns that Brunetti snatched it off and tossed it into their slipstream. Another fighter zoomed in from above and ahead. "I shot into him until he veered off smoking," said Jorgenson. Fortunately, the Zeros broke off at this moment, in search of other targets.[22]

Fritz Faulkner and Art Downing released from between two thousand and twenty-five hundred feet, but at ten thousand feet their sights began to fog. *Shokaku*—known in Japanese as the "flying crane"—was "maneuvering frantically and AA bursts made the sky resemble a tufted quilt," recalled Downing. *Shokaku*'s turns caused bombs to hit the ocean beside her, exploding in towering geysers of seawater that splattered her flight deck. Sixth to dive on *Shokaku*, Turner Caldwell was flying with Admiral Fletcher's gunnery officer, Commander "Jake" Schindler, in his rear seat.[23]

Schindler used his single Browning to fire whenever a Zero came within range. As Caldwell plunged on *Shokaku*, the first Zero on his tail flashed past. "The telescope and windshield both fogged up so heavily I couldn't see anything," Caldwell said. "I tried to put my head out and see where I was, but the force of the air was too great." He released his bomb and pulled out, looking back to see that it was a miss to the right and astern. Another Zero jumped onto Caldwell's tail during his recovery. He made a gentle turn as it approached, to offer Jake Schindler a better shot. This time, the commander could not miss. He blasted away until the Zero was so close that Caldwell felt he was "all engine." The fighter's 20mm cannons created white mist, which Schindler could see zipping past. He coolly returned fire until the Zero's engine began smoking. "His momentum carried him on and he zoomed over us," Schindler recalled as he watched the fighter head toward the sea. As Caldwell cleared the task force, he made a firing run on another Zero that was making a run on an SBD formation ahead. As the Zero turned away, Schindler called up in a slow drawl, "I think you got him, Turner."[24]

Caldwell's wingman, Elmer Maul, also missed with his thousand-pound bomb. After pullout, Maul survived a tangle with a Zero that his gunner, Jack McLain, claimed as a kill. Although they believed they had hit *Shokaku* three times, she successfully dodged all seven of Burch's squadron. In return, all seven VS-5 SBDs were hit, five in their fuel tanks, but the self-sealing rubber liners performed well. Burch's rear gunners believed they downed four Japanese fighters in the encounter, although Japanese records would not bear this out.[25]

Wally Short's seventeen VB-5 SBDs circled and aligned for attack while VS-5 was in its dives. Their gunners blazed away at Zeros as the unit commenced its attack at 1103. "The carrier was still at full speed with no apparent damage," said Bill Christie. Johnny Nielsen glanced fifty feet off his wingtip at his roommate, John Powers, before they pushed over. Jo Jo was "making monkey faces" in jest to his friend.[26]

Rockey Dickson crossed in front of Nielsen just as Short pushed over on *Shokaku*. Their ensuing turn enabled Jo Jo Powers to make a nice, easy approach on the target in line with its flight deck. As he pulled out, Nielsen could see explosions. He also saw another VB-5 plane plunging directly over the center of *Shokaku*'s flight deck at extremely low altitude. He felt that it could only be his roommate, Powers.[27]

Bill Guest, Ben Preston, and Hank McDowell had a good view of his SBD. They saw it was hit repeatedly by AA fire, which threw it off course. Powers radioed that both he and gunner Everett Hill were wounded, but he rolled his plane back on target and continued down. Powers's SBD was on fire, spewing gasoline from a hit in its fuel tanks, as it plunged down past two thousand feet and then beyond fifteen hundred. Wounded and flying a flaming dive-bomber, Jo Jo Powers reached a mere five hundred feet before he released and pulled out. He may have been as low as two hundred feet before his thousand-pounder ripped open *Shokaku*'s flight deck just aft of her island structure. His dive-bomber slammed into the Coral Sea a short distance away, killing both Powers and gunner Hill. Powers would be posthumously awarded the Medal of Honor for pressing home his attack almost to *Shokaku*'s flight deck.[28]

As Sam Adams's second division dived, Dave Berry opened his hood and peered over the side to see past the fog on his windshield. With a Zero right on his tail, Jeff Bigelow plunged down. His gunner, John Gardner, reported the fighter followed their SBD through its dive but did not open fire. Pulling out, Bigelow was surprised to see the Zero pilot pull alongside and wave before departing. Gunner Lynn Forshee blazed away at two Zeros and scored hits on one. His pilot, Bill Christie, believed they had scored a hit in spite of his fogged windshield and telescopic sight.[29]

Bombing Five claimed three direct hits on *Shokaku* and they did score two damaging hits with their thousand-pound bombs. Torpedo Five was last in to attack and their fighter escorts were kept fully engaged by Zeros. Three of their less reliable Mark 13, Model 1, torpedoes ran erratically, and *Shokaku* dodged the rest. Joe Taylor's squadron claimed three hits, but these were likely near-miss bomb explosions from the last of the VB-5 attackers.[30]

By 1115, the *Yorktown* strike was over and *Shokaku* was ablaze, her bow burning like an acetylene torch. Zeros slashed into the SBDs after they pulled out of their dives. Willie Burch collected five VB-5 planes in addition to his own seven Dauntlesses. Following just behind Burch's lead group was another pack of nine Bombing Five SBDs.[31]

"Glidewell, watch those fighters!" Burch called to his gunner.[32]

"I see 'em, Captain," he acknowledged.

Rocky Glidewell felt with the SBDs' slow pullout speed, the Zeros could literally "fly rings around us. Three fighters came right on us. Willie Burch had the pedal to the metal, so to speak, trying to get out of there." Burch was still closing his dive flaps when fighters tore into his plane. "It sounded like rain on the roof, the Zeros were pouring so many bullets into us," he recalled. "They were slapping the wings and the armor plate."[33]

Glidewell saw the first Zero fishtailing around behind the SBDs before it came in. He conserved his can of a hundred rounds of bullets as the Zero bore in with 20mm cannons firing through its prop—creating smoke rings from each bullet. "We were trained to shoot in short bursts of eight to ten shots," Glidewell said. "When he settled down and put his nose on us, that's when I started letting him have it."

Glidewell squeezed off several bursts. "As he passed over our tail more than twenty or thirty feet higher, he just blew up, so I got credit for a kill." The next Zero caught Glidewell with his ammo can three-quarters empty. He chose his shots wisely and emptied his remaining twenty-five or thirty rounds into the Mitsubishi. "He fell off and circled down toward the water," Glidewell stated. Rocky removed his empty can and, from his rack of six spares, reloaded a fresh hundred-round can. In perhaps six seconds, he had replaced his ammo can, charged his gun again, and was ready for action. The third Zero came in shooting on his tail, just as the lead pilot had done. "We were less than two hundred yards away," said Glidewell. The Zero came within a hundred feet, blasting away as Glidewell returned the favor with full force.

The third Zero finally rolled away and headed for the ocean. The brief but violent fight was over. Burch had bypassed the Japanese screening warships, but his plane was a mess. He called back on the intercom to announce that he had lost control of his left rudder.

"Let me look," Glidewell responded. He reached down, pulled on the braided wire in his rear cockpit, and announced that their left rudder control cable had been shot away. Burch called for an assessment of other damage. Glidewell could see a 20mm cannon hole in the vertical stabilizer big enough to throw a basketball through. For all the confidence he held in his skipper's flying abilities, Glidewell knew then that their return would be difficult at best.

"Let's head for home," Burch announced. He desired for his SBDs to close up for mutual firepower to fend off the melee of Japanese Zeros. Glidewell opened up on the radio and called to the other VS-5 pilots, "Scouts, close up."

Nineteen-year-old gunner Dayton Harp wondered if he would survive. Three Zeros were pressing in as his pilot, Leif Larsen, raced for cloud cover. *I promised my folks I'd come back home to Florida someday*, Harp thought. *So, it's get these three fighters or not come home.* He fired with a vengeance as red dots of machine guns flashed back from the Zeros' guns. Harp saw smoke pour from two of his pursuers, but as the third Zero came in on his SBD, his Browning jammed. Fortunately, another gunner poured lead into the fighter as Ensign Larsen dived into the cumulus banks.

Johnny Nielsen, Rockey Dickson, and Leif Larsen flew by their instruments when passing through the clouds. Once inside, they whipped around to fool their pursuers. Adams, Berry, and Bigelow also flew hellbent for the storm clouds, with Zeros on their tails. "Those SBDs plunged into that cloud from every direction," said Berry, "and why we didn't smack into each other, nobody knows." Ensign Ben Preston fought through a swirl of fighters as he hauled clear of *Shokaku*. His gunner, Harry Cowden, raked the fuselage of one Zero that flashed in so close that Cowden could see the pilot's sneering face. Preston evaded the other fighters in the rainstorm, but became separated from his squadron.[34]

Dave Chaffee was in peril. Known as "Red" to his VB-5 squadron mates, he was a former athlete and graduate of Baldwin-Wallace College in Berea, Ohio. "Although Davis had been in the squadron only a very short time, we were all impressed with his willingness and sincerity," recalled Lieutenant Keith Taylor. Chaffee's 5-B-16 suffered heavy damage after he completed his dive on *Shokaku*. Rocky Glidewell spotted Chaffee's SBD as it approached Bill Burch's little formation. Fuel was blowing from his burning right inboard wing tank and Rocky knew the young pilot was facing serious risk of an explosion as his wing burned down. Glidewell motioned frantically to Chaffee to make a water landing, but Red was likely wounded. He could see rear gunner Johnny Kasselman was already dead from a round that had hit him in the head.[35]

Turner Caldwell caught up with Burch's group and saw the skipper was struggling to keep his plane on a straight course. As Yogi Jorgenson joined up on the portside, Caldwell saw Yogi's plane was "shot up pretty bad; half his rudder and half of his engine cowling gone. There was a big V-shaped hole in his left wing." Red Chaffee then joined on Caldwell's starboard

U.S. Navy

Seaman 2c Wilburn Dayton Harp.

wing. He saw Kasselman slumped over in the backseat and that Chaffee's face was incredibly white as his SBD burned away with a pale blue flame. Caldwell, unable to get Chaffee to respond to radio calls, motioned for Jorgenson to fly alongside and take a look. At that moment, Chaffee lost his battle with his crippled SBD.[36]

"He hadn't flown another twenty or thirty seconds before his wing blew off and he went in," Glidewell said. Caldwell saw Chaffee's tail section sticking above the seas but there was no sign of life. Taylor and Larsen circled the bobbing wreckage long enough to see that no one had escaped.[37]

Scouting Five claimed two Japanese planes shot down and seven damaged. Bombing Five airmen claimed another three fighters shot down. Bombing Five had scored two hits on *Shokaku*, temporarily shutting down her flight operations. One bomb had hit near her bow, damaging the bow ramp and igniting gasoline storage tanks. Another explosion ripped through *Shokaku*'s engine repair workshop. She still managed thirty knots' speed, although her forward flight deck was burning furiously.[38]

Yorktown's Dauntlesses retired from the Japanese task force area, but the fight during their return flight was far from over.

*L*exington's divided forty-three-plane strike group was still trying to find the *Shokaku* and *Zuikaku* force. Only twenty-one managed to contact the enemy fleet: six Wildcats, four SBDs, and Jimmy Brett's eleven TBDs. Three of these F4Fs would be shot down while protecting the torpedo bombers.[39]

Bill Ault had the big carriers in sight fifteen miles away by 1130. Weldon Hamilton's frustrated VB-2 was unable to coordinate an attack. A half hour later, he finally had his pilots jettison their bombs and head for home. Commander Ault pushed forward with his attack with only four Dauntlesses as Brett's Torpedo Two made their runs from another direction. Zeros from *Shokaku* and *Zuikaku* engaged *Lexington*'s fighter pilots as Ault and wingman Harry Wood executed shallow glide-bombing runs on the closest carrier, *Shokaku*. At 1140, Ault's thousand-pound bomb struck *Shokaku* on her flight deck to starboard, just aft of the island structure. Ensigns Marvin Haschke and John Wingfield, separated from Ault's group, instead made similar lower-level bombing attacks on *Zuikaku*. Haschke's bomb exploded in the ocean close aboard

Zuikaku but caused no appreciable damage. Upon pullout, the duo joined up and Wingfield found his bomb had failed to release. He swung back around and headed back for *Zuikaku* to make a second attack. Wingfield and gunner Bill Davis were likely hit by AA fire or downed by the vigilant Zero patrol, as they were never seen again.[40]

Haschke retired alone, while Ault and Wood fought their way through the Zeros. Ault's SBD was heavily damaged, and both he and gunner William Thomas were wounded by bullets. Harry Wood's 2-S-5 made it through the fighters with less damage, but in the fray he became separated from CLAG. Ensign Wood headed for home alone as, behind him, Jimmy Brett's eleven Devastators made runs on *Shokaku*. Torpedo Two claimed five hits, but Captain Takaji Joshima turned and outran each of their erratic torpedoes. By 1150, the American strike was over.[41]

Ault had added a third thousand-pound bomb hit to *Shokaku*. On board *Shokaku*, 109 sailors perished and another 114 lay wounded. With his ship afire and his flight deck too damaged to land planes, Captain Joshima recommended a high-speed retreat to the north to seek repairs. His superiors agreed, leaving *Zuikaku* behind as the only undamaged Japanese carrier to continue the Battle of the Coral Sea. *Shokaku*'s damage would be enough to keep her out of the Pacific War for months.

W hen Bill Burch last saw *Shokaku*, she was blazing at the bow and aft of her island. If she could survive this damage, he felt, "she was tougher than any other carrier I've ever seen, including our own."[42]

Burch, Caldwell, and Jorgenson flew together in three badly riddled Dauntlesses. Caldwell was pleased that his fuel level had remained steady, indicating the self-sealing tanks were working as designed, even with numerous bullet holes through them. Bill Guest of VB-5 joined Burch's group next, but he slowly pulled ahead of them. Guest radioed Caldwell that he could manage only one speed with his badly shot-up engine. Art Downing, his SBD chewed up from his own tangle with Zeros, was next to catch up to the little formation.[43]

Burch soon spotted Japanese dive-bombers approaching from about five miles away. He headed for a large cumulus bank and called to Rocky Glidewell, "We're going to have to hide in these clouds." Rocky kept a running commentary to his skipper on the enemy formation as the SBDs flew in tight formation into the cover. "I coached him south about five miles before we turned east again toward our fleet," Glidewell said. "The fighters chased us in but they went on across a couple miles farther and waited for us to come out. But we didn't come out there."[44]

Burch's SBDs emerged from the clouds miles from where the Zeros were waiting for them. Low on fuel, the Japanese fighters turned for home. The Americans nursed their crippled planes toward Point Option, but Yogi Jorgenson knew he could not make it. "My engine began to lose power, missing on one or two cylinders," he said. Burch and Caldwell informed him that his landing gear had been shot away. Jorgenson told Tony Brunetti he had been shot in the leg and was weak. Another bullet had taken away the rubber heel from one of his shoes. Jorgenson managed to put a tourniquet around his leg with his belt while fighting his failing engine. He asked for help in controlling the aircraft, which was trying to flip to the left because of the large hole in their wing.[45]

Gunner Brunetti put his control stick into the hole between his legs in the rear cockpit and attempted to help fly the plane. "I did the best I could, looking out the side of the canopy, trying to hold formation with another SBD," Brunetti recalled. The young gunner had no flight training and admitted, "I'm not sure how much help I was."[46]

The *Yorktown* and *Lexington* aviators had battered the mighty *Shokaku*. Unfortunately, both Japanese fleet carriers had already dispatched their own strike groups. Willie Burch's bloodied Dauntless crews had no guarantee the U.S. flight decks would be intact when they found them again.

NINE

"A Real Rooster Fight"

Junior Behl's stomach was growling as he lined up in the groove to land on *Lexington*. His name had not been on the morning flight schedule when Lady Lex sent off her eighteen scouts. At the last minute, he had been tagged as a replacement. Three hours later, he was returning with thoughts of enjoying the breakfast he had missed.

Lexington's flight deck was cleared of her outbound strike group and at 0928 she began landing her morning scouts. First to snag arresting wires were the six from VB-2: Behl, Buchan, Williams, McDonald, Clarke, and Knapp. Within the half hour they were followed down by the first four from VS-2 to return—Hall, Willems, Edwards, and Woyke. The morning search pilots headed for their dual ready room–wardroom to relax and enjoy a meal. Gunner Lanny Wheeler learned that he would be without his pilot the rest of the day. *Lexington*'s flight surgeon, discovering that Everleigh Willems had been suffering with a severe head cold that might affect his flying abilities, grounded him from further flights. Wheeler and his 2-S-6 were assigned to another rookie pilot, Ensign Bob "Smitty" Smith, for the rest of the day.[1]

The first ten scout crews scarcely had time to settle back on board *Lexington* before word got around of an inbound Japanese strike. Junior Behl had gone below to finally eat while his Dauntless was being refueled. *Still no breakfast*, he thought as he raced topside to launch on anti-VT patrol.[2]

U.S. Navy

Ensign Arthur "Junior" Behl of VB-2.

Lexington turned into the wind at 1012 and tossed the ten scout SBDs back into the skies. Ensign Smith was the only one of the twenty aviators not to have made the morning search. Task force command soon found the incoming Japanese plane scare to be a false alarm. Admiral Fitch, however, prudently opted to keep them aloft to join the eight VS-5 anti-torpedo-plane SBDs that had already been established by *Yorktown*.[3]

The Battle of the Coral Sea was the first naval engagement in which the opposing surface forces struck each other while remaining many miles apart. One interesting highlight of this first carrier clash is that Dauntlesses were used as fighters, as Admirals Fitch and Fletcher deployed them for the specific purpose of engaging Japanese attack planes. The need stemmed from an insufficient number of Wildcat fighters to shepherd their own strike groups and fly CAPs. The SBDs were assigned to attack the Japanese torpedo bombers, which were assumed to be as slow as the U.S. Navy's obsolete Devastators. The nimble Wildcats were to handle any Val dive-bombers and Zero fighters. The Japanese torpedo planes, however, possessed faster airspeeds and more effective torpedoes than the American torpedo planes. Whereas the Devastators approached at speeds of around 110 knots and at only a hundred feet above the water before dropping their fish, the Kates came in much faster and at higher altitudes.

Thirty-nine SBD crews from *Lexington* and *Yorktown* had been sent to attack the Japanese carriers. Another twenty-three dive-bombers would be deployed defensively against the inbound Japanese strike forces. The Dauntless dive-bomber was very responsive to a pilot's controls but it simply was not intended to serve as a premier fighter plane. Capable of climbing at speeds of perhaps a thousand feet per minute, the SBD paled in comparison to the armanent and climbing abilities of the Japanese Zero.

The Japanese strike force numbered sixty-nine planes from *Shokaku* and *Zuikaku* under Lieutenant Commander Kakuichi Takahashi from *Shokaku*. He and thirty-two other pilots were flying Aichi Type 99 carrier dive-bombers—later known popularly to U.S. aviators as "Vals." The Japanese had also launched eighteen Zero fighters and eighteen Nakajima B5N2 Type 97 carrier attack planes—torpedo bombers later popularly known as "Kates."[4]

By 1050, *Lexington* had recovered seven more VS-2 SBDs from the morning patrol: Neely, Schultz, Swanson, Hale, Leppla, Joe Smith, and, finally, Hoyt Mann in the CLAG plane. Joe Smith, sixth to land, damaged his tail hook upon landing, and his 2-S-2 was struck below for repairs on the hangar deck. Only skipper Bob Dixon remained aloft from VS-2's morning search, directing in the two carrier strike groups toward the *Shokaku* group.[5]

At 1055, the CXAM radars on both U.S. carriers detected a large group of unidentified aircraft sixty-eight miles out. In *Lexington*'s wardroom, freshly returned VS-2 pilots were told to man their planes. "They refueled us and shoved us right back up in the air so we could be used as fighters," gunner Slim Colley recalled. "We were hurting for fighters at that time." Johnny Liska had only enough time to grab a sandwich before he was back in his rear cockpit.[6]

Lexington turned into the wind again at 1101 to clear her decks. Paul Ramsey led off with five available F4Fs. Five minutes later, the Wildcats were followed by five pilots of VS-2: Art Schultz, Roy Hale, Jack Leppla, Roscoe Neely, and Chandler Swanson. The morning scout crews had been on board for times varying between only fifteen and forty-five minutes. Without any formal briefing, these VS-2 pilots were only flashed a note of "port bow" on a chalkboard that was held up as they waited to take off.[7]

With their Dauntless struck down to the hangar deck, Joe Smith and Lefty Craft were left behind. The only other stranded crew from the early flight was that of Hoyt Mann and gunner Leslie Anderson, as the deck crews had insufficient time to refuel their SBD. Last off the deck, at 1112, was Lieutenant (j.g.) Swanson. *Lexington* then turned onto a course to place the incoming Japanese planes on her port bow.

The ten SBDs launched by *Lexington* at 1012 were equally balanced to either side of their carrier. The task force Wildcats were controlled by Lieutenant Frank "Red" Gill, the fighter director officer (FDO) on board *Lexington*. Gill's report, at 1109, of torpedo planes at a distance of thirty-five miles induced ten of the eighteen SBDs previously deployed to abandon their sectors and head toward the approaching enemy formation. Scouting Two's Pappy Hall, a veteran of three raids on enemy islands and the previous day's *Shoho* strike, found his new orders to deploy as a fighter pilot left him with more anxiety than fear. Hall later likened the scenario to a football star preparing for an important game—the difference being that "we trade slugs for life instead of a ball for yards." Hall, a slender man with red hair and blue eyes, stood only five feet five, but he was athletic—a former track star and bantamweight boxer. When *Yorktown* had escorted a convoy to England, Pappy Hall spent his spare time in the sail locker where the bosun's mate taught him how to tie knots, splice lines, weave belts, and tie hemp line boat fenders out of individual knots. Hall could hardly imagine that his newfound love for knot tying might come in handy this day for fashioning his own tourniquet.[8]

Lieutenant Roger Woodhull, leading eight of *Yorktown*'s anti-VT dive-bombers from VS-5, was directed to intercept enemy planes twenty miles north and east of his task force. Woodhull and second division leader Birney Strong organized their Dauntlesses into one loose formation of pairs and set out at fifteen hundred feet to meet the Japanese head-on. They stayed below the overcast, and by 1116 were about eight miles north of their own ships.[9]

More than eight thousand feet above Scouting Five, the sixty-nine-plane strike group from *Shokaku* and *Zuikaku* moved in. The Nakajima torpedo planes, led by Lieutenant Commander Shigekazu Shimazaki of *Zuikaku*, were far higher than expected by the SBD pilots. Only when they neared the American carriers would the Kates push over into shallow, high-speed dives from this superior altitude. The *Zuikaku* torpedo planes were unmolested by the American CAP, and they suddenly flashed through Woodhull's division. Dropping down at more than 180 knots, the Kates roared above and past before the *Yorktown* SBDs had a chance to react.[10]

Battle of the Coral Sea: May 8, 1942	
Yorktown VS-5 SBDs: Anti-Torpedo-Plane Patrol	
PILOT	REAR-SEAT GUNNER
FIRST DIVISION	
Lt. Roger Blake Woodhull	RM2c Albert Woodrow Garlow
Ens. Edward Blaine Kinzer*	Sea1c Charles Joseph Bonness*
Lt. (j.g.) Stanley Winfield Vejtasa	ARM3c Frank Barton Wood
Ens. Samuel Jackson Underhill*	RM3c Woodrow Andrew Fontenot*
SECOND DIVISION	
Lt. Stockton Birney Strong	RM2c John F. Hurley
Ens. Kendall Carl Campbell*	ARM2c Leon Hall*
Lt. (j.g.) Earl Vincent Johnson*	ARM3c Franklin Delano Richesin*
Ens. Walton Anderson Austin	ARM2c Joseph Ellsworth Roll
Fighting Forty-Two (VF-42)	Eight F4Fs under Lt. Cdr. James Henry Flatley Jr.

* Lost in action with Japanese planes.

The Zero escorts did not delay in attacking. Swede Vejtasa, leading the second section of Woodhull's division on the left, spotted Japanese fighters coming in from both sides. Three Zeros from *Zuikaku* ripped into the four-SBD division from above on the left. Swede had been looking back frequently to avoid being caught by surprise again as he had been during his second hop over Tulagi three days prior. This time, he "knew exactly what to do and how." His only good option was to turn hard left to throw off the Zero pilots' timing. At the same instant, he opened up on the radio and shouted to his division mates, "Turn! Turn! Turn!" Nobody turned with him, and for some of Swede's comrades the results were fatal.[11]

The agile Zero turned just as quickly as Swede did, lining up to make a firing run on his SBD. "I needed every bit of experience and every trick I could possibly think of, because not only was he damn good but he had that Zero, which scared the hell out of me," Swede said. Rear-seat man Barton Wood kept up a steady play-by-play of the position of the Japanese fighters as his pilot threw their plane into radical countermaneuvers. Another Zero soon joined the fight. "Every time I figured they were in position to fire, I'd slip and slide and dive, pull up and turn," Swede related.

After a series of violent maneuvers, Vejtasa was in position to open fire on one of the Zeros. He saw the fighter break away, trailing smoke, but his attention was immediately turned back to another Zero on his tail. The second fighter made overhead runs, firing away as Wood blazed back with his .30-caliber and continued his reports to his pilot. Vejtasa countered each overhead run. Well into the fight, he caught another Zero ahead in the clouds.

Pulling up into a stall, Vejtasa put himself into position to stitch the fighter with his forward .50-calibers. The Zero suddenly turned back toward the SBD in a desperate attempt to collide with Vejtasa. The Japanese pilot fired 20mm shells that passed so close to his cockpit that Swede "could hear the crack when they went by." He found that escaping the Zero's head-on run "at such close proximity was damn difficult." He knew that one shell in his engine would be the end. *I've got to do something drastic,* he thought. At the last moment, Vejtasa slammed his left rudder to the firewall to throw his SBD into a skid.

His nose slid left and his wingtip rose as the Zero slashed in. Swede braced himself for the inevitable collision. He was so close he could see the other pilot's goggles as their wingtips nearly scraped. Both pilots pulled their aircraft back around hard toward each other. This time the Zero did not bank around but was still flying away from Vejtasa. *He must be in communication with another fighter*, Swede thought. Sure enough, another Zero joined in. The odds were now stacked against him.

The two Zeros split to make their moves on the wily American. A third streaked in with guns blazing. Swede banked left and found the second Zero coming straight at him again. *The other is coming back around on me*, he thought. *They've got me in a scissors placement now.*

Each time Swede yanked the stick back and forced himself into a turn, he found himself heading toward another fighter. Bullets punched through his fuselage. He had to fight to keep his hands and feet on the controls in the tight turns. The 9-g force he experienced was equivalent to his body weighing more than a thousand pounds. The next instant, he would make a hard dive, creating negative g's that left his body hanging from his harness straps. The pressure left gunner Wood barely able to hold his head up, much less fire his guns effectively. Swede's hand became numb from snapping his controls so violently, but he had managed to escape serious damage.

The SBD of Sam Underhill, Swede's wingman, took heavy damage and quickly caught fire in the first pass of the *Zuikaku* Zeros. Underhill dropped off toward the ocean in flames. Neither he nor gunner Woodrow Fontenot survived. Woodhull's wingman, Ensign Ed Kinzer with Charles Bonness, were also killed when the Zeros raked their SBD. Gunner Al Garlow saw Bonness's plane plunge toward the ocean and thought of how his young buddy had shared his apprehensions about death the previous evening. Ironically, Kinzer had been a last-minute substitute for Link Traynor for this anti-VT patrol. "Talk about fate," Traynor said.

Vejtasa recalled Kinzer as "something of a character, an awful nice guy. He was always happy, always joking." He was even more crushed by the loss of Sam Underhill, his roommate on *Yorktown*. Underhill came from an influential Long Island family and had attended Harvard and Yale before flight school. "He gave up everything and joined the Navy,"

Vejtasa recalled. "I gave Sam hell every day about that. With his education and background, he had so much to offer."

Birney Strong saw Underhill drop away in flames. "The SBD is not a fighter plane," said Strong. He felt it was "disastrous to even have us out there." Strong saw the Kates roar by overhead, "and the next thing we knew we were mixed up with Japanese fighters." The *Zuikaku* Zeros then blasted Strong's wingman, Ensign Kendall Campbell, blowing off his tail section with 20mm cannon fire. Campbell and veteran gunner Leon Hall plunged toward the ocean and their deaths.[12]

The Zeros also disposed of another Dauntless from Strong's division on their first pass. Lieutenant (j.g.) Earl Johnson's plane plunged into the ocean, killing him and his gunner, Aviation Radioman Third Class Franklin Richesin. In an instant, only Strong and Johnson's wingman, Ensign Red Austin, remained in the desperate fight. Four planes from Scouting Five's anti-VT patrol had gone down quickly, taking eight airmen to their deaths.

Radioman Joe Roll had flown with Ensign Austin during 1941. Born in Three Rivers, Michigan, Roll had quit high school to join the Navy in 1937. His first service had been on a battleship but Roll had been with VS-5 since early 1941. His experiences during previous *Yorktown* island strikes had been sharpened by chatting it up with his fellow gunners who had engaged Zeros the previous day.

Radioman/gunner Joe Roll of Scouting Five stands on the dirt airstrip during the Louisiana Maneuvers in September 1941. Roll is wearing a battle helmet of the "Blue Army."

Courtesy of the Tailhook Association

Six Zeros from *Zuikaku*, under the command of Lieutenant Yuzo Tsukamoto, latched onto the tails of Austin and Vejtasa, who had become the objects of their attention. As fighters took turns making individual high-side or above-rear runs, keeping the SBDs under almost constant fire, Joe Roll conserved his ammunition. At one point, he fired a few bursts from his Browning, and then decided to trick the enemy pilot. He had heard that Zeros often moved in with deadly results after spotting an American gunner out of ammunition, so Roll opened the breech of his gun—pretending to be trying to open a new can of ammunition. Right on cue, the Zero zoomed in close for the kill but Roll surprised him by slamming his breech shut and stitching the fighter from close range.[13]

Roll's adversary fell away smoking as he reloaded and prepared to use the same trick on his next opponent. Swede Vejtasa had only occasional glimpses of Austin's Dauntless and he tried to coordinate his own countermoves by turning in Austin's direction. Swede encouraged Barton Wood to use his ammunition wisely. More often than not, Swede was lining up his own forward guns on a Zero instead of allowing one of them to get on his tail in Wood's line of fire.[14]

Lieutenants Woodhull and Strong evaded the Zeros by slipping into the cloud cover. Strong wished his SBD had more than a single .30-caliber rear gun for John Hurley to fire with. "I never want to go through a thing like that again," Strong said in 1943. The slashing Zero melee "sort of made a Christian out of me for a while."[15]

Woodhull's gunner, Al Garlow, was later credited with shooting down one of the Zeros. Some seven minutes into the fight, Jimmy Flatley's Wildcat Red division of VF-42 arrived to the aid of Red Austin. Moving in from high altitude, Flatley found several Zeros attacking Austin's SBD beneath at six thousand feet. His F4Fs shortly scattered them, claiming three fighters destroyed in return for Lieutenant (j.g.) Dick Crommelin being shot down.

Vejtasa remained locked in his fight with *Zuikaku* Zeros. *It is obvious that they have selected me as the target for the morning and they plan to dispatch me pretty quickly,* he thought. Swede's SBD was hit several times, and a piece of metal sliced into his leg. His fight had gone on for some fifteen minutes. He was waiting for the Zeros to make a mistake. He finally cut inside the turn of one of them and lined himself up for a good head-on shot. "What I was really trying to do was to get some bullets into their gas tanks by firing fairly low into the engine," he said. Instead, his slugs tore into the Zero's engine, and he saw smoke begin pouring out.

As this victim dropped away, Swede pulled up nearly vertically and latched onto another opponent. He got in a good burst and narrowly missed colliding with the enemy plane as it plunged toward the sea. Vejtasa soon lost track of any other Zeros and spotted Red Austin's Dauntless in the distance. Red had been slightly wounded, and as Swede joined up, he saw that his dive-bomber was in bad shape. Only Vejtasa, Austin, Woodhull, and Strong emerged from the fight near the task force. Woodhull reported that their leakproof tanks had saved three of the remaining four SBDS from gas loss or fire. Half of their division had been shot away. In return, Vejtasa and three gunners—Garlow, Roll, and Wood—claimed credit for destroying a Japanese fighter. The Nakajimas they had been launched to destroy had made it through *Yorktown*'s anti-VT patrol untouched.

Scouting Two's Ensign Art Schultz was the first of the *Lexington* dive-bombers to make contact. He was a little east of Scouting Five's fight when he spotted four of Lieutenant Commander Shimazaki's *Zuikaku* planes diving at him almost head-on. Schultz swung around to take them under fire as they passed. He made several passes with his forward guns and believed he had finished one off. Another *Zuikaku* fighter moved in on Schultz's tail, and gunner Wayne Colley fired back at it.[16]

Schultz pulled up to force the Zero to overrun and come into his forward gun range. The Japanese pilot climbed out of range too quickly and turned inside the SBD for a second pass. Schultz evaded with a tight spiral and sought protection in nearby cloud cover. "We rolled over upside down, heading for the ocean," recalled Colley. "I grayed out. I didn't black out, but I lost my vision. I could hear the bullets every now and then banging into the plane. Those that didn't bang in, you could hear them going by. They had a real sharp, vicious snap to them."[17]

Schultz righted his plane low on the water, and Colley began to get his vision back. One opponent had stuck with them through their maneuver and was closing again. At the same time, he saw a Wildcat from VF-2 diving in to their aid. Ensign "Doc" Sellstrom locked onto one of the torpedo planes close to the water. In short order, one Nakajima was certainly destroyed, the victim of either Sellstrom or Schultz's handiwork. Colley suddenly saw the plane on his tail erupt into flames, and felt deep gratitude toward Sellstrom for his intervention.[18]

The surviving Kates launched torpedoes at *Yorktown* at 1118, but Captain Buckmaster was able to dodge them. Antiaircraft fire accounted for two of the B5N2s. Lieutenant (j.g.) Max Woyke, flying with Lieutenant Tommy Edwards of VS-2 on *Lexington*'s starboard bow, claimed a kill on one of these Kates after it made its drop.[19]

Captain Ted Sherman managed to dodge the first torpedoes dropped by the Kates from *Zuikaku* and *Shokaku* that began assaulting his carrier. The next group of Nakajimas circled to attack from Lady Lex's starboard bow, where they were greeted by VB-2's Lieutenant (j.g.) Paul Knapp and Ensign John Clarke. Knapp's forward guns quickly jammed and then his gunner, Len DeSalvo, had to fight with a rear Browning gun mount that locked in one position. Fortunately for them, Ensign Bob Smith of VS-2 latched onto a Kate that Knapp's crew was unable to finish. Smith claimed two Nakajimas from *Shokaku*'s torpedo squadron.[20]

Battle of the Coral Sea: May 8, 1942		
USS Lexington *SBDs: Anti-Torpedo-Plane Patrol*		
PLANE	**PILOT / DEFENSIVE POSITION**	**REAR-SEAT GUNNER**
PORT BOW POSITION		
2-S-8	Lt. (j.g.) William Edward Hall+	Sea1c John Arthur Moore
2-S-6	Ens. Robert Edward Smith	ARM3c Lanois Mardi Wheeler

(continued)

PLANE	PILOT / DEFENSIVE POSITION	REAR-SEAT GUNNER
Battle of the Coral Sea: May 8, 1942		
Lexington SBDs: Anti-Torpedo-Plane Patrol		
PORT QUARTER POSITION		
2-B-1	Lt. (j.g.) Robert Boone Buchan	ARM2c Forest Glen Stanley
2-B-13	Ens. Frank Ronald McDonald+	RM3c Charles Harold Owen Hamilton+
2-B-6	Ens. Arthur J. Behl	ARM3c Joseph George Teyshak
STARBOARD BOW POSITION		
2-S-13	Lt. Thomas Elbert Edwards Jr.	ARM1c Clarence Halman Garlow
2-S-14	Ens. Max Einar Eric Woyke	ARM3c Raymond Eugene Reames
STARBOARD QUARTER POSITION		
2-B-5	Lt. (j.g.) Paul Joseph Knapp	ARM3c Leonard A. DeSalvo
2-B-4	Ens. Robert Pershing Williams	Sea1c Charles John Young
2-B-16	Ens. John M. Clarke	ARM3c Ralph H. Horton

STARBOARD AHEAD POSITION		
2-S-15	Ens. Arthur Joseph Schultz Jr.	ARM3c Wayne Carson Colley
PORT BOW POSITION		
2-S-18	Lt. (j.g.) Roy Orestus Hale Jr.*	ARM2c John Delmar Lackey*
2-S-12	Ens. John Arthur Leppla	ARM3c John Liska
STARBOARD BOW POSITION		
2-S-3	Ens. Richard Franklin Neely	RM3c Ralph Arthur Gowling
2-S-16	Lt. (j.g.) Chandler Waterman Swanson+	ARM2c John Owen Edwards*

+ Wounded in action
* Lost in action
Note: All of these airmen, except Ensign Smith, had made the morning scout mission.

In the meantime, Pappy Hall engaged the six other inbound Kates from the *Shokaku. This is like suicide, taking on this whole bunch,* he thought. *But here they come. This will be a real rooster fight.*[21]

The Nakajimas were approaching *Lexington* at six hundred feet in a dive for her port side. Hall rolled sharply left onto the tail of Lieutenant Norio Yano and set his B5N2 on fire with his forward .50-calibers. As both Hall and Yano passed over the destroyer *Dewey* and other escort ships, they came under heavy AA fire. Hall "saw the right wing of the enemy craft start to smoke and the plane went into a left rolling turn, plunging toward the water." Spotters on board *Lexington* saw Hall's victim hit the ocean before it reached its drop point. Pappy did not feel particularly brave. "I was just trying to keep myself in the air," he recalled. He promptly set fire to another torpedo plane piloted by Warrant Officer Saburo Shindo, who managed to release his torpedo and then tried to crash into the American carrier. Shindo's flaming plane slammed into the ocean with a fiery explosion a hundred yards short of *Lexington*'s starboard bow.[22]

The remaining two pilots of Yano's second section were attacked by VS-2's Lieutenant (j.g.) Roy Hale and Ensign Jack Leppla. Leppla and gunner Johnny Liska had claimed four aerial victories during the previous day's *Shoho* strike. Leppla dived after the incoming Nakajimas and overtook one. He fired into it, and then took a good shot at the other plane. Both *Shokaku* planes veered sharply right and away from *Lexington*, leading Leppla to believe he had shot them down. Both Japanese pilots dropped against the cruiser *Minneapolis*, but she evaded their torpedoes.[23]

At 1120, three remaining Kates from *Shokaku* made unopposed torpedo drops against *Lexington*'s port bow. One missed but the other two torpedoes hit home forward and amidships, causing tremendous explosions and shudders down *Lexington*'s length. Joe Smith had gone below to VS-2's ready room to ride out the attack. His carrier "shook like a toy boat" as explosions rocked her. The concussion from one blast momentarily knocked Smith unconscious, but he made it topside in time to see the last Japanese striker being shot down.[24]

In Bombing Two's combination ready room–wardroom, Lieutenant Hoyt Mann had sweated out the Japanese attack with his remaining pilots—Ensigns Tom Ball, Joe Riley, Alva Simmons, Herb Shonk, Roger Scudder, and Warren Schoen. A loud explosion suddenly swept flame and smoke into the room, knocking Simmons to the deck. The compartment became untenable, so Mann—who had been on board *Lexington* since 1939—led the junior pilots, stewards' mates, and gunners through the darkened officers' country. His men hung on to one another's shirttails while stumbling over bodies in the darkness. Mann's group reached the starboard AA platform and gulped fresh air as the ship's guns were still shooting at retiring Japanese aircraft.[25]

Jack Leppla, having shot up two Kates, was climbing for altitude when he was attacked by several *Zuikaku* Zeros. One began scoring hits on Jack's SBD while the other two took turns making firing runs from astern. "It was the biggest melee I've ever seen, with planes all over the sky," said Liska, who kept up a continual fire on the swirling Zeros. He could hear Leppla doing the same with his forward guns. The Zeros riddled Leppla's 2-S-12 and knocked out his starboard-side forward .50-caliber. Liska was certain, however, that he burned one of his opponents in the process.[26]

The *Zuikaku* Zeros also made firing runs on the Dauntlesses flown by Roy Hale and Bob Smith. Ensign Smith could not see his attackers but heard rear gunner Lanny Wheeler firing furiously, so he escaped by flying past *Lexington*'s bow to the starboard side. Paul Knapp latched onto one of the retiring Kates with his SBD and chased it more than six miles until his forward .50s jammed completely.[27]

Aichi Type 99 Val dive-bombers moved in on the American task force about five minutes after the Kates had completed their torpedo runs. Nineteen Vals swarmed *Lexington*, hit her with two bombs, and shook her hull with damaging near misses. Fourteen bombers from *Zuikaku* attacked *Yorktown*, hitting her with a 240-kilogram high-explosive bomb at 1127. It crashed through the flight deck, about fifteen feet from the island. Brothers Otis and Otto Phelps were sitting in the VB-5 ready room, listening to the attack, since they had not been assigned to the *Shokaku* strike group. The bomb literally passed between them as it slashed through the ready room and through three more decks before exploding in a storeroom below.[28]

As the Japanese recovered from their dives, some encountered the anti-VT patrol SBDs. One Val flew up alongside Ensign Robert Williams's SBD and opened fire. His rear gunner, Charles Young, briefly exchanged fire as the two bombers passed, and Williams's SBD took several hits in the tail section. Another VB-2 pilot, John Clarke, attacked a retiring Val and claimed it as a kill.[29]

Pappy Hall had claimed two torpedo plane kills in the early skirmishes. As he climbed back for altitude advantage, his SBD's engine suddenly began to cut out. In an instant he realized his mistake: "After taking off, I switched my gas line to the right tank to save the main tank's fuel for combat," he recalled. Hall shifted from auxiliary to main fuel tanks but had lost the altitude advantage he had hoped for. At this inopportune moment, he was jumped by four *Shokaku* Zeros that made repeated runs. The leading Zero dived onto Hall's tail. Bullets clanged and zipped by as they punched through the dive-bomber's thin skin and left entry and exit holes. Another bullet slashed through Pappy's front cockpit, severing the headphone cord to his flight helmet.[30]

As Hall commenced violent maneuvers, Johnny Moore blasted away from the rear seat. The first Zero passed under their Dauntless and came up in a shallow, climbing right turn. Hall poured in the lead. "I was able to get on his tail and he never pulled out of the shallow turn and went in," he said. In the twisting fight, Moore believed that he flamed one of the pursuing Zeros and damaged a second. Hall climbed for altitude after his firing run and spotted another Zero coming head-on with his guns blazing. "I returned the fire and did not turn away as we neared," said Hall. The Zero finally pulled out to the left in a slow downward slant toward the ocean. Hall made a climbing turn to the right to watch his latest victim head toward the wave tops. As he did so, another Zero latched onto his tail with devastating results.[31]

The Japanese pilot put a 20mm round through the fuselage of Hall's 2-S-8, just in front of the pilot's cockpit. The explosion nearly tore off Hall's right foot, peppered his leg with shell fragments, and knocked out his plane's hydraulics. "There was no pain but a sudden pressure on my foot," he recalled. Another piece of shrapnel tore into the back of his skull. It somehow punched a small hole in his head without tearing through his flight helmet. Hall was determined to stay in the fight despite the fact that he could not put his torn right foot on the rudder pedal. He instead steered with his left foot and worked the rudder trim tabs until the aerial fight was completed and he escaped into a cloud.

The surviving Zero disappeared as quickly as the pilot had shattered their plane. Moore was uninjured in the rear cockpit, but Pappy was in for the struggle of his life. A dull pain throbbed near the base of his skull. His cockpit was splattered with his own blood. His right foot had lost its function. With no hydraulic control, he began manhandling his tattered Dauntless toward a friendly flight deck, hoping to avoid a water landing that might prove fatal.

Jack Leppla and John Liska became wrapped up in a fresh fight. They came upon two Zeros attacking another SBD, so Leppla dived in and began hammering one with his only functional .50-caliber. He exhausted the last of his ammunition but drove off the Mitsubishi in the process, feeling confident he had shot it down. The pilot he likely saved was squadron mate Roy Hale.[32]

Hale tried to land his crippled SBD on *Lexington* at 1129 as the dive-bombing attack was ending. Although his 2-S-18 clearly sported white stars on its fuselage and wings, Hale's Dauntless was fired upon by *Lexington* and her screening vessels. By the time the observers below realized that an American dive-bomber was under fire, it was too late. Hale turned away from *Lexington* and flew toward the heavy cruiser *New Orleans* off her port bow. The *New Orleans* gunners hammered the misidentified SBD, and Hale slammed into the water under partial control near the cruiser's starboard bow. Neither Hale nor gunner John Lackey escaped their SBD before it sank. John Liska glimpsed a friendly plane splashing about this time, which was certainly Hale's. Leppla's own plane was taken under fire again by two *Shokaku* Zeros. Liska's return fire was enough to draw smoke from one of his opponents, after which the Zeros departed.[33]

Other *Lexington* SBDs were still fighting it out. With his forward guns, Ensign Roscoe Neely claimed two aerial victories against retiring *Shokaku* dive-bombers. Buck Buchan and his VB-2 wingmen, Frank McDonald and Junior Behl, had split up when the task force erupted into gunfire. Buchan engaged a retiring Kate torpedo bomber head-on with skipper Weldon Hamilton's 2-B-1, which had shot holes in its own propeller the previous day due to malfunctioning synchronization gear. This time Buchan poured lead into both Nakajimas and suffered only one hole through the prop. McDonald clashed with a shiny, new-looking lone Zero that got the better of their duel. McDonald's 2-B-13 was riddled with 7.7mm slugs and one round tore into his right shoulder. Painfully wounded, McDonald turned back toward *Lexington,* hoping to make it on board as soon as her flight deck was open for business.[34]

The last anti-VT patrol SBD to launch from *Lexington* before the Japanese strikes was piloted by Chandler Swanson. Scouting Two's communications officer had wanted to fly since early childhood. Swanson used to lie on the grass, looking at the stars at night in Minnesota with his brother, saying how he wanted to be a pilot, while his brother dreamed of becoming an astronomer. Now the Carleton College graduate was living his dream and facing two *Shokaku* Zeros that dived in from ahead of them. Swanson attacked the leader head-on at high speed and caught his opponent off guard.[35]

The second Zero jumped on his tail, forcing Swanson to conduct a tight turn and dive for the ocean. The Zero remained in hot pursuit as Aviation Radioman Second Class John Edwards opened up with his .30-caliber. Swanson suddenly heard Edwards shout, "They got me!"

A bullet ripped through the gunner's lower abdomen. Free from opposing fire, the Zero closed in and raked Swanson's 2-S-16, nearly severing the aileron control cables. Once the Zero broke off for home, the pilot called back for Edwards but heard no reply. Swanson then turned toward the task force to bring aid to his severely wounded rear gunner.[36]

Lexington and *Yorktown* had both been heavily damaged in the multiple rounds of Japanese carrier plane attacks. Of their twenty-three SBDs that took part in the anti-VT patrols, six had been destroyed and two others were jettisoned. Eleven pilots and radiomen were killed in action. Hall, McDonald, and Austin had been wounded. Aerial credits to VS-5 were four Zeros shot down, two probables, and seven damaged. Scouting Two pilots and gunners claimed seven torpedo planes and six fighters shot down, plus one fighter as a probable. Bombing Two claimed one Kate and one Val destroyed. Analysis of Japanese records by naval historian John Lundstrom showed actual kills by the SBDs were more likely five or six torpedo planes and one dive-bomber—although five airplanes returning to *Zuikaku* were so badly shot up they were dumped overboard and another was forced to ditch.[37]

TEN

"You Are on Your Own"

Rocky Glidewell turned to the little black Zed Baker box to guide Scouting Five home. This instrument received coded UHF (ultra-high-frequency) signals, broadcast straight out from their ship, that indicated various sectors. "At ten thousand feet, you could pick up these signals at about 100 miles," he recalled. "We had to memorize the codes for the sectors because they changed every couple of days."[1]

Glidewell picked up the homing signal at higher altitude and guided Burch toward the U.S. fleet. In the distance he could soon see *Lexington* burning with billowing black smoke. To Turner Caldwell, the "peculiar greenish-colored patches" of oil on the water's surface, each marking the location of a downed aircraft, indicated "there were an awful lot of them." At around 1130, the U.S. carriers began recovering their own aircraft as the last enemy attackers departed. Among the first to wobble into *Lexington*'s landing pattern was the anti-VT patrol SBD of wounded pilot Frank McDonald. His carrier was executing a hard turn to starboard as he came in at 150 feet. Black antiaircraft bursts and lines of red tracers arced toward his Dauntless. The LSO, Lieutenant Acquilla G. Dibrell, frantically waved off McDonald's SBD. Attempting to hold the stick with his right arm, McDonald lost control due to his shoulder wound.[2]

He cut the engine during his landing, but 2-B-13 hit the slanted ramp at a bad angle. His arresting gear snapped the number-two wire and McDonald's SBD cartwheeled across the flight deck, plunging over *Lexington*'s port side just aft of the barrier. Aviation Machinist's Mate Third Class Edgar R. Jones, who was manning the arresting gear, was swept over the side as well. Radioman Charles Hamilton escaped the sinking Dauntless without injury, but Ensign McDonald had suffered a bullet in his shoulder, and his right humerus bone was broken in two places. In spite of his lame arm, McDonald remained afloat until he and Hamilton were picked up by the destroyer *Morris*.[3]

Pappy Hall, bleeding heavily and in great pain, brought his badly shot-up SBD in on *Lexington* at 1139. While waiting to land, he used the radio cord severed from his flight helmet to improvise a tourniquet around his right leg. While approaching, he fired a red Very flare to warn the ships below that he was friendly. "I tried to drop my landing gear, and only one wheel came down, as I had no hydraulic action," Hall recalled. He also made a sharp left turn, hoping that his three acts would properly identify him as an approaching friendly plane.[4]

The left turn, the dropped landing gear, and the red signal flare, however, seemed only to excite the eager American gunners on the destroyer he was passing over. The tin can opened up with a full broadside of fire on Hall's 2-S-8. One five-inch shell ripped right through his cockpit. Hall was relieved that the shell apparently had not traveled far enough to arm its fuses, thereby not detonating. The shell ripped a hole through both sides of his front fuselage and tore the leg off his flight suit.

The Zeros nearly did me in, he thought, *but now I'm going to be killed by my own people!*

Hall continued his turn and dived to the wave tops to escape the destroyer's gunners. He then flew around the task force and made another approach from the direction of *Yorktown*. He made his way over to *Lexington* and did an emergency landing pass, flying past the flight deck while indicating to those on board that he needed to come down immediately. He banked around, flying past the stern before swinging around to come into the groove. He shook his plane violently all the while and finally managed to drop his other wheel. With his hydraulic system out, Hall was unable to use his landing flaps to check his airspeed during descent. He came in thirty knots faster than his ordinary landing speed. With his right foot useless, he kept the plane under control by using the hand tab controls.

Dibrell signaled a wave-off to Hall because of his excessive speed. "I knew I could not last another round, as my engine had long since exceeded the danger heat point," he recalled. Weak from blood loss, he was unable to open the engine-cooling flaps or the oil cooler, and his engine was about to go. Hall ignored the LSO's frantic waves, cut his engine, and dropped fast onto the deck. His SBD's tail hook snagged the second arresting wire and ripped it out of the deck. His Dauntless skipped over the next several wires before his hook caught the ninth and final wire. His plane jerked to a violent halt right in front of the crash barrier.

Looking over his wrecked mount in a daze, Hall noted that his SBD "had been so throughly riddled, it was a wonder it didn't break its back while we were landing." Gunner Johnny Moore was unhurt even though the armor plating surrounding him sported bullet dents. Flight-deck personnel swarmed over Pappy's plane and extracted the badly wounded pilot. Chandler Swanson's damaged 2-S-16 was already in the landing groove as Hall was hustled off to sick bay. Swanson's rudder controls were severed and John Edwards was dead in the rear seat. The flight-deck crew decided that Hall and Swanson's VS-2 planes were unflyable. They stripped them of their propellers and portable gear before dumping the SBDs over the side into the ocean.[5]

Skipper Bob Dixon, the last of the morning searchers to return, landed at 1145. He returned with a group of VS-2 dive-bombers (pilots Smith, Knapp, Edwards, Woyke, Leppla, Neely, and Schultz), along with Clarke and Buchan from VB-2's anti-VT patrol. Lieutenant (j.g.) Buchan encountered the squadron line chief, Aviation Chief Machinist's Mate Charles E. Brewster, who was annoyed to see another hole shot through 2-B-1's propeller.[6]

Junior Behl, Robert Williams, and two others of *Lexington*'s surviving anti-VT patrol SBDs later landed on *Yorktown* at 1400. "I certainly was hungry," recalled Behl, who visited *Yorktown*'s galley to grab a sandwich after having missed breakfast twice that day. Acting VB-2 exec Jim Newell felt that Buchan and Behl landed with "the most shot-up planes." Johnny Liska found his SBD had been holed in fourteen places, including both the horizontal and vertical stabilizers.[7]

Yorktown's returning dive-bombers approached TF-17 around noon. Cruising at six thousand feet, Willie Burch spotted six Zeros approaching his VS-5 formation from ahead. At 1204, he opened up on his radio to announce, "We need help!" Fleet FDO Red Gill sent Wildcats north to meet the returning American strike groups. Fortunately, the *Yorktown* planes avoided any confrontations with the last of the departing Japanese planes. The *Yorktown* SBDs bypassed *Lexington* and headed toward their own carrier, five miles beyond. Around 1215, *Yorktown* landed the damaged surviving planes of VS-5's anti-VT patrol: Woodhull, Vejtasa, Austin, and Strong. Red Austin, hobbled by shrapnel wounds to his foot, had to be assisted from his cockpit.[8]

As Woodhull approached the landing circle, gunner Al Garlow swung his Browning around and then swiveled in his seat to face forward for the landing. He forgot in his excitement, however, to properly lock the gun in position. As their SBD jerked to a halt, the heavy gun swung around and smashed Garlow in the head. He was knocked senseless and suffered a concussion. Woodhull sent his gunner to sick bay to get his head injury tended to. Climbing down one of the steel ladders, Garlow saw the death and destruction around him. As he reached for one of the ladder rungs, he spotted the severed scalp of another sailor. In sick bay, he saw men burned and bleeding and dying. Garlow decided his injury was not worthy, grabbed some aspirin for his splitting headache, and moved on.

By 1231, *Yorktown*'s first SBDs and TBDs from her *Shokaku* strike group were entering her landing circle. Only one VT-5 Devastator had suffered a bullet hole, but eighteen SBDs returned with varying degrees of damage. For Lieutenant Commander Burch, landing was no simple task, as his left rudder control cables had been shot away. "I don't know if anyone ever practiced that maneuver but he did it okay," recalled Rocky Glidewell of their safe landing.[9]

The damaged VS-5 SBDs of Hugh Nicholson, Fritz Faulkner, Art Downing, Turner Caldwell, and Elmer Maul were next to land. Nicholson, a former Indiana schoolteacher and graduate of Indiana University, was limping from the bullet that had cut through his heel. "I thought my plane was pretty badly shot up until I saw some of the other boys," Nicholson said. Viewing the hundreds of bullet holes in their SBDs, Downing reflected, "We separately offered a short prayer of thanks to the men who had put these 'flying tanks' together." Lieutenant Caldwell's plane was taken down on the forward elevator into the smoke-filled hangar. Scouting Five's leading engineering chief, Jake Ulmer, climbed onto Caldwell's wing after his engine stopped. "He told me about the bomb hit," said Caldwell, "and said that a young seaman attached to our squadron had been killed."[10]

Ensign Yogi Jorgenson could not land safely, as the landing gear in his badly damaged wings would not deploy. "The plane was uncontrollable," said Jorgenson, who raised his flaps and radioed *Yorktown* that he was making a water landing. "Yogi made a beautiful approach, touching down between two swells, and the airplane nosed down, starting to sink," said gunner Tony Brunetti. "I just barely got the rubber raft out of its compartment when we had to get clear as the airplane disappeared."[11]

Jorgenson had put his plane down near a destroyer at 1248. His intended rescue ship kept going but the nearby destroyer *Aylwin* moved in to effect the rescue. Weak from loss of blood, he was assisted into the raft by his gunner. Brunetti worried that sharks might be attracted by the blood as he pushed Jorgenson over the side. "When I finally got him in the raft, I was damned near too tired to get in myself," said Brunetti. "But, thank the Lord, we saw no sharks." *Aylwin* picked up the airmen at 1259 and soon transferred them back to *Yorktown*.[12]

Fourteen of Wally Short's VB-5 dive-bombers were next to land. As Bill Christie's plane was lowered to the hangar deck, his gunner, Lynn Forshee, could see "a pile of bodies stacked like cordwood. Someone came up and began counting holes in our plane. One had cut all but three strands of the rudder cable between my feet."[13]

Leif Larsen's gunner, Dayton Harp, survived his Zero battle with only a few minor burns but their plane had about fifty holes in it. In a letter to his father written after the Coral Sea action, Harp said he missed fishing and playing his guitar. He was eager to do some quail hunting again as well. "I surely would like to shoot at something once more that wasn't shooting back at me," he wrote.[14]

The fuel tanks of Floyd Moan's 5-B-19 had been riddled with twenty-two holes, and his flaps were inoperable. LSO Soupy Campbell gave him the cut, but Moan missed the wires and barrier and crashed at full speed into the island. Moan and gunner Bob Hodgens, both wounded during the *Shokaku* attack, were pulled from the wreck before deck crews shoved their Dauntless over the side. *Yorktown* next landed nine TBDs of VT-5, Ben Preston's shot-up VB-5 Dauntless, and five of their VF-42 escorts. Harry Cowden, Preston's gunner, emerged from his rear cockpit feeling like a blooded veteran. "On your first flight, you're excited as hell until you get a Zero in your sights, or feel the anti-aircraft pushing you around," Cowden said. "You're an old-timer when you climb out of the plane and nonchalantly poke your fingers in the bullet holes."[15]

Lexington had continued her own air operations. By 1233, her damage-control parties reported that all fires had been extinguished. On her deck, seven VS-2 Dauntlesses and two VB-2 bombers had landed in the past hour were quickly refueled and ready to launch. Disaster, however, stalled this effort as fumes from leaks in *Lexington*'s port stowage gasoline tanks were ignited by untended electric motors. At 1247, the mighty carrier was rocked by a tremendous explosion, which killed twenty-five sailors and hampered *Lexington*'s steering ability.

Captain Sherman ordered flight operations to proceed as his carrier shuddered and new fires raged belowdecks. *Lexington* was still under way and there was a need to clear the flight deck to make room for her returning strikers. At 1300, Bob Dixon, Bobby Edwards, Jack Leppla, Art Schultz, Hoyt Mann, Max Woyke, Roscoe Neely, and two others departed with the nine refueled SBDs. Lieutenant (j.g.) Joe Smith took over Bob Smith's plane but had anxious moments waiting to launch with the nine. His gunner, Lefty Craft, realized they were likely departing their carrier for the last time. He made a dash from the flight deck down to the crew's bunk area to retrieve his prized photo of his wife, Bee Bee. By the time Craft made it back to his rear cockpit, Smith and others were screaming at him. The explosion that rocked *Lexington* while Smith was waiting to take off had made him impatient to depart, and his disappearing radioman did little to soothe his nerves. Dixon's nine SBDs and four VB-2 SBDs that had remained on patrol were taken on board *Yorktown*.[16]

While *Lexington*'s crew continued to fight fires, Admirals Fletcher and Fitch contemplated sending out a second attack group against the Japanese. At the moment, Lady Lex's strike force had yet to return and *Yorktown* had only eleven SBDs, eight TBDs, and seven F4Fs that could be used for another strike. *Yorktown*'s intelligence staff had picked up enough radio intercepts to determine that *Zuikaku* was undamaged and was recovering *Shokaku*'s planes. At 1315, Fletcher signaled to Fitch to hold off on further strikes and retire. Fitch agreed, with both U.S. commanders hoping that a reassembled *Yorktown/Lexington* air group could possibly hit the Japanese again the following day.[17]

The *Lexington* strike force began arriving over TF-17 just after 1300. Weldon Hamilton's luckless eleven VB-2 SBDs were first to land. During their arrival, *Lexington* was shaken by a violent explosion, which filled her hangar deck with choking black smoke. Next to land were Marvin Haschke of VS-2, Noel Gayler of VF-2, and ten of Jimmy Brett's eleven VT-2 TBDs. The only loss was Lieutenant (j.g.) Leonard Thornhill, whose Devastator ran out fuel twenty miles short of *Lexington*. He and his gunner were seen climbing into their rubber boat, but the destroyer dispatched to rescue Thornhill's crew never found them.[18]

The renewed fires and damage-control efforts on *Lexington* forced fleet FDO Red Gill to turn over fighter direction duties to Pete Pederson on *Yorktown*. Pederson directed the efforts of the *Lexington* dive-bombers aloft on anti-VT patrol duty and in helping to guide in two of Lady Lex's lost SBDs. Shortly after 1400, Bill Ault radioed *Lexington* that he and gunner William Butler were wounded, Ault having been hit in the leg and arm. He asked if *Lexington* had him on radar, but his carrier had shifted the communications to *Yorktown*. Harry Wood, a former graduate of Eastern Illinois State Teachers College, then joined in on the radio reports that played over the loudspeakers of both carriers.[19]

"We are going to try to make the nearest land," called Wood. "Advise, please." Pederson, however, did not have Wood's Dauntless on his radar. Ault advised that he was flying on course 110 degrees, but he was also out of radar sight. In response to Ault, Wood radioed, "Bill, I received. You're strength two. So, I think you are a long way off. If you reported two hits, we would like to be given credit for one hit."[20]

Ensign Wood's transmissions soon faded away. He was fortunate to be flying near Rossel Island, where he managed to safely ditch his SBD. Wood and his gunner, Cyril Huvar, from Corpus Christi, Texas, broke out their rubber boat and made it ashore. They ate coconuts, slept under their parachutes in the rain, and spent four days crossing the island. Wood and Huvar were befriended by natives who helped maneuver them away from Japanese patrols and into Allied hands to coordinate their eventual return home.[21]

Wood's VS-2 squadron mate, John Wingfield, and his gunner, Bill Davis, were never heard from after their attack against the *Shokaku* and *Zuikaku* force. The radio calls between Commander Ault and *Yorktown* continued for nearly an hour, as the wounded air group commander ran through the last of his fuel. "Shall I circle? Do you want me to gain or lose altitude?" Ault finally asked at 1449.

Yorktown replied, "You are not on the screen. Try to make the nearest land." Ault realized his plight. "Nearest land is over two hundred miles away," he radioed. "We would never make it." *Yorktown* returned with, "You are on your own. Good luck." Ault then asked that a message be relayed to the *Lexington* that he had scored a thousand-pound bomb hit on a Japanese carrier. He then indicated that he had spotted enemy fighters and was changing course to the north.[22]

Pete Pederson promised to relay CLAG's message and again wished him good luck. At 1454, Bill Ault sent his final transmission before disappearing into the Coral Sea: "From CLAG. OK, so long people. We got a one-thousand-pound hit on the flattop."[23]

While this sad drama was carried out over the loudspeakers in the air plot areas, *Lexington*'s flight-deck crews optimistically respotted her strike aircraft on the after end of the flight deck. At 1442, however, another major explosion rocked *Lexington*, lifting her forward elevator by at least a foot and igniting intense fires below. At 1452, Captain Sherman signaled to *Yorktown*, "This ship needs help."[24]

Yorktown took over landing the remaining aircraft from both carriers. At 1525, *Lexington*'s fate was sealed by a huge explosion that caused water pressure to fail and forced the abandonment of her engineering spaces. Around 1630, her power plant was secured and the Lady Lex went dead in the water. The destroyer *Morris* came alongside to help fight fires and to remove the most seriously wounded personnel. Captain Sherman directed that excess squadron personnel should embark on the destroyer. Pilot Ralph Cousins, unable to go below to fetch one hundred dollars cash from his stateroom safe, slid down a line right onto the destroyer's deck. At 1707, Admiral Fitch finally ordered Sherman to begin abandoning his carrier.[25]

From Scouting Two, only Chandler Swanson, Bill Hall, Robert Smith, and radiomen Wheeler and Moore, who had flown the anti-VT patrol, had been unable to secure a serviceable SBD to fly over to *Yorktown*. They were joined on the flight deck by junior pilots Everleigh Willems, Jesse Walker, and Carl Thomas; gunner Ken Garrigan; and several other rear seatmen. Tom Ball of VB-2 was amused by the sight of grown men, pilots and gunners, eating gallons of ice cream from paper cups with wooden spoons on the deck of a burning, listing flattop. "Somebody said the geedunk shop was full of ice cream," recalled Garrigan. "So, we got it, went back up, and sat on the portside aft waiting for someone to give us orders." Pappy Hall, his foot cleaned and wrapped by the medics, hobbled to the air group abandon-ship station and ate ice cream from a helmet.[26]

Garrigan saw a sailor finally approach the air group personnel and ask them what they were doing there. "They passed orders a while ago to abandon ship," he said. With that, the aviators began climbing down lines and dropping into the ocean. Garrigan spent time fighting the drift of the burning carrier before he was picked up by a motor launch from the cruiser *Minneapolis*. Chandler Swanson was swimming off *Lexington*'s port stern when his ship was racked by another violent explosion that hurled airplanes and deck planking over the side. Swanson noted two balsa rafts, with about fifteen men on board, held close to the ship by suction force until a *Minneapolis* motor whaleboat arrived, freed them, and also scooped him from the ocean.[27]

Joe Teyshak of VB-2 also took to the water early and bobbed around for some time before he was rescued. Harold Nobis found many shipmates "seemed loath to leave" their beloved *Lexington*. Pilot Junior Behl lost a wallet containing fifty dollars in cash. Among other items left in his stateroom were the shellback credentials and diploma he had earned upon crossing the equator—meaning Behl would likely have to endure another future pollywog initiation.[28]

Chief Skip Gardner regretted the loss of his uniforms and $280 in cash he had stashed below. He dropped his plane's inflated rubber raft

and slid down a line, only to find another man in it and eight others clinging to the sides. The man in the raft finally swam for a nearby cruiser,
and Gardner, a non-swimmer, scrambled in to take his place until he
was rescued forty-five minutes later. Pappy Hall, wounded in the back of
the head and nursing a shredded right foot, struggled to slide down one
of the lines into the ocean. He clung to the side of a life raft in the swells
for nearly two hours before a cruiser whaleboat picked him up.[29]

Stanley Johnston, also picked up by a *Minneapolis* whaleboat, saw
VB-2's Ensign Shonk swimming with one hand raised high, clutching a
water bottle and a tin of fifty cigarettes, trying to keep them out of the
sea. Shonk handed them to the correspondent. Seconds later, he was
aboard and had an unlit cigarette in his lips. "Has anybody got a match?"
he called around. Jack Leppla, in abandoning *Lexington*, lost all of his
belongings, save "the clothes I was wearing, my naval aviator's ring, and
my dog tag."[30]

Around 1800, two massive explosions occurred on *Lexington*, toss-
ing aircraft into the air like toys. Link Traynor of VS-5 had spent the
early afternoon riding out the bombing attack of *Yorktown* from her
wardroom. After seeing that area transformed to a triage of burned and
maimed sailors, Link was relieved to be part of the evening patrol to escape the grisly sights and smells. He overflew *Lexington* as she burned
brightly while her crew was plucked from the ocean. "She was exploding
right and left," said Traynor.[31]

As dusk set in, *Yorktown* recovered the last of her SBDs. The doomed
Lexington burned brightly on the horizon. It was a sad sight for many
of the *Lexington* pilots who had taken refuge on *Yorktown*. Their morale was low until *Yorktown*'s exec, Dixie Kiefer, produced four bottles of Four Roses bourbon—enough for each pilot and gunner to have a
drink. Art Schultz of VS-2 felt the bourbon "couldn't have been timed
better."[32]

Task Force 17 vessels saved ninety-two percent of *Lexington*'s crew,
but their home carrier was finished. The destroyer *Phelps* fired five torpedoes into the carrier at 1915 to prevent her from being salvaged by the
Japanese. The 33,000-ton *Lexington* rolled over at 1952 and disappeared
beneath the Coral Sea with a final, violent underwater explosion.[33]

Lady Lex sank with half of her air group: fourteen SBDs, thirteen

TBDs, and nine Wildcats. The U.S. Navy earned a tactical victory during the first-ever duel between opposing carrier forces by turning back the Port Moresby invasion efforts. The Japanese lost nearly two-thirds of their planes, the light carrier *Shoho* had been sunk, and the heavy carrier *Shokaku* had been knocked out of the war effort for months with extensive bomb damage. In return, the United States lost the carrier *Lexington*, the destroyer *Sims*, and the tanker *Neosho*, along with seventy carrier aircraft. By the end of May 8, *Yorktown* had forty-nine operational aircraft out of seventy-one total that she had recovered from both air groups. In terms of SBDs, she had ten operational VB-5 planes out of fifteen on board, eight operational VS-2 SBDs, five operational VB-2 SBDs, and only five of twelve VS-5 SBDs that were immediately operational.[34]

The Dauntless dive-bomber aircrews had performed admirably at Coral Sea. Most of *Yorktown*'s pilots who had participated in the *Shoho* and *Shokaku* attacks would be awarded the Navy Cross for their actions. In addition, all eight of the VS-5 anti-torpedo-plane patrol pilots received the Navy Cross, half of them posthumously. All eight VS-5 rear gunners—Bonness, Garlow, Hall, Wood, Hurley, Fontenont, Richesin, and Roll—received the Distinguished Flying Cross for their "fighter" work. In addition, the *Yorktown* gunners credited with aerial victories at Coral Sea—Rocky Glidewell, Bob Hodgens, Lynn Forshee, Harry Cowden, Dayton Harp, and Tony Brunetti—also received DFCs.

Lexington's SBD pilots were also decorated for their Coral Sea actions. Foremost was Bill Hall, who later received a significant honor for defending his *Lexington* in the role of a fighter pilot. From Scouting Two, the Navy Cross was given to many anti-VT patrol pilots: Edwards, Swanson, Woyke, Schultz, Neely, Leppla, and Bob Smith. Roy Hale was posthumously awarded the Distinguished Flying Cross. Numerous Bombing Two pilots also earned Navy Crosses and DFCs, including several from the anti-VT patrol.[35]

Lexington's rear gunners were largely passed over for their actions. John Edwards received a posthumous DFC and Forest Stanley also received one. All others were passed over, including John Liska, with his numerous claims in two days of superb gunnery. On May 20, Rear Admiral Fitch called attention to the fact that more of VB-2's and VS-2's

gunners "should be considered in making any further recommendations." Captain Sherman somehow overlooked making any further medal
awards in the weeks following the Coral Sea battle.[36]

Sherman would defend his use of SBDs as fighters on May 8, saying
this was "amply justified as better than nothing." Many SBD crews, in
fact, had done well in preventing more damage to their carriers. The
broader lesson quickly employed by the Navy was to increase the number
of fighter planes on each carrier before the next major carrier battle.[37]

Turner Caldwell of Scouting Five found it difficult to sleep that night.
Like others, he was still "super excited" from the events of the previous two days and taxed with the worries of whether Japanese carriers
were still in pursuit of the damaged *Yorktown*.[38]

At dawn of May 9, *Yorktown* launched a mixed group of SBDs from
Scouting and Bombing Five to search northward for Japanese ships. Each
plane flew with a five-hundred-pound bomb under orders to scout his
sector, transmit a contact report, and make a solo dive-bombing attack if
a carrier was encountered. Some considered such a mission to be a "suicide patrol." Around 0900, Fritz Faulkner of VS-5 reported a carrier
force about 175 miles from TF-17. When his radio cut out during transmission, listeners on *Yorktown* wondered if he had been shot down. Fortunately, Faulkner's wingman, Link Traynor, relayed the report. The
returning searchers made their way back, picking up an oil slick being
trailed from *Yorktown*, a sign that eased their navigational concerns.
Lieutenant Caldwell worried, however, that this slick also provided "a
perfect trail for an unfriendly force to follow."[39]

Faulkner's sighting report caused a stir with Admiral Fletcher's staff,
who had only sixteen dive-bombers and seven TBDs in condition to fly an
attack. Joe Taylor's Devastators would have little chance of surviving a
long flight and Fletcher opted to hold off on sending them. Bob Dixon,
however, volunteered to lead a search-strike mission of four SBDs to pinpoint Faulkner's carrier force. Harry Frederickson of VB-5 noted in his
diary that TF-17 expected to be attacked, "and everyone was very down
hearted and scared." Despite such concerns, Dixon received the nod from
Fletcher to lead his group off, loaded with thousand-pound bombs. Around

1000, four VS-2 orphans departed: Dixon, Joe Smith, Hoyt Mann, and Jack Leppla.[40]

Link Traynor worried that he would not make it back. *Yorktown* was not at Point Option when he and Faulkner returned, and her homing beacon was not working. They followed her oil slick and found *Yorktown* around 1130 as their fourth fuel tanks were registering empty. Traynor noted that her flight deck was spotted aft with aircraft ready to launch.[41]

Traynor received a "Charlie" by blinker and dived for the landing pattern. *Yorktown* was in a hard turn to port to get into the wind. Soupy Campbell gave him a "Roger," and then Link received the cut motion from Soupy's paddles. He tried to keep his SBD as level as possible as he came in toward the tilting flight deck at 1152. "The hook caught the wire, the SBD shimmied and skidded to the low side, starboard, rolled inverted over the side, and landed in the water upside down," said Traynor. He was momentarily confused about which way was up, but released his seat belt. He swam up between the wing and fuselage of his borrowed VS-2 Dauntless. As he broke the surface, Link saw gunner Jim Cales floating with his .45-caliber pistol held high, looking for sharks. The destroyer *Morris* hauled Traynor and Cales on board. "I had a cracked rib and was given a stiff shot of brandy, which helped the pain on a rolling DD," Traynor said. "The officers and crew took great care of us, fed us, cut our hair, and made us comfortable."

Faulkner was called to brief Admiral Fletcher on his sighting. Fletcher turned to his staff gunnery officer, Butch Schindler, and said that he wanted him to fly immediately to Australia to request an air strike from Army Air Force bombers at Townsville. Schindler would fly as a passenger for Hugh Nicholson, who had been slightly wounded in the foot during the previous day's *Shokaku* strike. As Commander Schindler donned his flight gear, *Yorktown*'s bighearted executive officer, Dixie Kiefer, confronted him with several VS-5 pilots. Out of respect for his five combat flights at Coral Sea, they pinned aviators' wings on Schindler's chest.[42]

Nicholson and Schindler were ordered to stay ashore at the air base at Rockhampton overnight, located some 250 miles southwest of TF-17. Bob Dixon's scouting flight returned in the afternoon, having found only a coral reef whose white-water action resembled ship wakes. Admiral Fletcher received word at 1655 that Schindler had succeeded in getting a group of Army aviators to fly an attack mission on the rumored force. Faulkner was called to the flag bridge again to pinpoint on maps the exact location of his sighting. The VS-5 pilot acknowledged that it was possible he could have been mistaken and he was dismissed without reprimand. Fletcher decided he had most likely spotted Lihou Reef.[43]

Yorktown ran into the night with a load of fully fueled and armed aircraft, waiting for any other reports of Japanese forces. "We were running scared, if the truth be told," recalled VB-5 skipper Wally Short. *Yorktown*'s task group continued retiring from the area on May 10, although false reports kept nerves on edge. Nicholson and Schindler returned safely from their brief visit to Australia. Admiral Fletcher detached Rear Admiral Thomas Kinkaid with three cruisers and three destroyers on May 11 to proceed to Nouméa, where they were to join with Admiral Bill Halsey's *Enterprise* task force, which was approaching from the northeast. Low on fuel, Fletcher opted to take *Yorktown* and his remaining TF-17 ships to Tongatabu again to regroup.[44]

Yorktown entered Tongatabu's Nuku'alofa Harbor on May 15 for a quick patch-up of her battle damage. Bill Burch took off for Tonga Airfield about 0730 with his only ten flyable VS-5 SBDs—piloted by Red Austin, Skip Ervin, Rog Woodhull, Elmer Maul, Turner Caldwell, Walt Coolbaugh, Walt Brown, Art Downing, and Hal Buell. They flew with regular rear gunners Glidewell, Garlow, Hurley, Russ, and Jones, plus five aviation mechanics and loads of spare tools, plugs, and pumps. The native women, however, had been sent far into the hills by the queen of Nuku'alofa. "Ample beer was allotted and five idyllic days were spent with no work, no flying, [and] all the sun and fresh air we could use," said Burch.[45]

In addition to numerous Navy Crosses and DFCs handed out to the SBD pilots and gunners of the Battle of the Coral Sea, two Dauntless aviators would be awarded the nation's highest honors. One of them was Lieutenant John Powers of *Yorktown*'s VB-5, who received a posthumous Medal of Honor for his minimum-altitude hit on *Shokaku*. Commander Bill Ault, lost in action following his attack on *Shokaku* on May 8, was honored later in 1942 by the new Whidbey Island Naval Air

Station at Oak Harbor, Washington, being christened as Ault Field. The Navy would also later honor John Powers and Bill Ault by naming destroyers after them.[46]

The world's first aircraft carrier battle was over. The SBDs had achieved an overall bombing accuracy of nearly twenty percent in two days—sixteen direct hits for the eighty-odd bombs dropped on three carriers in two days by four Dauntless squadrons.

ELEVEN
Transitions

Swede Vejtasa and Fritz Faulkner knew their time with Scouting Five was over. They had both asked for and received extensions to fly in the big Coral Sea battle. Their previous orders were to report Stateside to the new Fighting Squadron Ten, a Wildcat unit that was to be commanded by fellow Coral Sea veteran Lieutenant Commander Jimmy Flatley.

Yorktown's battle damage was patched enough to make her seaworthy for the return trip to Pearl Harbor. Intelligence was pointing toward something big brewing near Midway, and Admiral Fletcher had orders from his boss, Chester Nimitz, to expedite his carrier's return. The *Lexington* Air Group was widely scattered. Chan Swanson, Pappy Hall, and others from Scouting Two had been plucked from the sea, while most of their squadron were able to land on *Yorktown* after their own flight deck had been disabled. The various cruisers and destroyers, along with *Yorktown*'s task force, that had made port in Nouméa, New Caledonia, and at Tongatabu after the Coral Sea battle returned the aviators.

Yorktown got under way from Tongatabu on May 19, and her air group departed midmorning for the flight back to their ship. Vejtasa and Faulkner of VS-5 were sent to join *Lexington*'s SBD crews and thirteen hundred members of the ship's company in boarding the 9,600-ton transport ship *Barnett* (AP-11) at Tongatabu. The transports departed in company toward San Francisco with the cruiser *Chester,* while *Yorktown*'s task group raced for Pearl Harbor.

Yorktown limped into Hawaii on May 27 and was immediately put into dry dock. Thousands of yard workers swarmed over the flattop, attending to bomb damage that would likely take weeks to mend. Chester Nimitz, the blue-eyed Texan commander in chief of the Pacific Fleet, sloshed around her hull in the dry dock with Captain Buckmaster. He declared that *Yorktown* must be ready for combat in just three days. Link Traynor heard the news while sharing a drink at an Oahu bar with VT-5 skipper Joe Taylor. "I guess we'll get a rest now," said Traynor. He was stunned when Taylor told him *Yorktown* would be going right back out.[1]

The effort to patch the carrier was a mighty one, but the floodgates were reopened some seventy-two hours later so that she could head for Midway. Code breakers on the staff of Nimitz had uncovered intelligence that dual landing forces, backed by most of the Imperial Japanese Navy's warships and flattops, were bound for the Aleutian Islands and Midway Atoll. Task groups centered around the carriers *Enterprise* and *Hornet* put to sea on May 28, followed two days later by *Yorktown.*

The scramble to properly organize new *Yorktown* squadrons meant that most of her Coral Sea air group was put ashore. In their place, she received three displaced *Saratoga* squadrons for temporary duty: Bombing Three, Fighting Three, and Torpedo Three. The only veteran squadron of *Yorktown* to be retained was Lieutenant Wally Short's Bombing Five, which was temporarily renamed Scouting Five to avoid the confusion of having two bombing squadrons on board. Short retained ten veteran pilots and took on ten new ACTG rookies to bolster his unit.

The rookies included Gerald Richey, Elmer Conzett, Ray Miligi, Dick Wolfe, and Bob "Hoot" Gibson. The latter was assigned to VB-5 as *Yorktown* departed for Midway after her hasty battle repairs. "At Ford Island, I jumped into an SBD and flew out to rendezvous with the air group for landing aboard the *Yorktown,* where I first met the pilots in the bombing squadron," said Gibson.[2]

In the battle that commenced near Midway on June 4, the U.S. carrier fleet achieved its greatest victory of the young war. By day's end, four Japanese aircraft carriers—*Akagi, Kaga, Soryu,* and *Hiryu*—were destroyed by Dauntless pilots from *Yorktown*'s VB-3 and *Enterprise*'s VS-6 and VB-6. Wally Short's Bombing/Scouting Five served with distinction at Midway as well. His pilots snooped out *Hiryu* and during the next two days participated in bombing attacks on other Japanese warships. The Dauntless units at Midway suffered heavy losses in terms of both planes and personnel. Among those lost from Short's squadron were two veterans of the early Scouting Five actions—Lieutenants Sam Adams and Charlie Ware—and several Norfolk Deck Dodgers—Johnny Lough, J. Q. Roberts, and Gene Greene.

Hoot Gibson participated in an early-morning search on June 4, but was caught on board *Yorktown* as she was pounded by Japanese torpedoes and bombs. He was forced to abandon ship that afternoon and was pulled from the ocean by the destroyer *Balch*. He spent that night sitting on a bench by the officers' wardroom while the ship's doctor worked endlessly on burned and wounded *Yorktown* survivors. "By morning the stench of medicine and the stronger smell of death was emblazoned on my senses," Gibson said.[3]

The "real" Scouting Five, under Lieutenant Commander Bill Burch, had been left behind at Pearl Harbor when the fleet sortied for Midway. On June 6, the carrier *Saratoga* arrived at Pearl Harbor, fresh from torpedo-damage repairs on the West Coast. She quickly reprovisioned, refueled, and dashed from Oahu the following morning to help with mop-up on the fleeing Japanese fleet. In addition to her air group, she took on ten of Burch's VS-5 planes and a nine-plane detachment under Lieutenant Keith Taylor of VB-5 orphans. *Sara* reached the Midway area too late to take part in the historic battle. She rendezvoused with *Enterprise* and *Hornet* on their return toward Pearl and ferried over Burch's ten scouts on June 11. "We conducted the usual ASPs and searches looking for enemy stragglers and downed pilots," said Hal Buell, who had also missed out on the carrier attacks at Coral Sea.[4]

The three carriers returned to Pearl Harbor on June 13 and the aviators settled into life ashore in the islands again. Scouting Five's Hal Buell was happy to leave the "Floating Dry Dock" behind when *Sara*'s pilots returned to Oahu. The Dauntless pilots found that Army B-17 pilots had been given all the credit for the victory. Four days after the carriers returned, Admiral Nimitz made a visit to the Big E. He held an awards ceremony on deck for a few pilots and submarine personnel. Edward Anderson, a VB-6 radioman, was among the aviators standing at attention as the admiral addressed the crew. Nimitz proclaimed that his men had achieved a great victory at Midway. Nimitz told the aviators that as soon as he received some new carriers from the shipyards, they would get some relief. For Anderson, the message was clear. *We are not going back to the States for a long time!*[5]

On June 2, the transport convoy reached San Diego, where Lieutenant Commander Bob Dixon assumed temporary duty with the advanced carrier training group at the naval air station. Dixon, scheduled to take command of the *Saratoga* Air Group at Pearl Harbor, was instead ordered to testify in federal court as to how correspondent Stanley Johnston had been leaked secret Midway war information by *Lexington*'s commander Mort Seligman. The Navy finally decided it best not to air its problem publicly, thereby jeopardizing the fact that they had broken the Japanese Navy's codes. Seligman was barred from future promotion, a minor slap on the wrist in the eyes of Bob Dixon—who missed out on returning right away to Pacific carrier action in the process.[6]

Fighter skipper Jimmy Flatley, unlike his buddy Dixon, went straight to work when *Barnett* disembarked her *Lexington* survivors on June 2. His new squadron, Replacement Fighting Ten (VRF-10), was commissioned as the "Grim Reapers" the very next day. He had only six pilots and three planes to start with, but he began with a solid nucleus. His Wildcat fighter squadron boasted four veteran Dauntless pilots: Bobby Edwards and Jack Leppla from VS-2, and Fritz Faulkner and Swede Vejtasa from VS-5. Leppla and Vejtasa, who had already achieved kills while flying dive-bombers, now had the chance to really tangle with the Zeros. The sixth member of Flatley's new Reaper unit was Lieutenant (j.g.) Dave Pollock, a former VS-2 pilot who had most recently served as *Lexington*'s air plot officer.

Leppla, Pollock, and Edwards got thirty-day leaves as Flatley sorted out his new VF-10. He also granted leave to Vejtasa and Faulkner as he sought airplanes, but only one week in their cases. They spent the week looking for houses in Coronado, where Swede soon located a sufficient place for his wife, Irene, and their young son, Gene.[7]

Flatley's Fighting Ten was one of the four units that would constitute Carrier Replacement Air Group Ten (CRAG-10), which had been formed on March 1, 1942, at NAS San Diego, along with CRAG-9. They were the first carrier air groups to be given separate numbers rather than a ship's name, such as *Lexington* Air Group. Three of CRAG-10's units—Replacement Scouting Ten (VRS-10), Replacement Bombing Ten (VRB-10), and Replacement Torpedo Ten (VRT-10)—were already taking shape by the time the *Lexington* survivors reached California on June 2. A new carrier, USS *Bon Homme Richard* (CV-10), later renamed USS *Yorktown*, was under construction and would eventually be in need of a full air group. The state of the carrier air groups following the Navy's losses at Coral Sea and Midway did not guarantee, however, that CRAG-10 would still be hanging around when the new flattop was put into service.

Many Coral Sea veterans from the *Lexington* group reached San Diego with a good amount of fanfare. The media had a field day with some of the Scouting Two crews. Art Schultz and gunner Wayne Colley were photographed beside a Dauntless at the air station while being interviewed by eager reporters. Jack Leppla and Johnny Liska got the same treatment, and California papers spread their stories that week.

Leppla had been credited with four Zero kills and Liska with three at Coral Sea. Their Scouting Two had been given a number of awards, including Navy Crosses, Distinguished Flying Crosses, and in one case even the Medal of Honor. Somehow in the paperwork shuffle, Liska's three fighter kills did not even earn him a Distinguished Flying Cross. *Oh, well,* he thought. *Better to be without a medal than to be a dead hero.* Liska and Leppla were honored as special guests on the NBC radio program *It Happened in the Service.* They were interviewed by commentator Hank McCune, and their story was dramatized for a network audience by NBC. Special audio effects were added for the show, broadcast on Wednesday, July 8, including the sounds of diving planes and machine-gun fire. Leppla mentioned his enthusiasm for joining the new Grim Reapers squadron, whose emblem was a skeleton diving at high speed with a scythe in his hands.

Ensign Don Wakeham of Bombing Two made a publicity appearance at the Douglas aircraft factory in Santa Monica during June. He credited the workers with building Dauntless planes that were rugged under fire. "They gave us everything they had," Wakeham said of the Japanese at Coral Sea. "You keep them rolling, and the Navy will keep them flying where they will do the most good."[8]

Most of the former *Lexington* dive-bomber pilots were given leave to visit their families before being assigned to new aviation duties. Chief Fred Sugar did not have such welcome news for his VS-2 enlisted gunners, however. They were under orders to remain at NAS North Island pending orders to the new replacement air group. Chief Skip Gardner heard similar grumbling from his VB-2 radiomen, who were also retained to join the new CRAG-10.

Johnny Liska, whose family lived in nearby Van Nuys, was able to visit his brother, Steve, who was still in high school, and his kid sisters, Mary and Alice. His leave was less than enjoyable when Liska became sidelined with a bad round of the flu that temporarily landed him in the naval hospital. Three of Liska's buddies—Lefty Craft, Slim Colley, and Lanny Wheeler—had hoped to be able to enjoy some Stateside leave. In that time, they planned to carry out their pact of visiting the family of J. B. Jewell, the member of their original quartet who had perished during the Lae strikes. Their quick assignment to the new CRAG-10, however, would postpone this quest for the time being.

Lieutenant (j.g.) Pappy Hall, one of Scouting Two's heroes of the Coral Sea battle, received neither home leave nor a new assignment. He had been badly wounded while defending *Lexington* on May 8, and he was in need of extensive rehabilitation. He was admitted into the Balboa Naval Hospital, where doctors worked to remove the majority of the shrapnel that had shredded his right foot and lower leg.

During his recovery, he took a strong liking to the pretty twenty-six-year-old head nurse in charge of his floor. She was Leah Christine Chapman, who had been raised on her father's farm near the tiny town of Anderson, Missouri. She had earned her nursing degree in Kansas City, was commissioned as an ensign in the U.S. Navy, and was ordered to report for duty at the Balboa Naval Hospital in San Diego.

Hall's feelings for Nurse Leah grew stronger the more they visited in the hospital. She had red hair, like him, and at five eight, she stood a good three inches taller than he. Leah tried to discourage him when he was finally well enough to ask her out. When Pappy came to pick her up at the nurses' quarters, she came down the stairs wearing a tall hat, tall feathers, and her tallest high heels—hoping to intimidate him.

Pappy was unruffled. "Don't you think I know you're taller than I am?" he said, laughing. "Take off that silly hat, and let's go out!"

Their romance blossomed as Lieutenant Hall began taking on light duty at NAS North Island. A short time later, he proposed and they were married on September 20, 1942, in Price, Utah. The newlyweds spent a weekend at Bright Angel Falls at the Grand Canyon. While they were away, far from radios and telephones, President Franklin Roosevelt made a big announcement during one of his chats. He was awarding the nation's highest honor, the Medal of Honor, to a pilot named William Edward Hall for his heroism in the Coral Sea battle.

Hall's parents were shocked by the news but had no way to reach him for days. Hall was completely oblivious to the announcement when he returned to duty on the naval air base at San Diego. He was confused when his commanding officer showered him with heavy congratulations. "Everybody must get married sometime," mumbled the confused newlywed lieutenant.[9]

His CO then shared the news about the impending Medal of Honor Award. "I thought some mistake must have been made and I was afraid to show my face until word finally came from the personnel center and verified the action," said Hall.

Reality soon set in. Hall was the first living Navy dive-bomber pilot to be given the nation's highest honor in World War II. Lieutenant Jo Jo Powers from *Yorktown*'s VB-5 had also been honored with the Medal of Honor, but had been killed in the course of earning it. Leah Hall stood proudly beside her husband as he was awarded his commendation in a small ceremony on his air base. By the direction of Admiral Nimitz, Hall was honored by Rear Admiral Ralston Smith Holmes, an aide to Nimitz and commandant of ships and aircraft of the Eleventh Naval District.

It was a short but moving ceremony as photographers snapped photos and filmed the proceedings. Bill Hall spent much of the next year instructing new dive-bomber pilots at NAS Daytona Beach. When pressed to brag about his Medal of Honor, he always politely brushed aside his own achievements in his usual, quiet, modest way. *Thousands of other people who gave their lives were real heroes,* he thought. He had merely done what he was trained to do with his Dauntless dive-bomber that day.

D uring the months when Bill Hall recovered from his injuries, other Dauntless heroes were in the making nearby in California.

Two replacement dive-bomber squadrons were coming together at San Diego. One of them was Scouting Ten, still officially VRS-10. It was commanded by sharp thirty-six-year-old James Richard Lee, a lieutenant commander who hailed from Greensboro, North Carolina. Lee, who had graduated third in his 1928 Annapolis class, was known to his peers as "Bucky." He had spent months pulling together aircraft, pilots, and enlisted men that would soon be called upon to see combat on the next available aircraft carrier. "Air Group Ten was the first carrier replacement air group formed and trained as such," said Lee.[10]

Some of Bucky Lee's men had been with him since the start of the year, including David John Cawley, an untested radioman-gunner. He came from hard upbringings in the brushy country of Clark County, Washington. Cawley's father died when he was young, leaving his mother to raise four kids. "Mother was bound and determined that all of us would get through high school," he said. Cawley did graduate from Battle Ground High School on May 28, 1941.[11]

Wages were only twenty-five cents an hour for jobs in his area, and even these were scarce. Toward the end of the summer after he graduated, Cawley enlisted in the Navy at the age of seventeen. He finished his basic training at San Diego in mid-September 1941, and decided the best way to work his way into flight duty was via the sixteen-week radio school at NAS North Island. Cawley entered with a class of thirty-five and finished fifth of the thirty who made it through. At the end of training in mid-January 1942, available billets were posted for the graduates. Those highest in their class standings had first choice. "There were five aviation billets listed," said Cawley. "I was fifth!"[12]

The two most coveted spots, flying in patrol squadrons that would be sent to Hawaii, were quickly snapped up. When his time came to choose, Cawley took the next best billet: joining Aircraft Training Group One (ACTG-1) at the south hangar of NAS North Island. The next few months passed with continual training and occasional guard duty for the young enlisted men, as the Navy began forming the nucleus of what would become Replacement Air Group Ten. In Cawley's opinion, the available aircraft were "just a rab-scrambled bunch of leftover airplanes"—two OS2Us, an SNJ trainer, and occasionally a borrowed J2F.[13]

During May, scuttlebutt made the rounds at North Island about a big carrier battle that had occurred in the Coral Sea. Cawley heard stories that the carrier *Lexington* had been sunk even though those details were semi-secret at the time. The rumors soon proved to be true. During early June, *Lexington* survivors began arriving at San Diego on board troop transports. Many of the *Lexington* air personnel were assigned to fill out Air Group Ten. Cawley felt that Lady Lex's airmen simply took over their group. "They were old salts, chiefs, first class, etc., while we were just kids," he said.

Bucky Lee's new Scouting Ten pulled heavily from the VS-2 gunners returning from the Coral Sea. Senior aviation radioman Sugar retained many of his veterans: Slim Colley, Lefty Craft, Ralph Gowling, Clarence Garlow, Johnny Liska, Doyle Phillips, Lanny Wheeler, John Moore, and Ray Reames. Their familiar pilots from the *Lexington* days were gone, but each gunner quickly fell in with one of the new VS-10 pilots during June.

Lee felt fortunate to draw such a veteran gunner pool, even if he believed it to be unfair on the enlisted men. He felt the backseaters "take a bad beating. They should be returned at the same time the pilot is." Lee would, in fact, recommend that in the future, gunners should be kept together with their pilot as a team, rotating Stateside together and returning to future squadron assignments together.[14]

He considered himself fortunate to have two "excellent" chief radiomen in Irby Sanders and Fred Sugar. They trained the newer radiomen until they knew their equipment inside out, and insisted that all rearseaters clean their own machine guns. Lefty Craft spent much of the month of June working with Chief Sugar on new equipment for their SBDs. Scouting Ten was assigned two AV(S) officers, non-flying specialists who helped handle air combat intelligence reports, operational issues, personnel welfare, and other odd jobs to help free up the skipper. Lieutenants Bill Boardman, a thirty-year-old Harvard graduate, and Ray

"Muddy" Waters were "ninety-day wonders," officers who had been hurried through basic training at NAS Quonset Point in Rhode Island. Despite their lack of extended naval training, Lee considered Waters and Boardman to be "outstanding" and "invaluable to us in every respect."[15]

Bucky Lee was slated to command an eighteen-plane squadron with roughly twenty-five percentage overage in pilots to fill in for any injured or sick aviators on any given day. His allotment of pilots were primarily ensigns fresh from ACTG training. His second in command, Lieutenant Bill Martin, was an academy graduate. Lieutenant Robert Conrad Frohlich, a twenty-nine-year-old North Dakota native and graduate of the University of Minnesota, also looked promising. The only VS-10 pilot who had seen any action was Ensign Tom Ramsay, who had flown with *Hornet*'s air group at the recent Midway battle. Four other junior pilots—Carl Thomas, Skip Ervin, Bob Edmondson, and William "Buddy" Edwards—had joined *Lexington* and *Yorktown* SBD squadrons in time for the Coral Sea battle but had not taken part in the carrier strikes.

Johnny Liska, recovered from his bout with sickness that had landed him in the hospital, was eager to get back to war. He had lost his long-time pilot Jack Leppla to Fighting Ten but he was soon pleased with his new regular pilot, who turned out to be a man whose character was as tough as his own. Liska was paired with Ensign Martin Doan Carmody, a stout athlete who had been a star tackle at San Jose State College in California. Doan's Spartans team had finished a perfect season with thirteen wins in 1939, but the former California fruit picker's aspirations were higher than playing sports for a living.

Aviation had long held his fancy. "I was infected by it," Carmody admitted. "It was very exciting for a young guy like me." He had first toured the carrier *Saratoga* in San Francisco at age thirteen with his friend's father, who was serving on the massive flattop. The following year, Doan and his buddy were able to crawl through the hangars of the Navy's first helium-filled airships *Akron* and *Macon*—each of which carried four Curtiss F9C Sparrowhawk biplane fighters. Carmody's interest in naval aviation was further piqued during his college football years, when a Spartans alumnius offered the team a tour of the Navy's first carrier, *Langley*, in the harbor at San Diego.[16]

Carmody joined the Navy in March 1941 and began flight training at the naval air station in Corpus Christi, Texas. Because of his bright red hair color, Carmody had inevitably become known as "Red" to his peers. One year later, with the war in full swing, he was carrier-qualified on *Saratoga*, the very flattop that had sparked his love for flying a decade before. His first landing was almost a failure, as Carmody failed to fully drop his landing hook. As soon as his dive-bomber was secured, he was ordered, "Get your ass to the ready room!" Carmody expected the worst, but he was given a second chance. He aced his next landings and was soon among the first pilots to be assigned to the next Carrier Replacement Air Group Ten.

Red Carmody and Johnny Liska became a tight team at North Island, as they put their SBD through the paces.

Ensign Leonard Robinson was part of Bombing Ten from the start. He and nine other pilots were in the first mustering of VRB-10 on June 1, 1942, at NAS San Diego at North Island. Robinson's original commanding officer was Lieutenant Commander Frank T. Corbin, who had served as XO of *Enterprise*'s Fighting Six during the early months of the war.

Corbin formed VB-10 with his second in command, thirty-two-year-old Lieutenant Commander James Alfred Thomas, a 1932 academy graduate from Columbus, Ohio. They were joined by a capable operations officer in the person of Lieutenant Warren Welch, who had joined *Lexington*'s VB-2 in October 1939 and had served through the early months of 1942 as its gunnery officer. When Welch, Thomas, and Corbin formed VB-10, they had one administrative personnel officer, Lieutenant Jack Dufficy, and seven other pilots—John Griffith, Len Robinson, Russell Hoogerwerf, Jim Leonard, Abraham Winegrad, Thomas A. Aspell Jr., and Bruce McGraw.

Len Robinson had fallen in love with flying while in college, after watching a carrier movie. He thought, *That's what I'd like to do.* He tried to sign up with the Army Air Corps, but failed because he was under twenty-one and his parents wouldn't sign the papers.[17]

Known to his peers as "Robbie," Robinson had been born in Brussels, Belgium, on July 12, 1920. His father was serving in the Army Red Cross, helping to set up recreational facilities for soldiers to help alleviate their combat stress. After the war, the Robinson family moved to Wax- ahachie, Texas, where Robbie attended school and sold newspapers, magazines, and rabbits. Robinson moved to El Dorado, Arkansas, to at- tend high school while his father taught history and coached football at El Dorado High School. He returned to Waxahachie to attend Trinity University, where he played tennis and was editor of the school paper.[18]

During college, Robinson flew in Aeroncas as part of the civilian pi- lot training program. "After I graduated from that I started building up time on my own as I thought I might be an airline pilot," he said. He then became interested in the Navy, and in April 1941, a Navy recruiter came through Dallas. Robinson passed all the tests and physicals and received the blessing of his parents to sign up.[19]

As soon as he graduated from Trinity University in June 1941, the Navy called Robinson to report to E-base at NAS Dallas. He had enough flight experience that it took him only four days to get out of E-base and head for Jacksonville, Florida, as a seaman, second class. There he became friends with another Texan, Bruce McGraw, and with Russell "Red" Hoogerwerf, both destined to be future squadron mates. In July 1941, they were transferred to NAS Corpus Christi. "I wanted fighters," said Robinson. "I was in an advanced fighter group, and just before we graduated, they changed the whole flight, twelve of us, to dive bombers."

Robinson and his group had been flying F3Fs, SNC-1s, N3N-3s, and mono-winged SNV-1s. When they were shifted to dive-bombers, they immediately began flying SBUs and later SBCs. Robbie earned his gold wings on January 27, 1942, and was married six weeks later to Jeanne Elizabeth McElroy. Two weeks later, on April 1, the newlywed ensign reported to ACTG in San Diego.[20]

Throughout his transition from flight training to Bombing Ten, Robbie Robinson remained close to Lieutenant (j.g.) Bruce McGraw. His parents had hoped for different career paths for young McGraw. "My mother wanted me to be a doctor and my dad wanted me to be a minis- ter," he said. "I didn't want to be either one." Once McGraw was inte- grated into the new VB-10, he formed tight bonds with his fellow pilots. "It was a real brotherhood and you became part of it and you were glad to be there," he recalled.[21]

During June, VB-10 inherited some *Lexington* VB-2 veterans: Ralph

Weymouth, Paul Knapp, Ralph Cousins, Don Wakeham, and Ralph Goddard. Of this group, only Goddard and Wakeham would remain with VB-10 through its training. More than half of the new squadron's rear-seat gunners came from Lexington's VB-2 bunch—Chief Skip Gardner, Joe Teyshak, Roy Haas, George Eiswald, Cliff Schindele, Jim Nelson, Harold Nobis, Bob Hynson, Forest Stanley, Arthur Margarido, Charles Hamilton, Len DeSalvo, Ralph Horton, and Leonard McAdams.

The VB-10 gunners began flying rotation with various pilots. By late July, Frank Corbin had received another ten pilots who would become permanent members of his squadron: Lieutenant Karl Border, and Ensigns Dan Frissell, Jeff Carroum, Paul Halloran, Richard Buchanan, Greg Nelson, Frank West, Nelson Wiggins, and Edwin Stevens. Border joined Air Group Ten at North Island on July 24, and was immediately struck by skipper Corbin and exec Jim Thomas. "They both seem fine and it looks like a good outfit."[22]

Twenty-seven-year-old Karl Border was in flight school at NAS Pensacola when the war commenced. He and his younger brother Bob, sons of a Navy captain, had graduated from Annapolis together in 1939. Both subsequently served on board the battleship Tennessee (BB-43), where Robert Lee Border was when Pearl Harbor was attacked. Karl Border earned his wings on April 4, 1942, during the week his younger brother Bob was flying his first training missions at Pensacola. Karl's ACTG training continued through May, a month in which one seven-day period saw five pilots killed in ACTG training accidents.[23]

Lieutenant Commander Corbin worked his pilots hard during the last week of July, as Bombing Ten conducted practice bombing missions and air group formation flights. Air Group Ten received orders on Sunday, August 2, to pack their bags and be prepared for immediate deployment to Hawaii. Ensign Dan Frissell, for one, knew that he might be gone quite a while before he saw the States again. He and his sweetheart had a hasty wedding just days before his group was deployed.

Air Group Ten, including three dozen Coral Sea veterans from the Lexington SBD squadrons, began moving toward San Francisco on August 5. Scouting Ten gunner Dave Cawley and his buddies boarded the "nickel-snatcher" train from North Island to the foot of Broadway. There, they marched over to board a troop train. The movement of personnel was done secretly and silently. The train moved east toward Yuma, then turned north to the Mojave Desert. The aviators spent a day and night packed in the hot boxcars in the sweltering desert before it moved on to Reno, Nevada. As they went right down the main tracks, Cawley saw a big sign that proclaimed Reno "The Biggest Little City in the World."[24]

The train carrying AG-10 slipped into San Francisco during the early morning of August 8. A gray blacked-out Navy bus shuffled the aviators to a blacked-out troopship, the USS *Republic*. The voyage from Frisco Bay to Hawaii commenced hours later. During the transit, VB-10 engineering officer Karl Border spent much of his free time thinking of his new bride, Mary, and writing to her. When the *Republic* arrived in Pearl on August 15, Border was happy to see his former ship *Tennessee* repaired and ready to fight again.[25]

At Pearl Harbor, Air Group Ten was split up for its final training phase. Scouting Ten, Bombing Ten, Fighting Ten, and Torpedo Ten each were equipped with about eighteen planes. The group spent its first days at NAS Kaneohe, but the field simply could not handle such a collection. "Someone made the decision to send the fighters to Maui, the torpedo guys stayed at Kaneohe, and the two SBD squadrons, VS-10 and VB-10, went to Ewa Field, which was a Marine Corps field," recalled Robbie Robinson.[26]

Scouting Ten was moved to a new field at Barbers Point on Oahu. The field was still under construction, with only the intersection of two runways complete thus far. VS-10 received a full complement of SBDs and began training in earnest. By late August, Bombing Ten had joined the scouts at Barbers Point.

The Air Group Ten Dauntless squadrons began sharpening the skills they would need once they were moved to the main action. War was raging around the Solomon Islands and on Guadalcanal. Dave Cawley, Slim Colley, Lefty Craft, and their fellow VS-10 gunners knew that their number would be called soon enough.

TWELVE
"I Hope I Won't Disappoint You"

Turner Caldwell could see the emotions bubbling over in his skipper. Standing before him and his fellow pilots was Lieutenant Commander Bill Burch, a man whose leadership abilities under fire could not be questioned. The resolute Kentuckian had earned his Navy Cross and Distinguished Flying Cross during some of America's darkest hours during the first six months of the Pacific War.

Burch's piercing pale blue eyes were welling up with tears as thoughts overwhelmed him. He had been a pilot for a dozen years and for one-third of that time he had been with the same squadron. He had led his Scouting Five on strikes against the Gilberts and Marshalls, against shipping at Lae and Salamaua, and on warships in Tulagi Harbor. At Coral Sea, Willie Burch had taken VS-5 on two attacks against Japanese carriers, sinking one and badly damaging another.

Rocky Glidewell was on a nickname basis with Willie, and had more insight into the skipper than most of VS-5's pilots. Rocky had treasured his time flying with Willie; together, they had scrapped their way through their fair share of aerial dogfights. On June 24, Rocky was emotional as his skipper prepared to pass the baton of leadership on Oahu. Lieutenant Art Downing was also moved by the ceremony. He had felt left out when his *Yorktown* was lost at Midway and Scouting Five's pilots and gunners were needed most to have been there to protect her.

Downing's squadron would have the chance, under new leadership.

Burch had orders to return to the U.S. mainland to the Operational Training Command. As his replacement, he had handpicked Lieutenant Caldwell, his executive officer. Of slight frame, with blue eyes and bright red hair, Caldwell stood tall with the pilots he had served with since 1939. The son of an academy man, he had a wealth of combat experience that earned him nearly as much respect as that conferred on Burch.

Scouting Five's officers and enlisted men were gathered in front of the operations building at Ford Island in Pearl Harbor. "We read our orders," said Caldwell. "Bill tried to make a speech. He had also been with the squadron for several years, and felt a deep emotion. His face screwed up. Tears came to his eyes. He could not talk." Caldwell stepped up and led his skipper inside. When Turner went back out, he was astonished as his men hoisted him onto their shoulders and carried him around. "I had not realized how deeply they felt about me, and I too was overcome," he said. "But many of them had been in the squadron a long time, too. We had been through much together. Our bond was strong."[1]

Once the emotions passed, the pilots celebrated the advancement of both Caldwell and Burch. Art Downing and the veteran pilots were pleased with the nod going to Turner Caldwell. "With over three years' service in Scouting Five, there was nothing of the unfamiliar in his new job," noted Downing. In the days that followed, Caldwell set about the serious business of preparing his squadron to deploy for a new campaign in the Pacific. He realized that Midway had made a real difference in the American war effort. "Most of us had a dim but persuasive sense that the war had turned around," Caldwell related. "We were starting from a long way back, and it would take time and much hard fighting, but the ultimate defeat and destruction of Japan seemed sure."[2]

In the weeks that followed, the VS-5 airmen saw air group buddies of VB-5, VF-42, and VT-5 sent home on thirty-day leaves prior to receiving new assignments. There would be no hometown reunions for VS-5, however. "To still our moans and grief-stricken cries, we were promised that we would receive a like reward when we had made 'one more' cruise," said Downing. "We turned our hats around" and settled down to the mission at hand.[3]

Willie Burch stayed in Hawaii for another month in his role as scout bombing training officer, Pacific Fleet. He helped the new AV(S)—aviation specialist—officers learn ways to make their squadrons more efficient in the combat zone. Burch also worked on solutions to the fogging-telescopic-sights issue VS-5 had experienced at Tulagi, Lae, and Coral Sea. He flew with an engineer from the National Research Laboratories to test a special anti-fogging fluid on sealed telescopic sights. "We installed a number of sights that way in Scouting Five before they left for the Solomon Islands and tried them out for a week," said Burch. The anti-fog liquid worked well enough that Burch had a bottle of the solution given to each SBD mechanic for use on the sights and to apply to the inside of each Dauntless windshield.[4]

Turner Caldwell and his key officers began working out new planes and adding personnel to get VS-5 ready for another combat cruise. He and eagle-eyed Rocky Glidewell became an item and they made their first flight on June 24, Caldwell's first day in command. Several other veteran teams remained in place: Tony Brunetti with pilot Yogi Jorgenson, Elmer Jones with Art Downing, Jim Cales with Link Traynor, and Al Garlow with Roger Woodhull. Birney Strong, Nick Nicholson, Walt Coolbaugh, Elmer Maul, and Red Austin—all Coral Sea veterans—were retained by Caldwell, along with three "new boys" who had joined just before the May carrier battle: Walt Brown, Skip Ervin, and Hal Buell. "We set up housekeeping at Kaneohe while awaiting further orders for return to combat," said Buell.[5]

Several new faces were pulled from the *Enterprise* radio gang and from *Yorktown*'s old VB-5 to fill out the enlisted gunner pool needed for Scouting Five. One was twenty-three-year-old Texan Clay Strickland, who had seen duty at Midway with pilot Hank McDowell of Bombing Five. Strickland became the regular gunner for VS-5's new flight officer, Birney Strong. He found the strapping, six-foot, blond-haired veteran officer to be a "no-nonsense" guy who could handle any situation "but chose to remain in the quiet background." Some of the squadron's veteran gunners found Strong to be overbearing and sullen. Clay Strickland's early impressions of this naval officer were somewhat different.[6]

Their first meeting came as VS-5 prepared to launch for a bombing and gunnery practice flight from NAS Kaneohe in late June. After a quick greeting, the pair stood aft of their SBD's starboard wing "and held a little question-and-answer session—his questions, my answers." Strickland dutifully answered the lieutenant's questions concerning his flight time, his previous pilot, and the action he had seen at Midway. Strickland's ears were still sore from having ruptured his eardrums during dives on Japanese warships at Midway, but he was not one to complain. Upon concluding the interview, Strong had a single-sentence reply that surprised his young gunner: "I hope I won't disappoint you."

Strong then went over their flight and requested that his gunner keep an eye on his rough spots and make suggestions for their improvement. In turn, Strong said he would do the same for his rear-seat man. *If this keeps up, we will become quite a team,* thought Strickland. The preflight talks would become a staple of his relationship with Strong.

Strickland found Strong was "the best all-around pilot that I had ever ridden with. There was nothing of which an SBD was capable that he couldn't perform with precision without overstressing the aircraft. It was just another side of his mild manner and positive attitude showing through his work." In the coming months, Stockton Birney Strong would have ample opportunities to shine.

The new air officer on *Enterprise* was making his presence felt. As the Big E spent late June in the Pearl Harbor Navy Yard undergoing repair and upkeep, Commander John Geraerdt Crommelin Jr. used the time to sort out and train the squadrons that would make the carrier's next war cruise.

Crommelin was a sandy-haired, plainspoken Alabaman who had graduated near the top of his academy class in 1923. He was an accomplished fighter pilot, and three of his four younger brothers who followed him through Annapolis also became naval aviators. Crommelin's tough expectations were matched by an equal compassion for the safety of his aviators that would make him known among the air group as their "Uncle John."[7]

Uncle John Crommelin sorted out *Enterprise*'s tattered air group, now headed by the Commander, *Enterprise* Air Group (CEAG), Max Leslie—who had led *Yorktown*'s Bombing Three at Midway. For the upcoming cruise, Lieutenant Louis H. Bauer was in command of Fighting Six's three dozen F4F Wildcat pilots. Torpedo Three, virtually wiped out at Midway, flying outdated Devastator torpedo bombers off *Yorktown*, was revamped with new model Grumman TBF Avengers. The new VT-3 became part of the *Enterprise* Air Group and was under Lieutenant Commander Charles M. Jett.

The Big E's two eighteen-plane Dauntless squadrons were a mix of veterans and rookies. Four of Wally Short's old VB-5 pilots from Midway— Carl Horenburger, Bob Gibson, Dick Wolfe, and Gerald Richey—were assigned to the new Bombing Six. Hoot Gibson, a flight-training buddy of VS-5's Hal Buell, returned to Pearl Harbor on the destroyer *Balch*, which had rescued him from the ocean after a tough swim. Hoot had lost one of his flight school buddies, Dave Chaffee, in the Coral Sea battle, but he was uplifted to find that another, Ensign Steve Czarnecki, would be joining him in VB-6. The revamped Bombing Six was put under command of Lieutenant Ray Davis, who had been flight officer of *Hornet*'s VS-8 at Midway. He retained only ensigns Harry Liffner and Don Ely from the old VB-6, plus five other *Enterprise* VS-6 Midway veterans—ensigns Eldor Rodenburg, Jim Dexter, Bill Pittman, Dick Jaccard, and Vernon Micheel.

Turner Caldwell's veteran VS-5 was ordered on board *Enterprise* to replace her decimated VS-6. His twelve veteran pilots were joined by six new ensigns fresh from ACTG: Howard Reason Burnett, Elmer Andrew Conzett, George Glenn Estes Jr., Jesse Theron Barker, Addison Charles Pfautz, and John Frazier Richey. They were new faces for only a short while. They soon acquired nicknames used in flight, just like their fellow pilots: Redbird, Spike, Rastus, Dog, A.C., and Rich. Of the newbies, only Conzett had seen service at Midway, as a backup pilot for Wally Short's SBD unit.

Ensign Barker was as disappointed as anyone for missing Midway. He had spent years pursuing the dream of flying as a means to escape life in rural Utah, where he once made two dollars per day pitching hay onto a wagon. Times were hard, but he became handy at repairing tractors and trucks on the farm. Since his father shared the same first name, Barker was known by his middle name, Theron, or Terry, as a youth. Terry Barker joined the Army Air Corps in 1934 after graduating from high school, hoping to become an aircraft mechanic. His pay rose to twenty-one dollars per month but he still found himself little more than a flunkie, rather than an aviation mechanic. Terry bought out the rest of his Army enlistment and went to school at Utah State University. He did not finish but instead took a job as a mechanic in 1940 while also earning his civilian pilot's license.[8]

Barker applied for service with the military, and in April 1941 was ordered to Pensacola as a naval aviation cadet. "I had no trouble at all and went right on through and finished up in September 1941," he recalled. In the Navy, his comrades began calling him by his first name, Jesse, and his boyhood nickname of Terry was dropped. He wanted to become a fighter pilot but found the Navy had other plans after Pearl Harbor. "I had orders to Fighting Two aboard the old *Lexington*," he said. "But after Pearl Harbor, everything was in turmoil. After a few months they decided they needed dive-bomber pilots more than they needed fighter pilots and I was dragged away from fighters—kicking and screaming."[9]

His training continued with the ACTG unit in California, and Jesse Barker was eventually transferred into Scouting Three on *Saratoga*. After Midway, he was shifted from VS-3 into Turner Caldwell's Hawaii-based Scouting Five. At age twenty-six, Barker was older than his fellow rookie pilots, who were training at NAS Kaneohe.

At the end of June, many of the VS-5 aviators were given a forty-eight-hour leave at the Royal Hawaiian Hotel on Waikiki Beach. The partying was legendary. Birney Strong was married to a local girl and the squadron celebrated by getting roaring drunk at his reception. Junior pilot Hal Buell shared a hotel room at the Moana Hotel with Art Downing and double-dated with two girls who lived in an apartment across from their hotel. Before shipping back to the war zone, others let off steam with liquor-infused parties that led to fighting in the hotel hallways.[10]

On July 8, Scouting Five reported on board *Enterprise* for three days of final training. Buell was happy to receive a stateroom with a porthole view he shared with pilot Walt Coolbaugh. Link Traynor and Yogi Jorgenson, both survivors of ditchings at Coral Sea, took up residence together. The Dauntless squadrons made simulated dive-bombing attacks and practiced defensive maneuvers with the fighter planes. The final day of practice was concluded with live bomb drops against a practice range on the southern coast of Hawaii. "This whole affair was practice for something coming," recalled Buell, "but no one was talking about what or where the action would be."[11]

Enterprise put to sea again that morning with the battleship *North Carolina*, the new antiaircraft cruiser *Atlanta*, the heavy cruiser *Portland*, and seven destroyers. Uncle John Crommelin worked out his pilots every day en route, flying two-hundred-mile searches. Admiral Thomas Kinkaid's TF-16 crossed the equator four days later, but this time there was no carefree crossing-of-the-line initiation ceremony for the ship's lowly pollywogs. Serious business was at hand. Pilot Hoot Gibson considered himself lucky to have been spared the hazing while still being issued a certificate of having accomplished the crossing. His paper was simply approved with "War Operations against Japan."[12]

Scouting Five was eager to get back to war after nearly two months ashore in Hawaii. "We were a happy, carefree bunch under the command of a great skipper, Turner Caldwell—good men with high spirits and an intense desire to engage the enemy," wrote Buell. "Just how good we were would be tested soon."[13]

The mission at hand for VS-5 and *Enterprise* involved the conquest of the Solomon Islands. Turner Caldwell's aviators had first seen action at Tulagi and the Guadalcanal area in early May, during the preliminaries to Coral Sea. The U.S. Navy was now gearing up to carry out its first offensive campaign of the Pacific War—known as Operation Watchtower—involving the landing of troops on Japanese-held soil in the Solomons.

The first Japanese troops had shifted from Tulagi to northern Guadalcanal on June 8 to establish an encampment area on Lunga Point. Two weeks later, an inspection team from Rabaul arrived to determine the difficulty of building a proper air base on Guadalcanal. Since the Midway operation had been a dismal failure, the Japanese military hoped to construct an airfield in the Solomons to disrupt the crucial United States–Australia lifeline. By July 1, some 257 Japanese troops were on Guadalcanal, and transports began offloading more men and equipment the following week. Artillery, supplies, trucks, a steamroller, four derricks, communications gear, radar, and construction teams were added to reinforce the efforts. Construction units began working night and day from opposite ends of the grassy field at Lunga Point. In addition to power equipment, troops used shovels, pickaxes, and reed baskets, and bicycle carts transported the rocks, coral gravel, and soil they dug.[14]

The new Japanese airfield was nearly complete by early August. Petty Officer Second Class Sankichi Kaneda—who had been working at Lunga for a month—wrote in his memoirs for August 4: "The first stage of construction on the runway is completed. 60m wide and 800m long. It is ready for fighter plane takeoffs and landing." For August 5, Kaneda wrote, "Guadalcanal Guard Unit sent an urgent request to the 8th Base Force [at Rabaul] to send airplanes, but the opinion at the highest levels of command was that the enemy would not mount a serious counterattack until 1943, so the request was denied." In a matter of hours, Kaneda and his comrades would find out just how wrong they were about American intentions.[15]

Admirals Ernie King and Chester Nimitz had been planning since shortly after Midway to contest the Imperial Japanese Army's occupation of Guadalcanal, Tulagi, and the adjacent, smaller islands of Gavutu and Tanambogo. The new 1st Marine Division arrived on July 10 at Nouméa, the capital of the French colony of the cigar-shaped island of New Caledonia. From there, the ground forces were loaded onto fast troop transports on July 27 to prepare for Operation Watchtower. Carrier air groups directed by Admiral Nimitz were to provide cover for the amphibious landing of the Marines in the Solomons on about August 1.[16]

The Guadalcanal landing group would comprise roughly eleven thousand men under the direct command of Major General Alexander Archer Vandegrift, while another 3,000 troops would seize Tulagi and the twin islands of Gavutu-Tanambogo. They would face a little over 3,400 Japanese troops stationed in the Guadalcanal-Tulagi area. The greatest resistance was expected on Guadalcanal Island, where the Japanese were building their new airfield.[17]

Life on Guadalcanal was no picnic. The island was ninety miles long and averaged about twenty-five miles in width. Its coconut plantations and occasional ridges were surrounded by dense, humid rain forests that were home to exotic birds, wild dogs, pigs, lizards, giant rats, and disease-carrying mosquitoes. Crocodiles slithered through the island's rivers and mangrove swamps near the shorelines. Over time, Japanese soldiers would come to despise their miserable ordeal on Guadalcanal, referring to the place as *Jigoku no Shima,* or "Hell's Island."[18]

Scouting Five's first test in the Solomons campaign came during intensive practice landings held in late July. *Enterprise*'s task force steamed toward the Tonga Islands to rendezvous with other task groups that had assembled there. The sobering realities of wartime operational casualties hit home four days out from Pearl. Bombing Six's Ensign Jim "Jamie" Dexter, who earned the Navy Cross at Midway, was lost on a routine mission on July 20. "Jamie's loss took the fun out of the cruise for quite a while," said a somber Ensign Fred Mears of VT-3, one of Dexter's close friends.[19]

The task force steamed southwesterly for ten days and reached Tongatabu's Nuku'alofa Harbor on July 23. There, the sailors were surprised to see an armada of transport ships loaded with green-clad Marines. It was apparent that America was about to launch its first offensive of the Pacific War. Three days later, *Enterprise* rendezvoused at sea some 350 miles south of Fiji with *Saratoga*'s TF-11 and *Wasp*'s TF-18. Eighty-two warships and transports were assembled in the most powerful naval force the Americans had yet assembled in their seven-month-old war. The armada conducted landing exercises on July 30 on Koro Island, where the transports practiced disembarking troops into landing boats. Fighters, SBDs, and TBFs flew practice air-support missions to sharpen the aviators' skills for the real landings that were scheduled in a week's time.

All three aircraft carriers would support the landings planned on Guadalcanal and Tulagi Islands in the Solomons. *Enterprise*'s Scouting Five and Bombing Six would work in close company with the other four Dauntless squadrons operating from *Saratoga* and *Wasp*. *Saratoga* had the veteran VB-3 under Midway veteran Lieutenant Commander DeWitt "Dave" Shumway and the as yet battle-untested Scouting Three. *Sara*'s scouts were commanded by Lieutenant Commander Louis Joseph Kirn, a thirty-five-year-old Milwaukee native. As a midshipman during his Naval Academy days, Kirn had played halfback for the Navy against

Knute Rockne's iron Notre Dame elevens. Despite his banged-up joints, Kirn had punched opponents' lines so hard he won the nickname of "Bullet Lou" among sports fans.

Wasp operated two scouting squadrons, VS-71 and VS-72, versus the typical arrangement of one group of scouts and one group of bombers. Scouting 72 was under Lieutenant Commander Ernie Snowden, a 1932 academy graduate who was a son-in-law of Army General Henry "Hap" Arnold. Scouting 71 was led by steadfast Lieutenant Commander John Eldridge Jr., a 1927 academy graduate who hailed from Norfolk. The *Wasp* pilots were itching for action, as most of their war had been spent escorting convoys and serving in the North Atlantic.

The airmen knew little about their mission. "On board our ship, the pilots enjoyed passing scuttlebutt about where we were headed," said Hoot Gibson. "The Navy was consistent in keeping the pilots in the dark."[20]

The three carrier task forces moved northwesterly from the Fiji Islands past Efate. They turned north toward Tulagi around noon on August 5 for the final run in toward the landing areas. The approach was slow while shepherding the lumbering troop transports. The Dauntless boys had the morning off from search duty on August 6 to prevent their planes from being spotted.

Ensign Jesse Barker knew that he might be called upon to fly types of missions other than what he had been trained for. Lieutenant Robin Lindsey, the senior *Enterprise* LSO, paid a visit to the VS-5 ready room shortly before the scheduled landings. Barker listened intently as Lindsey demonstrated his lighted landing signal wands and the signals they should understand if they were to make landings after dark. "Any questions?" Lindsey asked.[21]

"Of course, nobody had any questions," recalled Barker. As a green ensign, he knew better than to speak out and appear nervous. "That was our total night-flight training indoctrination," he said.

Overcast weather helped mask the massive American force bearing down on the Solomons. Guadalcanal was only eighty-five miles northeast by sunset and Tulagi another fifty miles beyond. "It appeared that

Providence was with the righteous," said Art Downing of VS-5 as his squadron made final preparations for their missions on the following morning. "Weather was almost ideal for our purpose—ceiling at 1,000 feet and visibility never more than five miles." *Wasp*, *Enterprise*, and *Saratoga* wielded 234 operational aircraft with which to execute the first Allied counteroffensive of the Pacific War.[22]

Air officer John Crommelin gathered the *Enterprise* aircrews to complete their pre-strike briefings. The next morning was known as "Dog Day"—landings of troops on Guadalcanal and Tulagi. The pilots were issued small maps for their plotting boards and were briefed on the objectives of their flights. "Show no quarter," Crommelin advised his men. He assured them that Japanese troops would give them the same treatment. American forces had been on the defensive throughout the Pacific War thus far. "Tomorrow, the tide is going to turn," Crommelin promised.[23]

As the *Enterprise* force made its final turn in toward the Guadalcanal area during the early hours of August 7, many pilots contemplated their fate. Dick Jaccard of Bombing Six joked with his buddies that he was a jinx. His roommate, Jim Dexter, had already been lost on this cruise, and his former SBD roommate had been lost on a cruise in May. Torpedo Three pilot Fred Mears spent time in the cabin of Hoot Gibson of VB-6, who was playing his favorite tune, "Blues in the Night." The popular song, recorded in 1942 by many popular artists, such as Woody Herman and Dinah Shore, included the line: "Whooee-a-whooee, ol' clickety-clack, I'm back on the track of blues in the night." Gibson vowed that he would give a "whooee-a-whooee" war whoop over the radio when he went into his first dive the next morning.[24]

Hal Buell of VS-5 knew he was scheduled to go in on the first attack wave before daybreak. He and roommate Walt Coolbaugh would be flying wing on skipper Turner Caldwell.[25]

I feel ready for whatever this invasion brings and am hoping that I can be lucky and get through the air-support raids okay, Buell thought. *I am not worried or scared—just hoping for the best.*

THIRTEEN
"Blood and Thunder" over Hell's Island

The trumpet call for flight quarters sounded at 0400 on Dog Day on the American carriers. Weary yet eager aviators donned their flight gear, gulped coffee, and choked down a fast breakfast before scurrying to their ready rooms for last-minute briefings. The carriers were slated to launch strike groups with numeric call signs for the use of the strike coordinators. Flights originating from *Wasp* would be numbered beginning with Flight 100; from *Saratoga*, the first flight would be Flight 200; and from *Enterprise*, the strikes would be numbered from Flight 300.

Dive-bombers, fighters, and torpedo bombers were to make simultaneous dawn attacks against positions on both Guadalcanal and Tulagi Islands. At around 0500 on all three flattops, more than ninety aircrews raced for their mounts. Gunner Bob Hansen of *Saratoga*'s VS-3 and his pilot, Ensign Jim Sauer, were buckled into their SBD, prepared to launch with the second strike group or as a fill-in for a faulty plane. In his diary, Hansen scrawled, "The big day ahead promised blood and thunder, the prime delight of unseasoned and ignorant warriors."[1]

At 0530, Sister Sara turned into the wind to begin the flight operations. Five miles south of *Saratoga*, *Wasp* followed suit, as did the Big E, some five miles north of *Saratoga*. It was still a full hour before sunrise. By a quarter moon on the horizon, only a sliver of light was available on the darkened ship. The first plane of the day, a Fighting Six Wildcat, was launched from *Enterprise* at 0535.[2]

Chief Rocky Glidewell was long past the pre-strike jitters. He had made so many island strikes that that was getting to be old hat. He climbed into Lieutenant Caldwell's plane, spotted at the front of the VS-5 strike group. Behind him, the deep-throated iron birds coughed and roared to life as their starters were fired. Ahead of him, the Big E was spitting forth her first CAP fighters into the dark sky. Skipper Caldwell throttled up to the starting line and checked his instruments one last time. The launching officer gave the signal, and he turned up his engine to 2,300 rpm.

Everything sounded in order. Glidewell knew it was a go. The starter dropped his flag and pointed toward the bow. Caldwell released his brakes and throttled down the flight deck at top speed at 0540. Behind their lead Dauntless, eight more VS-5 dive-bombers lifted off their carrier's bow into the darkness and clawed for altitude.

Caldwell's VS-5 was the most seasoned unit of the six Dauntless squadrons to see action during the Guadalcanal landings. Four pilots in his first flight—Walt Coolbaugh, Nick Nicholson, Yogi Jorgenson, and Art Downing—had been with him on the first strikes against Tulagi Harbor in May and against the Japanese carriers in the Coral Sea battle. The other four pilots of his Flight 303—Ensigns Hal Buell, Walt Brown, Howard Burnett, and Spike Conzett—were still combat virgins, although Buell and Brown had joined VS-5 in early May.

Lieutenant Downing, leading the second section, knew their orders were to bomb and strafe targets along the southwest coast of Tulagi. He was already familiar with the island, but reaching it was a whole different issue. Confusion reigned in the predawn skies. "The sky was a vortex of red, white, and green lights of hundreds of planes from the three carriers," Downing recalled. At long last, his squadron straightened away toward the coast of Tulagi some distance away.[3]

Redbird Burnett was unable to find his squadron mates during the rendezvous. The auburn-haired aviator who had earned his nickname during flight training in Florida hailed from the New Eden community east of Coldwater, Kansas. In school, Burnett excelled at academics and also at football, track, and basketball. When he graduated from the University of Kansas, he had been making two hundred dollars per month at the Kansas Electric Power Company in Lawrence, but gave it up to enlist as an aviation cadet. He earned his gold wings in November 1941 and had finished first in aeronautical acrobatics in his class of 181. Redbird would need all of his training now. He set out individually for Tulagi and would never find Scouting Five during his first combat mission.

Saratoga's VS-3 got off to a rocky start.

Ensign William Richard Bell, a heavyset rookie, pulled to the starting line with an engine that was coughing and spitting. Anxious to make his first strike, he lumbered down the deck, but

Lieutenant (j.g.) Howard "Redbird" Burnett.

could not gather enough speed. His 3-S-13 cleared the end of the flight deck, but it wobbled, rolled onto its back, and crashed into the ocean just ahead of *Saratoga*. Neither he nor his gunner, Seaman Second Class Robert Keith Cameron, was recovered. In fact, one third of Bullet Lou Kirn's scouts failed to launch and crashed, became lost, or lost their weapons without even getting in sight of an enemy.[4]

On *Wasp*, the virgin Scouting 71 sent up fifteen SBDs under Lieutenant Commander John Eldridge. "I had never seen a thousand-pound bomb, let alone take off with one," recalled Ensign Harold "Nate" Murphy of VS-71. "I managed to get in the air and join on my section leader's exhaust flames. This being my first combat mission, I was quite uptight and, frankly, scared. A couple of planes outboard of me decided they should try their guns to see if they worked. I almost spun in when I saw the flashes and the tracers. I thought for sure I was being shot at." Another young pilot, Ensign Robert Escher, lost his bomb due to an electrical malfunction. Eldridge's scouts flew in company with three divisions of fighters and their air group commander, Lieutenant Commander Wallace M. Beakley, who would serve as one of the morning's aerial coordinators.

Saratoga's SBDs proceeded to the north coast of Guadalcanal, in

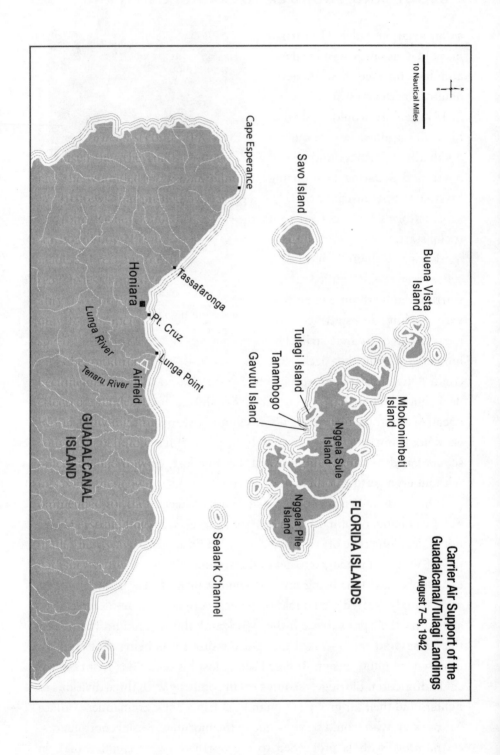

Carrier Air Support of the
Guadalcanal/Tulagi Landings
August 7–8, 1942

the vicinity of the Lunga River. Bullet Lou Kirn's Scouting Three commenced its attacks at 0625 under the lower clouds. They caused extensive damage to the AA installations and dumps in the Kukum area. Ensign Allard "Slim" Russell, flying wing on Lieutenant Ralph Weymouth, saw the fighters begin their strafing runs on Kukum ahead of him. Weymouth's division attacked first and he claimed the first bomb dropped on Guadalcanal.[5]

Hal Buell was excited to finally see action. As a rookie pilot of VS-5, he had sat out the Coral Sea battle in May, and his unit had arrived just days late to join the battle off Midway. Now, as Turner Caldwell's Flight 303 approached Tulagi's coast at fourteen thousand feet, Buell watched in awe as battleships, cruisers, and destroyers unloaded their big guns with flashes of fire toward Japanese targets ashore. His running lights were turned off but he was tucked in close enough to Caldwell and Coolbaugh to see their planes. They arrived over the southeast side of Tulagi at around 0615, to carry out a strike in coordination with Wallace Beakley's first *Wasp* group.[6]

Their objectives were specific targets and areas on Tulagi and two small linked islets—Gavutu and Tanambogo—about three thousand yards east of Tulagi. The other targets named for VS-5 and the *Wasp* pilots were Halavo, Port Purvis, Haleta, Bungana, and a radio station code-named "Asses' Ears." Lieutenant Commander Courtney Shands, head of *Wasp*'s VF-71, flew over the strike area as his passenger recorded four rolls of motion picture film of the strikes. The fighters moved in first to strafe, and then the dive-bombers headed toward their respective targets.

Buell followed his skipper into his dive on Tulagi. There was just enough light that he could make out the installations below. He noted with satisfaction that his big bomb landed right alongside Caldwell's on their target. He then joined his squadron mates in strafing enemy troop positions. *There is surprisingly little opposition*, Caldwell thought as he and Rocky Glidewell blazed away with their guns.[7]

The greatest danger for Art Downing came from overeager fellow pilots. While flying flat on the deck in a strafing run, he was startled by a nearby violent bomb explosion—courtesy of a VS-5 shipmate releasing from higher altitude. "Gun emplacements, troop concentrations, dugouts and revetments replaced the high-speed twisting and zig-zagging targets we had always attacked," said Downing. "We were treated to the unaccustomed luxury of diving on stationary targets."[8]

Redbird Burnett, separated from his eight VS-5 comrades since leaving the ship, made the most of his first combat. He coolly dived on a large coastal gun emplacement on Tulagi while under heavy AA fire. He then made strafing runs before finally heading back for his ship on his own. Caldwell's flight straggled back aboard *Enterprise* between 0805 and 0818.

Scouting Five came through without loss. The *Wasp* fighters had a field day strafing four-engined flying boats moored off Tulagi. Lieutenant Porter Maxwell reported that the other *Wasp* scout bombers "cleared out to keep from getting shot down by our own fighters, who were going wild and shooting at everything in sight."[9]

The airmen grabbed sandwiches, slurped coffee, and copied flight instructions as their SBDs were refueled and rearmed for follow-up strikes. It was only the beginning of what would be their longest day of continual bombing missions. As the aviators returned, squadron intelligence officers interrogated each pilot and carried the data forms to Air Plot, where the intelligence was transcribed onto a series of large charts covering the operating area.

For the *Enterprise* Air Group, Dog Day at Guadalcanal would be a day of endless flight duty. Every plane that would fly had been readied for action, either as part of strike groups, combat air patrols, IAPs, or anti-submarine patrols. Bombing Six, led by skipper Ray Davis, departed on its first Guadalcanal mission a half hour behind Caldwell's predawn strikers. Ensign Hoot Gibson was flying with Davis as they attacked Tulagi, Gavutu, and Tanambogo Islands. He had promised his fellow pilots he would sing from his favorite song "Blues in the Night" over his radio as he attacked. "The phrase I sang while in a split-S beginning the bomb run was *whooey, whooey*," Gibson recalled. "My gravel voice probably struck fear into the Japanese hearts all the way to Rabaul."[10]

The VB-6 group was back in the landing circle over the Big E by 0930. The *Enterprise* scouts and bombers tag-teamed each other throughout the morning as wave after wave of strike planes roared toward the

Canal. Scouting Five's second attack group had taken departure just after 0800, and was officially designated Flight 309.

Lieutenant Roger Woodhull, the VS-5 exec, led Coral Sea veteran wingmen Elmer Maul and Skip Ervin, trailed by the second section of Lieutenants (j.g.) Red Austin and Link Traynor. Armed with thousand-pound bombs, they received directives from *Wasp* Air Group commander Wallace Beakley and from the Air Support Director Group in the transport ship *McCawley*. Woodhull's crews bombed an antiaircraft position northeast of the light on Bungana Island, strafed the town and beaches of Halavo, and were back on board the Big E by 1023.

In the interim, Turner Caldwell and Rocky Glidewell launched for their second strike at 0902 in charge of Flight 312—leading Coolbaugh, Buell, Nicholson, Jorgenson, Richey, Downing, Brown, and Conzett. They dropped five-hundred-pound bombs on Gavutu Island and strafed Gavutu and Tanambogo. Hal Buell was strafing an ammunition dump when another dive-bomber landed a direct hit that exploded with an outstanding flash. The dump erupted in front of Buell "with debris flying up all around but not striking the plane."[11]

Caldwell's second flight landed back on their carrier by 1128. Launching just ahead of them at 1114 was Rog Woodhull with his four morning wingmen (Maul, Ervin, Austin, and Traynor) plus Birney Strong and his section of Glenn Estes, Dog Barker, and Redbird Burnett. Woodhull's VS-5 was split into three sections and also included two VB-6 crews under Troy Guillory and Harry Liffner. His eleven dive-bombers bombed and strafed along the northeast coast of Tulagi.

To Birney Strong, "the air work over those islands was not particularly difficult. I think the hardest thing was in spotting an objective." The air coordinator assigned him to drop on an AA gun a thousand yards northeast of a lighthouse on one of the small islands off Tanambogo. Strong flew low, searching for the lighthouse, but could make out only a navigational marker. Assuming it must be the intended point, he climbed for diving altitude and shifted his aim northeast of the marker. As he released and pulled out of his dive, he heard the coordinator calling, "Nice drop! Nice drop!" Strong turned and flew right back over the spot where he had dropped but could not make out anything.[12]

Ensign Jesse Barker was flying his first combat mission. "At the time, we didn't know enough to be scared," he said. His target was a radio station on Tanambogo. "I'm not sure if I hit the damned tower or not," said Barker, "but there was a huge secondary explosion—a bomb blast and an enormous fire."[13]

From *Wasp*, *Saratoga*, and *Enterprise*, many of the pilots were departing on their third missions by midday. They attacked targets of opportunity as assigned, including Japanese troop landing areas, buildings, suspected hideouts, warehouses, ammunition dumps, and tent villages. Petty Officer Sankichi Kaneda took cover near the new Japanese airfield at Lunga Point as the American warplanes bombed and strafed and warships shelled the area. "August 7 was the beginning of Hell," Kaneda recalled. "I found myself instinctively running barefoot through clouds of sand and gunpowder smoke, jumping head-first into an air raid shelter."[14]

By noon, most of Scouting Five's pilots had made two flights. Walt Brown and Spike Conzett had been left behind when Lieutenant Woodhull departed on his second mission. Their two planes, however, were soon grouped into a division of Bombing Six for Flight 319. Lieutenant Carl Horenburger, a decorated veteran of Midway, was in charge of this mixed flight. Horenburger departed at 1217 with eight planes. His lead division included Ensigns Bob Shaw and Hoot Gibson of his own squadron, plus Brown and Conzett. Bringing up the rear was the VB-6 section of Ensigns Eldor Rodenburg, Jerry Richey, and Steve Czarnecki.

As their flight approached Tulagi, Lew Jones, rear gunner for Shaw, took in the surroundings. Far below, as far as he could see, white wakes of troop transports streamed in toward the beach, while warships fired salvos into the island. *What a show!* Jones thought.[15]

The show so far had been fairly tame in terms of Japanese resistance. Things were about to change, however, for Jones and company.

Rear Admiral Sadayoshi Yamada, commanding the 25th Air Flotilla at Rabaul, put his air group in action. He had received word that American ships and aircraft were assaulting Tulagi and Guadalcanal. By 0930, a Japanese strike force began launching from Rabaul to attack the U.S. invaders. Yamada sent out twenty-seven Mitsubishi G4M Type 1 medium bombers (later known popularly as Bettys to the Allies), nine Aichi 99 "Val" dive-bombers, and seventeen Zero fighters from Rabaul's airfields.

Petty Officer First Class Saburo Sakai led the second *shotai* (three-plane section) of the third *chutai* (division) of Zeros. He was the Imperial Navy's top-scoring ace with some forty-eight aerial victories. Sakai, a pilot since 1937, had seen extensive combat in China, the Philippines, the East Indies, and around Port Moresby. Sakai now had the chance to engage the American planes that were ravaging his comrades in the Solomons. An Australian Coastwatcher on Bougainville Island spotted the inbound Rabaul strike group and radioed the intelligence ahead.[16]

The American carriers increased their CAP fighters and waited for the expected engagement. Yamada's bomber force was sighted over Savo Island at 1320, and was engaged. Wildcat divisions from *Enterprise*'s VF-6 and *Saratoga*'s VF-5 tore into the Betty bombers and began mixing it up with the Zeros. Planes from both sides began dropping into the ocean as the first big aerial clash over Guadalcanal ensued on August 7. Saburo Sakai locked into a deadly dogfight with Lieutenant James "Pug" Southerland of Fighting Five. Sakai won the match and blasted Southerland's F4F from the sky, forcing the American fighter pilot to bail out over Guadalcanal.

The Rabaul Zeros destroyed five of eight VF-5 Wildcats and then turned their attention to a flight of VS-71 SBDs from *Wasp*. At 1330, Lieutenant Commander John Eldridge was preparing to bomb positions off the Florida Island coast, a few miles southeast of Tulagi, when his group was attacked. His Dauntless crews climbed for altitude as Betty bombers began raining bombs down among the American transports in Group X-Ray.

Eldridge had reached 7,500 feet when five fighters attacked his SBDs. Lieutenant Dudley Adams fought back, smashing Saburo Sakai's rear canopy glass with one bullet before Japan's leading ace turned the tables on him. Sakai riddled the SBD of Adams, forcing him to ditch near the American transport forces at 1337. The destroyer *Dewey* picked up the wounded Dud Adams, but his gunner, Harry Elliott, was killed.[17]

Sakai then resumed his flight toward his bombers, but for the ace fighter pilot, targets proved to be plentiful. In the distance ahead, he next made out what appeared to be eight Grumman fighters flying in formation. Sakai moved in once again, feeling certain that he could ambush them.

USS *Enterprise* Flight 319 vs. Saburo Sakai		
Guadalcanal Landing Support, August 7, 1942		
PILOT	REAR-SEAT GUNNER	SQUADRON
Lt. Carl Herman Horenburger	AMM2c Herman Hull Caruthers	VB-6
Ens. Robert Douglas Gibson	RM3c Edward Rutledge Anderson	VB-6
Ens. Robert Carl Shaw	AOM2c Harold Llewellyn Jones	VB-6
Ens. Eldor Ernst Rodenburg	ARM3c James William Patterson Jr.	VB-6
Ens. Gerald S. Richey	RM3c Julian Alfred Johansson	VB-6
Ens. Stephen Joseph Czarnecki	ARM3c Paul N. Deadwiley	VB-6
Ens. Walter E. Brown Jr.	ARM2c Norbert Anthony Fives	VS-5
Ens. Elmer Andrew Conzett	ARM3c Eugene Clay Strickland	VS-5

The aggressive Sakai was making his first big mistake. His "prey" was not the Wildcat fighters but instead Carl Horenburger's mixed Bombing Six/Scouting Five dive-bombers of Flight 319. The eight *Enterprise* SBDs were holding a position at about 8,500 feet near Tulagi. The pilots awaited instructions from the ground coordinator on Tulagi as to which specific targets on their maps they were to bomb. "These instructions never came," said Horenburger.[18]

Ed Anderson was feeling quite at ease. There had been no aerial opposition on his first hop over the Solomons. He had closed his rear-seat hood during the flight from the ship because of the coldness above eight thousand feet. "Things had been going along so smoothly that we had more or less been sitting back and taking life easy," Anderson wrote in his diary. Suddenly, on the horizon, he saw a group of planes approaching. Uncertain of their identity, Anderson was first to slide his canopy back open. It was about 1320, just an hour into their flight.[19]

Horenburger conferred with his gunner, Herman Caruthers, about their likely target. Caruthers knew that his buddy Lew Jones had taken good briefing notes before the flight. He looked over to Jones's plane and asked where the target was. Caruthers communicated by using open-hand, closed-fist Morse code. "I looked at my notes and was just about to send the answer concerning the target when he pointed excitedly to the back of us," said Jones.[20]

Caruthers excitedly shouted over the intercom: "Fighters!"

Horenburger immediately signaled for his formation to tighten up. Eldor Rodenburg, leading the second section of VB-6, ordered Richey and Czarnecki—flying slightly astern and below—in tight on his wings. Horenburger then led their formation into a gradual turn to starboard.

Sakai moved in fast, thinking he had found an unsuspecting group of American fighters. His opponents headed for the nearest cumulus clouds. Hoot Gibson, Horenburger's wingman, had seen the fighters coming, too. The first one he spotted was just a little dot on the horizon but it was coming toward him at a high rate of speed. All of a sudden, Gibson saw shells streaking by in front of him as Sakai opened fire.[21]

Ed Anderson saw Sakai's first Zero diving in on his section from above and astern. He opened fire first, followed quickly by Jones and Caruthers from his section. All three gunners saw their rounds hitting home, causing the Zero to burst into flames. One of the bullets shattered Sakai's windscreen and tore into his head, temporarily blinding him.

Horenburger saw Sakai's Zero roll into an inverted position as it passed over the SBD formation. He quickly lost sight of it as Sakai's wingman, Petty Officer Second Class Enji Kakimoto, moved in from astern. The jubilant American rear gunners chalked up a kill to their credit, and they credited Lew Jones, in the closest SBD to Sakai, with scoring the hits.

Their attention immediately turned to Kakimoto's fighter. He opened fire on the left side of the Dauntless formation. Horenburger's and Bob Shaw's planes took hits but Hoot Gibson's bird took the brunt of the assault. "The second one made a belly run on our plane and planted a 20mm shell in our bomb and on up through my transmitter," said Anderson. The cannon shell struck the vane of Gibson's bomb and bounced off, ripping through the SBD's underside. After shredding Anderson's radio and passing practically between his legs, it exploded against the pilot's seat. Gibson's seat was heavily armored but it still felt like a swift kick in the pants. The plating saved his life.[22]

Shrapnel from the explosion made a mess of Gibson's plane. He could hear the rear gunners rattling away at their opponent. "I looked over my left shoulder and about twenty feet behind me, going straight up, was a Japanese Zero in a huge ball of flame," he said. From Gibson's rear seat, Anderson could see heavy smoke pouring from Sakai's Zero as it disappeared toward the horizon. "We all thought he was going to crash," Anderson said.[23]

Bob Shaw fell out of formation, struggling to fly his Dauntless with a damaged right elevator. Gunner Lew Jones learned that their plane had been hit by 232 rounds of 7.7mm bullets. They returned to the ship alone, and Jones later found that a pain in his left eye had been caused by a tiny sliver of metal he believed must have been acquired in his fight with Saburo Sakai.[24]

Horenburger's flight was ordered to return to *Enterprise* without having completed its bombing mission. Sakai was in pain from the bullet that had grazed his skull. He recovered from his plunge toward the ocean, which fortunately extinguished the flames that were enveloping his fighter. Sakai was blinded in one eye but struggled to return his Zero to Rabaul and complete a harrowing 560-mile flight. The *Enterprise* SBD gunners had succeeded in sidelining Japan's top ace for the next two years.

The remainder of the August 7 landing-support missions were less dra-
matic for the *Enterprise* bombers. Turner Caldwell was leading one
of his missions when he heard the excited call: "Tally-ho, many bogey
bombers!"

He tightened up his SBD formation to create a more formidable firepower from the rear gunners and headed back toward the ship at about
five thousand feet altitude. Suddenly an enemy fighter was spotted at five
o'clock, coming in at high speed.

Hal Buell watched in shock as the Zero raced straight for them. As it
came within a few hundred yards, he thought, *My God, he's going to
ram the formation!* At that instant, the Zero's 7.7mm guns began twinkling, followed by the slower puffs of a 20mm cannon. Caldwell's nine
rear-seat gunners opened fire with their .30-caliber Browning machine
guns. Buell saw pieces fly from the Zero's wings and fuselage, and it fell
away in a slow left spiral for the sea. Since no one actually saw the fighter
strike the water, Caldwell only chalked up a probable kill for his VS-5
gunners. Art Downing believed that Yogi Jorgenson's gunner, Tony Brunetti, had been dead-on in lacing the fighter with lead.[25]

By midafternoon, the scouts could see that the Marines had occupied
Gavutu Island and that additional equipment was being brought ashore
on Blue Beach, on Tulagi's west coast. Turner Caldwell and Rog Woodhull continued to lead groups of VS-5 crews to bomb targets on Tanambogo and Makambo Islands. The Solomons occupation was going so
well that some pilots simply could not find troop installations, AA nests,
or sampans worthy of the expending of their bombs. Art Downing was
the last of the scouts to return to *Enterprise* on August 7. Flying a photo
SBD, he became lost after dark and made it on board the Big E only at
1857 with the use of his ZB device.[26]

By day's end, the statistics were record-breaking. *Saratoga* had
launched 240 aircraft on various missions. They logged a collective 607
flight hours and dropped 316 one-hundred-pound bombs, a dozen five-
hundred-pound bombs, thirty-five incendiary clusters, and sixty-five
thousand-pound bombs. *Saratoga* lost six fighters and one SBD during
the day. *Wasp* was almost equal, having dispatched 223 total aircraft on
all kinds of missions, with only one SBD lost. *Enterprise* set a single-day

record for flight operations with 236 takeoffs and 229 landings. The pilots, gunners, and flight-deck crews were exhausted. Ensign Slim Russell of *Saratoga*'s VS-3 enjoyed a shot of bourbon and Coke and then a shower before crawling into his bunk.[27]

Air operations commenced again at daybreak on August 8—known as D-Day + 1. Ernie Snowden of *Wasp*'s VS-72 shot down a Japanese fighter seaplane about forty miles off Rekata Bay during the early morning. Seven of Turner Caldwell's scouts departed at 0800 with five-hundred-pound bombs. Split into two groups, they dropped on the western side of Tanambogo and on Mokamo Island. Woodhull and Downing led another six from VS-5 to scout for enemy submarines between Guadalcanal and Tulagi, and to search for two fighter pilots believed to be down southeast of Guadalcanal. They deposited some of their bombs on Mbangai Island and returned unscathed.

The only SBD crews to tangle with Japanese planes on August 8 were those of John Eldridge's VS-71. Six Zeros moved in to attack the group of *Wasp* SBDs. Lieutenant (j.g.) Robert Howard and his gunner, Seaman Second Class Lawrence Paul Lupo, fought back doggedly. Howard finally caught the Zero piloted by Petty Officer Third Class Yutaka Kimura in a head-on shoot-out. Kimura's Mitsubishi burst into flames and plowed into the water near Florida Island. Eldridge, Howard, and Porter Maxwell's planes all returned to *Wasp* with fresh bullet holes as souvenirs of their scrape with the Zeros.[28]

Scouting Five had flown three more bombing missions by early afternoon on August 8. The late-afternoon search planes returned after dark. Last to land was Ensign Fred Mears of VT-3, who became lost and had to be given a steer by radio to find *Enterprise* at 1835. He was waved off by the LSO for coming in too fast but finally landed on the last fumes of his fuel. His buddy Hoot Gibson of VB-6 was quick to rib him on his near loss: "You've got just enough dumb luck to fly over the carrier in the dark without knowing it and catch your hook in a wire."[29]

Admiral Fletcher, feeling the Japanese were fully alerted to his presence, decided to withdraw his three carriers from the Guadalcanal area earlier than planned. He needed to refuel his ships and worried about the fact that he had lost twenty percent of his fighters in two days of action. Admiral Kelly Turner's cargo ships and screening warships were still offloading supplies at Guadalcanal and were left exposed to attack from Japanese warships. Hoot Gibson, inspired by his first two days of combat flights, asked squadron skipper Ray Davis to allow him to land on Guadalcanal's airstrip with a flight of six SBDs to help protect Turner's transports. The reality of the situation, however, was that the fliers would not have extra fuel and bombs to resupply their dive-bombers. "My appeal was to no avail," said Gibson. "We turned tail and got the hell out of there and Kelly Turner was left holding the bag."[30]

That night, Japanese warships slid into the scene, and the Battle of Savo Island, one of the worst defeats in American naval history, ensued. One Australian and three American heavy cruisers were blasted to shreds and they sank to the depths off Guadalcanal that became known as Ironbottom Sound.

The American transport ships were forced to weigh anchor and haul clear of the area. The Marine command on Guadalcanal felt abandoned by Fletcher's decision to withdraw his carrier air support. The ground forces on Hell's Island were on their own for the time being, and the Japanese did not appear eager to hand over the bloody island anytime soon.

FOURTEEN
"We'd Better Go Get the Carrier"

The Japanese were never able to finish it. The U.S. Marines were quick to seize it. From August 7 for months to come, control of Guadalcanal's one little dirt airstrip would be hotly contested. Carrier airpower would play a key role in the struggle now in place to maintain possession of Hell's Island as a landlocked flight deck.

Major General Alexander Vandegrift's 1st Marine Division succeeded in overrunning the new Japanese airfield on Lunga Point by D-Day + 1, August 8. The airstrip was little more than 2,600 feet of hard-packed soil and crushed coral gravel on a broad, grassy savanna. The Japanese had been hard at work on their Solomons airfield, but when the Marines stormed ashore, they fled hastily. They left behind steamrollers, dump trucks, gasoline-powered locomotives, and shovels. The approach end of the field still had too many trees, and there was a large hole in the middle of the runway. Vandegrift immediately declared that his men would extend the runway by a thousand feet and make it suitable for Marine dive-bombers and fighters. The Marines set to work improving Guadalcanal's "landlocked carrier" field for future operations. By August 11 they had filled in a large bomb crater and had the strip usable to 160 feet wide by the full 2,600-foot length.[1]

On August 8, the 5th Marines also captured the Japanese communications control tower, a radio transmitter connected via a power cable to the Pagoda, a Korean-style building near the airstrip that the Japanese had planned as an officers' club. By the next day, the station was able to transmit messages to and receive messages directly from CINCPAC at Pearl Harbor. "Radio Guadalcanal," with the call letters NGK, had been born.[2]

Rear Admiral John Sidney McCain, commander, aircraft, South Pacific Area, sent one of his staffers in a Navy PBY-5A Catalina on August 12 to survey the Lunga Point airfield. The flying boat crew declared that the airstrip was suitable for fighter operations, and McCain moved quickly to forward Marine aircraft. The Marines renamed the former Japanese airfield Henderson Field, in honor of a well-known Marine SBD squadron commander, Major Lofton Henderson, who had been killed while attacking the Japanese carrier *Hiryu* at Midway.

Ground crews worked tirelessly—often under Japanese sniper fire and shelling from destroyers offshore—during the next week. The first U.S. aircraft to be based from Henderson Field flew in on August 20 from the auxiliary carrier *Long Island* (ACV-1). They were nineteen F4Fs of Marine Fighting Squadron 223 (VMF-223) under Major John Lucian Smith and a dozen SBDs of Marine Scout Bombing Squadron 232 (VMSB-232) under Lieutenant Colonel Richard C. Mangrum. First to kick up the dust on Henderson Field was Dick Mangrum as he brought his SBD in for a landing. As he climbed from the cockpit of his plane, General Vandegrift sprang forward to shake his hand excitedly.[3]

Guadalcanal was code-named "Cactus," and the aviators who began flying from the heavily contested airfield proudly considered themselves members of the "Cactus Air Force." Smith and Mangrum's aircrews slept in Marine tents near their planes and on their first night were treated to an artillery and infantry attack by Japanese forces. The next day, the Marine pilots of VMF-223 tangled with Japanese Zeros, and learned that aerial combat was to be an almost daily event for them. Two days later, on August 22, the first reinforcements arrived in the form of five Bell P-400 fighters (versions of the P-39 Airacobra), commanded by Major Dale D. Brannon, skipper of the U.S. Army Air Force 67th Pursuit Squadron.

The Cactus Air Force was formed under the most extreme conditions on an island held by the Imperial Japanese Army. The struggle to seize control of the Canal would be long and brutal. Rear Admiral Jack Fletcher had no false illusions of how easily the Japanese would hand over Guadalcanal. He had conservatively withdrawn his three aircraft carrier groups on the afternoon of August 8, and his actions in so doing had drawn heavy scorn from the Marines left ashore.

The *Enterprise*, *Wasp*, and *Saratoga* task groups refueled at sea southwest of Espíritu Santo while their aircrews enjoyed some much-needed downtime. The bomber squadrons from each carrier rotated duty days, flying scout flights, anti-submarine patrols, and inner air patrols (IAPs) from sunup to sundown to search for and protect against enemy shipping and aircraft.

The Big E was the duty carrier on August 12. She launched four VB-6 crews for IAP duty, followed by another dozen scouts of Turner Caldwell's VS-5 to search a sector out to 140 miles. Ensign Hoot Gibson and wingman Jerry Richey had scarcely retracted their wheels after takeoff when something caught Gibson's eye. He was just twenty miles south of the ship, but there below was the white wake of a Japanese submarine running on the surface. Gibson decided he had no time to climb to make a proper dive-bombing attack from higher altitude. *I'm under five hundred feet,* he thought. *At this altitude, I'll probably blow myself out of the air if I'm careless.*[4]

Gibson passed directly over the I-boat, dipped his nose, and toggled his bomb. It was a near miss, so he wheeled his Dauntless around to make a strafing run. He blasted away at the pigboat sailors he could see on deck, and rear gunner Ed Anderson did the same as they flew past. The I-boat seemed to be having difficulty submerging, so Gibson made repeated strafing runs. Richey landed another near miss with his bomb close to the hull. He and gunner Julian Johansson then joined Gibson's crew in making strafing runs. Personnel were seen lying on the deck and in the water. The submarine finally settled below the surface in a bow-down attitude, but without any apparent headway. Gibson and Richey were given credit for the sinking, although Japanese records failed to confirm the loss. Ed Anderson, who had seen combat at Midway, wrote in his diary that it was the "biggest thrill of the war so far for me."[5]

On the morning of August 17, *Enterprise*, *Saratoga*, and *Wasp* were about 275 miles southeast of Guadalcanal. The Task Force 61 carriers were the principal line of defense for the entire region, and were charged with protecting the vital shipping lanes. On August 18, they refueled west of Espíritu Santo as Admiral Fletcher prepared for a new mission. His carriers were ordered to escort the auxiliary carrier *Long Island* to within flight range of Guadalcanal. The little flattop had sailed from Fiji, loaded with thirty-one Marine aircraft from VMF-223 and VMSB-232. That afternoon, John Smith's fighters and Dick Mangrum's SBDs touched down on Henderson Field.

TF-61 retired southeast the following day while escorting *Long Island* from the area. It had been two weeks since the bombing missions that had supported the Guadalcanal landings. The grueling daily search flights had since created monotony for the SBD crews. "This past week [we] have done little except go around in circles," wrote Slim Russell of Scouting Three. Enemy contacts began heating up on August 22. Lieutenant (j.g.) Bill Henry and Ensign Robert Pellissier of *Saratoga*'s VS-3 encountered a Japanese two-stack destroyer north of Florida Island. The next day, Scouting Five had air duty, and its pilots found enemy submarines.[6]

Turner Caldwell launched shortly after 0630 with orders for his scouts to patrol out to 180 miles for signs of Japanese shipping. His unit was down to just nineteen pilots with the transfer of Ensign Addison Pfautz, leaving only one man more than VS-5's eighteen operational SBDs. Caldwell stayed at low altitude on August 23 due to intermittent rainsqualls. One hour out, he and Rocky Glidewell sighted the white wake of a vessel plowing along in the moderate seas. It was a Japanese submarine heading toward TF-61. Wingman Hal Buell pointed out the sub to gunner Jim Cales as they pushed over into glide-bombing runs. Alert lookouts spotted the shiny Dauntless bombers and the I-boat made a crash-dive.[7]

Caldwell landed his five-hundred-pound bomb about a hundred feet off the starboard bow. The deck was already awash as Buell realized he was in a poor position to bomb effectively. He hoped Caldwell's bomb would do enough damage to bring the I-boat back to the surface, but the undersea vessel disappeared for good. "My disappointment in being so ineffective in this, my first enemy ship contact, was almost unbearable," Buell admitted.[8]

It would not be long before Scouting Five would find another submarine, however. At 0815, Birney Strong and "Rich" Richey caught *I-17* running on the surface about eighty miles northeast of Caldwell's contact. They pushed into glide-bombing runs and released at a thousand feet. Strong's bomb landed sixty feet to starboard and Richey dropped his two lengths ahead of where the boat disappeared beneath the surface. The effects of the blasts forced the *I-17* back to the surface. Both pilots and their gunners, Clay Strickland and Mark Broussard, strafed the vessel until it dived again. Strong and Richey scoured the area for some time before heading for home, confident they had at least damaged the Japanese sub. The skipper of *I-17* was fortunate to escape with only bullet damage to her starboard main ballast tank cover.[9]

At 1400, *Enterprise* launched another ten SBDs to search sectors out to 200 miles. At 1530, Elmer Maul and Glenn Estes of VS-5 caught another submarine on the surface. They attacked as the I-boat began to crash-dive. Maul's bomb landed twenty-five feet from the conning tower before it was totally submerged. Estes landed his five-hundred-pounder near the conning tower just after it had passed beneath the surface. About ninety seconds after submerging, the submarine emitted an oil slick that began spreading on the surface as the planes left the location. The *Enterprise* scouts felt certain that they had sunk or badly damaged some of the submarines, but again Japanese records failed to verify the claims.

During the late morning, Admiral Fletcher received intelligence reports of Japanese ships approaching Guadalcanal. The *Enterprise* and *Wasp* planes were held in reserve while *Saratoga* sent out a strike force at 1440 under CSAG Don Felt. Felt set out with thirty-one SBDs from VB-3 and VS-3, plus a half dozen TBDs of Torpedo Eight. The mission was foiled by heavy storms and poor visibility. The force broke through the weather around 1700, but no enemy force was in sight where it should have been. Felt swept the area for a short while but finally decided to head for Guadalcanal, where he had orders to keep his planes overnight.[10]

Saratoga's planes arrived over Henderson Field about fifteen minutes after sunset in between passing rainsqualls. Lieutenant (j.g.) Bob Elder of VB-3 noted that Marines had positioned several jeeps so their headlights would help point out the runway. "The Marines knew more about the situation than we did, of course," he said. "They turned on the lights and ran like hell." The Navy SBDs and TBFs were dispersed around the field to be fueled by hand through the night and prepared for takeoff in the morning. "We had to spend the night in the cockpit of the airplane or under the airplanes," Lou Kirn said.[11]

Slim Russell of VS-3 ate stew, hardtack, pears, and peas right out of a Marine mess kit in a coconut grove. *Really the western front*, he thought. Lieutenant Harold Sydney Bottomley sampled a form of boiler-maker consisting of small bottles of rotgut Lejon California brandy and captured Asahi Japanese beer. Ensign Austin Merrill of VB-3 slept with his back against one of his SBD's wheel struts. He kept his service .45 ready as he listened to taunting voices coming from the brush during the night. Around 0200, their sleep was interrupted by the Japanese destroyer *Kagero* lobbing shells toward the airstrip for about ten minutes. Pilot Lefty Holmberg believed the Japanese commander fired on them "just to harass us and keep us awake. He succeeded."[12]

Admiral Fletcher dispatched the carrier *Wasp* and her escorts during the late afternoon of August 23 to refuel north of Espíritu Santo. He felt that *Enterprise* and *Saratoga*, with their 157 aircraft, could handle Japanese warships and transports being reported by Navy PBY snoopers. Fletcher did not yet have the knowledge that several Japanese forces were in fact converging upon Guadalcanal. These included Vice Admiral Chu-ichi Nagumo's *Kido Butai* carrier group, with the big flattops *Shokaku* and *Zuikaku*, and Rear Admiral Chuichi Hara's Detached Force. Hara's group included two destroyers, the heavy cruiser *Tone*, and the light carrier *Ryujo*, and it was positioned out ahead of the other forces.[13]

Fletcher kept his scouts busy during the morning hours while he awaited the return of Don Felt's SBDs and TBFs from Henderson Field. *Enterprise* sent out twenty SBDs to scout to the north and another three to handle IAP duties around the carriers. There were no contacts with the Japanese surface vessels, but Roger Woodhull of VS-5 did drop his bomb on another I-boat. It exploded twelve hundred feet ahead of the distur-bance where the submarine had dived, but no damage could be observed.

The *Saratoga* strike force on Guadalcanal unloaded their bombs for the use of the Marines and launched around 0930 back for their ship. Just after 0900 on August 24, the first of several scouting reports from PBYs from the tender *Mackinac* relayed information on the *Ryujo* Detached Force. *Enterprise* recovered her morning scouts shortly after 1000, and all but two of the *Saratoga's* dive-bombers were back from Cactus by 1140. By midday, Fletcher was ready to move. He directed Admiral Kinkaid on *Enterprise* to send out another search group and to ready a secondary load of aircraft for follow-up work. He was wary of making the same mistake he had made at Coral Sea—sending two entire air groups after the little carrier *Shoho*.

The Big E sent out twenty-two planes to pinpoint the various groups of Japanese ships. Clay Strickland was standing by with other VS-5 radiomen when a new squadron flight schedule was published. He and Lieutenant Strong would be going out again, this time in company with Rich Richey and gunner Mark Broussard as the second half of their search team. Strickland headed topside to check out his SBD while the pilots received last-minute directions. Some of the searchers penciled in for the second scouting effort had already made a long and fruitless morning search. Ray Davis was sending up six of his VB-6 planes, plus another seven SBDs from VS-5 and seven Avengers from VT-3. They were to search to a distance of 250 miles over nearly the entire northern perimeter: from 290 degrees through due east.[14]

Birney Strong was later than usual in making his way to the flight deck, but Strickland, busy in the rear seat of his SBD, did not notice until he heard his pilot call his nickname, "Strick."[15]

Rising, Strickland replied, "Yes, sir," as Strong climbed up on their wing and bent over the edge of the rear cockpit to speak more easily.

"Strick, I am sure that you know the Japs are somewhere in the area and it is our job to find them," Strong started. "I know where they are," he added confidently. "They are on the maximum extent of our cruise range. We will go directly to them, circle them on the horizon for type count, and make our contact report. Sure hope that radio works and we find them before they find us. Your CW fist ready?"

Strickland simply gave Strong a thumbs-up to indicate his readiness to send out a longer-range "CW" Morse code dot-dash-style transmission.

"Good," said Strong. "We will talk about it when we get home." With that, Strong climbed into the pilot's seat and buckled up. Here was a seasoned aviator, exuding full confidence that he would fly directly out to the Japanese fleet and be the first to report their location. "This ocean was beautiful and there wasn't a cloud in the sky," Strickland recalled. He had little reason to doubt that his pilot would do exactly what he intended.

Enterprise sent off Birney Strong and his comrades at around 1240. Three VS-5 crews—those of Redbird Burnett, Glenn Estes, and Red Austin—were retained for inner air patrol, and launched after the search group. During the next half hour, the task force combat air patrols tangled with a nearby Japanese snooper. Admiral Fletcher felt certain that his position had been compromised, so he ordered *Saratoga*'s air group to prepare for action. *Enterprise*'s remaining bombers under Turner Caldwell and VT-3's other torpedo bombers were held for a follow-up strike.

Saratoga Air Group commander Don Felt, however, requested Fletcher's staff to wait until the distance narrowed a little more. "Although we had not slept well nor had proper meals for the past twenty-four hours, we were keyed up enough to not mind," said VB-3's Lefty Holmberg. Lieutenant Commander Dave Shumway would lead the same VB-3 crews aloft that had spent the night on the Canal. Lou Kirn, on the other hand, opted to rest some of his crews in favor of some of the new boys who had gotten more sleep.[16]

Don Felt's strike force began launching from *Saratoga* at 1340, an hour behind the Big E's afternoon search force. The last solid fix on the Japanese carrier force placed them some 216 miles from the ship. Felt departed with twenty-nine SBDs, eight Avengers from VT-8, and no fighter escorts. One of the TBFs soon turned back, leaving Felt with three dozen strikers to attack whatever the *Enterprise* searchers could uncover.

Admiral Fletcher had largely shot his bolt. Only small groups of TBFs and SBDs remained on his two flattops. In the meantime, the Japanese had launched a strike force of their own. Rear Admiral Hara's Detached Force reached a point two hundred miles north of Guadalcanal by 1200, and his light carrier *Ryujo* soon sent off fifteen Zeros and six Type 97 carrier attack planes in two waves to attack American airplanes at

Henderson Field and to knock out gun positions. *Ryujo's* first fighters began strafing the Lunga airfield shortly after 1415. Marine fighters scrambled to engage the enemy aircraft, and a number of small dogfights ensued. Three Marine Wildcats were lost over the island in exchange for three bombers and four Zeros downed. The overall strike was a failure in terms of damaging the airfield or destroying artillery. The surviving *Ryujo* aircraft headed for home, unaware that two large forces of American planes were closing in on their own flattop.[17]

Birney Strong was right on the money. He had told Clay Strickland before takeoff that he knew right where the Japanese carriers would be found. His Scouting Five two-plane search team was the first of the *Enterprise* scouts to find a Japanese flattop on the afternoon of August 24.

Strong and wingman Rich Richey—with whom he had attacked a sub the day before—were in the 330- to 340-degrees sector. Richey, a young Texan, admired his resolute section leader. To him, Birney felt fear but "had a lot of courage. He was young looking and clean-cut, a Tom Sawyer–type–looking guy with freckles and rosy cheeks." About 1440, Strong noticed three ships about fifteen miles ahead and dropped down to investigate. He identified them as two cruisers and a destroyer. They were actually the heavy cruiser *Tone* and two destroyers from *Ryujo's* force, *Amatsukaze* and *Tokitsukaze*.[18]

Almost immediately, Strong sighted the carrier and approached to within five miles before sending his report. The message was sent in plain language, but the *Enterprise* didn't acknowledge for six minutes. It was just the first instance of communications problems that would plague the Americans all day. As the VS-5 team sent their report, Strong noted two Avengers from his carrier climbing away in the distance. He and Richey then headed for home, having successfully snooped out one of the Japanese flattops.

Birney Strong's courage could hardly be questioned. In the past seven months in the Pacific, he had bombed ships in the Gilberts, off New Guinea, and in Tulagi Harbor. He had helped sink the Japanese carrier *Shoho* at Coral Sea, survived vicious dogfights in an SBD against superior Zeros, flown numerous missions during the Guadalcanal landings,

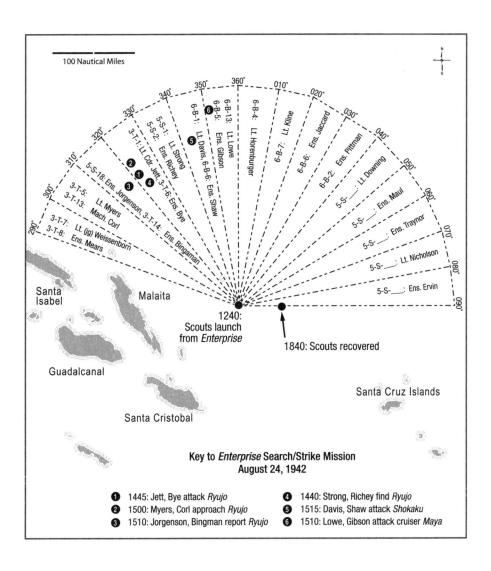

100 Nautical Miles

350° 360° 010°
340° 020°
330° 030°
320° 040°
310° 050°
300° 060°
290° 070°
080°
090°

6-B-13: Lt. Lowe
6-B-5: Ens. Gibson
6-B-1: Lt. Davis, 6-B-6: Ens. Shaw
5-S-1: Lt. Strong
5-S-2: Ens. Richey
3-T-1: Lt. Cdr. Jett, 3-T-6: Ens. Bye
5-S-18: Ens. Jorgenson, 3-T-14: Ens. Bingaman
3-T-5: Lt. Myers
3-T-13: Mach. Corl
3-T-7: Lt. (jg) Weissenborn
3-T-8: Ens. Mears

6-B-4: Lt. Horenburger
6-B-7: Lt. Kline
6-B-6: Ens. Jaccard
6-B-2: Ens. Pittman
5-S-___: Lt. Downing
5-S-___: Ens. Maul
5-S-___: Ens. Traynor
5-S-___: Lt. Nicholson
5-S-___: Ens. Ervin

Santa Isabel
Malaita
Guadalcanal
Santa Cristobal
Santa Cruz Islands

1240:
Scouts launch
from *Enterprise*

1840: Scouts recovered

**Key to *Enterprise* Search/Strike Mission
August 24, 1942**

❶ 1445: Jett, Bye attack *Ryujo*   ❹ 1440: Strong, Richey find *Ryujo*
❷ 1500: Myers, Corl approach *Ryujo*   ❺ 1515: Davis, Shaw attack *Shokaku*
❸ 1510: Jorgenson, Bingman report *Ryujo*   ❻ 1510: Lowe, Gibson attack cruiser *Maya*

and bombed an enemy submarine the previous day. He had already earned a Navy Cross and an Air Medal in the process. Yet Lieutenant Strong's decision to return without trying to plant a bomb on *Ryujo* would soon be criticized. It would be two months before another opportunity would present itself for Scouting Five's second in command to redeem himself.

One of the Torpedo Three search teams found *Ryujo* at the same moment as the Strong-Richey team. Lieutenant Commander Charlie Jett, skipper of *Enterprise*'s VT-3, was flying with Ensign Robert J. Bye in the search sector immediately to the west of Strong's quadrant. At about 1440, Jett spotted a carrier and what he believed were three destroyers on the horizon, and two more cruisers about two miles off the carrier's starboard beam. He sent a contact report and then braved the AA fire from below with Bye to drop their two pairs of five-hundred-pound bombs. *Ryujo* twisted sharply to starboard, and all four exploded in her wake just 150 meters astern. Three Zeros and one Type 97 anti-sub plane pursued Jett and Bye as they raced from the area.

Next to find *Ryujo* was Ensign Yogi Jorgenson of VS-5 and his wingman, Ensign Harold L. Bingaman of VT-3. Jorgenson had not even been slated to make this mission. He and gunner Tony Brunetti had been idling on standby on the flight deck when a VT-3 Avenger failed to start. Their SBD was tossed into the mix and departed with Bingaman to scout the 310 to 320 sector. Less than an hour into their flight, they spotted a twin-float observation plane. They gave chase but lost the plane in a cloud. They resumed their search and were within visual range of the *Ryujo* formation just as Strong and Richey had made contact from the adjacent sector. Jorgenson and Bingaman approached *Ryujo*'s force at five hundred feet without being detected by enemy planes they saw in the area. They observed bomb splashes about the carrier and two TBFs were seen to be attacking. At this point, Bingaman and Jorgenson were detected and attacked by Japanese planes, so they retired to the south. En route home, Jorgenson encountered the *Saratoga* attack group about fifty-five miles southeast of the Japanese fleet. The contact report was repeated to Don Felt's group and they acknowledged it.

B ill Rambur was developing a sore in his rear. He and pilot Martin McNair were still getting over the long flight the previous afternoon and their sleeplessness night on Guadalcanal. Rambur, a twenty-year-old who hailed from North Dakota, had been seated backward for ninety minutes while CSAG Felt led *Saratoga*'s SBDs at fifteen thousand feet toward the Japanese fleet.

One of Rambur's VS-3 enlisted comrades was suffering from pains of another sort. Radioman Bob Hansen was afraid he was having an attack of appendicitis. Since Ensign Jim Sauer had taken off from *Saratoga*, Hansen had felt like he had "a very decided stomachache and shooting pains in my groin." He shifted around continuously in his seat, trying to contrive some position that would relieve the stress in his guts. Finally, Hansen almost unconsciously unbuckled the leg straps of his parachute and noticed "a marked improvement" in the aches and pains. He realized in his hurry to put his chute on when leaving the ship, "I had unknowingly strapped my left testicle to the leg of the same side, giving undue pressure to that tender organ."[19]

Commander Felt led the *Saratoga* strike force farther north as radio chatter indicated that the Big E's scouts were continuing to find the Japanese ships. The VT-3 Avenger team of Lieutenant John Myers and Machinist Harry Corl came across the *Ryujo* force just moments behind Jorgenson and Bingaman. Corl was one of only three VT-3 aviators to survive the slaughter the squadron had suffered at Midway. His luck ran out this day. His TBF was blasted into the sea by Zeros before he and Myers could get close enough to drop their bombs on *Ryujo*. Corl was killed but his turret gunner, Radioman Third Class Delmar Wiley, survived fifteen days at sea before washing up on isolated Carteret Island. It would take Wiley another seven months to reach safety at Guadalcanal.[20]

The Scouting Five single-plane searchers flying the easternmost legs—Link Traynor, Art Downing, Elmer Maul, Nick Nicholson, and Skip Ervin—found nothing but empty ocean. While Birney Strong had sniffed out *Ryujo*'s group, it was the Bombing Six teams flying the centermost search sectors that found other Japanese warships. Lieutenant John Lowe, the VB-6 executive officer, and wingman Bob Gibson located Vice

Admiral Kondo's Advance Force around 1430, about 210 miles north-northwest of *Enterprise*. Their first two hundred miles of searching had passed silently as they droned above the ocean at a thousand feet. Lowe opted to extend their area by another twenty-five miles, and it paid off.[21]

Gibson and Lowe counted three heavy cruisers, several destroyers, and other ships on course 180 degrees, speed twenty knots. The pair circled to the east while Gabe Sellers tapped out a contact report from Lowe's rear cockpit. Lowe received no reply from *Enterprise*. "We then tried to climb to a higher altitude and send it again," said Lowe. "Still no answers." The VB-6 team climbed to eleven thousand feet, sent the report again, and then pushed home an attack on Kondo's warships. They selected what Lowe considered an *Atago*-class cruiser, actually the heavy cruiser *Maya*.

Maya's skipper kept his ship's beam to the planes, and while they were diving he made an abrupt turn to starboard, skidded around, and reversed course. Lowe struggled to keep his pipper on the twisting cruiser below as he made allowances for her course and speed. His five-hundred-pound bomb exploded about twenty yards off *Maya*'s starboard quarter. Hoot Gibson felt he was diving "by the books," keeping the sun behind him and facing a pullout in the direction of the warships. He was disappointed to see that his bomb was also a near miss. It landed within twenty-five feet of the port bow, blowing ocean spray over the cruiser's bow.[22]

"From then on I knew that a hit resulted from putting a saddle on the enemy ship and riding that baby down to release," said Gibson. Lowe sarcastically chalked up their two bomb drops as "Army hits," near misses that would have been counted as hits by Army Air Force flyboys at Midway. Sellers and Ed Anderson strafed the big cruiser during their SBDs' pullouts. Anderson felt amazed as they managed to escape the iron curtain of every big gun on every ship that was intent on knocking down the American dive-bombers.[23]

The seventh *Enterprise* search team to contact the Japanese warships found big prey. Lieutenant Ray Davis and Ensign Bob Shaw discovered the twenty-thousand-ton carrier *Shokaku*, a veteran of the Pearl Harbor attack and the Coral Sea battle. As Shaw climbed and circled to attack, his gunner, Lew Jones, counted eight planes amidships and another dozen spotted aft on the flight deck. Here was the chance to surprise another big carrier with planes on deck just like at Midway. The two diving SBDs were taken under fire only at the last moment, at 1414, as they pushed over on *Shokaku*.[24]

Captain Arima saved *Shokaku*'s deck by throwing her into a hard right turn that caused the VB-6 bombs to sail wide. Davis's bomb missed *Shokaku*'s starboard side by only thirty-five feet, but shrapnel from its explosion still killed six crewmen. *Shokaku* had just launched an attack group against the American carriers. Five of the Zeros escorting the strike group broke away and pursued Davis and Shaw. From Davis's rear seat, Chief Jack Trott tapped out contact reports to *Enterprise* of two flattops with their position, speed, and a bombing report. Radio reception was very poor this day; neither *Saratoga* nor *Enterprise* copied enough of Trott's report to determine the position of these carriers.

At 1536, twenty minutes after Ray Davis made his attack on *Shokaku*, Don Felt's *Saratoga* bunch finally sighted the smaller carrier *Ryujo* to the northwest. He had heard Lieutenant Commander Jett's sighting report and swung his group toward the north. The poor radio reception that was in place this day prevented his group from ever getting a solid fix on *Shokaku* and *Zuikaku*. It was Coral Sea all over again—*Ryujo* was as *Shoho* had been. Once again, *Shokaku* and *Zuikaku* were dodging a bullet while one of their smaller sister carriers took all the heat.

Felt directed all fifteen of Bullet Lou Kirn's scouts to work over *Ryujo*, along with five VT-8 Avengers and the first six-plane division of Dave Shumway's Bombing Three. The second division of VB-3, seven planes under Lieutenant Syd Bottomley, and two TBFs were to attack the heavy cruiser *Tone*. *Sara*'s air group commander would watch the show from overhead to make sure the targets were properly damaged. Kirn maneuvered his scouts to attack the carrier from two directions, while Captain Tadao Kato swung into the wind to launch two more fighters. Dave Shumway's first division of VB-3 approached from the northeast, climbing to sixteen thousand feet. It took some fifteen minutes after first sighting *Ryujo* that the Dauntless crews were in position to dive.

Kirn's first division started down at 1550. The antiaircraft fire was fairly light, but Captain Kato's expert ship handling spoiled the aim of the scouts. Kirn, Lieutenant (j.g.) Elwood Mildahn, Ensign Alfred Wright, Lieutenant Fred Schroeder, and Ensign Richard Balenti created only big fountains of water with the explosions of their thousand-pounders. Lieutenant Bob Milner and Lieutenant (j.g.) Bill Henry did little better against the rapidly twisting carrier. Ensign Roger Crow, eighth to dive, dropped his wheels and dive flaps to slow his dive to 165 knots to stay on target. Crow believed he landed a direct hit on *Ryujo*'s forward elevator, but his reduced airspeed made him a prime target for the Japanese gunners.[25]

Scouting Three's next trio of pilots—Lieutenant (j.g.) Alan Frank, Ensign Oran Newton, and Lieutenant Ralph Weymouth—added more near misses on *Ryujo*. Jim Sauer, hot on the heels of Weymouth, released his thousand-pounder and pulled out low on the water. Gunner Bob Hansen looked back and saw a bomb explode on the carrier's stern.[26]

Bill Rambur, gunner for Martin McNair in one of the last VS-3 SBDs to dive, also saw an explosion on *Ryujo*'s flight deck. Lou Kirn claimed two probable hits or hits along the side of the carrier from his fifteen pilots and a dozen misses within a hundred feet. Chief Carl Russ in Kirn's rear seat saw an enemy plane destroyed when it flew over an exploding bomb on the water. CSAG Don Felt, on the other hand, felt Kirn's scouts made nothing better than very close misses with their first ten drops. *Ryujo*'s starboard turn and the resultant change in wind drift across the target caused many to miss. Lieutenant Syd Bottomley of VB-3 watched bombs fall all around without any direct hits. He pulled out of his approach on the cruiser and radioed to his second section leader, Lieutenant Gordon Sherwood, "We'd better go get the carrier."[27]

Sherwood's section was approaching *Tone*, but Commander Felt also called them off. "Hey, Gordon, belay that," he radioed. "Come over here and hit that carrier."[28]

Dave Shumway abruptly pushed over on *Ryujo* with his first division of Bombing Three. His wingman, Lefty Holmberg, saw Shumway's bomb miss and tried to skid his own plane by depressing his left rudder pedal to fling his bomb closer to the target. He glanced back but saw only a tall geyser of water alongside *Ryujo*'s starboard quarter. Don Felt pushed over behind Shumway's division to use his own bomb, feeling certain that no direct hits had been made yet. The flak was accurate enough to shoot off his radio mast, but Felt continued coolly into his dive. He believed his bomb hit squarely on *Ryujo*'s flight deck, slightly port and aft of dead center.[29]

All that remained were seven SBDs of Syd Bottomley's second division that shifted from the cruiser *Tone*. Bottomley eyed *Ryujo*'s bridge all the way down before he pressed the electric bomb release on his stick and yanked the manual release under the instrument panel just to make sure. "That bomb hit target dead center," Bottomley said. Gordon Sherwood had a grandstand view of Syd's work. "It was as if you'd drawn a big cross exactly in the center of the carrier's deck and his bomb had landed right at the crosspiece." From Sherwood's rear seat, Aviation Radioman Second Class Harmon Bennett saw their bomb hit right behind that of Bottomley. Sherwood looked back as he pulled out and saw Lieutenant (j.g.) Roy Isaman land a third hit.[30]

Ryujo was smoking badly, with flames rushing out from under the flight deck on both sides for the entire length of the ship. The carrier was losing speed as Lieutenant Bruce Harwood's Avengers moved in to deliver the finishing touches. Ensign Aaron Katz, flying the tail-end Charlie TBF of VT-8, watched tracer bullets from an attacking Zero soar over the plane of Ensign Gene Hanson ahead of him. "It was exciting as hell," said Frank Balsley, turret gunner in Hanson's Avenger. Flak bounced the torpedo bomber crew around as they made their torpedo drops and roared right past the carrier's fantail. Balsley believed Hanson scored a hit on *Ryujo*. Harwood, with wingmen Bill Grady and Bert Earnest, made their drops from the carrier's starboard bow. Japanese records show that at least one torpedo slammed into *Ryujo*'s starboard side aft, crippling her steering control.

Zeros attacked the *Saratoga* planes as they retired. Ensign Bill Behr's Dauntless collected bullets in its horizontal stabilizer, another in the leading edge of the vertical stabilizer, and in its left wing. Other bullets pierced his rear cockpit and tore through Aviation Radioman Third Class James Q. Olive's ammunition can, exploding one .30-caliber tracer bullet.[31]

Don Felt flew just outside of the warship screen until 1620, watching *Ryujo* run in circles to the right, pouring out black smoke. The carrier was finished. *Ryujo* coasted to a stop with a twenty-three-degree starboard list. Two destroyers moved in to pick up her crew as they began abandoning ship. Shortly before sunset at 1810, three Army B-17s found the stricken carrier and bombed her from high altitude, claiming one hit. The Japanese scuttled the mortally wounded flattop after dark, taking 120 IJN sailors and officers down with her. She was the sixth aircraft carrier sunk by Dauntlesses in 1942 and would be the last sunk by American aircraft for two years.[32]

FIFTEEN
Battle off the Eastern Solomons

Turner Caldwell and Rocky Glidewell knew they were missing out on the action. Many of Caldwell's scouts and some of Ray Davis's VB-6 crews were sending in various contact reports with Japanese ships. Then the radios began crackling with excited chatter from *Saratoga*'s strikers as they worked over a Japanese carrier. Caldwell could only sit by in frustration with his remaining crews. *Enterprise* still had a small secondary strike group spotted for launch: the CEAG's TBF, seven more VT-3 Avengers, and eleven dive-bombers (seven of Caldwell's VS-5 and four from VB-6).

The two big undamaged Japanese carriers, *Shokaku* and *Zuikaku*, had dispatched strike groups to hit the American carriers. Just after 1600, the *Enterprise* and *Saratoga* CXAM radars began picking up large return blips closing on the task forces. The fighter director vectored Wildcat divisions out to investigate, and at 1610 Admiral Fletcher directed Admiral Kinkaid to begin clearing his flight decks.

"We sat in our ready rooms much of the day, with the ship at general quarters most of the time," said Caldwell. The approaching Japanese strike planes finally brought the call from the loudspeakers: "Pilots, man your planes!" *Saratoga* scrambled a half dozen fighters and the last of her strike planes: five fully armed and fueled VT-8 Avengers, plus the last two SBD crews that had returned home late from their overnight stay at Guadalcanal—those of VB-3's Lieutenant (j.g.) Bob Elder and Ensign

Bob Gordon. Lieutenant Swede Larsen, skipper of VT-8, jumped into the last TBF and climbed into the sky. Bob Elder was caught off guard by the launching order. He climbed into his cockpit without even his navigation board, thinking he was only going to taxi his SBD forward so that other planes could land.[1]

By 1630, the first strike from *Shokaku* was within thirty miles of TF-16 and the remaining strike planes were ordered off the deck. *Enterprise* sent off Flight 300, which included seven TBFs plus eight VS-5 planes and three from VB-6. Lieutenant Caldwell's SBD group was the last to come up from the hangar deck, and the crews were ill prepared for a long flight. "Inasmuch as all the rank in the squadron were out on a search, there was no briefing held," recalled Ensign Chris Fink. "We were told to join up on the skipper of Scouting Five and follow him." It was a frantic launch of available pilots and aircrews. Hal Buell of VS-5 took off with Johnny Villarreal of VB-6 filling in as a substitute for his usual VS-5 gunner. Gunner Jim Cales—who had flown with both Buell and Link Traynor in the past twenty-four hours—found himself in the rear seat of Ensign Spike Conzett's Dauntless.[2]

Air group commander Max Leslie was the last off, flying a fully loaded TBF. He lifted off at 1638, turned to port to follow the others, and looked back in time to see *Enterprise* under an enemy dive-bombing attack. Commander Mamoru Seki's eighteen *Shokaku* bombers approached from the Big E's port quarter as the carrier groups below tightened their formation. The skies were heavily congested with American planes— three VS-5 SBDs flying IAP duty, divisions and sections of CAP fighters, Caldwell and Leslie's group as it tried to rendezvous, *Saratoga*'s small strike group, and half of the *Enterprise* SBDs and TBFs returning from their search mission.

At 1640, *Enterprise* gunners opened fire on the first approaching enemy planes. One minute later, the first Val dive-bombers were pushing over on *Enterprise*, even as Wildcats flailed away at them. Geysers of water blasted skyward as bombs rained down near the twisting *Enterprise*. Ensign Rodey Rodenburg of VB-6 felt helpless sitting in his ready room, aft of the island structure just below the flight deck. "Hearing the 5-inch anti-aircraft guns, then the 40 millimeters, and smaller, you waited for the bomb," Rodenburg said. He did not have long to wait.[3]

At 1644, a 550-pound semi-armor-piercing bomb punched through the forward corner of the Big E's number-three elevator aft. Another bomb also landed near the aft elevator, just thirty seconds after the first hit. The next Val was hit during its approach and it exploded spectacularly directly over the ship in a flaming blast of metallic confetti. Another bomb exploded close to starboard of *Enterprise*'s bridge. Antiaircraft fire ripped apart yet another Val but its bomb tumbled free and hit the Big E amidships at 1646, just aft of her central aircraft elevator. The long-charmed *Enterprise* was directly hit by three bombs and she was blazing heavily as the surviving *Shokaku* attackers pulled clear. One of the bombs exploded close to Bombing Six's ready room. "The concussion was deafening," said Rodenburg.

The second strike from *Zuikaku* was ripped apart by the Wildcat CAP, but some of them made it through to release bombs toward *Enterprise* and the battleship *North Carolina*. At least ten Val bombers were destroyed before or during their attack runs. Some seventeen *Shokaku* and *Zuikaku* Vals survived, along with eight Zeros. In order to make it back to their own flight decks, however, they were forced to fight through a gauntlet of F4Fs, IAP Dauntlesses, newly launched strike groups, and returning search planes. *Saratoga* and *Enterprise* fighters claimed a number of the Japanese warplanes, but the American bomber crews were also quick to join in on the action.[4]

Glenn Estes was caught off guard. He had been airborne for four hours, leading Redbird Burnett and Red Austin of Scouting Five on an IAP flight near the task force.

"I was leading the flight down the starboard side of the *Enterprise* in preparation for joining the carrier's landing circle," said Estes. They had been making lazy circles off the starboard beam of the ship while allowing the CAP fighters to make their approaches first. Just as the Estes trio flew past the antiaircraft cruiser *San Juan*, she erupted into fire on the approaching Val dive-bombers. "We hauled tail out of there and flew out of the field of fire," Estes said.[5]

Harold Wilger, Burnett's regular gunner and a Coral Sea veteran, was equally surprised. "The first I knew of a battle in progress was when we saw the Jap planes diving on *Enterprise* on our return," he said. Red

Austin, who had been wounded in action flying the anti-VT mission at Coral Sea, followed Estes northward. The pair took up station there in hopes of catching some of the Japanese attackers as they pulled out of their dives.[6]

Redbird Burnett went right to work. He broke formation, rolled his 6-S-15 over, and dived onto the tail of one of the fleeing Aichis. He opened fire with his .50-calibers and set the enemy bomber aflame on his first pass. In his rear seat, Wilger watched the Val hit the water, burning. Their Dauntless was now very close to the water, heading away from their own ships. As they passed the nearby battleship, Wilger was stunned by the volume of AA fire. "The sky had turned black with puffs from shells," he said. "I was afraid we would be mistaken for enemy aircraft."

Burnett then got on the tail of another Val clearing the area and followed it away from the U.S. ships. Redbird chased the Japanese plane some sixty miles but could not overhaul it due to the five-hundred-pound bomb he was carrying. He finally broke off the chase and headed back for *Enterprise*. "I got sore and made up my mind I wanted to have a fighter plane so I could wrap it up pretty fast," Burnett later related.[7]

Glenn Estes engaged another Val in a head-on run. He saw his tracers lacing the dive-bomber's belly. "I was scoring hits on him when we had to break off the fight before we ran into one another," said Estes. "I could see his tracers going past me." Estes hoped he had poured in enough lead to cause his opponent's demise but he had lost contact with Burnett and Austin in the interim.[8]

Turner Caldwell's Flight 300 was still forming up as the Japanese planes attacked. Chris Fink of VB-6 looked back toward *Enterprise* and saw an enormous amount of AA fire and flaming planes plummeting into the water. "I led our little formation toward a great cumulus cloud and skirted its edge, trying to find a little concealment from Japanese fighters," said Caldwell. Rocky Glidewell, facing rearward, could see smoke rising from *Enterprise*'s flight deck from bomb damage. He wondered whether his ship would still be afloat when they returned hours later.[9]

Several *Enterprise* TBF pilots from the afternoon search tangled with Vals and Zeros. Air Group Commander Max Leslie had a scrape with a Val that his rear gunner chased away. By the time he was clear of the task force, however, Caldwell's Flight 300 had departed without him.

The surviving *Shokaku* and *Zuikaku* carrier planes headed west but ran afoul of even more returning American planes. Lieutenant Commander Seki and two of his dive-bomber comrades narrowly escaped heated shoot-outs with Lieutenants Rip Kline and Carl Horenburger of VB-6. About seventy-five miles northwest of TF-16, at around 1710, Seki's Vals then tangled with ten of Lou Kirn's VS-3 *Saratoga* scouts and a trio of VB-3 Dauntless crews. Kirn credited Ensign Oley Hanson, Chief Carl Russ, and Aviation Radioman Third Class Willard Wright with downing three Vals. Ensign Bob Campbell of VB-3 took on another dive-bomber, puncturing its right wing tank and causing it to burst into flames.[10]

As Lou Kirn's formation reached the U.S. task force around 1444, they charged into a group of *Shokaku* bombers under Lieutenant Keiichi Arima. Ensign Roger Crow chased one Val for twenty-five miles, exhausting his ammunition while starting fires in his victim's fuselage. His gunner, Aviation Radioman Third Class Thomas Miner, set fire to another dive-bomber. Lieutenant Bill Henry tried in vain to engage Arima. Destined to become the Navy's top night-fighter ace, Henry left this fight frustrated at his inability to get in some shots.[11]

*E*nterprise was burning aft and belowdecks, with many injured and dead sailors to tend to. Her two aftermost elevators were malfunctioning due to bomb damage while numerous fuel-starved aircraft circled overhead waiting for their flight deck to reopen. Another wave of Japanese strikers was showing on the radar screens by 1651. They were tracked during the next hour but missed a golden opportunity to follow up on the damaged American flattop. The strike leader erred in his navigation and missed TF-61 more than eighty miles to the south.[12]

During that hour, repair crews swarmed over the damaged flight deck and patched the bomb holes with steel plates. *Saratoga* spent forty minutes taking in the majority of the combat air patrol fighters from both carriers while the SBDs and TBFs continued to circle. Finally, at 1749, the Big E turned into the wind so that LSO Robin Lindsey could begin landing planes.[13]

Bombing Six searcher Carl Horenburger was down to only his eighteen-gallon reserve fuel tank. When he finally entered the groove to land, he was cut off by another aircraft making an unorthodox approach from the starboard quarter. Horenburger maintained his course and saw the other Dauntless veer off to make a water landing.[14]

The faltering SBD he had seen was that of squadron mate Bob Gibson. He was flying wing on VB-6 exec John Lowe, returning from their bombing attack on the cruiser *Maya*. They reached their task force just as the bombing attack on *Enterprise* was commencing. Lowe made a low pass over her flight deck so that gunner Gabe Sellers could toss a weighted beanbag message with their contact report. His note gave the enemy force's composition, course, and speed. It also included the sarcastic reference that he and Gibson had made "two Army hits"—two near misses—on their warship target.[15]

Ed Anderson, in Gibson's rear seat, saw a string of Vals plunging down on his ship. Lowe knew that the carrier *Wasp* was off to the south, refueling, so he led Gibson out in that direction during the attack. They found nothing, however, and were forced to turn back, low on fuel. They joined the other SBDs in gradual circles while they waited for the opportunity to land.

"We did not get by so lucky this time," Anderson logged in his diary. Ensign Gibson's 6-B-5 sputtered as the last of his fuel burned away. He headed for a nearby destroyer and hollered to Anderson to brace himself. Anderson could see the rollers below coming at him fast as Gibson ditched ahead of the cruiser *Minneapolis* by setting down on top of a wave. His five-ton SBD skipped once and then plowed headlong into the next wave. Gibson's head slammed into the bombsight and knocked him senseless. Anderson scrambled out of his rear cockpit to help tug his pilot free. As Gibson regained his composure, he found a new dilemma: his foot was jammed in between the rudder pedal and the floor.[16]

He struggled, fearing his Dauntless would sink in less than a minute. Gibson finally yanked his foot right out of his shoe and crawled out. He had the presence of mind to grab his chart board and managed to drop into their life raft without getting his feet wet. Heavy waves rocked their bobbing bomber, pinning the life raft between the tail and the wing. "With each wave we had to dive out of the lifeboat to avoid being killed by our thrashing SBD," said Gibson.

Fortunately for them, the destroyer *Farragut* moved in quickly. As the tin can slowed to a halt, a sailor dived into the water to assist with a line tied around his waist. Anderson grabbed the line and floundered in the rolling swells as sailors hauled him toward the warship's deck. On board *Farragut*, Gibson and Anderson traded their soggy flight gear and jackets for fresh clothes. They were later transferred to the destroyer *Balch*, which transferred them back to *Enterprise* on August 27.

John Lowe made it on board *Enterprise* with only fuel fumes to spare. Behind him, a steady string of SBDs, F4Fs, and TBFs were still coming in the landing pattern. Horenburger, Kline, Dick Jaccard, Bill Pittman, Bob Shaw, and skipper Ray Davis also made it home, making Gibson's SBD the only loss of the eight VB-6 searchers. Davis had only four gallons of fuel remaining in his 6-B-1.[17]

Eleven VS-5 SBDs and a handful from VB-3 were also fighting for their chance to land. The IAP section of Red Austin, Glenn Estes, and Redbird Burnett narrowly made it on board. Burnett, who had burned off his fuel chasing the Japanese bomber, landed with only ten gallons to spare. Harold Wilger climbed out of his rear cockpit and was stunned by the grisly scene in the after five-inch-gun gallery. "The pointers and trainers were still at their posts and burned to a crisp," he said.[18]

Estes could see "a hell of a big hump in the flight deck" from the bomb damage. He also noticed that Robin Lindsey brought them down "by cutting us slightly later than normal so that we could engage the number 4, 5, 6 or 7 wire." Estes considered Lindsey to be "a master craftsman" at his art of landing planes exactly where he wanted them. Estes proceeded below to the ready room to inform Lieutenant Muddy Waters, the ACI officer, about his engagement with a Val bomber.[19]

Enterprise was fortunate to have exceptional landing signal officers. Lieutenant Lindsey and his assistant LSO, Lieutenant (j.g.) Cleo Dobson, had joined the firefighting efforts until the flight deck was sufficiently patched to resume air operations. Lindsey calmly took his spot on the after flight-deck platform and used his paddles to cut the fuel-starved airplanes one after another. It was no small effort. "I never saw anything like that before in my life, and I hope never again," said Dobson.[20]

To Birney Strong, the sight of the burning *Enterprise* was "one of the most sickening sights I had ever seen." Link Traynor was among the

VS-5 search-scout pilots still awaiting his turn to land. Once the Big E's smoking flight deck reopened, he watched a free-for-all ensue. "No matter where any pilot was, he just dove for that carrier because he was so low on fuel," said Traynor. Lindsey masterfully coached many anxious returnees down on the aftermost number-one and -two arresting wires. "I thought it was really phenomenal," Traynor said of Lindsey's talents in the emergency situation.[21]

Traynor, Strong, Rich Richey, Art Downing, Elmer Maul, Nick Nicholson, and Skip Ervin from VS-5 all made it. The only scout that failed to land on *Enterprise* from the afternoon mission was Yogi Jorgenson. He and wingman Harold Bingaman of VT-3 made water landings when their fuel expired during the endless circling. Bingaman and his gunner were rescued by a PBY three days later while Jorgenson and gunner Tony Brunetti were quickly scooped up by the destroyer *Monssen.*

Last to land on *Enterprise* at 1813 was VB-3's Ensign Bill Behr, who was suffering from a slight leg wound. Behr caught an arresting wire just as the Big E suddenly went out of control. Captain Arthur Davis lost all steering control due to steering motors shorted out by water and Foamite used to fight the fires. The big carrier wheeled away like a careening bronco and very nearly collided with the destroyer *Balch* before Davis could slow her down. *Enterprise* engineers raced to restore the motors but flight operations were shut down again for the time being.[22]

Glenn Estes had made it to VS-5's ready room, where he was reliving their aerial encounters with Japanese planes. He felt the ship heel over in a sharp turn and heard her blowing her whistles. He heard that *Enterprise*'s wild ride and whistle blowing scattered the screening destroyers and cruisers around her "like a flushed covey of quail."[23]

All aircraft still in the skies were diverted to *Saratoga*, busy collecting her own jubilant *Ryujo* strike group and CAP Wildcats. Admiral Fletcher's carriers had survived the Eastern Solomons battle, but *Enterprise* was badly damaged. Pilot Link Traynor walked aft on the flight deck that evening to survey the damage. He looked down at one of the after starboard gun galleries in the catwalk. "All I could see were two forearms, severed at the elbows, still lightly grasping the gun handles," Traynor said. "I'll never forget that frightening sight."[24]

As evening approached, one hastily dispatched small strike group from each U.S. flattop was still seeking the Japanese warships.

From *Saratoga*, Lieutenant Swede Larsen had departed with five VT-8 TBFs and two VB-3 dive-bombers led by Bob Elder. They spotted Vice Admiral Kondo's Advance Force at 1735. It comprised the seaplane tender *Chitose*, cruisers, and destroyers. Larsen's Avengers made torpedo runs against a heavy cruiser and believed they scored a hit, although no ships were damaged. Elder and wingman Bob Gordon attacked *Chitose* through heavy antiaircraft fire and escaped with only a shrapnel hole in Gordon's dive flap. Their bombs closely bracketed *Chitose*, destroying three Type 0 reconnaissance seaplanes. The tender took on heavy flooding and was forced to Truk for repairs. Elder and Gordon returned to *Saratoga* with three of Larsen's TBFs at 1930. Two VT-8 crews ditched due to fuel shortage, but the aviators were recovered.[25]

Dauntless crews had dropped three dozen bombs on enemy ships during the Eastern Solomons carrier battle. Only four hits had been made on *Ryujo*, a disappointing eleven percent record, well below their performances at Coral Sea and Midway. The battle was far less conclusive than the glorious results that the SBDs had achieved at Midway in June, but the Americans had maintained protection for the Marines ashore on Guadalcanal. Had the Japanese destroyed both U.S. carriers, the struggle for Guadalcanal might have swung more in their favor. Only two SBDs had been lost to ditching, but the four squadrons suffered no casualties for a change. They had sunk a Japanese carrier, damaged a seaplane tender, and claimed at least five enemy planes shot down. *Enterprise* Air Group commander Max Leslie felt the only reason the Dauntless crews had not achieved more was their lack of practice against moving targets.[26]

Scouting Five, Bombing Six, and Bombing Three had been involved to some degree in sinking all six Japanese carriers destroyed in 1942 from Coral Sea to Eastern Solomons. These workhorse squadrons would be hard to replace in the Pacific. As the world's third-ever carrier conflict drew to a close late on August 24, one small contingent of two of these squadrons, led by VS-5 skipper Turner Caldwell, was still airborne and far from their carrier's flight deck.

SIXTEEN
Flight 300 on Hell's Island

Max Leslie had been the last to launch from *Enterprise* as the Japanese moved in to pound his carrier. His scattered strike group failed to find the Japanese carriers, and his Avengers landed on *Enterprise* and *Saratoga*. Commander Leslie finally found his own ship and landed at 2303, the last Eastern Solomons striker to return to an American carrier on August 24.

Lieutenant Turner Caldwell's eleven SBDs did not return. They had departed without sufficient intelligence on where to find the carriers that the others had attacked. Caldwell's mixed Flight 300 crews had varying degrees of combat experience. He had with him four pilots of Bombing Six—Lieutenant (j.g.) Troy Guillory and ensigns Harry Liffner, Harold "Buck" Manford, and Chris Fink. Guillory had flown against the Japanese at Midway but his balky plane had forced him into the ocean and out of action. Liffner, a blue-eyed junior pilot who had recently married, had made a strike against Japanese cruisers at Midway. Manford and Fink were newcomers to the veteran VB-6, but both had gained experience during the Guadalcanal landings weeks earlier. Fink, a rugged six-foot farm boy who hailed from the plains of Greybull, Wyoming, could speak a fair amount of German. He said that if he was ever shot down, he would shout "Heil Hitler!" to his Japanese captors and claim to be a Nazi.[1]

The seven VS-5 crews of Caldwell's flight were the most experienced. Caldwell, Rog Woodhull, Walt Coolbaugh, Hal Buell, and Walt Brown had flown together since the Battle of Coral Sea. Coolbaugh was fearless and ever eager for action. Broad-shouldered and stout, Woodhull had a straightforward approach to war. At twenty-eight, he had a few years on some of his junior pilots, and with a new wife, he hoped to make it back home to see her again. Brown, the shortest of his group, was a religious young man from Maine who did not smoke or drink. His love of hunting and fishing and for the cooler northeast climates back home was a frequent subject of his conversations. Jesse "Dog" Barker and Elmer "Spike" Conzett had joined during the squadron's re-formation period after Midway. Barker was the largest of the Flight 300 pilots and he was full of nerve. Conzett, on the other hand, was a tall, lean man of few words. He hailed from Iowa, the home state of boyish-looking Hal Buell.[2]

The eleven pilots and gunners of Caldwell's strike group could little imagine how well they would get to know each other in the weeks ahead.

Flight 300's mission was troubled from the start. Caldwell had only general information as to the Japanese fleet's bearing and distance, which was said to be about 140 miles out. Two hours of daylight remained when they set out. After two hours, they had sighted nothing and the moon was beginning to rise.

Where are the bastards? Hal Buell wondered. He desperately wanted to attack a Japanese carrier to make up for his missed opportunities at Coral Sea and at Midway. *Please, Lord, give us a chance to avenge our dead comrades and stricken ship*, he prayed.[3]

Caldwell flew another forty miles beyond the expected contact point but found only empty ocean. "I decided to break radio silence and tell the ship I was turning back," he said. There was no reply. Caldwell decided to reverse course. *It's getting late and it's already dusk*, he realized. *We will be in full darkness when we arrive back at the* Enterprise. Shortly into the return flight, Rocky Glidewell picked up a faint yet understandable message from the Big E: "Proceed to Guadalcanal." *Enterprise* was apparently damaged and unable to reach the Point Option position Flight 300 had been given.[4]

Caldwell directed his flight to jettison their thousand-pound bombs and turn their engines to a lean fuel mixture for maximum range. It was now completely dark. Scouting Five's skipper had two useful aids—his familiarity with the Solomon Islands and the full moon that was climbing higher into the night sky. Chris Fink was surprised to suddenly see the great cone of Savo Island, an excellent landmark ten miles east of Guadalcanal, to his right. Henderson Field lay fifty miles closer than Flight 300's own carrier and was much easier to find after dark. Only Woodhull, Coolbaugh, and Brown had night landing experience, so getting down safely was no certainty.[5]

As the Navy SBDs crossed the bay between Savo and Guadalcanal islands, Chief Glidewell struggled to raise the Marine command. Caldwell could make out Lunga Point, which helped him locate the airfield. "At last a faint message came from the ground that lights were being set up on the runway, and that we should approach over the water," he recalled.[6]

Caldwell circled over Guadalcanal's coast several times to give the pilots a chance to orient themselves with an airfield they had not seen in three weeks—the last time they had been over it, it was held by the Japanese. He radioed for them to go in one by one. Ensign Fink saw that the Marines below had set out kerosene lamps to roughly mark the runway of crushed coral, and jeeps, with their lights on, had been parked at each end of the field. As they skimmed in low over the western end, at the approach end of the runway, Caldwell's pilots were cautioned to watch out for tall palm trees.[7]

At 2020, Caldwell and Coolbaugh were the first to approach. Glidewell tried with his searchlight to signal to the Marines that they were friendly. His skipper made a long approach, realizing at the last instant that he was coming in from downwind. He pulled up sharply and warned his other pilots over the radio. Great clouds of dust swirled up behind his Dauntless when Caldwell finally touched down and turned off the gravel-topped runway. Taxi directors guided him to a safe spot to park his dive-bomber.[8]

During his final approach, Hal Buell was startled to suddenly see, just below his landing gear, treetops illuminated by his engine exhaust flares. Stuart Mason, gunner for Troy Guillory, was a seasoned veteran of the Pacific War who had been wounded at Midway. Still, he was unprepared for the scary experience of landing on a jungle strip at night by the light of jeeps. All eleven of Flight 300's SBD crews made it down without cracking up and became inhabitants of an island that was being fought over hourly by two countries.[9]

Lieutenant Caldwell stiffly climbed out of his cockpit and was led to the operations building, a wood-frame structure known as the Pagoda, constructed by the Japanese on a knoll that overlooked the airfield. Caldwell's Navy pilots were greeted by General Archie Vandegrift and Lieutenant Colonel Dick Mangrum, skipper of the resident Marine SBD squadron VMSB-232.

Mangrum was concerned over how narrowly the *Enterprise* pilots had missed the trees at the end of the runway. "Next morning, when I saw them, I understood his concern," said Caldwell. "They were great tropical hardwoods, towering on a ridge just beyond the end of the runway."[10]

USS *Enterprise* Flight 300 into Guadalcanal	
August 24, 1942	
SCOUTING FIVE (VS-5), 7 SBDs	
PILOT	**REAR-SEAT GUNNER**
Lt. Turner Foster Caldwell Jr.	ACRM Willard Ellis Glidewell
Ens. Walter Wesley Coolbaugh	ARM1c Charles A. Jaeger
Ens. Harold Lloyd Buell	ARM3c John Laughan Villarreal
Lt. Roger Blake Woodhull	ARM1c Albert Woodrow Garlow

(continued)

Enterprise Flight 300 into Guadalcanal	
August 24, 1942	
SCOUTING FIVE (VS-5), 7 SBDs	
Ens. Walter E. Brown Jr.	ARM2c Norbert Anthony Fives
Ens. Jesse Theron Barker	RM3c Eugene James Monahan
Ens. Elmer Andrew Conzett	ARM1c James Hedger Cales
BOMBING SIX (VB-6), 4 SBDs	
Lt. (j.g.) Troy Tilman Guillory	ARM1c Stuart James Mason
Ens. Harry Warren Liffner	ARM3c Eugene K. Braun
Ens. Harold Camp Manford	ARM3c Homer Lloyd Joselyn
Ens. Christian Fink	ARM3c Milo L. Kimberlin

The indoctrination meeting at the Pagoda was short, and then the Navy fliers were driven to a coconut grove that would become their new home. "The Marine mess cooks had a meal waiting for us, composed of a rare delicacy called Australian sheep's tongue," Chris Fink recalled. "Inasmuch as we thought we would be returning to either the *Sara* or back to the *Enterprise* the following morning, we politely declined the chow."[11]

The VS-5 and VB-6 pilots moved to a makeshift building that doubled as Henderson Field's hospital and tried to sleep on stretchers. "They gave us a blanket, a bowl, and a spoon," gunner Al Garlow said of the scant provisions. Pilot Jesse Barker found that his blanket came from a deceased soldier. "A man had been killed in it the night before," said Barker. "I had to spend the night on the ground in that bloody blanket." Caldwell felt his fliers were "all very keyed up, uncertain of everything, and nervous over our surroundings. It was well known that the Japanese were masters of night combat and infiltration, and all during the night there were terrifying rustlings in the trees." He learned the next morning that the noise was made by large numbers of parrots in the nearby rubber grove.[12]

The Flight 300 crews were in a palm grove northwest of the airfield. "As there was a shortage of cots, most of us prepared to sleep on Japanese matting spread on the ground," said Hal Buell. Rocky Glidewell would have been happy with a cot. He was ordered to stay near the skipper's plane. He flopped down in the dirt, placed his back against the landing gear, and tried to sleep. Marine crews began refueling the *Enterprise* SBDs with captured Japanese fuel that had been stored in fifty-gallon drums. Rocky found it was a long process, hand-pumping more than two hundred gallons of fuel at the rate of about two gallons per minute.[13]

During the night, a noise more frightful than the calls of jungle birds sent the *Enterprise* aviators scrambling. Ten minutes after midnight, the Japanese destroyers *Mochizuki*, *Yayoi*, and *Mutsuki* approached the Guadalcanal coastline and began bombarding the Lunga airfield and the surrounding areas. The Navy airmen raced for cover as shells whistled overhead and exploded in the trees. Red flares lit the jungle canopy as shards of bark and wood cascaded down. Chris Fink hid behind the trunks of coconut trees, while Walt Coolbaugh and Hal Buell leaped from their hospital stretchers and raced for a Marine dugout.[14]

The Marines were accustomed to the harassment ritual the Japanese Navy frequently bestowed upon the Americans, but for the new carrier boys it was terrifying. "When it was over, we went back to our stretchers, and found that they had been confiscated to take care of the wounded," said Fink. He and his buddies found some bags of rice and tried once again to get some sleep.[15]

The Cactus crews swarmed over the SBDs near the field to check for shelling damage. Colonel Louis Woods, chief of staff for the 1st Marine Air Wing, decided to send up a three-plane SBD flight to hit the departing warships. Dick Mangrum, skipper of Marine squadron VMSB-232, took off at 0230 with First Lieutenant Daniel Iverson Jr. and Second Lieutenant Lawrence Baldinus to attack their recent assailants. One of their three five-hundred-pound bombs dropped was a dud and the other two were near misses. Mangrum's flight strafed the warships and then returned to Lunga.[16]

Thirty-six-year-old Lieutenant Colonel Mangrum was enough of a veteran soldier to appreciate the gift he had been given in the persons of the fresh Navy dive-bomber crews. He had entered flight training in 1929 and had since accumulated more than three thousand flight hours with the Marine Corps, some of that time spent as an instructor. Turner Caldwell's eleven Navy SBDs doubled the size of Dick Mangrum's force at Henderson Field. "They kind of adopted us and took us in," Jesse Barker said of Mangrum's VMSB-232. "We operated quite closely with them."[17]

Upon returning to the field, Mangrum described the situation to Lieutenant Caldwell, who agreed to send a few of his boys out to hit the ships. At around 0345, five seaplanes that had launched from Japanese cruisers came over the airfield and dropped bombs. The pilots gathered in the air operations Pagoda scrambled to dive into nearby slit trenches.

Caldwell offered his only three VS-5 pilots with night experience to make the next flight. Roger Woodhull took off at 0400 with Walt Coolbaugh and Walt Brown. They found the destroyers retiring through Indispensable Strait and made their climb to attack, with the aid of a quarter moon. Two of their bombs were misses, but Brownie was credited with a direct hit. Rear gunners Al Garlow, Charles Jaeger, and Tony Fives strafed the warships upon pulling out. Woodhull led his group back for more strafing runs before deciding it was time to return to Henderson Field.

Ensign Brown had managed to cause minor damage to the destroyer *Mochizuki*, which experienced three sailors wounded. He became separated from the group and was soon disoriented. Brown flew along the coast but could not locate Henderson Field. He made a water landing off the coast of Malaita Island when his fuel supply—never completely replenished on the Canal—was exhausted. He and his gunner, Aviation Radioman Second Class Fives, were found by island natives and escorted to the local missionaries. He gave the natives his flight gear, and the women were thrilled with the silk parachute for their own use in making clothing. In exchange, Brown and Fives were fed much better food than the chow their comrades had to endure at Henderson Field. It would be some two weeks before an amphibious aircraft located and rescued Brown's downed crew.[18]

If the first eight hours on Hell's Island were any indication of how things would go for Flight 300, then they would be grueling. They had been shelled, had gone out to attack warships, and had lost one plane and one crew in action.

Thirty minutes after Woodhull's trio departed, General Vandegrift received a contact report that a Japanese carrier, a light cruiser, and five destroyers had been spotted 180 miles north of Cactus. Vandegrift, as commander of Marine Air Group 23 (or MAG-23), directed a dawn strike against the carrier force. He sent up eight dive-bombers escorted by eight of Major John L. Smith's VMF-223 Wildcats. The convoy, commanded by Rear Admiral Raizo Tanaka, included his flagship light cruiser *Jintsu*, three troop transports, seven destroyers, and four gunboats. Tanaka was under orders to land a thousand fresh troops outside of the American perimeter defense positions around the airfield.

Admiral Tanaka would prove to be an almost constant opponent for the Cactus Air Force and the Marines ashore on Hell's Island. Fifty-year-old Tanaka, a decorated torpedo expert with a tenacious personality, graduated from the Imperial Japanese Naval Academy in 1913 and had a long career in surface ships. He had commanded destroyers, his current flagship *Jintsu*, and even the battleship *Kongo* before he was promoted to rear admiral in 1941 and placed in charge of the 2nd Destroyer Squadron. In August, Tanaka was designated "Commander Reinforcement Group" in charge of shuttling troops and supplies to Guadalcanal after the American landings. In the early hours of August 19, some 917 fresh troops had been landed at Taivu Point. Within a week, the majority of these men had been killed while attempting to overrun Henderson Field.

On August 24, Tanaka's next group of reinforcements was heading for Guadalcanal as the Eastern Solomons battle played out.[19]

Three of Tanaka's destroyers—*Mutsuki, Yayoi,* and *Mochizuki*—had been detached during the night to shell Henderson Field. Three transports loaded with fifteen hundred Japanese troops continued toward Guadalcanal during the early-morning hours of August 25 with their destroyers and four patrol boats. These reinforcement groups shuttling supplies and troops to the Canal would soon become known to the Cactus aviators as either a "Tokyo Express" or a "Rat Patrol."

Lieutenant Caldwell reported to the Pagoda with ensigns Chris Fink and Jesse Barker of VB-6 for flight instructions. They would accompany five of Major Mangrum's Marine bomber crews for the attack on Tanaka's Tokyo Express. As Barker climbed into his Dauntless, he was relieved to find that the Marines had refueled their planes during the night. The sixteen strikers roared down the dusty, bomb-cratered airstrip at 0600. Rocky Glidewell was apprehensive of his first takeoff from Henderson Field. Their Dauntless had been fueled with captured Japanese gasoline. "We needed one hundred octane and they had eighty," he said. "This meant we had to have a little longer runway than we were accustomed to, especially with a heavy load."

Most of the airstrip was hard-packed dirt laid on a coral gravel base. The Navy Seabees of the 6th Naval Construction Battalion had only enough steel Marston mats to cover the most unstable areas in the center of the field. The runway was oriented southwest to northwest toward the prevailing sea winds. After making their rendezvous, the planes flew past Savo Island and then turned toward a north-northwest heading.[20]

Ensign Fink was completely in the dark as to their mission. It was the same feeling he had experienced when launching from *Enterprise* the previous afternoon. *Caldwell may know where we're going,* he thought, *but all I've gotten is, "Follow me."*[21]

Dick Mangrum's group searched far to the north but found no signs of a carrier task group. Major Smith's fighters, not equipped with fuel drop tanks, finally had to turn back for the Canal. Mangrum shifted his returning search path fifty miles to the west of the path they had taken outbound. At around 0800, they found the only force in the area, Rear Admiral Tanaka's Reinforcement Convoy, 150 miles out. Mangrum split

Prewar photo of the Scouting Five (VS-5) Dauntless dive-bomber of Fritz Faulkner, in flight near the Hawaiian islands. NAVAL AVIATION MUSEUM, PENSACOLA

Sister aircraft carriers *USS Saratoga* (CV-3) and beyond her USS *Lexington* (CV-2) seen in 1933 off Diamond Head, Oahu. In service since 1927, these two carriers were the largest of the U.S fleet at the time. U.S. NAVY

Prewar view of USS *Yorktown* (CV-5), home to Scouting Squadron Five. U.S. NAVY

Yorktown's Dauntless dive-bombers participated in three strikes against Japanese installations and shipping in the Marshalls on February 1, 1942. This view of Bombing Five SBDs preparing to launch was taken during operations in the Coral Sea during April 1942. This SBD's plane number 3 is visible on the cowl. U.S. NAVY

The SBD of VS-5 skipper Bill Burch is seen moving across the shore of Makin Island during *Yorktown*'s second strike of February 1. View taken by photographer John Pflaum from Tom Reeves's Dauntless. U.S. NAVY

Scouting Five skipper Bill Burch (*right*), seen in a photo taken June 6, 1942. He is standing with *Yorktown*'s Torpedo Five skipper, Lieutenant Commander Joe Taylor, who was a 1927 Naval Academy classmate of Burch.
U.S. NAVY

The armed merchant cruiser *Kongo Maru*, hit by both *Lexington* and *Yorktown* dive-bombers, burns off the coast of Lae.
U.S. NAVY

The 6,863-ton Japanese seaplane tender *Kiyokawa Maru*—as viewed under attack from high above—maneuvers while under bombing attack by *Yorktown* planes on March 10.
U.S. NAVY

A Japanese "Betty" bomber crashes into the ocean near *Lexington* on February 20, 1942. Fighter pilot Butch O'Hare earned the Medal of Honor by shooting down five of these land-based bombers this day.
U.S. NAVY

The wreckage of the Japanese destroyer *Kikuzuki*, in August 1943 in Tulagi's harbor. *Kikuzuki* was pounded by *Yorktown*'s aircraft on May 4, 1942.
U.S. NAVY

Yorktown Dauntlesses head back to their carrier from Tulagi on May 4, 1942, through heavy cloud cover, their bombs having been dropped on shipping.
U.S. NAVY

ARM3c John Liska (*left*) shakes hands with his pilot, Ensign Jack Leppla from *Lexington*'s Scouting Two, in a publicity photo taken after the Coral Sea battle. This pilot/gunner team was credited with four aerial victories in an SBD on May 7 during the *Shoho* strike and they would use their Dauntless as a fighter plane again the following day.
U.S. NAVY

The Japanese carrier *Shoho* ("Happy Phoenix") seen under way and burning from VB-2 bomb hits as Torpedo Two scores a direct hit on her starboard side. This photo was taken by a *Lexington* aircraft at about 1119.
U.S. NAVY

This photo by RM3c Eugene W. Jones of Torpedo Five captures *Shoho* as she is undergoing a two-pronged torpedo attack from *Yorktown*'s VT-5. Note the TBD in the foreground and other torpedo planes in the distance beyond *Shoho*.   U.S. NAVY

The Japanese carrier *Shokaku* under attack by Bill Burch's VS-5 *Yorktown* dive-bombers during the battle of the Coral Sea on May 8, 1942.   U.S. NAVY

Seen late in the *Yorktown* attack, the bow of the twisting *Shokaku* is blazing and she is belching black smoke from John Powers's direct hit.   U.S. NAVY

Scouting Two's Wayne Colley (*left*) and his pilot, Ensign Art Schultz, shake hands during a publicity photo taken in San Diego in June 1942.
U.S. NAVY

Scouting Two pilot Lieutenant (j.g.) Bill "Pappy" Hall (*left*) receives the Medal of Honor for his actions at Coral Sea. He has just returned from his honeymoon in late September 1942. His new wife, Leah Christine Chapman Hall, looks on with pride as Rear Admiral Ralston Holmes (*right*) reads the citation.
U.S. NAVY

Lieutenant (j.g.) Pappy Hall earned his Medal of Honor for his defense of *Lexington* while wounded on May 8.
COURTESY OF GWEN HALL

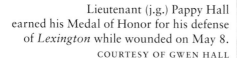

Lieutenant John James "Jo Jo" Powers was awarded the Medal of Honor for diving so low on *Shokaku* to ensure a hit that his plane was lost.
U.S. NAVY

This photo from May 8 is believed by historian John Lundstrom to show Pappy Hall's crippled SBD flying over the destroyer *Dewey* (DD-349).
U.S. NAVY

Late in the afternoon of 8 May, *Lexington* is listing heavily and ablaze, with aircraft still spotted on her flight deck.
U.S. NAVY

Lexington's internal explosions began tearing her apart in the afternoon. The destroyer *Hammann* backs away as a spectacular blast around 1800 blows an aircraft overboard.
U.S. NAVY

Scouting Five skipper Turner Caldwell and gunner Rocky Glidewell roar off the end of the *Enterprise* flight deck for Guadalcanal on August 7, 1942. This view was taken during Caldwell's second launch of the morning.
U.S. NAVY

This view, taken from an SBD on August 8, shows the wrecked facilities at the Japanese seaplane base on Tanambogo Island, east of Tulagi. Note the burned-out pier in foreground, the fuel drums piled to the left, and the wreckage of a seaplane among the trees in the center. U.S. NAVY

Gunner John Liska (*left*) and pilot Jack Leppla (*right*) record a radio program in July with NBC commentator Hank McCune (*center*). They are reliving their fights with Japanese Zeros at Coral Sea. COURTESY OF MICHAEL LISKA

The dirt-and-coral gravel airstrip at Henderson Field, soon known as Bomber One. U.S. MARINE CORPS

The crude airstrip of Henderson Field on Guadalcanal. This view was taken from a *Saratoga* SBD during the initial assault on August 7, 1942. U.S. NAVY

A *Wasp* SBD of VS-72 seen in flight near the Solomons on August 24, 1942. This plane, S-14, had been flown by Ensign Thomas Reeves during the initial Guadalcanal landings on August 7. Reeves would be lost with *Wasp* weeks later. NATIONAL ARCHIVES

Enterprise landing signal officer Robin Lindsey artfully waves in another returning SBD as assistant Cleo Dobson looks on. U.S. NAVY

A Japanese bomb explodes on *Enterprise*'s flight deck during the Eastern Solomons battle. Turner Caldwell's Flight 300 SBDs had just taken off moments before their carrier was hit. Photographer's Mate 2c Robert Frederick Edmondson died while photographing this attack on the Big E on August 24.   U.S. NAVY

The 10,150-ton Japanese carrier *Ryujo*.   U.S. NAVY

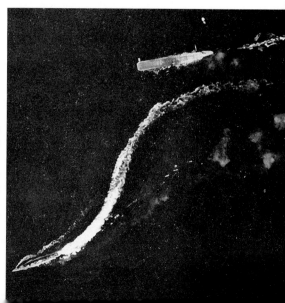

Ryujo is dead in the water while abandoning ship after the *Saratoga* air group's attack on August 24. The destroyer *Amatsukaze* is under way and maneuvering as USAAF B-17 bombers attack *Ryujo*. The destroyer *Tokitsukaze* is closer to the stricken carrier, getting under way.
U.S. NAVY

The newly arrived *Enterprise* SBD pilots gathered at the Pagoda at Henderson Field on Guadalcanal. This templelike wooden building served as the air operations building for the Cactus Air Force until it was later destroyed. U.S. MARINE CORPS

Navy and Marine ground crews used damaged SBDs for spare parts to keep the Cactus Air Force flying. This is a damaged Dauntless of Marine VMSB-233, while other battle-damaged planes can be seen near the Guadalcanal palms. U.S. NAVY NATIONAL MUSEUM OF NAVAL AVIATION PHOTO NO. 1996.253.752.

Cactus Air Force airmen are driven toward the Pagoda in about the second week of October 1942. Ensign Bob Mohler of VS-71 is seated on the left (*looking to the right*). COURTESY OF ROBERT MOHLER

Overnight bombardments and midday air strikes against Henderson Field slowly wiped out many of the Cactus Air Force planes. This was all that was left of one SBD near the field after a Japanese bombardment. Turner Caldwell's Dauntless was destroyed in a September 27 air raid.
NATIONAL ARCHIVES

Wildcat F4F fighters seen dispersed near the open-air repair area off Henderson Field's new Fighter One airstrip. Note the Army tents on the hill in the distance.
U.S. MARINE CORPS

The carrier *Wasp* is blazing out of control on September 15 from torpedo damage. Four SBD pilots were killed in the inferno.
U.S. NAVY

Pilots Birney Strong and Chuck Irvine made direct hits on *Zuiho* at Santa Cruz. The 11,262-ton Japanese carrier, capable of carrying thirty aircraft, is seen here in 1940.
U.S. NAVY

As the nine VT-10 Avengers and three VS-10 Dauntlesses of the small Enterprise strike group roll to the launch point at 0750 on October 26, a sailor holds up a card telling the pilots to "Proceed Without Hornet." U.S. NAVY

The Japanese cruiser *Chikuma* under attack from *Hornet*'s planes around 0930. This photo was taken from air group commander Walt Rodee's TBF. Three VS-10 *Enterprise* SBDs also attacked *Chikuma* moments later. U.S. NAVY

Hornet, smoking from bomb and torpedo damage, is about to be slammed by the diving Japanese Val bomber of Warrant Officer Shigeyuki Sato. U.S. NAVY

Dauntless overboard! Captain Hardison threw *Enterprise* into a violent turn while under Japanese attack so that brave deck crewmen could help push Don Wakeham's dangling B-1 SBD over the side. U.S. NAVY

Former dive-bomber pilot Swede Vejtasa
achieved seven kills in one mission
on October 26 at Santa Cruz.
U.S. NAVY

The last Kate torpedo plane, crippled
by the bullets of Vejtasa's Wildcat,
plowed into the destroyer *Smith* as
Swede was still giving chase.
U.S. NAVY

The destroyer *Russell* maneuvers
alongside *Hornet* to take off her
wounded and her aviators,
including three stranded
Enterprise dive-bomber crews.
U.S. NAVY

Enterprise viewed on November 10 at Noumea, New Caledonia. Her bomb-damaged
Number 1 elevator has been lowered for testing, but it would not be used for the
upcoming naval battle for Guadalcanal.   U.S. NAVY, COURTESY OF BILL SHINNEMAN,
VIA JAMES T. RINDT

Dust clouds swirl as SBD and TBF engines are started in the mud on Henderson Field. The flight action was constant on November 14 as the Cactus Air Force attempted to turn back both Japanese warships and troop transports.
U.S. MARINE CORPS

Beached Japanese troop transport ships *Hirokawa Maru* and *Kinugawa Maru* blaze from bomb damage off Guadalcanal in this photo taken from Bob Gibson's SBD on November 15. NATIONAL ARCHIVES

The 6,936-ton transport *Kinugawa Maru*, beached on Guadalcanal at the mouth of the Bonegi River near Tassafaronga. Although partially salvaged in the 1960s, the remains of *Kinugawa* are still a popular wreck-diving site today.
NATIONAL ARCHIVES

An *Enterprise* VB-10 Dauntless flying off the coast of Guadalcanal on the afternoon of November 15. Taken from Bob Gibson's SBD, this view shows several Japanese troop ships burning on the beach. U.S. NAVY

Scouting Ten SBD S-13 seen with its tailhook down as it prepares to land on the *Enterprise* below. The carrier *Saratoga* is seen in the distance, circa December 1942 in the Solomons. NATIONAL ARCHIVES

his VMSB-232 dive-bombers between the transports and the warships. Larry Baldinus laid his thousand-pounder on the flagship *Jintsu*, damaging her badly enough to force her back to Truk for repairs. Admiral Tanaka was knocked unconscious by the bomb blast and soon transferred his flag to the destroyer *Kagero*. Mangrum scored a damaging near miss on one of the transports, *Boston Maru*.[22]

Turner Caldwell selected the large transport *Kinryu Maru* for his three Navy SBDs. "My bomb skimmed the starboard side, and I hope did underwater damage," he said. Chris Fink saw his skipper's bomb explode close to the troopship. He kept her decks lined up in his sights as Milo Kimberlin called out the altitude from the rear seat. Fink released his thousand-pounder and pulled out low on the water. His bomb landed amidships and just aft of *Kinryu Maru*'s bridge. "A sheet of flame and smoke went right up to the clouds," Kimberlin said. "I could see the stack and bridge lift out of the ship and go kerplunk into the ocean. She was still burning when we left. You could see the smoke for about forty miles."[23]

Fink was not able to see his bomb hit, but the shouts of Kimberlin said it all. He glanced back and saw debris in the air and one of the warships smoking heavily. "The antiaircraft fire wasn't particularly heavy and I got only one hole in my plane," said Jesse Barker. Dick Mangrum saw that Fink's transport was blazing furiously, with personnel and wreckage in the water. *Kinryu Maru* was later scuttled but fate played a cruel twist for Tanaka's Rat Patrol. As the destroyer *Mutsuki* came alongside *Kinryu* to remove its crew, B-17s from Espíritu Santo came over and dropped a cluster of bombs, sinking the destroyer. Two of Tanaka's ships had been sunk in one morning, one by Scouting Five.[24]

The three Flight 300 crews escaped the convoy attack without loss, although Caldwell's SBD was closely rocked by the concussions of heavy shells from the cruiser during his pullout. Caldwell's trio made a running rendezvous and hand-signaled to each other to check fuel status. "Both Barker and Caldwell indicated that they only had about twenty-five gallons left, while I had forty left," said Fink. He was amazed to have such a supply remaining, as he had flown with a thousand-pound bomb during the previous day's mission. He was the only one of this Cactus flight who had gone out with such a heavy payload.

On the ground at Cactus, the Dauntless crews were congratulated by General Vandegrift. They had sunk or damaged ships of the invasion force and forced it to turn back, thus sparing many lives on Guadalcanal. Admiral Tanaka's reinforcement group retired toward Truk, but his Tokyo Express would not be long in making more supply runs toward Hell's Island.

Fink's, Barker's, and Caldwell's planes were refueled by the Cactus ground crews. "We rolled fifty-gallon drums near the plane and poured the gas into twelve-quart buckets and strained it through a chamois skin," Fink said. One captured Japanese gas truck was reserved for the use of the fighter planes. In the dust and heat, gunner Stuart Mason of VB-6 used Marines to help hoist new bombs on the Dauntlesses and put in the fuses. "There wasn't a bung wrench on the field and we had to take the bung out with a chisel and hammer," said Mason. Jesse Barker and his gunner, a small-framed Boston Irishman named Gene Monahan, helped the meager ground crews refuel their SBDs. "They'd drop off a fifty-gallon drum next to our aircraft along with a three-gallon bucket," said Barker. He and Monahan used the bucket to scoop fuel from the drum and strained it through a chamois cloth by hand into their airplane's tanks. "It was very primitive."[25]

Caldwell's crews had not been back on the ground long before another follow-up raid was called for. Dick Mangrum took off at 1120 with a mixed Marine-Navy Dauntless group to make another visit to the Japanese invasion force. Dog Barker was back in the air with this group, along with Hal Buell and Gil Guillory. Thirty minutes after this bombing group departed, warning flags went up over Henderson Field.

The incoming Japanese air raid was the first scramble the Flight 300 airmen faced, but the procedure would soon become old hat. The Navy pilots learned from Mangrum's Marine crews to watch the flagpole on the Pagoda. Radio Guadalcanal, the Lunga Point station set up only a week prior, monitored Coastwatcher warnings and relayed them to Generals Vandegrift and Geiger at the airfield. Japanese planes or shipping departing from Bougainville, Rabaul, or Shortland Island would inevitably pass within sight of Coastwatchers stationed on Bougainville, New Georgia Island, Santa Isabel Island, or western Guadalcanal. The Pagoda flag system included readiness colors of green, yellow, and red. Condition green was the all-clear condition, indicated by a white flag.

Yellow meant that Coastwatchers had spotted Japanese aircraft inbound perhaps an hour away. Four enlisted men at the Pagoda watch would then crank a captured hand siren and run up a red flag that indicated condition yellow. When the red flag for condition yellow was hoisted, all pilots scurried to their planes to take off while the siren wailed. The precious dive-bombers and fighters were subject to bomb damage or strafing if they remained on the ground during the noon bombing raid. Condition red, signaled by a black flag and the siren, meant that Japanese planes were already over the island. Maintenance crews and any aviators caught on the ground were to take cover in foxholes immediately.[26]

With the departure of Barker, Buell, and Guillory, Turner Caldwell was caught with six other Flight 300 crews as the air raid siren howled. Coolbaugh, Woodhull, Conzett, Liffner, Manford, Fink, and their gunners raced for their planes. Chris Fink, one of the last to clear the field, found himself alone, so he explored the Tulagi area until the raid was over. Twenty-one Japanese bombers made a high-altitude attack at 1155 from 27,400 feet. About forty well-grouped bombs landed near the field-operations building. All but three aircraft were sufficiently fueled in order to get airborne in time before this bombing strike. Minor damage was sustained to the runway and aircraft dispersal areas, but none of the three grounded planes were destroyed. Best yet, the busy Marines made temporary patches to the runway in time to enable landings later by the returning strikers.[27]

Mangrum and Guillory's flight reached the area where Fink had blasted his transport earlier in the morning. They found immense oil slicks and some debris. Three of the pilots lost their bombs on this flight while searching for worthwhile targets. The Marine air command believed the trouble had been caused by the extreme dampness of the electrical release system. En route home, this group found a lone destroyer about 150 miles northwest of Guadalcanal. Guillory led his six bomb-armed SBDs down to the attack.

Hal Buell observed a good deal of AA fire from the destroyer, and saw that two bombs from the leading section ahead of him had missed. Buell's bomb was a close miss to starboard and Dog Barker landed his close to the port side. "Buell said there was a flash and a fire amidships," recalled Barker. "I am not sure whether it was a hit or a near miss. Anyway, I didn't claim it." The destroyer appeared to be badly damaged by the near misses, leaving debris and a heavy oil slick in its wake.[28]

Guillory led his flight back toward Guadalcanal low on the water. Their route took them past the little island of Gavutu, just off Florida Island. As they cruised past, Jesse Barker came head to head with a light-colored float Zero. "He was right on my altitude and we were both just looking at each other's eyeballs," he said. The equally surprised pilots zipped past each other and then both made hard turns to come back at each other. Barker only squeezed off three rounds with one of his forward .50-calibers before it jammed. The second wing gun stubbornly refused to fire at all. The short burst, however, was enough to convince the Japanese pilot to turn tail.[29]

After a long first day with two combat flights, Barker hoped for decent chow upon his return to the field. He was less than overwhelmed to learn that captured Japanese rice would be the only form of sustenance he would be offered. The Marine ground crews had a primitive field kitchen south of the runway, near the group of rickety Japanese-built hangars where they had set up shop. A Marine cook was standing next to a big pot of rice boiling over a fire. The soldier stirred the rice with a shovel, cracking jokes about the food all the while. "He kept pointing out that we were going to have fresh meat with our rice," Barker said. "When I looked closer I could see that the rice was just crawling with maggots. I couldn't eat for several days after that."[30]

During the day, Japanese snipers perched in high treetops took shots at the airmen moving about the field. "When we get a line on one, we grab our weapons and go into the edge of the woods and fire a hail of bullets up into the tree," Army Air Force fighter pilot Robert Ferguson wrote in his diary. "They are usually tied up in the tree. They just stay there with their blood running down the tree."[31]

The Flight 300 fliers, having slept on stretchers or the ground and been shelled the first night, moved into more long-term "housing" during their first full day at Guadalcanal. They would bivouac with Dick Mangrum's VMSB-232 Dauntless fliers in a tent city in a rubber tree grove. Jesse Barker happily traded the ground and his bloody blanket for a cot in an eight-man tent. Marine pilots doubled up to provide tent space for the *Enterprise* aviators, and even helped outfit them with clothes and shoes. "Part of my outfit was several pairs of Japanese tropical underwear, of good-quality cotton," said Caldwell. "I kept them for years."[32]

The night hours were relatively quiet at Henderson Field. The next day, August 26, included the usual noon raid with its half-hour warning as the Japanese were spotted coming over New Georgia Island. Caldwell's crews learned that Betty bombers launched from Rabaul were a daily ritual—dubbed "Tojo Time"—for their airfield. "We took off just beforehand so that our aircraft wouldn't be destroyed, and then we'd get out of the way while the Marine fighters shot them down," said Barker. John Smith's Marine fighters scrambled to attack, but the bombers damaged some grounded aircraft with fragmentation bombs and set a nest of two thousand gallons of aviation fuel on fire. The blaze cooked off two thousand-pound bombs dispersed on the field, but no one was injured in the violent blasts.[33]

To say that conditions were trying for the *Enterprise* Flight 300 men was an understatement. The MAG-23 war diary states that air operations for this week "were carried on during the most primitive operating conditions and despite an acute shortage of personnel. Food was prepared over open fires, washing and bathing done in the Lunga River, and practically all hands kept their clothes on continuously except when at the river bathing."

Jim Cales was becoming weary of the scant rations of Japanese-style rice and fish or the Australian sheep's tongue. To top it off, he had developed a bad sunburn from sitting around his SBD, waiting for action. His buddy Al Garlow was dark-complected and had little issue with the sun. Cales and others were beginning to feel sick from the poor food and were developing dysentery, an uncomfortable ailment derived from poor living conditions.[34]

Hal Buell found more than just poor food and sunburn to frustrate him with Cactus life. Night missions were "quite hazardous with little in the way of rewards. Japanese snipers crept close to the field to fire at planes and aircrews both on the ground and during takeoff and landing," said Buell. "Everyone was living under siegelike conditions, with soaring temperatures, torrential rains, and humidity for weather."[35]

Courtesy of Nate Murphy

Ensign Nate Murphy of VS-71,
sporting a full beard upon his return
to San Francisco from Guadalcanal in
1942.

Turner Caldwell still held out hope that his SBD crews would be rejoining *Enterprise* at any time.

Enterprise and her sister carriers had moved beyond the Guadalcanal area in the wake of the Eastern Solomons battle. *Wasp* sent out a strike group in the afternoon to follow up on hitting the Tanaka convoy that Caldwell's Flight 300 fliers had plastered northwest of Malaita Island. Outbound, the American strikers were shadowed by a four-engine Kawanishi flying boat (code-named "Mavis") that continued to edge nearer to their formation. Four VS-71 pilots—Lieutenant Morris "Mo" Doughty, Ensign Nate Murphy, Lieutenant (j.g.) Chuck Mester, and Ensign Bob Escher—rolled in to attack. "I was the number three man on Mo's wing, so I was closest to the flying boat," said Murphy. He could see the enemy's guns firing back at him as he commenced firing from the Kawanishi's starboard quarter. Murphy's .50-calibers flamed the Mavis' number-three engine, while Escher rolled in and flamed the number-two engine. "Shortly thereafter the plane exploded and four flaming engines fell into the sea," said Murphy. The two *Wasp* scouting squadrons had shot down six enemy aircraft since August 8, while their VF-71 counterparts had not even seen a Japanese plane in the air.[36]

The *Wasp* attack force failed to find the transport ships. *Enterprise* and *Saratoga*'s task forces had spent most of the day refueling from tankers 150 miles northwest of Espíritu Santo. Admiral Fletcher, still riding his flagship *Saratoga*, decided that Kinkaid should take the Big E into Nouméa for temporary repairs of the bomb damage sustained in the Eastern Solomons.

Glenn Estes of Scouting Five made two submarine attacks while the carrier groups refueled. He found his first I-boat shortly after 0930, and landed his bomb just aft of its conning tower. Estes then made two strafing runs on the crippled boat as its bow slipped beneath the surface. Oil and debris littered the surface as Estes headed to *Saratoga* for gunner Floyd Stamey to make a message drop on her deck. He was back over the attack area around 1030 and spotted another submarine near the scene of his first attack. Estes strafed the waterline forward on the submarine. It crash-dived, leaving a light trail of oil, and Estes returned to land on *Saratoga*.

During the afternoon, all hands not on duty were mustered on the hangar deck of *Enterprise* to dispose of the ship's Eastern Solomons victims. On August 26, *Enterprise* was ordered to Tongatabu, where the repair ship *Vestal's* specialists could work over her bomb damage. The majority of her air group was divided up to help bolster the other carriers and local island defense. *Saratoga* took on eighteen F4Fs, one SBD, and five TBFs from the *Enterprise* Air Group. Some of the *Enterprise* pilots remained on the *Saratoga* and their records and personal gear (including that of the Flight 300 airmen) were shuttled over by the destroyer *Maury* in the afternoon. Nick Nicholson and Link Traynor of VS-5 were spotted on deck in the late afternoon of August 26, with orders to fly into Efate to arrange for some of the *Enterprise* aircraft to operate from that base.

"We waited in our aircraft for hours before we finally got the message we were to take to Efate," said Traynor. It was nearly dark when he and Nicholson took off, and it was nighttime when they arrived over the jungle airstrip. Traynor could barely see the outline of the coral runway from the landing lights. "I followed Nick and came in very close to the trees to make the landing," he said. Traynor taxied his Dauntless to a parking area, as directed by a young soldier. As he climbed from his cockpit, the soldier put a flashlight on his face.[37]

"Are you Traynor?" he asked with surprise. "You look just like the pilot who left here today."

"What was his name?" Link asked.

"Traynor," replied the soldier.

Link explained that it had probably been his older brother, Lieutenant (j.g.) Raymond H. Traynor, a patrol plane pilot for the Navy who was based in the Pacific. The vast world suddenly seemed a little smaller to Link, who would regret missing the chance to see his brother. Ray would be killed in service in 1943.

Nicholson and Traynor returned to *Enterprise* the following morning. Their carrier flew off another large group of aircraft for Efate as she prepared to make port in Tongatabu for battle damage repairs. Ray Davis departed with fourteen VB-6 crews and Charlie Jett set out with his five remaining Avengers. The TBFs of Jett and wingman Ed Holley were overloaded and crashed into the ocean during takeoff, although the crews were recovered. Many of the seventeen aircrews that did make it to Efate would soon see service on Guadalcanal. From Bombing Six, only Exec John Lowe and Ensign Steve Czarnecki remained with the ship.

Bombing Six was directed to supply six SBDs and crews to the *Wasp* Air Group per Carl Horenburger. "Pilots and radiomen drew straws, with the short straws drawing the assignment. I drew a short straw and led the formation to New Caledonia," Horenburger said. He, Dick Jaccard, Don Ely, Dan Dopuch, Bob Shaw, and Warren Bolt thus became temporary members of the two *Wasp* scouting squadrons.[38]

Enterprise retained only Fighting Six skipper Lou Bauer with eight Wildcats and eight SBDs of Scouting Five. Redbird Burnett and Elmer Maul of VS-5, on standby during the launching, were held back and remained with the ship as well. They were left with Birney Strong, Downing, Nicholson, Traynor, Austin, Ervin, Estes, Richey, and Jorgenson. Lieutenant Strong became acting commander of VS-5 since Caldwell and Woodhull had joined the Cactus Air Force. Strong remained grounded for several days as air officer Crommelin tried to contain his anger with the pilot who had not followed through on attacking *Ryujo* days before. Strong had seven of his own SBDs and one VB-3 plane that had taken refuge on his ship at Eastern Solomons with which to conduct the routine IAP flights.

Ensign Hoot Gibson and gunner Ed Anderson, pulled from the ocean at Eastern Solomons by the destroyer *Farragut*, arrived at Tongatabu on August 27. They went ashore to the grass airfield of Tonga Field while the Big E was patched up. Gibson spent time with other VS-5 and Army Air Corps fighter pilots, as well as Australian and New Zealand servicemen.

"The only thing to drink was Australian beer that they had in tremendous quantities," he said. "The Aussies were very good imbibers. Their objective was to stay seated at a table all evening without getting up to go to the bathroom. The real test of how much of a man you were was how much beer you could drink without leaving the table to get rid of it."[39]

Gibson and his VS-5 buddies tried their best to hold their beer. Around two in the morning, Hoot and Glenn "Taterhead" Estes decided it would be fun to empty their .45 service revolvers into the air outside their Quonset hut. "The military police started a frantic search for the culprits, who by this time had dashed across a thirty-yard space, jumped into their cots, and pulled the blankets up over themselves, clothes and all, and pretended to be asleep," said Gibson.

Enterprise, having remained at Tongatabu for several days, licking her wounds, departed the next morning. She had been ordered to Pearl Harbor for more extensive navy yard repairs. Estes and Gibson had only three hours of sleep and were terribly hungover when they manned their SBDs for the obligatory scouting mission and flight out to their departing carrier. "I was thankful for the pilot's relief tube in the cockpit," said Gibson. "Those were the longest six hours of my entire life."[40]

Enterprise would be out of the Guadalcanal campaign for nearly two months, leaving her Eastern Solomons Flight 300 airmen stranded at Henderson Field. By the time the Big E returned to action, her air group would be completely overhauled as well.

Chris Fink, a farm boy from the open plains of Wyoming, was quite impressed with the greenery of their tropical environment. The Guadalcanal airfield went from one extreme to the other. If it rained, the airstrip was a mud bog. When it was dry, the prop wash from the SBDs raised blinding dust clouds. "Coconuts were plentiful and the captured Jap workers would shinny up the trees like monkeys and throw them down," Fink said.[41]

In VMSB-232's camp north of the runway, the Navy enlisted gunners slept four to an assigned tent, with mosquito netting in the coconut grove. Bathroom facilities were slit trenches that served as latrines. Multi-throne toilet chairs suspended over the latrines served as seats for the sick who suffered from "fluid drive"—persistent diarrhea brought on by dysentery.

Hal Buell and several pilots visited the battle area near the Tenaru River during one period of downtime. Marines had used bulldozers to clean up the carnage, burying the enemy troops in one mass grave. Frontline Marines let the fliers pick souvenirs from the piles of Japanese gear. Buell collected a rifle, bayonet, helmet, canteen, short knife, flag, and other small items.[42]

One of the most disturbing encounters for the SBD airmen was with Sergeant Major Jacob Vouza, chief scout for Australian Coastwatcher Martin Clemens. Chris Fink learned that Vouza had been "bayoneted several times in the throat after being captured by the Japanese and left for dead." The patrol that captured Vouza on August 20 was unable to get him to talk. They tied him to a tree, beat him, stabbed him, and slashed his throat. The forty-eight-year-old scout summoned enough strength later to gnaw through his ropes and crawl to a Marine outpost near the mouth of Alligator Creek. Hal Buell encountered Vouza, the most famous survivor of Japanese barbarism on the Canal, recovering in the makeshift hospital near Henderson Field. He realized what he could expect if he was shot down and captured.[43]

Coastwatchers on New Georgia Island sent a warning at 1035 on August 27, and the aviators scrambled their planes. The expected noon air raid during Flight 300's third full day on the Canal fortunately failed to materialize. The bright spot of the day was the arrival of nine U.S. Army P-400 fighters of the 67th Fighting Squadron to help with low-level strafing missions.

The next afternoon, the scout patrol of Dog Barker and Harry Liffner sighted four Japanese destroyers—*Amagiri*, *Yugiri*, *Asagiri*, and *Shirakumo*. The Rat Patrol of troop-carrying destroyers was seventy miles from Cactus and closing, so Barker climbed and called back to Henderson Field. He then joined the other SBDs in pushing over against the rearmost tin can of the Tokyo Express group. "These ships didn't try to circle, or turn, or evade at all," said Barker. "They just stayed in line." Other pilots credited Barker with a direct hit on the stern of one of the destroyers, causing it to lose headway and begin trailing oil.[44]

Word of this inbound bombardment force set Henderson Field in motion like a kicked-over ant pile. Dick Mangrum took off with eleven SBDs from VMSB-232 and VS-5 to attack these warships. Caldwell, Coolbaugh, Conzett, Fink, and Buell had the vessels in sight and were ready to attack in half an hour. At 1805, Caldwell and Mangrum led their SBDs down on the ships about fifteen miles north of Ramos Island. Caldwell landed his bomb on the destroyer *Shirakumo*, while Fink hit the leading destroyer, *Asagiri*, directly amidships with his thousand-pounder. Fink's victim exploded and sank, carrying down her division commander, Captain Yuzo Arita. *Shirakumo* was heavily damaged and spewing oil badly. Spike Conzett and Hal Buell pushed over on the second ship on the right, the destroyer *Yugiri*. Buell released at two thousand feet. He wrote in his diary that night: "I saw my bomb explode almost amidships—a direct hit. She started exploding in her magazines and I saw heavy red fire burst out of her."[45]

Asagiri went down quickly, *Yugiri* was moderately damaged (out of the war for months), and *Shirakumo* was taken in tow by the undamaged destroyer *Amagiri*. One Marine SBD was lost on this strike to antiaircraft fire while strafing *Amagiri*. Due to poor visibility and adverse weather conditions after dark, a second mission was not attempted. Admiral Tanaka, based on Shortland Island, was not pleased that his latest Rat Patrol was turned back without landing any troops.

The marooned *Enterprise* crews received a welcome gift on August 28. Lieutenant John Myers and Ensign Corwin Morgan of VT-8 made a supply flight in to Cactus from *Saratoga* in Avengers carrying the personal gear of the orphaned VS-5 and VB-6 airmen. They landed at around 1100, in the middle of an air raid. Myers and Morgan opened their bomb-bay doors, dumped parachute bags, turned and taxied to the end of the runway, and departed.[46]

"The parachute bags contained our belongings, one bag for each plane crew member," recalled Lieutenant Caldwell. "In my room aboard *Enterprise*, I had a gallon of whiskey, unopened. I was anxious to get it, as it was worth its weight in cut diamonds as trading material for souvenirs." Caldwell found the bottle in his bag, all right, but only an inch of whiskey remained. The furious skipper decided not to further investigate the event. "It could only have led to an assault with intent to harm," he said.

Gunner Stuart Mason was happy to have some of his clothes and personal gear. He was taken aback when Colonel Mangrum made it clear that they were not leaving Guadalcanal to return to another carrier. "You can have all the gas and ammo you need to help us, but you can't have one drop of gas to go to the *Saratoga*," he announced. "Of course, Vandegrift backed him up 100 percent," Mason said.[47]

It is now clear that we have been abandoned by the Navy, Caldwell thought. *We will be serving with the Marines for an indefinite time.*[48]

The Cactus Air Force had turned back the latest bombardment mission for the night of August 28–29. During the predawn hours, however, the Japanese sent a night bombing strike that put craters around the runway and killed three Marines. This was followed by a noon air raid that forced all fliers to scramble their planes to safety. Two of Henderson Field's hangars were set on fire, torching a grounded F4F and SBD. Crews rushed around with trucks to dump dirt in the fresh bomb craters that pockmarked the runway. The aviators helped beat down the fresh grass fires with blankets, shovels, and even handfuls of dirt—while taking potshots from Japanese snipers.[49]

U.S. Navy

Ensign Elmer "Spike" Conzett of VS-5.

Daily life revolved around flight schedules, Japanese raids, and meals. "Rations were short, and consisted of two meals a day of canned Australian sheep's tongue, canned butter, and Japanese rice," Caldwell reflected. "Only the latter was in good supply. I must say the Marine cooks did everything they could to vary the menu, but there was just so many ways of preparing sheep's tongue, and only one for rice." Some mornings, there were Marine hotcakes, but most breakfasts consisted of plain, unsweetened oatmeal slopped into mess kits. The persistent dust around Henderson Field settled upon a man's oatmeal and turned the tastless paste a dark color before it could be consumed. Afternoon meals of captured Japanese rice were occasionally flavored with canned sausage or Spam.[50]

Night flying, a necessity for the Cactus aviators, was often perilous. Gunner Jim Cales and his best friend, Al Garlow, old-timers with VS-5, had seen their share of action. But nothing could prepare Cales for his most harrowing flight, one he experienced just a week after his arrival on Hell's Island. Shortly before midnight on August 30, his pilot, Spike Conzett, summoned him.

"Cales, they're sending up two SBDs tonight, and we're one of them," said Conzett. "The Coastwatchers have spotted some Jap destroyers coming down the Slot toward us. They're probably carrying troops. It's our job to turn 'em back."[51]

Dick Mangrum and Turner Caldwell offered up one Marine and one Navy crew for the mission in the Slot—the nickname for New Georgia Sound, which runs roughly through the middle of the Solomon Islands. Major Fletcher L. Brown Jr. of VMSB-232 and Ensign Conzett were to fly as a team along the beaches of Guadalcanal to look for destroyers unloading troops. They took off at 0030 on August 30 with a dozen other SBDs that fanned out to cover other sectors. In a testament to their pilots' abilities, all of the night-flying SBDs made it back to Henderson Field. Conzett's plane made it home only because of the tenacity of rear-seat gunner Jimmy Cales.

"The island was covered with clouds from the shore up to three miles," said Cales. A partial moon penetrated the clouds periodically. Conzett had flown only eight minutes along Guadalcanal's southwest coast when Cales spotted five ships close to the beach through a small hole in the clouds off their left wing. They appeared to be dead in the water, likely unloading troops. Cales blurted over the intercom to Conzett that they had just overflown some Japanese ships.[52]

"What?" Conzett called back.

He and Conzett were a new team, and the pilot struggled to understand his gunner's thick West Virginia drawl. Cales repeated his excited report two more times. Conzett finally got the message and radioed Major Brown, who relayed word to Henderson Field. Cactus ordered them to investigate further.

Brown and Conzett dropped below the clouds and reversed direction. Cales felt they might not have even spotted the ships again except for the fact that the destroyers opened fire with their AA guns. Major Brown dropped his bombs on freshly landed supplies and strafed the warships until his ammunition was exhausted. He was later awarded the Navy Cross for boldly pressing home his attacks in the early hours of August 30 in poor visibility.

Spike Conzett never saw his Marine wingman again once the destroyers opened fire on them. He pulled into a wingover and dived on one of the ships while Cales chattered away from the rear seat with his .30-calibers. Neither man was able to determine what effect their bomb had but Conzett quickly climbed again to make a second dive.[53]

During their second dive, a shell ripped through Cales's transmitter and passed through their SBD's front cockpit. The plane's intercom system was shot away and other bullets chewed up the insides of their Dauntless. "They shot out my instrument panel, filled the cockpit full of holes, and scared the hell out of me," Conzett said. He heard the shell hit and then he felt a chunk of shrapnel strike him in the back of the leg and lodge in his shinbone.

Conzett lapsed into a state of delirium from heavy blood loss. Cales quickly became alarmed at how erratic their plane was flying. He stowed his machine guns and installed the control stick in the flying position and locked it. "He spent the next few minutes flying around over the area, diving and climbing, without any sense of purpose," Cales said.[54]

Conzett then seemed to settle down. He headed south and started climbing above the hills while moving out to sea. Their SBD clawed from 3,500 feet up to 5,000. From his rear seat, Cales could see Guadalcanal disappearing in the distance. *We're going the wrong way!* Cales shook his rear-seat control stick vigorously. Conzett acknowledged the maneuver and let go of his main control stick to let his radioman fly from the rear seat. Fortunately, Cales had practiced the maneuver in more peaceful times. He turned the SBD around and headed back, cruising over the hills toward Henderson Field. He let down under the clouds and started a right turn to make an approach. Conzett suddenly shook his control stick, and Cales let him resume control.

For some reason, Conzett banked their Dauntless around and headed back out to sea again. *What the hell is he thinking?* Cales wondered. *Maybe he is wounded.* After a couple of minutes, Conzett turned ninety degrees to the left into a heavily clouded area. Cales stayed on the controls to help with the turns. As they approached the clouds, they flew back into range of one of the Japanese warships. The ship erupted into antiaircraft fire. Conzett flew them right through the flak, turned, and flew through it again. "He did this once more and I was sure he had lost some of his marbles," said Cales.[55]

They were down to about 800 feet when Conzett suddenly began climbing sharply to about 7,500 feet. At that moment, the destroyer found their range. A five-inch shell exploded just to the left and ahead of their left wing. The concussion tore Cales's pants leg and left small pieces of shrapnel in his leg. "What it did to Ensign Conzett, I can only guess that the shock knocked him out, as he was seen to be out part-time before," he said.

Their dive-bomber was rocked mightily by the concussion and then began a spiraling plunge toward the ocean. Cales shook the stick to see if Conzett was consciously performing some strange stunt. There was no response. *Mr. Conzett must have been knocked across the left rudder control,* he thought. *It seems locked. We're dead if I can't correct this. He's just bent over the stick, not moving.* Cales went to work on the controls, booted the right rudder, and tried to move the stick to center and forward.[56]

He found very little response to his stick movements. His plane was loosely spiraling down from high altitude. *It's time to bail out,* he thought. Another image of all the sharks he had seen in the water during the daylight compelled Cales to give it one more shot to save himself. He grabbed the controls and tugged with all his strength. "The stick and rudder moved a bit and suddenly the pressure was gone," he said. "I had control."

Conzett was still unresponsive, so his gunner flew their plane from the rear seat back to Guadalcanal. Cales climbed through eight hundred feet of broken clouds along the way and finally had the island in sight.

Conzett suddenly became coherent again. He shook his forward control stick, indicating he wanted control. "I gave it to him, but not completely," said Cales. *There's no way in hell I'm going to let this delirious pilot take us back out over the ocean.* This time, they lined up on Henderson Field and landed their damaged SBD with the aid of jeep headlights. Cales stayed on his controls the whole way, just to make sure.[57]

As they rolled to a halt, Cales climbed onto the wing to help Ensign Conzett out. It was a struggle for the short, small-framed gunner to tug his tall, bloodied pilot free. Cales dumped him unceremoniously in the mire alongside their wing. He hoisted Conzett onto his back and dragged him through the muck for fifty yards. The tower sent some Marines to assist, and they hauled Conzett off to the first-aid tent. Cales headed for his tent, feeling lucky to be alive. He intended to quiz his pilot later as to what exactly he was thinking during all of the unorthodox flying.

Spike Conzett's buddies came to visit him in the hospital tent the next morning. Chris Fink saw that he was heavily wrapped below the knee and learned that Conzett still had chunks of shrapnel embedded in his leg. War correspondent Dick Tregaskis, future author of *Guadalcanal Diary,* also visited with the wounded VS-5 pilot. "One of his long legs was bandaged, in the region of the knee, and he looked a bit drawn," Tregaskis wrote.[58]

Conzett told Tregaskis he had tried to fly the plane back home on instruments, "and that didn't work out very well." He admitted that he was not in his element when he did find Guadalcanal. "I was pretty feeble when I reached there," Conzett said, "and I couldn't find the runway. I was lucky to get in at all."

SEVENTEEN
"Heroes All"

Hal Buell figured he was in the clear. On August 30, the Pagoda's warning flags and siren had correctly alerted the Cactus Air Force of Tojo Time. At 1145, eighteen Zeros swept in, fighting a fierce engagement with Dale Brannon's P-400s and John Smith's Marine Wildcats. Four Army fighters were downed in the engagement, but the Japanese lost twice as many Zeros.

Once the all-clear was signaled, the fighters pancaked on the field to refuel. Buell and several other Scouting Five airmen then waded into the Lunga River stark naked to wash their bodies and their stinking clothes. Everyone at Henderson Field was in for a rude surprise, however, as the Japanese uncharacteristically followed up with a second group of eighteen Betty bombers with thirteen Zero escorts. The destroyer transport *Colhoun* was caught off Lunga Point and was sunk by four bomb hits that killed fifty of her men.[1]

Other bombs rained down near the airfield. "Everyone got out of the water, and took cover as best he could—each bare as the day he was born," recalled Ensign Buell. One cluster of bombs hit close enough to shake up the Flight 300 airmen. Another bomb touched off an ammo dump, "causing a fireworks display rivaling any Fourth of July celebration I had ever seen," said Buell.[2]

The second Japanese air strike had caught Cactus completely off guard. The one bright spot for General Geiger's 1st MAW was the arrival of reinforcements. Nineteen Wildcat fighters from Major Robert Edward Galer's VMF-224 flew in from Espíritu Santo (code name "Button") with a dozen SBD-3 dive-bombers from VMSB-231, under Major Leo R. Smith. Scouting Five's and Bombing Six's airmen would enjoy a bit of a breather, thanks to some of the new Marine crews.

Spike Conzett was airlifted out of Cactus on September 1 to Espíritu Santo, where he could undergo proper surgery to remove the remaining shrapnel from his leg. More troubling than the personnel losses—Conzett, Brown, and Fives, so far—was the airplane attrition. Navy and Marine crews alike manned whatever SBDs were ready when strikes were ordered, and some of Flight 300's dive-bombers had been lost by Marines. Jim Cales learned that there would be no quick departure from the Canal for him, according to Lieutenant Caldwell.

"Skipper says we stay here as long as planes last," Cales wrote in his diary. "Our planes are going fairly fast but not fast enough for this boy."[3]

During the Tojo Time air raid on September 1, the Japanese bombers torched another of Henderson Field's aircraft hangars and set fire to three SBDs. Several crews were ordered to take off at about 2100 under fire to attack warships that were shelling the airfield. Hal Buell was roaring down the runway, preparing to pull up into the air when a shell exploded under his SBD. His plane was thrown off course to the left. He frantically tried to pull his bomber into the air to miss Dog Barker and Buck Manford in SBDs that were taxiing to take off.[4]

Buell had insufficient flying speed, however, and stalled. His Dauntless hit a small steamroller parked near the runway and splintered as it flew, slid, and rolled another fifty yards before coming to a halt. "I was out of the crash almost before it stopped moving, fearing fire," he said. His engine was torn free from its firewall, and both wheels were broken off. Only stubs remained of his two wings. Rear gunner Johnny Villarreal was stunned and left dangling by his safety belt from the wreckage of his rear cockpit. Blood spurted from a laceration around Buell's left eye and his thighs were sore from the beating they had taken from his control stick as the wings were shorn off. Marines loaded the battered VS-5 aviators into a jeep and took them to the field hospital. Buell passed out from blood loss as doctors helped him onto the table.[5]

When he came to in a stretcher, his left eye was bandaged. "My body was a mass of contusions and scratches, and mammoth bruises stretched from my crotch to my knees on the insides of both legs, and along each arm from wrists to elbows," he said. Walt Coolbaugh brought Buell a change of clothing to replace the flight suit the Marine medics had cut off him.

One bright spot on the next day was the return of Walt Brown and Tony Fives to Henderson Field, recovered from their water ordeal. Turner Caldwell's only pleasure at Guadalcanal was an occasional bath or doing laundry in the cool Lunga River to the west. "The only soap available was that captured in the landing, and it did not lather too well, but it was better than nothing," he said. Caldwell, accustomed to shaving with an electric razor on *Enterprise*, decided to let his beard grow out. "Though my hair is an undistinguished brown, my beard came in a pleasant red," he wrote. "In time I grew proud of it, in spite of the continuous itch."[6]

Marines warned the Navy fliers any nick suffered while shaving could lead to dengue fever. The men scratched themselves raw from mosquito bites and suffered painful rashes from the chafing of sweaty skin. Large rats and ants carried off anything not properly covered. Even those who ventured into the Guadalcanal streams had to be mindful of leeches and snakes. "We ate our Atabrine and hoped for the best," said Chris Fink. "Even at that, several still were shipped out with malaria. Liffner lost so much weight that if he swallowed an olive he'd have looked pregnant," said Fink.[7]

The *Enterprise* Dauntless crews felt abandoned by their Navy on Guadalcanal, but other squadrons soon became orphaned during the campaign.

Saratoga and *Wasp* were still patrolling the Solomon waters, and their task force was joined on August 29 by *Hornet*'s Task Force 17. Two days later, Admiral Fletcher learned why the waters near Guadalcanal were becoming known as Torpedo Junction. His flagship *Saratoga* collected a submarine torpedo for the second time in 1942. Gunner Bill Rambur of VS-3 was sitting on the flight deck mule, the little tractor used to tow airplanes into position, when he spotted a warhead streaking in. The resulting explosion shook the deck and blew a wall of oily water high into the sky. As the sea crashed down around him, Rambur held tightly to a chain guardrail to keep from being swept from the deck. It was his second experience with *Saratoga* catching a torpedo.

Sister Sara was effectively out of the Guadalcanal campaign. Most of her VS-3 and VT-3 planes were flown off to Espíritu Santo and *Saratoga* headed for Pearl Harbor and repairs. Espíritu, the largest island of the New Hebrides chain, was code-named Button by the Allies. Construction crews had opened the new airfield there only at the end of July by hacking a strip 4,500 feet long by 200 feet wide from the jungle. Bullet Lou Kirn's scouts began building a VS-3 camp, but their new home at Button would soon be exchanged for camping at Cactus, located some 558 miles away.[8]

The Cactus Air Force received a big boost on September 2 in preparing its aviators for the routine Tojo Time attacks. The Marine Air Wing placed a big SCR-270-B air-search radar unit, received from the 3rd Defense Battalion, near aviation headquarters at the main field. With an extreme range of 150 miles, the radar could now detect incoming Japanese planes still over New Georgia Island. Seabees of the 6th Naval Construction Battalion had come ashore at Cactus and assumed the maintenance duties at Henderson Field.[9]

Turner Caldwell's Flight 300 was back in action that night. His Navy crews launched at 0100 to bomb and strafe landing boats on Santa Isabel Island and the northwest tip of Guadalcanal. Caldwell led Woodhull, Guillory, Coolbaugh, Buell, Brown, Barker, Fink, Liffner, and Manford. Jim Cales returned to the air as a substitute for Ensign Coolbaugh, whose regular gunner, Jaeger, was suffering from sickness. "The weather was miserable—misty and foggy—and it was a very dark night," said Jesse Barker. "But the decision was made to send us out anyway." The *Enterprise* flight found the landing boats covered and camouflaged on the beach. Barker unleashed his small bombs from low altitude on the landing barges. Results were difficult to judge in the dark, although Marine intelligence credited them with extreme damage inflicted.[10]

Later that day, Lieutenant Caldwell led an afternoon mission with four Marine SBDs to bomb and strafe landing barges and shore installations on northwest Guadalcanal. Dick Mangrum took out eleven of his Marine SBDs the following morning, September 3, to continue smashing the Japanese landing boats that were ferrying troops to Guadalcanal.

Caldwell led four Marine SBDs that afternoon to hit barges and shore installations in the Cape Esperance area of Guadalcanal.

The biggest news of the day was the arrival of new Marine air command at Cactus: Major General Roy Stanley Geiger, Colonel Louis E. Woods, his chief of staff, and Lieutenant Colonel John Calvin "Toby" Munn, the 1st Marine Air Wing (1st MAW) intelligence officer. General Geiger, known for his cold stare and frank manner, had earned his wings in 1917 as Marine Aviator No. 5 and had fought in World War I. Geiger, Woods, and Munn now controlled all aviation on Guadalcanal under General Vandegrift, the commanding general on Cactus.[11]

Malaria, dysentery, and other tropical ailments took their toll on the Navy boys. Jim Cales was sidelined with severe sickness and a burning 104.4-degree fever. He slept outdoors in the makeshift sick bay, which he found more comforting than the coconut tree leaf bed he had first slept on. Cales helped keep his fever down by lying in the cool Lunga River waters during the day, but it would be days before he was strong enough to fly as a relief crewman again.[12]

Turner Caldwell led a strike at 1005 on September 4. He had Fink, Coolbaugh, Woodhull, and Guillory from his command, plus another eight Marine SBDs under Dick Mangrum and eight Wildcat escorts. They went to hit thirty-nine Japanese landing boats on Santa Isabel Island, five miles northwest of Ortega Channel, and on San Jorge Island.

Approximately one-third of the beached and camouflaged Japanese landing craft were seventy feet long and the rest about forty feet long. Each Dauntless was armed with one five-hundred-pound bomb and two smaller hundred-pound wing bombs. Caldwell signaled his Navy bombers to attack as best they could. He flew in low over a hill and down through an inlet straight to the barges. He dumped his loads of smaller bombs on the boats while firing his forward .50s into the surrounding area. From his rear cockpit, Rocky Glidewell blazed away at boats and installations with his twin .30s. They were barely a hundred feet above the barges. Glidewell saw flak rising from the small-arms fire below and concentrated on firing into the brush line where he assumed troops were hiding.

As Caldwell came back around for his second bombing and strafing pass, the Japanese got their range on his plane. Automatic fire struck the bottom side of his Dauntless several times, knocking out a few of the sway braces that had held his ordnance. "It was the first time I had bullets close enough to hear them," said Glidewell. He heard the zip of bullets flying by and then suddenly felt a sharp sting in his right arm.

Caldwell was alarmed when Glidewell called up faintly over their intercom, "I've been hit." Blood streamed from his arm but he realized the bullet had not shattered any bones. He informed Caldwell that he was okay and then continued firing his Brownings. Caldwell dropped his big bomb and decided it was time to seek help for his veteran gunner. His SBDs had splintered three of the boats with bomb hits, and had chewed up the others with machine-gun bullets. Caldwell's strike was back safely at Henderson Field by 1355, straggling in behind their fighter escort.

On the ground, Glidewell was sent to the little hospital tent near the field. The doctor assured him he had only been grazed by a small bullet of about .30 caliber. He cleaned out the wound, sprinkled it with sulfa powder, and wrapped his arm in bandages. With that, Glidewell was sent back to rejoin his squadron. There was no downtime on Henderson Field for him. Al Garlow filled in for him on one flight with the skipper, but resilient former boxer Glidewell was back in the ring in his cockpit the following day.

The Cactus Air Force endured another heavy shelling during the early hours of September 6. Five Japanese warships worked over the beachhead and airfield for about an hour. Buck Manford jumped into a foxhole as the shelling started, only to have a Marine jump in right behind him and land a boot on his face. The next day, Manford sported a fresh black eye as a souvenir of the night bombardment.[13]

At 1050, eleven SBDs under Major Smith and six VMF-224 Wildcats took off to bomb Gizo Harbor ships and shore installations. Harry Liffner and Gene Braun were the only members of Flight 300 to make this strike. Heavy weather forced two Marine SBDs to return, but the balance of Smith's flight carried out their mission. Turner Caldwell took five Marine SBD crews out in the afternoon to attack a destroyer reported at Russell Island, but found only a seventy-foot boat, which they laced with machine-gun bullets.

The Tojo Time raid this day was effective in hitting Hangar No. 4

Albert Garlow collection, courtesy of David Massicot

The *Enterprise* Flight 300 rear gunners pose in early September 1942 near Guadalcanal's Henderson Field: (*front row, left to right*) Rocky Glidewell (his arm bandaged due to a bullet wound), Homer Joselyn, Tony Fives, and Al Garlow; (*back row, left to right*) Milo Kimberlin, Jim Cales, Gene Monahan, Gene Braun, Stuart Mason, Charles Jaeger, and Johnny Villarreal. Note that most of the radiomen are wearing service revolvers and are clutching Japanese souvenirs obtained from their Marine buddies. Villarreal is wearing a Japanese samurai sword.

and in burning up an SBD parked near it. Fortunately, Caldwell's VS-5 and VB-6 Navy unit at Guadalcanal were reinforced by Scouting Three SBDs on September 6. At Button, Lieutenant Commander Bullet Lou Kirn asked for six volunteer SBD crews. Lieutenant Bob Milner led the crews of Lieutenant (j.g.) Alan Frank and Ensigns Roger Crow, Bob Pellissier, Oran Newton, and Emory Wages from Espíritu to Cactus. "We had to depend on the Marines for everything except combat crews because we didn't bring our own ground crew in to Guadalcanal," Milner said. Jesse Barker had a mini-reunion with some of the VS-3 pilots and gunners, whom he had flown with prior to joining VS-5.[14]

Al Garlow and his fellow radiomen struggled to keep their planes patched up enough to fly. One day he found they didn't have the right tools for some repairs, so he slipped into a Marine supply hut to liberate some gear. Garlow spotted a toolbox on a bench, glanced around to make sure no one was looking, and then made a grab for it. The toolbox refused to move. Some wise Marine had fastened it securely to the bench.

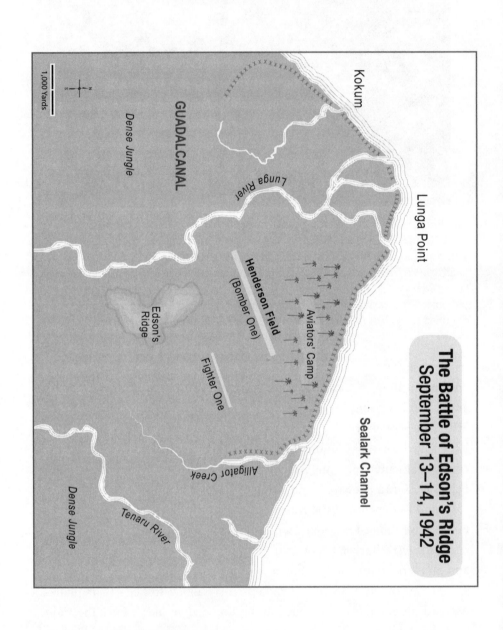

The Battle of Edson's Ridge
September 13–14, 1942

Kokum

Lunga Point

Sealark Channel

GUADALCANAL

Dense Jungle

Lunga River

Henderson Field
(Bomber One)

Edson's
Ridge

Fighter One

Aviators' Camp

Alligator Creek

Tenaru River

Dense Jungle

1,000 Yards

The local Seabees were making progress on Hell's Island. During early September they cut the high grass of a meadow about a mile to the east of Henderson Field and tamped it down to create a new airstrip. The "cow pasture" was soon dubbed Fighter Field No. 1 (or Fighter One), and on September 9 the Marine fighter squadrons began operating from it. With Fighter One now in place, the original Henderson airstrip became known as Bomber One.

The arrival of the first six VS-3 crews provided Lieutenant Caldwell some relief in the flight schedules. Heavy rains on September 8 and 9 made Bomber One a muddy mess, even with the additional Marston matting laid down by the Seabees. Caldwell's next mission was with Buck Manford and Chris Fink on September 10 against shore installations. The following day, Manford and Coolbaugh went out with Dick Mangrum's Marine SBDs to attack installations on Gizo. During their absence, Cactus was pounded by about twenty-six Japanese bombers during the noon hour. They destroyed one Army P-400 on the ground, killed eleven Marines, and injured seventeen more. In the swirling dogfights with the Zeros, Major Robert Galer was shot down but managed to swim ashore.[15]

The Tojo Time noon raid on September 11 destroyed three SBDs caught on the ground and damaged Henderson Field's radio shack. One wounded VF-5 pilot cracked up his F4F while trying to make a dead-stick landing and was killed. The afternoon scouts that day found two destroyers and a cruiser only a hundred miles northwest of Guadalcanal. Turner Caldwell, Coolbaugh, Buell, and Fink were included in the thirteen-SBD group that took off to attack them. Only four planes managed to make contact due to lousy visibility, and the frustrated pilots claimed only one near miss. "A thorough .50-caliber strafing was all we could do," Caldwell said.[16]

The Cactus Air Force received a morale boost that afternoon when an entire Wildcat squadron arrived as reinforcement. Lieutenant Commander Leroy "Roy" Simpler brought in two dozen F4Fs from his old *Saratoga* VF-5 from Button at 1620. The next afternoon, September 12, brought indications that the Japanese were beefing up their strike efforts. Bob Milner's VS-3 search team reported another Japanese Rat Patrol in the vicinity. Cactus veterans knew what to expect: They would probably be crouching in foxholes before the night was over. "We are fighting for our very lives," Ensign Francis Register of VF-5 wrote in his diary this day. "May God give us the strength and help us."[17]

As expected, the Japanese destroyers made their presence known during the early-morning hours of September 13. "We knew we were in for it when an overhead plane dropped a flare on top of our bivouac area," said Hal Buell. Gunner Stuart Mason and tent mate Milo Kimberlin scrambled for cover. They had dug a foxhole large enough for two outside their tent and had covered it with boards and dirt. As the heavy shells screamed overhead, Mason and Kimberlin were joined by gunners Homer Joselyn and Gene Braun, making for very tight quarters. Explosions rained down with accuracy more alarming than usual. "The shells were coming right through our camp and sounded like railroad locomotives," said Mason.[18]

Al Garlow and tent mate Jim Cales were caught off guard by the sudden shelling. They simply hit the deck out in the open. Cales locked arms with Garlow and lay facedown in the dirt, expecting the worst. "Chris Fink and I dug a slit trench outside our tent between a pair of palm trees," said Jesse Barker. "Everyone made fun of us." Tent mate Buell and pilots Woodhull, Guillory, and Coolbaugh from the next tent were happy to jump into Barker and Fink's trench. Coolbaugh methodically counted the explosions as they erupted nearby. "The shells were cutting trees off right over our heads, and the shrapnel was falling around us like hailstones," said Buell. Lieutenant Caldwell cheated death by diving into the shared foxhole just as a large-caliber shell exploded over the tent area. "The aiming point was our grove of rubber trees, which was marked prominently on the maps," Caldwell said. Just yards away, Larry Baldinus and Second Lieutenant Donald V. Rose of VMSB-232 were killed and two others were wounded as shrapnel shredded their tent.[19]

"We have had shellings before, but this one is beyond belief," fighter pilot Bob Ferguson wrote in his diary. When the shelling finally stopped, Caldwell was unable to sleep due to a persistent quivering of the muscles in one of his legs. "I thought it must be a nervous reaction to the shelling," he said. "But it persisted." At last, he got up and felt around inside his blanket, where he found a small lizard trying to wriggle free. "He probably was more frightened than I." After daylight, Caldwell found that his tent was riddled—its tent pole halved by a shell—and his cot had a hole blasted right through it.[20]

Artillery, mortar, and small-arms fire continued in the hills just south of Henderson Field. More than 2,100 Japanese troops were intent on overrunning the airfield. Lieutenant Colonel Merritt "Red Mike" Edson's Raiders were engaged in a serious fight through the night as soldiers charged them. The Japanese suffered heavy casualties although a few of the soldiers did make it to Henderson Field before they were killed. Caldwell and his aviators were approached by a Marine who warned them that the fighting was getting close. He told them if they heard a certain signal, they were to run to a Quonset hut to be issued a rifle. Gunner Al Garlow became nervous when he heard the Marines say, "It will be every man for himself." "Things were so bad on the front lines, we were all issued two bandoleers of ammo and a rifle," said Stu Mason. "I hadn't fired a rifle since boot camp."[21]

The intense three days of fighting along Lunga Ridge became known at the time as the Battle of the Ridge. After the battle, Lunga Ridge was known to the Marines as Edson's Ridge, although war correspondents dubbed it Bloody Ridge. The Japanese had one purpose in their fight on Guadalcanal—to recapture their airfield. One of their battalion commanders, Major Yukichi Kokusho, passed the word to his troops, "We must sacrifice our lives to serve our emperor and our country." Kokusho and an estimated one thousand of his troops did just that in the multi-day assault on Bloody Ridge.[22]

Just before daybreak, word reached the Flight 300 aviators that their field had been secured. Hal Buell and Johnny Villarreal, scheduled for the dawn search, were dropped off at their assigned SBD in the parking area southwest of the runway. Buell noticed a young Marine seated in the front cockpit, cleaning his automatic weapon as he approached. "In the darkness, I did not notice the dead Japanese soldier until I almost tripped over him," Buell said.[23]

The body was lying on the ground a few feet from the aircraft's tail on the starboard side. The Marine explained that Red Mike had assigned one Raider to each aircraft to prevent the enemy from trying to destroy them. He had given the Japanese soldier a burst of fire into the chest when he jumped up onto the SBD's wing in the darkness. "A large, bloody smear ran down the wing from the cockpit to the trailing edge of the flaps," said Buell. He and Villarreal thanked the Marine for his vigilance and warmed up their bloodstained Dauntless for its next mission.

Three P-400s of the 67th VF took off at first light to strafe Japanese troops advancing over Bloody Ridge toward the airfield. The Marines held the line through the day while Henderson Field endured the expected Japanese air raids. Twenty-eight Wildcats scrambled to engage a late-morning fighter sweep. They dropped four Zeros in aerial combat, but the Cactus Air Force lost two pilots and two planes, plus two other pilots wounded. Right behind this strike came the usual Tojo Time bombing raid, comprising twenty-six Bettys and a dozen Zeros. Seven Marine fighters and nine of Roy Simpler's VF-5 Navy Wildcats knocked down a Zero and a Betty at the cost of four Wildcats and one pilot lost.[24]

Later that afternoon, another group of former *Saratoga* aviators came to join the Cactus Air Force. Bullet Lou Kirn led twelve of his VS-3 scouts on the four-hour flight, along with six of Lieutenant Swede Larsen's Torpedo Eight TBFs. The *Saratoga* planes arrived at 1740, the worst possible moment. Ten minutes earlier, two float-type Zero fighters had killed Second Lieutenant Owen D. Johnson, just as he was approaching the landing strip after a scout mission in his Marine SBD.[25]

"They were more than a little upset," Kirn said of the Marines on Henderson Field. "I was suddenly challenged over the radio to identify myself immediately or I would be fired upon." Kirn's radioman and others called Cactus command frantically to advise them that they were flying Dauntless dive-bombers. After landing, Lieutenant Commander Kirn learned that one of his young pilots, Ensign Emory Wages, had been lost that afternoon when he was forced to ditch at sea. Kirn's fresh SBDs were thus a welcomed sight after the loss of two crews from the Canal in a matter of hours.

The replacement *Saratoga* crews were treated to a late-night bombardment from the Japanese and the chattering of machine guns at all hours. On September 14, Lou Kirn's VS-3 crews set up five tents and dug their foxholes nearby while he partnered with Turner Caldwell to understand the situation they faced. The Cactus Air Force now sported

Scouting Squadron Three (VS-3)			
Aircrews Deployed to Henderson Field			
PILOT	**RADIOMAN/ GUNNER**	**DATE IN**	**DATE OUT**
Lt. Robert Miller Milner	ARM2c Gerald J. Farrell	9/6/42	10/12/42
Lt. (j.g.) Alan Stetson Frank	ARM2c Darrell H. Beaman	9/6/42	10/17/42
Ens. Roger Curtis Crow	ARM3c Thomas H. Miner	9/6/42	10/6/42
Ens. Oran Newton Jr.	ARM3c Robert Sarrel Thornton	9/6/42	KIA 9/16
Ens. Robert Edmund Pellissier	ARM3c William T. Stafford Jr.	9/6/42	9/16/42
Ens. Emory Speer Wages Jr.	Sea2c James Henry	9/6/42	MIA 9/13
Lt. Cdr. Louis Joseph Kirn	ACRM Carl Edgar Russ	9/13/42	10/17/42
Lt. Martin Paul McNair	ARM2c William Michael Rambur	9/13/42	10/17/42
Lt. Frederick John Schroeder	ARM2c Alfred Wayne Dobson	9/13/42	9/20/42
Lt. Ralph Weymouth	ARM3c Clyde R. Simpson	9/13/42	10/17/42

(continued)

Scouting Squadron Three (VS-3)			
Aircrews Deployed to Henderson Field			
PILOT	**RADIOMAN/ GUNNER**	**DATE IN**	**DATE OUT**
Lt. (j.g.) William Earl Henry	ARM3c Willard L. Wright	9/13/42	10/17/42
Lt. (j.g.) Elwood Charles Mildahn	ARM2c Balford A. Sumner	9/13/42	10/17/42
Ens. Daniel W. Byerly	ARM3c Edward Ladwick	9/13/42	10/17/42
Ens. Richard C. Purdum	ARM3c Morton Lachowitz	9/13/42	10/17/42
Ens. Allard Guy Russell	ARM3c Gordon D. Bradberry	9/13/42	10/17/42
Ens. Francis James Sauer	ARM3c Robert Hansen	9/13/42	10/17/42
Ens. Neil Scott Weary	ARM3c Marvin K. Taylor	9/13/42	10/17/42
Ens. Alfred Wright	ARM3c Melvin M. Bryson	9/13/42	10/17/42
Lt. (j.g.) Richard P. Balenti	ARM3c K. L. Johnson	9/28/42	10/17/42
Lt. (j.g.) James Jennings Davidson	ARM3c Charles M. Gunter	9/28/42	10/17/42
Lt. (j.g.) William James Foley Jr.	ARM1c John W. Schliekelman	9/28/42	10/17/42

portions of five different SBD units: VMSB-141, VMSB-142, VS-5, VB-6, and VS-3. One of Kirn's pilots, Bill Henry, recalled: "We took very little in clothes with us and at Guadalcanal it didn't make much difference. Everybody looked like bums in no time."[26]

Jesse Barker flew most missions with his regular VS-5 gunner Gene Monahan, but sickness and rapid scrambles sometimes made for mixed crews. On other occasions, the Navy boys were happy to take a Marine comrade up for a hop. "One afternoon, I took up a Marine major who was just busting a gut to go up and encounter some Jap shipping," said Barker. "I put him in the rear seat and he flew with his Thompson submachine gun in his lap along with his two .30-caliber machine guns. We didn't run into a thing on that flight, so he just had a ride."[27]

Chris Fink and Hal Buell of VS-5 were included in a thirteen-SBD strike led by Bullet Lou Kirn that departed in the late afternoon of September 16. Two destroyers and two cruisers were coming down the Slot. Buell and two other pilots claimed three near misses against one of the cruisers, while the other pilots reported one hit and three near misses on a destroyer. In return, AA fire claimed the lives of VS-3 pilot Oran Newton and gunner Robert Thornton. Japanese troops clashed with Marines around the perimeters of Henderson Field that night. Buell scribbled in his diary, "The nights are tough, as we never know what to expect from these yellow bastards."[28]

On the morning of September 17, the Cactus Air Force had twenty-nine F4Fs, twenty-six SBD-3s, five TBFs, and three P-400 fighters considered airworthy. Four SBDs were sent out by Hal Buell that evening to attack two warships reported twenty miles from the northeast corner of New Georgia Island. No hits were made and a larger bombing mission to Gizo Island that evening was equally frustrated. Bad weather and poor visibility prevented the Cactus force from attacking Japanese ships in the harbor. During the return flight, Second Lieutenant Alan Miller Smith of VMSB-231 and his gunner were lost.

By day's end, three ill pilots—Buck Manford and Roger Woodhull of Flight 300, plus Bob Pellissier of VS-3—were evacuated from Guadalcanal via transport plane to Espíritu Santo. Despite suffering from extreme sickness and weight loss for days, Woodhull had continued to give his all until Lieutenant Caldwell made the call to ship out his ailing XO.

Manford was equally bony after losing thirty-five pounds. "Everyone is sick," Jim Cales wrote in his diary. "I haven't flown last few days but always standing by ready."[29]

Dauntless strength on Hell's Island dropped to twenty-four planes when a VMSB-232 SBD was shot down on September 18. The Avenger count increased this day, however, as Lieutenant Bruce Harwood arrived with six new TBFs from Button and seven pilots. Fred Mears, one of the new VT-8 pilots, had been briefed on what he could expect at Guadalcanal by Buck Manford, one of Flight 300's evacuees.

"He looked like a worn-out bum," said Mears. "His eyes were prominent and circled, he was thin as a bunch of sticks, his clothes were filthy, and he needed a shave." Manford detailed the daily bombing attacks, the inferior food, the illnesses on the island, the countless scouting missions flown by the Marine and Navy crews at Cactus, and the nightly artillery and warship bombardments.[30]

Lou Kirn believed that pilots carried out their missions "with fervor when they went out." When they returned, however, "they would think about it and then wonder whether the next flight was going to be the one from which they were not to come back."

Torpedo Junction, the deadly waters off the Solomon Islands, continued to live up to its nickname. Japanese submarines in this dangerous alley had picked off a number of Allied ships, including the carrier *Saratoga* at the end of August. The next victim was the carrier *Wasp*.

Wasp had departed Nouméa on September 7. While there, her air group had taken on spare Bombing Six pilots recently detached from *Enterprise*. Ensigns Dick Jaccard, Don Ely, and Warren Bolt helped round out VS-71, while VB-6 pilots Carl Horenburger, Bob Shaw, and Dan Dopuch were assigned to VS-72. One week out to sea, *Wasp* was operating in conjunction with the *Hornet* Air Group. Ensign Cook Cleland of VS-72 was flying IAP on September 15 to watch for submarines near his task force with two other pilots. Cleland spotted a diving submarine and swooped in so that his gunner, Seaman Second Class James Pein, could drop a smoke light to mark its location. Cleland flew in low over *Wasp*'s deck as Pein dropped a beanbag message with the submarine's coordinates.[31]

By 1320, Cleland's section was due to be relieved on anti-submarine patrol. They circled near *Wasp* as she turned into the wind some 150 miles southeast of San Cristobal. The carrier first launched the next IAP group and Lieutenant Commander John Eldridge with fourteen VS-71 SBDs for an afternoon scout mission. Cookie Cleland landed and taxied to the elevator, and his Dauntless was lowered to the hangar deck to join thirty-seven other parked aircraft. On the flight deck were a number of armed and gassed aircraft ready for deployment: a dozen F4Fs, ten TBFs armed with torpedoes, ten Dauntlesses, and an unarmed amphibious J2F Duck.[32]

TF-61 turned to starboard at 1342 to resume its base course. Cleland had scarcely left his Dauntless behind on the hangar at 1345 when shouts went up that torpedoes were spotted headed toward the starboard bow. They came from Commander Kinashi Takaichi's *I-19*, which had launched a spread of six torpedoes. Three of them connected with *Wasp* with devastating effects. The explosions flooded bomb and powder magazines, ruptured aviation gasoline tanks, and triggered a blast that blew the bomb elevator's armored hatch cover onto the flight deck. *I-19*'s other torpedoes plowed through TF-18 and toward Admiral Murray's TF-17 five to seven miles away. The destroyer *O'Brien* was rocked by a torpedo and her damage was so severe that she would later sink en route to Pearl Harbor. Another torpedo ripped a large hole in the battleship *North Carolina*'s bow. She was damaged but would continue with the task force.[33]

Thick, black smoke rolled from *Wasp*'s hangar deck, where gasoline fires erupted from Wildcat fighters knocked from the hangar's overhead storage. A number of black mess attendants, officers' cooks, and stewards from the two scouting squadrons and from VF-71 were killed when the second torpedo blew up directly below the officers' galley. Two former VB-6 *Enterprise* pilots on temporary duty with VS-71, Ensigns Warren Guy Bolt and Midway veteran Dick Jaccard, were killed in their staterooms. From VS-72, Ensigns Charles Cecil Littel and Thomas Center Reed also perished.

The explosions and sweeping fires forced Captain Forrest Sherman to order abandon ship only thirty-five minutes after the first torpedo explosion. Cook Cleland swam through burning oil and ended up clinging to a little wood-slat life raft with sixteen others. During his four-hour ordeal in the ocean, Cleland saw destroyers make depth-charge runs on suspected Japanese submarine contacts. The charges were "so close that the underwater explosions were shoving water up our bungs. The water straightened out your guts. It was like a hose whipping around in your stomach." They resorted to a tactic they had been taught to help lessen the chances of internal injuries. "We all shoved our fingers up our butts and swam like hell," Cleland said. "If you got tired, you changed fingers."[34]

Wasp's circling airplanes were in a quandary. "We were outside of land range and low on fuel," said Ensign Nate Murphy of VS-71. "Luckily, some smart soul on the *Hornet* envisioned our predicament and sent their planes to the *Wasp* to lead us to the *Hornet*." Pilot Porter Maxwell could see that his *Wasp* was "burning fiercely and huge explosions rocked her hull at frequent intervals." Maxwell, Eldridge, Murphy, and most of VS-71 were taken aboard Captain Charles P. Mason's *Hornet*, with the exception of Ensign Bob Escher—who ran out of fuel and ditched. The destroyer *Duncan* retrieved Escher and his gunner, although in the forced landing the pilot had permanently damaged an eye on his gun sight. *Hornet* then flew off fifteen SBDs, five VT-6 TBFs, and eight VF-72 Wildcats to Espíritu Santo some two hundred miles away while *Wasp* was being abandoned. The blazing *Wasp* slipped beneath the waves at 2100, aided by torpedoes from the destroyer *Lansdowne* to prevent the carrier from being salvaged by the Japanese. The overcrowded *Hornet* sent more SBDs and F4Fs into Espíritu Santo on September 16. The loss of *Wasp* left only *Hornet* and *Enterprise* available for service in the Solomons, but the VS-71 airmen marooned at Button would soon become a valuable resource for the Cactus Air Force.

Turner Caldwell's Flight 300 aviators had been on Guadalcanal for nearly a month. Many of the planes they had arrived in had been lost due to ditchings, bomb damage, and enemy bombardments. Ensign Chris Fink of VB-6 lost another of the group's SBDs on September 19.

He was flying an afternoon scouting sector with Walt Coolbaugh when at 1600 the pair spotted a large Japanese convoy near Gizo. Fink and Coolbaugh were chased off by four enemy floatplanes, and Fink ran out of gas before he could reach Cactus. He put his Dauntless down in the water at 1700 and scrambled into his life raft with Milo Kimberlin.

A Marine amphibious plane crew was unable to recover them before dark. Lieutenant Colonel Charles Fike returned in the J2F Duck the following morning, however, and discovered them drifting between Savo Island and Cape Esperance. Fike retrieved the uninjured Kimberlin and Fink and returned them to Guadalcanal.

Pilots Hal Buell, Troy Guillory, and Harry Liffner were evaced by a DC-3 transport plane to Button on September 19. Liffner's five-foot-eleven frame was thin, as he had lost some twenty-five pounds. "Emotions ran high as the jungle hellhole faded from view beneath the wingtips," said Buell. "I had the elation of a survivor combined with the sorrow of leaving behind so many friends and fellow CAF [Cactus Air Force] pilots still engaged in the unequal struggle."[35]

Those still roughing it near Henderson Field endured another naval bombardment during the early minutes of September 20. Night scouts were ordered out to patrol, but Roger Crow of VS-3 destroyed his SBD as he tried to take off in the dark. He cracked up, smashing into a parked DC-3 and tearing the wing off an R4D hospital aircraft parked on the runway. Crow suffered broken ribs and an injured back in the crash but was back on the flight schedule the following day. Such was the seriousness of the situation on the Canal, where the airmen had to dodge potshots from Japanese snipers near the field again that day.[36]

Turner Caldwell's remaining crews had turned over the bulk of the flight duties to Bullet Lou Kirn's fresher Scouting Three. Scouting Five gunner Jim Cales, bored with the inactivity by September 21, hiked up to the front lines with Walt Brown and Walt Coolbaugh to watch some of the Marines pounding away at the Japanese with their artillery.[37]

During the early hours of September 22, Scouting Three made night attacks on Tokyo Express destroyers. Three of Torpedo Eight's TBFs made bombing attacks to help the Marines and General Geiger even took an SBD up the same day to drop a thousand-pound bomb. Squadron leaders Dick Mangrum and Caldwell were visited that afternoon by war correspondent Dick Tregaskis. Their units had been largely idle since fresh SBD crews arrived, but both leaders continued to fly when needed. "They had both grown thin as scarecrows and their faces were haggard," Tregaskis wrote. "They told me they were exhausted from the night-and-day stint of work they had been doing."[38]

Caldwell admitted that the constant strain of life on the Canal had worn down some of the crews. He had originally scoffed at medics who cautioned about the potential of pilot fatigue. "Now I know what they meant," said Caldwell. "There's a point where you just get to be no good; you're shot to the devil—and there's nothing you can do about it."

Flight 300's time at Cactus was winding to a close. On September 23, Lieutenant Colonel Albert Dustin Cooley arrived at Henderson Field as the new commanding officer of Marine Air Group 14. Colonel William J. Wallace took on Fighter Command with the Marine fighter squadrons, the 67th Pursuit Squadron, and VF-5 from *Saratoga*. Cooley led Strike Command—comprised of Caldwell's Flight 300, VMSB-231, VMSB-232, Lou Kirn's VS-3, and Swede Larsen's VT-8. Two days later, Seabees began widening Bomber One and adding newly received Marston matting to finish covering Henderson's original airstrip.[39]

Walt Coolbaugh, flying the afternoon B Sector search the following day, radioed a report at 1500 of four enemy destroyers and a cruiser two hundred miles from Cactus. Coolbaugh and Second Lieutenant Donald E. McCafferty attacked, landing one bomb about twenty feet from the light cruiser. Other SBDs manned by Marine and VS-3 crews bombed destroyers during the late afternoon. Ensign Alfred Wright survived a brush with two Japanese biplane float fighters and returned a badly shot-up Dauntless to Henderson Field.

Colonel Cooley ordered out another mixed bag of SBDs at 2135 to try to slow the incoming Cactus Express. Turner Caldwell and Walt Brown of VS-5 took part in this strike of nine SBDs, led by Bullet Lou Kirn. In the darkness, only Kirn, Neil Weary, and two other pilots managed to make contact with the warships. Slim Russell of VS-3 landed his thousand-pounder next to the port bow of one destroyer, while a Marine crew was believed to have scored a direct hit. As Russell pulled out of his dive, his SBD was hit by a heavy shell. He could not see any fire but his plane was sluggish to respond. As he headed toward Cactus, low on the water, Lieutenant Caldwell flew up alongside the VS-3 plane to inspect the damage.[40]

"I can see stars through your elevator," Caldwell announced.

During his return, Russell was able to climb his plane slowly, and Henderson Field was cleared for an emergency crash landing. He came in nose heavy, using half flaps, and made a hard landing. "We were really lucky, and I mean lucky," he wrote in his diary that night.

Over the next two days, Caldwell's *Enterprise* aviators saw little action. Martin McNair of VS-3 strafed a small sailing schooner, *Daiwa Maru No. 2*, off Moe Island on September 27. His gunner, Bill Rambur, experienced jammed guns, so McNair returned to Cactus to obtain another Dauntless. He flew back with Chris Fink of Bombing Six. They attacked the little vessel again with machine guns just as it was reaching the beach of Moe Island, killing an estimated half dozen of those on board. For Fink, it was his last combat hop from Guadalcanal. Bombing Six gunner Stu Mason made his last SBD flight on the afternoon before he was airlifted out. A Marine pilot was about to take off without a gunner, so he jumped in the rear cockpit and flew a night patrol with him.[41]

That day, the noon bombing raid on Henderson Field was effective. Eighteen bombers came in at around 1330 with a heavy covering force of thirty-seven Zeros. They were greeted by mixed divisions of Marine fighters and seventeen Fighting Five Navy F4Fs, but only two bombers were destroyed over Guadalcanal. The Japanese bombers damaged five TBFs, six F4Fs, and five SBDs caught on the ground. Their bombs wiped out Turner Caldwell's SBD as it sat on the strip. Slim Russell, watching the attack from a foxhole, saw the SBD's bomb explode, blowing the Dauntless "into thousands of pieces." Jim Cales noted in his diary that the *Enterprise* crews had finally been relieved of their last SBDs. "All planes are blown up or lost," he wrote.[42]

The long-awaited word finally reached Lieutenant Caldwell that afternoon. It was time to take his boys out. The remaining Flight 300 aviators boarded a DC-3 transport plane for the flight to Button. Their five weeks of hell had finally ended. Boarding the outbound flight from VS-5 were Caldwell, Walt Coolbaugh, Dog Barker, Walt Brown, Jim Cales, Charles Jaeger, Gene Monahan, Tony Fives, Rocky Glidewell, and Al Garlow, plus the last of VB-6's aviators—Chris Fink, Homer Joselyn, Stuart Mason, Johnny Villarreal, Milo Kimberlin, and Gene Braun.

At 105 pounds, Coolbaugh was a walking skeleton, having lost more than 50 pounds of his normal body weight since the start of the war. "So much has happened in this past year that I can hardly remember life as it used to be," Coolbaugh wrote to his mother soon after leaving Hell's Island. Stu Mason had gone from 145 pounds down to 129.[43]

Only Fink, Barker, and Brown were still flying at the very end. "Everyone else had dysentery and malaria and the trots," said Barker. "It was really bad." Fink added, "I damn near missed the flight out on an R4D as I was tooling around the Russells jousting with a boatload of Japs which had just landed. But Cactus Tower ordered me home on the double. I landed, taxied near the Pagoda, and went out to the end of the runway, and boarded the plane. Goodbye Guadalcanal."[44]

Gunner Al Garlow was the last to climb into the transport and he was glad to be leaving. Boarding the DC-3 was the brightest moment of his Cactus ordeal for Jim Cales. Colonel Mangrum pulled aside some of the *Enterprise* rear gunners and thanked them for their tireless service during the past month. "You're the best damn bunch of Marines I ever saw in bell-bottom trousers," said Mangrum.[45]

The DC-3 carrying the last of the *Enterprise* crews from Henderson Field landed at Nouméa late on September 27. Lieutenant Caldwell, still sporting his bushy red beard, called on Rear Admiral John Sidney McCain, the commander of the Southwest Pacific Forces. He recommended that the patrol planes be equipped with new airborne radar to detect the Tokyo Express, although McCain was not convinced it would work.

Garlow, Coolbaugh, Barker, Fives, and Cales left on September 30 on the first Martin PBM Mariner to Espíritu Santo. Caldwell and the others followed on a second PBM patrol bomber flying boat. They spent the night at Button on the tender *Curtiss*. Their journey continued the following day, with flights to Suva, Fiji, and on to Canton. Along the way, Cales was chagrined to find that someone had managed to steal most of their liquor supply.[46]

On October 2, the Flight 300 men flew on to Palmyra. During the flight, Caldwell kept company with Captain Forrest Sherman, who had lost his carrier *Wasp* during the campaign. "He was very gloomy," said Caldwell, who tried to encourage the skipper that he had done everything possible to save his ship. During the flight, Caldwell had time to reflect on his weeks at Guadalcanal. He thought of the "fine people" from his *Enterprise* squadrons who had given their all to help hold the line at Cactus. Some would never see home again due to future deployments, but to Caldwell, they were "heroes all."[47]

The Flight 300 veterans arrived at Pearl Harbor on October 3 and spent the night at the CASU 1 hangar. The following day, they were sent to the Royal Hawaiian for proper R&R for several days before receiving new assignments. The enlisted men straggled in on various flights. On October 5, Stu Mason was the last VB-6 gunner to arrive in Hawaii in a PBY.[48]

At Pearl Harbor, the red-bearded, skinny Scouting Five skipper paid a visit to Admiral Bill Halsey on Ford Island. As he poked his grizzled head in the admiral's door, he was greeted by "Who the hell are you?"

"Turner Caldwell, Admiral."

Halsey growled back, "Get rid of that beard and come back to see me."

Caldwell dropped by his parents' home in Kailua, where he gave himself his first clean shave in nearly two months. He returned to see Halsey, asking to be given another tour of duty with a new command. The admiral told him he was needed instead to train a new crop of pilots in Jacksonville, Florida. Caldwell was disappointed, but found that Halsey had a tender spot for him in his heart. "As the recommendations for awards came across his desk, he had mine copied and framed," he recalled. Turner Caldwell was given a Gold Star in lieu of a third Navy Cross for his time on Guadalcanal.[49]

On September 28—the day after the last of *Enterprise*'s Flight 300 were evaced from Henderson Field—more Navy replacements from displaced *Saratoga* and *Wasp* units arrived. Lieutenant Commander John Eldridge began bringing up the first three of his dozen VS-71 SBD crews from Button, and the remaining TBDs of VT-8 were ferried up for use with the Cactus Air Force. On October 2, Bob Milner of VS-3 led six SBDs and five of Lieutenant Bruce Harwood's torpedo-loaded TBFs to attack an inbound Japanese destroyer force. The Cactus strikers achieved nothing better than near misses, and during the return three VT-8 crews became lost in the overcast. Pilots Bill Dye, Andy Divine, and Larry Engel were forced to make water landings. Eighteen-year-old Aviation Radioman Third Class John King, Engel's rear gunner from Springfield,

Illinois, narrowly escaped his ditching. "As soon as we hit the water, I popped my safety belt," he said. Their heavy Avenger bounced on the concrete-hard ocean surface and skipped back into the air. Looking out to sea, King suddenly saw stars twinkling on the horizon. When his torpedo bomber hit the water again, he was standing up. His face was slammed into the bombsight and he suffered a badly injured ankle. Fortunately, the destroyer *Grayson* prowled the coast until all nine downed Torpedo Eight airmen had been rescued.

John Eldridge lost two SBDs on October 2, along with pilots Warren Garrett and Herb Perritte, and Perritte's gunner, Irvin Newsome. Fortunately, VS-71 exec Porter Maxwell arrived from Button with six fresh SBDs and their crews to supplement Cactus. "It was decided that the fairest way to pick who would go was to draw cards for it, the six low ones to go," recalled Ensign Nate Murphy. "Naturally, I drew the deuce of clubs, so the die was cast. We left that day for a four-hour flight and arrived in the middle of a Japanese bombing attack."

The constant combat through all types of weather conditions was brutal on the aircraft. Torpedo Eight lost two more Avengers in the next week and two more SBDs (one from VS-71 and one from VMSB-141) were chalked up to losses as well. Skipper John Eldridge and gunner Lester Powers were picked up by friendly natives after ditching their aircraft on October 5 and they were returned to the Canal via its amphibious rescue plane. Of the six men who went down with the VT-8 crews of Ensign John Taurman and Chief Red Doggett, only one enlisted man (Aviation Radioman Third Class Russell J. Bradley) survived two days drifting in the ocean. In his diary on Guadalcanal, frustrated VS-3 pilot Slim Russell wrote, "Seems like someone lost every day."

Nate Murphy, one of the VS-71 pilots who reached Guadalcanal on October 3, was quickly in the thick of the action. On the night of October 5, he accompanied Lou Kirn's mixed Navy-Marine SBD force to bomb destroyers unloading cargoes west of Lunga Point. Kirn laid a crippling hit on the destroyer *Minegumo*, while Murphy's section landed three damaging near misses on the destroyer *Murasame*. A week later, on October 12, Murphy also participated in one of the biggest achievements for the Cactus fliers: Admiral Tanaka's Rat Patrol was intercepted during

Scouting Squadron 71 (VS-71)			
Aircrews Deployed to Henderson Field			
PILOT	RADIOMAN/ GUNNER	DATE IN	DATE OUT
Lt. Cdr. John Eldridge	ACRM Lester Alvis Powers Jr.	9/28/42	Eldridge KIA 11/2; Powers evaced 11/8
Lt. (j.g.) Herbert Hoover Perritte	ARM2c Irvin Ellison Newsome Jr.	9/28/42	MIA 10/2/42
Ens. Warren K. Garrett	ARM3c Charles Evans Spires	9/28/42	Garrett KIA 11/2; Spires evaced 11/8
Lt. Porter Wilson Maxwell	ARM3c Frank Edward Wise Jr.	10/3/42	11/8/42
Lt. William Perry Kephart	ARM3c John William Phillips	10/3/42	Kephart KIA 10/13; Phillips evaced 11/8
Lt. (j.g.) Chester Vincent Zalewski	ARM2c Lyle Henry Faast	10/3/42	11/8/42
Lt. (j.g.) Harold Nathan Murphy	Sea1c Thomas Panno	10/3/42	11/8/42
Lt. (j.g.) Gene Martin Lerman	ARM3c John Cephas Swann	10/3/42	MIA 11/2/42
Lt. (j.g.) Robert J. Mohler	ARM3c Thomas Jesse Turner Jr.	10/3/42	11/8/42
Lt. Morris Russell Doughty	ARM1c Charles Francis Patton	10/14/42	11/8/42

(continued)

Scouting Squadron 71 (VS-71)			
Aircrews Deployed to Henderson Field			
PILOT	RADIOMAN/ GUNNER	DATE IN	DATE OUT
Lt. (j.g.) Charles Herman Mester	ARM2c Elsworth Leo Forewood Jr.	10/15/42	11/8/42
Lt. (j.g.) Harlan Judson Coit	ARM3c George Yanick	10/15/42	Coit evaced 11/8; Yanick KIA 11/2

the night hours, and a major naval engagement was fought off Cape Esperance. Multiple strike groups from Henderson Field attacked Japanese
warships as they moved out during the morning. "John Eldridge was
leading the first three planes and I was leading the second three," Murphy said of his attack that day. "John made a direct hit on the number
one destroyer." Murphy was certain that his own thousand-pound bomb
helped finish off a second destroyer. Eldridge, Lou Kirn, and Swede Larsen's Navy crews celebrated a double kill of destroyers as their bombs
and torpedoes removed *Natsugumo* and *Murakumo* from Tanaka's in-
ventory of Tokyo Express warships.[50]

Torpedo Junction had robbed the Guadalcanal Marines of any carrier support for the time being. They had only the Cactus Air Force for
support until a new carrier air group could join the campaign to hold
Hell's Island.

Carrier Replacement Air Group Ten was still in training in Hawaii
when the final members of VS-5 and VB-6 returned from Guadalcanal by September 3. Ensign Hal Buell reached Pearl Harbor and spent
a liberty at the Moana Hotel catching up on booze and local girls. He
then reported to Ford Island, where he learned that VS-5 was being dis-
banded. Buell said good-bye to Cactus comrades Troy Guillory and
Harry Liffner of VB-6, who both had orders to go Stateside.[51]

National Archives

The pilots of *Enterprise*'s Scouting Ten (VS-10), October 23, 1942, days before the Battle of Santa Cruz: (*front row, left to right*) Lieutenant (j.g.) William Edwards, Ensign Leonard Lucier, Lieutenant (j.g.) Glenn Estes, Lieutenant (j.g.) Bill Johnson, Lieutenant (j.g.) John Richey, Lieutenant Commander Bucky Lee, Lieutenant Bill Martin, Lieutenant Bill Boardman, Lieutenant Bob Frohlich, Lieutenant (j.g.) Bob Edmondson, Lieutenant (j.g.) Joseph Bloch, Ensign Tom Dardis; (*back row, left to right*) Lieutenant (j.g.) Howard Burnett, Lieutenant (j.g.) Tom Ramsay, Lieutenant (j.g.) Doan Carmody, Lieutenant (j.g.) Leslie Ward, Lieutenant Birney Strong, Lieutenant (j.g.) Kenneth Miller, Ensign Max Mohr, Lieutenant (j.g.) John Finrow, Ensign Charles Irvine, Lieutenant (j.g.) Henry Ervin, and Lieutenant Ray Waters.

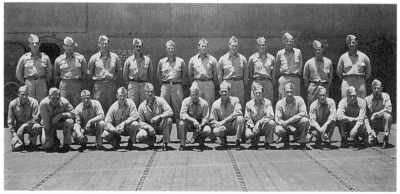

National Archives

The pilots of Bombing Ten (VB-10): (*front row, left to right*) Ensign Nelson Wiggins, Lieutenant (j.g.) Hal Buell, Ensign Dan Frissell, Ensign Leonard Robinson, Ensign Ed Stevens, Lieutenant John Dufficy, Lieutenant (j.g.) James G. Leonard, Lieutenant Warren Welch, Lieutenant (j.g.) Bruce McGraw, and Lieutenant Commander Jim Thomas (CO); (*back row, left to right*) Lieutenant (j.g.) Don Wakeham, Lieutenant (j.g.) John Griffith, Ensign Russell Hoogerwerf, Lieutenant (j.g.) Ralph Goddard, Lieutenant (j.g.) Bob Gibson, Ensign Paul Halloran, Ensign Richard Buchanan, Ensign Gregory C. Nelson, Lieutenant (j.g.) Rupert Allen (ACIO), Lieutenant (j.g.) Frank West, and Ensign Jeff Carroum.

Buell and five of his VS-5 peers, however, were pulled to bolster the new Air Group Ten. For Lieutenant Birney Strong, it was a chance at redemption. He had been the object of air boss John Crommelin's ire during *Enterprise*'s return trip to Pearl for his failure to attack *Ryujo* at Eastern Solomons. "Birney asked for a second chance and was *ordered* to return to immediate combat," said Buell. Strong—along with Redbird Burnett, Glenn Estes, John Richey, and Ralph Goddard—were ordered into the new Scouting Ten. Buell, newly promoted to lieutenant (j.g.), was sent to Bombing Ten with VB-6 veterans Bob Gibson and Steve Czarnecki, as well as Ensign Roger Scudder from *Lexington*'s old Scouting Two unit.[52]

Birney Strong's squadron had been out for eight months and VS-5's aviators were in need of rest. Even still, Strong considered it a good thing that several seasoned pilots were mixed in with VS-10. "I don't think a squadron should go to sea with absolutely green people," he reflected. "I feel sure that the five of us were really a tremendous help in getting Scouting Ten into the right condition for combat work." He and the other VS-5 veterans shared "some very practical information about operations on the *Enterprise* itself" with his new VS-10 skipper and exec, Bucky Lee and Bill Martin.[53]

Scouting Ten and Bombing Ten were based at Barbers Point during early September when the *Enterprise* veterans joined them. Their ship was finishing up repairs in the navy yard while her new air group prepared to come aboard for its first combat cruise. Dave Cawley was just a teenage kid, one of the green young gunners of Scouting Ten. To him, a milk shake was heaven, but it required walking halfway back to Pearl Harbor to get one at Ewa.[54]

Lieutenant Commander Frank T. Corbin welcomed Hoot Gibson, who had been through both the Midway and Eastern Solomons carrier battles. However, he had not yet had the chance to bomb a Japanese carrier. *When will I get that chance?* Gibson wondered. *It keeps gnawing at me. The sole purpose of being a dive-bomber pilot is to help quicken the end of the war by sinking the enemy's ships.* The frustration was driving him nuts. *How many more carrier battles will there be while I'm still out in the Pacific?*[55]

Gibson caught a flight to Barbers Point, the new airfield on the southwest corner of Oahu. He arrived with "little beyond the khakis on my back." Much of his personal gear had gone down with *Yorktown* at Midway. Corbin's VB-10 and Bucky Lee's new Scouting Ten spent much of early September in dive-bombing, glide-bombing, gunnery, and formation tactic training. Lieutenant Karl Border, Bombing Ten's engineering officer, was impressed with the performance of his gunner, Coral Sea veteran Arthur Margarido, at shooting up aerial target sleeves towed by other planes on September 14. "I hope he'll be able to do as well on the Jap Zeroes," Border noted in his diary.[56]

By September 18, Border had command of VB-10's second division. He worked to whip his division into shape for a tight defense against Zeros and for a quick, accurate dive-bombing attack. Border's wingmen were VS-5 veterans Hoot Gibson and Ralph Goddard. His second section comprised Ensigns Steve Czarnecki, Jim Leonard, and Abraham Winegrad. They practiced night flying, and he was particularly pleased with the performance of wingman Gibson. "Bob is a veteran with two subs to his credit and is an excellent flier and a good fellow," Border wrote.[57]

Fate was not kind to Karl Border's team, however. Bombing Ten suffered its first fatality on Sunday, September 30. Jim Thomas led his first division in a dive-bombing attack on a target boat off Barbers Point, followed by Lieutenant Border's second division. Ensign Leonard "Robbie" Robinson, flying in another division, witnessed the performance of Border and was not impressed. *The Navy is rushing academy boys through aviation training at a fast clip,* thought Robinson. Some of the men Border led into the dives on the target ship had more flight hours but were junior in rank to him.[58]

Robinson saw that Border fouled up as he led his division. "He made a terrible breakup on the initial dive," said Robinson. The sloppy lead forced Steve Czarnecki out of position as he pulled up. His SBD climbed straight into the whirling propeller of Ralph Goddard, the number-three wingman. Goddard's prop slashed through the fuselage of Czarnecki's bomber, cutting it apart just aft of the rear cockpit. Czarnecki's gunner, Aviation Radioman Third Class Edward Peter Bode Jr., was unable to deploy his chute and went in with the plane. Czarnecki jumped free and popped his chute, but a piece of his shredded wing or his tail section sliced through his head. Robinson and his gunner, Joe Teyshak, saw that the ensign was nearly decapitated and that his limp torso was left drifting down with his parachute.[59]

Goddard and gunner Charles Hamilton jumped to safety and another Dauntless crew nearly did the same. A big chunk of either Goddard's prop or of Czarnecki's plane slammed into the adjacent SBD of Hoot Gibson. "As I looked out, I saw the end of my wing and other pieces of airplane parts flying through the air," he said. Part of Hoot's starboard wing was sliced away. He saw parachutes popping open nearby, and Gibson hollered back to Cliff Schindele to prepare to bail out. Before he could completely exit his cockpit, Gibson noticed his airplane still seemed to be holding its composure.[60]

Schindele opted to stay as well when Gibson sat back down. He tested his flaps, landing gear, and other controls. Hoot then radioed his emergency situation and headed straight for Barbers Point. He came in from the west over the ocean as the tower cleared the runway for the dive-bomber with only a partial right wing. "I touched down at the end of the runway at a higher landing speed than normal," said Gibson, "but I still had plenty of runway to come to a stop."

Border assessed the losses in his diary that night: "Tough luck for two good fellows." Junior pilot Robinson was more direct in his assessment of Border's leadership. *To hell with rank!* Robinson thought. *Put experience ahead of rank when assigning section and division leaders.*[61]

Just one day after VB-10's first loss, Air Group Ten was put on notice that it was heading to the war zone. *Enterprise* was completing repair work on her Eastern Solomons bomb damage, and her services were badly needed at Guadalcanal. "We are all working like hell and I expect we will be in fair shape by the time we go aboard," Border wrote.[62]

Steve Czarnecki's body was retrieved and sent to the morgue at Pearl Harbor. Frank Corbin ordered Hoot Gibson—who had known the victim since flight school—to make proper identification. He flew to Ford Island and was driven to the morgue. The terrible image of seeing what was left of his friend's head was one that he was forced to tuck "into a deep dark corner of my brain." The sight would linger with Gibson for decades.[63]

The new air group continued with heavy flight training and night operations practice over the next several days. On October 6, Air Group Ten left Kaneohe and flew to the big island of Hawaii. Tragedy struck VB-10 again on Sunday, October 11. Once again, it involved Lieutenant Border. Several crews were scheduled to make a dive-bombing training mission to drop live bombs. Border took off in B-7 with Arthur Margarido as his rear-seat gunner. He revved up his engine and started down the runway at NAS Barbers Point at 0910. Pilots Len Robinson and Warren Welch stood on the flight line watching.

Robinson realized the inexperienced division leader was attempting to lift off with his SBD's engine in high blower. "It was sputtering something awful," he said. "We watched in horror and disgust as the SBD tried to rise more than a few feet."[64]

Border barely cleared the bushes at the end of the runway as he retracted his landing gear. He immediately made a starboard turn toward nearby Ewa Field, straight ahead, and tried to make a forced landing. His wheels had just been tucked away, so his B-7 skidded down the runway some five hundred feet on its belly, dragging its live bomb all the way. Border's SBD came to a screeching halt directly in front of the Marine Corps's flight tower.

Border leaped from his cockpit to help Margarido, who was struggling to exit his rear cockpit. Suddenly, there was a loud explosion and blinding flash. The Dauntless was obliterated as its five-hundred-pound bomb detonated, throwing the bodies of Margarido and Border more than twenty feet. *Four VB-10 personnel killed in ten days!* Ensign Robinson was both stunned and angered. *All Border had to do at any time was to slap one lever from high to low blower.*[65]

As a much-shaken air group prepared to ship out to the war zone, there were several last-minute changes for Bombing Ten. Skipper Frank Corbin received orders back to a new assignment in the States, and turned over command of the unit to Jim Thomas. He elevated senior pilot Warren Welch to the XO position and seized the opportunity to tighten up his group. On October 14, he transferred Lieutenant (j.g.) Benjamin R. Petrie Jr., who had somehow shot himself in the foot with a .45-caliber pistol. "He was accused of doing it deliberately," said Len Robinson. Thomas also gave the boot to Ensigns Abe Winegrad (who had failed to carrier-qualify on two consecutive days) and Roger Scudder for poor performance.[66]

Bucky Lee felt prepared when his VS-10 finally went out on *Enterprise*. On Hawaii, he had constantly been short of planes, but still managed to get each of his pilots to average of eighty flying hours per month. "I am convinced that six weeks was what put us on our feet," he said of his Hawaii training.[67]

For the first time since Midway, *Enterprise* was carrying an air group in which all of her squadrons carried the same number. Lieutenant Commander Jimmy Flatley's Fighting Ten, known as the Grim Reapers, sported five former SBD pilots. Jack Leppla, Dave Pollock, and Thomas "Bobby" Edwards had joined from *Lexington*'s old VS-2, along with Swede Vejtasa and Fritz Faulkner from *Yorktown*'s VS-5. Their experience with Japanese fighters would go a long way in helping to shape their new fighter squadron.

During the second week of October, *Enterprise* got under way for a short shakedown to carrier-qualify the newbies of Air Group Ten. Each day, there were four-hour anti-submarine and IAP hops for the SBD crews. Eighteen-year-old Dave Cawley had become the regular gunner for youthful-looking Ensign Ken Miller of VS-10. "We were so junior in the squadron, we'd get all the dirty assignments," said Cawley. There were two ASP or search flights on many days. In between air time, Cawley was tasked with debriefings, working on radio equipment, cleaning machine guns, and more squadron meetings. Most days were fifteen or more hours of awake time.[68]

Hoot Gibson became shipboard roommates with Lieutenant (j.g.) Rupert Allen, a VB-10 intelligence officer who had joined the squadron in late September. Allen was one of Quonset Point's "Ninety-Day Wonders," officers rushed through training to join the fleet for non-flying administrative roles. "Rupert was a true scholar," said Gibson. "He was a graduate of a major private university, after which he had earned a graduate degree from Oxford University in England." Gibson was still aching to contribute to the ending of the war by blasting a major Japanese warship or aircraft carrier. "Running through my head was my strong resolve to make this cruise really count," he said.[69]

Senior landing signal officer Robin Lindsey handled the task of carrier-qualifying the young pilots of the new squadrons. In two days, he coached in 274 aircraft landings without a single mishap. Captain Arthur Davis gave his new air group a "well done" on October 12 as the car-qual process was wrapped up. His *Enterprise* moved back into Pearl Harbor for final loading and provisioning for a combat cruise to the Solomons.[70]

The pilots had one last romp at the Royal Hawaiian Hotel before they headed back to war. Hoot Gibson and others continued drinking in their rooms well past the hour when the hotel was blacked out for the night. They tied their bedsheets together to make a fabric barricade across the hallway in order to stop any man trying to sneak a female into his darkened room. "This was all in fun, and only once did I see a fist hit a chin," said Gibson. "Then a few of us decided to go outside and have a little more fun." Gibson, with Paul Halloran, Don Wakeham, and a couple other pilots, headed out onto Kalakaua Avenue, the main drag on Waikiki, with whiskey bottles in hand. "We were roaming up and down in front of the hotel whooping and hollering and raising hell, drinking," said Gibson. They were out of uniform and out past curfew, which inevitably brought the shore patrol after them. The officers took down the pilots' names, but Gibson and company told the shore patrol to go to hell before racing back into the Royal Hawaiian and jumping into bed. Fortunately for them, *Enterprise* put to sea before any charges could be filed.[71]

Lieutenant Jack Leppla, the new material officer for Fighting Ten, put his career at risk in equipping the Grim Reapers for combat. *Enterprise* and her task force were scheduled to depart the following morning, October 15. Near midnight, Leppla grabbed Ensign Edward "Whitey" Feightner and told him to follow him ashore to obtain new starters for their planes. They took a pickup to a spare aircraft compound on the base, where Leppla pulled his pistol on the Marine sentry. After taking the Marine's rifle and identifying himself, Leppla told him, "We have a little work to do here."[72]

Leppla and several enlisted men liberated their desired aircraft parts, and then returned the Marine's rifle before departing. "I suggest you forget we were here," Leppla told him. To Feightner, he added, "The skipper doesn't need to know about this. If they want me, they'll have to come after us in the Solomons. We've got work to do."

EIGHTEEN
Strong's Salvation

It was ninety-eight minutes past midnight on October 14 when all hell broke loose on Henderson Field. The Cactus Air Force members had been shelled plenty of nights in the past, but this attack packed unusual ferocity and accuracy.

Fourteen-inch and twelve-inch shells rained down near the airfield and the aviators' camps. "Shells and shrapnel, coconut trees, and dirt were flying in all directions," said Porter Maxwell of VS-71. General Archie Vandegrift was flung to the floor of his dugout by the concussion of a near miss. The battleships *Haruna* and *Kongo* laid down 973 large-caliber shells for ninety minutes while land-attack planes from Rabaul occasionally bombed illuminated targets. Bullet Lou Kirn, skipper of VS-3, crouched in a foxhole with six other pilots, listening to field mice running around the entrance to their hole. The next morning, Kirn saw "one mouse running around in circles that had been shocked by the shell fire."[1]

Lieutenant Bill Kephart of VS-71 was decapitated by a shell that hit his dugout shelter. From VMSB-141, Major Gordon A. Bell and three of his senior pilots were killed, along with four enlisted men of MAG-23. Torpedo Eight gunner Frank Balsley felt fortunate. "Our tent was decimated and not a one of us wound up with a scratch," he said. The VT-8 TBFs did not fare as well, however. "Every aircraft in our squadron was destroyed," said pilot Aaron Katz. Lieutenant (j.g.) Nate Murphy of VS-71, temporarily sidelined with malaria and a fever of 104 degrees, dived into a foxhole near his hospital tent during the shelling. "I crouched against the dirt wall shivering as if I had the plague, probably a combination of my fright and fever," Murphy admitted.

Only five SBDs were in commission at daybreak, along with a handful of the Marine and Navy fighters. Even the distinctive flight operations Pagoda on the field had been hit. When planes began launching at 0540, a distant artillery piece dubbed "Millimeter Mike" began shelling the area—a danger that would become a routine in their daily misery. First Lieutenant Akio Tani's 2nd Company of the 7th Heavy Field Artillery Regiment had arrived on October 14 via the Rat Patrol transport ship *Sado Maru*. Tani brought four Type 92 105mm Osaka arsenal guns, which he set up near the White River to harass the airplanes and pilots of Henderson Field. The collective Marines, Army Air Force, and Navy personnel would label the new artillery menace Hillside Harry, Millimeter Mike, and Pistol Pete. As Pete Coit and Nate Murphy of VS-71 scrambled to get their SBDs airborne, Murphy had the misfortune of taxiing into one of Millimeter Mike's fresh shell holes. Lieutenant (j.g.) Bob Mohler of VS-71 was another who made it into the air. Conditions on Guadalcanal were a far cry from his youth in North Canton, Ohio, when Mohler aspired to be like his aviation hero Charles Lindbergh. At Cactus, he often found himself flying patched-together SBDs. "If the plane captain said it was a go," recalled Mohler, "I never hesitated. I got in it and flew."[2]

The Cactus Air Force survivors endured more bombing raids over the ensuing days, while conducting scouting missions and strikes against Japanese transport groups and warships. The familiar Pagoda was torn down when Marines realized its galvanized roof was reflecting moonlight and flares, providing a good sighting point for Washing Machine Charlie (the persistent evening Japanese planes that buzzed the field) and enemy warships.

Lieutenant Ray Davis flew in eight fresh dive-bomber crews of his orphaned VB-6 to help with the aircraft losses on Guadalcanal. They were welcomed by an early-morning warship pounding on October 15, in which the heavy cruisers *Chokai* and *Kinugasa* bombarded the Henderson Field area with 752 eight-inch shells for half an hour. After daybreak, the Cactus planes carried out a series of attacks on Japanese transport ships and destroyers that were found near Guadalcanal and Savo Islands. Three enemy transports were left burning fiercely after attacks by SBDs, B-17s, P-39s and even a PBY.[3]

Bombing Squadron 6 (VB-6)			
Aircrews Deployed to Henderson Field			
PILOT	**RADIOMAN/ GUNNER**	**DATE IN**	**DATE OUT**
Lt. Cdr. Ray Davis	ACRM John Warren Trott	10/14/42	11/3/42
Lt. Raymond Phillip Kline	ARM1c Edward Joseph Garaudy	10/14/42	11/3/42
Lt. (j.g.) William Robinson Pittman	AMM2c Sherman Lee Duncan	10/14/42	11/3/42
Lt. (j.g) Vernon Larson Micheel	AMM1c Herman Hull Caruthers	10/14/42	11/3/42
Lt. (j.g.) Richard Harold Mills	AOM2c Harold Llewellyn Jones	10/14/42	Ditched 10/21; later recovered
Lt. (j.g.) Eldor Ernst Rodenburg	ACMM Walter E. Schwartz	10/14/42	11/3/42
Lt. (j.g.) Gerald S. Richey	ARM1c Harold French Heard	10/14/42	11/3/42
Lt. (j.g.) Richard Frederick Wolfe	AMM1c James V. Lawless	10/14/42	11/3/42

Admiral Tanaka's destroyers returned with the heavy cruisers *Myoko* and *Maya* during the early minutes of October 16. They shelled Henderson Field for the third straight night, and the Cactus Air Force paid dearly. Thirteen SBDs were destroyed and another thirteen were damaged and repaired. Another ten Dauntlesses were in need of major overhauls. Four P-39s were destroyed, along with six Wildcats and five TBFs, putting Swede Larsen's VT-8 out of business for the moment.

A late-afternoon Japanese bombing attack on October 16 was even more deadly. Anchored off Lunga Point, the seaplane tender *McFarland* was unloading drums of aviation gasoline, ammunition, and a dozen torpedoes onto a barge moored alongside her. Many of the non-essential aviation enlisted men had gone on board *McFarland* to be evaced. One bomb landed squarely on the volatile barge and another hit *McFarland*'s crowded fantail. Scouting Three and Torpedo Eight each lost an enlisted man; twenty-five other men were killed.

With the evacuation of many aviators of the old Marine Air Group 23, tactical command of operations at Henderson Field was turned over to MAG-14. The following day, October 17, Lou Kirn and the last of his VS-3 pilots and gunners boarded a transport plane to be flown out of Guadalcanal. The departure of *Saratoga*'s VS-3 left only a small group of Navy fliers as part of the Cactus Air Force: several Torpedo Eight crews, plus the Dauntless groups of John Eldridge's VS-71 from *Wasp* and Ray Davis's VB-6 group from *Enterprise*. Chuck Mester and his VS-71 gunner, Elsworth Forewood, were wounded and forced to make a water landing in the ocean that afternoon after their SBD was blasted by Japanese float Zeros. Friendly natives, however, enabled the *Wasp* aircrew to eventually make their way back to Cactus by October 29.

Pistol Pete, the new gun crews under Lieutenant Tani, flat-trajectory artillery firing on the airfield after daybreak on October 18 and Bomber One had to be curtailed from constant use due to this danger. "We were now getting it from the sea, from the air, and from the hills," said Porter Maxwell of VS-71. During the next few days, the Cactus fliers bombed key Japanese positions around Guadalcanal and attacked another shipping group 175 miles out.

On October 19, John Eldridge led a flight of a dozen SBDs to attack three destroyers bearing down on the Canal. His pilots chalked up one hit and one near miss but were attacked by a group of Japanese float Zeros. Nate Murphy of VS-71 had been flying with a young gunner, Seaman First Class Thomas Panno, since the day his *Wasp* was torpedoed. "He had only gone on our scout flight that day because he needed four hours in the air to earn flight pay," said Murphy. "Once we got to Guadalcanal, the other gunners had to teach Panno the radio and Morse code." After a month of flying with Murphy, Panno earned his keep that day by shooting up one of the more aggressive floatplanes harassing Eldridge's flight. "Panno kept firing until this fighter drifted off and lost altitude," said Murphy. "His pontoon hit the water, he bounced back into the air, and then went inverted and crashed into the sea." Another of the Zeros riddled the Dauntless of VS-71's Bob Mohler, who felt the bullets "sounded like somebody pounded the airplane with a ball bat. When we got back to the field and landed, they gave me directions to the junkyard. The airplane was full of holes in the fuselage and wings, and our tail was in shreds." On the afternoon of October 21, Bombing Six pilot Dick Mills and rear-seater Lew Jones—who had wounded Saburo Sakai during the Guadalcanal landings—were forced to make an emergency water landing east of Savo. For Mills and Jones it was the beginning of a two-week odyssey in dodging Japanese patrols before they were returned to Hell's Island.[4]

By this point, Nate Murphy found the Cactus Air Force "had sprinklings of SBDs from everywhere—from the Marines, from our squadron, and from other carriers. When you were assigned to a strike, you just flew any plane that could fly. If it had holes in it, they just patched it up." Murphy, Mo Doughty, Pete Coit, Bob Mohler, and Chester Zalewski of VS-71 made numerous bombing and strafing attacks on Japanese forces to keep them at bay. Mohler recalled "flying back and forth over the Jap lines dropping a single bomb at odd intervals and sometimes throwing over an empty Coke bottle. We had been told that it made a sound similar to a bomb dropping."

During the night of October 24, the Japanese started another ground offensive, pushing through the hills south of Henderson Field. Sergeant John Basilone became the first enlisted Marine to earn the Medal of Honor by helping to hold off the charging Japanese soldiers. A few

Japanese broke through the lines during the night, sparking Tokyo to boast that their troops had gained control of the airfield. "That is true if a bunch of dead Japs lying on the field can be called 'Control,'" said Porter Maxwell.[5]

By dawn of October 25, heavy rains had turned both Henderson Field and the fighter strip into a quagmire. Some SBDs could not be moved from their dispersal area to the runway. During the day, there were several spectacular dogfights. In the afternoon, John Eldridge and Ray Davis led Dauntless strikes against three cruisers and two destroyers, claiming a hit and several near misses. By day's end, Cactus had only thirty planes in flying condition. Another bloody ground battle ensued during the night. The situation at Henderson Field was becoming more desperate.

Meanwhile at sea, a major clash was brewing between Japanese and U.S. carrier forces.

B irney Strong made it known that he was on a personal mission. Hal Buell, one of Bombing Ten's young pilots, stopped by the lieutenant's stateroom after evening chow one night. *Enterprise* was under way from Pearl Harbor, on a new mission in support of the Guadalcanal offensive. She had taken aboard her new Air Group Ten, which sported plenty of rookie pilots itching for their first action.

There were also plenty of old hands. Buell and four other pilots of his VB-10—Warren Welch, Hoot Gibson, Ralph Goddard, and Don Wakeham—had experienced combat in early 1942, at the Coral Sea battle or during the previous Eastern Solomons battle. Most of the enlisted rear gunners of VB-10 and VS-10 had flown in *Lexington*'s Dauntless squadrons at the Coral Sea battle. Scouting Ten similarly had six combat-tested pilots: Birney Strong, Redbird Burnett, Skip Ervin, Glenn Estes, and Rich Richey were VS-5 veterans, while Tom Ramsay had flown with *Hornet*'s Bombing Eight at Midway.

Birney Strong was by far the most seasoned of the Dauntless pilots heading back into the war zone with the Big E. He had attacked Japanese carriers at the Coral Sea battle, participated in the August landing-support missions on Guadalcanal, and made attacks against Japanese ships and installations at New Guinea, Tulagi, and in the Gilbert Islands. But his courage had been called into question most recently during the Eastern Solomons carrier battle. Strong had reported the Japanese carrier *Ryujo* but did not press home an attack.

Uncle John Crommelin had come down hard on him and ordered him back out with Bucky Lee's VS-10 to prove his worth. Buell could see the frustration and desire welling up in his third senior officer's piercing blue eyes as they chatted in Strong's stateroom that night. "He was a man determined to attack and hit a Japanese carrier if the opportunity ever came his way again," Buell said. "He did say that he intended to show Commander John that he was not afraid to attack the Japanese, even by himself if necessary."[6]

Rear Admiral Tom Kinkaid was flying his flag on board *Enterprise* for this war cruise. His Task Force 16 had sailed from Pearl Harbor with ninety-five aircraft: thirty-six fighters, forty-four dive-bombers, and fifteen Avengers, plus eight SBDs and two TBFs earmarked for Air-SoPac replacements. Jim Thomas's VB-10 and Bucky Lee's VS-10 each sported twenty-two SBDs, with fifteen per squadron in regular flying rotation.[7]

Vice Admiral Bill Halsey took over as Commander South Pacific on October 18, and he wasted no time in organizing a fighting carrier force. His intelligence indicated that the Imperial Japanese Navy was mobilizing a strong carrier force to support the Guadalcanal offensive, and he intended to meet them head-on. Halsey ordered Kinkaid's *Enterprise* force out from Pearl Harbor the next day to rendezvous with Rear Admiral George Murray's TF-17, built around the carrier *Hornet*, northeast of the New Hebrides on October 24. Halsey ordered Kinkaid's force to sweep past the Santa Cruz Islands and engage any Japanese convoys or carrier forces. Jim Thomas kept the nineteen pilots and two non-flying officers of Bombing Ten grumbling but in shape with flight-deck calisthenics every afternoon.[8]

On October 24 at 1245, *Enterprise*'s TF-16 contacted Murray's TF-17, which included the carrier *Hornet*, four cruisers, and six destroyers. Rear Admiral Kinkaid took overall command of the combined TF-61 and ordered the *Hornet* group to operate five miles southeast of his own TF-16. The carriers rotated each day in providing the search teams and combat air patrols. Kinkaid increased his fleet's speed to twenty-three knots as he headed for the waters north of Santa Cruz and awaited solid scout plane intelligence on the whereabouts of the Japanese forces.

Several large Japanese forces were at sea to support a powerful thrust to overtake Cactus airpower. Admiral Nagumo had three carriers, the large *Shokaku* and *Zuikaku*, along with the smaller flattop *Zuiho*, one cruiser, and eight destroyers. Vice Admiral Nobutake Kondo was in charge of the Advance Force, built around the new carriers *Junyo* and *Hiyo* and operating a hundred miles west of Nagumo. Their job was to support the larger surface force, but *Hiyo* turned back for Truk on October 22 due to an engine-room fire. A third force, Rear Admiral Hiroaki Abe's Vanguard Group, was composed of the battleships *Hiei* and *Kirishima*, four cruisers (*Tone*, *Chikuma*, *Suzuya*, and *Nagara*), and seven destroyers. Kondo and Nagumo were awaiting word from the Japanese Army that they had captured the airfield on Guadalcanal. Then they would move in to destroy U.S. naval forces operating near Cactus with either their carrier airpower or their powerful surface ships.

The Japanese 17th Army on Guadalcanal radioed Admiral Yamamoto's Truk headquarters in the early hours of October 25 that ground forces had succeeded in capturing Henderson Field from the Americans. The truth was revealed later in the morning, but Admiral Nagumo's carrier force made a turn to the south toward Guadalcanal.

Three destroyers moved in toward Koli Point, east of the airfield, to land fresh Japanese troops during the daylight on October 25. Another force of the cruiser *Yura* and five destroyers was to furnish gunfire support to the army forces ashore, while Kondo's ships moved in to crush any resistance. It was an all-out assault to retake Henderson Field. The destroyers sank an American tugboat and patrol craft near Lunga Point, but the Cactus Air Force came to the rescue. John Eldridge, the VS-71 skipper, landed a thousand-pound bomb on *Yura*, knocking the old cruiser to a halt. Cactus fliers, including Ray Davis's VB-6 SBDs, assaulted the warships throughout the day, heavily damaging destroyer *Akizuki* and forcing the Japanese to scuttle *Yura*.

The Japanese had failed to retake Henderson Field and no fresh troops had been landed. Admiral Kinkaid hoped to add to the Japanese losses by crushing the carriers of Nagumo and Kondo. On October 25, from Espíritu Santo, dawn searches of PBYs and B-17s fanned out to search for

U.S. Navy

Lieutenant Bill Martin of VB-10.

the flattops. By late morning, contact reports began filtering in of Admiral Abe's Vanguard Force. Admiral Spruance's first order of business that day was to find the Japanese forces and keep a steady balance of warplanes available between both U.S. carriers.

Lieutenant Bill Martin, second in command of Scouting Ten, was given the nod to bolster *Hornet*'s aircraft arsenal. Born in the Ozark hills of Missouri, he had attended both the University of Oklahoma and the University of Missouri before being appointed to the Naval Academy. Martin was a big man with an infectious smile below his dark, pencil-thin mustache. He became a master of instrument flying and would soon help pioneer aerial radar use. For the moment, however, Martin was tasked with a ferry flight that would unwittingly sideline him.

"*Enterprise* had taken additional airplanes out of Pearl Harbor," he said. "We had them hoisted up in the overhead of the hangar deck, intended to replace the losses the Marines had had at Guadalcanal." Martin pulled one of his junior pilots, Lieutenant (j.g.) Jack Finrow, to help him shuttle two of the planes. *Hornet*, having sent all of her spare planes to Guadalcanal previously, was short on SBDs and TBFs.[9]

At 0603, *Enterprise* commenced launching nineteen morning scout SBDs, led by Bucky Lee and Jim Thomas. Around 0630, *Enterprise* launched some of her spare planes to be delivered to *Hornet* as replacements. Martin led the flight of three SBDs, accompanied by Finrow and Robbie Robinson of VB-10. Right behind the spare SBDs, Jerry Rapp and Johnny Boudreaux of VT-10 flew a patrol and then landed on *Hornet* to give them two spare TBDs. The *Enterprise* orphans settled in with their sister carrier's aviators, fully expecting to be shuttled back to their own carrier during the day.

Lee and Thomas's morning scouts and IAP fliers made no enemy contacts and began returning to their ship. During the recovery process, a VF-10 Wildcat piloted by Lieutenant (j.g.) Bill Blair crashed and knocked a VB-10 Dauntless overboard. He destroyed three other SBDs in the crash, making Commander Crommelin regret having sent over the spares to *Hornet*. Blair's Grim Reaper buddies quickly dubbed him a "Japanese ace" for destroying five U.S. planes. Two more of the damaged SBDs were shoved overboard. This left the *Enterprise* Air Group with thirty-six fighters, forty-one dive-bombers, and thirteen Avengers. Of these, however, only twenty-seven SBDs were in operation, with others reserved as spares on the hangar deck.[10]

At 1150, word came from the scouts that they had sighted two Japanese carriers about 355 miles away. Admiral Halsey immediately ordered an attack. On deck, *Enterprise* had a full strike group of forty-eight planes loaded and ready for a potential strike. Kinkaid felt the Japanese ships were at extreme range, so he plowed ahead for several hours to cut the distance. He planned to send two dozen SBDs out as part of his scout-and-attack mission. The first twelve Dauntless crews were to scout out to 150 miles and then return before dark if no suitable targets were found.

At 1336, Bucky Lee took off with a dozen VS-10 crews to conduct this search. Behind him on deck were spotted another thirty-five planes of an attack group. Jim Thomas of VB-10 was slated to lead it, and his strikers began launching at 1408. A great deal of confusion ensued in the launching process. Grim Reapers XO Bill Kane planned to launch with sixteen fighters, including his own division and those of former SBD pilots Swede Vejtasa and Fritz Faulkner. Faulkner's three wingmen missed their rendezvous and returned to the ship, leaving him to join up with "Killer" Kane. In the end, only eight Wildcats—half the number that had been intended—departed on the mission.

Swede Vejtasa was pissed off. By his calculations, the largely inexperienced Air Group Ten pilots were going on an "impossible mission." Their SBDs, and even his Wildcats, with their extra wing tanks, simply had insufficient fuel to reach the Japanese force and return. The U.S. and Japanese carrier forces were still reckoned to be more than 250 miles apart. Swede slammed down his chart board, announced that Admiral

Kinkaid was a "stupid ass," and headed for the flag bridge to share his thoughts. "I didn't give a damn if they court-martialed me," he said.[11]

Vejtasa dramatically aired his complaints. He pointed out that the length of the mission would end with rookie pilots making their first night landings upon their return. He was later surprised when no action was taken against him by the admiral's staff. Upon his return, VB-10 skipper Jim Thomas tried to calm him. "Don't be so hasty," said Thomas. "We'll do an out and in."

Swede agreed with Thomas. To satisfy the brass, they would simply fly out, scan the area, and fly back to the ship—even if both of them believed it to be a fruitless effort. Swede's ire was not abated as he rendezvoused above the ship and found that only half of the scheduled Grim Reapers were able to join up. The snafu was even greater for Bombing Ten. Instead of a dozen SBDs, Thomas got away with only his plane and four others. Lieutenant Albert "Scoofer" Coffin followed with six torpedo-armed Avengers, making the entire strike group only nineteen planes, as opposed to the intended thirty-five. CEAG Dick Gaines followed the group in his command TBF, flying as a strike evaluator with no payload. The mission was jinxed from the start.

Outbound, Killer Kane's fighters climbed to high altitude while the VT-10 and VB-10 contingent cruised slightly lower. After flying out 150 miles, Thomas was unable to locate any enemy ships, and opted to continue on another fifty miles. Due to garbled radio orders he received after launching, Thomas believed his outbound leg was to be two hundred miles, instead of Kinkaid's intended 150 miles. Finally, the VB-10 skipper added a further eighty-mile leg to the north before deciding it was well past time to head back. By 1800, as darkness began to settle, *Enterprise* had landed the last of the afternoon scouts. The strike group of Gaines, Thomas, Kane, and Coffin was still nowhere to be seen.[12]

Thomas had four junior pilots with him, including wingmen Dan Frissell and Paul Halloran. Ensign Frissell had wanted to fly from a young age. He had grown up quick in Chaffee, Missouri, after his father died when he was just sixteen. He was still finishing college in 1941 when he elected to pursue his dream of flying. He earned his wings in March 1942 and shifted from NAS Corpus Christi to San Diego to join Bombing Ten.

Section leader Hoot Gibson had previously flown scouting missions with *Yorktown*'s air group at Midway, but his wingman Tiny Carroum was green.

Jefferson Haney Carroum, the shortest pilot of VB-10, nicknamed "Tiny," hailed from the little town of Smackover, Arkansas. The extra hour the group spent flying beyond the prescribed 150-mile search had consumed precious fuel. By the time Thomas decided to return, the strikers had flown well beyond the Santa Cruz Islands.

Ensign Jeff "Tiny" Carroum of VB-10.

U.S. Navy

Carroum could barely keep his eyes open. His oxygen system had developed a leak during the outward leg, so he had flown at high altitude with little to no oxygen and a splitting headache. To add to his frustrations, Ensign Carroum's gunner, Bob Hynson, announced that their YE-ZB homing device had malfunctioned—preventing them from receiving *Enterprise*'s directional signals.[13]

Hoot Gibson had turned twenty-three just six days previous as his task force crossed the International Date Line. He was making his second flight of the day, the first being "hot as hell" flying so close to the equator. As Thomas led his SBDs to high altitude, Gibson wished he had worn his flight jacket. "I've never been so cold in my life, as there's no effective cockpit heater in an SBD," he said.[14]

The Wildcats had been sent out with auxiliary wing tanks for the long mission. Swede Vejtasa had trouble transferring fuel from the spare tank due to poor suction. In the laborious process of pumping out the entire wing tank by hand, he ruined his flying gloves. The moon had not yet risen as the strikers flew in darkness. Fritz Faulkner, VF-10's engineering officer, had an uncanny sense of navigation. Listening carefully to the YE signals coming from the Big E, he carefully plotted the correct course home. Faulkner slid up to skipper Killer Kane and signaled him to turn.

Assuming that Kane had turned over the lead to him, Faulkner changed course and headed straight in for his carrier. His homing technique was dead-on, but he soon found that no one had followed him back to *Enterprise*.[15]

The rest of the formation followed each other in the darkness only by keeping track of the red exhaust fires of their companions. As the SBDs dropped to lower altitudes, Tiny Carroum's oxygen deprivation issue became less painful. At 1814 and about forty miles northwest of Task Force 61, Lieutenant Don Miller's Wildcat lost power and dropped back through the formation. Miller was seen to bail out before his Wildcat splashed into the ocean, but was never found.

When the group reached Point Option, there was nothing but empty ocean. Jim Thomas ordered his pilots to jettison their thousand-pound bombs. Hoot Gibson swerved away from Thomas to release his payload, thankful he would not have to try landing on his ship with the bomb still attached. He lost sight of his skipper but continued on with other planes tucked in tight behind him.[16]

One of the bombs exploded on the ocean with a mighty flash. Swede Vejtasa had been unable to pick up the Big E's YE homing device but the bomb flash gave him a sudden inspiration. "That morning, flying endless circles around the fleet, I noticed an oil slick from the *Enterprise*." He dropped down low to the ocean and switched on his bright lights. "Whitey turned his on, which gave much better visibility," said Swede. "We flew twelve to fifteen miles, weaving gently, searching." He thought, *If I can find that damned oil slick, we can make it.*[17]

Luck was on their side. Swede soon spotted an oil slick and began following it, with other planes of the strike group trailing along with him. A new fear struck him. *Am I going in the right direction? If it gets wider, I'm in deep trouble. If it gets narrower, I'm going in the right direction.* Fortunately, the oil slick became narrower as Vejtasa led the straggling strike group back toward their carrier. The shimmering wakes of the task force soon appeared ahead. Tiny Carroum had big worries. He had only made fifteen previous carrier landings and none at night. Added to this was his fatigue. Having flown a morning patrol, Carroum had now been in the air some ten hours.

It was after 1830 when Vejtasa and the F4F pilots safely dropped into the landing circle. "It was one of the scariest days of my life," Ensign Whitey Feightner recalled. "I flew ten minutes with my fuel gauges reading zero." Vejtasa snagged the third arresting wire and was shocked as one of his young wingmen landed at the same instant, nearly plowing into his Wildcat's tail. LSO Robin Lindsey also gave the cut to Doc Norton's TBF, which dropped its right wheel into the starboard 20mm gun gallery and fouled the deck for precious minutes.[18]

In the interim, two SBDs finally ran out of fuel. At 1905, Paul Halloran was forced to make a water landing with his borrowed S-15, and he and Earl Gallagher scrambled into their life raft. They were quickly retrieved by the destroyer *Cushing*. Time also expired for Dan Frissell, who similarly had to put his B-10 into the drink ten minutes after Halloran. Frissell split open his forehead upon landing and was momentarily knocked senseless. Chuck Otterstetter, his twenty-year-old gunner from San Antonio, helped his pilot until the destroyer *Porter* spotted the pair bobbing in the water around 1955. *Porter* maneuvered to pick up the VB-10 crew, and her sailors hustled them below, where one of her doctors sewed up Frissell's split forehead.[19]

Bob Gibson made his first night landing approach when flight operations resumed. *I can't even tell if this is the* Hornet *or* Enterprise, he thought. *Well, it really doesn't matter at this point. I've got about five gallons of gas left.* Gibson took the cut from LSO Lindsey and landed. Just as crewmen released his tail hook from the arresting gear and he applied full throttle to move forward past the protective crash barrier, he heard the blaring of the warning klaxon. Another plane was coming in hot, having ignored a wave-off. "I tried to bend the throttle forward to get one more ounce of power," said Gibson. "Ten more feet could save my life."[20]

Behind Gibson, Tiny Carroum came into the groove at 1909 with all fuel gauges reading empty. Robin Lindsey waved his paddles excitedly, indicating that the rookie ensign was coming in too high. Carroum knew another pass would force his Dauntless into the dark waters, so he gave himself the "cut" and continued in. Carroum's tail hook failed to snag even the ninth and final arresting wire. His SBD slammed into *Enterprise*'s island structure with a terrific flash, sheering off his right wing and right wheel. Carroum's prop shredded Gibson's SBD as the klaxon continued to blare and Hoot clawed to release his seat and shoulder belts. "His propeller cut off the rear of my plane like slicing salami and ended up within three feet of my cockpit, but fortunately three inches short of my gunner Cliff Schindele's cockpit," said Hoot. Gibson, having lost part of his right wing weeks before to another wingman's negligence, was left feeling "I was getting chopped up all around." Flight-deck personnel extracted young Carroum and gunner Bob Hynson from the wreckage uninjured. To his surprise, Carroum received no chastisement for making such a dangerous, unauthorized landing.[21]

"Both planes were tossed overboard," said Gibson. The time spent clearing Carroum and Gibson's wrecks cost the *Enterprise* Air Group dearly. Three Buzzard Brigade Avengers ran out of gas and dropped into the water. The crews of Lieutenant Scoofer Coffin, Lieutenant (j.g.) Bob Nelson, and Ensign George Wilson were all recovered by the destroyers *Maury* and *Mahan*, with the exception of one young airman who drowned. The mission beyond darkness cost *Enterprise* two men, one fighter, four SBDs, and three TBFs. Another three SBD and two TBF crews were marooned on *Hornet* for the night.

Swede Vejtasa considered the entire mission an absolute disaster. Bob Gruebel, a young VT-10 turret gunner who had flown the mission, thought otherwise. "If the PBYs had found the carriers, we wouldn't have gone out searching. There was a damn good chance we could have found them with a strike group just before nightfall and alleviated any need to hit them again the next day," Gruebel said.

Air officer John Crommelin addressed the aircrews that night in the *Enterprise* wardroom. He spoke at length on the training that prepared them for combat, and of the Marines ashore who were depending on them. He stressed that they were to hit their targets.[22]

"There is no room for waste," said Crommelin, "and no excuse for misses." Guadalcanal must be held in order to maintain the Australian lifeline. The Japanese carrier forces operating nearby must be knocked out. "If you're going to miss with your bomb, you might as well stay home and let a *good* pilot take your place." Crommelin then encouraged his aviators to rest and in the morning be prepared to "knock the sons-of-bitches off the face of the earth."[23]

Uncle John's words rang particularly sharp with VS-10's Birney Strong, who had found *Ryujo* at the Eastern Solomons. He had done his job in reporting her, but he knew now that if he found a Japanese carrier again, he would attack it—with a group or on his own.

Johnny Liska was feeling confident. *The* Enterprise *is a well-trained ship,* he thought. *Most everyone on board has been with her since well before the war started. Now it's our job to take care of those enemy carriers.* His former Coral Sea pilot, Jack Leppla of the Grim Reapers, was feeling a higher degree of anticipation. He wrote a letter to his mother

U.S. Navy

Commander John Crommelin, the *Enterprise* air officer.

back in Lima, Ohio—to be mailed in the event he did not return from the mission off Santa Cruz.[24]

"The battle must be decisive," Leppla wrote. "I hope I can do my part well before I go. Some must die so that others may live. I am glad to be able to give my life in the hope that someday men will learn to stop fighting and live together peaceably."

Bucky Lee reviewed the day's objectives long before dawn on October 26. In case of positive contact with enemy carriers, he told his scouts to use voice radio, attempt to rendezvous, and then attack—provided that planes had enough fuel to still return to base. The *Enterprise* scouts were to search from southwest by west through due north to a distance of two hundred miles.

Gunner Dave Cawley listened intently. Lee pointed to a spot on the blackboard where he presumed the Japanese would be found. *Miller and I are going right to them!* he thought. *That's two hundred miles out, fifty miles across, and another two hundred miles back!* He had never flown such a stretch.[25]

By the looks of Lee's assigned search sectors, Birney Strong was almost certain his would not contain enemy ships—but he knew what he would do if the Japanese were discovered in time. The loudspeakers blared the order for the scouts to man their planes, and Lee's crews scurried toward the flight deck. En route, Birney spoke to his skipper.[26]

"Captain, I think you'll find the yellowbellies are in your sector," said Strong. "When you discover them, give us the word, loud and clear."

Scouting Ten had only fifteen SBDs in operation to start the day on October 26 after pulling two spares from the hangar reserves. Jim Thomas's VB-10 was down to ten operational Dauntlesses, having lost four the previous night. At 0512, the morning CAP was launched, followed by eight pairs of SBDs. Bombing Ten provided six planes to search the three southernmost sectors, fifteen degrees each instead of the usual ten degrees, while the scouting squadron launched ten SBDs to cover the five northern sectors. Each SBD was loaded with a five-hundred-pound bomb. "The weather was almost perfect for a search, with visibility clear as far as the eye could see," said Hal Buell, who was teamed with Red Hoogerwerf.[27]

Immediately after launching the sixteen scouts, *Enterprise* sent up six SBD crews for IAP duty. From VB-10, Buck Buchanan, Ralph Goddard, and John Griffith would handle inner air patrols for TF-17, while Lieutenant Bob Frohlich of VS-10 was sent up with Bud Lucier of his squadron and Frank West of VB-10 to conduct IAP for TF-16. The sun rose at 0530, bringing good weather as the U.S. carrier forces steamed some 120 miles north of the Santa Cruz Islands.

The first group to make enemy contact was VB-10 XO Warren Welch and Bruce McGraw. Eighty-five miles out from their launch point, they spotted a Nakajima Kate torpedo plane flying an opposite course three miles away. Welch and McGraw continued their search course for another twenty minutes before they made visual contact with Japanese warships. At 0630, radioman Harry Ansley keyed Welch's contact back to *Enterprise*, reporting two battleships, a cruiser, and seven destroyers, all moving north at twenty knots.

At 0700, Welch had Ansley sent an amplifying report to his ship as they passed back over the warship group they had previously reported.

The enemy ships were making twenty-five knots on a westerly course. The Big E acknowledged receipt, and Welch decided it was time to head home. "The air was full of puffy, black little clouds," McGraw recalled of the warships' long-range antiaircraft shells that were bursting all about his Dauntless.[28]

Welch and McGraw passed the same Mitsubishi Type 97 plane flying an opposite course while still a hundred miles from *Enterprise*. All three planes again opted to hold their fire and the Dauntless scouts landed on their carrier at 0931. Welch's team was the only pair of the six VB-10 crews to contact Japanese ships. They had found Admiral Abe's force of two battleships, four cruisers, and seven destroyers. Scouting Ten's five pairs of morning searchers were in for a considerable amount of action.

Redbird Burnett and Ken Miller began climbing after they heard the first warship contacts. At around 0645, just fifteen minutes after Welch's first report came from the adjacent search sector, Burnett's team approached Admiral Abe's heavy ships. Dave Cawley, flying in Miller's rear seat, first saw just some odd-looking bumps on the horizon almost dead ahead. As they closed the distance, he made out ship silhouettes. Two had distinctive pagoda-style masts. *Battleships!* Cawley thought.[29]

Cawley used his continuous-wave radio to key out the ship types, course, speed, and other vital information. He then signaled via Morse

Gunner Dave Cawley.

code to Bob Wynn in Burnett's rear seat. Wynn acknowledged that Cawley's report had gone out, and then rebroadcast it. Cawley sent their contact report a third time just to be sure.

Burnett, one of the Eastern Solomons veterans, pulled ahead in his more powerful SBD-3, while Miller trailed in his Dash-2 older-model Dauntless. There was no AA fire as they climbed to fourteen thousand feet while heading for the center of Abe's task group. Cawley noticed one of the cruisers turn toward them and begin blinking recognition signals with a large searchlight. He pulled out his Aldis light, put a green cover on it, and started sending dots and dashes in response. Cawley knew his "answer" would mean nothing to the Japanese below, but for a moment it seemed to delay them down from firing.[30]

Then every ship in the task force seemed to open fire at once. The antiaircraft fire was fairly accurate as Burnett led the section down on the cruiser *Tone*. One of the first bursts nearly blew off Miller's right wing. The concussion flipped his plane on its back and left him spinning out of control straight down for some four thousand feet. Burnett believed his five-hundred-pounder was a hit, but *Tone*'s crew chalked up only a near miss. By the time Miller wrestled back control of his spinning SBD, his aim was farther off the mark. He pulled out low on the waves with heavy guns booming all around and phosphorus shells spiraling madly past. Dave Cawley, who had never been shot at in his life, was so scared it took him an extra moment to think to fire back with his rear Brownings. The ocean around him erupted into mighty pillars of dirty seawater as trios of battleship shells exploded near the departing American dive-bombers.[31]

Burnett and Miller retired toward their task force, feeling confident they had damaged their heavy cruiser target due to smoke rising from her stern. *Tone* escaped with only minor damage from their near-misses.

In the end, it was scouts skipper Bucky Lee who found the Japanese carriers first. He and wingman Bill Johnson made first contact around 0645. From thirty-five miles out, Lee closed the distance to make positive identification of the ships. He and Johnson moved to within fifteen miles, where they began circling. With one carrier in sight, Lee changed course and clawed for altitude to get off a contact report.

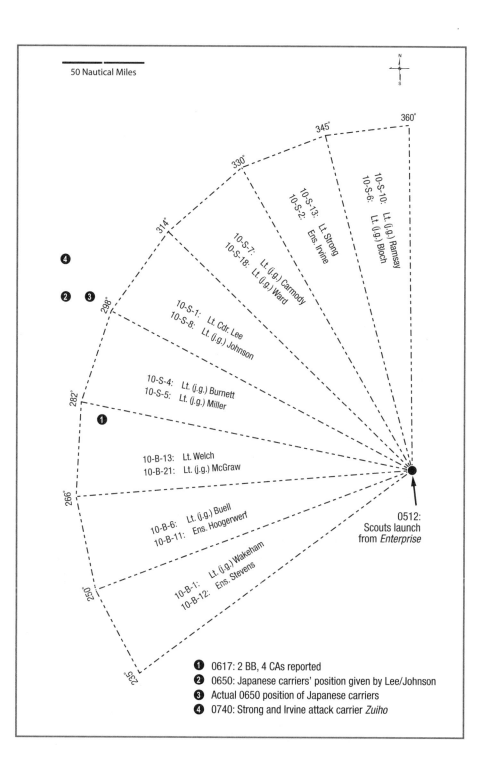

50 Nautical Miles

N

360°
345°
330°

10-S-10: Lt. (j.g.) Ramsay
10-S-6: Lt. (j.g.) Bloch

10-S-13: Lt. Strong
10-S-2: Ens. Irvine

314°

❹

❷ ❸

298°

10-S-7: Lt. (j.g.) Carmody
10-S-18: Lt. (j.g.) Ward

10-S-1: Lt. Cdr. Lee
10-S-8: Lt. (j.g.) Johnson

282°

10-S-4: Lt. (j.g.) Burnett
10-S-5: Lt. (j.g.) Miller

❶

10-B-13: Lt. Welch
10-B-21: Lt. (j.g.) McGraw

266°

0512:
Scouts launch
from *Enterprise*

10-B-6: Lt. (j.g.) Buell
10-B-11: Ens. Hoogerwerf

250°

10-B-1: Lt. (j.g.) Wakeham
10-B-12: Ens. Stevens

235°

❶ 0617: 2 BB, 4 CAs reported
❷ 0650: Japanese carriers' position given by Lee/Johnson
❸ Actual 0650 position of Japanese carriers
❹ 0740: Strong and Irvine attack carrier *Zuiho*

From his rear seat, Chief Irby Sanders keyed their first report of one Japanese carrier, course 330 degrees, speed fifteen knots. During the next fifteen minutes of circling Nagumo's fleet, the VS-10 team caught sight of both *Shokaku* and *Zuikaku*, veterans of both the Coral Sea and Eastern Solomons battles. Sanders keyed additional contact reports of the two big carriers and their accompanying vessels. The Japanese sailors below spotted the American search planes and scrambled additional fighters to raise their combat air patrol to twenty Zeros.[32]

Sanders was unable to obtain an acknowledgment from *Enterprise* of his contact reports before two Zeros caught up to the SBDs around 0705. The warships below commenced evasive maneuvering while making a smoke screen. Zeros approached Lee and Johnson head-on with guns blazing. A burst of small-caliber fire shattered Lee's windscreen, but VS-10's skipper was blasting away as well. He felt certain that his .50-caliber rounds knocked down the leading assailant, as he watched it explode while passing below him. Bill Johnson was equally sure that his guns took out the other of the first two Zeros.[33]

Two more Zeros latched onto Lee's tail, forcing him to gun his throttle and race for the clouds. He and Johnson entered the cumulus banks while Sanders and Hugh Hughes in their rear seats blazed back at their assailants. Lee hoped to dodge the Zeros in the clouds, rendezvous with more of his scouts, and make an attack on the carriers. As Johnson emerged from his cover, he blasted away a second Zero. When five more appeared to take its place, he wisely called off the fight and poured on the throttle to head for home. In the process, Johnson became separated from his skipper, who was pursued by fighters for some forty miles. Unable to regroup or to shake the heavy fighter cover, they headed for the Big E independently.

Their hopes of driving home an attack were spoiled, but Lee and Johnson had uncovered the big prizes. Their contact reports quickly stirred some of their fellow scouts into action.

The search sector just to the south of Bucky Lee's team was flown by VS-10 Lieutenants (j.g.) Martin "Red" Carmody and Leslie James Ward. They were flying without the benefit of radar, so Carmody had been diligent in his search efforts. "Everything was by eyeball and we did everything by plotter boards," he said. He and Ward were about a hundred miles away from the position of the Japanese carriers when they picked up Lee's contact report.[34]

Since radio silence was in effect, Johnny Liska hand-signaled directions from Carmody to Nick Baumgartner by tapping on the side of his plane. *If separated, we will rendezvous above the clouds,* he tapped. Carmody climbed to nine thousand feet and headed for the Japanese ships to the north. In an area free of cloud cover, he could make out black smoke on the horizon from enemy ships. Once in this open area, he signaled to Les Ward that they should climb to gain a favorable attack position. Rear-seat gunners Baumgartner and Liska suddenly announced that Zeros were approaching their SBDs.

Carmody commenced evasive maneuvers and Ward tried to stay tight on his wing. Liska called up to Carmody, telling him which way to turn based on how the enemy fighters were approaching. "He could see clearly," said Carmody. "I couldn't."[35]

"Pull right! Pull right!" Liska yelled as a Zero zoomed in.

Carmody veered sharp to starboard, causing the Zero to roar by. The fighter flashed past and pulled into a fancy wingover to come back around.

"They made one long firing run way out of range to about seventy-five yards upon us," said Liska. "I fired about three hundred rounds into one Zero that came right on me. I could see the tracers go right into him. He was still going straight down when I last saw him."[36]

Liska's plane was not hit but another Zero was coming in. He opened fire with his twin .30-caliber Brownings. Carmody felt that Liska "burned him right out of the sky. You could see him going down as we were turning." Two more Zeros moved in, forcing Carmody and Ward into sharp countermaneuvers to throw off their aim. Baumgartner poured lead into one fighter and saw it fall off in flames. Following the skirmish with *Zuiho* and *Shokaku* fighters, Liska looked back and saw Ward's plane approaching from astern sporting a 20mm hit in one wing.

The heavy fighter presence prevented this duo from attacking. Carmody finally shook off the last pursuing fighter in the cloud cover but lost Les Ward in the process. Red dumped his bomb into the ocean and plotted the course for home. Ward did the same, and along the return route, he and Carmody managed to regroup. Both SBDs sported bullet damage but they were free of fighters for the rest of their flight back toward *Enterprise*.

Birney Strong and wingman Chuck Irvine were flying the search sector two slots to the north of Bucky Lee. So far, they had spotted nothing and Strong was beginning to wonder if he would ever get the chance to prove his valor again.

Shortly after 0700, Clarence Garlow, in the rear cockpit of Strong's S-13, picked up Warren Welch's early report of warships. Birney used his plotting board to figure out the navigational challenge. They were already near the end of their search sector, and the ships were about 150 miles away. He decided his fuel situation was sufficient enough to head for this contact.

Strong led Ensign Irvine into a turn to port and the pair climbed for altitude while heading southwest. En route, they copied the contact report from Bucky Lee of Japanese carriers. *The skipper has found the flattops in his sector, just as I expected*, thought Birney. Lee's new report still placed the carriers about a hundred miles away, but Birney's navigation was right on the money, for about twenty minutes later he began seeing the ships below.

U.S. Navy

Ensign Chuck "Skinhead" Irvine.

Large cumulus clouds at high altitude helped conceal the ships at times, but the big prizes soon became evident. Strong and Irvine moved through the cover. As Birney came around one large cumulus bank, he saw "two very large carriers separated by about fifteen miles, launching aircraft." They had found the big *Shokaku* and the smaller *Zuiho*, while the third carrier *Zuikaku* was momentarily obscured by the cloud cover.[37]

At the moment, the pair was enjoying the absence of fighter attacks.

Later on, they would find that two of their companions, Ward and Carmody, were keeping the fighter cover occupied. At 0740, Strong looked over to Irvine and tapped the top of his flying helmet to indicate, *I've got it.* Irvine allowed his SBD to slide away from his leader's as Strong nosed up. Then Strong pushed over into a dive on the nearest of the two carriers. Irvine followed suit from fourteen thousand feet.[38]

"[As] I approached, the sun was also in my favor, being directly behind my back, and I slid in," Strong said. "As I got close, I moved over to the wind line and made a downward dive which in effect gave me just about a no-wind dive because we had about a twenty-four-knot wind, and these carriers were going downwind at about twenty-five knots. It was just a dive bomber's paradise, something that you dream about, hope to see maybe once in your life."[39]

Strong and Irvine had no opposition from fighters or AA fire. Although Birney believed he was diving on the large *Shokaku*, he was in fact leading his team down on *Zuiho*, the sister carrier to *Shoho* that his VS-5 had attacked at Coral Sea. At fifteen hundred feet, Strong yanked back on the double-handled bomb release. He aimed for the red circle on the flight deck, and Irvine followed suit right behind him. Their dives were picture perfect. Birney strafed the portside gun positions on *Zuiho*'s deck as he pulled out. Both five-hundred-pounders slammed into *Zuiho*'s stern, ripping a fifteen-meter hole through her after flight deck and rendering it useless for further flight operations.

As he pulled out under heavy AA fire, Strong found the Japanese "had a reception committee waiting for us of twelve Zeros at the bottom of the hill." Irvine was a quarter mile away from Strong when the Zeros hit. "We both turned south," said Strong. "I made a report of our success to the *Enterprise*, which they heard and broadcast again their position." Three *Zuikaku* Zeros pursued Strong and Irvine in a fight that would continue fifty miles beyond the warships.[40]

The SBDs stayed tight, weaving back and forth to allow Garlow and Williams in the rear seats to make good shots. Williams struggled to stay on target as Irvine jinked and weaved radically to avoid the Zero fire. His first shots were off the mark. "I was just a bit hasty in firing," he said. "I was on an empty stomach not having more than an orange I ate just before we got into battle."[41]

The Zeros shot up Strong's tail section, knocking out gunner Garlow's radio equipment. Seaman First Class Koichi Nakagami of *Zuikaku* misjudged the range, ceasing his firing too far out and pulling around for another pass. "Right then, I laced in a burst of fire," said Garlow. "The gasoline started shooting out and he hit the water hard and burst into flames." Williams in Irvine's plane felt certain that he sent another Zero blazing toward the ocean. The Zeros scored their own hits, shooting up Irvine's tail and puncturing his starboard main fuel tank. As they retreated, Williams sent a contact report announcing to *Enterprise* that they had scored two hits on a carrier. At around 0830, after a forty-five-minute pursuit, the Dauntlesses shook the Zeros in a cloud formation. Williams said the rainsquall "was the prettiest sight I hope to see this side of heaven." Once they felt safe, Irvine called back over the intercom: "I feel like a smoke, what about you?" The jubilant pilot and gunner enjoyed a cigarette as they winged for home.[42]

Bucky Lee would write in his report that the actions of Strong and Irvine were "the most outstanding demonstration of intrepidity and determination of the entire naval engagement." He found their attacks to be "in accordance with the highest traditions of the naval service."

The final VS-10 search duo of Tom Ramsay and Joe Bloch, flying the farthest sector to the east, did not make contact with the Japanese forces. Still, the morning search effort had been a tremendous success. *Enterprise*'s sixteen Dauntlesses had made four different contact reports on the Japanese naval forces. They had crippled an aircraft carrier in addition to claiming seven Zeros and one Kate shot down. Better yet, all thirty-two SBD crewmen would eventually return to their fleet without loss.

And, for Birney Strong, the morning of October 26 was a day of redemption. But the Battle of Santa Cruz—as this fourth-ever confrontation in the Pacific between American and Japanese carrier fleets came to be known—was only getting started.

NINETEEN
Action at Santa Cruz

Robbie Robinson wanted his shot at the Japanese carriers, too. The VB-10 pilot was one of three *Enterprise* dive-bomber crews marooned on board *Hornet* after ferrying over spare SBDs the previous day.

Robinson, Lieutenant Bill Martin, and Lieutenant (j.g.) Jack Finrow of VS-10 were preparing to return to their own flattop. Just as a destroyer approached *Hornet* to transfer them via highlines on bosun's chairs, VS-10's reports of the Japanese fleet began coming in. "The destroyer was told to resume its position in the screen," said Martin. The TBF and SBD pilots were thus resigned to ride out the impending action on *Hornet*. *What a miserable feeling*, Martin thought. *A pilot is supposed to be flying, where he has so much to do. Now we're just passengers.*[1]

Task Force 61's command staff decided to send the *Hornet* Air Group out to pound the reported Japanese carriers, since the Big E's striking power was stretched thin from the morning scouting missions. Lieutenant Commander William J. "Gus" Widhelm, skipper of VS-8, was enthusiastic to be heading out on the offensive. He had shared his shipboard quarters with Ensign Robinson of VB-10, while Bill Martin had spent the night in the quarters of Bombing Eight skipper Lieutenant James "Moe" Vose. Widhelm offered to let Robinson fly as part of VS-8's strike group, and Vose had made the same offer for Jack Finrow to fly with VB-8.[2]

Lieutenant Martin, however, was not in agreement.

"No," he said. "We've given the *Hornet* these planes, and they've got them now."

Finrow and Robinson pleaded their desire to make the strike. They pointed out that Jerry Rapp and Johnny Boudreaux of Torpedo Ten, who had similarly ferried over TBFs the following day, were being allowed to join Torpedo Six for the strike. Martin was not giving in.

"Bill, you're in Scouting Ten," challenged Robinson. "You're not in my chain of command. I'm in Bombing Ten."

Martin dressed down the ensign, making sure he was aware that he held rank among the three *Enterprise* SBD pilots. It did not matter which squadron Robinson was in. He and Finrow were both grounded. Robinson was angry but reluctantly gave up the fight.

Hornet began launching her first wave of strikers at 0732. Gus Widhelm led the twenty-nine-plane group, which included seven VS-8 Dauntless crews. Trailing Widhelm's scouts were eight SBDs of VB-8, led by skipper Moe Vose. The Japanese formation was estimated to be about two hundred miles out as Widhelm climbed to eleven thousand feet. At around 0830, about seventy-five miles northwest of TF-17, a formation of twenty-five enemy planes was sighted two thousand feet above—flying in a directly opposite direction. "But they continued on their way toward the *Hornet* without making a run on us," said Lieutenant Fred Bates of VB-8.[3]

Lanny Wheeler made one last check of his instruments as Lieutenant (j.g.) Skip Ervin turned up their engine. Wheeler was slightly out of sorts in a different plane. In the scramble to prepare a meager strike group, the *Enterprise* air command had ordered three Scouting Ten crews to man the three ready VB-10 SBDs that were spotted on deck. Glenn Estes would head the small group, which included Ervin and Rich Richey.

Dick Gaines, commander of the *Enterprise* Air Group, led the small force of twenty-one planes that began lifting off at 0750. Gaines flew his command TBF, while Lieutenant Commander Jack Collett led nine other torpedo-armed Avenger crews of his Torpedo Ten. His group was escorted by two Grim Reaper fighter divisions under skipper Jimmy Flatley and former SBD pilot Jack Leppla. The three SBD crews under Estes were last off the deck. As Ervin's Dauntless rolled to the starting line, gunner Wheeler noted two placards that were being held up. One announced the enemy force's speed to be twenty-five knots. The other said simply,

PROCEED WITHOUT *HORNET*. Wheeler realized their small force would be flying independently to seek out the enemy carriers.

All told, three small strike groups would head in toward Nagumo's fleet separately. Following the first two strike groups from *Hornet* and *Enterprise*, *Hornet* turned back into the wind. Commander Walt Rodee, in a bombless TBF, took command of twenty-five strikers of the second *Hornet* group. Seven Wildcats launched to cover the nine bomb-armed Avengers of VT-6 and nine SBDs of this group. Lieutenant John Lynch of Bombing Eight had a trio of three-plane sections of SBDs. All nine pilots, three from VS-8 and six from VB-8, were veterans of the Battle of Midway.

The American fleet had dispatched seventy-three warplanes in three straggling groups to hit an enemy formation that was about two hundred miles away—well within their striking range. It was fair to assume that Japanese warplanes were already en route to the U.S. fleet. In the next few hours, the victory of the Santa Cruz carrier battle would be determined by which forces found their opponents first, and by the side that did the most with its weapons.

The Japanese carriers had indeed sent out their own strikers in the interim. From the decks of *Shokaku*, *Zuikaku*, and *Zuiho*, sixty-four planes of an initial strike wave were en route to the reported position of the American fleet by around 0730. Only minutes later, Birney Strong and Chuck Irvine delivered their punishing blows to the flight deck of *Zuiho*, effectively shutting down her flight operations for the battle. Admiral Nagumo, worried that he might take another pounding with aircraft still on deck as he had suffered at Midway, opted to fling a second strike group at the American carriers. Shortly after 0800, *Shokaku* and *Zuikaku* each launched follow-up strike groups.

With so many opposing aircraft passing each other en route to their respective targets, it was only a matter of time before they began to mix it up.

The small *Enterprise* strike force bore the brunt of the first major clash with passing Zeros.

For Jack Leppla, it was his chance to finally engage Japanese fighter planes in a fighter plane. At Coral Sea, he and gunner Johnny Liska had performed admirably in two days of dogfighting with a Dauntless dive-bomber. Leppla had four enemy kills to his credit. With his more nimble F4F Wildcat, he hoped to add more feathers to his war bonnet. Leppla also had old scores to settle. During the first five months of the Pacific War, operational mishaps and enemy combat had cost him close squadron mates—Robert Weinzapfel, Pappy Hunter, Joe Johnson, Edward Allen, John Wingfield, and Roy Hale. Just one kill away from attaining "ace" status, Leppla and his Grim Reapers were in for plenty of action on October 26.

At around 0835, just over sixty miles out from the ship, the *Enterprise* force was still climbing for altitude. Leppla's "Reaper Six" division of Wildcats was cruising slightly to the left and about one thousand feet above Jack Collett's Torpedo Ten Avengers. To the right and above was Lieutenant Commander Jimmy Flatley's four-plane "Reaper One" flight of F4Fs.

At that moment all hell broke loose: Nine *Zuiho* Zeros came diving down from fourteen thousand feet on the unsuspecting American formation. Jack Collett's leading TBF was blasted from the skies almost immediately. Only his radioman, Aviation Radioman First Class Thomas Nelson, parachuted safely from their blazing torpedo bomber. Other *Zuiho* fighters ripped through the Buzzard Brigade and finished off Ensign John Reed's TBF. His turret gunner, Aviation Radioman Third Class Murray "Mick" Glasser, dived out an open hatch, pulled his ripcord, and began floating down just as his Avenger blew apart in midair.

Leppla, spotting the onslaught, was in a tough situation. Only moments before, he had test-fired his forward Brownings. He signaled his wingman, Ensign Albert Mead, that only one gun was functioning. Unfazed, Leppla pushed forward to assault the Zeros ripping through the Buzzard Brigade. He ordered his division to drop their auxiliary wing tanks before leading them into a hard right turn back toward the TBFs. As Leppla and Mead moved in on the last of the Zeros recovering from their runs on VT-10, they were attacked by six more Zeros from above and behind.[4]

Mead was astonished that Leppla did not assume the defensive Thach Weave—the crisscrossing defensive maneuver developed by Reaper Leader Thach—but instead seemed to fly straight ahead. Mead assumed he had been wounded by some of the first bullets. In the rolling, twisting dog-fight that ensued, Mead claimed three Zeros before his Wildcat was finished. He made a dead-stick water landing and scrambled from his sinking F4F. Jack Leppla was last seen with a Zero blasting at his tail and another diving in from ahead. Mead and Leppla were each given credit for a kill, finally making former SBD pilot Leppla an ace on the day he lost his life.[5]

Leppla disappeared forever, one of three Wildcat pilots shot down. Reapers Al Mead and Ensign Raleigh "Dusty" Rhodes would be retrieved from the ocean by Japanese ships, as were VT-10 enlisted men Mick Glasser and Tom Nelson. Leppla and Flatley's division had polished off three Zeros, while VT-10's gunners knocked down another three. In return, Dick Gaines's strike force suffered five men killed, five planes shot down, and another two cripples that were forced to turn back. The decimated *Enterprise* group continued toward the Japanese fleet with only four Wildcats, five Avengers, and three Dauntlesses remaining.

Gus Widhelm, heading up *Hornet*'s first strike group SBDs, began noticing ship wakes ahead at around 0845. This group was Rear Admiral Chuichi Hara's 8th Cruiser Division of *Tone* and *Chikuma*, escorted by a pair of destroyers.

Pushing twenty miles farther, Widhelm found Admiral Abe's Vanguard Force. It included the battleships *Hiei* and *Kirishima*, cruisers *Suzuya* and *Nagara*, and four destroyers. Passing east of the Vanguard Force warships, the *Hornet* Air Group was jumped by the alerted Japanese combat air patrol. The warning went over the radio at 0910 from an SBD crew: "Tally ho! Dead ahead. Tally ho! Down below, two Zeros!"[6]

Zuiho fighters ripped into Mike Sanchez's VF-72 divisions. Two Wildcats were downed, another was crippled, and one F4F pilot was wounded. Gus Widhelm's dive-bombers pressed on and he soon spotted the big prize—Japanese carriers. Closest in view was the larger *Shokaku* with several escorting warships. Several miles beyond her was a smaller carrier, *Zuiho*, still streaming black smoke from Birney Strong's bomb hits ninety minutes earlier. Widhelm tried unsuccessfully to raise Commander Gaines and the TBFs, but his luck ran out at 0918.

Shokaku and *Zuiho* fighters rolled in against the Dauntless bombers from ahead, overhead, and from the sides. Widhelm's 8-S-1 was worked over by several Zeros and he was finally forced to ditch his SBD at about 0925, within sight of the Japanese carriers. Lieutenant (j.g.) Ken White of VB-8 was shot through the left arm and hand in the fierce dogfight. He dumped his bomb and nursed his crippled Dauntless back toward the American fleet. Lieutenant (j.g.) Ralph Hovind of VS-8 collected at least a hundred slugs in his SBD and marveled that it was still able to fly. Ensign Clay Fisher's 10-B-8 was hit by 20mm shells that knocked out his hydraulic system. Fisher sought refuge in the clouds after he and gunner George Ferguson were wounded by bullets and shrapnel fragments.[7]

Bombing Eight section leader Fred Bates saw Lieutenant (j.g.) Phil Grant's SBD falling away. He noted a belt of .30-caliber ammunition peeling out of Ensign Grant's rear cockpit as his gunner, Floyd Kilmer, lost it. Kilmer and Grant were killed as their SBD smashed into the sea. Four *Hornet* SBDs had been shot down or forced to limp home. Ralph Hovind, now in the lead of the *Hornet* dive-bombers, was relieved when VB-8 skipper Moe Vose flew up alongside him. Vose gave Hovind a big grin and the *I'll take over* signal. Hovind felt that Vose was "as cool as could be. He looked just like a deacon driving a buckboard to church."[8]

Moe Vose cued his group up on the mighty *Shokaku*, veteran of the Pearl Harbor assault, the Coral Sea battle, and the Eastern Solomons carrier battle. At 0927, the six surviving planes of VS-8 commenced their dives. Bill Woodman, first down on *Shokaku*, laid his thousand-pound bomb on the after flight deck behind the island structure. Lieutenant Ben Moore, VS-8's chubby operations officer, and Lieutenant (j.g.) Don Kirkpatrick landed their big bombs just aft and close to *Shokaku*'s stern. Lieutenant (j.g.) Jimmy Forbes, fifth to dive, was credited with a hit on the carrier's port bow on the flight deck.[9]

Moe Vose's VB-8 group was hot on the heels of the VS-8 pilots. Vose landed his thousand-pounder on *Shokaku* as well. An antiaircraft burst exploded below the cockpit of Vose's wingman, Lieutenant (j.g.) Doug Carter—whose gunner, Slim Moore, was hit in the right leg by a bullet. Moore spent the return flight trying to stop the bleeding, using supplies from his first-aid kit. Chunks of *Shokaku*'s flight deck were blasted skyward and slammed into the cockpit of Fred Bates as he dived down with the flattop square in his sights. Two of the last VB-10 pilots to attack,

Lieutenants (j.g.) Roy Gee and Joe Auman, were credited with additional direct hits.[10]

Shokaku was blazing from bow to stern as the *Hornet* dive-bombers cleared the area. The Japanese could only estimate that she had taken between three and six bomb hits. The eleven *Hornet* survivors tuned their YE homing gear en route home, confident that they had knocked one enemy flattop out of the battle.[11]

The second *Hornet* strike force made its attack on Japanese shipping at almost the same time that Vose and company were pounding *Shokaku.*

Commander Walt Rodee's group approached Admiral Hara's small force of two cruisers and two destroyers. Lieutenant John Lynch, leading the nine VB-8 and VS-8 SBDs, attacked the cruiser *Chikuma.* Lynch planted his big bomb just aft of the cruiser's forward smokestack, setting off a large explosion, flames, and black smoke. Lieutenants (j.g.) Joe King and Tom Wood also claimed hits on *Chikuma* with their thousand-pound bombs. Lieutenant Ed Stebbins, bringing in the VS-8 section of Lieutenants (j.g.) Phil Rusk and Al Wood, claimed an additional two hits and a near miss.[12]

Chikuma was hit by at least two bombs that demolished her bridge and created havoc belowdecks. At least two near misses were close enough to rock the big ship heavily. In the meantime, Lieutenant Ward Powell's nine bomb-armed Avengers attacked the second cruiser, *Tone,* but failed to score any direct hits. With that, the two *Hornet* strike groups had shot their bolt and turned for home.[13]

The scattered *Enterprise* strike group, decimated by Zeros, followed up with their own separate attacks. At around 0920, Lieutenant Mac Thompson, leading the Torpedo Ten survivors, noticed Admiral Abe's ships off to the west. He swung his Avengers toward them, with CEAG Dick Gaines and Jimmy Flatley's fighters following.

Lanny Wheeler, flying rear seat in Skip Ervin's SBD, noted the majority of his group's planes peeling away. Glenn Estes, leading the trio of VS-10 bombers, missed the turn to the west made by the F4Fs and TBFs. His small Dauntless group kept flying northwest toward a large cumulus cloud mass. In their absence, the VT-10 group and Flatley's fighters pounced on the cruiser *Suzuya* at around 0930. The Avengers were unable to drive home their torpedoes, and *Suzuya* escaped with only strafing damage left by Flatley's Wildcats.[14]

After observing the Japanese ships from the advantage of cloud cover, Estes turned his SBDs back toward the *Chikuma* force that had just been hit by *Hornet*'s second attack group. From twelve thousand feet, Estes surmised that they had a *Kongo*-class battleship below them. It was in fact the wounded *Chikuma*, which became the focal point of the three VS-10 crews that pushed over against her at 0939.

John Richey landed his thousand-pound bomb just off *Chikuma*'s starboard bow. Ervin followed closely and gunner Wheeler believed they made a direct hit on the warship's number-two turret. Bringing up the rear, Estes claimed a direct hit on her starboard side amidships. In actuality, two of their bombs hit close enough to *Chikuma*'s starboard side only to rip open a large hole that flooded a fire room and slowed her speed.[15]

The antiaircraft fire, which had been fairly light during their dives, became intense as the VS-10 pilots retreated. After their attack, the trio effected a rendezvous, and Zeros made one more pass at them. Wheeler, Ralph Gowling, and Jay Pugh all opened fire in unison as the Zeros converged behind Ensign Richey's dive-bomber. They believed their combined fire had downed one of the Japanese fighters, and for their actions in saving their own planes, the three VS-10 radiomen would all be recommended for the Air Medal.

The straggling formations of *Hornet* and *Enterprise* strike planes made their way back toward TF-61, hoping that their own flight decks had survived whatever Admiral Nagumo had sent out against them.

TWENTY
Ace in a Day

What a hell of a place to be stuck in, thought Robbie Robinson.

He and Jack Finrow of VS-10 had been denied permission to join *Hornet*'s morning strike groups against Nagumo's carriers. Now they and Lieutenant Bill Martin were resigned to riding out enemy air attacks in their sister carrier's ready room with unassigned VS-8 pilots Ivan Swope, Harold White, and Ben Tappan. Radio transmissions at 0843 indicated a Japanese attack group was moving in on the U.S. carriers. The cruiser *Northampton*'s radar was first to lock in on bogeys closing from seventy miles out. The U.S. fighter director officers urgently vectored Wildcat fighters out to intercept the incoming strike. Dogfights ensued between F4F and Zero opponents while the carriers commenced high-speed evasive maneuvering.

The first *Zuikaku* strikers moved in against *Hornet* at around 0905 as Captain Mason zigzagged his big carrier at twenty-eight knots. Minutes later, Robinson could hear *Hornet*'s five-inch-gun batteries above open fire as Japanese dive-bombers moved into range at 10,500 yards distant. The standby pilots continued chatting to pass the time. One minute later, the smaller 1.1-inch-gun batteries and then the 20mms started firing as the Val dive-bombers flew directly overhead.[1]

The first Val's bomb threw up a geyser of water to the starboard side of *Hornet*'s bow. The second Japanese pilot landed a 551-pound semi-armor-piercing bomb at the center of *Hornet*'s flight deck. The next Val was hit by AA fire, and the plane, with its bomb still on board, slammed into the ocean just off *Hornet*'s starboard bow. The next section of *Zuikaku* dive-bombers quickly landed two more devastating direct hits. One explosion wiped out thirty sailors in *Hornet*'s starboard after-gun gallery.

Nakajima Kate torpedo bombers from *Shokaku* assaulted *Hornet* next. Two torpedoes exploded in *Hornet*'s engineering spaces at 0914, flooding fire rooms, knocking out power, inducing a 10.5-degree list, and killing her headway. There was no break for the luckless flattop, as more *Zuikaku* dive-bombers came plunging down from above. Warrant Officer Shigeyuki Sato, likely wounded, plunged straight down and did not release his bomb. His Val slammed into the island structure, ripping off its starboard wing in the signal halyards, and spraying burning gasoline over the signal bridge. The remains of the dive-bomber smashed through the flight deck, penetrated all the way to VS-8's ready room, and spread fire and chaos below.[2]

Pilot Ben Tappan undogged the door at the rear of the ready room and was nearly stampeded by the airmen who rushed out. The only injury in VS-8's room was Lieutenant (j.g.) Ivan Swope, who suffered burned flesh on his left leg below the knee and on his left hand and foot. Jack Finrow and Robbie Robinson fought their way through the frenzy of airmen as the room filled with thick black smoke and sprinklers went off. Finrow and others headed toward the open hangar deck, while Robinson led another group toward the flight deck. *Hornet* had been reduced to a flaming, listing wreck. Robbie helped pass ammunition to 20mm gun crews and administered morphine to critically injured sailors carried up to the flight deck.[3]

The CAP fighter pilots tangled with the various groups of Japanese warplanes that had wrecked *Hornet*. Some of the *Enterprise* morning scout planes, reaching their task force at about the time of these attacks, mixed it up with enemy warplanes as well.

Ken Miller of VS-10 used dead-reckoning navigation for the early part of his return after bombing the Japanese warships. Miller then climbed to 3,500 feet, so that gunner Dave Cawley could direct their course using his ZB homing gear. They finally reached *Hornet* first and made a deck-level pass above her before turning toward his own carrier in the distance. Suddenly, the carrier's guns boomed into action. Cawley swung his rear guns into position and looked up in time to see Japanese dive-bombers coming down directly on *Hornet*. The screening cruisers and destroyers joined in the shooting. Miller's wingman, Redbird Burnett, saw a burst of flames on *Hornet*'s flight deck as one of the Japanese scored a direct hit.[4]

Miller cleared the heavy AA fire and headed for the Big E. His SBD was critically low on fuel. Burnett lingered closer around the *Hornet* task force, where he was swept up in the action with the Japanese strikers. One plane got on his tail and shot out a cylinder in his engine and his hydraulic system. His gas system was punctured, and gasoline puddled in his bullet-riddled cockpit. Burnett spotted a Nakajima 97 Kate torpedo plane just fifty feet above the water, and made a pass on it in spite of his plane's damage. His slugs forced the Kate into the ocean, where the crew scrambled into their rubber raft. For Burnett, attacking enemy planes was becoming old hat: he had downed a Val at the Eastern Solomons battle. He and gunner Bob Wynn fired on the downed crew until they had deflated the life raft before moving on.

Tom Ramsay of VS-10 also engaged several Japanese planes. Gunner Lefty Craft felt certain he accounted for some damage with his Brownings. He was firing on one plane when another opened up on Ramsay's SBD with a 20mm cannon. One of the shells exploded in his rear cockpit, throwing shrapnel into Craft's left leg.[5]

The first Japanese strike group had included fifty-three aircraft. Nine Val dive-bombers were destroyed by fighters and antiaircraft fire, as were several Nakajima torpedo bombers, and three Zeros. Burnett had downed one departing Kate with his SBD, while F4Fs piled onto several others. All told, twenty-four Japanese strikers were lost in the target area, including the two planes that slammed into *Hornet*. Fourteen others would eventually ditch due to battle damage or fuel exhaustion, leaving only fifteen of the fifty-three first-wave strikers to make it home.[6]

Unknown to the sailors fighting for their lives on the stricken *Hornet*, a second Japanese strike group was already inbound to add to Task Force 61's miseries.

Ken Miller and Dave Cawley reached the Big E about 0930. Most of the sixteen SBDs from the morning search-strike group, plus the six IAP dive-bombers, were already waiting to land. Among them was VB-10's Don Wakeham, whose only contact had been with an American PBY patrol plane. Frank West, flying an IAP bomber, had chased another PBY that failed to answer his recognition signals until he closed in tight on the big seaplane. All of the returning SBDs were low on fuel and five had suffered battle damage. *Enterprise* obligingly turned into the wind and Lieutenant (j.g.) Jim Daniels began landing the first of the returning VS-10 and VB-10 dive-bombers.

Birney Strong, returning from his triumphant pounding of the carrier *Zuiho*, made it on board with less than five gallons of fuel remaining. Bucky Lee's S-1 had a smashed windshield, bullet holes in its prop, and holes in its left gas tank. Chuck Irvine's S-2 had bullet holes in the right main tank, a badly riddled tail section, and more bullets in his right wing. Redbird Burnett's S-4 had bullet holes in the right outboard tank and its flap operating mechanism was destroyed.

Slim Colley was flying with Lieutenant Bob Frohlich, a senior pilot with whom he had never flown. Frolich called the ship and said that his plane and that of Bud Lucier were very low on fuel and they had better do something fast. "The ship called back and said for us to land the best we could," said Colley. "They couldn't straighten out to take us aboard as they were doing their high speed maneuvers." Frohlich chased the Big E around in a full circle. As they entered the groove, Colley noted that the carrier "was cocked at an angle because of the turn. We landed and almost rolled off the side because of the steep angle." As Frohlich taxied out of the barrier around 0943, his SBD was gasping its last fumes of fuel.[7]

Hal Buell and wingman Red Hoogerwerf circled *Enterprise* until they received the "Charlie" signal that indicated they could land. Buell landed first, and the deck crews moved his Dauntless forward to a spot just left of the center bow edge of the flight deck. As Buell and gunner George Eiswald scrambled out, deck crews tied down their SBD. Hal saw incoming Japanese planes as he ran across the flight deck to take cover in the starboard-side forward gun mount.[8]

Scouting Ten searchers Red Carmody and Les Ward were getting tense as they approached the spot where Point Option should be. *How had we navigated?* Red wondered. At first, there was nothing but lonely ocean, but they followed the ZB signals in toward the task force. Carmody and Ward spotted the flaming *Hornet* but did not yet have *Enterprise* in sight. Red was feeling the "pucker factor" as their fuel gauges dropped toward empty. "We agreed to ditch together at the same time," said Carmody. "Then all of a sudden, the *Enterprise* came out from under a squall." He and Ward were among the last of the morning group to land on mere fuel fumes. "Both Les and I had to be pushed out of the arresting gear," Carmody said.[9]

The final SBD to make the cut was that of Miller and Cawley. They caught the third arresting wire and waited while the deck crews cleared their tail hook. It was 0948, and LSO Daniels had brought down all twenty-two of the morning *Enterprise* scouts and seven Grim Reaper CAP fighters. The flight deck was a gaggle of activity as the Big E next prepared to land some of the other returning fighter planes from both *Hornet* and *Enterprise*. The flight deck was temporarily shut down as the planes were hurriedly respotted. Most airmen went below to give intelligence reports and grab some coffee and food. Captain Osborne Hardison proposed to Jim Thomas that he take a strike of ten of his VB-10 crews (Welch, Gibson, Stevens, West, Nelson, Carroum, McGraw, Griffith, and Hoogerwerf) back into the air as quickly as possible. They would fly out without fighter plane cover, strike the enemy ships previously reported, and then continue on to Henderson Field on Guadalcanal.[10]

The *Enterprise* radar team was already reporting the second Japanese strike group to be only forty-five miles out and approaching. At 0959, two TBFs and one F4F from Dick Gaines's tattered strike group approached to land. Dick Batten was forced to put his Avenger in the water and at 1004, his errant torpedo—knocked loose in his ditching— circled around and blasted his own rescue destroyer *Porter*. Those on board *Porter*, including VB-10 airmen Paul Halloran and Earl Gallagher, were recovered by the destroyer *Shaw*.

Ken Miller's Dauntless was lowered on the number one elevator to the hangar deck, where ready hands shoved his SBD aft. As Dave Cawley jumped out of his rear cockpit, he heard his ship's five-inch guns booming away at enemy aircraft overhead. Then the smaller 40mm and 20mm guns erupted. The action was getting too close for comfort. Cawley's throat was parched, however, and his first thought was to find a drink of water.[11]

Gunner Johnny Liska had been on the flight deck getting some fresh air. As the bombers moved in, he heard over the loudspeaker that everyone was to take cover. Liska headed for his ready room and lay down on the deck. "This was one time I sure wanted to be in the air," he said.

Captain Hardison, forced to commence evasive maneuvers, did not have time to launch Jim Thomas's VB-10 strike group. One SBD was still spotted aft on her flight deck, while others that had been hurriedly refueled and rearmed with bombs were parked on the forward end of her flight deck. Down below in the hangar deck, other SBDs had been readied for the next strike and were just waiting to be hoisted topside.

Lookouts spotted the first Vals pushing over at 1015, and heavy AA fire erupted from the battleship *South Dakota*. Wayne Colley had spent several minutes going over his instruments in the rear cockpit after his SBD was parked up on the port bow. When he finally strolled across the flight deck toward the ready room below, all hell was breaking loose. The ship's guns opened up with a frightening roar as dive-bombers screamed down. Colley and other airmen raced for cover belowdecks.

The first strike group to assault *Enterprise* was led by Lieutenant Commander Mamoru Seki of *Shokaku* and included nineteen Val dive-bombers with five Zero escorts. A murderous hail of TF-16 gunfire shredded Seki's leading Aichi. His Val was disintegrated by the AA fire and plunged into the sea. His bomb exploded close amidships off *Enterprise*'s side as Captain Hardison heeled the Big E into a hard left turn.

The first dive-bombers failed to score a hit, but *Enterprise*'s good luck thus far had reached its end. At 1017, Petty Officer First Class Kiyoto Furuta landed his 551-pound bomb through the center of the flight deck. The bomb punched through *Enterprise*'s deck and forecastle and detonated in midair near her port bow. The bomb's concussion blew Bucky Lee's VS-10 SBD, numbered S-1, off the bow. In its rear seat, Aviation Machinist Mate First Class Sam Davis Presley was killed as he fired away with its twin .30-caliber machine guns. The blast also badly wounded a gunnery officer, Ensign Marshall Field IV, son of the Chicago businessman who started the department store of the same name. The VS-10 SBD of Frohlich and Colley, S-11, began leaking burning gasoline and was shoved overboard.[12]

Dave Cawley was slurping from a drinking fountain on the hangar deck when the Japanese bomb punched through within fifty feet of where he was standing. The force of its blast knocked Cawley to the deck. Unhurt, he headed topside. He became stuck on a hanging chain ladder en route and decided to just stay put while the ship's guns pounded away.

One minute after the first hit, a second bomb struck *Enterprise* ten feet abaft the number-one elevator in the center of the flight deck. There were two distinct explosions. The first blast set afire three SBDs strapped to the hangar deck overhead and threatened to ignite five others being armed and gassed nearby. The three burning aircraft (one from VB-10 and two VS-10 spares) were lowered and jettisoned, along with three other VS-10 planes being serviced nearby.

Cawley made his way back to the hangar deck but found it completely ablaze. Burning gasoline quickly surrounded him and he panicked. *I'll have to jump overboard*, he thought. To do so, however, he realized that he would have to get across some of the burning fuel. An alert bosun's mate activated the hangar's sprinkler system. Cawley dived into a six-foot-wide gear locker with a group of men as jets of water sprayed from the four-inch pipes overhead. Torrents of water poured into the locker as *Enterprise* heeled over sharply to starboard in one of Captain Hardison's violent maneuvers. Cawley found himself fighting from the bottom of a pile of sailors as water filled the tight space. *I'd better get off this hangar deck!* he thought. The perils of fire and water below were enough. Cawley decided to take his chances topside.[13]

"It was really something for a greenhorn to feel those bombs when they hit near the ship," said Red Carmody, who made his way to the VS-10 ready room. "The whole ship would just shake." Radioman Slim Colley, who had just landed, was playing acey-deucey with a pilot while sweating out the attack. "You had to do something," he said. "Everyone was almost a basket case at the end of the attack." With each near miss, *Enterprise* would bounce sharply, sending boards and checkers flying. "We'd grab them and put them back," said Colley. "That's how we occupied our time during the attack."[14]

Bombing Ten's Hoot Gibson, who had flown the previous night's late mission, had slept in on October 26. He, Warren Welch, and other pilots dived for the steel deck as the explosions started. "The policy was to hit the deck to save our lives," said Gibson. The first to the floor was Lieutenant John Dufficy, the non-flying, pudgy intelligence officer from Long Island, who lay spread-eagled under a pile of pilots. "Someone with a sense of humor, and less regard for the accuracy of Japanese bombing, took that moment to draw an outline around the prostrate officer," said Hal Buell. In block letters, the chalk outline drawing was labeled RE-SERVED FOR LT. DUFFICY.[15]

The violent gyrations of the twisting carrier did little to soothe the fliers sprawled for protection in VB-10's ready room. "We had a huge fifty-cup coffee urn sitting on a table, which tipped over," said Gibson. "We were all swimming around on the deck in hot coffee." At 1020, a near miss exploded just ten feet from *Enterprise*'s starboard quarter. The concussion rocked *Enterprise* so violently that one Wildcat parked forward on the flight deck bounced over the side. Don Wakeham's VB-10 Dauntless was bounced into the starboard 20mm gun gallery, where it was left perched precariously on the edge. Willing hands, including senior LSO Robin Lindsey, attempted to rock the SBD over the side. Captain Hardison, seeing the danger, alertly threw *Enterprise* into a violent turn to port and helped toss the dangling SBD into the sea.

Fully armed and fueled aircraft had ensured the destruction of Japanese carriers at the Battle of Midway. Alert thinking by many *Enterprise* personnel helped save her from a similar fate this day. Thus, of thirty-one SBDs on board during the attack (twelve VB-10 and nineteen VS-10), nine had gone overboard due to fire, damage, or the force of explosions. Red Carmody marveled at how efficiently the Big E's damage control men shored up the damage and tended to the wounded. In the aftermath of such destruction, the battle veteran–former California fruit picker could only think, *I'm no longer a hick.*[16]

Bombing Ten pilot Bruce McGraw and his scouting section leader, Warren Welch, had landed back on board before the bombs hit. After his ship was hit, McGraw made his way to a first-aid station and asked what he could do to help.

"Go sit by that sailor right there and talk to him," one of the doctors advised. "Ask him if there's anything you can do for him."

McGraw found that the badly burned sailor was crying out for morphine. Moved by the young man's pitiful wails, the pilot asked the doctor to administer more morphine for his pain.

"He's had all that we can give him," McGraw was advised. "He has less than ten minutes to live, so just do what you can."[17]

McGraw returned to comfort the dying sailor, who finally slumped over against him and passed away. The scene of death and blood running freely across his own carrier's deck was more than the Texan could handle. He found himself moved to tears and a new resolve. *This war is too terrible a thing to have to go on any longer than necessary. The quickest way to get it over with is to kill as many Japanese as I can in my role as a dive-bomber pilot.*

Why in the hell am I once again stuck aboard ship when I should be bombing a carrier? thought Hoot Gibson. At Midway, he had ridden out the Japanese air attacks when his *Yorktown* was destroyed.[18]

As smoke poured into VB-10's ready room, Gibson decided, *To hell with this! I'm going up to the flight deck.* He arrived in time to see the next wave of Japanese planes attack his ship. At 1035, just fifteen minutes after *Enterprise* had been damaged with bombs, her radar picked up another inbound Japanese strike group. This second wave included seventeen Type 97 Kate torpedo planes from *Zuikaku*, escorted by four Zero fighters.

The Grim Reapers of Fighting Ten moved in to intercept. Swede Vejtasa, leading the Reaper Seven Wildcat division, had already torched one Val during the first strike against *Hornet*. Minutes later, as Kate torpedo planes attacked *Hornet*, Swede spotted a lone Val searching for his companions. Vejtasa scored his second kill by cutting down the dive-bomber at low altitude.[19]

Around 1045, Swede was pumping fuel from his auxiliary wing tank and climbing for higher altitude. His division mate Hank Leder was first to spot the next attackers, eleven *Zuikaku* Type 97 torpedo bombers. "Tally ho, nine o'clock down!" Leder called.[20]

Swede blasted away one of the dark-green Kates, and his wingman, Lieutenant Leroy "Tex" Harris, nailed another. Then they teamed up to down a third Kate. Swede ducked under the tails of the torpedo bombers to avoid the fire from their rear gunners and began sending one after another down in flames as he chased them into a cloud bank. After disposing of an entire section of them with short, effective bursts, Vejtasa broke out of the clouds and found another Kate heading toward *Enterprise* with a torpedo. He closed in and let loose with his .50s. "I kept figuring he'd release his torpedo as he got lower on the water, but he never did," said Swede. "Finally, he caught a wingtip in the water and cartwheeled." It was Vejtasa's fifth Kate to splash and his seventh kill of the mission.[21]

Swede was very low on ammo as another Kate flew over his top. "I almost had heart failure," he said. "All he had to do was drop down and fire his forward machine guns and I was a goner." Instead, Swede emptied his guns into the torpedo plane. The Kate was losing altitude, but Swede was now out of bullets as he continued to chase his foe. The Japanese pilot headed straight for the battleship *South Dakota* as AA fire pounded at both aircraft. "I gave serious consideration to cutting off his tail with my prop as we had discussed in our training," Vejtasa related. As he closed in, his SBD was caught in the turbulent stream of fire pouring off the Kate and he was forced hard to the right by the blast.

Vejtasa was later credited with a probable kill of this plane, but the doomed pilot, Seaman First Class Kiyomi Takei, made a last-minute dive for a U.S. warship. Swede watched in horror as the Kate plowed into the destroyer *Smith*, still wielding a torpedo. Dozens of sailors were killed in the spectacular blast and in the explosion of the Kate's torpedo moments later. *Smith* staggered out of formation, belching smoke and losing speed as other Kates tried to polish off the damaged *Enterprise*.

Just prior to the attack, the *Enterprise* flight deck crews had spotted six Dauntlesses aft to move them from the fires burning forward. LSOs Robin Lindsey and Jim Daniels jumped into the two rearmost SBDs and blazed away with the .30-calibers. One of the Kates they were firing upon rolled into a steep wingover and smashed into the ocean in flames.

Swede Vejtasa had accounted for five Kates in one mission and an amazing seven total kills for the day. It was a feat unmatched by any other Navy Wildcat pilot in a single day—making him an ace and a half in one flight! His skipper, Jimmy Flatley, was beyond impressed with his star pupil. He wrote in the margin of Swede's flight logbook, "Greatest single combat flight record in the history of air warfare," and signed his name. Months earlier, Swede's shipmate Butch O'Hare was given the Medal of Honor for downing five Japanese planes while defending *Lexington*. Flatley recommended Vejtasa for a Medal of Honor as well for his Santa Cruz victories, but in the end he was given his third Navy Cross.[22]

Elements of the U.S. strike forces began straggling back at around 1045, as the latest wave of Japanese planes cleared out from TF-61.

The first wave of *Hornet*'s strikers were the first to return. Clay Fisher of VB-8 ran out of fuel and ditched near the cruiser *Juneau*. Both he and his gunner, George Ferguson, were wounded but the cruiser pulled them on board. Al Wood of VS-8 traded fire with a departing Kate and hammered it into the ocean. Several other returning *Hornet* SBD crews slugged it out with Japanese warplanes, including Joe Auman of VB-8. In the process, his dive-bomber was riddled, but he was credited with destroying a *Zuiho* Kate near TF-17.[23]

Before *Enterprise* could take aboard any of the returning *Hornet* strike planes, a third strike group from *Junyo* approached TF-16. The Big E's flight deck finally reopened at 1115, after a ninety-minute hiatus due to Japanese attacks and jammed elevators. Jim Daniels brought down some of the CAP fighters before the *Junyo* strikers attacked at 1121. They landed one bomb squarely on the battleship *South Dakota* and another glanced off *Enterprise*'s port bow and exploded at her waterline. Several *Hornet* VB-8 Dauntless crews tangled with the *Junyo* strike group, and they claimed several kills.[24]

The *Enterprise* strike group led by Dick Gaines also returned during this time. All three radiomen in Glenn Estes's VS-10 section—Pugh, Garlow, and Wheeler—blazed away at what they thought was a Zero. It was actually the *Hornet* SBD of Stan Holms. Although Estes would later apologize to his fellow bomber pilot, he was disturbed that his gunners had not only failed to recognize an American plane but had also missed their target.[25]

As the last *Junyo* strikers moved out, Admiral Kinkaid decided that he must break off the action in order to avoid losing his last carrier, *Enterprise*. He informed Murray that he was retiring toward "Roses," the code name for Efate. The fight was on to save *Hornet* as the cruiser *Northampton* attempted to take her under tow. By 1140, some seventy-three aircraft from both the *Hornet* and Air Group Ten were circling above, waiting to land on the Big E. Among this group were two dozen SBDs (twenty-one from *Hornet* and Estes's three VS-10 strikers), very low on fuel.

Ralph Hovind of VS-8 could see his own *Hornet* lying dead in the water. The Big E was also smoking, but it was his only hope. "Any port in a storm," said Hovind. Moe Vose led his SBDs through the day's proper recognition signal—left-hand turns, made while dipping the port wingtip twice—but the aviators were still greeted by heavy AA fire from jittery U.S. gunners. Hovind's Dauntless was so shot up that *Enterprise* deck crews shoved it overboard to make room for other circling planes to land. "Five planes were completely unfit for further service on landing," Vose noted. Pilot Fred Bates returned with a chunk of *Shokaku*'s flight deck. He greeted his astonished VB-8 skipper, and presented the charred chunk of wood with jagged edges to Vose.[26]

Jim Daniels, coached by boss Robin Lindsey, signaled down all the circling planes. Benny Moore of VS-8 returned with most of his canopy shot away. His borrowed *Enterprise* S-16 was pushed overboard to make room for more returnees. Moore's gunner, ACRM Ralph Phillips, was taken below for treatment of a broken right radius and ulna. Slim Moore, gunner for Doug Carter of Bombing Eight, suffered from a bullet in his right leg. Pilot Ken White had a lacerated arm and hand, and gunner Dick Woodson had a gunshot wound to his left knee.

Daniels had landed more than sixty planes without mishap since 0930, and the flight deck was now severely crowded. Senior LSO Lindsey stepped in and continued landing planes even after the bridge ordered him to stop. The previous evening, John Crommelin had promised his pilots, "If you get back to the ship and into the groove, we'll get you aboard!" The red flag for no more landings was flying, but Crommelin made sure the Big E kept steaming into the wind. The rest was up to Lindsey, who wisely took Uncle John's hint to keep on landing war birds as long as he had an open wire.[27]

Daniels bet his boss a dime for every plane he could bring down on the number-one arresting wire. Five SBDs and three of Swede Vejtasa's Wildcat division soon made the cut safely. Grim Reaper pilot Russ Reiserer was next, and he was able to taxi forward only a few feet before his prop was nearly touching the next plane. The flight deck was packed nearly to its aft end, yet one fighter plane still circled above. It was Swede Vejtasa, the valiant fighter who had scored seven kills.

At 1222, Swede dropped in and hooked the number-one wire on the aft end of the flight deck. "Robin was the best," said Swede. "There were no barricades, and he brought me in easy." His Wildcat was chocked right there on the spot. That was it: forty-seven planes had landed in forty-three minutes without a crash. Vejtasa walked over to thank Lindsey, who was collecting ten dimes from his assistant Daniel.[28]

Commander, *Hornet* Air Group, (CHAG) Walt Rodee, still circling overhead, decided to head for Espíritu Santo, where he landed his TBF at 1600. To make room for other planes, deck crews hustled aircraft below as *Enterprise* began launching Wildcats to free the flight deck. In the interim, nine Avengers from VT-10 and VT-6 were forced to ditch, but task force warships rescued all of the downed airmen. At 1507, thirteen hastily refueled *Hornet* SBDs were launched under John Lynch for Espíritu Santo to help clear the congestion.

The fight to save *Hornet* continued for hours. Admiral Nagumo, not satisfied he had finished off the American carriers, had sent seven *Junyo* Kate torpedo planes with eight Zero escorts off at 1313. *Zuikaku* sent out another two Vals, seven Kates, and five Zeros at about the same time. *Junyo* would follow two hours later with a final small strike of six Zeros and four Vals.[29]

Hornet was being towed by *Northampton* at three knots while her engineers labored to restore power to the stricken carrier. Admiral Murray ordered his wounded sailors and all non-essential aviators to be transferred to the destroyer *Russell*, which had come alongside to help fight the fires. "The rolling of the two ships made a shambles of the starboard bridge wing on the *Russell*," said VB-8 gunner Billy Cottrell. *Enterprise* SBD aviators Bill Martin, Jack Finrow, Robbie Robinson, Buck Bevier, and Fred Sugar eased down lines and nets and dropped into the ocean. Their swim was only about thirty feet before they scrambled up netting lowered over *Russell*'s side.[30]

Radar soon picked up the groups of inbound Japanese strike planes, forcing *Russell* to cast off with the excess personnel. *Northampton* cast off her towlines at 1513 as the first Kate torpedo planes began making their runs. One of the *Junyo* Type 97s slammed another torpedo into *Hornet*'s starboard side, adding to her dangerous list. Captain Mason was finally forced to order his crew to abandon ship.

Bill Martin watched *Russell*'s skipper maneuver his destroyer to help rescue the carrier crewmen swimming in the ocean. "A lot of them were so black when they came to the surface from the oil that they were hard to find," Martin said. Others were terribly burned and had suffered all sorts of injuries during the many attacks on their ship.[31]

In the abandon-ship process, *Zuikaku* planes appeared and dropped their 1,760-pound bombs in a close pattern. One detonated aft on her flight deck, while the rest exploded in the sea astern. Martin watched the Japanese planes diving down to drop their bombs and then strafe the U.S. escort ships as they pulled out. One *Hornet* sailor was being pulled from the water by *Russell* destroyermen as Martin watched. Just as he was being brought aboard, he was struck in the head by a bullet from a strafing Japanese plane. Martin could only think how cruel fate was "after all that."

Junyo's final strike force of ten planes appeared over TF-17 at 1650. One of their 551-pound bombs penetrated *Hornet*'s flight deck and exploded in the hangar, causing another fire. The decks on *Russell* were packed end to end with survivors. "It was standing room only," pilot Robbie Robinson said. "There was maybe another twelve hundred of us on there, not counting the wounded."

Captain Mason was the last to leave his carrier, which had lost 118 men. Admiral Murray ordered the destroyers *Mustin* and *Anderson* to finish off *Hornet* with torpedoes and gunfire, to prevent the Japanese from capturing the battered flattop. When last seen, the stubborn flattop was blazing from stem to stern as her escort warships limped away. Japanese warships found *Hornet* during the night and, deeming her unworthy of salvage, finally put her out of her misery with four more torpedoes.

Enterprise continued to retire toward Roses. That evening, her wardroom served as both a makeshift operating room and busy cafeteria due to damage to her main sickbay. "Strong smells of chloroform, antiseptics, and death permeated the multiple surgical operations going on," said Hoot Gibson. He and other weary pilots sloshed through standing water with their food trays and sat down to eat evening chow.[32]

In the final accounting of damage caused by *Enterprise* dive-bombers at Santa Cruz, credit for fighter kills was given to Bucky Lee, Bill Johnson (two), Clarence Garlow, Elgie Williams, John Liska, and Nick Baumgartner. A combined kill was credited to gunners Jay Pugh, Ralph Gowling, and Lanny Wheeler from the Gaines strike. Redbird Burnett was acknowledged for shooting down a torpedo bomber.

The *Enterprise* fliers were honored with numerous awards. Among them was John Liska, who was recommended by *Enterprise*'s skipper for an Air Medal for shooting down another Japanese Zero at Santa Cruz. Liska, a hero of the Coral Sea battle in May, serving with *Lexington*'s VS-2, had been bypassed for awards previously. Captain Hardison of the Big E considered Liska's actions "outstanding performance of duty," duly acknowledged by former *Lexington* skipper Ted Sherman in his previous intent to award him. Birney Strong was recommended for the Medal of Honor for taking out *Zuiho*, an award VF-10 skipper Jimmy Flatley believed Strong "richly deserved." Instead, Birney would eventually add another Navy Cross to his collection for his bravery at Santa Cruz.[33]

Jimmy Flatley's Grim Reapers had contributed heavily to the final tally of some four dozen Japanese planes destroyed. Former VS-2 pilot Dave Pollock was credited with a torpedo plane, and Jack Leppla achieved ace status by adding one more kill to his previous four. Swede Vejtasa was the hero of the day, with seven confirmed kills. Eleven Reaper Wildcats had gone down on October 26, with only six pilots rescued—two by the enemy. Leppla was not among those fortunate enough to be rescued. Gus Widhelm, skipper of *Hornet*'s Scouting Eight, and gunner George Stokely were recovered the following afternoon by a PBY from Espíritu Santo.

Santa Cruz was a tactical defeat for the U.S. Navy. Two Japanese carriers and a heavy cruiser had been damaged, but the Americans had lost one of their precious carriers, a destroyer, and seventy-four aircraft.

More than twenty Dauntlesses were lost from all causes, including eleven blown overboard or jettisoned on *Enterprise*. In return, the SBD crews claimed twenty-three Zeros, three Vals and two Kates shot down, although the true number was much lower. The SBDs bomb-hit ratio was much higher than what had been accomplished at Eastern Solomons. On August 24, they had scored eleven percent versus forty percent hits at Santa Cruz. They had dropped twenty-seven bombs on five enemy ships and made at least eleven hits on four of them.[34]

Enterprise limped away toward Efate to lick her wounds and to piece her air group back together following her third carrier battle in five months. The difference this time was that she had been seriously damaged and was now the sole U.S. Navy aircraft carrier in the Pacific to defend the Marines in the Solomons with her Air Group Ten.

TWENTY-ONE
"Back to Sea in a Pitiable Condition"

The Cactus Air Force was struggling to hold the line at Henderson Field as *Enterprise* limped back to Nouméa to tend to her battle damage. The orphaned Navy Dauntless aviators still at Cactus included Scouting 71 crews from the lost *Wasp* and a half dozen VB-6 crews under Ray Davis.

During late October and early November, Dauntless crews on Guadalcanal were frequently called upon to bomb Japanese artillery pieces and troop concentrations. They used everything in their arsenal at Cactus: 100-pound wing bombs, 500-pounders, and even 325-pound depth charges. Bob Mohler of VS-71 dropped anti-submarine ordnance "that had eighteen-inch fuses on the noses so that when the depth charges hit, they would explode eighteen inches off the ground and not dig a crater— thus doing much harm. It would take out shrubs and trees and leave a bare spot in the jungle."

General Geiger's crews struggled to keep sufficient quantities of aircraft in service each day. On October 29, Mohler, Gene Lerman, and several other aviators rode the DC3 medical evac plane to Espíritu Santo to bring back more SBDs. "The evac plane had bunks three tiers high on one side and bucket seats on the other side," said Mohler. "All the bunks held terribly wounded Marines and soldiers. The nurses had their hands full the entire five-hundred-mile trip." Mohler and his companions returned to the Canal two days later with fresh Dauntlesses, flying wing on a B-24 bomber loaded with vital supplies. "We were feeling sort of put out that they wouldn't let us go it alone, for we could easily find an island that was ninety miles long and thirty miles wide," Mohler related. "Our routine searches were longer than that and any of us could find a carrier that was 741 feet long."

At 1500 on November 2, a contact report from B-17s reported a Japanese force of seventeen destroyers, and a cruiser 215 miles from Cactus. Despite heavy rain and thunderheads, Lieutenant Commander Eldridge volunteered to lead two other VMSB-132 SBDs to hit the enemy before dark. All three Dauntless crews were lost, including the indomitable John Eldridge and his VS-71 gunner, Aviation Radioman Third Class George Yanick. Natives on the southeastern tip of Santa Isabel said that at around 2300 they saw a plane with running lights on crash into the sea just outside the reef from Tannibuli Bay. Native pearl divers found the plane the next day. The front half was badly crushed and detached from the after part. They were unable to extricate the body of John Eldridge but Yanick's remains were buried near Tannibuli Bay in a grave marked by a large white cross.[1]

Another VS-71 crew, Lieutenant (j.g.) Gene Lerman and Aviation Radioman Third Class John Swann, was forced to make a water landing during the night off Lunga Point. PT boats that searched the area found no trace of the SBD or its crew. Lieutenant Porter Maxwell assumed acting command of Wasp's old VS-71. The next major threat to Henderson Field was detected by Maxwell's scouts on the afternoon of November 7: eleven troop-laden destroyers were bearing down on Guadalcanal just 170 miles out. Admiral Tanaka, under orders to remain at Shortland, put Captain Torajiro Sato in command of this latest Tokyo Express.

Major Joe Sailer led a division of VMSB-132 and VMSB-141 dive-bombers, along with fighters and three VT-8 Avenger crews, in to attack. They lost one SBD to Japanese float biplanes and damaged destroyers Naganami and Takanami with near misses. It was not enough, however, to prevent the Rat Patrol from depositing eighty percent of its soldier passengers at Tassafaronga and Esperance.[2]

Admiral Halsey made a brief visit to Guadalcanal on November 8. He met with General Geiger, the Marine air commander who was being given a short leave to rest, and Brigadier General Louis Woods, who was taking over his role as senior aviator in command of the Cactus Air Force. Also on this day, the last fifteen of *Wasp*'s VS-71 pilots and gunners and the balance of *Enterprise*'s VB-6 crews boarded a DC-3 transport plane for Espíritu Santo. Nate Murphy considered himself lucky: five of the twelve VS-71 pilots had been lost in action on the Canal. "We were a sorry-looking group, completely exhausted and a little psyched out," Murphy admitted of the surviving *Wasp* crews. Bombing Six pilot Eldor Rodenburg believed his faith had gotten him by on Guadalcanal. He could not imagine an atheist being in his bunch after the many nights they had spent huddled in bombardment shelters.[3]

Jim Thomas gathered his VB-10 pilots in the ready room on October 27, the day after the big Santa Cruz battle. He had a dispatch forwarded from fleet command at Pearl Harbor. The Hawaiian shore patrol had a list of infractions committed by a group of drunken *Enterprise* pilots the night before their carrier had departed Pearl. "It called for strong disciplinary action against the jackasses involved, including me," said Hoot Gibson. Lieutenant Commander Thomas finished reading the charges, looked at Gibson, and laughed. "Consider that you have been severely punished," he said with a wink. The episode would be swept under the rug by the next time the Big E reached Hawaii, as some of the airmen in question would no longer be living.[4]

Enterprise dropped anchor in the mountain-rimmed little anchorage of Nouméa, New Caledonia, on October 30. One day before arriving in port, Lieutenant Commander Mike Sanchez flew ahead with four fighters and Warren Welch of VB-10. They landed at Tontouta Field, located more than forty miles northwest of Nouméa.[5]

Many of Air Group Ten's pilots and gunners were moved ashore via liberty boats once the carrier was anchored in the French harbor. There were simply not enough airworthy planes to go around. Lieutenant Bob Frohlich of VS-10 had orders transferring him to new duty, but the balance of the SBD aviators were shuffled toward Tontouta as repairs to *Enterprise*'s Santa Cruz battle damage commenced. Vice Admiral Halsey was told it would take three weeks to make the lone U.S. carrier in the

Pacific battle-ready again, but he wanted that time reduced by ten days. Seabees and shipfitters from the repair ship *Vestal* swarmed on board to shore up compartments and patch the flight deck and hangar deck.

Hoot Gibson marveled at the lush green vegetation, towering hills, and sandy beaches as they moved through the harbor town. The culture of the local free French citizens, including sidewalk urinals, was a new experience. "It didn't take much to please our jaundiced servicemen that were emerging from the stark fear of hell," Gibson related. "As usual, we had to set up camp," said Birney Strong of Tontouta Airfield. "We operated our planes there and got new airplanes and took over some of the *Hornet*'s airplanes so we actually got the squadrons into some semblance of fighting condition."[6]

Air Group Ten's personnel settled into a hillside about three miles from grassy, Marston-matting-covered Tontouta Field, where their airplanes were based. Aircrews flew the morning scout missions and enjoyed the afternoons off. The pilots slept four to a tent. "We licked our wounds, told a few stories, and drank lots of beer," said Red Carmody. Hoot Gibson found that "modesty flew out the window" with the local toilet being a forty-hole, open-air sensation. "Living conditions were almost as bad as at the Canal, but without the bombing and shelling," said Hal Buell.[7]

There were mini-reunions during the first day in port as rescued aviators, plucked from the ocean by the busy destroyers and cruisers, were returned to the ship. Torpedo Ten suffered the most, with five men killed, two captured by the enemy, and only nine TBFs left in operation. Bombing Ten and Scouting Ten had lost plenty of aircraft, but were fortunate to have escaped the Santa Cruz action without personnel losses. Paul Halloran, Earl Gallagher, Dan Frissell, and Bill Otterstetter had been forced into the ocean. Bill Martin, Jack Finrow, Robbie Robinson, Chief Sugar, and Buck Bevier had been stuck on board *Hornet* when she was bombed and torpedoed. Forced to abandon ship, they rode back to Nouméa on the destroyer *Russell*.

The returned aviators hitched rides on jeeps and Army trucks down forty-four miles of dusty roads from the harbor out to Tontouta. The squadrons took up quarters in Army tents with wood floors and rolled-up flaps. The pilots and gunners slept on cots that were draped with mosquito netting that helped fend off the malaria-carrying insects. Mechanics worked to keep the SBDs, TBFs, and F4Fs airworthy at Tontouta Field (code-named "White Poppy"). Meals were largely Spam and powdered eggs, with the rare treat of fresh meat coming from pilots who ventured into the jungles to shoot the wild deer. A clear, cool mountain stream near the tent camp served as a recreational swimming hole, bathing facility, and laundry. Many of the airmen resorted to growing rough beards in their jungle home. Those who shaved, like Hoot Gibson, did so by feel, without a mirror, using cold water.

Jim Thomas and Bucky Lee's pilots helped check out the new pilots of a freshly arrived Marine bombing squadron that was en route to Guadalcanal. Major Joe Sailer had departed Tontouta the previous day with a handful of his VMSB-132 pilots for Henderson Field. The balance of his squadron under Major Louis B. Robertshaw, Sailer's exec, had just reached Nouméa. Robertshaw took advantage of the seasoned carrier SBD pilots to help whip his scouting squadron into shape. Within a week, the balance of VMSB-132's Dauntless crews would make their way to Henderson Field as well.[8]

During the morning hours, Air Group Ten flew search flights and conducted maintenance on their aircraft. Red Carmody got permission from skipper Bucky Lee to make a sightseeing flight around New Caledonia's coastline. The afternoons were clear for recreation and relaxation. Bruce McGraw, out on a hunt with VB-10 pilot Don Wakeham, managed to kill a young doe with his service pistol on November 9. Hoot Gibson ended one evening craps game with a pocketful of several thousand francs after a gambling session with French soldiers. While the bomber crews were able to unwind, work continued around the clock back at Nouméa's harbor to make *Enterprise* battle-worthy once again. Bill Halsey visited his freshly returned fleet at Nouméa, and saw the beating that his last carrier had taken. The work to repair seamless flight operation had a major hitch: the bomb-damaged number one aircraft elevator was tested while at Nouméa, and it was found to be still malfunctioning.[9]

Halsey returned to Nouméa on November 10, and was met by his chief of staff, Captain Miles Browning. He had been informed by Admiral Nimitz's code breakers of another major Japanese push planned against Guadalcanal. It appeared that a significant landing force was planned to reinforce the Japanese army on the Canal and that the transport convoy carrying the troops to Hell's Island would be shepherded by an armada of warships and two light carriers.

Admiral Yamamoto began forming his plans in early November to support the army buildup on Guadalcanal. The Battle of Santa Cruz had forced his carriers *Shokaku*, *Zuikaku*, and *Zuiho* to head for Japan to repair battle damage and supplement their depleted air groups. He would instead rely upon his Second Fleet, built around the light carriers *Hiyo* and *Junyo*, to provide cover for his other forces. One warship force, which included the battleships *Hiei* and *Kirishima*, was directed to bombard Henderson Field on the night of November 12. Vice Admiral Gunichi Mikawa's Eighth Fleet was to protect Admiral Tanaka's transport convoy while thousands of fresh troops and supplies were off-loaded. All told, Yamamoto planned to move nearly five dozen warships and troop transports in a massive push to turn the tide on Hell's Island.[10]

Admiral Halsey had few options. *Enterprise* was his last operable flight deck in the area, although by his estimates she needed nearly another two weeks to effectively repair her battle damage. The choice was painful but obvious. He met with Admiral Kinkaid that afternoon and warned him that his Air Group Ten should be ready to depart on short notice. *Enterprise* was placed on a one-hour sailing notice, beginning at 0900 on November 11.[11]

The news reached Commander Dick Gaines at 1800 on November 11 that his aviators must be prepared to move out quickly. Action was imminent again and word was passed that all non-flying personnel and spare pilots would leave camp in the morning for *Enterprise*.

At midnight, however, Air Group Ten was roused from its camp by a bugler and told that non-flying personnel were to depart for the ship immediately. Jack Dufficy, Rupert Allen, and spare pilots Jim Leonard, Buck Buchanan, and Nelson Wiggins supervised the moving of VB-10's gear to the carrier at the Nouméa docks on Army trucks. Their carrier was putting to sea with her escort ships to take station about two hundred miles south of San Cristobal Island by daybreak on November 13. The spare aviators without planes barely made it to *Enterprise* in time. Radioman Jack Glass enjoyed a warm shower, good food, and ample cold water, for a change.[12]

The air group began taking off during the early-morning hours of November 11, only to be grounded again when the Big E did not sail at 0900. She finally sortied from Nouméa at 1100, only about twenty-four hours after Halsey had been briefed on the major Japanese offensive that was unfolding. Selected Seabee personnel remained on board *Enterprise* to continue the repair work. Captain Hardison made the decision to keep his forward-most elevator out of commission. He simply could not take the gamble on its becoming stuck in the down position. If it should stick, aircraft launching would be shut down. Scouting Ten skipper Bucky Lee summed up their plight: "We got word that the Japs were winding up to throw the works at us. We were the only carrier in that area; so we put back to sea in a pitiable condition."[13]

Bombing Ten's Hoot Gibson was determined to make his bombs count during this next action. *This is going to be my battle!* he thought. *I will not be denied.* Gibson assumed the Japanese were also rushing to prepare for the next engagement. *By God,* he declared to himself, *I am going to be the person in the middle of this next action.*[14]

The Big E collected her air group as she moved out to sea. The carrier now sported seventy-seven aircraft, including eight Avengers of VT-10, Dick Gaines's CAG-10 TBF, thirty-seven F4Fs, and thirty-one dive-bombers. Bucky Lee had sixteen operational Dauntlesses, while Jim Thomas's VB-10 had fifteen SBDs in operation. The SBD and TBF squadrons were each operating below their normal capacity, but their skippers were determined to make each one count.

As *Enterprise* sailed toward Guadalcanal, another fierce naval surface battle erupted during the night hours of November 12–13. Rear Admiral Hiroaki Abe's bombardment force of two battleships, one light cruiser, and eleven destroyers was intercepted by Rear Admiral Dan Callaghan's force of two heavy cruisers, two light antiaircraft cruisers, and eight destroyers. In the bloody big-gun duel, one Japanese destroyer was sunk, and another, *Yudachi*, was left helpless near the U.S. fleet's own cripples. Callaghan lost two destroyers in the fight, and three others— *Cushing, Monssen,* and *Aaron Ward*—were left battered and powerless. The cruisers *Atlanta* and *Portland* were crippled so badly that they could only limp away from the fight at greatly reduced speed the following morning. The behemoth IJN battleship *Hiei*, pounded by more than eighty-five direct shell hits, suffered a flooded steering room, which crippled her steering control. By dawn of October 13, *Hiei* lay just off Guadalcanal as a prime target while the surviving battleship *Kirishima* and her destroyers headed north toward safety.

The stage had been set for nonstop rounds of shipping attacks the likes of which the Cactus Air Force had never experienced in its nearly three months of existence.

Rear gunner Wayne Colley was getting used to the nightly intelligence briefings. Muddy Waters, VS-10's intelligence officer, used the ready room to describe the latest information about the Japanese offensive against Guadalcanal. On a map, he placed blue pins for carriers, red pins for battleships, and so on. Colley noted that there was only one blue pin for the United States. *Enterprise* was the only carrier in the vicinity to check the enemy's latest advance. Uncle John Crommelin addressed the air group that evening, just as he had done before Santa Cruz. He played up the importance of helping to hold Guadalcanal and how important their individual roles would be. The pilots even learned that Crommelin had ordered mess attendants to cook every steak in the lockers that night for them "because tomorrow evening they may be on the bottom of the ocean."[15]

By dawn of November 13, *Enterprise*'s task group was still too far from the scene to play a direct role with her dive-bombers. At about 270 miles from Guadalcanal, her SBDs did not have the range to strike the crippled and fleeing Japanese warships and make it back to their own flight deck. Colley and his comrades knew that they would have to wait it out.

By 0700, the ten dawn-search SBDs had not made a sighting report. Air boss Crommelin thus implemented an emergency plan to send all of his Avengers on an offensive sweep to attack any cripples they could find. Captain Hardison and Admiral Kinkaid could not risk using their errant forward elevator, so dispatching Lieutenant Scoofer Coffin's Torpedo Ten would help free up the carrier for other flight operations. Armed with a map to Henderson Field, Coffin and his flight of nine TBFs could see the green jungles of Guadalcanal's southern coast by 0930.

In the meantime, General Louis Woods sent his Cactus Air Force Marine units to attack a crippled survivor of the overnight warship battle near Savo Island. It was the battleship *Hiei*, heavily damaged and left steaming slowly in circles. Woods sent fighters, Avengers from Captain George Dooley's VMSB-131, and Marine SBDs from Major Robert Richard's VMSB-142 and Major Joe Sailer's VMSB-141 against the battlewagon in a merry-go-round series of attacks.

Scoofer Coffin's *Enterprise* flight also found *Hiei*. His Buzzard Brigade pilots claimed three torpedo hits before landing at Henderson Field to refuel and rearm. *Hiei*'s sailors fired broadsides from her big guns as the Avengers came in low, but Coffin calmly ignored the threat. Bucky Lee talked to some of VT-10's younger pilots the next day about their harrowing attack runs. "They told me that if it had been anyone other than their commander leading them, they didn't think they would have gone in," Lee recalled.[16]

By noon, more than one hundred sorties had been flown against *Hiei* by Marine and Navy SBDs, torpedo bombers, and fighter planes, as well as Army Air Force B-17s. The jubilant airmen claimed five bomb hits and eight torpedo hits during the morning. Six of Coffin's *Enterprise* TBFs were back at 1330 and they ripped the battlewagon with three more torpedo hits. Captain Masao Nishida ordered his battleship abandoned after dark. *Hiei* slipped under the waves during the night, carrying down 450 officers and men. Launched in 1912, *Hiei* was the first Japanese battleship to be lost in World War II, and the first battleship sunk by the U.S. Navy since 1898.[17]

The *Enterprise* Dauntless crews missed the big action off Guadalcanal on Friday the thirteenth, flying only inner air patrols and anti-sub missions. Swede Vejtasa's CAP division disposed of a Kawanishi Type 97 flying boat during late morning fifty miles out from the carrier. He awarded equal credit to his quartet who, in Swede's words, "cut the plane into rag dolls."[18]

Late that evening, *Enterprise* headed in closer toward Guadalcanal. Admiral Halsey's intelligence pointed toward the following day as the day when the Japanese would try to land major reinforcements. Two of Vice Admiral Gunichi Mikawa's heavy cruisers, *Suzuya* and *Maya*, pounded the Henderson Field area with about a thousand rounds of eight-inch shells during the early minutes of November 14 and damaged a number of the Cactus Air Force planes. Out at sea, Scouting Ten and Bombing

Ten's crews hit their bunks to catch some rest. All signs pointed toward heavy action in the morning. They would not be disappointed.

Rear Admiral Raizo Tanaka was an old hand at reinforcing Guadalcanal. His Tokyo Express destroyers had been making nightly runs for months to off-load fresh soldiers. Tanaka sailed at 1730 from the Shortland Islands with eleven troop transports, escorted by an equal number of destroyers. His ships were loaded with 31,500 artillery shells, supplies for thirty thousand troops for twenty days, and seven thousand khaki- and green-clad soldiers to reinforce his countrymen's efforts to wrestle Guadalcanal from American hands.[19]

As the sun rose over the Solomons, Mikawa's warships were pulling away from the area as Tanaka's transport force steadily moved in. Admiral Kinkaid's TF-16 was approximately two hundred miles south-southwest of Guadalcanal by daybreak. Kinkaid decided to send out early search groups while holding back an attack force to pounce on any contacts that were made.

Enterprise had flown off nine Avengers and six Wildcats to Henderson Field the previous day. She was left with sixty-two available aircraft to handle the vast quantities of Japanese ships that were operating in the vicinity. Scouting Ten and Bombing Ten collectively had thirty-one operable SBDs, and the Grim Reapers had an equal number of F4Fs. The dawn takeoffs were delayed due to heavy rains, but shortly after 0600 the flight deck came alive.[20]

The morning's CAP was followed by ten search SBDs. John Griffith and Greg Nelson of VB-10 were assigned to search the arc from 285 to 315 degrees out to two hundred miles. Another four pairs of searchers would scour 250 miles in northwest and northerly sectors (315 to 015 degrees), where enemy shipping was most likely expected. From Bombing Ten, the two search teams were composed of Red Hoogerwerf with Paul Halloran and Bob Gibson with Richard Buchanan. Scouting Ten's four-plane contribution included the search teams of Red Carmody with Bill Johnson and Bill Martin with Chuck Irvine. The scout groups were advised by air boss John Crommelin that they might be ordered to fly into Cactus at the conclusion of their searches, rather than back to *Enterprise*.

Right behind the ten scouts, Buddy Edwards and Bob Edmondson of VS-10 with Jim Leonard of VB-10 launched at 0620 for anti-sub patrol. The IAP flight was a first for nineteen-year-old radioman Jack Glass, who had been servicing the fighters' radio gear for months. He felt comfortable enough with the rear-seat electronics to seize the opportunity to begin flying with VB-10. "I didn't want to be on that flight deck anymore," said Glass, who had ridden out the enemy attacks at Santa Cruz. "It just seemed like flying was the best way to be."[21]

The *Enterprise* scout group soon found evidence of enemy forces. At 0707, less than an hour into his flight, Scouting Ten exec Bill Martin made the first contact. He reported ten unidentified planes about 140 miles to the north, heading in the direction of Task Force 16. The planes he spotted may have been an optical illusion, for no further sightings of the bogeys developed and they never appeared on task force radar. Martin's mere report of Japanese aircraft was enough, however, to send Admiral Kinkaid into motion.

A dozen F4Fs scrambled to augment the morning CAP. The admiral also decided to fling his standby strike group into the air and guide them toward the most suitable targets, based on further radio reports. *Enterprise* was thus committing the lion's share of her remaining Dauntless crews with no solid direction on enemy shipping.

"Pilots, man your planes!" blared from the loudspeakers. Jim Thomas and Bucky Lee's SBD crews raced for the flight deck, knowing that the fate of Guadalcanal rested largely upon what they might accomplish.

TWENTY-TWO
Desperation in the Slot

R obbie Robinson hoped the brass knew what they were doing. This time, he could not offer gunner Joe Teyshak much solid info on the mission at hand. Admiral Kinkaid was sending out a strike group, and their 10-B-11 was spotted toward the rear of the pack.

Robinson revved up his engine as he watched eleven planes of Bucky Lee's first two divisions of Scouting Ten taking off ahead of him. Jim Thomas's VB-10 was adding a six-plane division, followed by ten of Jimmy Flatley and Swede Vejtasa's Grim Reaper escorts. *We don't know where we are going*, Robinson thought as he circled above the ship to form up on his squadron mates. *We don't even have target assignments.*

By 0800, the twenty-seven-plane strike group was on its way. Uncle John Crommelin had given strike leader Lee the best direction he could: head north, monitor the search net for sightings, and select the best shipping targets that develop within reach.[1]

Bucky Lee's group encountered an Aichi Type 0 reconnaissance seaplane about sixty miles out from the ship. Two of Flatley's fighters peeled off to give chase, but the Japanese snooper escaped into the clouds. Robbie Robinson kept his section close to with Lieutenant Commander Thomas's lead section as the SBDs continued on their remaining eight Wildcat escorts. Robinson kept an eye on his fuel gauges throughout the flight as they neared Guadalcanal. He knew that they stood an equal chance of either returning to the ship or being sent on to land at Henderson Field at the end of their mission.

Everything hinged on what kind of enemy forces the dawn scouts ahead of him would find. The Cactus Air Force had been busy during the morning of November 14 as the *Enterprise* scouts were searching and the Big E's main strike group made its departure.

Major Joe Sailer had taken out six Marine SBDs, six TBFs, and eight fighters. They overtook a Japanese cruiser raiding force near Rendova off New Georgia and attacked at 0830. The torpedo bombers made drops against the cruiser *Chokai*, while Sailer's dive-bombers crippled the heavy cruiser *Kinugasa* with near misses and one direct thousand-pound-bomb hit. This force of cruisers and destroyers became prime targets for other search and strike groups prowling the area.

Bombing Ten scouts Hoot Gibson and Buck Buchanan had these ships in sight long before Sailer's Cactus force attacked them. Admiral Mikawa's force came into view at 0750, at first as just white ship wakes far to the northwest. Gibson led his team in closer, climbing to seventeen thousand feet while taking cover in clouds to the south of the ships. Gibson wanted to make sure that he properly alerted the other strikers before committing to his own attack. He had full confidence in his regular gunner, self-reliant North Dakotan Cliff Schindele. "He was a serious, smart friend and companion, and one to be relied upon when things got tough," said Gibson.[2]

Hoot was fully aware of the perils facing the Marines on Guadalcanal with the current all-out thrust by the Japanese. "The situation was boiling down to the last two minutes of the game, and the team that had last possession of the ball was going to win," he recalled thinking. He also believed his search group had a great possibility of finding the enemy. "I had made my mind up before takeoff not to return to the ship," Gibson said. "I had learned too many times that to return to the ship would spell the end to my opportunity." He was encouraged that both he and wingman Buchanan were of Scottish ancestry. "I felt that I would need all the good luck possible this day, and Buchanan would be part of that good luck."

Now his good luck was holding firm. In three straight actions against

Japanese naval forces, Hoot Gibson had helped locate the enemy fleet. The warships below had the VB-10 search team in sight and they fired at the distant SBDs. Gibson instructed Schindele to transmit a contact report at 0810. The voice transmission was garbled, so Schindele keyed contact reports of the nine ships in sight below—one of which appeared from altitude to be a possible converted carrier. At 0821, Gibson reported the weather to be good and favorable for dive-bombing. At such high altitude, he and Buchanan were unable to see the Marine attacks being made on Mikawa's warships.

Enterprise Dawn Scout Mission (Six VB-10, Four VS-10)			
Naval Battle for Guadalcanal: November 14, 1942			
SECTOR	PLANE	PILOT	REAR-SEAT GUNNER
285–300	10-B-2	Lt. (j.g.) John L. Griffith[1]	ARM3c Roy J. Haas[1]
300–315	10-B-7	Ens. Gregory C. Nelson[1]	ARM3c James C. Bennett[1]
315–330	10-B-5	Ens. Russell A. Hoogerwerf[1]	ARM2c Harold Sidney Nobis[1]
	10-B-14	Ens. Paul Mathew Halloran[2]	ARM3c Earl Gallagher[2]
330–345	10-B-3	Lt. (j.g.) Robert Douglas Gibson[3]	ARM2c Clifford Ernest Schindele[3]
	10-B-8	Ens. Richard M. Buchanan[3]	ARM3c David Otto Herget[3]
345–000	10-S-13	Lt. (j.g.) Martin Doan Carmody[1]	ARM2c John Liska[1]

	10-B-6	Lt. (j.g.) William Edward Johnson[2]	ARM3c Hugh Price Hughes[2]
000–015	10-S-10	Lt. William Inman Martin[3]	ACRM Ferdinand John Sugar[3]
	10-S-11	Ens. Charles Boyd Irvine[3]	ARM3c Elgie Pearl Williams[3]

[1] Returned to *Enterprise*.
[2] Killed in action during mission.
[3] Landed at Cactus.

Enterprise Strike Group 1 (17 SBDs, 10 F4Fs)

Launched 0737, November 14; landed at Henderson Field (Cactus)

PLANE	PILOT	REAR-SEAT GUNNER
SCOUTING TEN, FIRST DIVISION		
10-S-1	Lt. Cdr. James Richard Lee	ACRM Irby Andrew Sanders
10-S-12	Lt. (j.g.) John Frazier Richey	ARM2c Ralph Arthur Gowling
10-S-3	Lt. (j.g.) Leslie James Ward	ARM3c Nick Baumgartner Jr.
10-S-14	Lt. (j.g.) Thomas Wesley Ramsay	ARM2c Lawrence Sargent Craft
10-S-5	Ens. Max D. Mohr	ARM3c John Edgar Criswell
10-S-6	Ens. Leonard Lucier	ARM2c John Arthur Moore

(continued)

PLANE	PILOT	REAR-SEAT GUNNER
Enterprise Strike Group 1 (17 SBDs, 10 F4Fs)		
Launched 0737, November 14; landed at Henderson Field (Cactus)		
SCOUTING TEN, SECOND DIVISION		
10-S-7	Lt. Stockton Birney Strong	ARM1c Clarence Halman Garlow
10-S-8	Lt. (j.g.) George Glenn Estes Jr.	ARM3c Jay Burnett Pugh
10-S-9	Lt. (j.g.) Joseph Bloch	ARM3c H. C. Blalock
10-S-2	Lt. (j.g.) Howard Reason Burnett	ARM3c Robert F. Wynn
10-S-15	Lt. (j.g.) John Henry Finrow	ARM3c John DuBois Bevier
BOMBING TEN DIVISION		
10-B-1	Lt. Cdr. James Alfred Thomas	ACRM Gordon Chester Gardner
10-B-13	Lt. Vivian Warren Welch	ARM1c Harry Claude Ansley Jr.
10-B-12	Lt. (j.g.) J. Donald Wakeham	ARM1c Forest Glen Stanley
10-B-11	Ens. Leonard Robinson	ARM2c Joseph George Teyshak
10-B-15	Ens. Jefferson Haney Carroum	ARM3c Robert C. Hynson Jr.

10-B-10	Ens. Edwin J. Stevens	ARM3c James Warren Nelson
FIGHTER ESCORT: 10 F4Fs, Lt. Cdr. James Henry Flatley		

One of Schindele's reports that was received by *Enterprise* at 0844 placed the Japanese ships south of New Georgia Island. Although somewhat garbled, the message listed two battleships, two heavy cruisers, a possible carrier, and four destroyers. The ship relayed the information to Bucky Lee's strikers, giving them the position and the fact that a carrier might be included. John Crommelin and Captain Hardison ordered Lee to attack this force and then land at Guadalcanal. Gibson's position placed Mikawa's group some 270 miles from the carrier, far out of fuel range for the SBDs and F4Fs to return safely.[3]

Gibson and Buchanan spent more than an hour snooping about to the south and sending reports. Gibson repeated some of Schindele's keyed reports by voice, making sure the word was getting out. At 0915, Gibson decided their fuel supply was low and they had done their part in calling in reinforcements. It was time to make their bombs count and go back for more. *I'm not going to miss this one*, Gibson thought as he recalled his near miss on a cruiser in August. He selected for his target the lone, battered cruiser *Kinugasa*, spewing an oil slick and listing from the bomb damage she had sustained at the hands of the Marines. She was accompanied by the destroyers *Makigumo* and *Kazegumo* as the Dauntlesses from *Enterprise* pushed over from twelve thousand feet. The Japanese gunners came alive in hopes of throwing off the Americans' aim.[4]

Gibson kept his telescopic sight on *Kinugasa* as she tried to twist away from his plunging dive-bomber. Still thinking of his near miss against the cruiser *Maya* months before, Hoot locked in on *Kinugasa*. He felt as if he were ten years old again, out with his father lining up a flying squirrel with his rifle. "I swore I was going to hit this squirrel and rode on its back as though in a saddle," he said.

He released his bomb at two thousand feet, pulled out hard, and recovered at about a thousand feet above the ocean. Buck Buchanan was right on Gibson's tail. Gunners Schindele and Herget strafed the heavy cruiser's decks as their pilots hauled clear. Gibson claimed a hit forward on *Kinugasa*'s superstructure, while Buchanan's crew felt they had scored just aft of amidships on her port side. Both VB-10 bombs actually missed their mark slightly, but were lethal still. The powerful concussions knocked out *Kinugasa*'s steering and added dangerously to the flooding on her port-side belowdecks. Looking back, Gibson saw several explosions from the cruiser. Now unable to maneuver, *Kinugasa* was left as a sitting duck.[5]

Gibson maneuvered his Dauntless radically as he retired. "I learned that when you saw the antiaircraft big black puffs, you head for those because instantly they were changing their aim," he said. He wanted to be right where the enemy had "missed" with their last shot. As they raced away low on the water, Buchanan's B-8 was damaged by a close shell burst. The blast punched a hole eight inches in diameter through the fuselage below his horizontal stabilizer. Although his rudder controls were wrecked, Buck was able to maintain flight control.[6]

At 0944, as Hoot led Buchanan toward Guadalcanal, he transmitted, "Dove on *Nachi*-class cruiser. Left ship burning. Continuing to Cactus." En route, he repeated the message of his cruiser attack at 0958 and again a minute later to make sure that it was heard.[7]

The first *Enterprise* search team to spot Rear Admiral Tanaka's Reinforcement Force was led by VS-10's Red Carmody. His wingman was Bill Johnson, who had spotted the Japanese carriers with Bucky Lee at Santa Cruz.

It had been two hours of flying before Carmody could make out Guadalcanal to his right and then the Russell Islands. Birney Strong, searching a nearby sector, recalled, "I think that was the longest flight in one direction that has ever been made off a carrier." Carmody and Johnson, flying the sector north of Bob Gibson, were in the center of the Slot off New Georgia Island when they began seeing white wakes on the blue seas below them at 0849.[8]

Carmody used hand motions to signal Johnson as they ducked in and out of cloud cover. They studied the vast array of Japanese ships below and counted numerous troop transports with escorting warships. There were eleven modern ex-merchant ships, bearing some seven thousand

17th Army troops, supplies, and ammunition, and more than eighty landing craft. Eleven sleek destroyers shepherded Tanaka's transports, which were scheduled to unload near Cape Esperance and at Tassafaronga.

Carmody ordered his regular gunner, John Liska—whom he considered a real "crackerjack," with four aerial kills to his credit—to transmit a contact report. Liska sent the force's speed, position, and course, and reported "many enemy transports, 2 CA, 3 CL, 6 DD." Although some of the destroyers were mistaken for cruisers, the contact was nonetheless riveting: a significant troop force was some 120 miles from Guadalcanal. If unchecked, thousands of fresh troops could be storming ashore on the Canal by nightfall.[9]

Red Carmody was fully aware of his orders. *As soon as you make the report, attack.* He hand-signaled to Johnson again to prepare to attack. The Scouting Ten team circled back toward the welcome cumulus cover. "We called them 'SBD clouds,'" said Carmody. *A refuge in the sky!* Johnny Liska was carrying one of four cameras assigned to VS-10 rear gunners for this strike. Hughes, Wynn, and Sugar had the others. As his plane headed in to attack, Liska took five photos at the start of their dive. After their dive, Liska took another dozen photos of the ships under attack.

Carmody came in from nine thousand feet and lined up on a big transport. Tracers lined the sky and concussions rocked his S-13. Reality

Gunner John Liska (*left*) and VS-10 pilot Doan "Red" Carmody.

suddenly hit home. *This is for real! I've never dived on a moving target in my life!* Red believed he hit his target on the stern. Liska saw it otherwise, calling up, "You missed on the stern." After pullout, Carmody strafed a destroyer in his path and heard his gunner do the same. Liska saw Johnson dive on a second transport and his bomb also landed just short of its mark.[10]

Before their dive, Carmody had spotted about seven Zeros approaching fast from the distance. Now, as he pulled out, he and his wingman were separated by about half a mile. *Here they come!* thought Carmody. They latched onto Johnson's rearmost SBD and hammered him. The Japanese fighters, acutally six in number from a base at Buin, lost one of their number to the gunfire of either Johnson or his rear gunner, Hugh Price Hughes. But there were simply too many Zeros for them to escape. The Japanese pilots raked Ensign Johnson's B-6 with 7.7mm bullets and 20mm cannon bursts. Seconds later, Liska announced that their wingman was going into the water. The Zeros returned to make strafing runs on the ditched Dauntless as he watched in horror. Neither VS-10 airman survived.[11]

Carmody applied throttle and used the cloud cover to make a hasty retreat for *Enterprise*. The return flight of about 280 miles exhausted the remainder of his fuel. Red anguished over his lost comrades and vowed to do better when given his next opportunity. Carmody and Liska landed at 1133, having been in the air for five hours and twenty-one minutes. The last miles had been "nip and tuck, using the wobble pump to get the last bit out of my tank," Carmody said. His plane had only five gallons remaining when it was chocked on the flight deck. Red headed below to be debriefed by aviation specialists Muddy Waters and Bill Boardman. He was dehydrated from the long flight. He "drank gallons of water and tried to get a little food down" while the air department sorted out the scouts' reports. Carmody then went down to his balmy stateroom and flopped into his bunk, exhausted.[12]

Johnny Liska was the only VS-10 gunner carrying a camera to return to the ship. Chief Sugar had snapped all of his pictures before the enemy was engaged. Hughes's camera was lost when the Zeros downed his SBD. Bob Wynn's camera was taken by someone on Guadalcanal and never

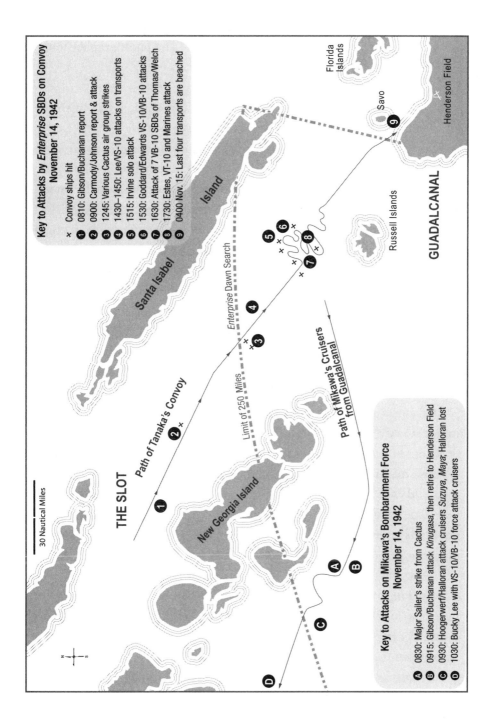

Key to Attacks by *Enterprise* SBDs on Convoy November 14, 1942

× Convoy ships hit
1 0810: Gibson/Buchanan report
2 0900: Carmody/Johnson report & attack
3 1245: Various Cactus air group strikes
4 1430–1450: Lee/VS-10 attacks on transports
5 1515: Irvine solo attack
6 1530: Goddard/Edwards VS-10/VB-10 attacks
7 1630: Attack of 7 VB-10 SBDs of Thomas/Welch
8 1730: Estes, VT-10 and Marines attack
9 0400 Nov. 15: Last four transports are beached

30 Nautical Miles

THE SLOT

Path of Tanaka's Convoy

Santa Isabel

Island

Enterprise Dawn Search

Limit of 250 Miles

New Georgia Island

Path of Mikawa's Cruisers from Guadalcanal

Russell Islands

GUADALCANAL

Florida Islands

Savo

Henderson Field

Key to Attacks on Mikawa's Bombardment Force November 14, 1942

A 0830: Major Sailer's strike from Cactus
B 0915: Gibson/Buchanan attack *Kinugasa*, then retire to Henderson Field
C 0930: Hoogerwerf/Halloran attack cruisers *Suzuya*, *Maya*; Halloran lost
D 1030: Bucky Lee with VS-10/VB-10 force attack cruisers

seen again. *Enterprise* photographers, eager to develop Liska's photos of the convoy attack, were bitterly disappointed. "The photographer found that he had put the film in wrong," Liska said.

W ith his fuel situation becoming dire, Hoot Gibson was intent on reaching Cactus. As he approached Savo Island, his fuel gauges were reading almost empty. *I may be making another water landing,* he thought as he and Schindele monitored their situation. To top off his poor luck, as he finally came in low for a landing, Gibson found that Henderson Field was enduring a Japanese bomber attack. There was insufficient time to continue circling. "I held the Dauntless' nose in a glide, straight for the field, and put her down," said Gibson. Before his SBD came to a complete halt, his engine sputtered and died from fuel exhaustion.[13]

Gibson's SBD had taken a number of bullet holes but his controls were still in good shape. His dive-bomber was met by eager young Marines who immediately set to work refueling his plane with five-gallon buckets and attaching a new bomb. "They looked like old men," said Hoot. "All Marines were most anxious to help us because we were keeping the enemy away from them."

Gibson was met by two Marines in a jeep who asked him to jump in. He was driven directly to the operations tent, with the Marine driver dodging rifle and mortar shells en route. Gibson met Generals Louis Woods and Archie Vandegrift and their staffs. He described what he had seen and what was moving in on Guadalcanal. The Marine staff announced that they were preparing another strike of their own SBDs. Vandegrift asked the Navy pilot if he would like to join some of his Marines on the next strike.[14]

"Absolutely," said Gibson. "They are getting my plane ready."

No longer will I be the frustrated dive-bomber pilot cheated from participating in the early raids and the Coral Sea battle, he thought. *This is what I came out here for. No Japanese will touch shore on Guadalcanal if I can help it.*

Wingman Buck Buchanan had an even more eventful landing. His B-8 was a wreck from the AA burst it had sustained. He struggled mightily against a lack of proper rudder, flap, and brake control. Buchanan forced his crippled SBD down at the beginning of the landing strip. With-

out brake control, his plane raced the full length of the field and continued on into the dirt before grinding to a halt. It had been a hair-raising
flight, but Buchanan and gunner Dave Herget emerged uninjured.

The Mikawa warship force attacked by Gibson and Buchanan was
next found by VB-10 searchers Red Hoogerwerf and Paul Halloran.
They spotted the wakes of two heavy cruisers, one light cruiser, and four
destroyers at 0923, just minutes after the previous *Enterprise* team had
pounded *Kinugasa*. Hoogerwerf noted that the heavy cruiser was listing
and dead in the water with two destroyers alongside to pick up her personnel. The remaining warships appeared to be making twenty-five
knots, moving westbound south of Rendova Island.[15]

Hoogerwerf and Halloran climbed to 17,500 feet to attack. The two
cruisers still under way, *Suzuya* and *Maya*, were about ten miles west
of the crippled *Kinugasa* and each were in company with a destroyer.
Hoogerwerf attacked the undamaged *Suzuya*, the flagship of Rear Admiral Shoji Nishimura, but his bomb landed about fifteen feet directly astern
of his ship. Paul Halloran made his dive on *Maya* and was thereafter not
seen again by his wingman. Japanese records indicate he came in from
astern and missed the ship with his five-hundred-pound bomb. His plane
was likely hit by AA fire in its dive, for Halloran's starboard wing struck
Maya's mainmast. His B-14 slammed into the warship's superstructure
near the portside number-two twelve-centimeter gun mount. Ready ammunition exploded from the SBD's gasoline, wrecking gun mounts and
searchlights, and killing thirty-seven sailors. *Maya*'s crew was forced to
jettison sixteen torpedoes when fire threatened their mounts.[16]

Hoogerwerf believed Halloran scored a direct hit on *Maya*, but had
no idea the hit came from his wingman's Dauntless. Thick black smoke
was pouring from the Japanese cruiser as Hoogerwerf retired toward
Enterprise. Upon landing, he was chastised for not properly radioing in
his contact report and subsequent attack.

The other four *Enterprise* dawn searchers had less luck in finding
either Mikawa's transport force or Nishimura's warships. By 1033, Bill
Martin of VS-10 had completed a thorough search of Guadalcanal, Florida Island, the Russell Islands, and the southeast tip of Santa Isabel
Island. He duly submitted a radio report that he had found no enemy

surface vessels in the vicinity of any of these islands. Martin's SBD had developed engine troubles during his long flight. "I couldn't get suction on one tank," he said. "I didn't have enough gas that I could use with the one tank that I could get suction on." To make things worse, he and wingman Chuck Irvine encountered an equatorial front between them and the carrier. Unable to penetrate the storm front, Martin's engine problems compelled him to head for Guadalcanal. He and Irvine arrived at Cactus at 1145.[17]

They made their landings at Henderson Field under friendly fire. "The Marines were really trigger-happy," said Martin. "I made every turn I could think of, lowered my wheels, made a turn to the right and a turn to the left and they continued to shoot at me going in there." Under the circumstances of the day's chaos, he could hardly blame them. *I'm not on their schedule. I'm not supposed to be here.*[18]

Once Irvine and his XO had parked, Marine ground crews went to work on Martin's balky dive-bomber. They discovered a stopped-up fuel line and effected quick repairs to get him ready for another strike. Every plane would be needed this day to slow the advance of the incoming Japanese troop convoy. Martin was left feeling a "great admiration for the Marines for that effort on Guadalcanal."

The morning searchers had shot their bolt. Two *Enterprise* Dauntlesses and four airmen had been lost. Now Bucky Lee's strike group was left to make the most of their opportunities. Monitoring the available intelligence, he changed his heading around 0930 to intercept the battleship-cruiser force reported by Gibson in the vicinity of Rendova Island.

As they continued to fly at fifteen thousand feet, Robbie Robinson of Jim Thomas' VB-10 division was concerned. He flew up alongside his skipper and signaled that his two auxiliary fuel tanks were empty. Thomas ordered the ensign to return to the ship. Robinson, however, knew that the Big E would likely be out of his range. The air staff had indicated that *Enterprise* would be turning away from the area after launching the SBDs. Robinson communicated to Thomas that he would instead stay in formation. If no Japanese ships were sighted by the time his fuel situation became critical, he would then peel off and land at Henderson Field.[19]

Gunner Lefty Craft spotted two incoming Zero floatplanes—likely launched from the nearby Japanese cruisers—moving in on Lee's lead division. Lefty rattled away at them with his twin .30s, but one of his adjacent comrades drove them off. Johnny Moore, blasting away from Ensign Leonard "Bud" Lucier's 6-S-6, believed he downed one of the float Zeros with his free guns. About the time Lieutenant Commander Lee turned his formation to head for Gibson's force, Robinson was forced to drop out of formation. His fuel situation was finally critical. He blew a good-bye kiss signal to his skipper and peeled away to head for Henderson Field. Two of Jimmy Flatley's Grim Reapers followed suit.[20]

Southwest of Rendova, at 0950, Bucky Lee finally sighted the crippled *Kinugasa* with her two destroyers standing by. The tin cans opened up with surprisingly accurate AA fire. Lee opted to search for undamaged warships and continued on a northwest track. About twenty minutes later, his sixteen remaining SBD crews began seeing the wakes of more Japanese warships under a large cumulus cloud cover. Lee's SBDs were now a good 330 miles from Task Force 16—far beyond the possibility of returning to their own flight deck.

But good targets were finally at hand, some thirty miles west of Rendova. The *Enterprise* strikers had found Admiral Mikawa's main warship force of three heavy cruisers (*Chokai*, *Suzuya*, and *Maya*), light cruisers *Isuzu* and *Tenryu*, and two destroyers. The Japanese were steaming to the northwest at high speed. Lee directed Jim Thomas's five remaining VB-10 bombers to attack the heavy cruisers and Birney Strong's five-SBD second division of VS-10 to go after the light cruisers. Lee took VS-10's first division of six SBDs further to search for a reported carrier as they dropped altitude to search under the big cumulus cloud.

At 1030, Thomas led his division down on *Chokai* through thick AA fire. He and Don Wakeham landed their thousand-pounders wide of the twisting cruiser. Ed Stevens achieved a near miss about thirty feet off *Chokai*'s starboard side. Warren Welch was then farther off the mark with his drop. Tiny Carroum, flying the tail-end Charlie position for Bombing Ten, was the closest, with his big bomb exploding about ten feet off the heavy cruiser's starboard bow. *Chokai* was able to continue at twenty-nine knots, although the near misses by Carroum and Stevens flooded some compartments. Skipper Thomas collected his small flock and headed northeast for Henderson Field, two hundred miles away. En route, they spotted Tanaka's large transport force in the distance before reaching Guadalcanal safely.

Birney Strong led his VS-10 division down on the light cruiser *Isuzu*. He felt his thousand-pounder was a close near miss, as was wingman Glenn Estes's drop. Ensign Joe Bloch was unable to release his bomb—likely due to poor arming on board *Enterprise*. Birney felt certain his final two pilots, Redbird Burnett and Jack Finrow, achieved direct hits on the twisting cruiser. *Isuzu* actually escaped any direct hit but did suffer flooding and steering-control problems due to buckled plates from near misses. Evidence of the close AA fire was noticed upon the division's landing at Cactus. "I had a few holes in my plane when I got back," said Burnett.[21]

Bucky Lee's first division did not find anything in their westward search, so he swung back and climbed to 7,500 feet to attack. Considerable AA fire rose to greet Lee's six planes as they plunged on the light cruiser *Tenryu*. Arming problems also robbed Rich Richey of his chance to release his bomb. Max Mohr missed wide, while Lee, Les Ward, and Tom Ramsay claimed three near misses on *Tenryu*. Ensign Leonard Lucier was making his first combat dive. The former high school football and basketball star had picked up the nickname Bud while attending Saint Ambrose University in Iowa. Bud Lucier's first bomb drop was another near miss close to the twisting *Tenryu*. As Bud pulled out of his dive, the bolt holding his seat in place failed, forcing him so low in the cockpit that he could not see out of his windshield from a sitting position. Gunner Lefty Craft—injured by shrapnel in the Santa Cruz battle—strafed the decks of the warships with a vengeance as Scouting Ten pulled away.[22]

Both Thomas and Lee saw *Kinugasa* dead in the water and listing as they departed. The heavy cruiser continued to take on water and finally rolled over and sank at 1122. Mikawa's Eighth Fleet had thus suffered one heavy cruiser sunk, and two other cruisers damaged in the morning's air strikes. The balance of Mikawa's ships retreated to Shortland to refuel.

Jim Thomas's VB-10 quintet reached Cactus first around 1310. The other eleven VS-10 strikers under Lee and Strong reached Henderson Field minutes later. "We were given instructions to land with caution, as the Japs were shelling the field with heavy artillery," said Craft. Marine ground crews rushed to refuel and rearm the Navy dive-bombers and fighters. A great sense of urgency was felt by all.

John Finrow's gunner, Buck Bevier, was typical of the resolve everyone shared to continue the fight. A year before, he had been attending San Mateo Junior College in California and was also holding down a job as a bank teller. Buck, part of the Navy Reserves, watched his older brothers Bill and Bob enlist in the Navy in 1941 and soon followed suit. College classes and banknotes were far removed from Buck's mind now as he toiled in the tropical heat on Hell's Island. Bevier jumped right in with the Marine crews to help fuel and rearm his group's SBDs. Control over the Solomons had come down to individual actions. The faster warplanes could be reserviced and put back in the air, the better the odds were of turning back the Japanese strikers.[23]

Cactus Air Force crews and the two *Enterprise* groups had concentrated on Mikawa's retreating warships during the morning hours. As the noon hour approached, the focus shifted to a new objective: stopping the inbound troop transport invasion force.

Brigadier General Lou Woods and Lieutenant Colonel Al Cooley, commanding the available Navy and Marine aircraft available at Cactus, decided it was time to drop the hammer on the Japanese transports. Beginning at about 1100, a strike force of thirty-eight planes—including a dozen Marine F4Fs and P-39s plus seven of Scoofer Coffin's *Enterprise* VT-10 Avengers—roared off the runways at Henderson Field and Fighter One. Major Joe Sailer of VMSB-132 led ten Marine SBDs, and Major Robert Richard of VMSB-142 took another nine SBDs.

The first two *Enterprise* SBDs to reach Cactus ahead of Lee's force were included in Major Richard's division of this strike force. Robbie Robinson of VB-10 had landed on Guadalcanal on his own after he was forced to break from Jim Thomas's division due to fuel shortage. Upon landing, Robinson had been quizzed by General Woods as to whether he had seen any troopships coming up the Slot. He had not. Woods had his crews quickly refuel the VB-10 ensign's Dauntless, which was still toting its bomb load.

Landing shortly after Robinson came Hoot Gibson and VB-10 wingman Buck Buchanan. The latter's SBD was so damaged that it could not be quickly prepared but ground crews hung a thousand-pound bomb on Gibson's bomber and finished refueling it from five-gallon cans. The sixteen *Enterprise* strikers under Lee and Thomas landed during the interim.

Robinson bumped down the dusty airstrip and departed at about 1140—less than thirty minutes after landing—in company with Staff Sergeant Albert C. Beneke of VMSB-142. Gibson's SBD was finally refueled and he departed fifteen minutes later, forcing him to gun his throttle to catch up to the big Cactus strike force about fifty miles out. "We got about halfway to the target and I saw an SBD coming up from behind," said Robinson. He was relieved to find that it was shipmate Gibson, making them the only carrier Dauntless pilots on this strike.[24]

The mixed group was about a hundred miles out from Lunga Point by 1245 when they began spotting Tanaka's transports and warships coming up the Slot. Lieutenant (j.g.) Gibson, being the senior aviator, took command of the tail-end Charlie section of Ensign Robinson and Sergeant Beneke. The Japanese below had split their convoy into three columns, and were covered by a half dozen Zero fighters as the Americans moved in.

Marine fighter pilots engaged the Zeros as Joe Sailer's ten SBDs attacked the southernmost of the three transport columns. They claimed six bomb hits—more than were actually made—but did succeed in crippling the 7,180-ton transport *Sado Maru*. Major Richard's first six Dauntless pilots were less successful against the troopships they dived on in the second column. The last section of Cactus SBDs to dive was that of Gibson, Robinson, and Beneke. Gibson watched the first two divisions brave the intense AA fire and pesky Zeros as they drove home their attacks.

One of the Zeros doggedly clung to Robbie Robinson's tail during their approach to dive. Gibson settled on the center column of troop transports—*Yamazuki Maru, Yamaura Maru,* and *Kinugawa Maru*—as his targets. His section dived from stern to bow from down-sun from the west. Gibson made a standard seventy-degree dive but wingman Robinson went down at only sixty degrees due to the Zeros blasting at his tail. Because of his lesser angle, Robinson caught up with Gibson during his dive. He then opened his flaps and dived the rest of the way at seventy degrees.

The Zeros chewed up Robinson's B-11 at the start of his dive. Bullets clanged into the underside of his wing and blasted away his antenna. Cliff Schindele, rear gunner for Gibson, finally unleashed a burst from his twin .30s that scared away the fighter. The transport in Gibson's sights below was lined with Japanese troops wearing khaki green and standing shoulder to shoulder. "I knew I couldn't miss," he said. He released at two thousand feet, just a split second before Robinson and both pilots strafed the transport's decks as they roared by. Both VB-10 pilots claimed direct hits amidships on their transport. Joe Teyshak, riding rear seat in Robinson's SBD, observed a large plane on board the ship they attacked blown overboard by the concussion of their bomb hits.[25]

Accurate assessment of which dive-bombers hit which transports became confused at best on November 14, but Robinson and Gibson felt certain they had contributed greatly to the demise of one troopship. The Japanese, for their part, would later claim little serious damage from this attack. There was no denying, however, the success of Scoofer Coffin's seven Buzzard Brigade TBFs with the last torpedoes available from Henderson Field. Coffin led George Welles, Doc Norton, and Dick Batten against the 7,198-ton transport *Nagara Maru* and scored two hits on her port side. Lieutenant Macdonald "Tommy" Thompson took wingmen Jerry Rapp and Bob Oscar in against the 6,477-ton transport *Canberra Maru*. At least one torpedo ripped open *Canberra Maru*'s starboard side, and she staggered out of formation. Welles suffered a shattered windshield from AA fire. A chunk of shrapnel landed in his lap, and it became his "go to hell, you yellow bastards" artifact. Three of Tanaka's transports were rendered useless in the attack, but the other eight steamed stubbornly on with nine destroyers toward Guadalcanal. Two destroyers were detached to recover survivors from the sinking *Nagara Maru* and *Canberra Maru*, after which they departed to escort the crippled *Sado Maru* back toward their Shortlands anchorage (although she subsequently sank).

At about 1330, less than two hours after departing, Hoot Gibson and Robbie Robinson landed with their VT-10 and Marine comrades. Cactus ground crews raced to rearm and refuel them to go right back out again.

*E*nterprise meanwhile had continued operating her CAP fighters after her search and strike groups departed. Morning SBD search pilots Griffith, Nelson, and Hoogerwerf returned to the ship by late morning. At 1130, six of Jimmy Flatley's strike group fighters had also arrived, with VS-10's Red Carmody tagging along. These planes were recovered and refueled while Captain Hardison and air boss John Crommelin made plans to send a second small strike group against the transports northwest of Guadalcanal.

Flatley, though just in from a long flight, was eager to lead it. Crommelin briefed the pilots before they launched. Bruce McGraw listened intently as the air group commander explained the terrible plight the U.S. Marines on Guadalcanal would face if the transports were able to land their fresh troops. "It will be the worst massacre for the United States," Crommelin said. "You get those transports!" McGraw at least felt some comfort in the fact that a dozen veteran Grim Reaper fighters would be sent as escorts, led by their skipper, Jimmy Flatley.[26]

Red Carmody's efforts to get some rest had been short-lived. He was summoned from his stateroom by Crommelin. "He wanted me to lead the group back to the transports because I already knew where they were," Carmody recalled. He tried saying that he and gunner John Liska had been up since 0400 and had already made an attack and a five-and-a-half-hour flight. "Oh, no, you're going to take them back," Crommelin told him. Liska had been back on board just long enough to enjoy a sandwich and cup of coffee. Carmody, who agreed to navigate for the group, felt, *We're throwing everything at them, even the kitchen sink.*[27]

Carmody would navigate for a three-plane VS-10 section led by Lieutenant (j.g.) Buddy Edwards. Two of the three, Edwards and Edmondson, had already spent the morning hours flying IAP duty. They began taking off at 1305 behind a five-plane VB-10 division led by Lieutenant (j.g.) Ralph Goddard. In company with Flatley's VF-10 Wildcats, this smaller second attack group was ordered to hit the Japanese transport force east of New Georgia Island and then land at Guadalcanal. Each SBD was armed with a thousand-pound bomb. *Enterprise* turned south at twenty-seven knots after they departed and headed for a storm front for protection. She had only eighteen fighters remaining on board, having sent off all of her flyable Avengers and Dauntlesses.

During the two hours it would take the second strike group to reach Tanaka's transports, other *Enterprise* SBDs operating from Henderson Field were sent on follow-up strikes. General Woods and Al Cooley were in desperation mode, flinging small collections of Navy and Marine fliers to hit the convoy as quickly as they could be assembled.

Lieutenant Commander Bucky Lee was back in the air at 1345, just a half hour after he had landed at Cactus with his first strike group. He departed with only wingman Glenn Estes and two VMSB-132 Marine dive-bomber crews. Minutes later, Lieutenant (j.g.) Rich Richey of VS-10 took off with several more Marine dive-bombers. The Dauntless crews had the transport force in sight within forty-five minutes northwest of the Russell Islands. The destroyers opened up with a heavy barrage of AA fire as Lee's group dived from ten thousand feet.

Lee claimed a direct hit on one of the transports, but Estes was unable to release his bomb—likely due to poor arming by the Cactus ground crews. Richey, with his Marine division, also claimed a direct hit on one of the transports. The two-pronged attack was completed by 1445, and all of the SBDs returned safely to Henderson Field by 1530.

The other first-strike VS-10 SBDs that had landed at Cactus with Lee were launched shortly after the mixed Marine group of Lee, Estes, and Richey. The *Enterprise* Air Group "operated sort of on a merry-go-round" the entire day, according to Birney Strong. He said it was "take off, fly out a hundred miles, drop bombs, return to Henderson Field, gas, rearm, fly out again, and attack again."[28]

Lieutenants Strong and Bill Martin were the senior pilots of this strike group. Martin had been on the ground just long enough for Marine crews to repair his clogged fuel line and refuel his Dauntless. As they did so, he had conferred with General Woods in his operations tent.[29]

"Where will we sleep tonight, General?" Martin mused.

"Don't worry about that, son," Woods returned. "We'll worry about that when you get back from this next mission."

Martin took to the air shortly after 1345 with the lion's share of his remaining squadron mates—Strong, Tom Ramsay, Max Mohr, Bud

Lucier, Redbird Burnett, Jack Finrow, and Joe Bloch. They were accompanied by eight Wildcats led by Lieutenant John "Jock" Sutherland of VF-10. Martin spotted Tanaka's convoy plodding along southeast of the Russells, but searched further for any possible Japanese carriers that might be lurking in the area. Finding nothing, Martin wheeled his flight around and began attacking the transports at around 1450. Martin, Mohr, Lucier, and Bloch were each credited with a direct hit on the two transports singled out by the scouts. Ramsay added a near miss against the side of one of the destroyers.

"I was just flying along just fat, dumb, and happy," Birney Strong said. "I had already dropped my bomb, and pulled out to the west. The other planes had pulled out to the east and I was just flying along watching the show when a destroyer let go with a salvo. He put it about ten feet behind my tail right on in range and right on in elevation. I moved."[30]

Ramsay's gunner, Lefty Craft, recalled, "We continued strafing anything and everything of the enemy that we thought might harm us later." Toward the end of the attack, a six-plane division of Zeros from Rabaul dived in to engage Jock Sutherland's F4Fs. The Wildcat pilots claimed two kills in the quick scrap, and Lieutenant (j.g.) Hank Carey of VF-10 suffered a 7.7mm bullet wound in his leg.[31]

Bill Martin's strikers completed their attacks by 1500 and headed back for Henderson Field. Yet another Scouting Ten crew moved in on Tanaka's convoy just as this group was finishing up. Ensign Chuck "Skinhead" Irvine had lifted off late from Cactus at about 1355 after struggling with a balky engine. Undeterred, he headed for the transport group completely on his own. He and gunner Elgie Williams faced concentrated AA fire and the attention of several CAP Zero fighters as they bore in. Williams claimed a kill on a float-type Zero, and Irvine chalked up a direct hit on a transport with his thousand-pound bomb.

When Irvine and Williams landed back at Cactus at about 1545, the field was still in a frenzy as General Woods continued to return both Marine and Navy crews to the attack.

There was little rest for the weary soldiers and sailors of Tanaka's determined convoy. During the previous small waves of attacks, the 5,425-ton transport *Brisbane Maru* had been pounded with bombs and its crew was forced to abandon ship. By 1515, the second small *Enterprise*-launched strike group under Jimmy Flatley and SBD leaders Ralph Goddard and Buddy Edwards was moving in.

Goddard could see Tanaka's force up toward Santa Isabel Island as his eight SBDs approached at eighteen thousand feet. Flatley directed the group to turn west in a long approach to take position astern of the ships. Several transports were burning in the distance, and the goal now was to knock out more of the troop carriers. At around 1530, Flatley assigned targets to the scout bombers, and they dropped to 15,400 feet to attack while their fighter escorts followed from above.[32]

USS *Enterprise* Strike Group 2 (8 SBDs, 12 F4Fs)		
Launched 1305, November 14		
PLANE	**PILOT**	**REAR-SEAT GUNNER**
BOMBING TEN DIVISION		
10-B-9	Lt. (j.g.) Ralph Hays Goddard	ARM2c Charles Harold Owen Hamilton
10-B-16	Lt. (j.g.) Bruce Allan McGraw	ARM3c Ralph H. Horton
10-B-2	Lt. (j.g.) Frank Russell West	ARM3c Leonard T. McAdams
10-B-5	Ens. Dan Hartzell Frissell	ARM3c Charles Henry Otterstetter
10-B-4	Ens. Nelson Eugene Wiggins	ARM3c Claude V. Mayer

(continued)

Enterprise Strike Group 2 (8 SBDs, 12 F4Fs)		
Launched 1305, November 14		
PLANE	PILOT	REAR-SEAT GUNNER
SCOUTING TEN SECTION		
10-S-4	Lt. (j.g.) William Clarence Edwards	ARM2c Wayne Carson Colley
10-S-13	Lt. (j.g.) Martin Doan Carmody	ARM2c John Liska
10-B-7	Lt. (j.g.) Robert Frederick Edmondson	ARM2c Raymond Eugene Reames
FIGHTER ESCORT: 12 F4Fs, Lt. Cdr. James Henry Flatley		

Goddard's five VB-10 planes fanned out against three Japanese transports steaming in column—*Nagara Maru*, *Hirokawa Maru*, and *Nako Maru*. Goddard dived on the transport on the far right flank of the force and missed, his bomb landing about forty feet to the starboard side. Nelson Wiggins dived on the same transport with the luxury of no AA fire against him but achieved only a near miss close off her starboard side amidships.

Dan Frissell released on the centermost transport of the column. He believed his big bomb hit the extreme portside of the well deck, probably going out through the side of the ship and exploding in the water. A geyser of water with large pieces of debris thrown into the air was observed—likely a near miss. During his withdrawal, Frissell's gunner, Chuck Otterstetter, strafed the smaller transport ahead of them.

Bruce McGraw, lining up on the transport southwest of the one Frissell had attacked, was relieved the enemy fire "wasn't concentrated all on one guy. They were shooting at all of us," he said. The divided bursts spared him. As he rolled into his dive on the transport, McGraw had a startling realization. *I've got a problem. I have no dive brakes! Instead of diving at about 250 knots, I'm going much faster with no flaps or dive brakes. I'll have to pickle my bomb earlier than normal or I'll reach the end of my dive way too fast. Well, I'm going to find out how tough this old airplane really is!*[33]

Aborting the dive was not an option for McGraw. He had comforted a dying sailor on *Enterprise* at Santa Cruz and had seen the blood of his comrades spilled on his ship's steel decks. He had vowed that as a dive-bomber pilot he would kill as many of the enemy as possible the next time the chance arrived. His errant plane quickly reached terminal velocity as he plunged downward nearly three miles on the troop transport. The negative G's gripping his body pushed him close to the blackout point.

With his aim steady, McGraw released his bomb at 2,500 feet and yanked back hard on the stick. He narrowly cleared the transport. Gunner Ralph Horton announced that their bomb was a direct hit—dead-on amidships. The explosion blasted out the side of the transport, which quickly caused her to go dead in the water. Horton opened fire with his twin .30s as McGraw flew right past one of the destroyers.

Frank West was the last VB-10 pilot to dive. Although small in size, he was an athletic man who had once been a football player and wrestler for Muhlenburg College. Seeing the right-flank transport sustain one miss and one near miss, he chose that as his target. West nailed his ship directly amidships. Rear gunner Leonard McAdams fired about 150 rounds at the AA battery of a cruiser that was firing on their plane. West felt his bomb hit stopped his transport dead in the water and a heavy fire was seen to have broken out. The Zeros did not molest Goddard, McGraw, West, and Frissell during their dives. Claude Mayer, rear gunner for Wiggins, scored some .30-caliber hits on a Zero that made a side run on their SBD during their withdrawal.

Buddy Edwards found that his dive flaps would not open as he led his VS-10 section in for the attack. At that inopportune moment, the Zeros slashed into his Dauntlesses. "I had two that came up underneath on my side," recalled Slim Colley, in Edwards's rear seat. Standing up, Colley fired his twin .30-calibers down on top of the Zeros that zoomed in from behind. *They are just hanging on their props,* he thought. *Their planes should be stalling out, but they're not. They're just coming right on up! It's amazing how they can maneuver.*[34]

Edwards's section was fortunate. Colley, Ray Reames, and John Liska in the rear seats were all decorated heroes of the Coral Sea battle in May and each had faced Zeros before. Reames, blazing away from Bob Edmondson's rear seat, was credited with downing one of the Japanese fighters. Liska and Colley felt certain they had disposed of another.

As Edwards struggled with his dive flaps, he motioned Edmondson and Carmody to proceed with their attacks on separate undamaged transports. Red Carmody knew what he had done wrong during his first morning attack. "The ship was moving away and I got too flat," he said. "I screwed it up the first time." Changing his dive tactic, Carmody landed a direct hit this time on the leading transport, the 7,504-ton *Shinanogawa Maru.* Johnny Liska, who had been firing at Zeros all the way in to the dive point, saw their bomb land on the starboard stern. "There was corruption flying as high as 500 feet," he said.[35]

As Carmody pulled out, he was immediately hit by two Zeros. *Santa Cruz all over again!* he thought. He found himself alone in the swirling dogfight. The first Zero slashed past, doing some fancy aerobatics as he passed. The second Zero came down on his SBD while Liska called out from the backseat, offering instructions to his pilot on which way to maneuver. Carmody was pulling heavy G's close to the water at about a thousand feet. Liska opened up with his machine guns and caused the second Zero to erupt in flames. "I saw him crash in the water," said Carmody.

Buddy Edwards was left alone with his battle against his SBD's controls. Slim Colley, in the rear seat, noticed four more Zeros approaching that had punched through Jimmy Flatley's fighter screen. The trailing Zero latched onto their tail and Colley opened fire. "I got a good burst into his engine," he said. "Then he came right up alongside and I think I hit the pilot. I kept shooting at him."[36]

Colley saw the Mitsubishi burst into flames, hang momentarily, and then roll off into a spin out of view. Colley frantically opened up on the mike to his pilot: "You'd better do something. I've got four fighters back here and my guns are jammed."

Edwards shot back: "I can't get my dive flaps split!"

We're in a bad position, Colley thought. *Everyone else has left us and made their dives. Our fighters have their hands full and we're the only ones up here. Everywhere I look, there's Zeros.* Suddenly, Edwards's finagling with his levers paid off. With a muttered, "Okay," he pushed into his dive as his flaps finally split. During their dive, they streaked past the spinning Zero Colley had nailed with his rear guns. "He was completely out of control, a ball of flame," he recalled. "He came within 100 feet of smacking us."

Edwards released at about two thousand feet and pulled up sharply. In his efforts to corkscrew his SBD back onto his target, his recovery took him right through the midst of the escorting Japanese warships. "We were real close," said Colley. "I could see the troops on the deck, just loaded." He knew that every soldier that made it ashore to Guadalcanal would claim American lives. He raked the decks with his Brownings until it was "a bloody damn mess."[37]

Like Carmody and Edwards, Edmondson was also credited with a hit on his transport target. Three for three for Scouting Ten. It just didn't get any better than that. Japanese records indicate that the VS-10 trio was indeed the most successful of the day: they scored direct hits on both *Shinanogawa Maru* in the lead of the column and the largest transport, the 9,685-ton *Arizona Maru*, at the rear of the column.[38]

Edwards pulled out so low and so close to one destroyer that her gunners could not bring their guns to bear on his plane. As they pulled away, the Japanese began walking their antiaircraft bursts toward the retiring SBDs. Colley shouted to Edwards to pull up each time he saw the five-inch barrels erupt in flame. Just as Edwards pulled clear of the destroyer gunners, another Zero was on his tail. It was the only time in the war that Slim Colley had a fighter catch him totally off guard. "He was shooting before I even knew he was there," he said.[39]

His guns were in full operation, so Colley rattled back at his opponent. Edwards was only a hundred feet above the water as he hauled clear with the Zero still pursuing. They passed directly over a tiny islet, just a piece of sand with a half dozen coconut trees on it. The setting sun was a ball of fire on the horizon. Colley had to hold his fist up to the sun to block it out while trying to monitor the pursuing fighter. The sea suddenly boiled with splashes directly behind his SBD as the Zero came in from the left. Red tracers zipped by to his right. All at once, the fighter pulled out away from his plane.[40]

There was no time or need to aim. The Zero was less than a hundred feet straight back. Colley's slugs tore through the fighter's fuel tanks. A vapor trail of fuel spewed from the Zero's belly but it did not catch fire. The Zero banked to make another run on the Dauntless formation but Colley was relieved to see him taken under fire by one of their Wildcat escorts. In the end, Ray Reames was given credit for one Zero kill and Colley was credited with downing two. Postwar analysis by historian John Lundstrom shows that two Zeros were lost in this frantic battle against the American SBDs and F4Fs.[41]

Carmody grouped his remaining SBDs for mutual firepower and headed southeast for Guadalcanal. A second group of Zeros attacked and much of their fire was concentrated on Carmody's plane. He was thus much relieved to see Ensign Whitey Feightner and Lieutenant Fritz Faulkner's Wildcats "smoke" the Zeros.[42]

The attack was concluded at 1520 and the VS-10–VB-10 flight reached Cactus at about 1615. Carmody could see tracers coming up from the ground as gunners fired at the Bombing Ten planes landing ahead of him. As Buddy Edwards approached, Slim Colley could also see firing going on below. He called Henderson Field and asked for permission to land. The SBDs were told to land with caution because the airfield was under artillery fire. Colley could see dust clouds puffing up all around the runway as the SBDs landed. As he climbed out of his cockpit, he heard the whistling rush of an incoming round. Instinctively, Colley hit the deck and lay prone in the dust. *Welcome to Guadalcanal*, he thought.[43]

Johnny Liska's SBD was guided to an open field dispersing area. Carmody was greeted by a Marine who jumped up onto his wing to offer instructions even as Pistol Pete's shells exploded nearby. Liska ducked in his rear cockpit as artillery rounds whistled in. "You could hear it coming but you didn't know in what direction," he said. "I had to get in the bilges of my plane S-13 to change coils and clean the empty cartridges out, which was an awful feeling with shells flying around."

The *Enterprise* afternoon strike group was still fighting its way out from Admiral Tanaka's transport force while General Woods was sending off his next strike group from Henderson Field.

The harrowing dilemma was all too obvioius to those rearming the returning planes on Guadalcanal. The broadcast sent by Admiral Nimitz to all task force commanders at 1500—"Looks like an all-out attempt now underway to recapture Guadalcanal regardless of losses"—was not an epiphany to Woods and his squadron leaders.[44]

Shortly before 1530, the Cactus Air Force had readied another strike force of *Enterprise* Dauntless crews. Robbie Robinson and Hoot Gibson, both freshly returned from their second combat missions of the day, were among this group. Robinson encountered skipper Jim Thomas and learned that his buddy Paul Halloran was among the missing crews from the morning's strikes. Robbie found his commander eager to take another swing at the Japanese convoy, with or without escorting fighter planes.

Robinson, however, was not ready to suffer more losses without a fighting chance. Sensing some hesitation, Thomas ordered his junior pilot to hurry up with getting his SBD refueled.[45]

"We've got to wait for fighter cover," Robinson insisted. He noted that some of the *Enterprise* fighters were still in the process of being refueled.

"No, we gotta go now," Thomas insisted. "We need the sun to our advantage. We've got to come in out of the sun."

"Look, Skipper," said Robinson. "We're dive-bombers, not torpedo bombers."

Thomas was not impressed with his wingman's smart-ass remark. He barked at Robinson to get his plane ready on the double. The ensign, however, continued to insist that the Zeros they had encountered warranted this next strike group taking along fighter cover.

Lieutenant Commander Thomas was irate. "If you're afraid to go," he snapped, "you just stay here and the rest of us will go!"

"You son of a bitch!" Robinson yelled. "I'm going, but I'm never going to fly on your wing again!"

Robinson and Thomas had long enjoyed a close relationship, but the strain of the day was taking its toll. Robinson paired up with Exec

Warren Welch, as one of his wingmen and reluctantly joined the VB-10 group that departed Cactus at 1530 without fighter cover. For him and Gibson, it would be their third combat mission of the day. Thomas's first section included wingmen Gibson and Ed Stevens, while Warren Welch headed the second section with wingmen Don Wakeham, Robinson, and Jeff Carroum.

By this point, it was only a fifty-mile hop to reach the enemy ships. Thomas circled around for a short time, thinking that perhaps some fighter escorts would indeed join them. He finally headed west, climbing to only nine thousand feet en route to the transports.

In their absence, things were not calm at Henderson Field. Around 1600, Millimeter Mike and Pistol Pete opened up on Bomber One and Fighter One. Lieutenant Tani's men were again firing two of their 150mm howitzers, which were soon joined by some 75mm mountain howitzers. As shells began exploding around the airfields on Guadalcanal, air operations continued.[46]

Bruce McGraw and Ralph Horton were sitting in their SBD as shells began landing. As a shell whistled by overhead, they sprawled out on the ground. Enduring shell fire in a dive-bombing attack was one thing; being fired at on the ground by howitzers was another. McGraw noticed Marines jeering at the Navy fliers lying prone in the dirt. *For them,* he decided, *it must be just another day at the office.*[47]

Steeling his nerve, McGraw picked himself up and moved over to the observation tower, where General Vandegrift was observing the bombardment. "General, may I join you?" he called up.

"Be my guest," Vandegrift replied.

McGraw climbed the ladder into the observation tower. By this point, he was over his fear of the shell fire. *I'm not going to let any damn Marine laugh at me ever again about dodging from a shell,* he thought. Together they watched puffs of dust erupt where the howitzer shells struck the edges of the runways. McGraw listened to the general explain how his men were dwindling in numbers due to casualties and mosquito-borne viruses such as malaria. "We're hanging by tooth and nail," Vandegrift told him. "We can barely hold on against what's out there."

Lieutenant (j.g.) McGraw felt at least some satisfaction for his bombing efforts this day. *I feel better because I know I hit my transport dead center. They were not coming ashore.*

Jim Thomas's VB-10 group sighted Tanaka's transports shortly after 1600, about ten miles northeast of Russell Island. Two troopships were burning furiously to the northwest and others were dead in the water. Four or five others, however, were still under way with destroyer escorts, heading in toward Guadalcanal.

Lieutenant Commander "Tommy" Thomas had reached only nine thousand feet with his seven SBDs. Hoot Gibson was becoming irritated at how slowly and casually his skipper was climbing while leading them out to attack. "This was a trait that Tommy had shown since I joined the squadron," Gibson said. "Barely flying above stalling speed reduces the controls to a mushy feeling, creating dangers of falling out and hitting another plane."[48]

Robbie Robinson, toward the back of the formation, wanted to go straight in, since they had no fighter protection. Thomas, however, wanted to get the sun at his back before diving. Warren Welch wanted more altitude, so he split his section from Thomas and began climbing to twelve thousand feet. Hoot Gibson and Ed Stevens were left struggling to stay in formation behind Thomas.

Bombing Ten Afternoon Strike Group 2 (7 SBDs)		
Launched 1350, November 14, from Henderson Field		
PLANE	**PILOT**	**REAR-SEAT GUNNER**
10-B-1	Lt. Cdr. James Alfred Thomas	ACRM Gordon Chester Gardner
10-B-3	Lt. (j.g.) Robert Douglas Gibson	ARM2c Clifford Ernest Schindele

(continued)

Bombing Ten Afternoon Strike Group 2 (7 SBDs)		
Launched 1350, November 14, from Henderson Field		
PLANE	**PILOT**	**REAR-SEAT GUNNER**
10-B-10	Ens. Edwin J. Stevens	ARM3c James Warren Nelson
10-B-13	Lt. Vivian Warren Welch[1]	ARM1c Harry Claude Ansley Jr.[1]
10-B-12	Lt. (j.g.) J. Donald Wakeham[1]	ARM1c Forest Glen Stanley[1]
10-B-11	Ens. Leonard Robinson	ARM3c Joseph George Teyshak
10-B-15	Ens. Jefferson Haney Carroum[2]	ARM3c Robert C. Hynson Jr.[1]

[1] Killed in action during mission.
[2] Downed, later recovered.

Gibson felt they were "way below an optimum altitude" to commence a dive-bombing attack. *Come on, Tommy!* he thought. *We should have gotten up to altitude over the airfield since the enemy ships are so close to Guadalcanal. Then we could come in at high speed, hit our targets, and get our asses out of there.*[49]

Welch's planes were still reaching their desired altitude when the peace was shattered. Robinson saw them first. Six Zeros were coming in at their altitude from his left side. Welch's quartet was now at a distance from the leading three-plane section of Thomas. The first Zero locked onto the tail of Robinson and Don Wakeham first. A second Zero blazed head-on toward Robinson from a slightly lower altitude. Robinson opened up with his forward .50s and the Zero did the same. Robbie saw his tracers scoring hits. At the same time, he saw tracers from the Zero on his tail making hits on Wakeham's right wing and chewing through his own port wing.

Robinson pulled away slightly to avoid being hit, as he had been flying extremely close to Wakeham.

Joe Teyshak, rear gunner for Robinson, suffered jammed guns during this exchange. In Wakeham's rear seat, Coral Sea veteran Forest Stanley also ceased firing. The first exchange was merely seconds long but seemed an eternity. The Zero coming head-on, piloted by Petty Officer Second Class Shigeo Motegi, then scored a direct hit. A 20mm shell slammed into Robinson's engine, starting a fire and knocking out his engine power. Shrapnel from the blast wounded Teyshak.[50]

Robinson had a moment of satisfaction as his plane began plunging down. He had scored hits on his head-on adversary. "I saw parts of his plane flying all over the place," he said. The steep dive did manage to put out the blaze in his engine as well as the one that had started in Teyshak's rear cockpit. Even better, Robbie was able to restart his engine during the plunge.[51]

The persistent Zero piloted by Motegi clung to Robbie's tail end as he went down. Tracers zipped past his SBD and clattered off his wings. Robinson decided to use an old trick Lieutenant Welch had taught him to save his life: He headed straight down, racing through the remaining altitude. As he approached the ocean, he popped his dive brakes and made a ninety-degree aileron roll to the right. He then pulled up hard and made another sharp turn. These radical maneuvers forced the Zero to corkscrew to stay on his tail.

"Every time his tracers started hitting me, I pulled my maneuver," Robinson said. For an instant, the thought flashed through his brain, *Poor old Joe back there! He must think we're dead.* Teyshak hung on as his young ensign made sharp turns to throw off Motegi's aim. Robinson pulled out of his no-flap dive with his thousand-pound bomb still on his plane while at 2,500 feet to give him speed. He headed for nearby Russell Island. The pesky Zero refused to be shaken and got on his tail again.

Robinson made a split-S maneuver and pulled out at about 240 knots. He flew low among the coconut trees on Russell Island, zipping up and over the hills with the Zero clinging to him and firing all the way. Robinson then dived at a thirty-degree angle to gain speed and then went up toward some clouds. Motegi fired until he expended all 110 of his 20mm cannon shells and 600 rounds of 7.7mm bullets. As Robinson approached the clouds, the Zero flew up along his starboard side. "It was a beautiful airplane, sort of a chartreuse color with a big red sun on the side," said Robinson. "He gave us quite a show."[52]

The Zero barrel-rolled around Robinson, showing off. Motegi slow-rolled, flying upside down for a few seconds as he made his final salute. Robinson thought to reach for his service .45 revolver but found that the tip of his weapon had been struck by the Zero's bullets. Teyshak could do nothing but watch the aerobatic show, as his Brownings were still jammed and useless.

The Zero finally rocked his wings and turned back toward the ships he was to protect. Robinson and Teyshak decided it was time to seek the safety of Henderson Field. The steel plate behind Robinson's seat showed dents from the bullets it had spared him from. His entire instrument panel had been shot away and his wingmen were nowhere to be seen. Warren Welch and Don Wakeham had not survived the attack.

Tiny Carroum saw eight Zeros coming directly out of the sun. He had lost track of Robinson and Wakeham in the action, as he stayed snugged tightly near Lieutenant Welch's plane. Rear gunners Harry Ansley and Bob Hynson kept their attackers occupied with heavy fire. Welch fired his guns once when a Zero made a head-on pass against him and Carroum.[53]

Welch and his wing mate went directly over the largest transport, right in the middle of her screening destroyers. Welch pushed over straight down on this ship. Carroum saw his exec's bomb strike it directly amidships, and it appeared to blow out the sides of the ship. As Hynson shouted, "Fifteen hundred feet!" he released his own bomb.

Tiny recovered nine hundred feet above the water, but half a minute later a direct hit plowed through his engine cowling. He had cleared the warships but his engine began to miss badly, spewing smoke and oil that fouled his forward vision. He eased the throttle back but was quickly overtaken by another Zero. Carroum shoved his throttle forward and zoomed up just as the Zero opened fire. "We each got a good burst in, but I doubt if either of us was hit," he said.[54]

Carroum's engine gave out and he made a forced landing in the ocean. His Dauntless entered the water crosswind to the waves and the impact knocked him senseless. Hynson tugged their inflatable life raft from its compartment, while the dazed pilot scrambled from his rapidly flooding cockpit. The SBD's radio antenna caught on Carroum's .45-caliber pistol and began taking him down with the plane. Carroum shucked his gun belt, popped the CO_2 bottles to inflate his life jacket, and was carried to the surface. He glanced at his wristwatch as he gasped for air with a throbbing head. It was 1805.

The tail of their Dauntless snagged the yellow raft and dragged it down to the depths. Hynson and Carroum were left treading water without survival provisions some twenty-five miles from the nearest land, the Russell Islands. Behind them, two Japanese transports were burning brightly. Darkness settled over the tropical waters, leaving the two VB-10 aviators to their lonely fate.

Lieutenant Commander Thomas's section was hit hard as well.

What a find for the Zeros, thought Hoot Gibson. His skipper was climbing toward attack altitude at a slow speed. To Gibson, the seven SBDs seemed just like the cliché of sitting ducks—caught unaware in a perfect setup, to be picked off by skilled hunters.[55]

Within seconds of the attack on Welch's quartet, two Zeros pounced Thomas's trio. Thomas's B-1 was attacked from behind and also by another Zero making a head-on run. Hoot Gibson's B-3 took the brunt of the fighters' attention before he could reach the transports. From his rear seat, gunner Cliff Schindele observed two Zeros come in low on the portside of the formation. Sitting high over the SBD's tail, their bellies exposed for a second or two, they would then turn and make a high-side run on the portside and withdraw to Gibson's starboard side. "They made six or seven attack runs in rapid succession," said Gibson. One Mitsubishi made a run on the low side of Ed Stevens's SBD while another flashed by in an overhead run. The fighters then moved from Stevens and concentrated on Gibson's plane, on the left side. Bullets ripped through his controls and forced him out of position. *I'm in a bad spot,* Gibson thought.[56]

Schindele kept up a rapid fire and saw smoke come out of the engine of one of his assailants. Lieutenant Commander Tadashi Kaneko, the Zero group leader, finally made a fatal mistake after making a run underneath Gibson's plane. He happened to cross behind Thomas's tail, providing Chief Skip Gardner in B-1 with an exposed belly shot. Gardner opened up with his twin .30s and Tadashi's fighter burst into flames. The leading Zero rolled onto its back and plunged into the sea. Schindele's rapid fire also forced Chief Petty Officer Jiro Tanaka to drop away, trailing smoke, and ditch in the ocean. But Tanaka and Kaneko pounded Gibson's Dauntless before falling out of the fight.[57]

Hoot's riddled Dauntless finally stalled and fell out of position into a spin. "At the same time, I encountered a Japanese Zero heading at me head-on from below," he said. Gibson opened fire with his forward guns as his enemy blazed back at him. "As he shot past me, I rolled from a spin into a dive," he said. Gibson quickly reached terminal velocity in his dive. He decided to make a right aileron roll of 180 degrees to test whether the Zero's wings could hold up to the pressures exerted on them at such high speed. "He kept coming straight down and picked me up on the way out of the dive."[58]

Gibson used the weight of his heavy bomb to help accelerate through the dive, and then released it at low altitude. Throughout his dive, he noted that his rear guns were silent. *Schindele must have shaken off the Zeros,* he thought. But as he flattened out after releasing their bomb, Gibson was startled to see a stream of tracers zip past his wing.

Reaching the denser, low-altitude air, Gibson realized that he had forgotten to shift back from high blower to low blower. "I looked at the engine mercury pressure gauge and it read twenty," said Gibson. *My God!* he thought. *The engine will explode. There's seventy pounds of pressure against the engine cylinders and the red line is fifty inches!* He kicked his supercharger setting back into low and reduced his throttle setting. To his relief, his overtaxed engine returned to more normal settings. As Gibson pulled free of the warships, he discovered that Schindele had ceased firing because the rear guns had jammed.[59]

Free of two of the Zeros, Jim Thomas and Ed Stevens dived on a transport on the southern edge of the convoy. Thomas believed he made a hit on its starboard side amidships. Gardner strafed the transport as VB-10's skipper roared out low at eight hundred feet. Right on their tail, Stevens released at 2,500 feet and sensed that his thousand-pound bomb exploded amidships in the same area as Thomas's bomb. Stevens pulled out low on the water while gunner Jim Nelson strafed the bows on two nearby transports.

Thomas and Stevens made a hasty retreat toward Guadalcanal, now free of fighter opposition. But Hoot Gibson had to fight his way out from the convoy. He had shucked his bomb but still had a Zero blasting on his tail as he pulled out of his terminal-velocity dive. "I could see and feel bullets and cannon shells hitting my wings, fuselage, and underneath my seat," Gibson said. He knew the Zero had a speed advantage over his SBD. His only hope was to juke violently enough to spoil the Japanese pilot's aim.

I'm not going to let him get on target, he thought. *He has to fire on me based on my flight plan, so my job now is to keep him from knowing what my flight plan is for more than a split second.* Gibson was so low on the water that at least the Zero could not fire from underneath at his exposed belly. The slower Gibson flew, the more difficult he made it for his opponent. "He was reduced to very short firing periods that enhanced my chances to skid through his fire with less hazard," Hoot recalled.[60]

Gibson swung his plane violently from side to side. Occasionally, Schindele was able to get in some bursts before his guns would jam again. The Zero hung on, not more than 150 yards astern as Gibson raced across the Russell Islands. Each time Hoot saw bullets tearing into his wing and working toward his cockpit, he slammed on full rudder and full opposite stick. He then quickly lifted his legs as bullets raked through his lower cockpit and thumped into his engine firewall. Gibson felt that time was standing still. Moments before, he had seen other SBDs spinning away toward the ocean. Now he felt a strange sense of confidence through each violent maneuver he made. *I'm doing it right and I am going to live through this,* he told himself.

At last, his jinking did the trick. The Zero pilot exhausted the last of his ammunition on Gibson's B-3. His Dauntless was riddled. Vapor trails of fuel sprayed from all four gas tanks. *He must be thoroughly dismayed that I'm still flying,* thought Hoot. The Zero pilot then flew up on Gibson as if flying in formation on him, just four feet off his left wingtip. "The two of us flew straight ahead while we looked eyeball to eyeball for more than a minute," said Gibson. "I had everything firewalled for maximum speed, but when he decided to leave, he rocked his wings. I waved and off he went. Jamming on his throttle, he rapidly and smoothly pulled up into an Immelman—a half loop followed with a slow roll—now a thousand feet above me, and headed home."[61]

It took all he had to wrestle his wounded bird back to Cactus. All four of his fuel tanks were punctured, and the port side of his fuselage was riddled. "Many of the bullets had entered my cockpit on an angle that would have hit my legs had I not lifted the proper leg at the right time," he recalled. Gibson arrived at Henderson Field around 1630 and landed his wreck. "When I got out of the plane they just looked at it and shoved it over into the graveyard ditch," Gibson said. "It wasn't worth repairing." An exhausted Robbie Robinson made it back about the same time. Ground crews counted sixty-eight bullet holes in his shattered Dauntless. Gunner Joe Teyshak, suffering from shrapnel wounds, was taken off further flight duty for treatment.[62]

Rear Admiral Tanaka did not credit any direct bomb hits against his transports during this violent encounter with VB-10's seven planes. In return, his Zeros polished off the SBDs of Welch, Wakeham, and Car-roum—the heaviest loss of the day for the Cactus Air Force. Stevens and Thomas were the last to return to Guadalcanal, landing around 1700.

The last strike group of the day to depart from Cactus was a mixed group of Marine and Navy SBDs, TBFs, and F4Fs. The *Enterprise* Air Group contributed three bomb-armed Avengers under Lieutenant Scoofer Coffin and one VS-10 Dauntless piloted by Glenn Estes. The thirty-four planes encountered heavy fighter opposition that knocked down two Marine Wildcat pilots. Three Zeros failed to return, one of them likely shot down by turret gunner Clarence Wall of VT-10.

Estes claimed a direct hit around 1730 against one of the transports, and the Marines believed they landed an additional five bombs on two transports. *Nako Maru* was badly damaged, left ablaze with ammunition cooking off, soon forcing her crew to abandon ship. One of the returning fighter pilots reported to General Lou Woods that two transports were dead in the water and two more were burning as destroyers stood by them. Rear Admiral Tanaka would report that the day's savage attacks had cost him two transports sunk outright, 450 men lost, and four transports dead in the water. The crippled *Sado Maru* had limped back toward the Shortlands under destroyer escort, leaving only four undamaged transports still making for Guadalcanal by day's end.[63]

As night fell over Henderson Field, General Woods took stock of his situation. He had lost two Marine fighters during the day and five *Enterprise* SBDs. Half of his thirty-two Dauntless bombers available at the end of the day's action were too badly damaged for immediate operation the next day.

Slim Colley, Johnny Liska, and Ray Reames were the last VS-10 gunners to arrive on Guadalcanal that afternoon. They checked in at the operations tent and were told to get some chow. "We were shown where we were to bunk up that night," said Liska. They were assigned cots in a tent with their Marine counterparts in the coconut grove. "There wasn't a tree in the whole grove that didn't have shrapnel in it, and a lot of them had their tops cut off." Liska and his companions inspected some nearby foxholes—assuming that they might be needed before morning—before they finally dozed off to sleep.

Everyone now part of the 1st Marine Air Wing was exhausted. Food was scarce, namely just Spam and Vienna sausage. Scouting Ten exec Bill Martin joined a group of Seabees to partake in some brandy before going to sleep in one of their foxholes. Bombing Ten pilot Bruce McGraw was taken in tow by one of the Marines as darkness fell. "I'll show you where you're gonna live," the Marine said. McGraw was led along a path into the edge of the jungle. Tents had been pitched to either side of the little path. As they approached the second tent to their right, the Marine announced, "This is your tent."[64]

McGraw was warned not to use any lights during the night and not to strike any matches. The aviator still carried his .45-caliber pistol and a knife. He was left with the unsettling instructions, "If anybody comes into your tent during the night, kill him and we'll work it out tomorrow."

TWENTY-THREE
"Unflinching Courage"

Tiny Carroum was exhausted. He had been swimming for hours. Once the sun went down on November 14, he and gunner Bob Hynson could just make out the faint outline of the distant Russell Islands. They kept their bearings on them by using the light from two Japanese troop transports burning in the distance.[1]

Carroum found that Hynson was falling behind as they swam through the night. Tiny swam on his stomach to keep track of the stars, which helped orient him to the islands. At around 0300 on November 15, a rain-squall blotted out the distant land and even the stars. When the squall lifted two hours later, the pilot and gunner began arguing over which direction to swim toward the islands. Daylight helped alleviate the drowsiness that Carroum had been feeling.[2]

He continued swimming hard for the distant land and eventually lost sight of his gunner. He figured if he could make it, he could send natives or American troops back out to look for Hynson. The morning sun was rising higher but the islands did not seem any closer.

The *Enterprise* aviators on Guadalcanal did not enjoy a restful night's sleep after their long day of blasting transports and warships. Shortly before midnight, another major naval engagement erupted in Ironbottom Sound near Cape Esperance. The Japanese lost the battleship *Kirishima* and a destroyer, while the U.S. Navy suffered the sinking of three destroyers and heavy damage to the battleship *South Dakota*.

At Henderson Field, the aviators were awakened from their tents by the distant booming of warships and an extraordinary display of red shells. "We could see the flash from the big battleship cannons and the cruisers' cannons and the lesser ones, down to five-inch, going off," said Bruce McGraw. "It was a horrendous battle." Hoot Gibson thought the huge shells sounded "like big trucks rambling in at high speed." Red Carmody of Scouting Ten took refuge. The former football star, weighing more than two hundred pounds, dived right into a slit trench beside his tent. "I went into that slit trench sideways," said Red. He lay wedged in the tight spot in physical discomfort yet with the mental comfort of knowing he was fairly well protected from any shrapnel.[3]

Johnny Liska could see the entire sky light up and hear the booming of distant guns. Most of the airmen crouched in their foxholes, fearing another naval bombardment of the airstrip. Liska and some of his companions, however, were so tired from the day's action they chose to stay in their cots and sleep through the excitement.

Admiral Nimitz, assessing the incoming reports at Pearl Harbor from the two days of heavy naval action, believed that his forces had gallantly thwarted the Japanese offensive to retake Guadalcanal. "This may be *the* decisive battle of this campaign," he noted.[4]

Rear Admiral Tanaka continued in toward Guadalcanal with his surviving troop transports and escorting destroyers during the early-morning hours of November 15. At around 0400, they headed past Savo Island and aimed for the anchorage on the Canal's north coast. The last four transports—*Yamazuki Maru*, *Yamaura Maru*, *Kinugawa Maru*, and *Hirokawa Maru*—beached themselves before dawn and began unloading their supplies and Army troops. Tanaka then rounded up his destroyers and steamed past Savo to retreat.

Gunner Wayne Colley was up bright and early on November 15. The night's action had prevented him from getting any solid sleep. At daybreak, the Japanese artillery pieces known as Millimeter Mike began shelling the field. Colley made his way to his Scouting Ten Dauntless to check it over. It was a far cry from carrier life. There, he had teams of personnel that checked over the planes, made repairs, and ensured that they were properly fueled and armed.[5]

Colley made sure that all was in order for his expected search flight. There were no close revetments to protect him from the shells that occasionally exploded near Henderson Field. He felt vulnerable and exposed as he went through his checklist. He was pulling the prop through to turn up the engine when he heard the *zoop!* of another round. The shell from Millimeter Mike landed right in front of him, only about three feet away.

Colley saw the dirt fly and then felt a sting as a piece of coral struck him in the face. He thought, *Geez! That's a dud. It hasn't exploded.* Colley hurried into the operations tent and told command that there was a two-foot-long live round underneath his dive-bomber. Marines moved in with a bulldozer and attached it to the tow bar on Buddy Edwards's SBD. They towed the plane out of the way and then dug up and defused the artillery shell. Colley considered himself fortunate: had the shell exploded, his world would have ended. Had the dud carried a few feet farther, he would have been sliced in half.[6]

Johnny Liska went down to where the VS-10 planes were dispersed and helped with warming up the engines. "Chief Sugar went to turn up his plane and, after seeing that most of the shells were hitting around his plane, he just returned on the double without ever turning his prop through," said Liska. "I had two dud shells hit only about fifty feet away from me."

Mopping-up operations against the Japanese transports that had beached themselves commenced early. The first Marine scouts from Henderson Field found the merchant ships shortly after dawn, and Marine artillery was hauled in to begin pounding the vessels. Tom Ramsay of Scouting Ten, with wingmen Max Mohr and Chuck Irvine, took off at 0630. They were followed by Scoofer Coffin of VT-10 in a bomb-armed TBF. It was a short flight to the two nearest transports, *Kinugawa Maru* and *Hirokawa Maru*, beached outside Tassafaronga. Coffin went straight in to make a bombing attack with his load of four quarter-ton bombs, while Ramsay led his flight up to twelve thousand feet.

The VS-10 section was met by a flight of eight Type 0 observation seaplanes, but the SBDs pushed into their dives before the Zeros could stop them. Ramsay landed a direct hit on one of the beached ships, while his wingmen achieved one near miss and another hit. Ramsay's flight turned back for Henderson Field to collect more bombs and were on the ground within an hour of taking off.

It was to be another busy day.

At 0700, Birney Strong and Glenn Estes of Scouting Ten took off to make the squadron's ninth attack mission in two days. They had been ordered to make a local search of the beaches of Guadalcanal and the nearby islands and to attack the most favorable targets presented. Their search turned up only the beached transports to the north of Lunga Point and four burning transports about a hundred miles to the northwest of Lunga. Strong sent a contact report on the conditions of the transports and then attacked targets on Guadalcanal's beach. He scored a direct hit on a transport, but Estes did not find it necessary to waste any more ordnance on the lifeless troop carrier. He had instead sighted a concentration of enemy stores salvaged from the transports and scattered the salvaged material with his bomb at 0915. Strong and Estes were back at Henderson Field within fifteen minutes of their attack.

In the meantime, other *Enterprise* SBD crews pounded the remnants of Tanaka's beached ships. Bill Martin and Redbird Burnett launched at 0730, dropped near misses against the transports, and were back on the ground in less than an hour. Bruce McGraw and Frank West of VB-10 departed at 0815 in company with two Marine SBDs. "Just as soon as you got your landing gear up and could see over the trees, you could see the transports," recalled McGraw.[7]

At about 0930, the group selected one of the four beached ships that appeared to be still unloading troops from its bow. West missed the ship but he and gunner Leonard McAdams scattered the Japanese soldiers with their bullets. McGraw was satisfied to see his bomb hit directly amidships. His transport erupted in fire, secondary explosions, and a great deal of black smoke. Upon landing around 1030, McGraw was congratulated by Marines who were elated with the pounding that the Navy boys had put on the Japanese transports. One of them handed him a square Japanese flag that was covered with Japanese inscriptions. "They say that when the Japs were issued these flags, their friends would write notes of good-bye and good luck," McGraw said. "I had never gotten such a welcome and such an expression of appreciation as I got from those Marines who were down there on the front line." The Texan came away with a "tremendous respect" for the valor of the United States Marine Corps.

Bill Martin's dive-bomber was quickly rearmed, and he took off at 0845 to hit the transports again. He flew in company with Les Ward, and both pilots scored direct hits. When they returned to Cactus at 0945, Scouting Ten had completed its share of the November 15 mop-up action.

Four Avengers took off at 1020 to help finish off some of the crippled transports Birney Strong had spotted during his early scout mission. George Welles and Bob Oscar of VT-10 made good drops on one transport but their Mark 13 aerial torpedoes failed to explode on contact. Swede Larsen and Lieutenant (j.g.) Larry Engel lined up on the bomb-battered and abandoned *Nako Maru*. Gunner John King of Engel's crew saw that "Larsen missed by a mile" with his torpedo, but Engel's war fish exploded directly amidships on *Nako Maru*, blowing a column of oily water high above the abandoned transport. As the four Avenger crews circled to watch, the ship bubbled under the waves shortly thereafter.

As the morning attacks played out, Hoot Gibson had moved from the tent area to the operations area where the Pagoda once stood. "The Japanese on the hill across the river were lobbing shells in from mortars," he recalled. Gibson had heard the saying, "You never hear the one that gets you," but the sound of one close round whistling in was enough to make him hit the dirt. *Why take any chances?* Hoot thought.[8]

At 1350, Lieutenant (j.g.) Gibson took three VB-10 planes from Henderson Field to hit the beached transports one more time. He approached *Kinugawa Maru* and released his thousand-pounder from a mere eighteen hundred feet. As he pulled out low on the water to the north, Gibson and gunner Cliff Schindele saw their bomb hit the transport thirty feet from the bow on the starboard side. Subsequent explosions ripped out *Kinugawa*'s starboard side and blasted flames out of a hatch forward of her bridge. Gibson made another pass to strafe soldiers who had been busy unloading the ship's cargo. He and Schindele returned from the flight with dozens of photos of the wrecked troopships on Guadalcanal's coast. One of Schindele's photos captured the burning transports in the distance as another SBD flew in the foreground. "The picture was printed in *Life* magazine as one of the top ten war pictures of 1942," recalled Gibson.[9]

Wingman Ed Stevens attempted to add his big bomb on the transport, but it failed to release during his dive. Ralph Goddard had been ordered to hit an enemy AA battery located on the beach near Tassafaronga. Unable to find the gun, Goddard noticed a road leading from the beach two miles south of Tassafaronga up to a circle. He dived on the area around the circle, and his thousand-pound bomb apparently hit an ammunition storage dump. The area erupted with a tremendous explosion and columns of smoke rising up to two thousand feet. Guadalcanal Radio announced, "Greatest sight ever seen on Guadalcanal. Still burning sixteen hours later. Heavy black smoke, estimated to be oil, ammunition, and stores." Goddard then strafed the nearby woods and the trio returned to Henderson at 1520.

Some *Enterprise* aviators were used on November 15 for mercy missions. Ensign Robbie Robinson and gunner Skip Gardner (replacing the wounded Joe Teyshak) took off at around 1100 to search for American survivors in the waters off Savo Island. En route, Robinson strafed one of the beached troopships. Off Savo, he flew inner air patrol for the destroyer *Meade* as her crew rescued wounded sailors. Robinson zoomed low to point out survivors for Guadalcanal's amphibious single-engine JRF planes, whose crew scooped up oily swimmers and deposited them with *Meade*.[10]

PT boats moved out to assist in the recovery of survivors, some of whom were pointed out by Robinson by dropping smoke bombs. He and Gardner helped spot at least a hundred men who were pulled on board *Meade*. Gardner was later cited for his exceptional spotting ability in pointing out at least a dozen isolated swimmers who might otherwise have perished. At 1500, the SBD crew returned to Cactus, feeling great accomplishment in their mission of mercy.

Air Group Ten had played a major role in saving Guadalcanal from Japan's largest offensive push. Historians would come to call this mid-November crisis the Naval Battle for Guadalcanal. It had cost Imperial Japan two battleships, a heavy cruiser, three destroyers, eleven troop transports, about sixty-four aircraft, and thousands of lives. In exchange,

Japan had landed only a small quantity of supplies and fresh troops. The American defense of Hell's Island during this period had cost them two light cruisers, seven destroyers, and thirty-six aircraft.[11]

By midafternoon on November 15, General Woods was comfortable enough with the secure conditions on Guadalcanal to release some of his carrier aviators. He radioed Admiral Kinkaid that he would forward the *Enterprise* members of his Cactus Air Force to Button, leaving the airfield in the capable hands of his Marine aviators.

Around 1400, Bucky Lee took off from Henderson Field with twelve of his VS-10 SBDs and eight of Lieutenant Coffin's Buzzard Brigade Avengers. One TBF was forced to return because of bad weather, and Lieutenant Jim McConnaughhay had to ditch his torpedo bomber due to a faulty engine. The remaining eighteen carrier planes continued south toward Espíritu Santo—a 558-mile distance—into formidable weather. Red Carmody soon became uneasy with the flight. "Our maps were terrible, everything about them," he recalled. "We wanted to stay at 1,000 feet so we could keep track of our navigation all the way down."[12]

A large squall, some three hundred miles by fifty miles in size, was in their path. The overcast was solid, and although Carmody knew San Cristobal Island was below, all he and wingman Rich Richey could do was climb for altitude to avoid it. They were in their climbing speed of ninety-five knots when Carmody hit a patch of rough air and spun out. His plane was suddenly spinning out of control. "I worried about that 4,000-foot mountain and finally, after kicking over this way and hitting right rudder, I came straight down," he said. "When the elevator took effect, I pulled out below the overcast at 300 feet. Shit!"[13]

Carmody lost all of his section mates during his recovery. He proceeded on toward Espíritu using his calculated dead-reckoning route. Hours later, he was pleasantly surprised to see Richey appear at his side. They stayed tight on each other and continued flying until they ran into another rainsquall. Richey finally opened up on his radio and announced, "I'm running out of gas." A few minutes later, Richey called, "I've got to go in." Carmody turned with him and they started down into the storm. The cloud cover enveloped the SBDs and Carmody lost all sight of him. Richey and gunner Ralph Gowling ditched off Espíritu Santo and took to their raft. Carmody and Liska could do nothing but continue on.

After almost six hours airborne, Carmody pulled out of the bad weather just east of Espíritu Santo. He eased back on his throttle to the near-stalling speed of 125 knots. He ordered Liska to dump his guns over the side, get ready, and hold on tight. All Carmody knew was that they were near Banks Island or Espíritu Santo. They suddenly hit an unexpected nice break in the weather, so Carmody encouraged his radioman to send an SOS to any ship in the area.

There was no answer, but Liska continued calling. He finally raised the seaplane tender *Curtiss* (AV-4) at Button. He communicated their predicament and the tender offered them a steering course. Carmody flew on their course direction for about a half hour before he received a stunning transmission from *Curtiss*, "Whoops, that wasn't you." He decided to go back to the point where he had turned on *Curtiss*'s directed steer and do everything by the numbers. *Now I'm really lost*, he thought. *I better get down and go through my ditching procedure.*

Carmody dropped near to the water level, getting his plane below the overcast. For once, he could actually see stars. He thought he could see something in the distance but wasn't sure. At about that time, his engine began coughing and he went down to about fifty feet off the water. "I hit my wobble pump just enough to keep my nose up, went in, and hit," he said. "I don't know which side of the swell I was on." As his Dauntless plowed into the water, Carmody's face slammed into the long telescopic dive bombing sight in front of him. The impact lacerated his forehead.[14]

Liska felt as though they had hit a brick wall. Survival instincts took over as the ocean water poured into their cockpits. Liska pulled the two-man life raft from the back of the fuselage. Before he had it out, Carmody had climbed out of his cockpit and helped him. "Our plane stayed up only about forty-five seconds," said Liska. Carmody, loaded with his .45-caliber pistol, a canteen, and a Very pistol, was exhausted in the process of joining Liska in their life raft. Fortunately, strong southwest winds were pushing their rubber boat toward the dark landmass Carmody had seen.

They had hit the drink around 2000, and after an hour of drifting, they could see the island each time their raft topped a crest. In the distance, white foam frothed where breakers were crashing over a rocky shoreline. Liska and Carmody battled through the surf and collapsed on the beach. Both men had finished off the last water from their canteens and were parched. They were exhausted, but decided to pull their raft up past the rocks in case they needed it again.

The next morning, November 16, Carmody tore up his T-shirt and used it to clean off his .45-caliber and his bullets. They crawled through the jagged rocks in search of water until Carmody finally used his pistol to shoot two coconuts out of a nearby palm tree. They used their survival knives to open the coconuts, a skill they had perfected during their previous stay at Espíritu Santo. "We drank the milk even though I was worried about the 'trots' afterward, because you know green coconut milk will do that to you," Carmody recalled. He and Liska continued hiking along the coast until they came upon a crude fish trap sitting up on the rocks.

The Scouting Ten aviators followed a narrow trail that led into the hills and jungle. They eventually reached an opening in the jungle where they found a small, crude shack made of palm fronds with smoke coming out of it. They met a little pygmy islander who was feeding his baby by the fire. Hoping to prove their friendly nature, Red prompted his gunner several times with, "Smile, John." Unable to communicate with him, Carmody and Liska decided to follow the native as he led them into the jungle.

The hike took hours through the damp, steamy jungle. At length, the native led them down a hill to his village of shacks beside a beautiful stream of water. The villagers were greatly entertained by the site of a redheaded giant and his radioman, both wearing flight gear and their "Mae West" life vests. "Flaming red hair had not been seen before, so there was a big curiosity," said Carmody. His forehead was still dripping blood from the gash he had suffered during the ditching, but the native children just wanted to touch his hair.

In a mixed charade of words and hand gestures, they described to the native chief that they were a downed American aircrew and needed water from the stream. "He took us over there, and John and I lay on our stomachs and sucked water—we were so exhausted," said Carmody. They had been going for about seventeen hours continuous without sleep. The natives led them to a small, open thatch-covered lean-to, where they slept until the next morning. The natives fed them papayas and bananas, and seemed delighted to have visitors.

The next day, a Coastwatcher who spoke some English arrived and told them that there was another white man on the next island. Liska and Carmody followed the man on a lengthy hike into the hills to the Coastwatcher's camp. He had a hand-cranked radio, with which they successfully raised the tender *Curtiss*. The VS-10 duo was told to wait it out. Sure enough, word came the next day with directions to where they were to proceed to meet a Catalina PBY seaplane.

The ordeal of Carmody and Liska was but one of many that played out during the Solomons campaign as natives and Coastwatchers alike did their best to save numerous downed American airmen. Five days after their ditching, the Dauntless crewmen hiked back down the mountain and were given a farewell by their friendly villagers. "We gave them a knife and other trinkets to show our thanks, and told them where we had left our life raft," said Carmody.

Their rescue PBY could not come closer than about one hundred yards from the rough beach breakers, so Carmody and Liska swam out to it. Red, still weak from his ordeal, was unable to pull his heavy frame up into the seaplane without assistance from its crew. "I flopped onto the floor of that PBY and thanked the good Lord for looking after me," he said. The Catalina taxied off, took to the air, and returned them to Espíritu Santo. The medical staff on board *Curtiss* checked over the aviators during the night before returning them back to their carrier *Enterprise* at Nouméa. Carmody felt great relief when he learned that Richey and Gowling of his squadron had also survived their ditching and subsequent ordeal.

By daybreak on November 16, Ensign Tiny Carroum of VB-10 had been swimming for some thirty-six hours. Hallucinations set in as his body suffered the effects of exhaustion, dehydration, and exposure. Bombing Ten skipper Jim Thomas took to the air from Henderson Field on November 16 to search the Russell Islands area for traces of missing pilots. Flying with Bob Gibson, Ralph Goddard, and Robbie Robinson, he scoured the bays and inlets. While passing through one rainsquall, Robinson unknowingly flew right over Carroum. Carroum later told him that his SBD had flown low enough for him to make out its side number, but Robinson did not spot him.[15]

At length, Gibson and Robinson did spot a tall, naked white man swimming in the ocean. A canoe of natives was paddling toward him. Skip Gardner, flying rear seat for Robinson, reported the downed American back through the command channels so that a PBY could be dispatched. Gibson later saw that the natives had paddled the white man back to their village of Loun nearby. Gibson dropped cigarettes and dungarees for him.

Carroum opened his eyes at daybreak on November 17. He had finally fallen asleep in his Mae West during the night. He had been suffering from the effects of the water and sun for more than sixty hours. His body was shivering and his teeth were chattering hard. Hallucinations set in again but he forced himself to begin swimming again toward native huts he could now see on one of the islands.[16]

By midday on November 17, Carroum could barely see the island right ahead. His eyes were swollen and his face was badly blistered from the sun. His burned skin felt like leather. It was painful even to force his eyes open. By 1700, his right eye had swollen completely shut. Carroum swam the last two miles half-blind and losing his mental faculties. He finally crawled ashore and slumped to the sand.

He was discovered by five native boys in canoes the next morning as he dried his clothes on a log and tried to open a coconut. Carroum was taken to a native village, where his saltwater sores were cleaned, he was fed, and he was allowed to rest. A native minister arrived with a note from a Marine fighter pilot, Staff Sergeant Thomas C. Hurst of VMF-112. He had also been shot down by Zeros on November 14, had bailed out of his Wildcat ten miles northwest of the Russells, and had spent forty-seven hours in the ocean. He had been seen by Hoot Gibson and Robbie Robinson's SBD flight as natives effected his rescue.[17]

Carroum was united with Sergeant Hurst and the two spent five days in the village of Hi. The next afternoon, a PBY Catalina circled over the village as Carroum and Hurst waved their shirts madly to attract its attention. The aviators were taken first to Tulagi and then were flown on to Espíritu Santo, where Jeff Carroum's infected sores were treated at the base hospital. The next day, November 28, he was flown on another PBY to Nouméa, where he was finally reunited with *Enterprise* shipmates.

The remainder of Air Group Ten's personnel were airlifted from Guadalcanal on November 17. Boarding an R4D transport plane, Wayne Colley was happy to leave behind the chaos of Henderson Field. His VS-10 buddy Lefty Craft was worn down, fighting the onset of malaria. Ten pilots and rear gunners of VB-10 were also flown out to Espíritu Santo, along with the balance of Jimmy Flatley's Grim Reapers and several members of VT-10. Jim Thomas's Bombing Ten left eleven of their SBDs at Henderson Field, and Flatley contributed fifteen of his fighters. Robbie Robinson, who missed the flight on November 17, followed the next day on board a DC-3. He took with him a Japanese battle flag and two rifles for which he had traded a small bottle of medicinal brandy with frontline Marines.[18]

The spare Air Group Ten planes were a godsend to the ragtag Cactus Air Force until the *Enterprise* group could draw new planes at Tontouta Field. As Colley, Gibson, Robinson, and the other Dauntless airmen watched Guadalcanal fade into the distance as they flew south, they felt relief to be moving on to a more civilized base but also a great pride in what they had accomplished. *Enterprise* had contributed nine torpedo planes, thirty-one dive-bombers, and twenty fighters to the defense of Guadalcanal during its most desperate hours. Through their perseverance, they had helped turn back convoys of both warships and troop transports.

Only about two thousand of Admiral Tanaka's troops had straggled ashore on Hell's Island. They carried about 260 cases of ammunition and 1,500 bags of rice, only a four-day supply, and Cactus aviators had been quick to pound much of this with bombs. In the same week, Admiral Turner had delivered 5,500 fresh U.S. troops. The difference would cost Japan dearly. The role of the aviators in turning back Japanese reinforcements allowed the U.S. ground troops to maintain the upper hand. The Cactus Air Force had decimated the Imperial Japanese Army's transport force and the Tokyo Express destroyers were being whittled down as well. By the end of November 1942, the thirty thousand Japanese soldiers on Guadalcanal had only forty-two hundred men fit for fighting. One regiment of three thousand soldiers could count no more than seventy men capable of service.[19]

The campaign to win Guadalcanal would continue until February 9, 1943, when the last Japanese survivors were evacuated. But the outcome of the Solomons campaign had been assured during November by the U.S. soldiers on the ground, the sailors on the sea, and the aggressive Cactus Air Force crews. The three-day air and naval Battle of Guadalcanal was a decisive American victory. The conflict had cost the U.S. Navy nine warships in two overnight surface actions and more than seventeen hundred sailors, Marines, and airmen over three days. Japan lost at least nineteen hundred men, two battleships, a heavy cruiser, three destroyers, and eleven troopships. The Cactus Air Force had played a crucial role in the pivotal struggle to hold Hell's Island.

Guadalcanal historian Richard Frank wrote, "The Japanese planning erred seriously in the failure to anticipate the possible intervention by *Enterprise* and her air group." On the morning of November 13, Henderson Field had only thirty-one attack planes in the form of twenty-three SBDs and eight TBFs. Air Group Ten had more than doubled this arsenal by donating another thirty-one SBDs and their skilled crews from VS-10 and VB-10, plus nine TBFs of its Torpedo Ten. The air and naval Battle of Guadalcanal was, per Frank, "decisive for the campaign, and in retrospect, it became clear that it was decisive for the Pacific War as a whole."[20]

Guadalcanal was strongly in American control. In his VS-10 action report, skipper Bucky Lee recommended Bill Martin be given command of his own squadron, based on the "ability, leadership, resourcefulness, and aggressiveness" he had shown in the fight for Guadalcanal. CEAG Dick Gaines offered high praise for his entire Air Group Ten in the November action: "Each officer and man has shown aggressive spirit and unflinching courage." On November 17, Admiral Halsey sent his command a dispatch commending all aircraft units on Guadalcanal that had participated in the battle. "You have written your names in golden letters on the pages of history and won the undying gratitude of your countrymen," said Halsey. "My pride in you is beyond expression. No honor for you could be too great."

Brigadier General Woods wrote to his command, "After five days of furious fighting we have, almost unaided, beaten off this formidable force by our airpower." Woods concluded by saying that his Cactus Air Force aviators had surpassed "the finest traditions of our flying force, and has thereby insured us the possession of this island, and the final defeat of the enemy."

Hoot Gibson of Bombing Ten boarded the outbound flight from Cactus to Button feeling rightfully proud of his accomplishments. In two days of combat, he had located the Japanese bombardment group, helped sink the cruiser *Kinugasa*, and bombed two troop transport ships. "The Battle of Midway was an incredible victory, but the turning point was the Guadalcanal period, and the pivotal point was mid-November 1942," Gibson reflected. "No longer was the Imperial Japanese Navy the conqueror of all the seas."[21]

TWENTY-FOUR
Hard Losses and Hard Promises

Bucky Lee's VS-10 flight from Cactus landed on the Marston matting field of Bomber One at Button still wearing the ragged clothing they had slept in at Guadalcanal. Air Group Ten's part in the Guadalcanal campaign was largely complete. Lee and Glenn Estes wasted little time in swiping an Army jeep for an area reconnaissance. They drove the dusty, jungle-bordered roads until they found what they were looking for: a hilltop repair base known as "Red Two," which could serve as the VS-10 temporary base.[1]

The scouts ate well and even enjoyed good U.S. whiskey at their new base for three days before shuffling 470 miles southwest to Nouméa, New Caledonia (code-named "White Poppy"). The air group was then based ashore at Tontouta Field as replacement aircraft slowly arrived in small groups on the decks of landing craft, transport ships, and the jeep carrier *Nassau*. Navy Seabees had improved the facilities at Tontouta by building wooden decking under the four-man tents and even installing open-air showers made from fifty-five-gallon oil drums. Life ashore, which involved fighting swarms of mosquitoes, spiders, and scorpions, was still a far cry from the comparatively pampered life aboard an aircraft carrier.

Gunner Wayne Colley found life in the tropics to be far from pleasant. "First, they gave you a tent and it rained all the time," he said. The airmen were responsible for digging their own protective foxholes near their tents. Air raids by Japanese planes were frequent. The persistent tropical showers meant that the foxholes were always filled with standing water or at least mud. Colley grew tired of diving into his foxhole every time the air raid alarm sounded at night. "Of course, some guy would come along and crap in it and use it as a latrine, so when you had to jump in it headfirst, that wasn't good," he said. Colley resorted to digging a new hole under the flap of his tent to prevent such vile surprises.[2]

Bucky Lee had more than his share of challenges at Tontouta. The men came down with colds, malaria, dysentery, dengue fever, and ear fungus from the tropical conditions they endured. "I had to count on having at least twenty percent of the pilots incapacitated," he said. His ground crews struggled to maintain sufficient backup parts to repair their SBDs. "We soon ran out of almost everything," said Lee. "After a couple of months, we were operating just a bunch of junk." The heat, rain, and coral dust were hell on the engines. On any given day, he figured his squadron was doing good if six of its planes were in the air flying.[3]

Bombing Ten and Scouting Ten each received replacement pilots at Tontouta. For the next few months, Jim Thomas's VB-10, having lost its XO and three other pilots, operated with Lieutenant John Dufficy, a non-flying aviation specialist, as its second in command. On December 4, Enterprise put to sea for a week of operations in the Coral Sea to break in her air group's new planes. The carrier returned to Espíritu, where her airmen would continue to live off and on in between brief voyages at sea.[4]

On December 23, Scoofer Coffin of VT-10 and Bill Martin of VS-10 flew Avengers down to Efate (code-named Roses) to collect some Christmas cheer. They returned with wine, gin, brandies, and other beverages to distribute among the Enterprise squadrons. Eighty-four bags of mail arrived on board Enterprise on Christmas Eve, adding extra good cheer to the airmen who partook liberally of the newly acquired booze on Christmas Eve.[5]

The fleet had established an officers' club bar about twenty minutes from the airfield. "Air Group Ten decided we'd have our own bar," said Hoot Gibson. "A tent was assigned to such proper duty, and the Bar and

Beach Club came into being. We snitched an ice maker from aboard the ship." Rum drinks were mixed with the ice, local limes, and ever-present coconut juice. The pilots found their Quonset huts infested with rats, which inevitably became targets after heavy drinking at the B&B Club. "We'd sneak into the hut with our .45 revolvers," said Gibson. "One man would turn on the lights and we'd start pot-shooting at rats."[6]

The strain of island life and boredom were the tropical routines were broken by various training exercises. One such drill on night strike operations turned deadly on January 13, 1943. Navigation in foul weather was impossible. It was nearly impossible in *good* weather. "There wasn't a compass rose in the whole South Pacific," said Bucky Lee. "We had no real compass check; and when we got out on a search, we considered we were lucky if we got back." Hoot Gibson recalled, "The corrections for compass calibration were printed on a card affixed to the compass near the windshield." Commander Crommelin's staff nonetheless pushed forward with training their pilots in night operations, first individually, and then by sections and divisions. The final test on January 13 would be a graduation exercise of thirty-two planes in a combined fighter, SBD, and torpedo plane simulated strike from the field at Espíritu Santo. Hal Buell made a late-afternoon test flight and returned to report a large storm front approaching. The brass shrugged off his request to cancel the night mission, and planes were manned after sunset. Bombing Ten was to contribute six planes to the mission and VS-10 added another half dozen.[7]

Buell led one VB-10 section, and his shipboard roommate Ralph Goddard headed the other. Just as Buell had feared, the night group ran right into a nasty storm front. Several planes were smashed up during landings on both the fighter and bomber airstrips. Two dive-bombers simply disappeared in the interim of circling in the storm. Lieutenant (j.g.) Skip Ervin of VS-10 and his gunner, Lanny Wheeler, were never found. Goddard and his VB-10 gunner, Coral Sea veteran Charles Hamilton, crashed in the Segond Channel harbor and their bodies were buried on a hill the next morning.[8]

Hoot Gibson mourned the loss of his best friend, Goddard. "Ralph was a tall, lanky, quiet boy from Minnesota whose father was the superintendent of an Indian reservation in that area. Ralph had sort of an

Abraham Lincoln manner—very witty and extremely intelligent." Section leader Buell stormed into the operations shack that night and confronted several senior air group officers, including skipper Jim Thomas. He proceeded to tell them off "using language liberally sprinkled with four-letter words. To me it was a disgrace—a breach of honor—to lose young men in this manner." Buell would long wonder how he escaped a court-martial over his venting.[9]

Lefty Craft and Wayne Colley were stunned by the tragedy. Their prewar quartet had been cut in half. Jewell perished early in the war during the Lae strikes, and now Lanny Wheeler was gone in a senseless training crash. "I lost a real close friend," said Colley. He and Craft somberly agreed that they would stick to their long-standing pledge of visiting the families of their best friends. With heavy hearts, they realized that there would now be two gut-wrenching hometown visits in their future.[10]

Colley and Craft still had to make it through their tour of duty first.

On January 28, *Enterprise* sailed out of Espíritu Santo as Rear Admiral Ted Sherman's flagship. Her mission was to ensure that a convoy of troops and equipment arrived safely at Guadalcanal. During the early hours of January 30, Sherman was notified that Japanese bombers had crippled the U.S. cruiser *Chicago* south of Guadalcanal during the night. Hoot Gibson, Red Hoogerwerf, Hal Buell, and Dan Frissell found *Chicago* after daybreak under tow about 120 miles from *Enterprise*, just off the eastern tip of Rennell Island.[11]

Enterprise Wildcats flew CAP over the crippled warship throughout the day. Jimmy Flatley's Grim Reapers intercepted a dozen torpedo-armed Betty bombers in the afternoon and downed several of them. The surviving Bettys further ripped open *Chicago* with four torpedoes and nailed one of her destroyers as well. The American cruiser was lost and Grim Reaper Bobby Edwards, another former SBD pilot, perished when his F4F crashed in the ocean during his landing.

Enterprise and Air Group Ten returned to Espíritu Santo, where her air group operated into the early spring with only occasional brief voyages to hunt for Japanese forces. During February, air officer John Crommelin fleeted up to executive officer of *Enterprise*, and Reaper leader Jimmy Flatley was rotated Stateside to a new command.

On March 16, VS-10 skipper Bucky Lee was ordered back to the States to command the revamped Air Group Six. Lee handed command to his XO, Bill Martin, during a little assemblage of his pilots in the squadron's crowded Quonset hut. Lee believed it was more important "to pick a squadron commander for qualities of leadership and ruggedness" versus a pilot's Naval Academy ranking. Martin expressed the deep loyalty and pride his men had shared while serving under Lee, and then opened the squadron's bar to toast their beloved former skipper.[12]

Lefty Craft was still thinking of how Lanny Wheeler had been lost in a senseless night mission when he got the word that Air Group Ten would be conducting more night training. During the morning of March 17, rookie SBD pilots were carrier-qualified during landings on the Big E. Six new VB-10 ensigns—James E. Keefe, Gordon V. Marlow, Ben E. Shefchik, Walter Finger, Robert E. Pine, and Jesse R. McCann—passed the test. The only pilot who failed to carrier-qualify was Roger Scudder, who hit the barrier on his first landing and blew out a tire on his second attempt. That evening, Craft was part of a VS-10 group led by Bill Martin scheduled to become qualified in night landings while the Big E was at sea.[13]

Lieutenant Tom "Bird Dog" Ramsay took off with a flight of six Dauntlesses for an intermediate air patrol. At the end of the patrol, his flight was to rendezvous with skipper Martin and fly back to Bomber One. Somehow, they missed the rendezvous, using an hour's fuel in the attempt, and then found their route to Espíritu blocked by a black, turbulent storm, which they were unable to penetrate or circumnavigate. Glenn Estes led the second section of planes. Lefty Craft, rear gunner for Ramsay, was in awe of the powerful storm. Lightning illuminated the heavy clouds from multiple directions and severe winds tossed the planes about. The VB-10 group was about 125 miles west of the New Hebrides, but without enough fuel to make it back to the ship.[14]

Ramsay had Craft flash messages to the other pilots to ditch their bombers while they were still able to maintain control. Bird Dog's flight came upon a group of U.S. destroyers operating near Efate and signaled for course information. Lieutenant (j.g.) Jack Finrow, however, was out of fuel. He landed his Dauntless in the water about four hundred yards from the destroyer *Cony*, which moved in quickly to effect a rescue. Finrow and gunner Buck Bevier scrambled into their life raft and watched their SBD sink in eighty seconds.[15]

Cony would deposit Finrow and Bevier safely at Havannah Harbor in Efate the following morning. Ramsay attempted to drop a beanbag message on the destroyer *Kankakee*, but Craft missed the mark by about fifty feet. *Kankakee*'s signalman tried blinkering the course to Efate (sixty miles away) and to Espíritu Santo (one hundred miles distant), but received no acknowledgment before the remaining five VS-10 SBDs disappeared into the cloud cover astern.

Ramsay's pilots flew down the southwest coast of Malekula, the next island south of Espíritu Santo. Ramsay opened up on the radio, reminding his men of rumors about a French hospital located in the area. Should they be able to ditch nearby, he suggested that they could recuperate with the lovely French nurses who were also rumored to be on duty at the facility. Their fuel gauge needles pegged eastward to the empty mark, however, before any of the remaining five planes had a chance.

Glenn Estes, Bud Lucier, and Joe Bloch put their SBDs into the calm waters of the lagoon at Hambi, one of the many small islands off the coast of Malekula. Ramsay and his wingman got a few miles farther along and also ditched near one of the small islets.

Ramsay plowed his Dauntless into the ocean about a half mile from one of the little islands. Both pilot and gunner were knocked unconscious, with Ramsay smashing his face into the controls. The ocean water revived Craft in a matter of seconds and he took stock of his situation. "Two bones were cracked in my left wrist and a couple of ribs were broken," he said. Skinned up and bleeding, Craft scrambled out of his rear cockpit. He grabbed at their rubber life raft, but it snagged on something, creating a large tear that caused it to sink. "I reached for Ramsay, who was unconscious with a cut over his forehead," Craft said. He pulled his pilot out of the cockpit, removing his parachute and harness. Craft inflated both of their Mae West life jackets and moved them about 150 feet away from their sinking dive-bomber.

Their SBD soon bubbled under toward the ocean bottom, leaving the young gunner struggling to keep his dazed pilot's face out of the

water. As irony would have it, Ramsay was the one with the most survival experience: during the Battle of Midway, he had been forced to
make a water landing. He and his gunner had survived a week in their
raft before they became the last SBD crew to be recovered by PBYs after
the historic battle. Ramsay's only chance at survival now rested with
Lefty Craft, who kept a strong grip on his pilot's life jacket while kicking toward a distant island. They had gone down near Malekula Island,
south of Espíritu.

"I realized the tide and wind were moving us away from land," Craft
said. He kicked and pulled with all his strength but made little headway.
About ninety minutes later, the winds graciously shifted direction and
made the task much easier. Ramsay finally regained some of his senses
and attempted to swim, although his efforts were of little help to his
weary gunner. Craft managed to keep them both afloat for more than
three hours before his feet finally kicked against the shoreline.[16]

The VS-10 airmen struggled through the surf and flopped onto a
beach on Malekula. A large native assisted Craft with taking Lieutenant Ramsay to a small building made out of small poles and vines. The
airmen enjoyed freshwater and Craft found a small testament left by a
Baptist organization. Fortunately, Espíritu Radio had heard Ramsay's
chatter about the French hospital and his intentions to ditch near the
island. Search groups were out in force the next day, and Lefty observed
a PBY patrol plane. The downed *Enterprise* scouts were retrieved by a
PT boat on March 19, and they were returned to Espíritu Santo. Lieutenant Ramsay recommended Craft for both the Legion of Merit and the
Navy and Marine Corps Medal for saving his life in the hours following
their ditching.

Lefty took a nose ring as a souvenir from one of the friendly natives. "In reward for his kindness, I gave him my pocket knife and a few
dollars in coin I had." The other five aircrews returned with numerous goodies they had obtained from the local natives, including a pair
of shrunken human heads they kept on display in Air Group Ten's bivouac area at Button. "The natives had some secret process that enabled
shrinking a head while retaining all the physical features," recalled Hoot
Gibson.[17]

———

B irney Strong had not seen his wife, Mani, in five months. Added to that longing was a frustration with the mounting losses of personnel and aircraft in noncombat situations. "Frankly, I'm becoming very much fed up with this war," he wrote to his sister Catherine in March. With eight hundred flight hours, Birney felt that he was overdue in receiving Stateside leave, but "I'm taking it with as good grace as possible."[18]

As his tour of duty wound down, Birney continued to climb the ranks in Air Group Ten. In early April, Dick Gaines was transferred, and his place as commander, *Enterprise* Air Group, was filled by Lieutenant Commander Jim Thomas. Strong, second in command of the scouts, was given the nod to shift to Bombing Ten and take over for Thomas on April 6. For Strong, who had been with VS-5 and VS-10 in almost constant combat since the start of the war, it was a big step. He was not short on confidence. One of the new replacement pilots Birney received in the spring was Lieutenant (j.g.) James David "Jig Dog" Ramage, a 1939 Annapolis graduate. "Ramage, I am going to make you the second best dive-bomber in the Pacific Fleet," Strong said when Jig reported. Birney knew talent when he saw it: in a year's time Jig Ramage would take command of VB-10.[19]

Training newer pilots took up almost all of Birney's time, and three weeks into his new command, one of them nearly took him out: Ensign Scudder, firing his forward .50s at a towed target sleeve, accidentally scored hits on his skipper's SBD.[20]

Air Group Ten's tour of duty drew to a close at Espíritu in the spring of 1943. Changes were in store for the veteran airmen once they returned to the United States. The Navy had redesignated carrier scouting squadrons to become bombing units effective March 1, while the VS designator was reserved for land-based scouting squadrons only. On paper, Scouting Ten became VB-20, although the members of VS-10 continued to operate separately from VB-10 while *Enterprise* was still in the combat zone.

Lefty Craft had cheated death in the mass ditching, but he and his last remaining "promise club" buddy, Wayne Colley, were not out of the woods in surviving their deployment. A seemingly innocuous gathering at the Bomber One airstrip on Monday, April 12, turned deadly. Robbie Robinson had been hoping to get up a poker game with fellow pilots

Dan Frissell and Red Hoogerwerf. They couldn't get enough players because of everyone's keen interest in seeing Rosalind Russell's movie *My Sister Eileen*, scheduled to start at 1900. They headed for the movie, where Air Group Ten's officers and enlisted men had arrived early to get good seats.[21]

Most of the airmen sat on coconut tree logs, but two enlisted men chose to drag a hundred-pound bomb to the movies for a seat. It had been off-loaded from an Army B-24 and was still fused. "One sailor who had been rotating the bomb propeller felt it get hot," said Robinson. "He yelled and dove toward the movie screen."

The bomb began to smoke, and then exploded with a terrific roar, blowing apart one of the two sailors and horribly wounding the other. Sixteen men were killed, including Radioman Second Class Joseph Victor Rybinski of VB-10, and another thirty were wounded, some suffering severed limbs and shattered faces. Scouting Ten pilots Bud Lucier and Buddy Edwards were sitting next to each other when the bomb erupted. Edwards survived with an eight-inch gash in the side of his head and Lucier's gut was ripped open by a chunk of shrapnel that lodged near a kidney. Lucier's radioman, John Criswell, was also wounded. Hoot Gibson was not injured but his good buddy Lucier would suffer for a long time. "For the next twenty-five years, he had pieces of shrapnel working their way out of his body," said Gibson.[22]

Slim Colley and Lefty Craft had taken a seat together to watch the show. Colley had a glimpse of "red hot stuff" coming at him. When the heat wave passed, he saw that his left hand was bleeding from an embedded chunk of metal. He and Craft crawled furiously on their hands and knees away from the carnage, looking for a place to hide.[23]

They reached a coconut tree and Craft asked, "Are you hurt?"

"Yeah," said Colley. "I don't know how bad, but I've been hit."

His left side felt odd and his hand throbbed. "I'm going to go to my foxhole," he mumbled.

Craft raced off to get medical help as Colley crawled to his tent and lay down in his foxhole. He saw that his dungaree shirt was saturated with his own blood. He reached up to his neck and ran his finger into a gaping hole. *I'm really in bad shape,* he thought. He tried yelling for help but was unable to make a sound. Lefty Craft was gone only for a moment, but to Colley it seemed like hours. Darkness was starting to settle among the coconut trees when Craft returned with a corpsman and helped lay Colley on a folding cot. They hustled him to a first-aid station, where his wounds were treated with sulfa powder. His neck and arm were wrapped with bandages.

Craft and gunner Ray Reames tried to comfort Colley but he was slipping into shock. Colley took a cigarette and tried to calm himself while chatting with his buddies. "All of a sudden, I just went limp, like somebody had hit me over the head," he said. The lit cigarette landed on his stomach and Craft had to flick it away. Craft then screamed for a doctor. A medic came over and checked his eyes with a light. He could not find a pulse. The words the doctor uttered stunned Colley to the core: "He's dead."

Craft began crying, torn up over the loss of his best friend. Slim wanted to tell him that it was just a mistake. He was okay. He felt sorry for his buddy but could do nothing to ease his suffering. Slim could not speak or move. He lay in shock, untreated and helpless for more than half an hour. His mind remained sharp and functioning all the while. *I'm not dead,* he thought. *You people made a mistake.* He watched a bright moon come up through the coconut trees near the beach. After a while, Colley tried to rationalize his plight. *You stupe, you're really dead. This is the way it really is. I'm really gone.*

Something told Slim that he was not really gone, however. He finally decided he had to signal his friends that he was still with them. He summoned his wits enough to make a slight movement. "He moved!" yelled Craft. "He's still alive!" A doctor raced over and hollered for assistance in transporting him to the nearby hospital. Colley's cot was loaded onto a dump truck and he was driven a few miles down the road. There were casualties all around him in the hospital. The man beside Colley had a tourniquet tied around a bloody stump that had been his leg. Slim had regained enough strength to talk. As the doctor began to work on Colley, he muttered, "Doc, take some of these other guys. They're worse off than I am."[24]

Slim was advised to stop talking and relax as a medical team placed him on the operating table to clean his wounds. They removed a four-inch piece of shrapnel that had torn through his collarbone. It came to rest against his jugular vein, just centimeters away from ending his life. Another metal shard had come to rest about two inches above Colley's heart. The doctors decided to leave it. Additional cutting and probing to retrieve it would do more damage than good.

Three days later, on April 15, Scouting Ten lost two more airmen. One of the new pilots, Ensign Thomas John Kelly, was taking off from Bomber One for a predawn scout mission. His wing clipped a crash truck and his SBD slammed into the runway and erupted into flames. Kelly and gunner John Crisswell were injured and could not escape the flames. Glenn Estes and others who tried to rescue them could not get past the fierce fire that burned their squadron mates to death.[25]

Crisswell had just been returned to flight status after recovering from his shrapnel wounds from the bomb explosion. He was not scheduled to fly with Ensign Kelly, and had protested when Chief Sugar ordered him into the air. "If I don't come back, I'll haunt you for the rest of your life," Crisswell barked at Sugar. Chuck Shinneman of VT-10, who had witnessed this exchange and the SBD's blazing crash, recalled, "I have often wondered if his ghost really did haunt that old boy."[26]

Slim Colley was still lying in his Espíritu hospital bunk when Crisswell was lost. Captain Samuel P. Ginder took command of *Enterprise* on April 16, and announced to his new shipmates that they would soon be rewarded with leaves back home. The Big E was due for an overhaul Stateside, and her air group would finally get to see their families. Colley's medical staff advised the new VS-10 skipper Bill Martin that the young radioman should be flown to New Zealand for better medical care. Martin, knowing the air group was due to be relieved in about a week, had other plans. "I don't want you to get separated from the squadron," he told Colley in confidence.[27]

Lieutenant Commander Martin had Slim moved back on board *Enterprise* to her hospital area. Colley was grateful for his skipper's action because he was able to ride with the ship when she departed the New Hebrides for Pearl Harbor on May 1. At Pearl, he was transported to a local hospital while Air Group Ten enjoyed a week at the Royal Hawaiian

Hotel. Colley's pilot, Buddy Edwards, snuck in fifths of whiskey to help his gunner get through his suffering.

Enterprise remained at Pearl Harbor for about six weeks while she broke in a new air group. During the interim, many of her Air Group Ten pilots and gunners were put on the transport ship *Kenmore* (AP-62) on May 17 for the slow voyage back to San Francisco. By that point, Wayne Colley's wounds were healed enough so that he could join his squadron for its return. He and Lefty Craft considered themselves fortunate indeed, as so many of the young men they had trained with and fought with had not survived the past year in the Pacific zone.

From Coral Sea to the Slot, SBDs had sunk six Japanese carriers and had badly damaged others on three occasions. A battleship, three cruisers, and four destroyers had gone down under SBD bombs, though torpedo planes had done their share in destroying some of these ships. The SBDs could claim more than 140,000 combatant tons sunk unassisted and nearly 50,000 tons shared. Heavy damage to two carriers and four cruisers amounted to another 80,000 tons. In six months' time, nearly one-third of Japan's prewar naval strength in carriers, battleships, and cruisers were sunk or disabled by Dauntless dive-bombers. This figure does not include some fifteen transports or merchantmen sunk, of which SBDs could claim eight exclusively. The SBDs also claimed nearly eighty Japanese aircraft destroyed.[28]

The course of the war in the Pacific had been changed by the Dauntless aviators who helped hold Hell's Island. As the war continued, many would return to help form the nucleus of new carrier air groups. Many others had given all during their first year of Pacific action. Air Group Ten had played a major part in changing the Pacific War's direction for the United States. "The tides of war had changed drastically," recalled Hoot Gibson. "America was on the move."[29]

It had been a year and a half since Lefty Craft and Wayne Colley had made a solemn promise with their two best friends of Scouting Two. *Whoever of us survives must promise to go visit our families and tell them about what we did.*

J. B. Jewell and Lanny Wheeler from their quartet had perished along the odyssey. Now, quite full of life and eager to visit loved ones at home,

Colley and Craft had some hard promises to fulfill in May 1943. Lefty's wife, Bee Bee, was keeping home in Coronado, where they were reunited. Lefty met his daughter, Judi, born weeks earlier on April 9. Then he went touring with Colley. They boarded a train in San Francisco for the cross-country ride toward their hometowns in the Carolinas and in Virginia. J. B. Jewell's mother and family lived in rural Horse Cave, Kentucky, where they had been grieving their son's loss for quite some time. Jewell had been officially listed as "missing in action" after his SBD was lost in the March 1942 Lae–Salamaua raid. There were many questions finally answered for the Jewells and some final closure. As fate would have it, Slim Colley would later become friends with J.B.'s brother when he was later assigned as a radio instructor in Memphis. Slim and his own family would remain close to Jewell's mother and pay occasional visits to her farm. "She always treated me just like I was her son," said Colley.[30]

Lefty and Slim rode the train to Illinois in spring 1943 to visit the Wheeler family in Rockford, just north and west of Chicago. They described their close relationship with Lanny, their promise, and how they were carrying through on it. They explained the situation at Espíritu Santo, the night operations training of their air group, and how Lanny's SBD had vanished one night. They described how heroic Lanny had been in all of his actions: his attack on Lae harbor in March, his dogfights with Japanese Zeros at Coral Sea, his attack on warships at Santa Cruz, and his part in their squadron's efforts to help hold Guadalcanal in November.

"They liked to have never let us go," said Colley. He and Craft spent two full days of their leave consoling the Wheeler family. "We lived up to our commitments," he said.[31]

Craft, Colley, Johnny Liska, Ray Reames, and Chief Sugar had been with VS-2 and VS-10 from their first days of wartime service. They had lost many good friends along the way. Five rear gunners and three pilots of VS-2 perished in the Coral Sea battle alone. Two more of Scouting Two's original pilots, Jack Leppla and Bobby Edwards, had given their lives in the Solomons as fighter pilots.

Chandler Swanson later commanded VT-84 during its torpedo attack on the Japanese super-battleship *Yamato* in 1945. Pete Aurand, one of VS-2's early pilots, commanded the Navy's second operational night fighter squadron, Night Fighting Squadron 76, on the carrier *Bunker Hill* through a number of island campaigns. Aurand retired as a vice admiral. Bill Hall, the VS-2 pilot who earned the Medal of Honor at Coral Sea, showed his heroism another time while serving as a flight instructor. Hall's plane erupted in flames near the town of Dalton, Georgia, and he selflessly flew it into the face of a hill to avoid killing anyone else. He survived, but badly injured his wrist in the crash. He and his wife, his former nurse, Christine, had two beautiful daughters, Gwendolyn and Linda Kay, by 1945. Pappy Hall helped promote the U.S. military efforts even past the end of the war by accepting speaking engagements, at which he was often in company with mayors, governors, and senior military leaders. During such public appearances, Hall played down his achievements in his usual quiet, modest way.

Scouting Five, the sister squadron to VS-2 that served on both *Yorktown* and *Enterprise* during 1942, created many naval leaders who helped carry the torch of valor to other carrier air groups throughout World War II. Three of *Yorktown*'s early 1942 dive-bomber leaders—Curt Smiley, Pappy Armstrong, and Wally Short—finished their Navy careers as rear admirals. Bill Burch, the skipper of VS-5 through June 1942, also rose to the rank of rear admiral before retiring in 1962. Burch served as the executive officer of the new carrier *Ticonderoga* (CV-14) from May 1944 until June 1945. During that time, he earned his third Navy Cross for his heroic conduct—while burned and severely injured by shrapnel— in leading firefighters and damage-control men when *Ticonderoga* was struck by a bomb-loaded kamikaze.

Turner Caldwell, who took command of VS-5 from Burch, placed Fighter Squadron Seventy-Nine (later VFN-41) into commission in October 1942. He later earned the Distinguished Flying Cross and Legion of Merit for his role as skipper of the night-attack and combat-training unit at the Naval Air Station, Barbers Point, Oahu, from March to November 1945. Caldwell would earn a second Distinguished Flying Cross in 1947 for setting a new world's speed record of 640.7 miles per hour while flying a jet over Muroc Dry Lake, California. In 1949, he became the first Navy pilot to exceed the speed of sound while flying an experimental rocket-propelled plane. In addition to other aviation commands, Caldwell would serve as executive officer of the carrier *Franklin D. Roosevelt* and skipper of the USS *Valcour* and USS *Ticonderoga*. He retired in May 1971 with the rank of vice admiral.[32]

Swede Vejtasa, one of VS-5's most daring dogfighters, continued his war as a fighter pilot at Guadalcanal and completed the campaign with 8.25 aerial kills to his credit. He later led his own air group, commanded the super-carrier *Constellation* (CVA-64), and retired as a captain. Swede helped establish the Navy's famed Topgun weapon school in 1969. After his death in January 2013, Vejtasa's family planned to scatter his ashes at sea.[33]

Flight 300 veteran Jesse "Dog" Barker of VS-5 later flew with Turner Caldwell in VFN-41. He would continue his naval service in Korea and during his thirty-three years in the Navy Barker would fly 117 different models of naval aircraft. Red Austin and Elmer Maul were killed in flying accidents within months of being relieved at Guadalcanal. Walt Coolbaugh returned to flying with VB-12 but was killed in a midair collision on December 19, 1942. Elmer "Spike" Conzett perished in a hotel fire in Atlanta, Georgia, at age thirty-two during a one-night stopover while ferrying planes from Norfolk to Long Beach, California. Link Traynor went on to fly with VSB-12 on *Saratoga*, participating in strikes on Rabaul, Bougainville, New Britain, and the Gilbert Islands. After the war, he commanded Attack Squadron 9A, attached to USS *Philippine Sea*, and retired as a captain after thirty years of service.

Rocky Glidewell and some of his fellow Guadalcanal Flight 300 rear gunners—Jim Cales, Tony Fives, Al Garlow, Johnny Villarreal, Homer Joselyn, and Gene Monahan—reached Pearl Harbor by November 19 after their deployment on Hell's Island. They boarded the passenger ship *Henderson* and sailed for the West Coast, arriving in California on November 28. Just before the first anniversary of Pearl Harbor, Glidewell and his companions were given two weeks' leave.

Jimmy Cales reported to flight school in the spring of 1943 and earned his wings. He became carrier-qualified in December, and by the spring of 1944 he was serving as a fighter pilot with VF-6. He was married on May 19, 1944, but would see little of his new wife, Laurie. Ensign

Cales was deployed on the carrier *Hancock* in November 1944 and flew with VF-17. On April 2, 1945, he was shot down and became a POW. When he was liberated, he returned to the States to find that his wife had remarried.

Rocky Glidewell headed for Toronto, Canada. He had been corresponding with a young lady since he had met her in 1941 while at a Royal Air Force radar and electronics radar systems school. While on leave, he got married on December 15. He returned to San Diego in late December and was serving as an aviation gunnery instructor in early 1943. He ran into Bill Burch, who recommended that his former rear-seat man be commissioned as an officer. Ensign Glidewell rejoined *Enterprise* in 1944 as an aviation electronics officer. When the war ended, he was a lieutenant, junior grade, back in Oregon, working in air operations for fighter pilots. After retiring from the Navy, he settled in Arkansas, and in 2013 was the last of the Flight 300 gunners still living, at the ripe age of one hundred.

Flight 300 pilot Chris Fink of VB-6 later flew missions over Japan, the Philippines, Formosa, and Wake Island. He served on the new carrier *Essex* in VB-13, the squadron commanded by VB-6 alumnus John Lowe and also including SBD veterans Tex Conatser, John Bridgers, Ben Petrie, and Don Hoff. Fink, one of the Navy's first helicopter pilots, served in the Korean War, commanded Fighter Squadron 54, and retired from the Navy in 1966. The last Flight 300 pilot still living in 2014, at age ninety-five, was Hal Buell, who had served with both VS-5 and VB-10 during 1942. In 1991, he published his popular memoirs of being a World War II dive-bomber pilot, *Dauntless Helldivers*.

Many of the Dauntless aviators who served on *Lexington* and *Yorktown* in the war's early months became part of VS-10 and VB-10 on *Enterprise* for the Guadalcanal campaign. Pilots Redbird Burnett and Chuck "Skinhead" Irvine were killed in flight duty during the war. Jack Finrow earned a Navy Cross for bombing the battleship *Musashi* at Leyte Gulf, but he was killed the following day while attacking the carrier *Zuikaku*. Tom "Bird Dog" Ramsay was killed in 1947 during an armament test flight from a Maryland naval air station. From Bombing Ten, John Griffith resigned his commission during 1943 and enlisted in the Army. Jeff Carroum returned to the United States and spent nineteen months as a dive-bombing flight instructor at NAS Miami. He was flying Vought F4U Corsair fighters at the end of the war, and after completing a lengthy military career, he eventually retired to Florida. Robbie Robinson took command of Bombing Squadron 153 and flew SB2C Helldivers until the war ended. Robinson completed twenty years of Navy service, and in June 1961 went to work for Lockheed. Robbie's Guadalcanal gunner, Joe Teyshak, earned his second Purple Heart while flying support missions for Allied landings in 1944.

Soon after returning to California in 1943, Hoot Gibson, Bud Lucier, and Red Hoogerwerf appeared on the weekly radio program *The First Line*—aired on CBS through its Chicago affiliate station—to recount their experiences at Guadalcanal. Hoot was assigned to pilot training at NAS Corpus Christi in mid-June 1943 as XO of Training Squadron 16B. Gibson later served as commanding officer of Training Squadron 14A in Kingsville, Texas. He parted ways with the Navy in October 1945 and pursued various sales and commercial development projects in electronics, medical centers, stocks, and real estate. The former high school music teacher even returned to his love of music by working with the Tucson Symphony. At the time of his death in Arizona in 2002, Bob Gibson was working on a wartime memoir of his Dauntless experiences titled *Slow but Deadly*.

Scouting Ten pilots Red Carmody and Les Ward joined Bombing Eight on the carrier *Bunker Hill* and made another combat tour. After the war, Red became involved in electronics warfare with TBMs, took command of a Corsair squadron, and flew sixty-eight missions in Korea. Carmody, who later served in the Pentagon, retired as a rear admiral and died at the age of ninety in March 2008. Bill Martin, who became skipper of VS-10 in 1943, rose to the rank of vice admiral. He led Torpedo Ten through another combat cruise on *Enterprise*, and developed night carrier operations in the late stages of the war. Martin's record of four hundred night carrier landings stood for forty years, and he later commanded the Sixth Fleet in the Mediterranean.

Stockton Birney Strong, the tough aviator who worked his way up through VS-5 and eventually commanded VB-10, later commanded the second carrier *Lexington* (CV-16) in 1959. He earned three Navy Crosses, the Distinguished Flying Cross, ten Air Medals, the Distinguished Service Medal, and two Presidential Unit Citations. Strong retired from the Navy after thirty years as a rear admiral and died from cancer in 1977.

Scouting Ten gunner Dave Cawley flew his next tour on *Enterprise* again, this time as rear-seat man for VB-10's skipper, Lieutenant Commander "Jig Dog" Ramage. Cawley was ordered to flight school in the fall of 1944 and became a first-class aviation pilot by Christmas 1946.

Both Lefty Craft and Slim Colley returned to Seattle after their leaves in 1943. Craft went to shore duty but Colley went back out to flying. His new skipper was Lieutenant Commander Richard Longstreet Poor, who picked Colley to be his regular gunner because of his experience. Colley was promoted to chief aviation radioman and flew with Poor through mid-1944 in offensives at Saipan, Hollandia, New Guinea, and Truk. He finished the war flying from the carrier *Intrepid* and returned to the States in the fall of 1945. He earned the nickname "Ace" for his gunnery proficiency during the war, but always maintained his gentle and compassionate persona. Colley stayed in the Navy after the war, went through advanced electronics school and was in electronics during his twenty-year Navy career. Colley retired from the Navy in September 1959, and passed away in 2005.

Larry Craft, awarded two Air Medals and two DFCs, saw service in 1944 as a chief radioman, supervising radio and radar repair for carrier planes during the invasion of Tinian, Saipan, and Iwo Jima. He flew as a radioman-gunner in an Avenger from the carrier *Kalinin Bay* during the land attacks on Iwo Jima. He requested journalism school to change his rating and received new assignments, including a three-year stint as Armed Forces Radio station manager at Kodiak, Alaska. Lefty finished his Navy career aboard the USS *Independence* in June 1960. He became director of recreation at Langley Air Force Base in Hampton, Virginia, where he remained for eleven years before moving back to his home state of South Carolina. After ten years in Columbia, he accepted the job of CEO for Dan Maples Design in Pinehurst, where he retired in 1998. Larry and Bee Bee raised two daughters and two sons, and celebrated seventy years of marriage in March 2011, just weeks before Lefty passed away.[34]

These Dauntless aviators helped the Marines hold the line more than seventy years ago during the bloody Pacific campaign for control over Hell's Island. Dauntless pilot Nate Murphy, who earned a Distinguished Flying Cross while serving with the Cactus Air Force, reflected in 2014 on the meaning of Guadalcanal. "We didn't know if we were going to make it or not," said Murphy. "Some days we shot the hell out of them and other days they shot the hell out of us. In the end, we stopped the Japanese in the Solomons and kept them from ending up in Australia or New Zealand."

Today, Guadalcanal is home to more than a hundred thousand Melanesians who have little visual evidence remaining of the once-bloody battlegrounds that covered the vast island. During a recent civil war, most of the metal plaques were stripped from the monuments that described the 1942 battle sites.

In the waters of the Slot and Ironbottom Sound, rusting hulls of once-proud warships lie as silent testimony to the violence of that period when surface duels and aerial combat helped decide the course of America's first big offensive of World War II. More than 6,600 Marines, Army, and Navy men were killed during the Guadalcanal campaign and at least 6,000 more were wounded. The airport terminal at Henderson Field has but a few meager plaques to commemorate the once-proud Cactus Air Force. The most significant artifact still standing there is a control tower that gazes toward Bloody Ridge and Mount Austin in the distance—sites of two of the bloodiest battles that took place in 1942.

Snorkelers and scuba divers can still poke around in the submerged remains of several of the Japanese transport ships. *Hirokawa Maru, Kinugawa Maru, Yamazuki Maru,* and *Yamaura Maru* ran themselves aground during the early hours of November 15, and their rusted remains now rest on slopes from 15 to 140 feet deep. *Yamazuki Maru* and *Yamaura Maru* were largely scrapped in the 1960s, leaving little remaining below the water. An abundance of coral and fish life greet divers who swim along the rusted hulk of *Kinugawa Maru* and peer through the gaping holes into empty cargo holds that once held vital supplies.

The twisted metal bears testimony to the destructive force of the thousand-pound bomb dropped by SBD pilot Hoot Gibson on November

15. Violent surface duels between warships, two carrier conflicts, multi-day land battles, and daily aerial engagements failed to hand Guadalcanal over to the Imperial Japanese military. "Midway was not the turning point nor did we have superiority over the Japanese after Midway," Gibson wrote in 2002. "We didn't have air superiority until November 1942." The rusting hulk of *Kinugawa* is one of the few remaining pieces of visual evidence of the mid-November climax that determined the fate of Hell's Island. This ghost ship is testimony to the hard-fought victory achieved in large part by the valiant young men like Gibson who once flew Dauntless dive-bombers from a dusty coral airstrip in the most trying of times.

APPENDIX

Decorations Awarded to Dauntless Airmen for Action from December 7, 1941, to November 15, 1942

Note: This compilation pertains only to the airmen of the SBD squadrons of primary focus in this book: VB-2, VS-2, VB-5, VS-5, VB-10, and VS-10. It is based on the author's research of available records; any omissions or errors are regretted.

KEY TO DECORATIONS AWARDED	
MOH	Medal of Honor
NC	Navy Cross
SS	Silver Star
DFC	Distinguished Flying Cross
AM	Air Medal
GS	Gold Star, in lieu of second or third award of same
LC	Navy Letter of Commendation
PH	Purple Heart

NAME, RANK/RATE	SQUADRON(S)	DECORATIONS/NOTES
Adams, Lt. Samuel	VB-5, VS-5	NC, GS (2), PH
Allen, Lt. Edward Henry	VS-2	NC, PH
Ammen, Ens. John Neville, Jr.	VB-5	NC
Ansley, ARM1c Harry Claude, Jr.	VB-10	AM, PH
Armstrong, Lt. Cdr. Robert Gordon	VB-5	NC, AM
Ault, Cdr. William Bowen	CLAG	NC, KIA
Aurand, Lt. (j.g.) Evan Peter	VS-2	NC
Austin, Ens. Walton Anderson	VS-5	NC
Barker, Ens. Jesse Theron	VS-5	AM
Bass, Lt. (j.g.) Harry Brinkley	VB-2	NC, GS
Baumgartner, ARM3c Nick, Jr.	VS-10	AM
Bellinger, Lt. George Lieninberger	VB-5	PH
Berger, Lt. (j.g.) Nels Luther Alvin	VB-5, VS-5	NC
Berry, Lt. (j.g.) David Render	VB-5, VS-5	NC, GS (2)
Bevier, ARM3c John Dubois	VS-10	AM
Bigelow, Ens. Lavell Meldrum	VB-5	NC, GS
Bonness, Sea1c Charles Joseph	VS-5	DFC, PH
Brown, Ens. Thomas Eugene	VB-5	NC
Brunetti, RM3c Anthony William	VS-5	DFC
Buchan, Lt. (j.g.) Robert Boone	VB-2	NC, GS
Buell, Lt. (j.g.) Harold Lloyd	VS-5, VB-10	SS, DFC

NAME, RANK/RATE	SQUADRON(S)	DECORATIONS/ NOTES
Burch, Lt. Cdr. William Oscar	VS-5	NC, DFC
Burnett, Lt. (j.g.) Howard Reason	VS-5	SS, AM
Butler, ARM1c William Thomas	VS-2	AM, PH
Caldwell, Lt. Turner Foster, Jr.	VS-5	NC, GS (2)
Campbell, Ens. Kendall Carl	VS-5	NC, GS, PH
Carmody, Lt. (j.g.) Martin Doan	VS-10	DFC
Chaffee, Ens. Davis Elliott	VS-5	NC, PH
Christie, Lt. (j.g.) William Francis	VB-5, VS-5	NC, GS
Clarke, Ens. John M.	VB-2	NC
Clegg, ARM2c Earnest Alwyn	VS-5	DFC
Colley, ARM1c Wayne Carson	VS-2, VS-10	AM
Connally, Lt. (j.g.) Clem Brandon	VB-2	NC
Coolbaugh, Ens. Walter Wesley	VS-5	NC
Costello, RM1c Leonard Wilfred	VB-5	PH
Cousins, Lt. Ralph Wynne	VB-2	NC
Cowden, ARM2c Harold R.	VB-5	DFC
Craft, ARM2c Lawrence Sargent	VS-2, VS-10	DFC, AM
Davis, Sea2c William Priere	VS-2	PH
Dickson, Lt. Harlan Rockey	VB-5, VS-5	NC, GS

(continued)

NAME, RANK/RATE	SQUADRON(S)	DECORATIONS/NOTES
Dixon, Lt. Cdr. Robert Ellington	VS-2	NC, GS
Downing, Lt. (j.g.) Arthur Lewis	VS-5	NC, GS
Edmondson, Ens. Robert Frederick	VB-5, VB-10	NC, AM
Edwards, Lt. Thomas Elbert, Jr.	VS-2	NC
Edwards, Lt. (j.g.) William Clarence	VS-10	NC
Ervin, Lt. (j.g.) Henry Nichols	VS-5, VS-10	AM
Estes, Ens. George Glenn, Jr.	VS-10	NC, SS, AM
Faulkner, Lt. (j.g.) Frederic Lewis	VS-5	NC
Finrow, Lt. (j.g.) John Henry	VS-10	AM
Fishel, Lt. (j.g.) Myron Phillip	VB-5	PH
Fontenot, RM3c Woodrow Andrew	VS-5	DFC, PH
Forshee, ARM3c Lynn Raymond	VB-5	DFC
Frederickson, Ens. Harry Alvin	VB-5	NC
Frissell, Ens. Dan Hartzell	VB-10	AM
Gallagher, ARM3c Earl	VB-10	AM, PH
Gardner, ACRM Gordon Chester	VB-2, VB-10	AM
Garlow, ARM2c Albert Woodrow	VS-5	DFC
Garlow, ARM1c Clarence Harlow	VS-10	AM
Gibson, Lt. (j.g.) Robert Douglas	VB-6, VB-10	NC

NAME, RANK/RATE	SQUADRON(S)	DECORATIONS/ NOTES
Glidewell, ACRM Willard Ellis	VS-5	DFC
Goddard, Lt. (j.g.) Ralph Hays	VS-5, VB-10	DFC, SS
Gowling, ARM3c Ralph Arthur	VS-2	AM
Guest, Lt. William Selman	VB-5	NC
Hale, Lt. (j.g.) Roy Orestus, Jr.	VS-2	DFC
Hall, ARM2c Leon	VS-5	DFC, PH
Hall, Lt. (j.g.) William Edward	VS-2	PH, MOH
Halloran, Ens. Paul Mathew	VB-10	DFC
Hamilton, Lt. Cdr. Weldon Lee	VB-2	NC, GS
Harp, Sea2c Wilburn Dayton	VB-5	DFC
Haschke, Ens. Marvin Milton	VS-2	NC
Henry, Lt. Walter Franklin	VB-2	NC, GS
Hill, ARM2c Everett Clyde	VB-5	PH
Hodgens, Sea2c Robert John	VB-5	DFC
Hughes, ARM3c Hugh Price, Jr.	VS-10	AM, PH
Hynson, ARM3c Robert C., Jr.	VB-2, VB-10	AM, PH
Irvine, Ens. Charles Boyd	VS-10	DFC, AM
Jewell, ARM3c James Buford	VS-2	PH
Johnson, Lt. (j.g.) Earl Vincent	VS-5	NC
Johnson, Ens. Joseph Philip	VS-2	PH

(continued)

NAME, RANK/RATE	SQUADRON(S)	DECORATIONS/ NOTES
Johnson, Lt. (j.g.) William Edward	VS-10	DFC, AM
Jorgenson, Ens. Harry John	VS-5	NC, PH
Karrol, RM2c Joseph John	VB-5, VS-5	NC, PH
Kasselman, Sea1c John Anthony	VB-5	DFC, PH
Kinzer, Ens. Edward Blaine	VS-5	NC
Knapp, Lt. Paul Joseph	VB-2	NC
Larsen, Ens. Leif Walther	VB-5, VS-5	NC
Lecklider, Lt. (j.g.) Russell Paul	VB-2	NC
Lee, Lt. Cdr. James Richard	VS-10	NC, DFC
Leppla, Lt. (j.g.) John Arthur	VS-2, VF-10	NC, GS
Liska, ARM2c John	VS-2, VS-10	AM
Lucier, Ens. Leonard	VS-10	AM
Lynch, ARM2c Joseph Michael	VB-5, VS-5	DFC
MacKillop, RM1c Donald	VB-5	PH
Mann, Lt. Hoyt Dobbs	VS-2	DFC
Martin, Lt. William Inman	VS-10	DFC
Maul, Ens. Elmer	VS-5	NC
McDonald, Ens. Frank Ronald	VB-2	NC
McDowell, Lt. (j.g.) Henry Martin	VB-5, VS-5	NC, DFC
McGraw, Lt. (j.g.) Bruce Allan	VB-10	AM
Miller, Lt. (j.g.) Kenneth Ray	VS-10	NC

NAME, RANK/RATE	SQUADRON(S)	DECORATIONS/ NOTES
Moan, Lt. (j.g.) Floyd Edward	VB-5	NC
Mohr, Ens. Max D.	VB-10	AM
Moore, ARM2c John Arthur	VS-2, VS-10	AM
Neely, Ens. Richard Franklin	VS-2	NC
Nielsen, Lt. John Ludwig	VB-5, VS-5	NC, GS
Nelson, RM3c James Warren	VB-2	LC
Newell, Lt. James Harold	VB-2	NC
Nicholson, Lt. (j.g.) Hugh Wilbur	VS-5	NC, GS
Phelps, ACRM Otto Russell	VB-5, VS-5	DFC
Powers, Lt. John James	VB-5	MOH, AM, PH
Preston, Ens. Benjamin Gifford	VB-5	NC, DFC
Pugh, ARM3c Jay Burnett	VS-10	AM
Ramsay, Ens. Thomas Wesley	VB-8, VS-10	NC, AM
Reames, ARM1c Raymond Eugene	VS-2, VS-10	AM
Richesin, ARM3c Franklin Delano	VS-5	DFC, PH
Richey, Ens. John Frazier	VS-10	AM
Riley, Ens. Joseph Archer	VB-2	NC
Robinson, Ens. Leonard	VB-10	AM, GS
Roll, ARM3c Joseph Ellsworth	VS-5	DFC
Rountree, ARM1c Bruce	VS-2	LC

(continued)

NAME, RANK/RATE	SQUADRON(S)	DECORATIONS/ NOTES
Rouser, ARM2c Charles Wayne	VS-2	AM, PH
Rowley, Ens. John Windsor	VB-5	NC
Quigley, Ens. Anthony Joseph	VS-2	NC, GS
Sanders, ACRM Irby Andrews	VS-10	LC
Schindele, ARM1c Clifford Ernest	VB-2, VB-10	AM
Schindler, Cdr. Walter Gabriel	Staff	NC
Schultz, Ens. Arthur Joseph, Jr.	VS-2	NC
Sheridan, Lt. (j.g.) John Gracie	VB-2	NC
Short, Lt. Wallace Clark, Jr.	VB-5, VS-5	NC, GS (2)
Simmons, Ens. Alva Alton	VB-2	NC
Smith, Lt. (j.g.) Joseph Grant	VS-2	NC
Smith, Ens. Robert Edward	VS-2	NC
Sobel, ARM1c Alvin A.	VB-5, VS-5	DFC
Stanley, ARM1c Forest Glen	VB-2, VB-10	DFC, AM, PH
Stevens, Ens. Edwin J.	VB-10	AM
Straub, ARM1c Walter Dean	VB-5, VS-5	DFC
Strong, Lt. Stockton Birney	VS-5	NC, GS, AM
Swanson, Lt. (j.g.) Chandler Waterman	VS-2	NC
Taylor, Lt. Keith Eikenberry	VB-5	NC
Teyshak, ARM2c Joseph George	VB-2, VB-10	PH
Thomas, Lt. Cdr. John Alfred	VB-10	NC

NAME, RANK/RATE	SQUADRON(S)	DECORATIONS/ NOTES
Traynor, Ens. Lawrence Gilworth	VS-5	NC
Trott, ACRM John Warren	VB-5, VS-5	DFC
Underhill, Ens. Samuel Jackson	VS-5	NC
Vejtasa, Lt. (j.g.) Stanley Winfield	VS-5, VF-10	NC, GS
Wakeham, Lt. (j.g.) J. Donald	VB-2, VB-10	NC, AM, PH
Ward, Lt. (j.g.) Leslie James	VS-10	AM
Ware, Lt. Charles Rollins	VS-5, VS-6	NC, PH
Welch, Lt. Vivian Warren	VB-2, VB-10	NC
West, Lt. (j.g.) Frank Russell	VS-10	AM
Wheeler, ARM3c Lanois Mardi	VS-2, VS-10	AM
Whittier, Lt. (j.g.) Mark Twain	VB-2	NC
Willems, Ens. Everleigh Durwood	VS-2	DFC
Williams, ARM2c Elgie Pearl	VS-10	AM, GS
Williams, Ens. Robert Pershing	VB-2	NC
Wingfield, Ens. John Davis	VS-2	NC, PH
Wood, ARM3c Frank Barton	VS-5	DFC
Wood, Lt. (j.g.) George Orr	VB-2	NC
Wood, Ens. Harry	VS-2	NC
Woodhull, Lt. Roger Blake	VS-5	NC
Woyke, Ens. Max Einar Eric	VS-2	NC

SOURCES

My research for the book *Pacific Payback* produced such hoards of Pacific War material on the early Dauntless dive-bomber airmen that this book was a necessity. The families, veterans, and historians who generously shared their stories, scrapbooks, logbooks, photos, and various memories deserve to have this story related.

Starting with the naval historians, archivists, and some of my fellow authors, there are many to thank. John Lundstrom and James C. Sawruk are the leading experts on the first carrier battle in the Coral Sea and on naval aviation in the Guadalcanal campaign. Both generously fielded questions and helped with important documents, including Sawruk's sharing of the VB-10 war diary he originally obtained from Bob "Hoot" Gibson.

The vast *Yorktown* and *Enterprise* Dauntless archives of historian Mark Horan was again a major source for some of the firsthand accounts of 1942 dive-bomber crews. William J. Shinneman, with whom I coauthored my first book in 1996, shared some of his archived oral history interviews that he collected many years ago. Other historians who shared documents and transcripts or helped fill in key data were naval aviation author Barrett Tillman, Arnie Olson of the *Enterprise* Foundation, Lieutenant Colonel Jay Stout for sharing his interviews with VS-5 pilot Jesse Barker, Henry Sakaida, Dr. Keith Huxen of the National World War II Museum in New Orleans, Seth Paridon (manager of research services at the National World War II Museum), Alex D'Amore in Washington, Tim Frank of the Naval History Center, and Keegan Chetwynd of the CAF Airpower Museum in Midland, Texas.

Aviation biographer Ted Edwards shared documents and interview material he collected during his research with Stanley "Swede" Vejtasa for a forthcoming biography on the *Enterprise* ace. Author James Scott has continued to copy and share various requested documents during his research visits to Washington. From Pensacola's Naval Aviation Museum, volunteers Bill Addison, Bob Ammann, and Theo Elbert in the Emil Buehel Library graciously scanned numerous pilot photos for use in this book. Video archivist Steve Heffernan allowed me to review the museum's collection of audiotapes for interviews with SBD pilots. Additional thanks go to Doug Siegfried and Dennis Ireland of the Tailhook Association for granting me permission to reproduce images from the *Hook* magazine.

My friend and agent, Jim Donovan, and my editor at Penguin Books, Brent Howard, have continued to be first-rate mentors throughout the publishing process.

Families of many of the Dauntless crew contributed stories, photos, logbooks, and memoirs. Namely they were Janice Anderson-Gram, Jane Kirshenbaum, Jacqui Bally, Mary Birden, Henry Weinzapfel, Kent Craft, Sandy Dinnsen, Dan H. Frissell Jr., Donald Garlow, Dixie Lou Glidewell, Barbara Gwaltney, Connie Hedrick, Fred Houghton, Jean Koch, Michael S. Liska, Elizabeth "Devie" Ludlum, David Massicot, Cynthia Murphy, Richard Roll, Dennis Rodenburg, Mary Mason, Patrick Lombardi, Troy T. Guillory Jr., Leonard Otterstetter, Roger Woodhull Jr., and Blake Woodhull III. Two brothers who deserve special mention are Robert D. Gibson Jr. and James M. "Hoot" Gibson, sons of SBD pilot Hoot Gibson. They assisted greatly by tracking down photos of their father and a copy of his unpublished wartime memoirs.

The key contributors are those who were there in 1942, veterans who flew the SBD Dauntless at Coral Sea and during the campaign to secure Hell's Island. Those who shared their stories, logbooks, photos, and other memorabilia were Edward R. Anderson, Thomas J. Ball, Frank Balsley, Frederick P. Bergeron, Harold L. "Hal" Buell, Kenneth J. Garrigan, Jack

Glass, John M. Iacovazzi, Willard "Rocky" Glidewell, Robert W. Gruebel, Aaron Katz, John W. King, Milford A. Merrill, Oral "Slim" Moore, Harold "Nate" Murphy, Charles F. Patton, William M. Rambur, and Stanley "Swede" Vejtasa.

To these brave carrier warriors this book is dedicated.

BIBLIOGRAPHY

INTERVIEWS, ORAL HISTORIES, AND CORRESPONDENCE

CAF AMERICAN AIRPOWER HERITAGE MUSEUM,
THE ORAL HISTORY ARCHIVE, MIDLAND, TEXAS

David John Cawley (VS-10): interviews with William J. Shinneman, April 24, 1995, and July 2, 1998, transcript.

Wayne C. Colley (VS-2, VS-10): interview with William J. Shinneman, July 27, 1991, transcript.

Lieutenant Commander Robert D. Gibson (VS-5, VB-10), USNR (Ret.), interview with William J. Shinneman, July 10, 1993, transcript.

Stuart J. Mason Jr. (VB-6): interview with William J. Shinneman, August 9, 2000, transcript.

Oral L. Moore (VB-8).

Leonard Robinson (VB-10): interview with William J. Shinneman.

Tony F. Schneider (VB-6).

Captain Stanley W. Vejtasa (VS-5, VF-10), USNR (Ret.): interview with William J. Shinneman, October 7, 2000, transcript.

BRITTANY HAYS INTERVIEW

Robert J. Mohler (VS-71), June 7, 1999 (courtesy of Robert L. Mohler).

MARK E. HORAN, PERSONAL INTERVIEWS, CORRESPONDENCE, AND OTHER ARCHIVES

Captain Harold S. Bottomley (VB-3).

Anthony W. Brunetti (VS-5), August 21, 1986.

Harold L. Buell (VS-5, VB-5), October 25, 1986.

William F. Christie (VS-5).

Captain Troy T. Guillory (VB-8), April 27, 1967, to Colonel Robert E. Barde.

Harold L. Jones (VB-6), December 22, 1986.

Joseph M. Lynch (VB-5, VS-5), October 20, 1986.

Lieutenant Commander Stuart J. Mason (VB-6), October 20, 1987.

Captain Vernon L. Micheel (VS-6).

Captain William R. Pittman (VB-6), October 22, 1986.

Commander Eldor E. Rodenburg (VS-6), 1987.

WALTER LORD COLLECTION, INTERVIEWS DURING RESEARCH FOR
INCREDIBLE VICTORY BOOK. OPERATIONAL ARCHIVES, NAVAL
HISTORY AND HERITAGE COMMAND, WASHINGTON NAVY YARD,
WASHINGTON, DC. SPECIFIC QUESTIONNAIRES, INTERVIEW NOTES,
AND CORRESPONDENCE WITH SBD PILOTS AND GUNNERS THAT
WERE REFERENCED

Rear Admiral Paul A. Holmberg (VB-3).

Ralph Hovind (VS-8).

Lieutenant Commander Stuart J. Mason (VB-6).

Commander Milford A. Merrill (VB-3).

Captain Vernon L. Micheel (VS-6).

Commander Eldor E. Rodenburg (VS-6).

NATIONAL MUSEUM OF THE PACIFIC WAR, FREDERICKSBURG, TEXAS

Frederick P. Bergeron (VB-3): April 29, 2004, interview.

Dr. Norman Anderson Sterrie (VT-2): July 20, 1997, interview.

NAVAL AVIATION MUSEUM FOUNDATION, PENSACOLA, FLORIDA,
ORAL HISTORY COLLECTION

Evan Peter Aurand (VS-2) and Marion Carl joint interview, May 1, 1988.

Admiral Ralph W. Cousins (VB-2) interview, October 18, 1988.

GORDON W. PRANGE PAPERS, INTERVIEWS AND CORRESPONDENCE
WITH MIDWAY VETERANS FOR *MIRACLE AT MIDWAY* BOOK.
UNIVERSITY OF MARYLAND, HORNBAKE LIBRARY, COLLEGE PARK

Captain Charlie N. "Tex" Conatser (VS-5) interview, May 11, 1966.

HENRY SAKAIDA RESEARCH

Robert D. Gibson to Sakaida, August 18, 1982.

Carl H. Horenburger to Sakaida, December 18, 1981.

Harold L. Jones, narrative to Sakaida, August 2, 1983.

INTERVIEWS CONDUCTED BY JAMES C. SAWRUK. INFORMATION
SHARED WITH AUTHOR VIA E-MAILS IN FEBRUARY 2012.

James H. Cales (VS-5).

Floyd E. Moan (VB-5).

Captain Arthur J. Schultz Jr. (VS-2).

LIEUTENANT COLONEL JAY STOUT INTERVIEW/RESEARCH

Captain Jesse T. Barker (VS-5) from 1999.

RUSH RHEES LIBRARY, UNIVERSITY OF ROCHESTER,
DEPARTMENT OF RARE BOOKS AND SPECIAL COLLECTIONS

Stockton B. Strong correspondence, Lyman Herbert Smith Papers.

INTERVIEWS CONDUCTED BY THE AUTHOR

Armstrong, Robert B. (nephew of VB-5 skipper Robert G. Armstrong). E-mail
correspondence, photos, and biography of Armstrong provided to author
on March 6, 2011.

Ball, Thomas J. (VB-2). Telephone interview, January 31, 2011.

Balsley, Frank (VT-8). Telephone interview, 1997.

Bergeron, Frederick P. (VB-3). Telephone interview, February 4, 2011, and
subsequent follow-up conversations and e-mail correspondence.

Birden, Mary (sister of VS-2 pilot Robert Weinzapfel). E-mail correspondence
with author from February to April 2011, in which she supplied letters
from her brother, his shipmates, and her family, circa 1941–1942.

Buell, Harold L. (VS-5). Telephone interviews, January 9 and February 8,
2011, and additional correspondence.

Craft, Kent (son of VS-2 gunner Lawrence S. Craft). Telephone interview,
April 8, 2011.

Frissell, Dan H., Jr. (son of VB-10 pilot Dan H. Frissell). Telephone
interview, May 28, 2013.

Garlow, Donald (son of VS-5 gunner Albert W. Garlow). Telephone
interview, May 15, 2013, and additional correspondence.

Garrigan, Kenneth J. (VS-2). Telephone interview, January 29, 2011.

Gibson, Robert D., Jr., and James M. "Hoot" Gibson (sons of VB-6, VB-10 pilot). Telephone interviews and e-mail correspondence, December 2013–May 2014. Bob provided photos and an unpublished memoir from his father's collection.

Glass, Jack (VB-10). Telephone interviews, April 4, 2012, and July 30, 2013.

Glidewell, Willard E. (VS-5). Telephone conversations with his wife, Dixie Lou Glidewell, in February 2011, and DVDs, written biography, and flight log data supplied by Mr. Glidewell.

Gruebel, Dr. Robert W. (VT-10). Telephone interview, May 22, 2014, and previous correspondence in 1995–1996.

Gwaltney, Barbara (daughter of VS-2 gunner Lawrence Craft). Telephone interviews and e-mail correspondence during 2013, papers of her father, and interview Barbara conducted with her mother, Beatrice McLendon Craft.

Hedrick, Connie (daughter of VB-2, VB-10 gunner Joseph Teyshak). Telephone interview, September 14, 2013.

Houghton, Fred (son of VB-5 pilot Orest I. Houghton). Telephone interview, March 3, 2011.

Iacovazzi, John M. (VB-5, VS-5). Telephone interview, January 25, 2011.

Johnston, Earnest Ray (VS-8). Telephone interviews, June 3 and June 20, 2011.

Katz, Aaron (VT-8). Telephone interview, 1997.

King, John W. (VT-8). Telephone interview, 1997.

Koch, Jean (wife of the late VS-2 pilot Lincoln C. Koch). Telephone interview, April 25, 2011. Additional details of Koch provided by his daughter, Jane G. Kirshenbaum.

Liska, Michael S. (son of VS-2 gunner John Liska). Telephone interview, September 2, 2013, and subsequent e-mail and correspondence.

Lombardi, Patrick (daughter of VB-5 gunner Dayton Harp). Telephone interview, May 17, 2012, and subsequent e-mail correspondence.

Ludlum, Elizabeth "Devie" (daughter of VS-10 officer William D. Boardman). Telephone interview, February 3, 2014, and subsequent e-mail correspondence.

Massicot, David (grandson of VS-5 gunner Albert W. Garlow). Telephone interview, June 20, 2013, and subsequent e-mail correspondence.

Mohler, Robert L. (son of VS-71 pilot Robert J. Mohler). Telephone interview, July 2, 2014, and subsequent correspondence.

Moore, Oral L. (VB-8). Telephone interview, June 2, 2011.

Murphy, Harold N. "Nate" (VS-71). Telephone interview, June 22, 2014. Special thanks to Nate's daughters, Cynthia Murphy and Sandy Dinnsen, for their assistance in forwarding his memoirs, photos, and other papers.

Otterstetter, Leonard (brother of VB-10 gunner Charles Otterstetter). Telephone interview, May 30, 2013.

Patton, Charles F. (VS-71). Telephone interview, March 27, 2012.

Rambur, William M. (VS-3). Telephone interview, March 25, 2012.

Rapp, Captain Jerome A., Jr. (VT-10). Telephone interviews and correspondence in 1995.

Roll, Richard (son of VS-5 gunner Joseph E. Roll). Telephone interview, January 30, 2011, and subsequent e-mail correspondence.

Vejtasa, Stanley W. (VS-5). Telephone interview, January 7, 2011.

Weinzapfel, Henry (brother of VS-2 pilot Robert Weinzapfel). Personal interview, February 19, 2011. Henry also provided photos, diary, and flight logs of his brother.

Woodhull, Roger B., Jr. (son of VS-5 pilot). Telephone interview, August 31, 2013, and subsequent correspondence. Additional information shared by Woodhull's grandson, R. B. "Blake" Woodhull III.

OFFICIAL DOCUMENTS, STATEMENTS

"Action Against Japanese Forces Attempting the Recapture of Guadalcanal, November 13–14, 1942, Report of" (November 19, 1942); Scouting Squadron Ten action report, November 20, 1942; Bombing Squadron Ten Action Report, November 20, 1942.

Bombing Squadron Six, "Report of Action, August 24, 1942," August 31, 1942.

Bombing Squadron Ten, war diary, courtesy of James Sawruk.

Caldwell, Commander Turner F., Jr., USN. Interview with Air Intelligence Group Division of Naval Intelligence Office, March 23, 1945, National Archives, courtesy of Barrett Tillman.

CTF-17 to CINCPAC, "The Battle of the Coral Sea, May 4–8, 1942," May 27, 1942.

Dixon, Lieutenant Commander R. E. "Report of Action, Scouting Squadron Two, on May 7, 1942, in Coral Sea," undated. "Report of Action, Scouting Squadron Two, on May 8, 1942, in Coral Sea," undated.

Hamilton, Lieutenant Commander W. L. "The Battle of the Coral Sea: Report of Action, Bombing Squadron Two," May 14, 1942. "Supplementary Report of Bombing Squadron Two Action in the Battle of the Coral Sea," May 30, 1942.

Liska, Aviation Radioman Third Class John, in Navy Department Press Release, "Gunner of Dive Bomber Tells How He and Pilot Shot Down Seven Jap 'Zero' Fighters," July 21, 1942.

Scouting Squadron Five Action Report, August 31, 1942.

Scouting Squadron Ten Report of Action, October 16 to October 26, 1942 (released October 29, 1942). Bombing Squadron Ten "Report of Action, October 26, 1942," October 30, 1942.

Short, Lieutenant W. C., Jr. Bombing Squadron (VB) Five Aircraft Action Reports for Coral Sea Action: May 4, 1942, May 7, 1942, and May 8, 1942.

Strong, Lieutenant Commander Stockton B. Bureau of Aeronautics interview of August 3, 1943, Office of Naval Records and Library, National Archives, Record Group 38, Box 26. Courtesy of James M. Scott.

Yorktown Air Group Action Reports: March 12, 1942, "Attack Made by USS Yorktown Air Group, 10 March 1942"; February 5, 1942, "CO USS Yorktown to CinCPac, Attack of Yorktown Air Group on Jaluit, Mili and Makin in Marshall and Gilbert Islands"; CTF-17 to CINCPAC, "The Battle of the Coral Sea, May 4–8, 1942," May 27, 1942.

ARTICLES, MEMOIRS, REPORTS

"Alumnus Tells of Adventures at Charleston." Alton Evening Telegraph, August 8, 1942, 1.

Antigone, Susan. "Birney Strong, Navy Hero, Pilot, Dies." Washington Post, December 22, 1977, B6.

Armstrong, Robert Bryan. "Armstrong, Robert Gordon. 1904–1980." Privately published biography of Captain Armstrong written by his nephew, August 2007.

Aurand, Evan Peter. Biographical sketch, accessed on May 15, 2013, from http://airlifes.wordpress.com/2012/07/21/evan-peter-aurand/.

Bigelow, Captain Lavell M. "Utah WWII Stories." Oral history, April 20, 2005.

Boardman, William D. (VS-10 officer). Papers and photos provided by his daughter, Elizabeth Devens "Devie" Ludlam. Additional information obtained via telephone conversations and e-mails with Mrs. Ludlam in February 2014.

"Boy Survivor of Lexington Feted Here." San Mateo Times, September 29, 1942, 1–2.

Bridgers, John D., M.D. "On the Traveling Squad E-Base, Doolittle & Midway, 1941–1942." Privately published "Memoirs and Personal Remembrances." http://tk-jk.net/Bridgers/NavyYears/OnTheTravelingSquad.html, accessed on February 5, 2011.

Brown, Gary. "WWII: Then and Now. Flew Dive Bombers." Canton Rep, February 27, 2012.

"Describes Sinking of Jap Aircraft Carrier in Pacific," Joplin News Herald, November 12, 1942, 7.

"Dive Bomber Pilots Hold a Reunion," *Joplin Globe*, July 1, 1942, 7.

"Dive-Bomber Pilot Tells of Scoring Hit on Jap Carrier," *Sunday Times* (Zanesville, OH), September 13, 1942.

Dixon, Robert E. "War Diary, Scouting Squadron Two: 7 December 1941 to 27 June 1942."

Downing, Arthur L. Unpublished narrative of VS-5. Eric Hammell Papers, Naval Historical Center.

"Elmer Maul Is Awarded Navy Cross." *Greeley Daily Tribune*, November 30, 1942, 1.

"Family Reunion on Fathers' Day," *Clovis News-Journal*, June 22, 1942, 6.

Felt, Admiral H. D., USN (Ret.). "VB-2 Partaking in Army Field Maneuvers—1941," *Foundation* (Naval Aviation Museum) (Spring 1984), 10–13.

"Flier Relates How Crew Saw *Lexington* Sunk." *Port Arthur News*, June 19, 1942, 2.

"Flier Describes Bursting of Bomb. Plane Carrier Hit by California Boy." *Reno Evening Gazette*, June 16, 1942, 1.

"Flier Describes Carrier Attack. Zeros Fail to Stop Him." *Reno Evening Gazette*, July 2, 1942, 6.

"Former J.C. Student Receives Citation." *San Mateo Times*, May 21, 1943.

Forshee, Lynn R. *Standby! Mark! An Autobiography by WWII Naval Aviator.* Privately published, 2004. http://www.forshee.0sites.org/index .shtml, accessed on January 12, 2011.

Gibson, Robert Douglas. *Slow but Deadly. A Navy Dive Bomber Pilot Makes a Pact with the Moon. A True Adventure Story.* Unpublished memoir, courtesy of Robert D. Gibson, Jr.

Graetz, Ronald. "Memories from Navy Days." Memoirs of service with Torpedo Squadron Six, courtesy of Ron Graetz.

Green, Adinah. "Chandler Swanson Survived Pearl Harbor, Served Navy for 32 Years." *Orlando Sentinel*, December 8, 2003.

Hackett, Bob, Sander Kingsepp, and Peter Cundall, "IJN Subchaser CH-51: Tabular Record of Movement." http://www.combinedfleet.com/Shisaka_t .htm, accessed on August 21, 2009.

———. "IJN Minelayer *Maeshima*: Tabular Record of Movement." © 2008– 2009. http://www.combinedfleet.com/Maeshima_t.htm, accessed on December 4, 2009.

"The Highest Military Honor for a Moment of True Heroism." *Tulsa World Sunday Magazine*, October 28, 1979, 6.

Johnston, Stanley. "Eye-Witness," 6.

"Kingsport, Va., Youth Vividly Tells of Jap Plane Attack." *Kingsport (TN) Times*, August 4, 1942, 1.

"Lanark Youth Loses $50 on U.S.S. *Lexington*." *Freeport Journal-Standard*, June 23, 1942, 2.

Lane, Marica. "Veteran Recounts Service on USS *Enterprise*." *St. Augustine Times*, April 24, 2006. http://staugustine.com/stories/042406/ news_3789710.shtml, accessed on December 27, 2011.

Lee, Clark. "Ex–Indiana School Teacher Dive-Bombs Japs, Likes It." *Charleston Gazette*, June 13, 1942, 1–2.

"Letter Indicates Sandusky Hero Lost. Commander of Squadron Tells of Ens. Davis Chaffee in Coral Sea Battle." *Sandusky Register Star-News*, October 2, 1942, 1, 8.

"Lieutenant Knapp, Mason Cityan, Bombed Jap Carrier." *Mason City Globe-Gazette*, June 18, 1942, 1.

"Lieut. Knapp Writes About Big Sea Fight." *Mason City Globe-Gazette*, March 16, 1942, 11.

"Lieut. Tepas, Home After Crusoe Adventure, Is City's First to Win Flying Medal." *Portsmouth* [OH] *Times*, December 17, 1942, 1–2.

Lundstrom, John B., and James C. Sawruk. "Courage and Devotion to Duty. The SBD Anti-torpedo Plane Patrol in the Coral Sea 8 May 1942." *Hook* (Winter 1988), 24–37.

Machalinski, Raymond A. (VT-5) "Ray Machalinski's Devastator Adventures." Memoirs of 1942 service provided to Mark Horan.

"Madison Radioman Downs Attacking Jap Zero Fighter. Navy May Decorate Coral Sea Airman." *Wisconsin State Journal*, August 10, 1942, 7.

Mason, Robert. "Eyewitness." *Proceedings* (June 1982), 40–42.

Mohler, Robert J. Correspondence to Norm R. Watson, USS *Wasp Stinger*. Editor, September 5, 1995, of personal accounts of VS-71 at Guadalcanal. *USS Wasp CV-7 Stinger Newsletter* 56 (3) (December 1, 1955,), 73–77.

Murphy, Howard N. "Exploits and Memories of a Naval Aviator." Privately published.

"Navy Gunner Gets Award, Tells of Lively Fight," *Helena Independent*, November 25, 1942, 1.

"Oakland Flier Drifts 17 Days in Rubber Boat; Fails to Thumb Ride on Passing Jap Submarine." *Oakland Tribune*, September 9, 1942.

Prescott, Robert S. "*Lexington* Was Sunk by Own Torpedoes." *Evening Capital* (Annapolis, MD), June 13, 1942, 8.

Register, Francis Roland. Diary (VF-5), March 17, 1941, to October 14, 1942. www.daveswarbirds.com/cactus/diary.htm, accessed on December 6, 2013.

Rodenburg, Dennis. *Eldor E. Rodenburg, Lieutenant Commander, U.S.N.R. World War II Dive Bomber Pilot and Landing Signal Officer*. Privately published. Courtesy of Dennis Rodenburg.

Roemer, Captain Charles E., USN (Ret.). "*Lexington*'s First Day of War," *Foundation* (Naval Aviation Museum), (Spring 1997), 97–100.

"Rowley Given Navy Cross for Heroic Flying Attack." *Wisconsin State Journal*, November 12, 1942, 9.

"Two Lisbon, N.D. Youths Honored. Tell of Sinking Enemy U-Boat and Big Jap Carrier." *Bismarck Tribune*, June 25, 1942, 1, 3.

"Top Utah Hero Home, Asks, 'Why the Fuss?'" *Salt Lake Tribune*, October 4, 1945, 1, 20.

Vejtasa, Stanley W. Unpublished memoirs, courtesy of the Vejtasa family, via Ted Edwards.

"Wait Irked Utahn in Coral Battle." *Salt Lake Tribune*, June 21, 1942, 2B.

Whittier, Mark Twain. *Instead of Becoming a Doctor*. Privately published memoir, 1988.

Woodson, Richard T. "In the Rear Seat at Midway and Santa Cruz."

"Wounded Pilot Tells of Coral Sea Battle." *Salt Lake Tribune*, July 6, 1942, 6, 16.

"Yank Flyers Forced Down Aided by Island Natives." *News Palladium* (Benton Harbor, MI), August 27, 1942, 1.

VIDEO

Glidewell, Willard E. (VS-5). Oral history, videotaped in 2006, Veterans History Project, Library of Congress.

BOOKS/EBOOKS

Ambrose, Hugh. *The Pacific*. New York: NAL Caliber, 2010.

Belote, James H., and William M. Belote. *Titans of the Seas: The Development and Operations of Japanese and American Carrier Task Forces During World War II*. New York: Harper & Row, 1975.

Buell, Harold L. *Dauntless Helldivers: A Dive-Bomber Pilot's Epic Story of the Carrier Battles*. New York: Orion Books, 1991.

Cressman, Robert. *That Gallant Ship: U.S.S. Yorktown (CV-5)*. Missoula, MT: Pictorial Histories Publishing Company, 1985. Second printing, 1989.

Cressman, Robert, with Steve Ewing, Barrett Tillman, Mark Horan, Clark Reynolds, and Stan Cohen. *"A Glorious Page in Our History": The Battle of Midway, 4–6 June 1942*. Missoula, MT: Pictorial Histories Publishing Company, 1990.

Cummings, J. Glenn. *Trailing a Texas Eagle: The Life and Legacy of Lt. Commander Harry Brinkley Bass*. Virginia Beach: Donning Company Publishers, 2010.

Fisher, Commander Clayton E., USN (Ret.). *Hooked: Tales & Adventures of a Tailhook Warrior.* Denver: Outskirts Press, Inc., 2009.

Frank, Pat, and Joseph D. Harrington. *Rendezvous at Midway: U.S.S. Yorktown and the Japanese Carrier Fleet.* New York: John Day Company, 1967.

Griffin, Alexander. *A Ship to Remember: The Saga of the Hornet.* New York: Howell, Soskin, Publishers, 1943.

Hoehling, A. A. *The Lexington Goes Down: The Last Seven Hours of a Fighting Lady.* Englewood Cliffs, NJ: Prentice-Hall, Inc., 1971.

Hoyt, Edwin P. *Blue Skies and Blood: The Battle of the Coral Sea.* New York: Paul S. Eriksson, Inc., 1975.

Johnston, Stanley. *Queen of the Flat-Tops.* New York: Bantam Books, 1942. Eleventh printing, 1979.

Ludlow, Stuart D. (Ex-Lieutenant, AVS, USNR). *They Turned the War Around at Coral Sea and Midway: Going to War with Yorktown's Air Group Five.* Bennington, VT: Merriam Press, 2003.

Lundstrom, John B. *The First Team: Pacific Naval Air Combat from Pearl Harbor to Midway.* Annapolis: Naval Institute Press, 1984.

———. *The First Team and the Guadalcanal Campaign: Navy Fighter Combat from August to November 1942.* Annapolis: Naval Institute Press, 1994.

———. *Black Shoe Carrier Admiral: Frank Jack Fletcher at Coral Sea, Midway, and Guadalcanal.* Annapolis: Naval Institute Press, 2006.

McWilliams, Bill. *Sunday in Hell: Pearl Harbor Minute by Minute.* E-Reads e-book, 2011.

Mears, Lieutenant Frederick. *Carrier Combat: Battle Action with an American Torpedo Plane Pilot.* Garden City, NY: Doubleday, Doran and Co., Inc., 1944.

Mrazek, Robert J. *A Dawn Like Thunder: The True Story of Torpedo Squadron Eight.* New York: Little, Brown and Company, 2008.

Nesmith, Jeff. *No Higher Honor: The U.S.S. Yorktown at the Battle of Midway.* Atlanta: Longstreet, 1999.

Stafford, Commander Edward P., U.S.N. *The Big E: The Story of the USS Enterprise.* New York: Random House, Inc., 1962.

Tillman, Barrett. *The Dauntless Dive Bomber of World War II.* Annapolis: Naval Institute Press, 1976. Sixth printing, 1989.

CHAPTER NOTES

CHAPTER ONE: "IT'S ALL EXCITING AS HELL"

1 Robert Weinzapfel, letter to family, October 18, 1941. Courtesy of Mary Birden.

2 "Lieut. John Leppla Missing in Action." *Lima News*, November 20, 1942, 1–2.

3 Pete Aurand sketch, from http://airlifes.wordpress.com/2012/07/21/evan -peter-aurand/ (accessed May 15, 2013); Captain Evan P. Aurand oral history recorded May 1, 1988, Naval Aviation Museum Foundation.

4 Robert Weinzapfel, letter to Thomas Weinzapfel, October 25, 1941. Courtesy of Mary Birden.

5 Robert Weinzapfel, letters to family, November 8 and December 1, 1941. Courtesy of Mary Birden.

6 Captain Charles E. Roemer, USN (Ret.), "Lexington's First Day of War," *Foundation* (Naval Aviation Foundation Museum), Spring 1997, 99; Lundstrom, *The First Team*, 22–23; Weinzapfel diary.

7 Roemer, "*Lexington*'s First Day of War," 99.

8 Admiral Ralph W. Cousins, oral history for Naval Aviation Foundation Museum, October 18, 1988.

9 Roemer, "*Lexington*'s First Day of War," 99–100.

10 Wayne C. Colley, oral history recorded by William J. Shinneman, July 27, 1991, 2. Courtesy of the CAF Museum, Midland, Texas.

11 Ibid., 2.

12 USS *Lexington* War Diary, December 1941; Roemer, "*Lexington*'s First Day of War," 100.

13 Weinzapfel, diary.

14 John A. Leppla, letter to Weinzapfel family, December 11, 1941. Courtesy of Mary Birden.

15 Mrs. J. M. Weinzapfel, letter to John Leppla, January 5, 1942.

16 War Diary of VS-2, 1; Whittier, *Instead of Becoming a Doctor*, 35.

17 Norman Anderson Sterrie, oral history interview, July 20, 1997. Transcription courtesy of the National Museum of the Pacific War, 9–10.

18   Aurand, sketch.
19   Whittier, *Instead of Becoming a Doctor*, 38–41; USS *Lexington* War Diary, December 1941.
20   Tillman, *The Dauntless Dive Bomber of World War II*, 9; Whittier, *Instead of Becoming a Doctor*, 1–3, 18–23.
21   Ibid., 23–25.
22   USS *Lexington* War Diary, December 1941.
23   Aurand, sketch.

CHAPTER TWO: ROCKY, SWEDE, AND "THE MASTER"

1   Cressman, *That Gallant Ship*, 48.
2   William F. Christie, correspondence with Mark Horan; Cressman, "Blaze of Glory," 24–26.
3   J. R. Bailey, "1941 Louisiana Maneuvers: The Big One," *Military Trader News*, January 7, 2009.
4   Admiral H. D. Felt, USN (Ret.), "VB-2 Partaking in Army Field Maneuvers—1941," *Foundation* (Naval Aviation Museum), Spring 1984, 10–12; Whittier, *Instead of Becoming a Doctor*, 30.
5   "Mid-Air Plane Crash Gives Maneuvers Realistic Start," *Laredo Times*, September 15, 1941, 1.
6   Stuart D. Ludlow (Lieutenant [Ret.], AVS, USNR). *They Turned the War Around at Coral Sea and Midway. Going to War with Yorktown's Air Group Five* (Bennington, Vt.: Merriam Press, 2003), 14.
7   Ibid., 14.
8   Willard E. Glidewell, oral history (videotaped), Veterans History Project, Library of Congress, February 13, 2006.
9   Harold Wilger, letter to Eric Hammell, March 22, 1982, Hammell Papers; Nesmith, *No Higher Honor*, 14.
10   Strickland, letter to Hammell, July 1982.
11   Ludlow, *They Turned the War Around*, 9–10.
12   Capt. Lavell M. Bigelow, Utah World War II Stories, oral history, April 20, 2005; Traynor, oral history, undated.
13   Ted Edwards, *Swede Vejtasa: His Battle of Santa Cruz and Beyond*; unpublished.
14   "Frank Vejtasa and family," http://boards.ancestry.com/mbexec/msg/rw/1RC.2ACE/3487, accessed January 30, 2013.
15   Stanley W. Vejtasa, oral history by William J. Shinneman.
16   Ibid.; additional background on Vejtasa supplied by author Ted Smith.
17   Vejtasa, oral history.
18   Buell, Harold L. *Dauntless Helldivers: A Dive-Bomber Pilot's Epic Story of the Carrier Battles*. New York: Orion Books, 1991, 55.
19   Vejtasa, oral history.
20   Stanley W. Vejtasa, unpublished memoir, 8. Courtesy of the Vejtasa family via Ted Edwards.
21   Lawrence G. Traynor, oral history; interview with Larry Traynor Jr., undated.
22   Ludlow, *They Turned the War Around*, 9–10.
23   Ibid., 10.
24   Downing, memoirs of VS-5, 2.

25 Ludlow, *They Turned the War Around*, 23.
26 Cressman, *That Gallant Ship*, 49–53; Lundstrom, *The First Team*, 56.
27 Downing, memoirs of VS-5, 2.
28 Lundstrom, *The First Team*, 59.

CHAPTER THREE: "HIT-AND-RUN ATTACK IN IMPOSSIBLE WEATHER"

1   Cressman, *That Gallant Ship*, 58; Nesmith, *No Higher Honor*, 41, 46.
2   Armstrong, "Armstrong, Robert Gordon. 1904–1980." Privately published biography of Captain Armstrong, written by his nephew, August 2007, 1–3.
3   Ludlow, *They Turned the War Around*, 26–27.
4   Forshee, *Standby! Mark!*, chapter 5.
5   Ludlow, *They Turned the War Around*, 27.
6   Ibid., 27–28; Glidewell, videotaped oral history.
7   Ludlow, *They Turned the War Around*, 29; Cressman, *That Gallant Ship*, 58.
8   Ludlow, *They Turned the War Around*, 29.
9   Harrington and Frank, *Rendezvous at Midway*, 57; Forshee, *Standby! Mark!*, chapter 5.
10 Ludlow, *They Turned the War Around*, 28; Buckmaster report; Cressman, *That Gallant Ship*, 59.
11 Lundstrom, *Black Shoe Carrier Admiral*, 67. Six airmen from Torpedo Five—Lieutenant Jack Cobb Moore, AOM1c Harold Frank Omo, RM3c Harold Carl Schonborg, Lieutenant Francis Xavier Maher Jr., AMM1c Joe Capers Chitwood, and RM3c Roy Lee Ayers—were gone, officially listed as missing in action.
12 Commander Turner F. Caldwell Jr., USN, interview with Air Intelligence Group Division of Naval Intelligence Office, March 23, 1945, National Archives, courtesy of Barrett Tillman.
13 Cressman, *That Gallant Ship*, 59; Ludlow, *They Turned the War Around*, 30.
14 Ibid.
15 "Top Utah Hero Home," *Salt Lake Tribune*, 20.
16 Ludlow, *They Turned the War Around*, 30.
17 Cressman, *That Gallant Ship*, 59; Ludlow, *They Turned the War Around*, 30.
18 Ludlow, *They Turned the War Around*, 30.
19 Buell, *Dauntless Helldivers*, 56–57.
20 Cressman, *That Gallant Ship*, 59.
21 Ibid.; Arthur Downing, unpublished VS-5 narrative, 4. Tom Reeves would be detached from the squadron at Honolulu to allow time for his scalp wounds to heal.
22 Cressman, *That Gallant Ship*, 60–61; Lundstrom, *The First Team*, 80.
23 Lieutenant Commander Stockton B. Strong, Bureau of Aeronautics, interview, August 3, 1943, Office of Naval Records and Library, National Archives, Record Group 38, Box 26. Courtesy of James M. Scott.
24 Nesmith, *No Higher Honor*, 58–59.
25 Ludlow, *They Turned the War Around*, 30; Vejtasa, oral history.

26 Downing, unpublished narrative, 5.
27 Ludlow, *They Turned the War Around*, 33–34.

CHAPTER FOUR: "I WANTED TO HIT 'EM HARD"

1   "Lanark Youth Loses $50 on U.S.S. *Lexington*," *Freeport Journal-Standard*, June 23, 1942, 2; Stanley Johnston, *Queen of the Flat-Tops*. New York: Bantam Books, 1942, eleventh printing, 1979, 6–7.
2   Lundstrom, *The First Team*, 92–99.
3   Whittier, *Instead of Becoming a Doctor*, 43–44; "Clintwood, Va., Youth Vividly Tells of Jap Plane Attack," *Kingsport Times*, August 4, 1942, 1.
4   Lundstrom, *The First Team*, 100–101.
5   Ibid., 102–4.
6   Ludlum, *They Turned the War Around*, 35, 43; Downing, unpublished VS-5 narrative, 6.
7   Vejtasa, oral history.
8   Lundstrom, *The First Team*, 123.
9   Lundstrom, *Black Shoe Carrier Admiral*, 91–92.
10 Whittier, *Instead of Becoming a Doctor*, 45; Lundstrom, *The First Team*, 127.
11 Cressman, *That Gallant Ship*, 67.
12 Johnston, *Queen of the Flat-Tops*, 86; Ludlum, *They Turned the War Around*, 37; Whittier, *Instead of Becoming a Doctor*, 45–46.
13 Ibid., 46; Cressman, *That Gallant Ship*, 67.
14 Scouting Two War Diary, 3.
15 Colley, oral history, 17–18.
16 James Sawruk, interviews with Arthur J. Schultz Jr., e-mail to author, April 7, 2011.
17 Colley, oral history, 18.
18 Scouting Two War Diary, 3; Lundstrom, *The First Team*, 129.
19 Sawruk, e-mail to author, April 7, 2011.
20 Scouting Two War Diary, 2–3.
21 Lundstrom, *The First Team*, 129; Johnston, *Queen of the Flat-Tops*, 88; Whittier, *Instead of Becoming a Doctor*, 46–47.
22 Lundstrom, *The First Team*, 129.
23 Ludlum, *They Turned the War Around*, 37; Pat Frank and Joseph D. Harrington. *Rendezvous at Midway: U.S.S. Yorktown and the Japanese Carrier Fleet*. New York: The John Day Company, 1967, 67.
24 Ludlum, *They Turned the War Around*, 38–39; Taylor bombing result information via James C. Sawruk, who provided notes to author in 2014.
25 Moan, interview with Sawruk, notes; Cressman, *That Gallant Ship*, 67; Forshee, *Standby! Mark!*, chapter 7; Ludlum, *They Turned the War Around*, 39–40; Lundstrom, *The First Team*, 131.
26 Ludlum, *They Turned the War Around*, 37.
27 Ibid., 38.
28 James H. Cales, interview with James C. Sawruk, notes related to author.
29 Downing, VS-5 narrative, 7; Ludlum, *They Turned the War Around*, 38; Cressman, *That Gallant Ship*, 68.
30 Ludlum, *They Turned the War Around*, 40–41.

31 Sawruk, e-mail to author, April 7, 2011.
32 Cressman, *That Gallant Ship*, 68–69.

CHAPTER FIVE: DECK DODGERS FIND A HOME

1   Buell, *Dauntless Helldivers*, 45–49.
2   Ibid., 13–21.
3   Robert Douglas Gibson, *Slow but Deadly*, 9–11.
4   Ibid., 12.
5   Ibid., 16–17; Gibson, oral history, 1.
6   Gibson, *Slow but Deadly*, 18–21.
7   Buell, *Dauntless Helldivers*, 31–32; Gibson, oral history, 2.
8   Buell, *Dauntless Helldivers*, 34–35; Gibson, oral history, 3.
9   Gibson, oral history, 4; Gibson, *Slow but Deadly*, 31.
10 Buell, *Dauntless Helldivers*, 45–49.
11 Ibid., 46–49.
12 Gibson, oral history, 5.
13 Lundstrom and Sawruk, "Courage and Devotion to Duty," 32.
14 Gibson, oral history, 5–6; Gibson, *Slow but Deadly*, 38–39.
15 Buell, *Dauntless Helldivers*, 52–53.
16 Downing, VS-5 narrative, 9.
17 Lundstrom, *The First Team*, 159.
18 Glidewell, videotaped oral history; Ludlum, *They Turned the War Around*, 44–45.
19 Rear Adm. Wallace C. Short interview with Robert Barde, May 24, 1966; Bill Christie correspondence with Mark Horan.
20 Glidewell, videotaped oral history.
21 Ibid.
22 Cressman, *That Gallant Ship*, 76–79; Buell, *Dauntless Helldivers*, 52–53.
23 John Lynch to Mark Horan, October 20, 1986. Harold Buell to Mark Horan, October 25, 1986, confirms that ten pilots—not nine, per some published sources—were received on *Yorktown*. Bombing Five and Scouting Five rosters show ten new ensigns being received on April 28, 1942. According to pilot Bill Christie to Mark Horan, Houghton requested non-combat (non-flying) duties before the Coral Sea battle and Captain Buckmaster revoked his commission. Houghton went on to fly for Pan Am out of San Francisco and later flew out of Brownsville, Texas.
24 Buell, *Dauntless Helldivers*, 55–56.
25 Ibid., 56.
26 Cressman, *That Gallant Ship*, 79; "Enemy Submarine, Contact with." USS *Yorktown* Action Report, May 2. 1942.
27 Cressman, *That Gallant Ship*, 79.

CHAPTER SIX: FIRST STRIKES IN THE SOLOMONS

1   Interview with Lieutenant Commander William O. Burch, USN, commanding VS-5, USS *Yorktown*, Bureau of Aeronautics, September 3, 1942.
2   Lundstrom, *Black Shoe Carrier Admiral*, 146.
3   Ibid., 146; Cressman, *That Gallant Ship*, 79.

4   Lundstrom, *Black Shoe Carrier Admiral*, 146.
5   Cressman, *That Gallant Ship*, 79.
6   Lundstrom, *Black Shoe Carrier Admiral*, 147; Lundstrom, *The First Team*, 170–71.
7   Cressman, *That Gallant Ship*, 79; Ludlum, *They Turned the War Around*, 49.
8   Ludlum, *They Turned the War Around*, 49; Burch, interview, 3–4.
9   Mark 13, Model 0, research of Mark E. Horan; http://www.navweaps .com/Weapons/WTUS_WWII.htm, accessed February 29, 2012.
10 Cressman, *That Gallant Ship*, 81; Lundstrom, *Black Shoe Carrier Admiral*, 147.
11 Cressman, *That Gallant Ship*, 81; Forshee, *Standby! Mark!*, chapter 9.
12 Ludlum, *They Turned the War Around*, 50; Downing, VS-5 narrative, 10.
13 Burch, interview, 3.
14 Forshee, *Standby! Mark!*, chapter 10.
15 Cressman, *That Gallant Ship*, 81.
16 Ibid., 81.
17 Ibid., 83; Lundstrom, *Black Shoe Carrier Admiral*, 148.
18 Vejtasa, oral history.
19 Downing, VS-5 narrative, 10.
20 Ludlum, *They Turned the War Around*, 50–51; Machalinski, "Ray Machalinski's Devastator Adventures."
21 Cressman, *That Gallant Ship*, 83; Ludlum, *They Turned the War Around*, 51.
22 Cressman, *That Gallant Ship*, 83.
23 Ludlum, *They Turned the War Around*, 51.
24 Vejtasa, oral history.
25 Cressman, *That Gallant Ship*, 83–84; Lundstrom, *The First Team*, 174.
26 Lundstrom, *Black Shoe Carrier Admiral*, 148.
27 Wilburn Dayton Harp collection, courtesy of Patrick Lombardi. Some of Harp's wartime letters to his parents are quoted in a 1942 (date unknown) *Lakeland Ledger* newspaper article.
28 Ludlum, *They Turned the War Around*, 52; Lundstrom, *The First Team*, 175; Downing, VS-5 narrative, 10.
29 Cressman, *That Gallant Ship*, 84–85; Ludlum, *They Turned the War Around*, 53–77.
30 Cressman, *That Gallant Ship*, 85; Lieutenant Commander Strong, interview, August 3, 1943; Lundstrom, *Black Shoe Carrier Admiral*, 149.
31 Lundstrom, *Black Shoe Carrier Admiral*, 149.
32 Ludlum, *They Turned the War Around*, 54.
33 Lundstrom, *The First Team*, 188, 190.
34 Buell, *Dauntless Helldivers*, 64–65.
35 Cressman, *That Gallant Ship*, 90.
36 Vejtasa, oral history.
37 Lundstrom, *Black Shoe Carrier Admiral*, 160.
38 Ludlum, *They Turned the War Around*, 79.
39 Lundstrom, *The First Team*, 189; operational count per Mark E. Horan.
40 Lundstrom, *Black Shoe Carrier Admiral*, 162; Lundstrom, *The First Team*, 193.

41 Ludlum, *They Turned the War Around*, 80–82.
42 Lundstrom, *Black Shoe Carrier Admiral*, 165, 553; Lundstrom, *The First Team*, 190–92.
43 Cressman, *That Gallant Ship*, 91.

CHAPTER SEVEN: "SCRATCH ONE FLATTOP!"

1 "Two Lisbon, N.D. Youths Honored. Tell of Sinking Enemy U-Boat and Big Jap Carrier," *Bismarck Tribune*, June 25, 1942, 1, 3.
2 Lundstrom, *The First Team*, 195.
3 Vejtasa, oral history.
4 Ludlum, *They Turned the War Around*, 83.
5 Lundstrom, *The First Team*, 195–96.
6 Ibid., 196; Ludlum, *They Turned the War Around*, 82; Cressman, *That Gallant Ship*, 92; Lundstrom, *Black Shoe Carrier Admiral*, 165.
7 Johnston, *Queen of the Flat-Tops*, 142.
8 "Two Lisbon, N.D. Youths Honored," 3; Johnston, *Queen of the Flat-Tops*, 142.
9 Tillman, *The Dauntless Dive Bomber of World War II*, 37; Lundstrom, *The First Team*, 197.
10 Tillman, *The Dauntless Dive Bomber of World War II*, 37; Johnston, *Queen of the Flat-Tops*, 154–55; "Flier Relates How Crew Saw *Lexington* Sunk," *Port Arthur News*, June 19, 1942, 2.
11 Johnston, *Queen of the Flat-Tops*, 145–46; Tillman, *The Dauntless Dive Bomber of World War II*, 38.
12 "Pilot Who Fought in Coral Sea Visiting Parents Here," *Lima News*, June 18, 1942, 1.
13 John Liska, Aviation Radioman 3rd Class, in Navy Department Press Release, "Gunner of Dive Bomber Tells How He and Pilot Shot Down Seven Jap 'Zero' Fighters," July 21, 1942.
14 Lundstrom, *The First Team*, 199.
15 "Flier Relates How Crew Saw *Lexington* Sunk," 2; Lieutenant Commander R. E. Dixon, "Report of Action, Scouting Squadron Two, on May 7, 1942, in Coral Sea," undated, 2.
16 Lieutenant Commander W. L. Hamilton, "The Battle of the Coral Sea: Report of Action, Bombing Squadron Two," May 14, 1942, 2–3; Johnston, *Queen of the Flat-Tops*, 143, 147, 152; Robert S. Prescott, "*Lexington* Was Sunk by Own Torpedoes," *Evening Capital* (Annapolis, MD), June 13, 1942, 8.
17 "Madison Radioman Downs Attacking Jap Zero Fighter. Navy May Decorate Coral Sea Airman," *Wisconsin State Journal*, August 10, 1942, 7.
18 Ibid., 7; Johnston, *Queen of the Flat-Tops*, 143.
19 "Flier Describes Carrier Attack. Zeros Fail to Stop Him," *Reno Evening Gazette*, July 2, 1942, 6; Hamilton, "The Battle of the Coral Sea: Report of Action, Bombing Squadron Two," 4; "Flier Describes Bursting of Bomb. Plane Carrier Hit by California Boy," *Reno Evening Gazette*, June 16, 1942, 1.
20 "Two Lisbon, N.D. Youths Honored," 3.
21 Lundstrom, *The First Team*, 199; "Two Lisbon, N.D. Youths Honored," 3.

22   Lundstrom, *The First Team*, 199–201; Ludlum, *They Turned the War Around*, 84; "Boy Survivor of *Lexington* Feted Here," *San Mateo Times*, September 29, 1942, 1–2.
23   Glidewell, videotaped oral history.
24   Ludlum, *They Turned the War Around*, 84–85; Lundstrom, *The First Team*, 201.
25   Ludlum, *They Turned the War Around*, 85; "Elmer Maul Is Awarded Navy Cross," *Greeley Daily Tribune*, November 30, 1942, 1.
26   Ludlum, *They Turned the War Around*, 85; Glidewell, oral history.
27   Lundstrom, *The First Team*, 201.
28   Ludlum, *They Turned the War Around*, 88; Lundstrom, *Black Shoe Carrier Admiral*, 169.
29   Forshee, *Standby! Mark!*, chapter 10; Ludlum, *They Turned the War Around*, 85; Downing, VS-5 narrative, 11.
30   Harrington and Frank, *Rendezvous at Midway*, 100; Cressman, *That Gallant Ship*, 94; Traynor, oral history.
31   Cressman, *That Gallant Ship*, 94; Lundstrom, *The First Team*, 205.
32   Strong, interview, August 3, 1943; Lundstrom, *The First Team*, 205.
33   Forshee, *Standby! Mark!*, chapter 10; Christie to Horan.
34   Johnston, *Queen of the Flat-Tops*, 152; Johnston, Douglas article, 8.
35   Liska, Navy Department press release, July 21, 1942.
36   Vejtasa, oral history.
37   Johnston, *Queen of the Flat-Tops*, 153–54.
38   Cressman, *That Gallant Ship*, 95; "Rowley Given Navy Cross for Heroic Flying Attack," *Wisconsin State Journal*, November 12, 1942, 9; Harrington and Frank, *Rendezvous at Midway*, 101.
39   Tillman, *The Dauntless Dive Bomber of World War II*, 41.
40   Ludlum, *They Turned the War Around*, 88; Lundstrom, *Black Shoe Carrier Admiral*, 168.
41   Ludlum, *They Turned the War Around*, 88.
42   Cressman, *That Gallant Ship*, 96; Lundstrom, *The First Team*, 205.
43   Ludlum, *They Turned the War Around*, 90.
44   Traynor, oral history.
45   Lundstrom, *Black Shoe Carrier Admiral*, 180.
46   Cressman, *That Gallant Ship*, 97; Ludlum, *They Turned the War Around*, 93.
47   Forshee, *Standby! Mark!*, chapter 11.

Chapter Eight: "I Am Going to Get a Hit"

1   Frank and Harrington, *Rendezvous at Midway*, 109.
2   Lundstrom, *The First Team*, 221–22.
3   Tillman, *The Dauntless Dive Bomber of World War II*, 43.
4   Lundstrom, *The First Team*, 222–24.
5   Cressman, *That Gallant Ship*, 99.
6   Tillman, *The Dauntless Dive Bomber of World War II*, 43; Lundstrom, *Black Shoe Carrier Admiral*, 185; Lundstrom and Sawruk, "Courage and Devotion to Duty," 34.
7   Lundstrom, *The First Team*, 225.
8   Christie, to Mark Horan; Forshee, *Standby! Mark!*, chapter 11.

9   Ludlum, *They Turned the War Around*, 94–95; Downing, memoirs of VS-5, 12.

10 Lundstrom, *The First Team*, 226.

11 Johnston, *Queen of the Flat-Tops*, 165; Tillman, *The Dauntless Dive Bomber of World War II*, 44; Lundstrom, *The First Team*, 227.

12 Tillman, *The Dauntless Dive Bomber of World War II*, 45; Johnston, *Queen of the Flat-Tops*, 164.

13 Tillman, *The Dauntless Dive Bomber of World War II*, 45; Lundstrom, *The First Team*, 236.

14 Ludlum, *They Turned the War Around*, 95.

15 Ibid., 95.

16 Forshee, *Standby! Mark!*, chapter 11.

17 Ludlum, *They Turned the War Around*, 95; Cressman, *That Gallant Ship*, 100.

18 Ludlum, *They Turned the War Around*, 96–97; Glidewell, oral history; Lundstrom, *The First Team*, 230.

19 Nesmith, *No Higher Honor*, 142–43; Johnston, "Eye-witness," 6.

20 Nesmith, *No Higher Honor*, 143.

21 Cressman, *That Gallant Ship*, 100; Nesmith, *No Higher Honor*, 143; "Describes Sinking of Jap Aircraft Carrier in Pacific," *Joplin News Herald*, November 12, 1942, 7; Anthony Brunetti to Mark Horan, August 21, 1986; Johnston, "Eye-witness," 6.

22 Nesmith, *No Higher Honor*, 143–44; Johnston, "Eye-witness," 6.

23 Downing, memoirs of VS-5, 12; Cressman, *That Gallant Ship*, 100.

24 Ludlum, *They Turned the War Around*, 97, 100; Clark Lee, "Ex–Indiana School Teacher Dive-Bombs Japs, Likes It," *Charleston Gazette*, June 13, 1942, 1–2.

25 Tillman, *The Dauntless Dive Bomber of World War II*, 46; "Elmer Maul Is Awarded Navy Cross," *Greeley Daily Tribune*, November 30, 1942, 1; Lundstrom, *The First Team*, 231.

26 Tillman, *The Dauntless Dive Bomber of World War II*, 46; Christie to Horan; Cressman, *That Gallant Ship*, 100; Ludlum, *They Turned the War Around*, 97.

27 Ludlum, *They Turned the War Around*, 97–98.

28 Tillman, *The Dauntless Dive Bomber of World War II*, 47; Cressman, *That Gallant Ship*, 100.

29 Ludlum, *They Turned the War Around*, 98; Bigelow, oral history; Forshee, *Standby! Mark!*, chapter 11; Christie to Horan, 1986.

30 Cressman, *That Gallant Ship*, 100; Ludlum, *They Turned the War Around*, 99.

31 Lundstrom, *The First Team*, 235.

32 Glidewell, oral history.

33 Ludlum, *They Turned the War Around*, 96.

34 Ibid., 98–99; "Navy Gunner Gets Award, Tells of Lively Fight," *Helena Independent*, November 25, 1942, 1.

35 Ibid.; "Letter Indicates Sandusky Hero Lost. Commander of Squadron Tells of Ens. Davis Chaffee in Coral Sea Battle," *Sandusky Register Star-News*, October 2, 1942, 1, 8; Glidewell, oral history.

36 Ludlum, *They Turned the War Around*, 100.

37   Glidewell, oral history; Ludlum, *They Turned the War Around*, 100; "Letter Indicates Sandusky Hero Lost," 1, 8.
38   Cressman, *That Gallant Ship*, 101.
39   Tillman, *The Dauntless Dive Bomber of World War II*, 47.
40   Hamilton, "The Battle of the Coral Sea: Report of Action, Bombing Squadron Two," 5; Lundstrom, *The First Team*, 237–38; Lundstrom, *Black Shoe Carrier Admiral*, 195, 559.
41   Lundstrom, *The First Team*, 240–42.
42   Cressman, *That Gallant Ship*, 101.
43   Ludlum, *They Turned the War Around*, 100–101.
44   Glidewell, oral history.
45   Nesmith, *No Higher Honor*, 144; "Describes Sinking of Jap Aircraft Carrier in Pacific," *Joplin News Herald*, November 12, 1942, 7; Johnston, "Eye-witness," 8.
46   Brunetti to Horan, August 21, 1986.

Chapter Nine: "A Real Rooster Fight"

1   Lundstrom and Sawruk, "Courage and Devotion to Duty," 26.
2   "Lanark Youth Loses $50 on U.S.S. *Lexington*," *Freeport Journal-Standard*, June 23, 1942, 2.
3   Lundstrom and Sawruk, "Courage and Devotion to Duty," 28.
4   Lundstrom, *The First Team*, 246.
5   Lundstrom and Sawruk, "Courage and Devotion to Duty," 26.
6   Colley, oral history.
7   Lundstrom and Sawruk, "Courage and Devotion to Duty," 26.
8   Ibid., 27–29; "Wounded Pilot Tells of Coral Sea Battle," *Salt Lake Tribune*, July 6, 1942, 6.
9   Lieutenant R. B. Woodhull, action report, May 8, 1942.
10   Lundstrom and Sawruk, "Courage and Devotion to Duty," 30.
11   Vejtasa, oral history.
12   Lundstrom and Sawruk, "Courage and Devotion to Duty," 30; Lieutenant Commander Strong, interview of August 3, 1943.
13   Lundstrom and Sawruk, "Courage and Devotion to Duty," 30.
14   Ibid., 30.
15   Lieutenant Commander Strong, interview, August 3, 1943.
16   Lundstrom and Sawruk, "Courage and Devotion to Duty," 30.
17   Colley, oral history.
18   Lundstrom and Sawruk, "Courage and Devotion to Duty," 30; Colley, oral history.
19   Lundstrom and Sawruk, "Courage and Devotion to Duty," 32.
20   Ibid., 32; "Lieutenant Knapp, Mason Cityan, Bombed Jap Carrier," *Mason City Globe-Gazette*, June 18, 1942, 1; Hall, battle notes via Gwen Hall.
21   "The Highest Military Honor for a Moment of True Heroism," *Tulsa World Sunday Magazine*, October 28, 1979, 6.
22   Lundstrom and Sawruk, "Courage and Devotion to Duty," 32; "Wounded Pilot Tells of Coral Sea Battle," *Salt Lake Tribune*, July 6, 1942, 6; "The Highest Military Honor," 6.
23   Lundstrom and Sawruk, "Courage and Devotion to Duty," 32.
24   "Wait Irked Utahn in Coral Battle," *Salt Lake Tribune*, June 21, 1942, 2B.

25 Hoehling, *The Lexington Goes Down*, 94–95; "Family Reunion on Father's Day," *Clovis News-Journal*, June 22, 1942, 6.
26 Liska, Navy Department press release, July 21, 1942.
27 Lundstrom and Sawruk, "Courage and Devotion to Duty," 32–33.
28 Ludlum, *They Turned the War Around*, 105.
29 Lundstrom and Sawruk, "Courage and Devotion to Duty," 33.
30 Hall, notes.
31 Lundstrom and Sawruk, "Courage and Devotion to Duty," 33; "Wounded Pilot Tells of Coral Sea Battle," *Salt Lake Tribune*, July 6, 1942, 16; Hall, notes.
32 Lundstrom and Sawruk, "Courage and Devotion to Duty," 33.
33 Ibid., 33–34.
34 Ibid., 34; "Lanark Youth Loses $50 on U.S.S. *Lexington*," *Freeport Journal-Standard*, June 23, 1942, 2; "Flyer Describes Carrier Attack. Zeros Fail to Stop Him." *Reno Evening Gazette*, July 2, 1942, 6.
35 Adinah Green, "Chandler Swanson Survived Pearl Harbor, Served Navy for 32 Years," *Orlando Sentinel*, December 8, 2003; Lundstrom and Sawruk, "Courage and Devotion to Duty," 34.
36 Ibid., 34.
37 Tillman, *The Dauntless Dive Bomber of World War II*, 52; Lundstrom and Sawruk, "Courage and Devotion to Duty," 35.

CHAPTER TEN: "YOU ARE ON YOUR OWN"

1 Glidewell, oral history.
2 Ludlum, *They Turned the War Around*, 106; Lundstrom and Sawruk, "Courage and Devotion to Duty," 34.
3 Lundstrom and Sawruk, "Courage and Devotion to Duty," 34.
4 Ibid., 35; Hall, notes; "Wounded Pilot Tells of Coral Sea Battle," *Salt Lake Tribune*, July 6, 1942, 16.
5 Ibid., 16; Lundstrom and Sawruk, "Courage and Devotion to Duty," 35.
6 Ibid., 35; "Flier Relates How Crew Saw *Lexington* Sunk," *Port Arthur News*, June 19, 1942, 2.
7 "Lanark Youth Loses $50 on U.S.S. *Lexington*," *Freeport Journal-Standard*, June 23, 1942, 2; "Dive Bomber Pilots Hold a Reunion," *Joplin Globe*, July 1, 1942, 7.
8 Lundstrom, *Black Shoe Carrier Admiral*, 192.
9 Glidewell, oral history.
10 Ludlum, *They Turned the War Around*, 107; Clark Lee, "Ex–Indiana School Teacher Dive-Bombs Japs, Likes It," *Charleston Gazette*, June 13, 1942, 1–2; Art Downing, VS-5 narrative, 12.
11 Johnston, "Eye-witness," 8; Nesmith, *No Higher Honor*, 144.
12 Nesmith, *No Higher Honor*, 144; Cressman, *That Gallant Ship*, 110; Brunetti to Horan, August 21, 1986.
13 Forshee, *Standby! Mark!*, Chapter 11.
14 Harp's 1942 correspondence, courtesy of Patrick Lombardi. Using the nickname "Dixieland Drifter," Dayton Harp would record country-and-western music as an act for the Four Star recording company in 1952.
15 Ludlum, *They Turned the War Around*, 106; "Navy Gunner Gets Award, Tells of Lively Fight," *Helena Independent*, November 25, 1942, 1.

16 Lundstrom and Sawruk, "Courage and Devotion to Duty," 35; "Wait Irked Utahn in Coral Battle," *Salt Lake Tribune*, June 21, 1942, 2B; Craft account via Barbara Gwaltney.

17 Lundstrom, *The First Team*, 273–74.

18 Hamilton, "The Battle of the Coral Sea: Report of Action, Bombing Squadron Two," 5; "Two Lisbon, N.D. Youths Honored," *Bismarck Tribune*, June 25, 1942, 3; Lundstrom, *The First Team*, 274–75; Sterrie, oral history, 15.

19 Lieutenant Commander R. E. Dixon, "Report of Action, Scouting Squadron Two, on May 8, 1942, in Coral Sea," 1.

20 Edwin P. Hoyt, *Blue Skies and Blood: The Battle of the Coral Sea* (New York: Paul S. Eriksson, Inc., 1975), 148–50.

21 "Alumnus Tells of Adventures at Charleston," *Alton Evening Telegraph*, August 8, 1942, 1; "Yank Flyers Forced Down Aided by Island Natives," *News Palladium* (Benton Harbor, MI), August 27, 1942, 1.

22 Hoyt, *Blue Skies and Blood*, 150.

23 Lundstrom, *The First Team*, 277.

24 Ibid., 279.

25 Ralph Cousins, oral history; Lundstrom, *The First Team*, 280.

26 "Wounded Pilot Tells of Coral Sea Battle," *Salt Lake Tribune*, July 6, 1942, 16.

27 Hoehling, *The Lexington Goes Down*, 177–78.

28 "Two Lisbon, N.D. Youths Honored," *Bismarck Tribune*, June 25, 1942, 3; "Lanark Youth Loses $50 on U.S.S. *Lexington*," *Freeport Journal-Standard*, June 23, 1942, 2.

29 "Madison Radioman Downs Attacking Jap Zero Fighter. Navy May Decorate Coral Sea Airman," *Wisconsin State Journal*, August 10, 1942, 7; Hall, notes from Gwen Hall.

30 Johnston, *Queen of the Flat-Tops*, 219; "Pilot Who Fought in Coral Sea Visiting Parents Here," *Lima News*, June 18, 1942, 1.

31 Ludlum, *They Turned the War Around*, 108; Traynor, oral history.

32 Cressman, *That Gallant Ship*, 112.

33 "Lieutenant Knapp, Mason Cityan, Bombed Jap Carrier," *Mason City Globe-Gazette*, June 18, 1942, 1.

34 Tillman, *The Dauntless Dive Bomber of World War II*, 53; Lundstrom, *The First Team*, 280.

35 Lundstrom and Sawruk, "Courage and Devotion to Duty," 35.

36 Ibid., 35–36.

37 Ibid., 36.

38 Ludlum, *They Turned the War Around*, 110.

39 Lundstrom, *Black Shoe Carrier Admiral*, 204; Ludlum, *They Turned the War Around*, 110.

40 Lundstrom, *Black Shoe Carrier Admiral*, 205, 561.

41 Captain Lawrence Traynor, "WWII Sea Story," December 1, 2002.

42 Lundstrom, *Black Shoe Carrier Admiral*, 205.

43 Ibid.

44 Tillman, *The Dauntless Dive Bomber of World War II*, 53; Lundstrom, *Black Shoe Carrier Admiral*, 206; Lundstrom, *The First Team*, 284.

45 Ludlum, *They Turned the War Around*, 114–15.

46 Tillman, *The Dauntless Dive Bomber of World War II*, 54.

CHAPTER ELEVEN: TRANSITIONS

1   Traynor, oral history.
2   Gibson, *Slow but Deadly*, 44.
3   Ibid., 45–57, 80.
4   Buell, *Dauntless Helldivers*, 91.
5   Edward Anderson, "War Diary," 55.
6   Robert Mason, "Eyewitness," *Proceedings*, June 1982, 41–44.
7   Johnston, *Grim Reapers*, 24, 48.
8   Johnston, "Eye-Witness," 9.
9   "Top Utah Hero Home, Asks, 'Why the Fuss?'" *Salt Lake Tribune*, Thursday, October 4, 1945, 1, 20; Hall information from daughter Gwen Hall.
10 Lieutenant Commander J. R. Lee, interview, Bureau of Aeronautics, April 14, 1943, 1.
11 David J. Cawley, oral history, 1.
12 Ibid., 1–2.
13 Ibid., 3.
14 Lee, interview, 6.
15 Ibid., 5.
16 Rear Admiral Martin Doan Carmody, interview, Veterans History Project, May 16, 2002. Courtesy of the Library of Congress.
17 Leonard Robinson, oral history, 1.
18 Robinson obituary, July 13, 2012, *Union Democrat*, Sonora, CA; Edwards, *Waxahachie Warrior*, 5–6.
19 Robinson, oral history, 1.
20 Robinson, oral history, 1; Edwards, *Waxahachie Warrior*, 10–11.
21 *Battle 360*, episode 3, "Jaws of the Enemy."
22 McWilliams, *Sunday in Hell*, 924.
23 Ibid., 923.
24 Cawley, oral history, 4.
25 McWilliams, *Sunday in Hell*, 925.
26 Robinson, oral history, 2.

CHAPTER TWELVE: "I HOPE I WON'T DISAPPOINT YOU"

1   Caldwell, "The Stranded *Enterprise* Aviators on Guadalcanal," *Foundation*, 31.
2   Ibid., 31; Downing, VS-5 memoirs, 15.
3   Ibid., 15.
4   Burch, interview, 7, 16.
5   Buell, Dauntless Helldivers, 95.
6   Strickland to Hammell, 1982 correspondence.
7   Tillman, *Enterprise*, 89; Stafford, *The Big E*, 101.
8   Stout, interview with Jesse Barker; Stout, *Unsung Eagles*, 43–44.
9   Stout, Unsung Eagles, 44.
10 Buell, *Dauntless Helldivers*, 96; Lundstrom, *The First Team and the Guadalcanal Campaign*, 15.
11 Buell, *Dauntless Helldivers*, 95–96.
12 Gibson, *Slow But Deadly*, 60.
13 Buell, *Dauntless Helldivers*, 96.

14   Stanley Coleman Jersey, *Hell's Islands*, 67–75.
15   Ibid., 75–76.
16   Frank, *Guadalcanal*, 31–46.
17   Ibid., 46–50.
18   Jersey, *Hell's Islands*, 401.
19   Mears, *Carrier Combat*, 85–86.
20   Gibson, *Slow but Deadly*, 60.
21   Barker, interview with Stout.
22   Lundstrom, *The First Team and the Guadalcanal Campaign*, 33; Downing, VS-5 memoirs, 17.
23   Mears, *Carrier Combat*, 100.
24   Ibid., 88, 100.
25   Buell, *Dauntless Helldivers*, 97.

Chapter Thirteen: "Blood and Thunder" over Hell's Island

1   Hansen diary, Hammell Papers.
2   Lundstrom, *The First Team and the Guadalcanal Campaign*, 34.
3   Downing, VS-5 memoirs, 17.
4   Hansen, diary, Hammell Papers.
5   Russell, diary, August 8, 1942.
6   Buell, *Dauntless Helldivers*, 97.
7   Caldwell, "The Stranded *Enterprise* Aviators on Guadalcanal," *Foundation*, 31.
8   Downing, VS-5 memoirs, 17.
9   VS-71 War Diary, 17.
10   Gibson, *Slow but Deadly*, 63.
11   Buell, *Dauntless Helldivers*, 98.
12   Strong, interview, 7.
13   Stout, *Unsung Eagles*, 46.
14   Jersey, *Hell's Islands*, 113–14.
15   Jones to Sakaida, August 2, 1983.
16   Lundstrom, *The First Team and the Guadalcanal Campaign*, 45.
17   Ibid., 56.
18   Horenburger to Sakaida, December 18, 1981.
19   Anderson, "War Diary," 58–59.
20   Jones to Sakaida, August 2, 1983.
21   Gibson, oral history, 8.
22   Anderson, "War Diary," 59; *Battle 360* video, episode 3, "Jaws of the Enemy."
23   Gibson, *Slow but Deadly*, 64; Anderson, "War Diary," 59.
24   Hammell, *Guadalcanal: The Carrier Battles*, 29.
25   Buell, *Dauntless Helldivers*, 99; Downing, VS-5 memoirs, 18.
26   Downing, VS-5 memoirs, 17.
27   Russell, diary, August 8, 1942.
28   Lundstrom, *The First Team and the Guadalcanal Campaign*, 77.
29   Mears, *Carrier Combat*, 107.
30   Gibson, *Slow but Deadly*, 67–71.

Chapter Fourteen: "We'd Better Go Get the Carrier"

1   Hornfischer, *Neptune's Inferno*, 105; Lundstrom, *The First Team and the Guadalcanal Campaign*, 89.
2   Jersey, *Hell's Islands*, 186–87.
3   Miller, *Cactus Air Force*, 26.
4   Gibson, oral history, 9.
5   Anderson, "War Diary," 59.
6   Russell diary, August 20, 1942.
7   Buell, *Dauntless Helldivers*, 101–2.
8   Ibid., 102.
9   Bob Hackett and Sander Kingsepp, "HIJMS Submarine *I-17*: Tabular Record of Movement, 2001–11." http://www.combinedfleet.com/*I-17*.htm, accessed on June 17, 2013.
10 Kirn, interview, 3–4.
11 Russell, diary, August 23, 1942; Tillman, "Where Are They Now?," 13; Kirn, interview, 4.
12 Russell, diary, August 23, 1942; Bottomley to Hammell, March 14, 1982; Austin Merrill, interview with Seth Paridon, National World War II Museum; Holmberg to Hammell, May 23, 1982.
13 Lundstrom, *The First Team and the Guadalcanal Campaign*, 105, 110.
14 Davis to Hammell, April 16, 1982.
15 Strickland to Hammell, 4.
16 Felt to Hammell, April 2, 1982; Kirn, interview, 5; Holmberg to Hammell, May 23, 1982; Russell, diary, August 24, 1942.
17 Lundstrom, *The First Team and the Guadalcanal Campaign*, 116–18.
18 Susan Antigone, "Birney Strong, Navy Hero, Pilot, Dies," *Washington Post*, December 22, 1977, B6.
19 Hansen, diary, Hammell Papers.
20 Lundstrom, *The First Team and the Guadalcanal Campaign*, 120–21.
21 Lowe account recorded July 26, 1982, Hammell Papers.
22 Ibid.; Lundstrom, *The First Team and the Guadalcanal Campaign*, 147; Gibson, *Slow but Deadly*, 77.
23 *Battle 360*, episode 3, "Jaws of the Enemy."
24 Davis to Hammell, February 10, 1982, and an undated 1982 letter.
25 Milner, interview, 10; Henry to Hammell, November 27, 1982 and December 6, 1982; Crow to Hammell, n.d.
26 Hansen, diary, Hammell Papers.
27 Scouting Squadron Three, "Narrative Report of Action with Enemy on August 24, 1942, in Solomon Islands Areas," August 26, 1942; Tillman, *The Dauntless Dive Bomber of World War II*, 137; Bottomley to Hammell, March 14, 1982.
28 "Dive-Bomber Pilot Tells of Scoring Hit on Jap Carrier," *Sunday Times*, Zanesville, OH, September 13, 1942.
29 Holmberg to Hammell, May 23, 1982, September 6, 1982, and July 5, 1982; Tillman, *The Dauntless Dive Bomber of World War II*, 137.
30 Bottomley to Hammell, March 14, 1982, and March 20, 1982; Clark Lee, "Merchantville Pilot Scores Hit on Carrier," June 13, 1942.
31 Tillman, *The Dauntless Dive Bomber of World War II*, 139.
32 Ibid., 138; Lundstrom, *The First Team and the Guadalcanal Campaign*, 122.

CHAPTER FIFTEEN: BATTLE OFF THE EASTERN SOLOMONS

1   Caldwell, "The Stranded *Enterprise* Aviators on Guadalcanal," *Foundation*, 31; Holmberg to Hammell, September 6, 1982.
2   Christian Fink to Hammell, March 10, 1982.
3   Eldor Rodenburg to Hammell, April 2, 1982.
4   Lundstrom, *The First Team and the Guadalcanal Campaign*, 141.
5   Glenn Estes to James Sawruk, February 1987 correspondence.
6   Wilger to Hammell, February 24, 1982, and March 22, 1982.
7   "Lieut. H. R. Burnett Featured on Program," *Western Star*, January 14, 1944.
8   Estes to Sawruk, February 1987 correspondence.
9   Fink to Hammell, March 2, 1982; Caldwell, "The Stranded *Enterprise* Aviators on Guadalcanal," *Foundation*, 31–32.
10 Lundstrom, *The First Team and the Guadalcanal Campaign*, 145; Horenburger to Hammell, May 24, 1982; Kirn, interview, 6; Tillman, *The Dauntless Dive Bomber of World War II*, 139.
11 Lundstrom, *The First Team and the Guadalcanal Campaign*, 150; Tillman, *The Dauntless Dive Bomber of World War II*, 139; Crow to Hammell, n.d.; Henry to Hammell, November 27, 1982 and December 6, 1982.
12 Lundstrom, *The First Team and the Guadalcanal Campaign*, 151–52.
13 Ibid., 152.
14 Horenburger to Hammell, May 24, 1982.
15 Lowe account recorded July 26, 1982, Hammell Papers.
16 Anderson, "War Diary," 60; Gibson, oral history, 9; Gibson, *Slow but Deadly*, 79–80.
17 Davis to Hammell, 1982, undated letter.
18 Combat record of Lieutenant Howard Reason Burnett; Wilger to Hammell, February 24, 1982.
19 Estes to Sawruk, February 1987 correspondence.
20 Cleo J. Dobson, diary, August 24, 1942.
21 Antigone, "Birney Strong, Navy Hero, Pilot, Dies," *Washington Post*, December 22, 1977, B6; Traynor recollections from June 16, 2003, courtesy of Larry Traynor Jr.; Traynor, oral history.
22 Tillman, *The Dauntless Dive Bomber of World War II*, 139.
23 Estes to Sawruk, February 1987 correspondence.
24 Traynor recollections, June 16, 2003; Traynor, oral history.
25 Tillman, *The Dauntless Dive Bomber of World War II*, 141; Lundstrom, *The First Team and the Guadalcanal Campaign*, 153–55.
26 Tillman, *The Dauntless Dive Bomber of World War II*, 142–43.

CHAPTER SIXTEEN: FLIGHT 300 ON HELL'S ISLAND

1   Burns, *Then There Was One*, 94.
2   Ibid., 94.
3   Buell, *Dauntless Helldivers*, 107.
4   Caldwell, "The Stranded *Enterprise* Aviators," 32.
5   Ibid., 32; Fink to Hammell, March 10, 1982.
6   Caldwell, "The Stranded *Enterprise* Aviators," 32.
7   Fink to Hammell, March 10, 1982.

8   Caldwell, "The Stranded *Enterprise* Aviators," 32.
9   Buell, *Dauntless Helldivers*, 107; Stuart Mason, oral history, 6.
10   Caldwell, "The Stranded *Enterprise* Aviators," 32.
11   Fink to Hammell, March 10, 1982.
12   Ibid.; Stout, *Unsung Eagles*, 48; Caldwell, "The Stranded *Enterprise* Aviators," 32.
13   Buell, *Dauntless Helldivers*, 111.
14   Fink to Hammell, March 10, 1982; Burns, *Then There Was One*, 96.
15   Fink to Hammell, March 10, 1982.
16   Lundstrom, *The First Team and the Guadalcanal Campaign*, 158.
17   Hammell, *Starvation Island*, 144; Stout, *Unsung Eagles*, 48.
18   Frank, *Guadalcanal*, 189; Burns, *Then There Was One*, 96–98.
19   Frank, *Guadalcanal*, 146–58.
20   Lundstrom, *The First Team and the Guadalcanal Campaign*, 181–82.
21   Fink to Hammell, March 10, 1982.
22   Frank, *Guadalcanal*, 190; Lundstrom, *The First Team and the Guadalcanal Campaign*, 158.
23   Caldwell, "The Stranded *Enterprise* Aviators," 34; Tregaskis, *Guadalcanal Diary*, 144.
24   Fink to Hammell, March 10, 1982; Stout, *Unsung Eagles*, 48.
25   Fink to Hammell, March 10, 1982; Caldwell, "The Stranded *Enterprise* Aviators," 34; Stuart Mason, oral history, 6; Stout, *Unsung Eagles*, 49; Mason to Arnie Olsen, September 13, 2002.
26   Lundstrom, *The First Team and the Guadalcanal Campaign*, 185.
27   Fink to Hammell, March 10, 1982.
28   Stout, *Unsung Eagles*, 49.
29   Ibid., 50.
30   Ibid., 49; Lundstrom, *The First Team and the Guadalcanal Campaign*, 188.
31   Ferguson, *Guadalcanal: Island of Fire*, 78.
32   Stout, Barker interview; Caldwell, "The Stranded *Enterprise* Aviators," 32.
33   Stout, *Unsung Eagles*, 50.
34   Cales, war diary.
35   Buell, *Dauntless Helldivers*, 114–15.
36   Howard N. Murphy, "Exploits and Memories of a Naval Aviator," 10; Lundstrom, *The First Team and the Guadalcanal Campaign*, 159.
37   Traynor, oral history.
38   Horenburger to Hammell, June 16, 1982.
39   Gibson, *Slow but Deadly*, 87–88.
40   Ibid., 89.
41   Fink to Hammell, March 10, 1982.
42   Buell, *Dauntless Helldivers*, 115.
43   Fink to Hammell, March 10, 1982; Hammell, *Starvation Island*, 165; Buell, *Dauntless Helldivers*, 122.
44   Stout, *Unsung Eagles*, 51.
45   Miller, *The Cactus Air Force*, 59; Buell, *Dauntless Helldivers*, 117.
46   Caldwell, "The Stranded *Enterprise* Aviators," 32.
47   Mason to Arnie Olsen, September 13, 2002.
48   Caldwell, "The Stranded *Enterprise* Aviators," 32–33.
49   Ferguson, *Guadalcanal: Island of Fire*, 76–77.

50   Caldwell, "The Stranded *Enterprise* Aviators," 33; Mzarek, *A Dawn Like Thunder*, 315–16.
51   Cales, "Remembrances of Guadalcanal," 54.
52   Cales, war diary.
53   Tregaskis, *Guadalcanal Diary*, 158.
54   Cales, war diary; Cales, "Remembrances of Guadalcanal," 54.
55   Cales, war diary.
56   Cales, "Remembrances of Guadalcanal," 54.
57   Ibid.
58   Fink to Hammell, March 10, 1982; Tregaskis, *Guadalcanal Diary*, 158.

Chapter Seventeen: "Heroes All"

1   Frank, *Guadalcanal*, 201–2.
2   Buell, *Dauntless Helldivers*, 118–19.
3   Cales, war diary.
4   Ferguson, *Guadalcanal: Island of Fire*, 84.
5   Buell, *Dauntless Helldivers*, 120–21.
6   Caldwell, "The Stranded *Enterprise* Aviators," 33.
7   Fink to Hammell, March 10, 1982.
8   Russell, diary, September 1, 1942; Kirn, interview, 9.
9   Lundstrom, *The First Team and the Guadalcanal Campaign*, 185.
10   Cales, war diary; Stout, *Unsung Eagles*, 51. Cactus records show Conzett made this strike, but it is a mistake. He had already been evaced with injury. Rocky Glidewell's flight log shows that he flew a strike with Caldwell this day.
11   Lundstrom, *The First Team and the Guadalcanal Campaign*, 182–83.
12   Cales, war diary.
13   Burns, *Then There Was One*, 94.
14   Ferguson, *Guadalcanal: Island of Fire*, 87; Kirn, interview, 10; Crow to Hammell, n.d.; Russell, diary, September 10, 1942; Milner, interview, 9.
15   Ferguson, *Guadalcanal: Island of Fire*, 89, 96.
16   Ibid., 98; Caldwell, "The Stranded *Enterprise* Aviators," 33.
17   Diary of Francis Roland Register of VF-5, March 17, 1941, to October 14, 1942, www.daveswarbirds.com/cactus/diary.htm, accessed on December 6, 2013.
18   Buell, *Dauntless Helldivers*, 125; Stuart Mason, oral history, 6; Mason to Olsen, September 13, 2002.
19   Cales, war diary; Stout, *Unsung Eagles*, 51; Burns, *Then There Was One*, 108; Caldwell, "The Stranded *Enterprise* Aviators," 33.
20   Ferguson, *Guadalcanal: Island of Fire*, 102; Caldwell, "The Stranded *Enterprise* Aviators," 33; Burns, *Then There Was One*, 108.
21   Mason to Olsen, September 13, 2002.
22   Jersey, *Hell's Island*, 230–33.
23   Buell, *Dauntless Helldivers*, 125–26.
24   Frank, *Guadalcanal*, 234.
25   Kirn, interview, 11–12.
26   Henry to Hammell, December 6, 1982.
27   Barker, interview with Jay Stout.

28 Buell, *Dauntless Helldivers*, 127–28.
29 Cales, war diary; Burns, *Then There Was One*, 92, 94.
30 Mears, *Carrier Combat*, 121–22.
31 "An Interview with Cook Cleland," *Aerophile* 1, (2) (March/April 1977), 108.
32 Lundstrom, *The First Team and the Guadalcanal Campaign*, 223.
33 Ibid., 223–27.
34 "An Interview with Cook Cleland," 108.
35 Mason, *Then There Was One*, 92, 94; Buell, *Dauntless Helldivers*, 129.
36 Crow to Hammell, n.d..
37 Cales, war diary.
38 Tregaskis, *Guadalcanal Diary*, 221.
39 Lundstrom, *The First Team and the Guadalcanal Campaign*, 240.
40 Russell, diary, September 23, 1942.
41 Mason to Olsen, September 13, 2002; Jersey, *Hell's Islands*, 245.
42 Lundstrom, *The First Team and the Guadalcanal Campaign*, 244–49; Caldwell, "The Stranded *Enterprise* Aviators," 34; Russell, diary, September 27, 1942; Cales, war diary.
43 Stuart Mason, oral history, 6; Mason, *Then There Was One*, 92, 94.
44 Stout, *Unsung Eagles*, 52; Fink to Hammell, March 10, 1982.
45 Cales, war diary.
46 Ibid.
47 Caldwell, "The Stranded *Enterprise* Aviators," 34.
48 Cales, war diary; Mason to Olsen, September 13, 2002.
49 Caldwell, "The Stranded *Enterprise* Aviators," 35.
50 Miller, *The Cactus Air Force*, 115.
51 Buell, *Dauntless Helldivers*, 131.
52 Ibid., 147.
53 Strong, interview, August 3, 1943, 10.
54 Cawley, oral history, 5.
55 Gibson, *Slow but Deadly*, 92–93.
56 McWilliams, *Sunday in Hell*, 926.
57 Ibid., 928.
58 Ibid., 929; Robinson, oral history, 2.
59 Robinson, oral history, 2.
60 Gibson, *Slow but Deadly*, 95–96.
61 McWilliam, *Sunday in Hell*, 929; Robinson oral history, 2.
62 McWilliams, *Sunday in Hell*, 929.
63 Gibson, *Slow but Deadly*, 96, 98, 100.
64 Robinson, oral history, 3.
65 McWilliams, *Sunday in Hell*, 931–32; Robinson, oral history, 3.
66 Robinson, oral history, 2; Bombing Squadron Ten, war diary, October 11–12, 1942.
67 Lee, interview, 2.
68 Cawley, oral history, 5.
69 Gibson, *Slow but Deadly*, 103–4.
70 Lundstrom, *The First Team and the Guadalcanal Campaign*, 327.
71 Gibson, *Slow but Deadly*, 121–23.
72 Steve Ewing, *Reaper Leader*, 122.

CHAPTER EIGHTEEN: STRONG'S SALVATION

1   Lundstrom, *The First Team and the Guadalcanal Campaign*, 301; VS-71 War Diary, 27; Kirn, interview, 21.

2   Jersey, *Hell's Islands*, 235–36, 246; Robert J. Mohler interview with Brittany Hays, June 7, 1999.

3   VS-71 War Diary, 28; Frank, *Guadalcanal*, 322.

4   VS-71 War Diary, 30–31; Murphy, "Exploits and Memories of a Naval Aviator," 20; Mohler, interview with Hays; Rodenburg, "Eldor E. Rodenburg," 14–16; Mohler, reflections of Guadalcanal, *Wasp Stinger* newsletter, December 1, 1995, 76.

5   VS-71 War Diary, 34.

6   Buell, *Dauntless Helldivers*, 147.

7   Lundstrom, *The First Team and the Guadalcanal Campaign*, 328.

8   Ibid., 337–41; Bombing Squadron Ten, war diary, October 20–23, 1942.

9   William Martin, oral history, 53.

10   Edwards, Vejtasa article.

11   Edwards, unpublished biography of Swede Vejtasa, based upon his interviews with Vejtasa.

12   Lundstrom, *The First Team and the Guadalcanal Campaign*, 349–50.

13   Hammell, *Guadalcanal: The Carrier Battles*, 325–26.

14   Gibson, *Slow but Deadly*, 110.

15   Lundstrom, *The First Team and the Guadalcanal Campaign*, 351.

16   Gibson, *Slow but Deadly*, 111.

17   Edwards, Swede Vejtasa biography; Stanley Vejtasa, oral history interview with Seth Paridon for the National World War II Museum.

18   Lundstrom, *The First Team and the Guadalcanal Campaign*, 351; Edwards, Vejtasa biography; Vejtasa, interview with Paridon; Vejtasa and Feightner insisted this pilot was Ed Coalson, although VF-10's war diary does not list him on this flight.

19   USS *Porter* deck log, October 25, 1942; Bombing Squadron Ten war diary, October 25, 1942.

20   Bob Gibson, oral history, 10; Gibson, *Slow but Deadly*, 114.

21   Hammell, *Guadalcanal: The Carrier Battles*, 327; Gibson, oral history, 10; Gibson, *Slow but Deadly*, 115.

22   Tillman, *The Dauntless Dive Bomber of World War II*, 148.

23   Stafford, *The Big E*, 151; Hammell, *Guadalcanal: The Carrier Battles*, 328–29.

24   John Liska, notes on Santa Cruz battle, courtesy of Michael Liska; Johnston, *The Grim Reapers*, 14.

25   Cawley, oral history, 6.

26   Flatley, "The Bravest Man," 16.

27   Buell, *Dauntless Helldivers*, 140. John Lundstrom gives VS-10's strength of available SBDs as thirteen at the start of October 26 and VB-10 as ten planes. Based upon the number of SBDs launched in the next few hours, however, VS-10's number was fifteen, with two planes having been put into service from her spares. This number was confirmed thanks to Elizabeth "Devie" Ludlam, daughter of VS-10 officer William D. Boardman. She provided a copy of the October 26 flight schedule kept by her father. Buchanan

flew VB-10 plane B-20, while the other five flew VS-10 planes S-21 (Frohlich), S-20 (Lucier), S-9 (West), S-12 (Goddard), and S-11 (Griffith).

28   *Battle 360*, episode 3, "Jaws of the Enemy."
29   Cawley, oral history, 6–7.
30   Ibid., 9.
31   Ibid., 10.
32   Lundstrom, *The First Team and the Guadalcanal Campaign*, 358.
33   Tillman, *The Dauntless Dive Bomber of World War II*, 152.
34   Rear Admiral Martin Doan Carmody, "A Carrier Pilot's Story," narrative of Carmody's 1991 speech at a Smithsonian seminar, http://collectair.com/World_War_II.html, accessed on April 2, 2012.
35   Ibid.; Martin D. Carmody, interview of May 16, 2002, Veterans History Project, the Library of Congress.
36   Liska, notes on Santa Cruz battle.
37   Tillman, *The Dauntless Dive Bomber of World War II*, 152; Strong, interview, August 3, 1943, 12–13.
38   Tillman, *The Dauntless Dive Bomber of World War II*, 153.
39   Strong, interview, August 3, 1943, 12–13.
40   Ibid., 13.
41   Buell, *Dauntless Helldivers*, 149.
42   *Zuikaku* pilot loss per Lundstrom, *The First Team and the Guadalcanal Campaign*, 361; Buell, *Dauntless Helldivers*, 149.

CHAPTER NINETEEN: ACTION AT SANTA CRUZ

1   Martin, oral history, 54.
2   Robinson, oral history, 3.
3   "Air Battle Notes," 23; Bates to Hammell, May 26, 1982, 1.
4   Lundstrom, *The First Team and the Guadalcanal Campaign*, 366.
5   Ibid., 367–68.
6   Ibid., 372.
7   Hovind to Hammell, 1986; Fisher, *Hooked*, 117.
8   Bates to Hammell, May 26, 1982, 2; Hovind to Hammell, 1986.
9   "Air Battle Notes," 24–25; Hovind to Hammell, 1986.
10   Fisher, *Hooked*, 116; Bates to Hammell, May 26, 1982, 2; "Air Battle Notes," 25.
11   Tillman, *The Dauntless Dive Bomber of World War II*, 158; Bates to Hammell, May 26, 1982, 2.
12   "Air Battle Notes," 26–27.
13   Tillman, *The Dauntless Dive Bomber of World War II*, 160.
14   Lundstrom, *The First Team and the Guadalcanal Campaign*, 378.
15   Ibid., 380.

CHAPTER TWENTY: ACE IN A DAY

1   Swope to Hammell, February 3, 1986.
2   Lundstrom, *The First Team and the Guadalcanal Campaign*, 398.
3   Swope to Hammell, February 3, 1986; Robinson, oral history, 4.

4   Cawley, oral history, 10–11; Combat record of Lieutenant Howard R. Burnett.
5   "Thrilling Account of Pacific War Told by Lefty Craft," Winnsboro (SC) *News and Herald*, undated article, circa July 1943.
6   Lundstrom, *The First Team and the Guadalcanal Campaign*, 404.
7   Wayne Colley, oral history, 4–5.
8   Buell, *Dauntless Helldivers*, 141.
9   Carmody, "A Carrier Pilot's Story"; Carmody, interview, Veterans History Project.
10 Lundstrom, *The First Team and the Guadalcanal Campaign*, 409; Bombing Squadron Ten, war diary, October 26, 1942.
11 Cawley, oral history, 13.
12 Lundstrom, *The First Team and the Guadalcanal Campaign*, 415.
13 Cawley, oral history, 14.
14 Carmody, "A Carrier Pilot's Story," unpaginated; Wayne, Colley oral history, 5.
15 Gibson, *Slow but Deadly*, 116; Buell, *Dauntless Helldivers*, 143.
16 Lundstrom, *The First Team and the Guadalcanal Campaign*, 415; Carmody, interview, Veterans History Project.
17 *Battle 360*, episode 3, "Jaws of the Enemy."
18 Gibson, *Slow but Deadly*, 117.
19 Lundstrom, *The First Team and the Guadalcanal Campaign*, 397, 401–2; Edwards, unpublished Vejtasa biography.
20 Lieutenant Stanley W. Vejtasa, "Narrative of Events," combat report of October 26, 1942; Edwards, unpublished Vejtasa biography.
21 Edwards, Vejtasa article; Edwards, unpublished biography.
22 Edwards story; Tillman, *Wildcat*, 118.
23 Fisher, *Hooked*, 121–22; Lundstrom, *The First Team and the Guadalcanal Campaign*, 428–29.
24 Lundstrom, *The First Team and the Guadalcanal Campaign*, 436.
25 Ibid., 437.
26 Hovind to Hammell; "Air Battle Notes," 25; Tillman, *The Dauntless Dive Bomber of World War II*, 158; Bates to Hammell, May 26, 1982, 3.
27 Lundstrom, *The First Team and the Guadalcanal Campaign*, 442–43.
28 Edwards, Vejtasa article.
29 Lundstrom, *The First Team and the Guadalcanal Campaign*, 446–47.
30 Cottrell to Hammell, 1982.
31 Martin, oral history, 55–56.
32 Gibson, *Slow but Deadly*, 120.
33 Flatley, "Bravest Man," 18.
34 Tillman, *The Dauntless Dive Bomber of World War II*, 160–61.

CHAPTER TWENTY-ONE: "BACK TO SEA IN A PITIABLE CONDITION"

1   Mohler, Guadalcanal reflections, 75; VS-71 War Diary, 38.
2   Miller, *The Cactus Air Force*, 178; Frank, *Guadalcanal*, 422.
3   VS-71 War Diary, 39; Murphy, "Exploits and Memories of a Naval Aviator," 21; Rodenburg, "Eldor E. Rodenburg," 18.
4   Gibson, *Slow but Deadly*, 121.

5   Lundstrom, *The First Team and the Guadalcanal Campaign*, 452.
6   Gibson, *Slow but Deadly*, 125–26; Strong, interview, 14.
7   Gibson, *Slow but Deadly*, 130; Buell, *Dauntless Helldivers*, 150.
8   Stafford, *The Big E*, 183; White, *Dauntless Marine*, 76.
9   Gibson, *Slow but Deadly*, 130; Bombing Squadron Ten war diary, November 9, 1942.
10 Miller, *The Cactus Air Force*, 175–76.
11 Lundstrom, *The First Team and the Guadalcanal Campaign*, 467–68.
12 Bombing Squadron Ten, war diary, November 11, 1942.
13 Lee, interview, Bureau of Aeronautics, April 14, 1943, 2.
14 Gibson, *Slow but Deadly*, 124, 131.
15 Colley, oral history, 10; Ewing, *Reaper Leader*, 148.
16 Lee, interview, 9.
17 Hammell, *Guadalcanal: The Carrier Battles*, 342.
18 Lundstrom, *The First Team and the Guadalcanal Campaign*, 484.
19 Ibid., 470; Frank, *Guadalcanal*, 428.
20 Ibid., 491.
21 *Battle 360*, episode 3, "Jaws of the Enemy."

Chapter Twenty-two: Desperation in the Slot

1   Lundstrom, *The First Team and the Guadalcanal Campaign*, 492.
2   Gibson, *Slow but Deadly*, 131, 133–34.
3   Lundstrom, *The First Team and the Guadalcanal Campaign*, 494.
4   Gibson, *Slow but Deadly*, 135–36.
5   Lundstrom, *The First Team and the Guadalcanal Campaign*, 495. Lunstrom credits Gibson and Buchanan with near misses, although Gibson felt certain his bomb was a hit. Gibson, *Slow but Deadly*, 138.
6   Gibson, oral history, 11.
7   Gibson, *Slow but Deadly*, 138.
8   Strong, interview, August 3, 1943, 14.
9   Carmody, "A Carrier Pilot's Story."
10 Carmody, Veterans History Project interview.
11 Carmody, "A Carrier Pilot's Story."
12 Carmody, Veterans History Project interview.
13 Johnston, *The Grim Reapers*, 177.
14 Gibson, oral history, 11; Gibson, *Slow but Deadly*, 143–45.
15 Johnston, *The Grim Reapers*, 178.
16 Lundstrom, *The First Team and the Guadalcanal Campaign*, 495.
17 Martin, oral history, 56.
18 Ibid., 57.
19 Robinson, oral history, 5.
20 Lundstrom, *The First Team and the Guadalcanal Campaign*, 496.
21 Strong, interview, August 3, 1943, 15; Lundstrom, *The First Team and the Guadalcanal Campaign*, 496; "Lieut. H. R. Burnett Is Decorated," *Western Star*, March 12, 1943.
22 Gibson, *Slow but Deadly*, 208.
23 "Former J.C. Student Receives Citation," *San Mateo Times*, May 21, 1943.
24 Robinson, oral history, 5.
25 Johnston, *The Grim Reapers*, 179–80; Gibson, *Slow but Deadly*, 147–48.

26   *Battle 360*, episode 3, "Jaws of the Enemy."
27   Carmody, "A Carrier Pilot's Story"; Carmody, Veterans History Project interview.
28   Strong, interview, August 3, 1943, 14.
29   Martin, oral history, 58.
30   Strong, interview, August 3, 1943, 15.
31   Lundstrom, *The First Team and the Guadalcanal Campaign*, 504.
32   Ibid., 504.
33   *Battle 360*, episode 3, "Jaws of the Enemy."
34   Wayne Colley, oral history, 11.
35   Carmody, "A Carrier Pilot's Story."
36   Colley, oral history, 11.
37   Ibid., 12.
38   Lundstrom, *The First Team and the Guadalcanal Campaign*, 505.
39   Colley, oral history, 13.
40   Ibid., 13–14.
41   Lundstrom, *The First Team and the Guadalcanal Campaign*, 506.
42   Carmody, "A Carrier Pilot's Story"; Carmody, Veterans History Project interview.
43   Colley, oral history, 14.
44   Lundstrom, *The First Team and the Guadalcanal Campaign*, 506.
45   Robinson, oral history, 6.
46   Lundstrom, *The First Team and the Guadalcanal Campaign*, 509.
47   *Battle 360*, episode 3, "Jaws of the Enemy."
48   Gibson, *Slow but Deadly*, 149.
49   Ibid., 150.
50   Lundstrom, *The First Team and the Guadalcanal Campaign*, 507.
51   Robinson, oral history, 7.
52   Lundstrom, *The First Team and the Guadalcanal Campaign*, 507.
53   Jeff Carroum, "Diary of the South Pacific," *Foundation* (Fall 2007), 63–68.
54   Ibid., 64.
55   Gibson, *Slow but Deadly*, 151.
56   Johnston, *The Grim Reapers*, 182.
57   Lundstrom, *The First Team and the Guadalcanal Campaign*, 508.
58   Gibson, *Slow but Deadly*, 151–52.
59   Ibid., 152; Johnston, *The Grim Reapers*, 183.
60   Gibson, *Slow but Deadly*, 152–54.
61   Gibson, oral history, 11; Gibson, *Slow but Deadly*, 155–56.
62   Gibson, oral history, 11; Gibson, *Slow but Deadly*, 156.
63   Lundstrom, *The First Team and the Guadalcanal Campaign*, 511–12.
64   Martin, oral history, 58; *Battle 360*, episode 3, "Jaws of the Enemy."

Chapter Twenty-three: "Unflinching Courage"

1   Carroum, "Diary of the South Pacific," 65.
2   Ibid., 66.
3   *Battle 360*, episode 3, "Jaws of the Enemy"; Gibson, *Slow but Deadly*, 157; Carmody, Veterans History Project interview; Carmody, "A Carrier Pilot's Story."

4   Lundstrom, *The First Team and the Guadalcanal Campaign*, 514–15.
5   Colley, oral history, 15.
6   Ibid., 16.
7   *Battle 360*, episode 3, "Jaws of the Enemy."
8   Gibson, *Slow but Deadly*, 157–58.
9   Ibid., 158.
10   Robinson, oral history, 7.
11   Ibid., 522–23.
12   Carmody, "A Carrier Pilot's Story."
13   Ibid.
14   The key sources for the Carmody-Liska episode are Carmody, "A Carrier Pilot's Story,"; Carmody, Veterans History Project interview; and John Liska, recollections, courtesy of Michael Liska.
15   Carroum, "Diary of the South Pacific," 67; Robinson, oral history, 7.
16   Carroum, "Diary of the South Pacific," 67.
17   Ibid., 68; Lundstrom, *The First Team and the Guadalcanal Campaign*, 509.
18   Edwards, *Leonard "Robbie" Robinson: Waxahachie Warrior*, 26.
19   Hornfischer, *Neptune's Inferno*, 368, 395; Frank, *Guadalcanal*, 490.
20   Frank, *Guadalcanal*, 490–91.
21   Gibson, *Slow but Deadly*, 181.

Chapter Twenty-four: Hard Losses and Hard Promises

1   Stafford, *The Big E*, 213.
2   Colley, oral history, 20.
3   Lee, interview, 3–4.
4   Buell, *Dauntless Helldivers*, 162.
5   Moore, *The Buzzard Brigade*, 96.
6   Gibson, *Slow but Deadly*, 165–67.
7   Lee, interview, 3; Gibson, *Slow but Deadly*, 129; Buell, *Dauntless Helldivers*, 168.
8   Ibid., 170.
9   Gibson, *Slow but Deadly*, 165; Buell, *Dauntless Helldivers*, 168.
10   Colley, oral history, 17.
11   Buell, *Dauntless Helldivers*, 173–75; Stafford, *The Big E*, 217–22.
12   Lee, interview, 6; Stafford, *The Big E*, 223–24.
13   Bombing Squadron Ten, war diary, March 18, 1943.
14   Ibid., 224; Craft, service summary, April 6, 2001, courtesy of Barbara Gwaltney.
15   USS *Kankakee*, war diary, March 1–31, 1943, 26.
16   Craft, service summary, April 6, 2001.
17   Buell, *Dauntless Helldivers*, 176–77; Gibson, *Slow but Deadly*, 173–74.
18   Stockton B. Strong to Catherine Strong, March 16, 1943, Lyman Herbert Smith Papers, Rush Rhees Library, University of Rochester Department of Rare Books and Special Collections.
19   Tillman, *Enterprise*, 151.
20   Bombing Squadron Ten, war diary, April 27, 1943.
21   Robinson, oral history, 10.
22   Gibson, *Slow but Deadly*, 168.
23   Colley, oral history, 19–23.

24   Ibid., 24.
25   Stafford, *The Big E*, 225.
26   Moore, *The Buzzard Brigade*, 107.
27   Colley, oral history, 25–26.
28   Tillman, *The Dauntless Dive Bomber of World War II*, 161.
29   Gibson, *Slow but Deadly*, 180.
30   Colley, oral history, 18.
31   Ibid., 19, 27.
32   Caldwell, "The Stranded *Enterprise* Aviators," *Foundation*, 35.
33   Tillman, *Enterprise*, 260.
34   "Southern Pines Couple Celebrate 70th Anniversary," *Pilot*, March 12, 2011.

INDEX